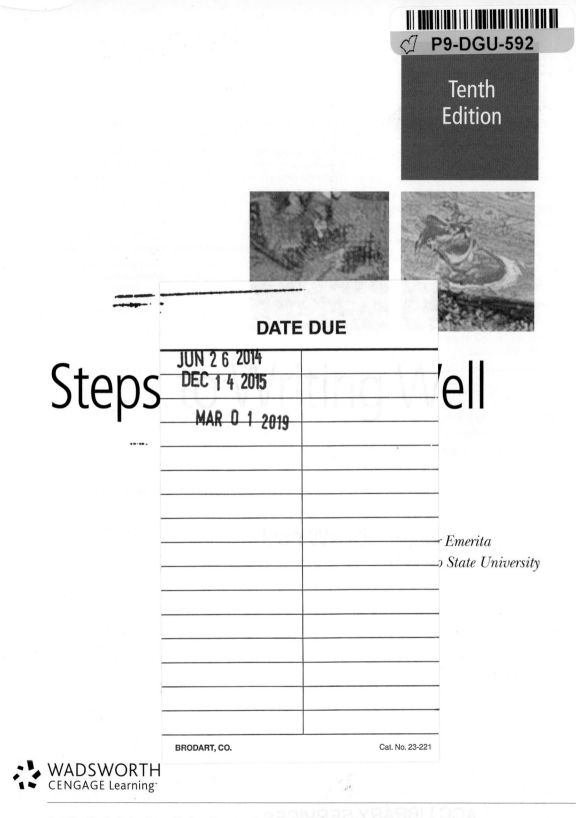

P9-DGU-592

Tenth
Edition

Steps to Writing Well

Emerita
State University

WADSWORTH
CENGAGE Learning

Australia • Brazil • Japan • Korea • Mexico • Singapore • Spain • United Kingdom • United States

WADSWORTH
CENGAGE Learning

Steps to Writing Well, Tenth Edition
Jean Wyrick

Publisher: Lyn Uhl

Acquisitions Editor: Aron Keesbury

Development Editor: Camille Adkins/
  Cheryl Forman

Technology Project Manager: Joe Gallagher

Managing Marketing Manager: Mandee
  Eckersley

Marketing Communications Manager:
  Stacey Purviance

Content Project Manager: Karen Stocz

Senior Art Director: Cate Rickard Barr

Print Buyer: Betsy Donaghey

Rights Acquisition Account Manager:
  Ron Montgomery

Permissions Researcher: Karyn Morrison

Production Service: Hearthside Publishing
  Services

Photo Manager: Sheri Blaney

Photo Researcher: Cheri Throop

Cover Designer: Gary Ragaglia

Compositor: GEX Publishing Services

For product information and technology assistance, contact us at
Cengage Learning Customer & Sales Support, 1-800-354-9706

For permission to use material from this text or product, submit all requests online at **cengage.com/permissions**
Further permissions questions can be emailed to
permissionrequest@cengage.com

Library of Congress Control Number: 2 006939181

ISBN-13: 978-1-4130-3230-7

ISBN-10: 1-4130-3230-3

Wadsworth
25 Thomson Place
Boston, MA 02210-1202
USA

Cengage Learning is a leading provider of customized learning solutions with office locations around the globe, including Singapore, the United Kingdom, Australia, Mexico, Brazil, and Japan. Locate your local office at: **international.cengage.com/region**

Cengage Learning products are represented in Canada by Nelson Education, Ltd.

For your course and learning solutions, visit **academic.cengage.com**

Purchase any of our products at your local college store or at our preferred online store **www.ichapters.com**

Cover Image: *The Walk*, 1890 (oil on canvas), Alfred Sisley (1839–99)/Musee d'Art et d'Histoire, Palais Massena, Nice, France, Lauros/Giraudon/The Bridgeman Art Library International

Credits appear on pages 577–580, which constitute a continuation of the copyright page.

Printed in China
3 4 5 6 7 09 08

Contents

21 A Concise Guide to Punctuation 545

22 A Concise Guide to Mechanics 569

List of Artworks

List of Advertisements

To the Teacher

The tenth edition of *Steps to Writing Well* has been written for teachers of composition who have had trouble finding a textbook that students can easily understand. Too many books on today's market, these teachers rightfully complain, are still unnecessarily complex, dry, or massive for the majority of students. Written simply, in an informal style and addressed to the student, this textbook offers a step-by-step guide to writing a variety of 500-to-800-word essays. The combination of concise, practical advice, a number of student and professional samples, and a brief handbook should provide more than enough helpful information for students enrolled in a one-semester course, without intimidating them. Teachers of this new edition may appreciate the book's four-color design and additional artwork, including fifty paintings and photographs, many used as writing prompts for today's visually oriented students.

Although many parts of the book have been revised or expanded for this edition, its organization remains essentially the same. Part One offers advice on "The Basics of the Short Essay"; Part Two discusses "Purposes, Modes, and Strategies"; Part Three focuses on "Special Assignments"; and Part Four presents "A Concise Handbook." This textbook still begins with the essay "To the Student," which not only argues that students can learn to write better with practice and dedication but also gives them a number of practical reasons why they *should* learn to write better.

Part One, containing eight chapters, moves students through the process of writing the short essay. Chapter 1, on prewriting, stresses finding the proper attitude ("the desire to communicate") and presents helpful suggestions for selecting a subject. This chapter then offers students ten methods for finding a significant purpose and focus for their essays. In addition, a section on using the journal explains more than a dozen ways that students may improve their skills by writing a variety of nonthreatening—and even playful—assignments. The section on audience, including new exercises addressing the appeals of advertising, should also help student writers identify their particular readers and communicate more effectively with them. After finding a topic and identifying their audience, students are ready for Chapter 2, devoted almost entirely to a discussion of the thesis statement. This chapter first explains the role of the "working thesis" in early drafts and then clearly outlines what a good thesis is and isn't by presenting a host of examples to illustrate the advice. Also included in this chapter is an explanation of the "essay map," an organizational tool that can help students structure their essays and plan their body paragraphs.

Chapter 3 discusses in detail the requirements of good body paragraphs: topic sentences, unity, order and coherence, adequate development, use of specific detail, and logical sequence. Over forty paragraphs illustrate both strengths and weaknesses of student writing. These paragraphs are not complex literary or professional excerpts but rather well-designed, precise examples of the principles under examination, written on subjects students can understand and appreciate. This chapter twice provides the opportunity for students to see how a topic may progress from a working thesis statement to an informal essay outline, which in turn helps produce well-developed paragraphs in the body of an essay. To complete the overview of the short essay, Chapter 4 explains, through an *EXPANDED* expanded number of samples, the creation of good introductions, conclusions, and titles.

Chapter 5, "Drafting and Revising: Creative Thinking, Critical Thinking," focuses on the revision process. Because too many students still think of revision as merely proofreading their essays rather than as an essential, recursive activity, this chapter emphasizes the importance of revision in all good writing. These pages offer a system for revising drafts in stages, including a discussion of drafting and revising on a word processor. A section on critical thinking shows students how to analyze and evaluate their ideas and those of others and stresses the role of critical thinking skills in the selection of evidence for all writing assignments. Chapter 5 also offers advice for participants in "peer workshops" (instructors may also find useful advice on organizing effective peer workshops in the Instructor's Manual for this edition). Also included in this chapter is a student essay, annotated to show how a writer (or a workshop partner) might use the questions suggested in the discussion of the revision process. This chapter ends with a list of suggestions for beating Writer's Block.

Chapter 6, on effective sentences, emphasizes the importance of clarity, conciseness, and vividness, with nearly one hundred and fifty sample sentences illustrating the chapter's *NEW* advice. A new section on fragments offers help resolving this common problem. Chapter 7, on word choice, presents practical suggestions for selecting accurate, appropriate words that are specific, memorable, and persuasive. This chapter also contains sections on avoiding sexist language and "bureaucratese." Chapter 8, "The Reading-Writing Connection," maintains that by learning to read analytically, students can improve their own writing skills. The chapter contains step-by-step directions for reading and annotating essays and suggests many ways students may profit from studying the rhetorical choices of other writers. A professional essay, annotated according to these steps, is included, as well as guidance for writing summaries of reading selections. Another section offers students suggestions for effective participation in class discussions, with advice for improving comprehension and note-taking skills. Teachers may wish to assign this chapter before asking students to read the professional essays that appear throughout this textbook.

Each chapter in Part One contains samples and exercises, many new to this edition. As in the previous editions, the "Practicing What You've Learned" exercises follow each major section in each chapter so that both teacher and students may quickly discover if particular material needs additional attention. Moreover, by conquering small steps in the writing process, one at a time, students should feel more confident and should learn more rapidly. Assignments, which also follow each major section in these chapters, suggest class activities and frequently emphasize "peer teaching," a useful method that asks students to prepare appropriate exercises for classmates and then to evaluate the results. Such assignments, operating under the premise that "you don't truly learn a subject until you teach it," provide engaging classroom activity for all the students and also remove from the teacher some of the burden of creating exercises.

Throughout the chapters in Part One, activities called "Applying What You've Learned to *Your* Writing" follow the exercises and assignments. Each of these activities encourages students to "follow through" by incorporating into a current draft the skill they have just read about and practiced. By following a three-step procedure—reading the advice in the text, practicing the advice through the exercises, and then applying the advice directly to their own prose—students should improve their writing processes. In addition, each of the chapters in Part One concludes with a summary, designed to help students review the important points in the material under study.

Part Two presents discussion of the kinds of essays students are most often asked to write. Chapter 9, on exposition, is divided into separate discussions of the expository strategies: example, process, comparison/contrast, definition, division and classification, and causal analysis. Discussions in Chapter 9 and the chapters on argument, description, and narration follow a similar format by offering the students (a) a clear definition of the mode (or strategy), explained with familiar examples; (b) practical advice on developing each essay; (c) warnings about common problems; (d) suggested essay topics; (e) a topic proposal sheet; (f) sample student essay(s) with marginal notes; (g) professional essay(s) followed by questions on content, structure, and style, writing suggestions, and a vocabulary list; (h) a revision worksheet to guide student writers through their rough drafts; and (i) progress report. In the lists of suggested essay topics, each #20 offers one or more

EXPANDED

of the pictures in this book as a writing prompt. Teachers may now choose from an expanded selection of paintings, photographs and advertisements to encourage thoughtful essays organized in a variety of ways.

The seventeen student essays in this text should encourage student writers by showing them that others in their situation can indeed compose organized, well-developed essays. The student essays that appear here are not perfect; consequently, teachers may use them in class to generate suggestions for still more revision. The twenty-two professional readings were also selected to spur class discussion and to illustrate the rhetorical principles presented throughout the text. (The process analysis and comparison/contrast sections of Chapter 9 contain two professional essays so that students may see examples of two commonly used methods of organization; both division and classification are also illus-

NEW

trated by professional writing.) Those professional readings most popular with the users of the last edition have been retained; eight selections are new to this edition.

NEW

Chapter 10 discusses the argumentative essay, presenting a new pair of professional essays with opposing views and new advertisements, selected to help students analyze rhetorical appeals and supporting evidence. Chapters 11 and 12, on writing description and narration, may be assigned prior to the expository strategies or may be used as supplementary material for any kind of writing incorporating descriptive language or extended example. Chapter 11 presents essays that illustrate description of a person, a

NEW

place, and a common object. Both chapters contain visual art designed to help students understand the importance of vivid details in support of a dominant effect.

Although this text shows students how to master individual rhetorical strategies, one essay at a time, experienced writers often choose a combination, or blending, of strategies to best accomplish their purpose. "Writing Essays Using Multiple Strategies," Chapter 13, concludes Part Two by offering advice to writers who are ready to address more complex topics and essay organization. This chapter also contains both student and professional essays to illustrate clear use of multiple strategies to accomplish the writer's purpose.

Part Three, called "Special Assignments," allows instructors to design their composition courses in a variety of ways, perhaps by adding a research paper, a literary analysis, an in-class essay, a review of an artwork or movie, or a business writing assignment. Chapter 14, "Writing a Paper Using Research," shows students how to focus a topic, search for information in a variety of ways, choose and evaluate evidence, avoid plagiarism, and effectively incorporate and cite source material in their essays. This edition contains updated discussions of electronic sources and continues a subscription offer to *InfoTrac College Edition*, an easy-to-use online database of full-text artcles from magazines, journals, newspapers, and other sources. To provide students with another avenue for collecting information, a new section on primary research has been created, adding guidance for designing questionnaires to the advice on interviewing. This chapter also presents updated MLA and APA documentation styles, with a student essay illustrating MLA citations and excerpts from that essay illustrating APA references.

Chapter 15 "Writing in Class: Exams and 'Response' Essays," is designed to help students respond quickly and accurately to a variety of in-class assignments by understanding their task's purpose and by recognizing key directional words. Advice for successfully organizing and completing timed writing should also help decrease students' anxiety. Because so many composition courses today include some variation of the "summary-and-response" assignment (used not only as an in- or out-of-class essay but also as a placement or exit test), this chapter also addresses that kind of writing and offers a sample student essay.

"Writing about Literature," Chapter 16, discusses multiple ways literary selections may be used in the composition class, either as prompts for personal essays or for papers of literary analysis. Students are offered a series of suggestions for close reading of both poetry and short fiction. The chapter contains an annotated poem, an annotated short story, and two student essays analyzing those works. Additional poems and stories, without marginal notes, have been included for classroom discussion or assignment.

An entirely new Chapter 17, "Writing about Visual Arts," encourages critical thinking and good writing practice in discussions of paintings, photographs, and sculpture. To illustrate the guidelines for analysis, this chapter includes a student's prewriting notes and subsequent essay on Edward Hopper's popular painting *Nighthawks*. Composition students may choose their own subject matter from more than twenty artworks reproduced in this chapter and throughout the text, more than twice the number in the previous edition. Artists such as Vincent Van Gogh, Frida Kahlo, Jacob Lawrence, Claude Monet, Dorothea Lange, Edvard Munch, Ansel Adams, Francisco Goya, Salvador Dali, and many others, offer a variety of styles from social realism to abstract expressionism. Teachers may also wish to use the new art in this edition as prompts for other kinds of assignments, such as descriptive paragraphs or comparison/contrast essays. (For quick reference, a complete list of the artworks appears at the end of the Table of Contents.)

Chapter 18, "Writing about Film," offers an opportunity for students to practice good writing skills in essays using movies as subject matter in a variety of ways. Suggestions for critical thinking and writing about films and a glossary of cinematic terms are included, as well as a student essay and a brief movie review that may be critiqued in class.

Chapter 19, "Writing in the World of Work," allows students to practice composing business letters, office memos, electronic mail, and résumés. With the increasing use of technology in the workplace, students may also profit from a section discussing "netiquette" that encourages writers to cultivate a sense of civility and professionalism, as well as clarity, in their electronic communications.

Part Four presents a concise handbook with accessible explanations and examples showing how to correct the most common errors in grammar, punctuation, and mechanics. To satisfy requests from teachers, the number of grammar and punctuation entries and exercises has been expanded.

~EXPANDED~

Once again, readers of this edition may note an occasional attempt at humor. The lighthearted tone of some samples and exercises is the result of the author's firm belief that while learning to write is serious business, solemn composition classrooms are not always the most beneficial environments for anxious beginning writers. The author takes full responsibility (and all of the blame) for the bad jokes and even worse puns.

~UPDATED~

Finally, a complimentary Instructor's Manual, updated for this edition by Colleen Schaeffer, is available, containing suggestions for teaching and answers to exercises and essay questions. Teachers interested in additional information regarding the *InfoTrac College Edition* subscription offer should contact their Cengage Learning sales representative or visit academic.cengage.com.

Although a new edition of this textbook has allowed its author to make a number of changes and additions, the book's purpose remains as stated in the original preface: "While there are many methods of teaching composition, *Steps to Writing Well* tries to help inexperienced writers by offering a clearly defined sequential approach to writing the short essay. By presenting simple, practical advice directly to the students, this text is intended to make the demanding jobs of teaching and learning the basic principles of composition easier and more enjoyable for everyone."

Acknowledgments

Many thanks to all the outstanding people at Thomson Wadsworth for their help with this revision. I greatly appreciate the support of Senior Acquisitions Editor Aron Keesbury, whose good counsel kept the project on the right track and whose generosity provided the wonderful artwork that makes this edition so special. Special thanks to Cheryl Forman, Assistant Editor, for her hard work, long hours, and careful supervision guiding this text through the many hoops, from the user reviews all the way to production. As always, I could not have produced a manuscript without the wisdom of Camille Adkins, Development Editor, whose insight improved every chapter. Thank you, Camille, for once again patiently walking with me on this long road. Another big thank you to Karyn Morrison, who again secured the text's many literary permissions with amazing speed, efficiency, and good cheer. Cheri Throop again successfully located and negotiated the complex art permissions from a variety of sources. I'm so grateful to Content Production Manager Karen Stocz, whose flexibility, patience, and dedication knew no bounds as she directed the team through a challenging production schedule. Huge thanks to Anne Seitz of Hearthside Publishing Services for her tireless help organizing the production services. Barbara Willette's careful copyediting and Grace Skinger's expert proofreading were also appreciated.

On-going gratitude is due the students at Colorado State University who allowed me to reprint their writing and also to Sharon Straus, whose essay "Treeclimbing" was a prize winner at the College of Charleston.

I would like to thank my colleagues from across the country whose helpful feedback informed the revision process:

Sandra Albers, *Leeward Community College*
Morgan Andaluz, *Maui Community College*
Janna Anderson, *Fullerton College*
Don Asay, *Treasure Valley Community College*
Ann Avery, *Central Wyoming College*
Susan Bailor, *Front Range Community College*
Dean Bartow, *Laramie County Community College*
Gregg Berlie, *Blue Mountain Community College*
Roland Eric Boys, *Oxnard College*
Muriel M. Brennan, *College of San Mateo*
Christy Bruemmer, *University of Northern Colorado*
Joyce Coleman, *Treasure Valley Community College*
Carol Cooper, *Jackson State University*
Ken Cox, *Florence-Darlington Technical College*
Huey Crisp, *University of Arkansas at Little Rock*
Susan Cunningham, *Ohlone College*
Martha Dede, *California State University, Long Beach*
V. Diaz-Cox, *Victor Valley College*
Steven A. Dolgin, *Schoolcraft College*
Scott Douglass, *Chattanooga State Technical Community College*
Marie Eckstrom, *Rio Hondo College*
Roberto Figueroa, *Columbia Basin College*

Mary Fister, *University of Hartford*
Robert Galin, *Pueblo Community College—Southwest Center*
Elizabeth Gilliland, *San Jose State University*
Ryan Gilpatrick, *University of Northern Colorado*
Susan Goldstein, *Mount Wachusett Community College*
Darryl Goncharoff, *Schoolcraft College*
Karen Hedgepeth, *York Technical College*
Beulah S. Hemmingway, *Florida A & M University*
Julie Hopgood, *University of Northern Colorado*
Frances Ilnicky, *Texas State Technical College—Harlingen*
Ron Israel, *San Diego Mesa College*
Kathleen M. Jennings, *Front Range Community College*
Susan A. Johnson, *Sierra College*
Deb Jones, *Columbia Basin College*
Kathleen Kidd, *University of Maryland, Baltimore County*
Noel Kinnamon, *Mars Hill College*
Tom Mantey, *Ohio University*
DaNita McClain, *Spelman College*
Judith McFadden, *Goucher College*
Michele McIver-Bell, *Fayetteville State University*
Rosemary McTier, *Waynesburg College*
Angela Medina, *Rio Hondo College*
Elaina Meiners, *Columbia Basin College*
Sally Michlin, *Sacred Heart University*
Donna Miguel, *Everett Community College*
Emily Moorer, *Hinds Community College*
Michael Morris, *Eastfield College*
Joyce Munro, *Schoolcraft College*
Amy Otis, *University of Northern Colorado*
Lori A. Paige, *Westfield State College*
Mary Alice E. Palm, *Schoolcraft College*
Joan Reeves, *Northeast Alabama Community College*
Holly Roberts, *Sullivan University*
Rita Rogers, *Roanoke-Chowan Community College*
Paul Rottenberg, *Broward Community College*
Rosalinda Ruiz, *Fullerton College*
Frances Stallworth, *Florida A & M University*
Bonnie Startt, *Tidewater Community College*
Kathryn Thompson, *Antelope Valley College*
Lori Wolf, *Los Angeles Pierce College*
Mary Wright, *Florida International University*

Special thanks go to Joan Beam, former Professor of Library Science at Colorado State University, and to Scott Douglass, of Chattanooga State College, for their thoughtful suggestions and valuable contributions to the updating of Chapter 14; and to Colleen Schaeffer at California State University, Northridge, for updating and expanding the useful Instructor's Manual with new advice for class discussions and writing assignments.

Finally, thanks to my husband, David Hall, and to our children, Sarah, Kate, and Austin, for their patience and flexibility during the many phases of this revision process.

To the Student

Finding the Right Attitude

If you agree with one or more of the following statements, we have some serious myth-killing to do before you begin this book:

1. I'm no good in English—never have been, never will be.

2. Only people with natural talent for writing can succeed in composition class.

3. My composition teacher is a picky, comma-hunting old fogey/radical, who will insist I write just like him or her.

4. I write for myself, not for anyone else, so I don't need this class or this book.

5. Composition classes are designed to put my creativity in a straitjacket.

The notion that good writers are born, not made, is a widespread myth that may make you feel defeated before you start. But the simple truth is that good writers *are* made—simply because *effective writing is a skill that can be learned.* Despite any feelings of insecurity you may have about composition, you should realize that you already know many of the basic rules of good writing; after all, you've been writing since you were six years old. What you need now is some practical advice on composition, some coaching to sharpen your skills, and a strong dose of determination to practice those skills until you can consistently produce the results you want. Talent, as the French writer Flaubert once said, is nothing more than long patience.

Think about learning to write well as you might consider your tennis game. No one is born a tennis star. You first learn the basic rules and movements and then go out on the court to practice. And practice. No one's tennis will improve if he or she stays off the court; similarly, you must write regularly and receive feedback to improve your composition skills. Try to see your teacher not as Dr. Frankenstein determined to reproduce his or her style of writing in you, but rather as your coach, your loyal trainer who wants you to do the very best you can. Like any good coach, your teacher will point out your strengths and weaknesses; she or he will often send you to this text for practical suggestions for improvement. And while there are no quick, magic solutions for learning to write well, the most important point to remember is this: with this text, your own common sense, and determination, *you can improve your writing*.

Why Write?

"OK," you say, "so I can improve if I try—but why should I bother? Why should I write well? I'm not going to be a professional writer."

In the first place, writing helps us explore our own thoughts and feelings. Writing forces us to articulate our ideas, to discover what we really think about an issue. For example, let's suppose you're faced with a difficult decision and that the arguments pro and con are jumbled in your head. You begin to write down all the pertinent facts and feelings, and suddenly, you begin to see that you do, indeed, have stronger arguments for one side of the question than the other. Once you "see" what you are thinking, you may then scrutinize your opinions for any logical flaws or weaknesses and revise your argument accordingly. In other words, writing lays out our ideas for examination, analysis, and thoughtful reaction. Thus when we write, we (and the world at large) see who we are, and what we stand for, much more clearly. Moreover, writing can provide a record of our thoughts that we may study and evaluate in a way that conversation cannot. In short, writing well enables us to see and know ourselves—our feelings, ideas, and opinions—better.

On a more practical level, we need to write effectively to communicate with others. While some of our writing may be done solely for ourselves, the majority of it is created for others to share. In this world, it is almost impossible to claim that we write only for ourselves. We are constantly asked to put our feelings, ideas, and knowledge in writing for others to read. During your college years, no matter what your major, you will be repeatedly required to write essays, tests, reports, and exercises (and possibly e-mail or letters home). Later, you may need to write formal letters of application for jobs or graduate training; your writing may make that important first impression. At work you may have to write numerous kinds of reports, proposals, analyses, and requisitions. To be successful in any field, you must make your correspondence with business associates and co-workers clearly understood; remember that enormous amounts of time, energy, and profit have been lost because of a single unclear office memo.

There's still a third—more cynical—reason for studying writing techniques. Once you begin to improve your ability to use language, you will become more aware of the ways others write and speak. Through today's mass media and electronic highways, we are continually bombarded with words from politicians, advertisers, scientists, preachers, teachers, and self-appointed "authorities." We need to understand and evaluate what we are hearing, not only for our benefit but also for self-protection. Language is frequently manipulated to manipulate us. For example, the CIA has long referred to the "neutralization" of enemies, and on occasion, Pentagon officials have carefully avoided discussion of times when misdirected "physics packages" (bombs) fell on "soft targets" (civilians). (One year not so long ago, the National Council of Teachers of English gave their Doublespeak Award to the U.S. officers who, after accidentally shooting down a plane of civilians, reported that the plane didn't crash—rather, it had "uncontrolled contact with the ground.") Some members of Congress have seen no recessions, just "meaningful downturns in aggregate output," so they have treated themselves to a "pay equalization concept," rather than a raise. Advertisers frequently try to disguise their pitches through "infomercials" and "advertorials"; realtors may promote dumps as "designer-ready" houses; the television networks treat us to "encore presentations" that are the same old summer reruns. And "fenestration engineers" are still window cleaners; "environmental superintendents" are still janitors; "drain surgeons" are still plumbers.

By becoming better writers ourselves, we can learn to recognize and reject the irresponsible, cloudy, or dishonest language of others before we become victims of their exploitation.

A Good Place to Start

If improving writing skills is not only possible but important, it is also something else: hard work. H. L. Mencken, American critic and writer, once remarked that "for every difficult and complex problem, there is an obvious solution that is simple, easy and wrong." No composition textbook can promise easy formulas guaranteed to improve your writing overnight. Nor is writing always fun for everyone. But this text can make the learning process easier, less painful, and more enjoyable than you might anticipate. Written in plain, straightforward language addressed to you, the student, this book will suggest a variety of practical ways for you to organize and write clear, concise prose. Because each of your writing tasks will be different, this textbook cannot provide a single, simple blueprint that will apply in all instances. Later chapters, however, will discuss some of the most common methods of organizing essays, such as development by example, definition, classification, causal analysis, comparison/contrast, and argument. As you become more familiar with, and begin to master, these patterns of writing, you will find yourself increasingly able to assess, organize, and explain the thoughts you have about the people, events, and situations in your own life. And while it may be true that in learning to write well there is no free ride, this book, along with your own willingness to work and improve, can start you down the road with a good sense of direction.

J.W.

Part 1

The Basics
of the Short Essay

The first section of this text is designed to move you through the writing process as you compose a short essay, the kind you are most likely to encounter in composition class and in other college courses. Chapters 1 and 2, on prewriting and the thesis statement, will help you find a topic, purpose, and focus for your essay. Chapter 3, on paragraphs, will show you how to plan, organize, and develop your ideas; Chapter 4 will help you complete your essay. Chapter 5 offers suggestions for revising your writing, and Chapters 6 and 7 present additional advice on selecting your words and composing your sentences. Chapter 8 explains the important reading-writing connection and shows how learning to read analytically can sharpen your writing skills. ■

Chapter 1

Prewriting

■ Getting Started (or Soup-Can Labels Can Be Fascinating)

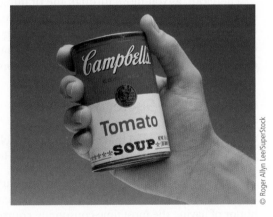

For many writers, getting started is the hardest part. You may have noticed that when it is time to begin a writing assignment, you suddenly develop an enormous desire to straighten your books, water your plants, or sharpen your pencils for the fifth time. If this situation sounds familiar, you may find it reassuring to know that many professionals undergo these same strange compulsions before they begin writing. Jean Kerr, author of *Please Don't Eat the Daisies*, admitted that she often found herself in the kitchen reading soup-can labels—or anything—to prolong the moments before taking pen in hand. John C. Calhoun, vice president under Andrew Jackson, insisted he had to plow his fields before he could write, and Joseph Conrad, author of *Lord Jim* and other novels, is said to have cried on occasion from the sheer dread of sitting down to compose his stories.

To spare you as much hand-wringing as possible, this chapter presents some practical suggestions on how to begin writing your short essay. Although all writers must find the methods that work best for them, you may find some of the following ideas helpful.

But no matter how you actually begin putting words on paper, it is absolutely essential to maintain two basic ideas concerning your writing task. Before you write a single sentence, you should always remind yourself that

1. You have some valuable ideas to tell your reader, and

2. More than anything, you want to communicate those ideas to your reader.

These reminders may seem obvious to you, but without a solid commitment to your own opinions as well as to your reader, your prose will be lifeless and boring. If *you* don't care about your subject, you can't very well expect anyone else to. Have confidence that your ideas are worthwhile and that your reader genuinely wants, or needs, to know what you think.

Equally important, you must also have a strong desire to tell others what you are thinking. One of the most common mistakes inexperienced writers make is failing to move past early stages in the writing process in which they are writing for—or writing to—themselves only. In the first stages of composing an essay, writers frequently "talk" on paper to themselves, exploring thoughts, discovering new insights, making connections, selecting examples, and so on. The ultimate goal of a finished essay, however, is to communicate your opinions to *others* clearly and persuasively. Whether you wish to inform your readers, change their minds, or stir them to action, you cannot accomplish your purpose by writing so that only you understand what you mean. The burden of communicating your thoughts falls on *you*, not the reader, who is under no obligation to struggle through confused, unclear prose, paragraphs that begin and end for no apparent reason, or sentences that come one after another with no more logic than lemmings following one another to the sea.

Therefore, as you move through the drafting and revising stages of your writing process, commit yourself to becoming increasingly aware of your reader's reactions to your prose. Ask yourself as you revise your drafts, "Am I moving beyond writing just to myself? Am I making myself clear to others who might not know what I mean?" Much of your success as a writer depends on an unflagging determination to communicate clearly with your readers.

■ Selecting a Subject

Once you have decided that communicating clearly with others is your ultimate goal, you are ready to select the subject of your essay. Here are some suggestions on how to begin:

Start early. Writing teachers since the earth's crust cooled have been pushing this advice—and for good reason. It's not because teachers are egoists competing for the dubious honor of having the most time-consuming course; it is because few writers, even experienced ones, can do a good job when rushed. You need time to mull over ideas, organize your thoughts, revise and polish your prose. Rule of thumb: Always give yourself twice as much time as you think you'll need to avoid the 2:00-A.M.-why-did-I-come-to-college panic.

Find your best space. Develop some successful writing habits by thinking about your very own writing process. When and where do you usually do your best composing? Some people write best early in the morning; others think better later in the day. What time of day seems to produce your best efforts? Where are you working? At a desk? In your room or in a library? Do you start drafting ideas on a computer or do you begin with paper or a yellow pad? With a certain pen or sharpened pencil? Most writers avoid noise and interruptions (TV, telephone, friends, etc.), although some swear by music in the background. If you can identify a previously successful writing experience, try duplicating its location, time, and tools to help you calmly address your new writing task. Or consider trying new combinations of time and place if your previous choices weren't as productive as you would have liked. Recognition and repeated use of your most comfortable writing "spot" may shorten your hesitation to begin composing; your subconscious may recognize the pattern ("Hey, it's time to write!") and help you start in a positive frame of mind. (Remember that it's not just writers who repeat such rituals—think of the athletes you've heard about who won't begin a game without wearing their lucky socks. If it works for them, it can work for you!)

Select something in which you currently have a strong interest. If the essay subject is left to you, think of something fun, fascinating, or frightening you've done or seen lately, perhaps something you've already told a friend about. The subject might be the pleasure of a new hobby, the challenge of a recent book or movie, or even the harassment of registration—anything in which you are personally involved. If you aren't enthusiastic enough about your subject to want to spread the word, pick something else. Bored writers write boring essays.

Don't feel you have nothing from which to choose your subject. Your days are full of activities, people, joys, and irritations. Essays do not have to be written on lofty intellectual or poetic subjects—in fact, some of the world's best essays have been written on such subjects as china teacups, roast pig, and chimney sweeps. Think: what have you been talking or thinking about lately? What have you been doing that you're excited about? Or what about your past? Reflect a few moments on some of your most vivid memories; special people, vacations, holidays, childhood hideaways, your first job or first date—all are possibilities.

Still searching? Make a list of all the subjects on which you are an expert. None, you say? Think again. Most of us have an array of talents we hardly acknowledge. Perhaps you play the guitar or make a mean pot of chili or know how to repair a sports car. You've trained a dog or become a first-class house-sitter or gardener. You know more about computers or old baseball cards than any of your friends. You play soccer or volleyball or Ping-Pong. In other words, take a fresh, close look at your life. You know things that others don't . . . now is your chance to enlighten them!

If a search of your immediate or past personal experience doesn't turn up anything inspiring, try looking in your local or campus newspaper for stories that arouse your strong feelings; don't skip the editorials or "Letters to the Editor" column. What are the current topics of controversy on your campus? How do you feel about a particular graduation requirement? Speakers or special-interest groups on campus? Financial aid applications? Registration procedures? Parking restrictions? Consider the material you are studying in your other classes: reading *The Jungle* in a literature class might spark an investigative essay on the hot dog industry today, or studying previous immigration laws in your history class might lead you to an argument for or against current immigration practices. News magazines on current display in your library might suggest timely essay topics on national or international affairs that affect your life. In addition, there are, according to the search engine Technorati, over fifty million online blogs, personal web logs that offer diverse—and often controversial—opinions on almost every subject, from politics to entertainment, hobbies, health, and home. Any one of these print or online sources might present an idea or argument that invites your thoughtful response.

In other words, when you're stuck for an essay topic, take a closer look at your environment: your own life—past, present, and future; your hometown; your campus and college town; your state; your country; and your world. You'll probably discover more than enough subjects to satisfy the assignments in your writing class.

Narrow a large subject. Once you've selected a general subject to write on, you may find that it is too broad for effective treatment in a short essay; therefore, you may need to narrow it somewhat. Suppose, for instance, you like to work with plants and have decided to make them the subject of your essay. The subject of "plants," however, is far too large and unwieldy for a short essay, perhaps even for a short book. Consequently, you must make your subject less general. "Houseplants" is more specific, but, again, there's too much to say. "Minimum-care houseplants" is better, but you still need to pare this large, complex subject further so that you can treat it in depth in your short essay. After all, there are many houseplants that require little attention. After several more tries, you might arrive at more specific, manageable topics, such as "houseplants that thrive in dark areas" or "the easy-care Devil's Ivy."

Then again, let's assume you are interested in sports. A 500-to-800-word essay on "sports" would obviously be superficial because the subject covers so much ground. Instead, you might divide the subject into categories such as "sports heroes," "my years on the high school tennis team," "women in gymnastics," "my love of running," and so forth. Perhaps several of your categories would make good short essays, but after looking at your list, you might decide that your real interest at this time is running and that it will be the topic of your essay.

■ Finding Your Essay's Purpose and Focus

Even after you've narrowed your large subject to a more manageable topic, you still must find a specific *purpose* for your essay. Why are you writing about this topic? Do your readers need to be informed, persuaded, entertained? What do you want your writing to accomplish?

In addition to knowing your purpose, you must also find a clear *focus* or direction for your essay. You cannot, for example, inform your readers about every aspect of running. Instead, you must decide on a particular part of the sport and then determine the main point you want to make. If it helps, think of a camera: you see a sweeping landscape you'd like to photograph, but you know you can't get it all into one picture, so you pick out a particularly interesting part of the scene. Focus in an essay works in the same way; you zoom in, so to speak, on a particular part of your topic and make that the focus of your paper.

Sometimes part of your problem may be solved by your assignment; your teacher may choose the focus of your essay for you by asking for certain specific information or by prescribing the method of development you should use (compare running to aerobics, explain the process of running properly, analyze the effects of daily running, and so forth). But if the purpose and focus of your essay are decisions you must make, you should always allow your interest and knowledge to guide you. Often a direction or focus for your essay will surface as you narrow your subject, but don't become frustrated if you have to discard several ideas before you hit the one that's right. For instance, you might first consider writing on how to select running shoes and then realize that you know too little about the shoe market, or you might find that there's just too little of importance to say about running paths to make an interesting 500-word essay.

Let's suppose for a moment that you have thought of a subject that interests you—but now you're stuck. Deciding on something to write about this subject suddenly looks as easy as nailing Jell-O to your kitchen wall. What should you say? What would be the purpose of your essay? What would be interesting for you to write about and for readers to hear about?

At this point, you may profit from trying more than one prewriting exercise, designed to help you generate some ideas about your topic. The exercises described next are, in a sense, "pump primers" that will get your creative juices flowing again. Because all writers compose differently, not all of these exercises will work for you—in fact, some of them may lead you nowhere. Nevertheless, try all of them at least once or twice; you may be surprised to discover that some pump-primer techniques work better with some subjects than with others.

■ Pump-Primer Techniques

1. Listing

Try jotting down all the ideas that pop into your head about your topic. Free-associate; don't hold back anything. Try to brainstorm for at least ten minutes.

A quick list on running might look like this:

fun	training for races
healthy	both sexes
relieves tension	any age group
no expensive equipment	running with friend or spouse
shoes	too much competition
poor shoes won't last	great expectations
shin splints	good for lungs
fresh air	improves circulation
good for heart	firming
jogging paths vs. streets	no weight loss
hard surfaces	warm-ups before run
muscle cramps	cool-downs after
going too far	getting discouraged
going too fast	hitting the wall
sense of accomplishment	marathons

As you read over the list, look for connections between ideas or one large idea that encompasses several small ones. In this list, you might first notice that many of the ideas focus on improving health (heart, lungs, circulation), but you discard that subject because a "running improves health" essay is too obvious; it's a topic that's been done too many times to say anything new. A closer look at your list, however, turns up a number of ideas that concern how *not* to jog or reasons why someone might become discouraged and quit a running program. You begin to think of friends who might have stuck with running as you have if only they'd warmed up properly beforehand, chosen the right places to run, paced themselves more realistically, and so on. You decide, therefore, to write an essay telling first-time runners how to start a successful program, how to avoid a number of problems, from shoes to track surfaces, that might otherwise defeat their efforts before they've given the sport a chance.

2. Freewriting

Some people simply need to start writing to find a focus. Take out several sheets of blank paper, give yourself at least ten to fifteen minutes, and begin writing whatever comes to mind on your subject. Don't worry about spelling, punctuation, or even complete sentences. Don't change, correct, or delete anything. If you run out of things to say, write "I can't think of anything to say" until you can find a new thought. At the end of the time period you may discover that by continuously writing you will have written yourself into an interesting topic.

Here are examples of freewriting from students who were given ten minutes to write on the general topic of "nature."

STUDENT 1:

I'm really not the outdoorsy type. I'd rather be inside somewhere than out in Nature tromping through the bushes. I don't like bugs and snakes and stuff like that. Lots of my friends like to go hiking around or camping but I don't. Secretly, I think maybe one of the big reasons I really don't like being out in Nature is because I'm deathly afraid of bees. When I was a kid I was out in the woods and ran into a swarm of bees and got stung about a million times, well, it felt like a million times. I had to go to the hospital for a few days. Now every time I'm outside somewhere and something, anything, flies by me I'm terrified. Totally paranoid. Everyone kids me because I immediately cover my head. I keep hearing about killer bees heading this way, my worst nightmare come true. . . .

STUDENT 2:

We're not going to have any Nature left if people don't do something about the environment. Despite all the media attention to recycling, we're still trashing the planet left and right. People talk big about "saving the environment" but then do such stupid things all the time. Like smokers who flip their cigarette butts out their car windows. Do they think those filters are just going to disappear overnight? The parking lot by this building is full of butts this morning where someone dumped their car ashtray. This campus is full of pop cans, I can see at least three empties under desks in this classroom right now. . . .

These two students reacted quite differently to the same general subject. The first student responded personally, thinking about her own relationship to "nature" (defined as being out in the woods), whereas the second student obviously associated nature with environmental concerns. More freewriting might lead student 1 to a humorous essay on her bee phobia or even to an inquiry about those dreaded killer bees; student 2 might write an interesting paper suggesting ways college students could clean up their campus or easily recycle their aluminum cans.

Often freewriting will not be as coherent as these two samples; sometimes freewriting goes nowhere or in circles. But it's a technique worth trying. By allowing our minds to roam freely over a subject, without worrying about "correctness" or organization, we may remember or discover topics we want to write about or investigate, topics we feel strongly about and wish to introduce to others.

3. Looping*

Looping is a variation on freewriting that works amazingly well for many people, including those who are frustrated rather than helped by freewriting.

Let's assume you've been assigned that old standby, "My Summer Vacation." Obviously, you must find a focus, something specific and important to say. Again, take out several sheets of blank paper and begin to freewrite, as described previously. Write for at least ten minutes. At the end of this period, read over what you've written and try to identify a central idea that has emerged. This idea might be an important thought that occurred to you in the middle or at the end of your writing, or perhaps it was the idea you liked best for whatever reason. It might be the idea that was pulling you onward when time ran out. In other words, look for the thought that stands out, that seems to indicate the direction of your thinking. Put this thought or idea into one sentence called the "center-of-gravity sentence." You have now completed loop 1.

To begin loop 2, use your center-of-gravity sentence as a jumping-off point for another ten minutes of freewriting. Stop, read what you've written, and complete loop 2 by composing another center-of-gravity sentence. Use this second sentence to start loop 3. You should write at least three loops and three center-of-gravity sentences. At the end of three loops, you may find that you have focused on a specific topic that might lead to a good essay. If you're not satisfied with your topic at this point, by all means try two or three more loops until your subject is sufficiently narrowed and focused.

Here's an example of one student's looping exercise:

SUMMER VACATION

Loop 1

I think summer vacations are very important aspects of living. They symbolize getting away from daily routines, discovering places and people that are different. When I think of vacations I think mostly of traveling somewhere too far to go, say, for a weekend. It is a chance to get away and relax and not think about most responsibilities. Just have a good time and enjoy yourself. Vacations can also be a time of gathering with family and friends.

Center-of-gravity sentence

Vacations are meant to be used for traveling.

Loop 2

Vacations are meant for traveling. Last summer my family and I drove to Yellowstone National Park. I didn't want to go at first. I thought looking at geysers would be dumb and boring. I was really

---

* This technique is suggested by Peter Elbow in *Writing Without Teachers* (New York: Oxford University Press, 1975).

obnoxious all the way up there and made lots of smart remarks about getting eaten by bears. Luckily, my parents ignored me and I'm glad they did, because Yellowstone turned out to be wonderful. It's not just Old Faithful—there's lots more to see and learn about, like these colorful boiling pools and boiling patches of mud. I got interested in the thermodynamics of the pools and how new ones are surfacing all the time, and how algae make the pools different colors.

Center-of-gravity sentence

Once I got interested in Yellowstone's amazing pools, my vacation turned out great.

Loop 3

Once I got interested in the pools, I had a good time, mainly because I felt I was seeing something really unusual. I knew I'd never see anything like this again unless I went to Iceland or New Zealand (highly unlikely!). I felt like I was learning a lot, too. I liked the idea of learning a lot about the inside of the earth without having to go to class and study books. I really hated to leave—Mom and Dad kidded me on the way back about how much I'd griped about going on the trip in the first place. I felt pretty dumb. But I was really glad I'd given the Park a closer look instead of holding on to my view of it as a boring bunch of water fountains. I would have had a terrible time, but now I hope to go back someday. I think the experience made me more open-minded about trying new places.

Center-of-gravity sentence

My vacation this summer was special because I was willing to put aside my expectations of boredom and learn some new ideas about the strange environment at Yellowstone.

At the end of three loops, this student has moved from the general subject of "summer vacation" to the more focused idea that her willingness to learn about a new place played an important part in the enjoyment of her vacation. Although her last center-of-gravity sentence still contains some vague words ("special," "new ideas," "strange environment"), the thought stated here may eventually lead to an essay that will not only say something about this student's vacation but may also persuade readers to reconsider their attitude toward taking trips to new places.

4. The Boomerang

Still another variation on freewriting is the technique called the "boomerang," named appropriately because, like the Australian stick, it invites your mind to travel over a subject from opposite directions to produce new ideas.

Suppose, for example, members of your class have been asked to write about their major field of study, which in your case is Liberal Arts. Begin by writing a statement that comes into your mind about majoring in the Liberal Arts, and then freewrite on that statement for five minutes. Then write a second statement that approaches the subject from an opposing point of view, and freewrite again for five minutes. Continue this pattern several times. Boomeranging, like looping, can help writers see their subject in a new way and consequently help them find an idea to write about.

Here's an abbreviated sample of boomeranging:

1. Majoring in the Liberal Arts is impractical in today's world.

    [Freewrite for five minutes.]

2. Majoring in the Liberal Arts is practical in today's world.

    [Freewrite for five minutes.]

3. Liberal Arts is a particularly enjoyable major for me.

    [Freewrite for five minutes.]

4. Liberal Arts is not always an enjoyable major for me.

    [Freewrite for five minutes.]

And so on.

By continuing to "throw the boomerang" across your subject, you may not only find your focus but also gain insight into other people's views of your topic, which can be especially valuable if your paper will address a controversial issue or one that you feel is often misunderstood.

5. Clustering

Another excellent technique is clustering (sometimes called "mapping"). Place your general subject in a circle in the middle of a blank sheet of paper and begin to draw other lines and circles that radiate from the original subject. Cluster those ideas that seem to fall together. At the end of ten minutes, see if a topic emerges from any of your groups of ideas.

Ten minutes of clustering on the subject of "A Memorable Holiday" might look like the drawing on page 12.

This student may wish to brainstorm further on the Christmas he spent in the hospital with a case of appendicitis or perhaps on the Halloween he first experienced a house of horrors. By using clustering, he has recollected some important details about a number of holidays that may help him focus on an occasion he wants to describe in his paper.

6. Cubing

Still another way to generate ideas is cubing. Imagine a six-sided cube that looks something like the figure on page 13.

Mentally, roll your subject around the cube and freewrite the answers to the questions that follow. Write whatever comes to mind for ten or fifteen minutes; don't concern yourself with the "correctness" of what you write.

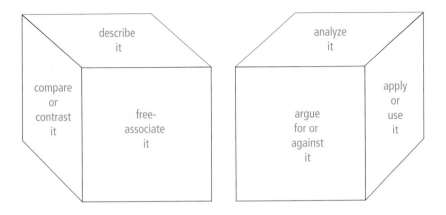

a. *Describe it:* What does your subject look like? What size, colors, textures does it have? Does it have any special features worth noting?

b. *Compare or contrast it:* What is your subject similar to? What is your subject different from? In what ways?

c. *Free-associate it:* What does this subject remind you of? What does it call to mind? What memories does it conjure up?

d. *Analyze it:* How does it work? How are the parts connected? What is its significance?

e. *Argue for or against it:* What arguments can you make for or against your subject? What advantages or disadvantages does it have? What changes or improvements should be made?

f. *Apply it:* What are the uses of your subject? What can you do with it?

A student who had recently volunteered at a homeless shelter wrote the following responses about her experience:

a. *Describe it:* I and five other members of my campus organization volunteered three Saturdays to work at the shelter here in town. We mainly helped in the kitchen, preparing, serving, and cleaning up after meals. At the dinners we served about forty homeless people, mostly men but also some families with small children and babies.

b. *Compare or contrast it:* I had never done anything like this before so it's hard to compare or contrast it to anything. It was different though from what I expected. I hadn't really thought much about the people who would be there— or to be honest I think I thought they would be pretty weird or sad and I was kind of dreading going there after I volunteered. But the people were just regular normal people. And they were very, very polite to us.

c. *Free-associate it:* Some of the people there reminded me of some of my relatives! John, the kitchen manager, said most of the people were just temporarily "down on their luck" and that reminded me of my aunt and uncle who came to stay with us for a while when I was in high school after my uncle lost his job.

d. *Analyze it:* I feel like I got a lot out of my experience. I think I had some wrong ideas about "the homeless" and working there made me think more about them as real people, not just a faceless group.

e. *Argue for or against it:* I would encourage others to volunteer there. The work isn't hard and it isn't scary. It makes you appreciate what you've got and also makes you think about what you or your family might do if things went wrong for a while. It also makes you feel good to do something for people you don't even know.

f. *Apply it:* I feel like I am more knowledgeable when I hear people talk about the poor or the homeless in this town, especially those people who criticize those who use the shelter.

After you've written your responses, see if any one or more of them give you an idea for a paper. The student who wrote the preceding responses decided she wanted to write an article for her campus newspaper encouraging people to volunteer at the shelter not only to provide much-needed help but also to challenge their own preconceived notions about the homeless in her college town. Cubing helped her realize she had something valuable to say about her experience and gave her a purpose for writing.

7. Interviewing

Another way to find a direction for your paper is through interviewing. Ask a classmate or friend to discuss your subject with you. Let your thoughts range over your subject as your friend asks you questions that arise naturally in the conversation. Or your friend might try asking what are called "reporter's questions" as she or he "interviews" you on your subject:

Who?	When?
What?	Why?
Where?	How?

Listen to what you have to say about your subject. What were you most interested in talking about? What did your friend want to know? Why? By talking about your subject, you may find that you have talked your way into an interesting focus for your paper. If, after the interview, you are still stumped, question your friend: if he or she had to publish an essay based on the information from your interview, what would that essay focus on? Why?

8. The Cross-Examination

If a classmate isn't available for an interview, try interviewing, or cross-examining, yourself. Ask yourself questions about your general subject, just as a lawyer might if you were on the witness stand. Consider using the five categories described on the next page, which are adapted from those suggested by Aristotle, centuries ago, to the orators of his day. Ask yourself as many questions in each category as you can think of, and then go on to the next category. Jot down brief notes to yourself as you answer.

Here are the five categories, plus six sample questions for each to illustrate the possibilities:

1. Definition
    a. How does the dictionary or encyclopedia define or explain this subject?
    b. How do most people define or explain it?
    c. How do I define or explain it?
    d. What do its parts look like?
    e. What is its history or origin?
    f. What are some examples of it?
2. Comparison and Contrast
    a. What is it similar to?
    b. What does it differ from?
    c. What does it parallel?
    d. What is it opposite to?
    e. What is it better than?
    f. What is it worse than?
3. Relationship
    a. What causes it?
    b. What are the effects of it?
    c. What larger group or category is it a part of?
    d. What larger group or category is it in opposition to?
    e. What are its values or goals?
    f. What contradictions does it contain?
4. Circumstance
    a. Is it possible?
    b. Is it impossible?
    c. When has it happened before?
    d. What might prevent it from happening?
    e. Why might it happen again?
    f. Who has been or might be associated with it?
5. Testimony
    a. What do people say about it?
    b. What has been written about it?
    c. What authorities exist on the subject?
    d. Are there any relevant statistics?
    e. What research has been done?
    f. Have I had any direct experience with it?

Some of the questions suggested here, or ones you think of, may not be relevant to or useful for your subject. But some may lead you to ideas you wish to explore in more depth, either in a discovery draft or by using another prewriting technique described in this chapter, such as looping or mapping.

9. Sketching

Sometimes when you have found or been assigned a general subject, the words to explain or describe it just won't come. Although listing or freewriting or one of the other methods suggested here works well for some people, other writers find these techniques intimidating or unproductive. Some of these writers are visual learners—that is, they respond better to pictorial representations of material than they do to written descriptions or explanations. If, on occasion, you are stuck for words, try drawing or sketching or even cartooning the pictures in your mind.

You may be surprised at the details that you remember once you start sketching. For example, you might have been asked to write about a favorite place or a special person in your life or to compare or contrast two places you have lived in or visited. See how many details you can conjure up by drawing the scenes or the people; then look at your details to see if some dominant impression or common theme has emerged. Your Aunt Sophie's insistence on wearing two pounds of costume jewelry might become the focus of a paragraph on her sparkling personality, or the many details you recalled about your grandfather's barn might lead you to a paper on the hardships of farm life. For some writers, a picture can be worth a thousand words—especially if that picture helps them begin putting those words on paper.

10. Dramatizing the Subject

Some writers find it helpful to visualize their subject as if it were a drama or play unfolding in their minds. Kenneth Burke, a thoughtful writer himself, suggests that writers might think about human action in dramatists' terms and then see what sorts of new insights arise as the "drama" unfolds. Burke's dramatists' terms might be adapted for our use and pictured this way:

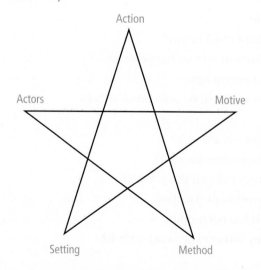

Action

Actors   Motive

Setting   Method

Just as you did in the cubing exercise, try mentally rolling your subject around the star and explore the possibilities that emerge. For example, suppose you want to write about your recent decision to return to college after a long period of working, but you don't know what you want to say about your decision. Start thinking about this decision as a drama and jot down brief answers to such questions as these:

Action: What happened?
What were the results?
What is going to happen?

Actors: Who was involved in the action?
Who was affected by the action?
Who caused the action?
Who was for it and who was opposed?

Motive: What were the reasons behind the action?
What forces motivated the actors to perform as they did?

Method: How did the action occur?
By what means did the actors accomplish the action?

Setting: What was the time and place of the action?
What did the place look like?
What positive or negative feelings are associated with this time or place?

These are only a few of the dozens of questions you might ask yourself about your "drama." (If it helps, think of your "drama" as a murder mystery and answer the questions the police detective might ask: what happened here? to whom? who did it? why? with what? when? where? and so on.)

You may find that you have a great deal to write about the combination of actor and motive but very little to say in response to the questions on setting or method. That's fine—simply use the "dramatists' approach" to help you find a specific topic or idea you want to write about.

> ✓ If at any point in this stage of the writing process you are experiencing *Writer's Block*, you might turn to the suggestions for overcoming this common affliction that appear on pages 112–115 in Chapter 5. You might also find it helpful to read the section *Keeping a Journal*, pages 26–28, because writing in a relaxed mood on a regular basis may be the best long-term cure for your writing anxiety.

■ After You've Found Your Focus

Once you think you've found the focus of your essay, you may be ready to compose a *working thesis statement*, an important part of your essay discussed in great detail in the next chapter. If you've used one of the prewriting exercises outlined in this chapter, by all means hang onto it. The details and observations you generated as you focused your topic may be useful to you as you begin to organize and develop your body paragraphs.

■ **PRACTICING WHAT YOU'VE LEARNED**

A. Some of the subjects listed below are too broad for a 500-to-800-word essay. Identify those topics that might be treated in short papers and those that still need to be narrowed.

1. The role of the modern university

2. My first (and last) experience with roller blading

3. The characters of William Shakespeare

4. Solar energy

5. Collecting baseball cards

6. Gun-control laws

7. Down with throwaway bottles

8. Computers

9. The best teacher I've ever had

10. Selecting the right bicycle

B. Select two of the large subjects that follow and, through looping or listing details or another prewriting technique, find focused topics that would be appropriate for essays of three to five pages.

1. Music

2. Cars

3. Education

4. Jobs

5. Television commercials

6. Politics

7. Animals

8. Childhood

9. Pollution

10. Athletics

■ Discovering Your Audience

Once you have a focused topic and perhaps some ideas about developing your essay, you need to stop a moment to consider your *audience*. Before you can decide what information needs to go into your essay and what should be omitted, you must know who will be reading your paper and why. Knowing your audience will also help you determine what *voice* you should use to achieve the proper tone in your essay.

Suppose, for example, you are attending a college organized on the quarter system, and you decide to write an essay arguing for a switch to the semester system. If your audience is composed of classmates, your essay will probably focus on the advantages to the student body, such as better opportunities for in-depth study in one's major, the ease of making better grades, and the benefits of longer midwinter and summer vacations. However, if you are addressing the Board of Regents, you might emphasize the power of the semester system to attract more students, cut registration costs, and use professors more efficiently. If your audience is composed of townspeople who know little about either system, you will have to devote more time to explaining the logistics of each one and then discuss the semester plan's advantages to the local merchants, realtors, restaurateurs, and so on. *In other words, such factors as the age, education, profession, and interests of your audience can make a difference in determining which points of your argument to stress or omit, which ideas need additional explanation, and what kind of language to adopt.*

■ How to Identify Your Readers

To help you analyze your audience before you begin writing your working thesis statement and rough drafts, here are some steps you may wish to follow:

1. First, see if your writing assignment specifies a particular audience (editors of a journal in your field or the Better Business Bureau of your town, for example) or a general audience of your peers (your classmates or readers of the local newspaper, for instance). Even if your assignment does not mention an intended audience, try to imagine one anyway. Imagining specific readers will help you stick to your goal of communicating clearly, in engaging detail.

2. If a specific audience is designated, ask yourself some questions about their motivation or *reasons for reading* your essay.

- What do these readers want to learn?
- What do they hope to gain?
- Do they need your information to make a decision? Formulate a new plan? Design a new project?
- What action do you want them to take?

The answers to such questions will help you find both your essay's purpose and its content. If, for example, you're trying to persuade an employer to hire you for a particular job, you certainly would write your application in a way that stresses the skills and training the company is searching for. You may have a fine hobby or a wonderful family, but if your prospective employer-reader doesn't need to hear about that particular part of your life, toss it out of this piece of writing.

3. Next, try to discover what *knowledge* your audience has of your subject.

- What, if anything, can you assume that your readers already know about your topic?
- What background information might they need to know to understand a current situation clearly?
- What facts, explanations, or examples will best present your ideas? How detailed should you be?
- What terms need to be defined? Equipment explained?

Questions like these should guide you as you collect and discard information for your paper. An essay written to your colleagues in electrical engineering, for instance, need not explain commonly used technical instruments; to do so might even insult your readers. But the same report read by your composition classmates would probably need more detailed explanation for you to make yourself understood. Always put yourself in your readers' place and then ask: what else do they need to know to understand this point completely?

4. Once you have decided what information is necessary for your audience, dig a little deeper into your readers' identities. Pose some questions about their *attitudes* and emotional states.

- Are your readers already biased for or against your ideas in some way?
- Do they have positive or negative associations with your subject?
- Are they fearful or anxious, reluctant or bored?
- Do they have radically different expectations or interests?

It helps enormously to know the emotional attitudes of your readers toward your subject. Let's suppose you were arguing for the admission of a young child with AIDS into a local school system, and your audience was the parent-teacher organization. Some of your readers might be frightened or even hostile; knowing this, you would wisely begin your argument with a disarming array of information showing that no cases of AIDS have developed from the casual contact of schoolchildren. In other words, the more you know about your audience's attitudes before you begin writing, the more convincing your prose, because you will make the best choices about both content and organization.

5. Last, think of any *special qualities* that might set your audience apart from any other.

- Are they older or younger than your peers?
- Do they share similar educational experiences or training?
- Are they from a particular part of the world or country that might affect their perspective? Urban or rural?
- Are they in positions of authority?

Knowing special facts about your audience makes a difference, often in your choice of words and tone. You wouldn't, after all, use the same level of vocabulary addressing a group of fifth-graders as you would writing to the children's teacher or principal. Similarly, your tone and word choice probably wouldn't be as formal in a letter to a friend as in a letter to the telephone company protesting your most recent bill.

Without question, analyzing your specific audience is an important step to take before you begin to shape your rough drafts. And before you move on to writing a working thesis, here are a few tips to keep in mind about *all* audiences, no matter who your readers are or what their reasons for reading your writing.

1. Readers don't like to be bored. Grab your readers' attention and fight to keep it. Remember the last dull movie you squirmed—or slept—through? How much you resented wasting not only your money but your valuable time as well? How you turned it off mentally and drifted away to someplace more exciting? As you write and revise your drafts, keep imagining readers who are as intelligent—and busy—as you are. Put yourself in their place: would you find this piece of writing stimulating enough to keep reading?

2. Readers hate confusion and disorder. Can you recall a time when you tried to find your way to a party, only to discover that a friend's directions were so muddled you wound up hours later, out of gas, cursing in a cornfield? Or the afternoon you spent trying to follow a friend's notes for setting up a chemistry experiment, with explanations that twisted and turned as often as a wandering stray cat? Try to relive such moments of intense frustration as you struggle to make *your* writing clear and direct.

3. Readers want to think and learn (whether they realize it or not). Every time you write, you strike a bargain of sorts with your readers: in return for their time and attention, you promise to inform and interest them, to tell them something new or show them something familiar in a different light. You may enlighten them or amuse them or even try to frighten them—but they must feel, in the end, that they've gotten a fair trade. As you plan, write, and revise, ask yourself, "What are my readers learning?" If the honest answer is "nothing important," you may be writing only for yourself. (If you yourself are bored rereading your drafts, you're probably not writing for anybody at all.)

4. Readers want to see what you see, feel what you feel. Writing that is vague keeps your readers from fully sharing the information or experience you are trying to communicate. Clear, precise language—full of concrete details and specific examples— lets your readers know that you understand your subject and that you want them to understand it, too. Even a potentially dull topic such as tuning up a car can become engaging to a reader if the right details are provided in the right places: your terror as blue sparks leap under your nose when the wrong wire is touched, the depressing sight of the screwdriver squirming from your greasy fingers and disappearing into the oil pan, the sudden shooting pain when the wrench slips and turns your knuckles to raw hamburger. Get your readers involved and interested—and they'll listen to what you have to say. (Details also persuade your reader that you're an authority on your subject; after all, no reader likes to waste time listening to someone whose tentative, vague prose style announces "I only sort-of know what I'm talking about here.")

5. Readers are turned off by writers with pretentious, phony voices. Too often, inexperienced writers feel they must sound especially scholarly, scientific, or sophisticated for their essays to be convincing. In fact, the contrary is true. When you assume a voice that is not yours, when you pretend to be someone you're not, you don't sound believable at all—you sound phony. Your readers want to hear what *you* have to say, and the best way to communicate with them is in a natural voice. You may also believe that to write a good essay it is necessary to use a host of unfamiliar, unpronounceable, polysyllabic words gleaned from the pages of your thesaurus. Again, the opposite is true. Our best writers agree with Mark Twain, who once said, "Never use a twenty-five-cent word when a ten-cent word will do." In other words, avoid pretension in your writing just as you do in everyday conversation. Select simple, direct words you know and use frequently; keep your voice natural, sincere, and reasonable. (For additional help choosing the appropriate words and the level of your diction, see Chapter 7.)

> ✓ **Don't Ever Forget Your Readers!**
> Thinking about them as you write will help you choose your ideas, organize your information effectively, and select the best words.

■ PRACTICING WHAT YOU'VE LEARNED

A. Practice identifying intended audiences by analyzing these advertisements reprinted in this text:

"Diamond Right-Hand Ring," page 220

"Gas Heat Makes Me Nervous," page 304

"Some Arguments for Nuclear Energy Are Smaller Than Others," page 306

"Pierce Brosnan's Choice," page 309

"PETA Anti-Fur," page 310

In each case, first determine the purpose of the ad and then describe the ad's target audience, explaining your reasons for your response. You may find it helpful to consider some of the following questions:

1. What age group does the ad target? Does it appeal primarily to males, females, or both? Is the intended audience of a particular social or economic class?

2. What concerns or strong interests might this audience have?

3. What kinds of arguments are used in the ad to persuade its intended audience?

4. What specific words or phrases are chosen to appeal to this particular audience?

B. Select an essay or feature story from a magazine or journal of your choosing and identify the intended audience. Explain how you arrived at this conclusion by showing ways the writer effectively addresses his or her audience.

■ **ASSIGNMENT**

The article that follows appeared in newspapers across the country some time ago. Read about the diet called "Breatharianism" and then write one or more of the assignments that follow the article.

The Ultimate in Diet Cults: Don't Eat Anything at All

1   CORTE MADERA, CALIF.—Among those seeking enlightenment through diet cults, Wiley Brooks seemed to have the ultimate answer—not eating at all. He called himself a "Breatharian" and claimed to live on air, supplemented only by occasional fluids taken to counteract the toxins of urban environments.

2   "Food is more addictive than heroin," the tall, gaunt man told hundreds of people who paid $500 each to attend five-day "intensives," at which he would stand before them in a camel velour sweatsuit and talk for hours without moving, his fingers meditatively touching at their tips.

3   Brooks, 46, became a celebrity on the New Age touring circuit. ABC-TV featured him in October, 1980, as a weight lifter; he allegedly hoisted 1,100 pounds, about 10 times his own weight. He has also been interviewed on radio and in newspapers.

4   Those who went to his sessions during the past six months on the West Coast and in Hawaii were not just food faddists, but also physicians and other professionals who—though not necessarily ready to believe—thought this man could be onto something important. Some were convinced enough by what they saw to begin limiting their own diets, taking the first steps toward Breatharianism.

5   In his intensives, Brooks did not recommend that people stop eating altogether. Rather, he suggested they "clean their blood" by starting with the "yellow diet"—24 food items including grapefruit, papaya, corn products, eggs, chicken, fish, goat's milk, millet, salsa piquante (Mexican hot sauce) and certain flavors of the Häagen Dazs brand ice cream, including "rum raisin." These foods, he said, have a less toxic effect because, among other things, "their vibrational quality is yellow."

6   Last week, however, aspirants toward Breatharianism were shocked by reports that Brooks had been eating—and what's more, eating things that to health food purists are the worst kind of junk.

7   Word spread that during an intensive in Vancouver, Brooks was seen emerging from a 7-Eleven store with a bag of groceries. The next morning there were allegedly room service trays outside his hotel room, while inside, the trash basket held empty containers of chicken pot pie, chili and biscuits.

8   Kendra Wagner, regional Breatharian coordinator, said she herself had seen Brooks drinking a Coke. "When I asked him about it he said, 'That's how dirty the air is here,'" she explained. "We (the coordinators) sat down with Wiley after the training and said, 'We want you to tell us the truth.' He denied everything. We felt tricked and deceived."

9   As the rumors grew, some Breatharians confronted their leader at a lecture in San Francisco. Brooks denied the story and said that the true message of Breatharianism did not depend on whether he ate or not, anyway.

10   The message in his promotional material reads that "modern man is the degenerate descendant of the Breatharian," and that "living on air alone leads to perfect health and perfect happiness." Though followers had the impression Brooks has not eaten for 18 years, his leaflets merely declare that "he does not eat, and seldom drinks any fluid. He sleeps less than seven hours a week and is healthier, more energetic and happier than he ever dreamed possible."

11   In a telephone interview, Brooks acknowledged that this assertion is not quite correct. "I'm sure I've taken some fruit, like an apple or an orange, but it's better in public to keep it simple." He again staunchly denied the 7-Eleven story.

12   Among those who have been on the yellow diet for months is Jime Collison, 24, who earlier tried "fruitarianism," fasting and other special regimens, and moved from Texas to the San Francisco Bay area just to be around the Breatharian movement. "Now I'm a basket case," he said. "My world revolved around Wiley's philosophy." He had thought Wiley "made the jump to where all of us health food fanatics were going," Collison said.

13   Other Brooks disciples, though disappointed, feel they nevertheless benefited from their experience. Said a physician who has been on the yellow diet for four months: "I feel very good. I still don't know what the truth is, but I do know that Wiley is a good salesman. So I'll be patient, keep an open mind and continue to observe."

14   "Breatharianism is the understanding of what the body really needs, not whether Wiley eats or doesn't," said James Wahler, 35, who teaches a self-development technique called "rebirthing," in Marin County. "I'm realizing that the less I eat the better I feel." He also suggested that Brooks may have lied for people's own good, to get them to listen.

15   "Everyone has benefited from what I'm saying," Brooks said. "There will be a food shortage and a lot of unhappy people when they realize that I was trying to save their lives."

Each of the assignments that follow is directed to a different audience, none of whom know much about Breatharianism. What information does each audience need to know? What kinds of details will be the most persuasive? What sort of organization will work best for each purpose and audience?

1. Write a brief radio advertisement for the five-day intensives. What appeals might persuade people to pay $500 each to attend a seminar to learn to eat air?

2. Assume you are a regional Breatharian coordinator. Write a letter to your city council petitioning for a parade permit that will allow members of your organization to parade down your main street in support of this diet and its lifestyle. What do council members need to know before they vote on such a permit?

3. You are a former Breatharian who is now unhappy with the diet and its unfulfilled promises. Write a report for the vice squad calling for an investigation into the organization. Convince the investigators that the organization is defrauding local citizens and should be stopped.

After writing these assignments, you might exchange them with those written by some of your classmates. Which ads, petitions, and reports are the most persuasive and why? ■

Homework, 1946, by Milton Avery

■ Keeping a Journal (Talking to Yourself Does Help)

Many professional writers carry small notebooks with them so they can jot down ideas and impressions for future use. Other people have kept daily logs or diaries for years to record their thoughts for their own enjoyment. In your composition class, you may find it useful to keep a journal that will help you with your writing process, especially in the early stages of prewriting. Journals can also help you to prepare for class discussions and to remember important course material.

You may have kept a journal in another class. There, it may have been called a "daybook" or "learning log" or some other name. Although the journal has a variety of uses, it frequently is assigned to encourage you to record your responses to reading material or class discussions as well as your own thoughts and questions. Often, the journal is kept in a notebook you can carry with you (spiral is fine, although a prong or ring notebook allows you to add or remove pages when you wish); some writers prefer to collect their thoughts in designated computer files or web logs. Even if a journal is not assigned in your composition class, it is still a useful tool.

Writers who have found journal writing effective advise trying to write a minimum of three entries a week, with each entry at least a half page. To keep a carry-around notebook organized, start each entry on a new page and date each entry you write. You might also leave the backs of your notebook pages blank so that you can return and respond to an entry at a later date if you wish.

Uses of the Journal

Here are some suggested uses for your journal as you move through the writing process. You may want to experiment with a number of these suggestions to see which are the most productive for you.

1. **Use the journal, especially in the first weeks of class, to confront your fears of writing, to conquer the blank page.** Write anything you want to—thoughts, observations, notes to yourself, letters home, anything at all. Best your enemy by writing down that witty retort you thought of later and wished you had said. Write about your ideal job, vacation, car, or home. Write a self-portrait or make a list of all the subjects on which you are (or would like to become) an "authority." The more you write, the easier writing becomes—or at least, the easier it is to begin writing because, like a sword swallower, you know you have accomplished the act before and lived to tell about it.

2. **Improve your powers of observation.** Record interesting snippets of conversations you overhear or catalog noises you hear in a ten-minute period in a crowded place, such as your student center, a bookstore, or a mall. Eat something with multiple layers (a piece of fruit such as an orange) and list all the tastes, textures, and smells you discover. Look around your room and write down a list of everything that is yellow. By becoming sensitive to the sights, sounds, smells, and textures around you, you may find that your powers of description and explanation will expand, enabling you to help your reader "see" what you're talking about in your next essay.

3. Save your own brilliant ideas. Jot down those bright ideas that might turn into great essays. Or save those thoughts you have now for the essay you know is coming later in the semester so you won't forget them. Expand or elaborate on any ideas you have; you might be able to convert your early thoughts into a paragraph when it's time to start drafting.

4. Save other people's brilliant ideas. Record interesting quotations, facts, and figures from other writers and thinkers. You may find some of this information useful in one of your later essays. It's also helpful to look at the ways other writers make their words emphatic, moving, and arresting so you can try some of their techniques in your own prose. (Important: Don't forget to note the source of any material you record, so if you do quote any of it in a paper later, you will be able to document it properly.)

5. Be creative. Write a poem or song or story or joke. Parody the style of someone you've heard or read. Become an inanimate object and complain to the humans around you (for example, what would a soft-drink machine like to say to those folks constantly beating on its stomach?). Become a little green creature from Mars and convince a human to accompany you back to your planet as a specimen of Earthlings (or be the invited guest and explain to the creature why you are definitely not the person to go). The possibilities are endless, so go wild.

6. Prepare for class. If you've been given a reading assignment (an essay or article or pages from a text, for instance), try a split-page entry. Draw a line down the middle of a page in your journal, and on the left side of the page write a summary of what you've read or perhaps list the main points. Then on the right side of the same page, write your responses to the material. Your responses might be your personal reaction to the content (what struck you hardest? why?) or your agreement or disagreement with a particular point or two. Or the material might call up some long-forgotten idea or memory. By thinking about your class material both analytically and personally, you almost certainly will remember it for class discussion. You might also find that a good idea for an essay will arise as you think about the reading assignments in different ways.

7. Record responses to class discussions. A journal is a good place to jot down your reactions to what your teacher and your peers are saying in class. You can ask yourself questions ("What did Megan mean when she said . . .") or note any confusion ("I got mixed up when . . .") or record your own reactions ("I disagreed with Jamal when he argued that . . ."). Again, some of your reactions might become the basis of a good essay.

8. Focus on a problem. You can restate the problem or explore the problem or solve the problem. Writing about a problem often encourages the mind to flow over the information in ways that allow discoveries to happen. Sometimes, too, we don't know exactly what the problem is or how we feel about it until we write about it. Remember the encouraging words of the philosopher Voltaire: "No problem can withstand the assault of thinking." Writing *is* thinking.

9. Practice audience awareness. Write letters to different companies, praising or panning their product; then write advertising copy for each product. Become the third critic on a popular movie-review program and show the other two commentators why your review of your favorite movie is superior to theirs. Thinking about a specific audience when you write will help you plan the content, organization, and tone of each writing assignment.

10. Describe your own writing process. It's helpful sometimes to record how you go about writing your essays. How do you get started? How much time do you spend getting started? Do you write an "idea" draft or work from an outline? How do you revise? Do you write multiple drafts? These and many other questions may give you a clue to any problems you might have as you write your next essay. If, for example, you see that you're having trouble again and again with conclusions, you can turn to Chapter 4 for some extra help. Sometimes it's hard to see that there's a pattern in our writing process until we've described it several times.

11. Write a progress report. List all the skills you've mastered as the course progresses. You'll be surprised at how much you have learned. Read the list over if you're ever feeling frustrated or discouraged, and take pride in your growth.

12. Become sensitive to language. Keep a record of jokes and puns that play on words. Record people's weird-but-funny uses of language (overheard at the dorm cafeteria: "She was so skinny she was emancipated" and "I'm tired of being the escape goat"). Rewrite some of today's bureaucratic jargon or retread a cliché. Come up with new images of your own. Playing with language in fun or even silly ways can make writing tasks seem less threatening. (A newspaper recently came up with this language game: Change, add, or subtract one letter in a word and provide a new definition. Example: intoxication/intaxication—the giddy feeling of getting a tax refund; graffiti/giraffiti—spray paint that appears on tall buildings; sarcasm/sarchasm—the gulf between the witty speaker and the listener who doesn't get it.)

13. Write your own textbook. Make notes on material that is important for you to remember. For instance, make your own grammar or punctuation handbook with only those rules you find yourself referring to often. Or keep a list of spelling rules that govern the words you misspell frequently. Writing out the rules in your own words and having a convenient place to refer to them may help you teach yourself quicker than studying any textbook (including this one).

These suggestions are some of the many uses you may find for your journal once you start writing in one on a regular basis. Obviously, not all the suggestions here will be appropriate for you, but some might be, so you might consider using a set of divider tabs to separate the different functions of your journal (one section for class responses, one section for your own thoughts, one for your own handbook, and so on).

You may find, as some students have, that the journal is especially useful during the first weeks of your writing course, when putting pen to paper is often hardest. Many students, however, continue to use the journal throughout the entire course, and others adapt their journals to record their thoughts and responses to their other college courses and experiences. Whether you continue using a journal beyond this course is up to you, but consider trying the journal for at least six weeks. You may find that it will improve your writing skills more than anything else you have tried before.

★ CHAPTER 1 SUMMARY

Here is a brief summary of what you should know about the prewriting stage of your writing process:

1. Before you begin writing anything, remember that you have valuable ideas to tell your readers.

2. It's not enough that these valuable ideas are clear to you, the writer. Your single most important goal is to communicate those ideas clearly to your readers, who cannot know what's in your mind until you tell them.

3. Whenever possible, select a subject to write on that is of great interest to you, and always give yourself more time than you think you'll need to work on your essay.

4. Try a variety of prewriting techniques to help you find your essay's purpose and a narrowed, specific focus.

5. Review your audience's knowledge of and attitudes toward your topic before you begin your first draft; ask yourself questions such as "Who needs to know about this topic, and why?"

6. Consider keeping a journal to help you explore good ideas and possible topics for writing assignments in your composition class.

Chapter 2

The Thesis Statement

The famous American author Thomas Wolfe had a simple formula for beginning his writing: "Just put a sheet of paper in the typewriter and start bleeding." For some writers, the "bleeding" method works well. You may find that, indeed, you are one of those writers who must begin by freewriting or by writing an entire "discovery draft"* to find your purpose and focus—you must write yourself into your topic, so to speak. Other writers are more structured; they may prefer prewriting in lists, outlines, or cubes. Sometimes writers begin certain projects by composing one way, whereas other kinds of writing tasks profit from another method. There is no right or wrong way to find a topic or to begin writing; simply try to find the methods that work best for you.

Let's assume at this point that you have identified a topic you wish to write about— perhaps you found it by working through one of the prewriting activities mentioned in Chapter 1 or by writing in your journal. Perhaps you had an important idea you have been wanting to write about for some time, or perhaps the assignment in your class suggested the topic to you. Suppose that through one of these avenues you have focused on a topic and you have given some thought to a possible audience for your paper. You may now find it helpful to formulate a *working thesis*.

---

* If you do begin with a discovery draft, you may wish to turn at this point to the manuscript suggestions on pages 94–95 in Chapter 5.

■ What Is a Thesis? What Does a "Working Thesis" Do?

The thesis statement declares the main point or controlling idea of your entire essay. Frequently located near the beginning of a short essay, the thesis answers these questions: "What is the subject of this essay?" "What is the writer's opinion on this subject?" "What is the writer's purpose in this essay?" (to explain something? to argue a position? to move people to action? to entertain?).

Consider a "working thesis" a statement of your main point in its trial or rough-draft form. Allow it to "work" for you as you move from prewriting through drafts and revision. Your working thesis may begin as a very simple sentence. For example, one of the freewriting exercises on nature in Chapter 1 (page 8) might lead to a working thesis such as "Our college needs an on-campus recycling center." Such a working thesis states an opinion about the subject (the need for a center) and suggests what the essay will do (give arguments for building such a center). Similarly, the prewriting list on running (page 7) might lead to a working thesis such as "Before beginning a successful program, novice runners must learn a series of warm-up and cool-down exercises." This statement not only tells the writer's opinion and purpose (the value of the exercises) but also indicates an audience (novice runners).

A working thesis statement can be your most valuable organizational tool. Once you have thought about your essay's main point and purpose, you can begin to draft your paper to accomplish your goals. *Everything in your essay should support your thesis.* Consequently, if you write your working thesis statement at the top of your first draft and refer to it often, your chances of drifting away from your purpose should be reduced.

■ Can a "Working Thesis" Change?

It's important for you to know at this point that there may be a difference between the working thesis that appears in your rough drafts and your final thesis. As you begin drafting, you may have one main idea in mind that surfaced from your prewriting activities. But as you write, you may discover that what you really want to write about is different. Perhaps you discover that one particular part of your essay is really what you want to concentrate on (instead of covering three or four problems you have with your current job, for instance, you decide you want to explore in depth only the difficulties with your boss), or perhaps in the course of writing you find another approach to your subject more satisfying or persuasive (explaining how employees may avoid problems with a particular kind of difficult boss instead of describing various kinds of difficult bosses in your field).

Changing directions is not uncommon: *writing is an act of discovery.* Frequently we don't know exactly what we think or what we want to say until we write it. A working thesis appears in your early drafts to help you focus and organize your essay; don't feel it's carved in stone.

A warning comes with this advice, however. If you do write yourself into another essay—that is, if you discover as you write that you are finding a better topic or main point to make—consider this piece of writing a "discovery draft," extended prewriting that has helped you find your real focus. Occasionally, your direction changes so slightly that you can rework or expand your thesis to accommodate your new ideas. But more frequently you may find that it's necessary to begin another draft with your newly discovered working thesis as the controlling idea. When this is the case, don't be discouraged—this kind of "reseeing" or revision of your topic is a common practice among experienced writers (for more advice on revising as rethinking, see Chapter 5). Don't be tempted at this point to leave your original thesis in an essay that has clearly changed its point, purpose, or approach—in other words, don't try to pass off an old head on the body of a new statue! Remember that ultimately you want your thesis to guide your readers rather than confuse them by promising an essay they can't find as they read on.

■ Guidelines for Writing a Good Thesis

To help you draft your thesis statement, here is some advice:

A good thesis states the writer's clearly defined opinion on some subject. You must tell your reader what you think. Don't dodge the issue; present your opinion specifically and precisely. For example, if you were asked to write a thesis statement expressing your position on the national law that designates twenty-one as the legal minimum age to purchase or consume alcohol, the first three theses listed below would be confusing:

Poor	Many people have different opinions on whether people under twenty-one should be permitted to drink alcohol, and I agree with some of them. [The writer's opinion on the issue is not clear to the reader.]
Poor	The question of whether we need a national law governing the minimum age to drink alcohol is a controversial issue in many states. [This statement might introduce the thesis, but the writer has still avoided stating a clear opinion on the issue.]
Poor	I want to give my opinion on the national law that sets twenty-one as the legal age to drink alcohol and the reasons I feel this way. [What is the writer's opinion? The reader still doesn't know.]
Better	To reduce the number of highway fatalities, our country needs to enforce the national law that designates twenty-one as the legal minimum age to purchase and consume alcohol. [The writer clearly states an opinion that will be supported in the essay.]
Better	The legal minimum age for purchasing alcohol should be eighteen rather than twenty-one. [Again, the writer has asserted a clear position on the issue that will be argued in the essay.]

If you want to write about a personal experience but are finding it difficult to find your clearly defined thesis idea, try asking yourself questions about the topic's significance or value. (Examples: Why is this topic important to me? What was so valuable about my year on newspaper staff? What was the most significant lesson I learned? What was an unexpected result of this experience?). Often the answer to one of your questions will show you the way to a working thesis. (Example: Writing for the school newspaper teaches time-management skills that are valuable both in and out of class).

A good thesis asserts one main idea. Many essays drift into confusion because the writer is trying to explain or argue two different, large issues in one essay. You can't effectively ride two horses at once; pick one main idea and explain or argue it in convincing detail.

Poor	The proposed no-smoking ordinance in our town will violate a number of our citizens' civil rights, and no one has proved that secondhand smoke is dangerous anyway. [This thesis contains two main assertions—the ordinance's violation of rights and second-hand smoke's lack of danger—that require two different kinds of supporting evidence.]
Better	The proposed no-smoking ordinance in our town will violate our civil rights. [This essay will show the various ways the ordinance will infringe on personal liberties.]
Better	The most recent U.S. Health Department studies claiming that secondhand smoke is dangerous to nonsmokers are based on faulty research. [This essay will also focus on one issue: the validity of the studies on secondhand smoke danger.]
Poor	High school athletes shouldn't have to maintain a "B" or better grade-point average in all subjects to participate in school sports, and the value of sports for some students is often overlooked. [Again, this thesis moves in two different directions.]
Better	High school athletes shouldn't have to maintain a "B" or better grade-point average in all subjects to participate in school sports. [This essay will focus on one issue: reasons why a particular average shouldn't be required.]
Better	For some students, participation in sports may be more valuable than achieving a "B" grade-point average in all subjects. [This essay will argue that the benefits of sports sometimes outweigh those of elective classes.]

Incidentally, at this point you may recall from your high school days a rule about always expressing your thesis in one sentence. Writing teachers often insist on this rule to help you avoid the double-assertion problem just illustrated. Although not all essays have one-sentence theses, many do, and it's a good habit to strive for in this early stage of your writing.

A good thesis has something worthwhile to say. Although it's true that almost any subject can be made interesting with the right treatment, some subjects are more predictable and therefore more boring than others. Before you write your thesis, think hard about your subject: does your position lend itself to stale or overly obvious ideas? For example, most readers would find the following theses tiresome unless the writers had some original method of developing their essays:

Poor	Dogs have always been man's best friends. [This essay might be full of ho-hum clichés about dogs' faithfulness to their owners.]
Poor	Friendship is a wonderful thing. [Again, watch out for tired truisms that restate the obvious.]
Poor	The food in my dorm is horrible. [Although this essay might be enlivened by some vividly repulsive imagery, the subject itself is ancient.]

Frequently in composition classes you will be asked to write about yourself; after all, you are the world's authority on that subject, and you have many significant interests to talk about whose subject matter will naturally intrigue your readers. However, some topics you might consider writing about may not necessarily appeal to other readers because the material is simply too personal or restricted to be of general interest. In these cases, it often helps to *universalize* the essay's thesis so your readers can also identify with or learn something about the general subject, while learning something about you at the same time:

Poor	The four children in my family have completely different personalities. [This statement may be true, but would anyone other than the children's parents really be fascinated by this topic?]
Better	Birth order can influence children's personalities in startling ways. [The writer is wiser to offer this controversial statement, which is of more interest to readers than the preceding one because many readers have brothers and sisters of their own. The writer can then illustrate her claims with examples from her own family, and from other families, if she wishes.]
Poor	I don't like to take courses that are held in big lecture classes at this school. [Why should your reader care one way or another about your class preference?]
Better	Large lecture classes provide a poor environment for the student who learns best through interaction with both teachers and peers. [This thesis will allow the writer to present personal examples that the reader may identify with or challenge, without writing an essay that is exclusively personal.]

In other words, try to select a subject that will interest, amuse, challenge, persuade, or enlighten your readers. If your subject itself is commonplace, find a unique approach or an unusual, perhaps even controversial, point of view. If your subject is personal, ask yourself if the topic alone will be sufficiently interesting to readers; if not, think about universalizing the thesis to include your audience. Remember that a good thesis should encourage readers to read on with enthusiasm rather than invite groans of "not this again" or shrugs of "so what."

A good thesis is limited to fit the assignment. Your thesis should show that you've narrowed your subject matter to an appropriate size for your essay. Don't allow your thesis to promise more of a discussion than you can adequately deliver in a short essay. You want an in-depth treatment of your subject, not a superficial one. Certainly you may take on important issues in your essays; don't feel you must limit your topics to local or personal subjects. But one simply cannot refight the Vietnam War or effectively defend U.S. foreign policy in Central America in five to eight paragraphs. Focus your essay on an important part of a broader subject that interests you. (For a review of ways to narrow and focus your subject, see pages 6–17.)

Poor	Nuclear power should be banned as an energy source in this country. [Can the writer give the broad subject of nuclear power a fair treatment in three to five pages?]

Better	Because of its poor safety record during the past two years, the Collin County nuclear power plant should be closed. [This writer could probably argue this focused thesis in a short essay.]
Poor	The parking permit system at this college should be completely revised. [An essay calling for the revision of the parking permit system would involve discussion of permits for various kinds of students, faculty, administrators, staff, visitors, delivery personnel, disabled people, and so forth. Therefore, the thesis is probably too broad for a short essay.]
Better	Because of the complicated application process, the parking permit system at this college penalizes disabled students. [This thesis is focused on a particular problem and could be argued in a short paper.]
Poor	African-American artists have always contributed a lot to many kinds of American culture. ["African-American artists," "many kinds," "a lot," and "culture" cover more ground than can be dealt with in one short essay.]
Better	Scott Joplin was a major influence in the development of the uniquely American music called ragtime. [This thesis is more specifically defined.]

A good thesis is clearly stated in specific terms. More than anything, a vague thesis reflects lack of clarity in the writer's mind and almost inevitably leads to an essay that talks around the subject but never makes a coherent point. Try to avoid words whose meanings are imprecise and those that depend largely on personal interpretation, such as "interesting," "good," and "bad."

Poor	The women's movement is good for our country. [What group does the writer refer to? How is it good? For whom?]
Better	The Colorado Women's Party is working to ensure the benefits of equal pay for equal work for both males and females in our state. [This tells who will benefit and how—clearly defining the thesis.]
Poor	Registration is a big hassle. [No clear idea is communicated here. How much trouble is a "hassle"?]
Better	Registration's alphabetical fee-paying system is inefficient. [The issue is specified.]
Poor	Living in an apartment for the first time can teach you many things about taking care of yourself. ["Things" and "taking care of yourself" are both too vague. What specific ideas does the writer want to discuss? And who is the "you" the writer has in mind?]
Better	By living in an apartment, first-year students can learn valuable lessons in financial planning and time management. [The thesis is now clearly defined and directed.]

A good thesis is easily recognized as the main idea and is often located in the first or second paragraph. Many students are hesitant to spell out a thesis at the beginning of an essay. To quote one student, "I feel as if I'm giving everything away." Although you may feel uncomfortable "giving away" the main point so soon, the alternative of waiting until the last page to present your thesis can seriously weaken your essay.

Without an assertion of what you are trying to prove, your reader does not know how to assess the supporting details your essay presents. For example, if your roommate comes home one afternoon and points out that the roof on your apartment leaks, the rent is too high, and the closet space is too small, you may agree but you may also be confused. Does your roommate want you to call the owner or is this merely a gripe session? How should you respond? On the other hand, if your roommate first announces that he wants the two of you to look for a new place, you can put the discussion of the roof, rent, and closets into its proper context and react accordingly. Similarly, you write an essay to have a specific effect on your readers. You will have a better chance of producing this effect if readers easily and quickly understand what you are trying to do.

Granted, some essays whose position is unmistakably obvious from the outset can get by with a strongly *implied thesis*, and it's true that some essays, often those written by professional writers, are organized to build dramatically to a climax. But if you are an inexperienced writer, the best choice at this point still may be a direct statement of your main idea. It is, after all, your responsibility to make your purpose clear, with as little expense of time and energy on the readers' part as possible. Readers should not be forced to puzzle out your essay's main point—it's your job to tell them.

Remember: an essay is not a detective story, so don't keep your readers in suspense until the last minute. Until you feel comfortable with more sophisticated patterns of organization, plan to put your clearly worded thesis statement near the beginning of your essay.

■ Avoiding Common Errors in Thesis Statements

Here are five mistakes to avoid when forming your thesis statements:

1. Don't make your thesis merely an announcement of your subject matter or a description of your intentions. State an attitude toward the subject.

Poor	The subject of this essay is my experience with a pet boa constrictor. [This is an announcement of the subject, not a thesis.]
Poor	I'm going to discuss boa constrictors as pets. [This represents a statement of intention but not a thesis.]
Better	Boa constrictors do not make healthy indoor pets. [The writer states an opinion that will be explained and defended in the essay.]
Better	My pet boa constrictor, Sir Pent, was a much better bodyguard than my dog, Fang. [The writer states an opinion that will be explained and illustrated in the essay.]

2. Don't clutter your thesis with such expressions as "in my opinion," "I believe," and "in this essay I'll argue that . . . ." These unnecessary phrases weaken your thesis statement because they often make you sound timid or uncertain. This is your essay; therefore, the opinions expressed are obviously yours. Be forceful: speak directly, with conviction.

Poor	My opinion is that the federal government should devote more money to solar energy research.
Poor	My thesis states that the federal government should devote more money to solar energy research.
Better	The federal government should devote more money to solar energy research.
Poor	In this essay I will present lots of reasons why horse racing should not be legalized in Texas.
Better	Horse racing should not be legalized in Texas.

3. Don't be unreasonable. Making irrational or oversimplified claims will not persuade your reader that you have a thorough understanding of the issue. Don't insult any reader; avoid irresponsible charges, name-calling, and profanity.

Poor	Radical religious fanatics across the nation are trying to impose their right-wing views by censoring high school library books. [Words such as "radical," "fanatics," "right-wing," and "censoring" will antagonize many readers immediately.]
Better	Only local school board members—not religious leaders or parents —should decide which books high school libraries should order.
Poor	Too many corrupt books in our high school libraries selected by liberal, atheistic educators are undermining the morals of our youth. [Again, some readers will be offended.]
Better	To ensure that high school libraries contain books that reflect community standards, parents should have a voice in selecting new titles.

4. Don't merely state a fact. A thesis is an assertion of opinion that leads to discussion. Don't select an idea that is self-evident or dead-ended.

Poor	Child abuse is a terrible problem. [Yes, of course, who wouldn't agree that child abuse is terrible?]
Better	Child-abuse laws in this state are too lenient for repeat offenders. [This thesis will lead to a discussion in which supporting arguments and evidence will be presented.]
Poor	Advertisers often use attractive models in their ads to sell products. [True, but rather obvious. How could this essay be turned into something more than a list describing one ad after another?]
Better	A number of liquor advertisers, well known for using pictures of attractive models to sell their products, are now using special graphics to send subliminal messages to their readers. [This claim is controversial and will require persuasive supporting evidence.]
Better	Although long criticized for its negative portrayal of women in television commercials, the auto industry is just as often guilty of stereotyping men as brainless idiots unable to make a decision. [This thesis makes a point that may lead to an interesting discussion.]

5. Don't express your thesis in the form of a question unless the answer is already obvious to the reader.

Poor	Why should every college student be required to take two years of foreign language?
Better	Chemistry majors should be exempt from the foreign-language requirement.

✓ **REMEMBER:** Many times writers "discover" a better thesis near the end of their first draft. That's fine—consider that draft a prewriting or focusing exercise and begin another draft, using the newly discovered thesis as a starting point.

■ PRACTICING WHAT YOU'VE LEARNED

A. Identify each of the following thesis statements as adequate or inadequate. If the thesis is weak or insufficient in some way, explain the problem.

1. I think *Schindler's List* is a really interesting movie that everyone should see.

2. Which cars are designed better, Japanese imports or those made in the United States?

3. Some people think that the state lottery is a bad way to raise money for parks.

4. My essay will tell you how to apply for a college loan with the least amount of trouble.

5. During the fall term, final examinations should be given before Winter Break, not after the holidays as they are now.

6. Raising the cost of tuition will be a terrible burden on the students and won't do anything to improve the quality of education at this school.

7. I can't stand to even look at people who are into body piercing, especially in their face.

8. The passage of the newly proposed health-care bill for the elderly will lead to socialized medicine in this country.

9. People over seventy-five should be required to renew their driver's licenses every year.

10. Having a close friend you can talk to is very important.

B. Rewrite the following sentences so that each one is a clear thesis statement. Be prepared to explain why you changed the sentences as you did.

1. Applying for a job can be a negative experience.

2. There are many advantages and disadvantages to the county's new voting machines.

3. Buying concert tickets online is one big headache.

4. In this paper I will debate the pros and cons of the controversial motorcycle helmet law.

5. We need to do something about the billboard clutter on the main highway into town.

6. The insurance laws in this country need to be rewritten.

7. Bicycle riding is my favorite exercise because it's so good for me.

8. In my opinion, Santa Barbara is a fantastic place.

9. The Civil Rights Movement of the 1960s had a tremendous effect on this country.

10. All my friends like the band Thriving Ivory, and it's too bad they don't play more venues around here.

■ Assignment

Narrow the subject and write one good thesis sentence for five of the following topics:

1. A political or social issue

2. College or high school

3. Family

4. A hobby or pastime

5. A recent book or movie

6. Vacations

7. An environmental issue

8. A current fad or fashion

9. A job or profession

10. A rule, law, or regulation

■ Using the Essay Map*

Many thesis sentences will benefit from the addition of an *essay map*, a brief statement in the introductory paragraph introducing the major points to be discussed in the essay. Consider the analogy of beginning a trip by checking your map to see where you are headed. Similarly, an essay map allows the readers to know in advance where you, the writer, will be taking them in the essay.

Let's suppose you have been assigned the task of praising or criticizing some aspect of your campus. You decide that your thesis will be "The Study Skills Center is an excellent place for first-year students to receive help with basic courses." Although your thesis does take a stand ("excellent place"), your reader will not know why the Center is helpful or

---

* I am indebted to Susan Wittig for this useful concept, introduced in *Steps to Structure: An Introduction to Composition and Rhetoric* (Cambridge, MA: Winthrop Publishers, 1975), pages 125–126.

what points you will cover in your argument. With an essay map added, the reader will have a brief but specific idea where the essay is going and how it will be developed:

Thesis

The Study Skills Center is an excellent place for first-year students to receive help with basic courses. <u>The Center's numerous free services, well-trained tutors, and variety of supplementary learning materials can often mean the difference between academic success and failure for many students.</u>

Essay map (underlined)

Thanks to the essay map, the reader knows that the essay will discuss the Center's free services, tutors, and learning materials.

Here's another example—this time let's assume you have been frustrated trying to read books your teacher has placed "on reserve" in your campus library, so you have decided to criticize your library's reserve facility:

Thesis

The library's reserve facility is badly managed. <u>Its unpredictable hours, poor staffing, and inadequate space discourage even the most dedicated students.</u>

Essay map (underlined)

After reading the introductory paragraph, the reader knows the essay will discuss the reserve facility's problematic hours, staff, and space. In other words, the thesis statement defines the main purpose of your essay, and the essay map indicates the route you will take to accomplish that purpose.

The essay map often follows the thesis, but it can also appear before it. It is, in fact, frequently part of the thesis statement itself, as illustrated in the following examples:

Thesis with underlined essay map

<u>Because of its free services, well-trained tutors, and useful learning aids,</u> the Study Skills Center is an excellent place for students seeking academic help.

Thesis with underlined essay map

For those students who need extra help with their basic courses, the Study Skills Center is one of the best resources <u>because of its numerous free services, well-trained tutors, and variety of useful learning aids.</u>

Thesis with underlined essay map

<u>Unreasonable hours, poor staffing, and inadequate space</u> make the library reserve facility difficult to use.

In addition to suggesting the main points of the essay, the map provides two other benefits. It will provide a set of guidelines for organizing your essay, and it will help keep you from wandering off into areas only vaguely related to your thesis. A clearly written thesis statement and essay map provide a skeletal outline for the sequence of paragraphs in your essay, frequently with one body paragraph devoted to each main point mentioned in your map. (Chapter 3, on paragraphs, will explain in more detail the relationships among the thesis, the map, and the body of your essay.) Note that the number of points in the essay map may vary, although three or four may be the number found most often in 500-to-800-word essays. (More than four main points in a short essay might result in underdeveloped paragraphs; see pages 58–62 for additional information.)

Some important advice: although essay maps can be helpful to both writers and readers, they can also sound too mechanical, repetitive, or obvious. If you choose to use a map, always strive to blend it with your thesis as smoothly as possible.

Poor   The Study Skills Center is a helpful place for three reasons. The reasons are its free services, good tutors, and lots of learning materials.

Better   Numerous free services, well-trained tutors, and a variety of useful learning aids make the Study Skills Center a valuable campus resource.

If you feel your essay map is too obvious or mechanical, try using it only in your rough drafts to help you organize your essay. Once you're sure it isn't necessary to clarify your thesis or to guide your reader, consider dropping it from your final draft.

▪ PRACTICING WHAT YOU'VE LEARNED

A. Identify the thesis and the essay map in the following sentences by underlining the map.

1. *Citizen Kane* deserves to appear on a list of "Top Movies of All Times" because of its excellent ensemble acting, its fast-paced script, and its innovative editing.

2. Our state should double the existing fines for first-offense drunk drivers. Such a move would lower the number of accidents, cut the costs of insurance, and increase the state revenues for highway maintenance.

3. To guarantee sound construction, lower costs, and personalized design, more people should consider building their own log cabin home.

4. Apartment living is preferable to dorm living because it's cheaper, quieter, and more luxurious.

5. Not everyone can become an astronaut. To qualify, a person must have intelligence, determination, and training.

6. Through unscrupulous uses of propaganda and secret assassination squads, Hitler was able to take control of an economically depressed Germany.

7. Because it builds muscles, increases circulation, and burns harmful fatty tissue, weightlifting is a sport that benefits the entire body.

8. The new tax bill will not radically reform the loophole-riddled revenue system: deductions on secondary residences will remain, real estate tax shelters will be untouched, and nonprofit health organizations will be taxed.

9. Avocados make excellent plants for children. They're inexpensive to buy, easy to root, quick to sprout, and fun to grow.

10. His spirit of protest and clever phrasing blended into unusual musical arrangements have made Bob Dylan a recording giant for over forty years.

B. Review the thesis statements you wrote for the Assignment on page 40. Write an essay map for each thesis statement. You may place the map before or after the thesis, or you may make it part of the thesis itself. Identify which part is the thesis and which is the essay map by underlining the map.

■ ASSIGNMENT

Use one of the following quotations to help you think of a subject for an essay of your own. Don't merely repeat the quotation itself as your thesis statement but, rather, allow the quotation to lead you to your subject and a main point of your own creation that is appropriately narrowed and focused. Don't forget to designate an audience for your essay, a group of readers who need or want to hear what you have to say.

1. "Opportunity is missed by most people because it is often dressed in overalls and looks like work."—Thomas Edison, inventor

2. "Sports do not build character. They reveal it."—Heywood Hale Broun, sportscaster

© Bettmann/CORBIS

Jackie Robinson stealing home base during the 1955 World Series.

3. "The world is a book and those who don't travel read only a page."—St. Augustine, cleric

4. "It is never too late to be what one might have been."—George Eliot (Mary Ann Evans), writer

5. "It is never too late to give up your prejudices."—Henry Thoreau, writer and naturalist

6. "When a thing is funny, search it carefully for a hidden truth."—George Bernard Shaw, writer

7. "I am a great believer in luck, and I find the harder I work the more I have of it."—Stephen Leacock, economist and humorist

8. "Noncooperation with evil is as much a moral obligation as is cooperation with good."—Martin Luther King, Jr., statesman and civil-rights activist

9. "When an old person dies, a library burns to the ground."—African proverb

10. "In this world there are only two tragedies. One is not getting what one wants, and the other is getting it."—Oscar Wilde, writer

11. "Education is the most powerful weapon. You can use it to change the world."—Nelson Mandela, former political prisoner and President of South Africa

12. "The journey is the reward."—Taoist proverb

13. "You can discover more about a person in an hour of play than in a year of conversation."—Plato, philosopher

14. "Nobody can make you feel inferior without your consent."—Eleanor Roosevelt, stateswoman

15. "Never doubt that a small group of thoughtful, committed people can change the world. Indeed, it is the only thing that ever has."—Margaret Mead, anthropologist

16. "If you are patient in one moment of anger, you will escape a hundred days of sorrow."—Chinese proverb

17. "We can never have enough of nature . . . we need the tonic of wilderness."—Henry David Thoreau, writer and naturalist

18. "Even if you are on the right track, you will get run over if you just sit there."—Will Rogers, humorist and writer

19. "No matter what accomplishments you make, somebody helps you."—Althea Gibson, tennis champion

20. "Human beings are like tea bags. You don't know your own strength until you get into hot water."—Bruce Laingen, U.S. diplomat

21. "Los secretos ni oirlos ni decirlos." [Don't listen to secrets, and don't tell them.]—Spanish proverb

22. "I took the [road] less traveled by, and that has made all the difference."—from "The Road Not Taken" by Robert Frost, poet (For the complete poem, see pages 463–464.)

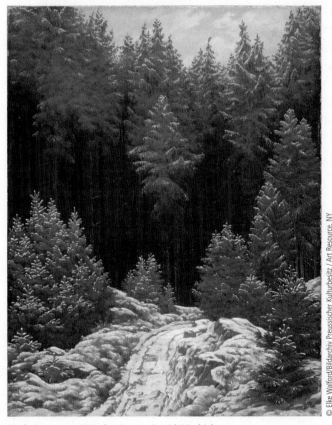

Early Snow, ca. 1827, by Caspar David Friedrich

© Elke Walford/Bildarchiv Preussischer Kulturbesitz / Art Resource, NY

CHAPTER 2 SUMMARY

Here's a brief review of what you need to know about the thesis statement:

1. A thesis statement declares the main point of your essay; it tells the reader what clearly defined opinion you hold.

2. Everything in your essay should support your thesis statement.

3. A good thesis statement asserts one main idea, narrowed to fit the assignment, and is stated in clear, specific terms.

4. A good thesis statement makes a reasonable claim about a topic that is of interest to its readers as well as to its writer.

5. The thesis statement is often presented near the beginning of the essay, frequently in the first or second paragraph, or is so strongly implied that readers cannot miss the writer's main point.

6. A "working" or trial thesis is an excellent organizing tool to use as you begin drafting because it can help you decide which ideas to include.

7. Because writing is an act of discovery, you may write yourself into a better thesis statement by the end of your first draft. Don't hesitate to begin a new draft with the new thesis statement.

8. Some writers may profit from using an essay map, a brief statement accompanying the thesis that introduces the supporting points discussed in the body of the essay.

Chapter 3

The Body Paragraphs

The middle—or *body*—of your essay is composed of paragraphs that support the thesis statement. By citing examples, explaining causes, offering reasons, or using other strategies in these paragraphs, you supply enough specific evidence to persuade your reader that the opinion expressed in your thesis is a sensible one. Each paragraph in the body usually presents and develops one main point in the discussion of your thesis. Generally, but not always, a new body paragraph signals another major point in the discussion.

■ Planning the Body of Your Essay

Many writers like to have a plan before they begin drafting the body of their essay. To help you create a plan, first look at your thesis. If you used an essay map, as suggested in Chapter 2, you may find that the points mentioned there will provide the basis for the body paragraphs of your essay. For example, recall from Chapter 2 a thesis and essay map praising the Study Skills Center: "Because of its free services, well-trained tutors, and useful learning aids, the Study Skills Center is an excellent place for students seeking academic help." Your plan for developing the body of your essay might look like this:

Body paragraph one:	discussion of free services
Body paragraph two:	discussion of tutors
Body paragraph three:	discussion of learning aids

At this point in your writing process you may wish to sketch in some of the supporting evidence you will include in each paragraph. You might find it helpful to go back to your prewriting activities (listing, looping, freewriting, mapping, cubing, and so on) to see what ideas surfaced then. Adding some examples and supporting details might make an informal outline of the Study Skills paper appear like this:

I. Free services
    A. Minicourse on improving study skills
    B. Tutoring
          composition
          math
    C. Weekly seminars
          stress management
          test anxiety
          building vocabulary
    D. Testing for learning disabilities
II. Tutors
    A. Top graduate students in their fields
    B. Experienced teachers
    C. Some bilingual
    D. Have taken training course at Center
III. Learning aids
    A. Supplementary texts
    B. Workbooks
    C. Audiovisual aids

Notice that this plan is an *informal* or *working outline* rather than a *formal outline*—that is, it doesn't have strictly parallel parts nor is it expressed in complete sentences. Unless your teacher requests a formal sentence or topic outline, don't feel you must make one at this early stage. Just consider using the informal outline to plot out a tentative plan that will help you start your first draft.

Here's an example of an informal outline at work: let's suppose you have been asked to write about your most prized possession, and you've chosen your 1966 Mustang, a car you have restored. You already have some ideas, but as yet they're scattered and too few to make an interesting, well-developed essay. You try an informal outline, jotting down your ideas thus far:

©Bettmann/CORBIS

    I. Car is special because it was a gift from Dad
   II. Fun to drive
  III. Looks great—new paint job
  IV. Engine in top condition
   V. Custom features
  VI. Car shows—fun to be part of

After looking at your outline, you see that some of your categories overlap and could be part of the same discussion. For example, your thoughts about the engine are actually part of the discussion of "fun to drive," and "custom features" are what make the car look great. Moreover, the outline may help you discover new ideas. For example, custom features could be divided into those on the interior as well as those on the exterior of the car. The revised outline might look like this:

I. Gift from Dad
II. Fun to drive
    A. Engine
    B. Steering
III. Looks great
    A. New paint job
    B. Custom features
        1. exterior
        2. interior
IV. Car shows

You could continue playing with this outline, even moving big chunks of it around; for example, you might decide that what really makes the car so special is that it was a graduation gift from your dad and that is the note you want to end on. So you move "I. Gift from Dad" down to the last position in your outline.

The important point to remember about an informal or working outline is that it is there to help you—not control you. The value of an outline is its ability to help you plan, to help you see logical connections between your ideas, and to help you see obvious places to add new ideas and details. (The informal outline is also handy to keep around in case you're interrupted for a long period while you're drafting; you can always check the outline to see where you were and where you were going when you stopped.) In other words, *don't be intimidated by the outline!*

Here's one more example of an informal outline, this time for the thesis and essay map on the library reserve facility, from Chapter 2:

Thesis-Map: Unpredictable hours, poor staffing, and inadequate space make the library's reserve facility difficult for students to use.

    I. Unpredictable hours
        A. Hours of operation vary from week to week
        B. Unannounced closures
        C. Closed on some holidays, open on others
    II. Poor staffing
        A. Uninformed personnel at reserve desk
        B. Too few on duty at peak times
    III. Inadequate space
        A. Room too small for number of users
        B. Too few chairs, tables
        C. Weak lighting

You may have more than three points to make in your essay. And, on occasion, you may need more than one paragraph to discuss a single point. For instance, you might discover that you need two paragraphs to explain fully the many services at the Study Skills Center. (For advice on splitting the discussion of a single point into two or more paragraphs, see page 62.) At this stage, you needn't bother trying to guess whether you'll need more than one paragraph per point; just use the outline to get going. Most writers don't know how much they have to say before they begin writing—and that's fine because *writing itself is an act of discovery and learning.*

When you are ready to begin drafting, read Chapter 5 for advice on composing and revising. Remember, too, that Chapter 5 contains suggestions for beating Writer's Block, should this condition arise while you are working on any part of your essay, as well as some specific hints on formatting your draft that may make revision easier (pages 94–97).

■ Composing the Body Paragraphs

There are many ways to organize and develop body paragraphs. Paragraphs developed by common patterns, such as example, comparison, and definition, will be discussed in specific chapters in Part Two; at this point, however, here are some comments about the general nature of all good body paragraphs that should help as you draft your essay.

> ✓ **REMEMBER:** Most of the body paragraphs in your essay will profit from a focused *topic sentence*. In addition, body paragraphs should have adequate *development, unity,* and *coherence.*

■ The Topic Sentence

Most body paragraphs present one main point in your discussion, expressed in a *topic sentence.* The topic sentence of a body paragraph has three important functions:

1. It supports the thesis by clearly stating a main point in the discussion.

2. It announces what the paragraph will be about.

3. It controls the subject matter of the paragraph. The entire discussion—the examples, details, and explanations—in a particular paragraph must directly relate to and support the topic sentence.

Think of a body paragraph (or a single paragraph) as a kind of mini-essay in itself. The topic sentence is, in a sense, a smaller thesis. It too asserts one main idea on a limited subject that the writer can explain or argue in the rest of the paragraph. Like the thesis, the topic sentence should be stated in as specific language as possible.

To see how a topic sentence works in a body paragraph, study this sample:

Essay Thesis: The Study Skills Center is an excellent place for students who need academic help.

Topic Sentence
1. The topic sentence supports the thesis by stating a main point (one reason why the Center provides excellent academic help).

The Center offers students a variety of free services designed to improve basic skills. Those who discover their study habits are poor, for instance, may enroll in a six-week minicourse in study skills that offers advice on such topics as how to read a text, take notes, and organize material for review. Students whose math or writing skills are below par

Topic Sentence
2. The topic sentence announces the subject matter of the paragraph (a variety of free services that improve basic skills).
3. The topic sentence controls the subject matter (all the examples—the minicourse, the tutoring, the seminars, and the testing—support the claim of the topic sentence).

can sign up for free tutoring sessions held five days a week throughout each semester. In addition, the Center presents weekly seminars on special topics such as stress management and overcoming test anxiety for those students who are finding college more of a nerve-wracking experience than they expected; other students can attend evening seminars in such worthwhile endeavors as vocabulary building or spelling tips. Finally, the Center offers a series of tests to identify the presence of any learning disabilities, such as dyslexia, that might prevent a student from succeeding academically. With such a variety of free services, the Center can help almost any student.

© ARS, NY/Smithsonian American Art Museum, Washington, DC / Art Resource, NY

The Library, 1960, by Jacob Lawrence

Here's another example from the essay on the library reserve facility:

Essay Thesis: The library's reserve facility is difficult for students to use.

Topic Sentence
1. The topic sentence supports the thesis by stating a main point (one reason why the

The library reserve facility's unpredictable hours frustrate even the most dedicated students. Instructors who place articles or books on reserve usually ask students to read them by a certain date. Too often, however, students arrive at the reserve desk only to find it closed. The

facility is difficult to use).
2. The topic sentence announces the subject matter of the paragraph (the unpredictable hours).
3. The topic sentence controls the subject matter (all the examples—the changing hours, the sudden closures, the erratic holiday schedule—support the claim of the topic sentence).

facility's open hours change from week to week: students who used the room last week on Tuesday morning may discover that this week on Tuesday the desk is closed, which means another trip. Perhaps even more frustrating are the facility's sudden, unannounced closures. Some of these closures allow staff members to have lunch or go on breaks, but, again, they occur without notice on no regular schedule. A student arrives, as I did two weeks ago, at the desk to find a "Be Back Soon" sign. In my case, I waited for nearly an hour. Another headache is the holiday schedule, which is difficult to figure out. For example, this year the reserve room was closed without advance notice on Presidents' Day but open on Easter; open during Winter Break but closed some days during Spring Break, a time many students use to catch up on their reserve assignments. Overall, the reserve facility would be much easier for students to use if it adopted a set schedule of operating hours, announced these times each semester, and maintained them.

Always be sure your topic sentences actually support the particular thesis of your essay. For example, the second topic sentence presented here doesn't belong in the essay promised by the thesis:

Thesis: Elk hunting should be permitted because it financially aids people in our state.

Topic Sentences

1. Fees for hunting licenses help pay for certain free, state-supported social services.
2. Hunting helps keep the elk population under control.
3. Elk hunting offers a means of obtaining free food for people with low incomes.

Although topic sentence 2 is about elk and may be true, it doesn't support the thesis's emphasis on financial aid and therefore should be tossed out of this essay.

Here's another example:

Thesis: During the past fifty years, movie stars have often tried to change the direction of America's politics.

Topic Sentences

1. During World War II, stars sold liberty bonds to support the country's war effort.
2. Many stars refused to cooperate with the blacklisting of their colleagues during the McCarthy Era in the 1950s.
3. Some stars were actively involved in protests against the Vietnam War.
4. More recently, stars have appeared in Congress criticizing the lack of legislative help for struggling farmers.

Topic sentences 2, 3, and 4 all show how stars have tried to effect a change. But topic sentence 1 says only that stars sold bonds to support, not *change*, the political direction of the nation. Although it does show stars involved in politics, it doesn't illustrate the claim of this particular thesis.

Sometimes a topic sentence needs only to be rewritten or slightly recast to fit:

Thesis: The recent tuition hike may discourage students from attending our college.

Topic Sentences

1. Students already pay more here than at other in-state schools.

2. Out-of-state students will have to pay an additional "penalty" to attend.

3. Tuition funds should be used for scholarships.

As written, topic sentence 3 doesn't show why students won't want to attend the school. However, a rewritten topic sentence does support the thesis:

3. Because the tuition money will not be used for scholarships, some students may not be able to afford this higher-priced school.

In other words, always check carefully to make sure that *all* your topic sentences clearly support your thesis's assertion.

Focusing Your Topic Sentence

A vague, fuzzy, or unfocused topic sentence most often leads to a paragraph that touches only on the surface of its subject or that wanders away from the writer's main idea. On the other hand, a topic sentence that is tightly focused and stated precisely not only will help the reader to understand the point of the paragraph but will also help you select, organize, and develop your supporting details.

Look, for example, at these unfocused topic sentences and their revisions:

Unfocused	Too many people treat animals badly in experiments. [What people? Badly how? What kinds of experiments?]
Focused	The cosmetic industry often harms animals in unnecessary experiments designed to test their products.
Unfocused	Grades are an unfair pain in the neck. [Again, the focus is too broad. All grades? Unfair how?]
Focused	A course grade based on one multiple-choice exam doesn't accurately measure a student's knowledge of the subject.
Unfocused	Finding the right job is important and can lead to rewarding experiences. [Note both vague language and a double focus: "important" and "can lead to rewarding experiences."]
Focused	Finding the right job can lead to an improved sense of self-esteem.

Before you practice writing focused topic sentences, you may wish to review pages 33–37, the advice on composing good thesis statements, as the same rules generally apply.

Placing Your Topic Sentence

Although the topic sentence most frequently occurs as the first sentence in the body paragraph, it also often appears as the second or last sentence. A topic sentence that directly follows the first sentence of a paragraph usually does so because the first sentence provides an introductory statement or some kind of "hook" to the preceding paragraph.

A topic sentence frequently appears at the end of a paragraph that first presents particular details and then concludes with its central point. Here are two paragraphs in which the topic sentences do not appear first:

Introductory sentence

Topic sentence

Millions of Americans have watched the elaborate Rose Bowl Parade televised nationally each January from Pasadena, California. *Less well known, but growing in popularity, is Pasadena's Doo Dah Parade, an annual parody of the Rose Bowl spectacle, that specializes in wild-and-crazy participants.* Take this year's Doo Dah Precision Drill Team, for instance. Instead of marching in unison, the members cavorted down the avenue displaying—what else—a variety of precision electric drills. In heated competition with this group was the Synchronized Briefcase Drill Team, whose members wore gray pinstripe suits and performed a series of tunes by tapping on their briefcases. Another crowd-pleasing entry was the Citizens for the Right to Bare Arms, whose members sang while carrying aloft unclothed mannequin arms. The zany procession, led this year as always by the All-Time Doo Dah Parade Band, attracted more than 150,000 fans and is already preparing for its next celebration.

In the preceding paragraph, the first sentence serves as an introduction leading directly to the topic sentence. In the following example, the writer places the topic sentence last to sum up the information in the paragraph:

Rumors certainly fly around Washington's Capitol Building—but ghosts too? According to legend, the building was cursed in 1808 by construction superintendent John Lenthall, crushed by a falling ceiling following a feud with his architect over the wisdom of ceiling braces. Some workers in the building swear they have heard both the ghostly footsteps of James Garfield, who was assassinated after only four months as president, and the spooky last murmurings of John Quincy Adams, who died mid-speech on the House floor. Others claim to have seen a demon cat, so large and terrifying that it caused a guard to suffer a fatal heart attack. Perhaps the most cheerful ghosts appear on the night of a new president's swearing-in ceremony when the statues in Statuary Hall are said to leave their pedestals and dance at their own Inaugural Ball. *Whether these stories are true or merely the products of rich imaginations, the U.S. Capitol Building boasts the reputation as one of the most haunted buildings in America.*

Topic sentence

As you can see, the position of topic sentences largely depends on what you are trying to do in your paragraph. And it's true that the purposes of some paragraphs are so obvious that no topic sentences are needed. However, if you are a beginning writer, you may want to practice putting your topic sentences first for a while to help you organize and unify your paragraphs.

Some paragraphs with a topic sentence near the beginning also contain a concluding sentence that makes a final general comment based on the supporting details. The last sentence of the following paragraph, for example, reemphasizes the main point.

Topic sentence

Of all nature's catastrophes, tornadoes may cause the most bizarre destruction. Whirling out of the sky at speeds up to 300 miles per hour, tornadoes have been known to drive broom handles through brick walls and straws into tree trunks. In one extreme case, a Kansas farmer reported that his prize rooster had been sucked into a two-gallon distilled-water bottle. More commonly, tornadoes lift autos and deposit them in fields miles away or uproot trees and drop them on lawns in neighboring towns. One tornado knocked down every wall in a house but Concluding sentence   one—luckily, the very wall shielding the terrified family. *Whenever a tornado touches the earth, spectacular headlines are sure to follow.*

Warning: Although topic sentences may appear in different places in a paragraph, there is one common error you should be careful to avoid. Do *not* put a topic sentence at the end of one body paragraph that belongs to the paragraph that follows it. For example, let's suppose you are writing an essay discussing a job you held recently, one that you enjoyed because of the responsibilities you were given, the training program you participated in, and the interaction you experienced with your coworkers. The body paragraph describing your responsibilities may end with its own topic sentence or with a concluding sentence about those responsibilities. However, that paragraph should not end with a sentence such as "Another excellent feature of this job was the training program for the next level of management." This "training program" sentence belongs in the *following* body paragraph as its topic sentence. Similarly, you would not end the paragraph on the training program with a topic sentence praising your experience with your coworkers.

If you feel that your paragraphs are ending too abruptly, consider using a concluding sentence, as described previously. Later in this chapter you will also learn some ways to smooth the way from one paragraph to the next by using transitional devices and "idea hooks" (pages 77–78). For now, remember: Do *not* place a topic sentence that introduces and controls paragraph "B" at the end of paragraph "A." In other words, always place your topic sentence in the paragraph to which it belongs, to which it is topic-related, not at the end of the preceding paragraph.

■ PRACTICING WHAT YOU'VE LEARNED

A. Point out the topic sentences in the following paragraphs; identify those paragraphs that also contain concluding sentences. Cross out any stray topic sentences that belong elsewhere.

Denim is one of America's most widely used fabrics. It was first introduced during Columbus's voyage, when the sails of the Santa Maria were made of the strong cloth. During our pioneer days, denim was used for tents, covered wagons, and the now-famous blue jeans. Cowboys found denim an ideal fabric for protection against sagebrush, cactus, and saddle sores. World War II also gave denim a boost in popularity when sailors were issued jeans as part of their dress code. Today, denim continues to be in demand as more and more casual clothes are cut from the economical fabric. Because of its low cost and durability, manufacturers feel that denim will continue as one of America's most useful fabrics.

Adlai Stevenson, American statesman and twice an unsuccessful presidential candidate against Eisenhower, was well known for his intelligence and wit. Once on the campaign trail, after he had spoken eloquently and at length about several complex ideas, a woman in the audience was moved to stand and cheer, "That's great! Every thinking person in America will vote for you!" Stevenson immediately retorted, "That's not enough. I need a majority!" Frequently a reluctant candidate but never at a loss for words, Stevenson once defined a politician as a person who "approaches every question with an open mouth." Stevenson was also admired for his work as the Governor of Illinois and, later, as Ambassador to the United Nations.

Almost every wedding tradition has a symbolic meaning that originated centuries ago. For example, couples have been exchanging rings to symbolize unending love for over a thousand years. Most often, the rings are worn on the third finger of the left hand, which was thought to contain a vein that ran directly to the heart. The rings in ancient times were sometimes made of braided grass, rope, or leather, giving rise to the expression "tying the knot." Another tradition, the bridal veil, began when marriages were arranged by the families and the groom was not allowed to see his bride until the wedding. The tossing of rice at newlyweds has long signified fertility blessings, and the sweet smell of the bride's bouquet was present to drive away evil spirits, who were also diverted by the surrounding bridal attendants. Weddings may vary enormously today, but many couples still include ancient traditions to signify their new life together.

You always think of the right answer five minutes after you hand in the test. You always hit the red light when you're already late for class. The one time you skip class is the day of the pop quiz. Back-to-back classes are always held in buildings at opposite ends of campus. The one course you need to graduate will not be offered your last semester. If any of these sound familiar, you've obviously been a victim of the "Murphy's Laws" that govern student life.

Want to win a sure bet? Then wager that your friends can't guess the most widely sold musical instrument in America today. Chances are they won't get the answer right—not even on the third try. In actuality, the most popular instrument in the country is neither the guitar nor the trumpet but the lowly kazoo. Last year alone, some three and one-half million kazoos were sold to music lovers of all ages. Part of the instrument's popularity arises from its availability, since kazoos are sold in variety stores and music centers nearly everywhere; another reason is its inexpensiveness—it ranges from the standard thirty-nine-cent model to the five-dollar gold-plated special. But perhaps the main reason for the kazoo's popularity is the ease with which it can be played by almost anyone—as can testify the members of the entire Swarthmore College marching band, who have now added a marching kazoo number to their repertoire. Louis Armstrong, move over!

It's a familiar scenario: Dad won't stop the car to ask directions, despite the fact that he's been hopelessly lost for over forty-five minutes. Mom keeps nagging Dad to slow down and finally blows up because your little sister suddenly remembers she's left her favorite doll, the one she can't sleep without, at the rest stop you left over an hour ago. Your legs are sweat-glued to the vinyl seats, you need desperately to go to the bathroom, and your big brother has just kindly acknowledged that he will relieve you of your front teeth if you allow any part of your body to extend over the imaginary line he has drawn down the back seat. The wonderful tradition known as the "family vacation" has begun.

B. Rewrite these topic sentences so that they are clear and focused rather than fuzzy or too broad.

1. My personality has changed a lot in the last year.

2. His date turned out to be really great.

3. The movie's special effects were incredible.

4. The Memorial Day celebration was more fun than ever before.

5. The evening with her parents was an unforgettable experience.

C. Add topic sentences to the following paragraphs:

Famous inventor Thomas Edison, for instance, did so poorly in his first years of school that his teachers warned his parents that he'd never be a success at anything. Henry Ford, the father of the auto industry, also had trouble in school with both reading and writing. But perhaps the best example is Albert Einstein, whose parents and teachers suspected that he was mentally disabled because he responded to questions so slowly and in a stuttering voice. Einstein's high school record was poor in everything but math, and he failed his college entrance exams the first time. Even out of school the man had trouble holding a job—until he announced the theory of relativity.

A 1950s felt skirt with Elvis's picture on it, for example, now sells for $150, and Elvis scarves go for as much as $300. Elvis handkerchiefs, originally 50 cents or less, fetch $150 in today's market; 1956 wallets imprinted with the singer's face have sold for over $400 each. Original posters from the Rock King's movies can sell for $500, and cards from the chewing gum series can run $30 apiece. Perhaps one of the most expensive collectors' items is the Emene Elvis guitar that can cost a fan at least $1000, regardless of musical condition.

When successful playwright Jean Kerr once checked into a hospital, the receptionist asked her occupation and was told, "Writer." The receptionist said, "I'll just put down 'housewife.'" Similarly, when a British official asked W. H. Auden, the award-winning poet and essayist, what he did for a living, Auden replied, "I'm a writer." The official jotted down "no occupation."

Cumberland College, for example, set the record back in 1916 for the biggest loss in college ball, having allowed Georgia Tech to run up 63 points in the first quarter and ultimately succumbing to them with a final score of 222 to nothing. In pro ball, the Washington Redskins are the biggest losers, going down in defeat 73 to 0 to the Chicago Bears in 1940. The award for the longest losing streak, however, goes to Northwestern University's team, who by 1981 had managed to lose 29 consecutive games. During that year, morale was so low that one disgruntled fan passing a local highway sign that read "Interstate 94" couldn't resist adding "Northwestern 0."

D. Write a focused topic sentence for five of the following subjects:

1. Job interviews

2. Friends

3. Food

4. Money

5. Selecting a major or occupation

6. Clothes

7. Music

8. Dreams

9. Housing

10. Childhood

■ **ASSIGNMENT**

Review the thesis statements with essay maps you wrote for the practice exercise on page 43. Choose two, and from each thesis create at least three topic sentences for possible body paragraphs. ■

■ **APPLYING WHAT YOU'VE LEARNED TO *YOUR* WRITING**

If you currently have a working thesis statement you have written in response to an assignment in your composition class, try sketching out an outline or a plan for the major ideas you wish to include. After you write a draft, underline the topic sentences in your body paragraphs. Do your topic sentences directly support your thesis? If you find that they do not clearly support your thesis, you must decide if you need to revise your draft's organization or whether you have, in fact, discovered a new, and possibly better, subject to write about. If the latter is true, you'll need to redraft your essay so that your readers will not be confused by a paper that announces one subject but discusses another. (See Chapter 5 for more information on revising your drafts.) ■

■ Paragraph Development

Possibly the most serious—and most common—weakness of all essays by novice writers is *the lack of effectively developed body paragraphs.* The information in each paragraph must adequately explain, exemplify, define, or in some other way support your topic sentence. Therefore, you must include *enough supporting information* or *evidence* in each paragraph to make your readers understand your topic sentence. Moreover, you must make the information in the paragraph clear and specific enough for the readers to accept your ideas.

The next paragraph is *underdeveloped.* Although the topic sentence promises a discussion of Jesse James as a Robin Hood figure, the paragraph does not provide enough specific supporting evidence (in this case, examples) to explain this unusual view of the gunfighter.

> Although he was an outlaw, Jesse James was considered a Robin Hood figure in my hometown in Missouri. He used to be generous to the poor, and he did many good deeds, not just robberies. In my hometown people still talk about how lots of the things James did weren't all bad.

Rewritten, the paragraph might read as follows:

> Although he was an outlaw, Jesse James was considered a Robin Hood figure in my hometown in Missouri. Jesse and his gang chose my hometown as a hiding place, and they set out immediately to make friends with the local people. Every Christmas for four years, the legend goes, he dumped bags of toys on the doorsteps of poor children. The parents knew the toys had been bought with money stolen from richer people, but they were grateful anyway. On three

occasions, Jesse gave groceries to the dozen neediest families—he seemed to know when times were toughest—and once he supposedly held up a stage to pay for an old man's operation. In my hometown, some people still sing the praises of Jesse James, the outlaw who wasn't all bad.

The topic sentence promises a discussion of James's generosity and delivers just that by citing specific examples of his gifts to children, the poor, and the sick. The paragraph is therefore better developed.

The following paragraph offers reasons but no specific examples or details to support its claims:

Living with my ex-roommate was unbearable. First, she thought everything she owned was the best. Second, she possessed numerous filthy habits. Finally, she constantly exhibited immature behavior.

The writer might provide more evidence this way:

Living with my ex-roommate was unbearable. First, she thought everything she owned, from clothes to cosmetics, was the best. If someone complimented my pants, she'd point out that her designer jeans looked better and would last longer because they were made of better material. If she borrowed my shampoo, she'd let me know that it didn't get her hair as clean and shiny as hers did. My hand cream wasn't as smooth; my suntan lotion wasn't as protective; not even my wire clothes hangers were as good as her padded ones! But despite her pickiness about products, she had numerous filthy habits. Her dirty dishes remained in the sink for days before she felt the need to wash them. Piles of the "best" brand of tissues were regularly discarded from her upper bunk and strewn about the floor. Her desk and closets overflowed with heaps of dirty clothes, books, cosmetics, and whatever else she owned, and she rarely brushed her teeth (when she did brush, she left oozes of toothpaste in the sink). Finally, she constantly acted immaturely by throwing tantrums when things didn't go her way. A poor grade on an exam or paper, for example, meant books, shoes, or any other small object within her reach would hit the wall flying. Living with such a person taught me some valuable lessons about how not to win friends or keep roommates.

By adding more supporting evidence—specific examples and details—to this paragraph, the writer has a better chance of convincing the reader of the roommate's real character.

Where does evidence come from? Where do writers find their supporting information? Evidence comes from many sources. Personal experiences, memories, observations, hypothetical examples, reasoned arguments, facts, statistics, testimony from authorities, many kinds of studies and research—all these and more can help you make your points clear and persuasive. In the paragraph on Jesse James, for example, the writer relied on stories and memories from his hometown. The paragraph on the obnoxious roommate was supported by examples gained through the writer's personal observation. The kind of supporting evidence you choose for your paragraphs depends on your purpose and your audience; as the writer, you must decide what will work best to make your readers understand and accept each important point in your discussion. (For advice on ways to think critically about evidence, see Chapter 5; for more information on incorporating research material into your essays, see Chapter 14.)

Having a well-developed paragraph is more than a matter of adding material or expanding length, however. The information in each paragraph must effectively explain or support your topic sentence. *Vague generalities or repetitious ideas are not convincing.* Look, for example, at the following paragraph, in which the writer offers only generalities:

> We ought to ban the use of cell phones in moving vehicles. Some people who have them think that's a really good idea, but a lot of us don't agree. Using a phone while driving causes too many dangerous accidents to happen, and even if there's no terrible accident, people using them have been known to do some really stupid things in traffic. Drivers using phones are constantly causing problems for other drivers; pedestrians are in big trouble from these people too. I think this is getting to be a really dangerous situation, and we ought to do something about it soon.

This paragraph is weak because it is composed of repetitious general statements using vague, unclear language. None of its general statements is supported with specific evidence. Why is car phone use not a "good" idea? How does it cause accidents? What are the "problems" and "trouble" the writer refers to? What exactly does "do something about it" mean? The writer obviously had some ideas in mind, but these ideas are not clear to the reader because they are not adequately developed with specific evidence and language.

By adding supporting examples and details, the writer might revise the paragraph this way:

> Although cell phones are a time-saving convenience for busy people, they are too distracting for use by drivers of moving vehicles, whose lack of full attention poses a serious threat to other drivers and to pedestrians. The simple act of dialing or answering a phone, for example, may take a driver's eyes away from traffic signals or other cars. Moreover, involvement in a complex or emotional conversation could slow down a driver's response time just when fast action is needed to avoid an accident. Last week I drove behind a man using his phone. As he drove and talked, I could see him gesturing wildly, obviously agitated with the other caller. His speed repeatedly slowed and then picked up, slowed and increased, and his car drifted more than once, on a street frequently crossed by schoolchildren. Because the man was clearly not in full, conscious control of his driving, he was dangerous. My experience is not isolated; a recent study by the Foundation for Traffic Safety has discovered that using a cell phone is far more distracting to drivers than listening to the radio or talking to a rider. With additional studies in progress, voters should soon be able to demand legislation to restrict phone use to passengers or to drivers when the vehicles are not in motion.

The reader now has a better idea why the writer feels such cell phone use is distracting and, consequently, dangerous. By using two hypothetical examples (looking away, slowed response time), one personal experience (observing the agitated man), and one reference to research (the safety study), the writer offers the reader three kinds of supporting evidence for the paragraph's claim.

After examining the following two paragraphs, decide which explains its point more effectively.

1   Competing in an Ironman triathlon is one of the most demanding feats known to amateur athletes. First, they have to swim many miles, and that takes a lot of endurance. Then they ride a bicycle a long way, which is also hard on their bodies. Last, they run a marathon, which can be difficult in itself but is especially hard after the first two events. Competing in the triathlon is really tough on the participants.

2   Competing in an Ironman triathlon is one of the most demanding feats known to amateur athletes. During the first stage of the triathlon, the competitors must swim 2.4 miles in the open ocean. They have to battle the constantly choppy ocean, the strong currents, and the frequent swells. The wind is often an adversary, and stinging jellyfish are a constant threat. Once they have completed the ocean swim, the triathletes must ride 112 miles on a bicycle. In addition to the strength needed to pedal that far, the bicyclists must use a variety of hand grips to ensure the continued circulation in their fingers and hands as well as to ease the strain on the neck and shoulder muscles. Moreover, the concentration necessary to steady the bicycle as well as the attention to the inclines on the course and the consequent shifting of gears causes mental fatigue for the athletes. After completing these two grueling segments, the triathletes must then run 26.2 miles, the length of a regular marathon. Dehydration is a constant concern, as is the prospect of cramping. Even the pain and swelling of a friction blister can be enough to eliminate a contestant at this late stage of the event. Finally, disorientation and fatigue can set in and distort the athlete's judgment. Competing in an Ironman triathlon takes incredible physical and mental endurance.

The first paragraph contains, for the most part, repetitious generalities; it repeats the same idea (the triathlon is hard work) and gives few specific details to illustrate the point presented in the topic sentence. The second paragraph, however, does offer many specific examples and details—the exact mileage figures, the currents, jellyfish, inclines, grips, blisters, and so forth—that help the reader understand why the event is so demanding.

Joseph Conrad, the famous novelist, once remarked that a writer's purpose was to use "the power of the written word to make you hear, to make you feel . . . before all, to make you *see*. That—and no more, and it is everything." By using specific details instead of vague, general statements, you can write an interesting, convincing essay. Ask yourself as you revise your paragraphs, "Have I provided enough information, presented enough clear, precise details to make my readers see what I want them to?" In other words, a well-developed paragraph effectively makes its point with *an appropriate amount of specific supporting evidence*. (Remember that a paragraph in a handwritten rough draft will look much shorter when it is typed. Therefore, if you can't think of much to say about a particular idea, you should gather more information or consider dropping it as a major point in your essay.)

■ Paragraph Length

"How long is a good paragraph?" is a question novice writers often ask. Like a teacher's lecture or a preacher's sermon, paragraphs should be long enough to accomplish their purpose and short enough to be interesting. In truth, there is no set length, no prescribed number of lines or sentences, for any of your paragraphs. In a body paragraph, your topic sentence presents the main point, and the rest of the paragraph must give enough supporting evidence to convince the reader. Although too much unnecessary or repetitious detail is boring, too little discussion will leave the reader uninformed, unconvinced, or confused.

Although paragraph length varies, beginning writers should avoid the one- or two-sentence paragraphs frequently seen in newspapers or magazine articles. (Journalists have their own rules to follow; paragraphs are shorter in newspapers, for one reason, because large masses of print in narrow columns are difficult to read quickly.) Essay writers do occasionally use the one-sentence paragraph, most often to produce some special effect, when the statement is especially dramatic or significant and needs to call attention to itself or when an emphatic transition is needed. For now, however, you should concentrate on writing well-developed body paragraphs.

One more note on paragraph length: sometimes you may discover that a particular point in your essay is so complex that your paragraph is growing far too long—well over a typed page, for instance. If this problem occurs, look for a logical place to divide your information and start a new paragraph. For example, you might see a convenient dividing point in a series of actions you're describing or a break in the chronology of a narrative or between explanations of arguments or examples. Just make sure you begin your next paragraph with some sort of transitional phrase or key words to let the reader know that you are still discussing the same point as before ("Still another problem caused by the computer's faulty memory circuit is . . .").

■ PRACTICING WHAT YOU'VE LEARNED

A. Analyze the following paragraphs. Explain how you might improve the development of each one.

1. Professor Wilson is the best teacher I've ever had. His lectures are interesting, and he's very concerned about his students. He makes the class challenging but not too hard. On tests he doesn't expect more than one can give. I think he's a great teacher.

2. Newspaper advice columns are pretty silly. The problems are generally stupid or unrealistic, and the advice is out of touch with today's world. Too often the columnist just uses the letter to make a smart remark about some pet peeve. The columns could be put to some good uses, but no one tries very hard.

3. Driving tests do not adequately examine a person's driving ability. Usually the person being tested does not have to drive very far. The test does not require the skills that are used in everyday driving situations. Supervisors of driving tests tend to be very lenient.

4. Nursing homes are often sad places. They are frequently located in ugly old buildings unfit for anyone. The people there are lonely and bored. What's more, they're sometimes treated badly by the people who run the homes. It's a shame something better can't be done for the elderly.

5. There is a big difference between acquaintances and friends. Acquaintances are just people you know slightly, but friends give you some important qualities. For example, they can help you gain self-esteem and confidence just by being close to you. By sharing their friendship, they also help you feel happy about being alive.

B. Practice developing paragraphs by choosing two of the three topics below, fleshing out each paragraph with an example from your own experience or that of a close friend. Use vivid, specific details to make each paragraph clear and interesting. (If you cannot think of an appropriate example, you may rework the topic sentence; for instance, in the first paragraph, you might change the topic to a product or service that exceeded your expectations rather than one that disappointed you.)

1. Too many products today have expensive advertising campaigns but simply don't live up to their claims. For instance,

2. Sooner or later, almost everyone experiences that dreaded moment when he or she suddenly forgets something familiar. Someone forgets a friend's name in the middle of an introduction; someone else experiences memory loss standing in front of the ATM or just after volunteering to answer a question in class. I too have temporarily "gone blank," but eventually regained my composure. For example,

3. Unexpected help is a miracle that often comes just in time to prevent a disaster or foolish move. Such help can come from a variety of sources—from friends, family, or even strangers. For example,

■ ASSIGNMENT

A. Find two well-developed paragraphs in an essay or book; explain why you think the paragraphs are successfully developed.

B. Select one of the paragraphs from Practice A (pages 62–63) and rewrite it, adding enough specific details to make a well-developed paragraph.

C. Exchange paragraphs with a classmate. Mark any weaknesses you see in the topic sentence or in the paragraph's development. Rewrite at least one problematic area so that the paragraph is stronger, with enough appropriate supporting detail. In a sentence or two, explain why you made the changes you did.

■ **APPLYING WHAT YOU'VE LEARNED TO *YOUR* WRITING**

If you are currently drafting an essay, look closely at your body paragraphs. Find the topic sentence in each paragraph, and circle the key words that most clearly communicate the main idea of the paragraph. Then ask yourself whether the information in each paragraph effectively supports, explains, or illustrates the main idea of the paragraph's topic sentence. Is there enough information? If you're not sure, try numbering your supporting details. Are there too few to be persuasive? Does the paragraph present clear, specific supporting material, or does it contain too many vague generalities to be convincing? Where could you add more details to help the reader understand your ideas better and to make each paragraph more interesting? (For more help revising your paragraphs, see Chapter 5.) ■

■ Paragraph Unity

Every sentence in a body paragraph should relate directly to the main idea presented by the topic sentence. A paragraph must stick to its announced subject; it must not drift away into another discussion. In other words, a good paragraph has *unity*.

Examine the following unified paragraph; note that the topic sentence clearly states the paragraph's main point and that each sentence thereafter supports the topic sentence.

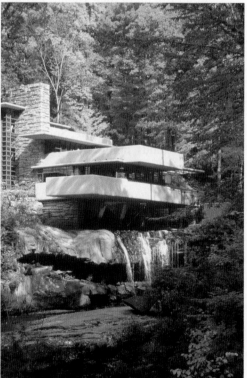

(1) Frank Lloyd Wright, America's leading architect of the first half of the twentieth century, believed that his houses should blend naturally with their building sites. (2) Consequently, he designed several "prairie houses," whose long, low lines echoed the flat earth plane. (3) Built of brick, stone, and natural wood, the houses shared a similar texture with their backgrounds. (4) Large windows were often used to blend the interior and exterior of the houses. (5) Wright also punctuated the lines and spaces of the houses with greenery in planters to further make the buildings look like part of nature.

Frank Lloyd Wright's Falling Water House in Bear Run, Pennsylvania

© Richard A. Cooke/CORBIS

The first sentence states the main idea, that Wright thought houses should blend with their location, and the other sentences support this assertion:

Topic Sentence: Wright's houses blend with their natural locations

(2) long, low lines echo flat prairie

(3) brick, stone, wood provide same texture as location

(4) windows blend inside with outside

(5) greenery in planters imitates the natural surroundings

Now look at the next paragraph, in which the writer strays from his original purpose:

(1) Cigarette smoke is unhealthy even for people who don't have the nicotine habit themselves. (2) Secondhand smoke can cause asthmatics and sufferers of sinusitis serious problems. (3) Doctors regularly advise heart patients to avoid confined smoky areas because coronary attacks might be triggered by the lack of clean air. (4) Moreover, having the smell of smoke in one's hair and clothes is a real nuisance. (5) Even if a person is without any health problems, exhaled smoke doubles the amount of carbon monoxide in the air, a condition that may cause lung problems in the future.

Sentence 4 refers to smoke as a nuisance and therefore does not belong in a paragraph that discusses smoking as a health hazard to nonsmokers.

Sometimes a large portion of a paragraph will drift into another topic. In the following paragraph, did the writer wish to focus on her messiness or on the beneficial effects of her engagement?

I have always been a very messy person. As a child, I was a pack rat, saving every little piece of insignificant paper that I thought might be important when I grew up. As a teenager, my pockets bulged with remnants of basketball tickets, hall passes, gum wrappers, and other important articles from my high school education. As a college student, I became a boxer—not a fighter, but someone who cannot throw anything away and therefore it winds up in a box in my closet. But my engagement has changed everything. I'm really pleased with the new stage of my life, and I owe it all to my fiancé. My overall outlook on life has changed because of his influence on me. I'm neater, much more cheerful, and I'm even getting places on time like I never did before. It's truly amazing what love can do.

Note shift from the topic of messiness

This writer may wish to discuss the changes her fiancé has inspired and then use her former messiness, tardiness, and other bad habits as examples illustrating those changes; however, as presented here, the paragraph is not unified around a central idea. On the contrary, it first seems to promise a discussion of her messiness but then wanders into comments on "what love can do."

Also beware a tendency to end your paragraph with a new idea. A new point calls for an entirely new paragraph. For example, the following paragraph focuses on the *origins* of Muzak; the last sentence, on Muzak's *effects* on workers, should be omitted or moved to a paragraph on Muzak's uses in the workplace.

Muzak, the ever-present sound of music that pervades elevators, office buildings, and reception rooms, was created over seventy years ago by George Owen Squier, an army general. A graduate of West Point, Squier was also an inventor and scientist. During World War I he headed the Signal Corps, where he began experimenting with the notion of transmitting simultaneous messages over power lines. When he retired from the army in 1922, he founded Wired Radio, Inc., and later, in 1934, the first Muzak medley was heard in Cleveland, Ohio, for homeowners willing to pay the great sum of $1.50 a month. That year he struck upon the now-famous name, which combined the idea of music with the brand name of the country's most popular camera, Kodak. *Today,*

Breaks unity *experiments show that workers get more done when they listen to Muzak.*

In general, think of paragraph unity in terms of the following diagram:

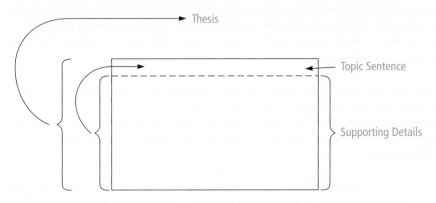

The sentences in the paragraph support the paragraph's topic sentence; the paragraph, in turn, supports the thesis statement.

■ PRACTICING WHAT YOU'VE LEARNED

In each of the following examples, delete or rewrite any information that interferes with the unity of the paragraph:

In the Great Depression of the 1930s, American painters suffered severely because few people had the money to spend on the luxury of owning art. To keep our artists from starving, the government ultimately set up the Federal Art Project, which paid then little-known painters such as Jackson Pollock, Arshile Gorky, and Willem de Kooning to paint murals in post offices, train stations, schools, housing projects, and other public places. During this period, songwriters were also affected by the Depression, and they produced such memorable songs as "Brother, Can You Spare a Dime?" The government-sponsored murals, usually depicting familiar American scenes and historical events, gave our young artists an opportunity to develop their skills and new techniques; in return, our country obtained thousands of elaborate works of art in over one thousand American cities. Sadly, many of these artworks were destroyed in later years as public buildings were torn down or remodeled.

After complaining in vain about the quality of food in the campus restaurant, University of Colorado students are having their revenge after all. The student body recently voted to rename the grill after Alferd Packer, the only American ever convicted of cannibalism. Packer was a Utah prospector trapped with an expedition of explorers in the southwest Colorado mountains during the winter of 1874; the sole survivor of the trip, he was later tried by a jury and sentenced to hang for dining on at least five of his companions. Colorado students are now holding an annual "Alferd Packer Day" and have installed a mural relating the prospector's story on the main wall of the restaurant. Some local wits have also suggested a new motto for the bar and grill: "Serving our fellow man since 1874." Another well-known incident of cannibalism in the West occurred in the winter of 1846, when the Donner party, a wagon train of eighty-seven California-bound immigrants, became trapped by ice and snow in the Sierra Nevada mountain range.

Inventors of food products often name their new creations after real people. In 1896 Leo Hirschfield hand-rolled a chewy candy and named it after his daughter Tootsie. In 1920 Otto Schnering gave the world the Baby Ruth candy bar, named after the daughter of former President Grover Cleveland. To publicize his new product, Schnering once dropped the candy tied to tiny parachutes from an airplane flying over Pittsburgh. One of our most popular soft drinks was named by a young suitor who sought to please his sweetheart's physician father, none other than old Dr. Pepper. Despite the honor, the girl's father never approved of the match, and the young man, Wade Morrison, married someone else.

States out West have often led the way in recognizing women's roles in politics. Wyoming, for example, was the first state to give women the right to vote and hold office, back in 1869 while the state was still a territory. Colorado was the second state to grant women's suffrage; Idaho, the third. Wyoming was also the first state to elect a woman as governor, Nellie Tayloe Ross, in1924. Montana elected Jeanette Rankin as the nation's first congresswoman in 1916. Former U.S. Representative from Colorado, Patricia Schroeder, claims to be the first person to take the congressional oath of office while clutching a handbag full of diapers. Ms. Schroeder later received the National Motherhood Award.

Living in a college dorm is a good way to meet people. There are activities every weekend, such as dances and parties where one can get acquainted with all kinds of students. Even just sitting by someone in the cafeteria during a meal can start a friendship. Making new friends from foreign countries can teach students more about international relations. A girl on my dorm floor, for example, is from Peru, and I've learned a lot about the customs and culture in her country. She's also helping me with my study of Spanish. I hope to visit her in Peru some day.

■ APPLYING WHAT YOU'VE LEARNED TO *YOUR* WRITING

If you have written a draft of an essay, underline the topic sentence in each body paragraph and circle the key words. For example, if in an essay on America's growing health consciousness, one of your topic sentences reads "In an effort to improve their health, Americans have increased the number of vitamins they consume," you might circle "Americans," "increased," and "vitamins." Then look closely at your paragraph. All the information in that paragraph should support the idea expressed in your topic sentence; nothing should detract from the idea of showing that Americans have increased their vitamin consumption. Now study the paragraphs in your draft, one by one. Cross out any sentence or material that interferes with the ideas in your topic sentences. If one of your paragraphs begins to drift away from its topic-sentence idea, you will need to rethink the purpose of that paragraph and rewrite so that the reader will understand what the paragraph is about. (For additional help revising your drafts, turn to Chapter 5.)

■ Paragraph Coherence

In addition to unity, *coherence* is essential to a good paragraph. Coherence means that all the sentences and ideas in your paragraph flow together to make a clear, logical point about your topic. Your paragraph should not be a confusing collection of ideas set down in random order. The readers should be able to follow what you have written and see easily and quickly how each sentence grows out of, or is related to, the preceding sentence. To achieve coherence, you should have a smooth connection or transition between the sentences in your paragraphs.

There are five important means of achieving coherence in your paragraphs:

1. A natural or easily recognized order

2. Transitional words and phrases

3. Repetition of key words

4. Substitution of pronouns for key nouns

5. Parallelism

These transitional devices are similar to the couplings between railroad cars; they enable the controlling engine to pull the train of thought along as a unit.

A Recognizable Ordering of Information

Without consciously thinking about the process, you may often organize paragraphs in easily recognized patterns that give the reader a sense of logical movement and order. Four common patterns of ordering sentences in a paragraph are discussed here.

The Order of Time

Some paragraphs are composed of details arranged in chronological order. You might, for example, explain the process of changing an oil filter on your car by beginning with the first step, draining the old oil, and concluding with the last step, installing the new filter. Here is a paragraph on black holes in which the writer chronologically orders the details:

> A black hole in space, from all indications, is the result of the death of a star. Scientists speculate that stars were first formed from the gases floating in the universe at the beginning of time. In the first stage in the life of a star, the hot gas is drawn by the force of gravity into a burning sphere. In the middle stage—our own sun being a middle-aged star—the burning continues at a regular rate, giving off enormous amounts of heat and light. As it grows old, however, the star eventually explodes to become what is called a nova, a superstar. But gravity soon takes over again, and the exploded star falls back in on itself with such force that all the matter in the star is compacted into a mass no larger than a few miles in diameter. At this point, no heavenly body can be seen in that area of the sky, as the tremendous pull of gravity lets nothing escape, not even light. A black hole has thus been formed.

The Order of Space

When your subject is a physical object, you should select some orderly means of describing it: from left to right, top to bottom, inside to outside, and so forth. For example, you might describe a sculpture as you walk around it from front to back. In the following paragraph describing a cowboy, the writer has ordered the details of the description in a head-to-feet pattern:

> Big Dave was pure cowboy. He wore a black felt hat so big that it kept his face in perpetual shade. Around his neck was knotted a red bandana stained with sweat from long hot days in the saddle. An oversized blue denim shirt hung from his shoulders to give him plenty of arm freedom, and his faded jeans were held up by a broad leather belt with a huge silver buckle featuring a snorting bronc in full buck. His boots, old and dirt-colored, kicked up little dust storms as he sauntered across the corral.

Deductive Order

A paragraph ordered deductively moves from a generalization to particular details that explain or support the general statement. Perhaps the most common pattern of all paragraphs, the deductive paragraph begins with its topic sentence and proceeds to its supporting details, as illustrated in the following example:

> If a group of 111 ninth-graders is typical of today's teenagers, spelling and social science teachers may be in for trouble. In a recent experiment, not one of

the students tested could write the Pledge of Allegiance correctly. In addition, the results showed that the students apparently had little understanding of the pledge's meaning. For example, several students described the United States as a "nation under guard" instead of "under God," and the phrase "to the Republic for which it stands" appeared in several responses as "of the richest stand" or "for Richard stand." Many students changed the word "indivisible" to the phrase "in the visible," and over 9 percent of the students, all of whom are Americans from varying racial and ethnic backgrounds, misspelled the word "America."

Inductive Order

An inductive paragraph begins with an examination of particular details and then concludes with a larger point or generalization about those details. Such a paragraph often ends with its topic sentence, as does the following paragraph on Little League baseball:

> At too many Little League baseball games, one or another adult creates a minor scene by yelling rudely at an umpire or a coach. Similarly, it is not uncommon to hear adults whispering loudly with one another in the stands over which child should have caught a missed ball. Perhaps the most astounding spectacle of all, however, is an irate parent or coach yanking a child off the field after a bad play for a humiliating lecture in front of the whole team. Sadly, Little League baseball today often seems intended more for childish adults than for the children who actually play it.

Transitional Words and Phrases

Some paragraphs may need internal transitional words to help the reader move smoothly from one thought to the next so that the ideas do not appear disconnected or choppy. Here is a list of common transitional words and phrases and their uses:

giving examples	for example, for instance, specifically, in particular, namely, another, other, in addition, to illustrate
comparison	similarly, not only . . . but also, in comparison
contrast	although, but, while, in contrast, however, though, on the other hand, nevertheless
sequence	first . . . second . . . third, finally, moreover, also, in addition, next, then, after, furthermore, and, previously
results	therefore, thus, consequently, as a result

Notice the difference the use of transitional words makes in the following paragraphs:

> Working in the neighborhood grocery store as a checker was one of the worst jobs I've ever had. In the first place, I had to wear an ugly, scratchy uniform cut at least three inches too short. My schedule of working hours was another inconvenience; because my hours were changed each week, it was impossible to make plans in advance, and getting a day off was out of the question. In addition, the lack of working space bothered me. Except for a half-hour lunch break, I was restricted to three square feet of room behind the counter and consequently felt as if I were no more than a cog in the cash register.

The same paragraph rewritten without transitional words sounds choppy and childish:

> Working in the neighborhood grocery store as a checker was one of the worst jobs I've ever had. I had to wear an ugly, scratchy uniform. It was cut at least three inches too short. My schedule of working hours was inconvenient. My hours changed each week. It was impossible to make plans in advance. Getting a day off was out of the question. The lack of working space bothered me. Except for a half-hour break, I was restricted to three square feet of room behind the counter. I felt like a cog in the cash register.

Although transitional words and phrases are useful in bridging the gaps between your ideas, don't overuse them. Not every sentence needs a transitional phrase, so use one only when the relationship between your thoughts needs clarification. It's also a mistake to place the transitional word in the same position in your sentence each time. Look at the paragraph that follows:

> It's a shame that every high school student isn't required to take a course in first aid. *For example*, you might need to treat a friend or relative for drowning during a family picnic. Or, *for instance*, someone might break a bone or receive a snakebite on a camping trip. *Also*, you should always know what to do for a common cut or burn. *Moreover*, it's important to realize when someone is in shock. *However*, very few people take the time to learn the simple rules of first aid. *Thus*, many injured or sick people suffer more than they should. *Therefore*, everyone should take a first aid course in school or at the Red Cross center.

As you can see, a series of sentences each beginning with a transitional word quickly becomes repetitious and boring. To hold your reader's attention, use transitional words only when necessary to avoid choppiness, and vary their placement in your sentences.

Repetition of Key Words

Important words or phrases (and their synonyms) may be repeated throughout a paragraph to connect the thoughts into a coherent statement:

> One of the most common, yet most puzzling, phobias is the *fear* of *snakes*. It's only natural, of course, to be afraid of a poisonous *snake*, but many people are just as frightened of the harmless varieties. For such people, a tiny green grass *snake* is as terrifying as a cobra. Some researchers say this unreasonable *fear* of any and all *snakes* is a legacy left to us by our cave-dwelling ancestors, for whom these *reptiles* were a real and constant danger. Others maintain that the *fear* is a result of our associating the *snake* with the notion of evil, as in the Garden of Eden. Whatever the reason, the fact remains that for many otherwise normal people, the mere sight of a *snake* slithering through the countryside is enough to keep them city dwellers forever.

The repeated words "fear" and "snake" and the synonym "reptile" help tie one sentence to another so that the reader can follow the ideas easily.

Pronouns Substituted for Key Nouns

A pronoun is a word that stands for a noun. In your paragraph you might use a key noun in one sentence and then use a pronoun in its place in the following sentences. The pronoun "it" often replaces "shark" in the description that follows:

> (1) The great white shark is perhaps the best equipped of all the ocean's predators. (2) *It* can grow up to twenty-one feet and weigh three tons, with two-inch teeth that can replace themselves within twenty-four hours when damaged. (3) The shark's sense of smell is so acute that *it* can detect one ounce of fish blood in a million ounces of water. (4) In addition, *it* can sense vibrations from six hundred feet away.

Sentences 2, 3, and 4 are tied to the topic sentence by the use of the pronoun "it."

Parallelism

Parallelism in a paragraph means using the same grammatical structure in several sentences to establish coherence. The repeated use of similar phrasing helps tie the ideas and sentences together. Next, for example, is a paragraph predominantly unified by its use of grammatically parallel sentences:

> (1) The weather of Texas offers something for everyone. (2) If you are the kind who likes to see snow drifting onto mountain peaks, a visit to the Big Bend area will satisfy your eye. (3) If, on the other hand, you demand a bright sun to bake your skin a golden brown, stop in the southern part of the state. (4) And for hardier souls, who ask from nature a show of force, the skies of the Panhandle regularly release ferocious springtime tornadoes. (5) Finally, if you are the fickle type, by all means come to central Texas, where the sun at any time may shine unashamed throughout the most torrential rainstorm.

The parallel structures of sentences 2, 3, and 5 ("if you" + verb) keep the paragraph flowing smoothly from one idea to the next.

Using a Variety of Transitional Devices

Most writers use a combination of transitional devices in their paragraphs. In the following example, three kinds of transitional devices are circled. See whether you can identify each one.

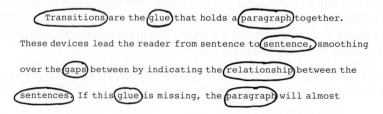

Transitions are the glue that holds a paragraph together. These devices lead the reader from sentence to sentence, smoothing over the gaps between by indicating the relationship between the sentences. If this glue is missing, the paragraph will almost

inevitably sound choppy or childish, even if every sentence in it
responds to a single topic commitment. However, transitions are
not substitutes for topic unity: like most glue, they are most
effective when joining similar objects, or, in this case, similar
ideas. For example, in a paragraph describing a chicken egg, no
transition could bridge the gap created by the inclusion of a
sentence concerned with naval losses in the Civil War. In other
words, transitions can call attention to the topic relationships
between sentences, but they cannot create those relationships.

transitional words	repetition of pronouns	repetition of key words

Avoiding Whiplash

The preceding example not only illustrates a variety of transitional devices but also makes an important point about their use—and their limitations. Transitional devices show connection between sentences, but they alone cannot create a logical flow of ideas if none exists. For example, notice in the following sample the "disconnect" between the first three sentences and sentence 4:

> (1) Despite our growing dependency on computers, one of our most useful household tools is still the lowly pencil. (2) Cheap, efficient, and long-lasting, the pencil may be operated by children and adults alike, without the necessity of a user's manual or tech support. (3) According to the Incense Cedar Institute, today's pencil can draw a line 70 miles long, be sharpened 17 times, and write an average of 45,000 words. (4) Chinese factories don't have to follow as many environmental regulations, and their workers are paid less than their American counterparts. (5) Many pencils used in this country are still manufactured in China because of the cheaper cost.

Did you suffer "reader's whiplash" as your mind experienced the sudden jerk from the discussion of pencil use to "Chinese factories"? No addition of a simple transitional word will fix this problem; the writer needs to revise the paragraph's internal logic and flow or perhaps even consider a new paragraph on cost or production. In other words, don't rely on transitional devices when deep-structure revision for coherence is needed. Make your reader's trip through your prose an enjoyable one by avoiding sudden stops and starts in thought, and then smooth that ride with appropriate transitional devices when they are necessary.

■ **PRACTICING WHAT YOU'VE LEARNED**

A. Identify each of the following paragraphs as ordered by time, space, or parallelism:

My apartment is so small that it will no longer hold all my possessions. Every day when I come in the door, I am shocked by the clutter. The wall to my immediate left is completely obscured by art and movie posters that have become so numerous they often overlap, even hiding each other. Along the adjoining wall is my sound system: CDs and tapes are stacked several feet high on two long, low tables. The big couch that runs across the back of the room is always piled so high with schoolbooks and magazines that a guest usually ends up sitting on the floor. To my right is a large sliding glass door that opens onto a balcony—or at least it used to, before it was permanently blocked by my tennis gear, golf clubs, and ten-speed bike. Even the tiny closet next to the front door is bursting with clothes, both clean and dirty. I think the time has come for me to move.

Once-common acts of greeting may be finding renewed popularity after three centuries. According to one historian, kissing was at the height of its popularity as a greeting in seventeenth-century England, when ladies and gentlemen of the court often saluted each other in this affectionate manner. Then the country was visited by a strange plague, whose cause was unknown. Because no one knew how the plague was spread, people tried to avoid physical contact with others as much as possible. Both kissing and the handshake went out of fashion and were replaced by the bow and curtsy, so people could greet others without having to touch them. The bow and curtsy remained in vogue for over a hundred years, until the handshake—for men only—returned to popularity in the nineteenth century. Today, both men and women may shake hands upon meeting others, and kissing as a greeting is making a comeback—especially among the jet-setters and Hollywood stars.

Students have diverse ways of preparing for final exams. Some stay up the night before, trying to cram into their brains what they avoided all term. Others pace themselves, spending a little time each night going over the notes they took in class that day. Still others just cross their fingers, assuming they absorbed enough along the way from lectures and readings. In the end, though, everyone hopes the tests are easy.

B. Circle and identify the transitional devices in the following paragraphs:

Each year I follow a system when preparing firewood to use in my stove. First, I hike about a mile from my house with my bow saw in hand. I then select three good-size oak trees and mark them with orange ties. Next, I saw through the base of each tree about two feet from the ground. After I fell the trees, not only do I trim away the branches, but I also sort the scrap from the usable limbs. I find cutting the trees into manageable-length logs is too much for one day; however, I roll them off the ground so they will not begin to rot. The next day I cut the trees into eight-foot lengths, which allows me to handle them more easily. Once they are cut, I roll them along the fire lane to the edge of the road, where I stack them neatly but not too high. The next day I borrow my uncle's van, drive to the pile of logs, and load as many logs as I can, thus reducing the number of trips. When I finally have all the logs in my backyard, I begin sawing them into eighteen-inch lengths. I create large piles that consequently have to be split and finally stacked. The logs will age and dry until winter, when I will make daily trips to the woodpile.

Fans of professional baseball and football argue continually over which is America's favorite spectator sport. Though the figures on attendance for each vary with every new season, certain arguments remain the same, spelling out both the enduring appeals of each game and something about the people who love to watch. Football, for instance, is a quicker, more physical sport, and football fans enjoy the emotional involvement they feel while watching. Baseball, on the other hand, seems more mental, like chess, and attracts those fans who prefer a quieter, more complicated game. In addition, professional football teams usually play no more than fourteen games a year, providing fans with a whole week between games to work themselves up to a pitch of excitement and expectation. Baseball teams, however, play almost every day for six months, so that the typical baseball fan is not so crushed by missing a game, knowing there will be many other chances to attend. Finally, football fans seem to love the half-time pageantry, the marching bands, the cheers, and the mascots, whereas baseball fans are often more content to concentrate on the game's finer details and spend the breaks between innings filling out their own private scorecards.

C. The following paragraph lacks common transitional devices. Fill in each blank with the appropriate transitional word or key word.

Scientists continue to debate the cause of the dinosaurs' disappearance. One group claims the _____ vanished after a comet smashed into the Earth; dust and smoke _____ blocked the sun for a long time. _____ of no direct sunlight, the Earth underwent a lengthy "winter," far too cold for the huge _____ to survive. A University of California paleontologist, _____, disputes this claim. He argues that _____ we generally think of _____ living in swampy land, fossils found in Alaska show that _____ could live in cold climates _____ warm ones. _____ group claims that the _____ became extinct following an intense period of global volcanic activity. _____ to killing the _____ themselves, these scientists _____ believe the volcanic activity killed much of the plant life that the _____ ate and, _____, many of the great _____ who survived the volcanic eruptions starved to death. Still _____ groups of _____ claim the _____ were destroyed by acid rain, by a passing "death star," _____ even by viruses from outer space.

D. The sentences in each of the following exercises are out of order. By noting the various transitional devices, you should be able to arrange each group of sentences into a coherent paragraph.

Paragraph 1: How to Purchase a New Car

a. If you're happy with the car's performance, find out about available financing arrangements.

b. Later, at home, study your notes carefully to help you decide which car fits your needs.

c. After you have discussed various loans and interest rates, you can negotiate the final price with the salesperson.

d. A visit to the showroom also allows you to test-drive the car.

e. Once you have agreed on the car's price, feel confident that you have made a well-chosen purchase.

f. Next, a visit to a nearby showroom should help you select the color, options, and style of the car of your choice.

g. First, take a trip to the library to read the current auto magazines.

h. As you read, take notes on models and prices.

Paragraph 2: Henry VIII and the Problems of Succession

a. After Jane, Henry took three more wives, but all these marriages were childless.

b. Jane did produce a son, Edward VI, but he died at age fifteen.

c. The problem of succession was therefore an important issue during the reign of Henry VIII.

d. Still hoping for a son, Henry beheaded Anne and married Jane Seymour.

e. Thus, despite his six marriages, Henry failed in his attempts to produce a male heir for the British throne.

f. In sixteenth-century England it was considered essential for a son to assume the throne.

g. Henry's first wife, Catherine of Aragon, had only one child, the Princess Mary.

h. Anne and Henry also produced a daughter, the future Queen Elizabeth I.

i. Consequently, he divorced Catherine and married Anne Boleyn.

■ Paragraph Sequence

The order in which you present your paragraphs is another decision you must make. In some essays, the subject matter itself will suggest its own order.* For instance, in an essay designed to instruct a beginning runner, you might want to discuss the necessary equipment—good running shoes, loose-fitting clothing, and a sweatband—before moving to a discussion of where to run and how to run. Other essay topics, however, may not suggest a natural order, in which case you must decide which order will most effectively reach and hold the attention of your audience. Frequently, writers withhold their strongest point until last. (Lawyers often use this technique; they first present the jury with the weakest arguments, then pull out the most incriminating evidence—the "smoking gun." Thus the jury members retire with the strongest argument freshest in their minds.) Sometimes, however, you'll find it necessary to present one particular point first so that the other points make good sense. Study your own major points, and decide which order will be the most logical, successful way of persuading your reader to accept your thesis.

■ Transitions between Paragraphs

As you already know, each paragraph usually signals a new major point in your discussion. These paragraphs should not appear as isolated blocks of thought but rather as parts of a unified, step-by-step progression. To avoid a choppy essay, link each paragraph to the one before it with *transitional devices*. Just as the sentences in your paragraphs are connected, so are the paragraphs themselves; therefore, you can use the same transitional devices suggested on pages 70–73.

The first sentence of most body paragraphs frequently contains the transitional device. To illustrate this point, here are some topic sentences lifted from the body paragraphs of a student essay criticizing a popular sports car, renamed the 'Gator to protect the guilty and to prevent lawsuits. The transitional devices are italicized.

Thesis: The *'Gator* is one of the worst cars on the market.

- When you buy a *'Gator*, you buy physical inconvenience. [repetition of key word from thesis]

- *Another* reason the *'Gator* is a bad buy is the cost of insurance. [transitional word, key word]

- You might overlook the *inconvenient* size and exorbitant *insurance* rates if the *'Gator* were a strong, reliable car, *but* this automobile constantly needs repair. [key words from preceding paragraphs, transitional word]

- When you decide to sell this *car*, you face *still another* unpleasant surprise: the extremely low resale value. [key word, transitional phrase]

- The most serious drawback, *however*, is the *'Gator*'s safety record. [transitional word, key word]

---

* For more information on easily recognized patterns of order, see pages 69–70.

Sometimes, instead of using transitional words or repetition of key words or their synonyms, you can use an *idea hook*. The last idea of one paragraph can lead you smoothly into your next paragraph. Instead of repeating a key word from the previous discussion, find a phrase that refers to the entire idea just expressed. If, for example, the previous paragraph discussed the highly complimentary advertising campaign for the 'Gator, the next paragraph might begin, "This view of the 'Gator as an economy car is ridiculous to anyone who has pumped a week's salary into this gas guzzler." The phrase "this view" connects the idea of the first paragraph with the one that follows. Idea hooks also work well with transitional words: "This view, however, is ridiculous. . . ."

If you do use transitional words, don't allow them to make your essay sound mechanical. For example, a long series of paragraphs beginning "first . . . second . . . third . . ." quickly becomes boring. Vary the type and position of your transitional devices so that your essay has a subtle but logical movement from point to point.

■ APPLYING WHAT YOU'VE LEARNED TO *YOUR* WRITING

If you are currently working on a draft of an essay, check each body paragraph for coherence, the smooth connection of ideas and sentences in a logical, easy-to-follow order. You might try placing brackets around key words, pronouns, and transitional words that carry the reader's attention from thought to thought and from sentence to sentence. Decide whether you have enough ordering devices, placed in appropriate places, or whether you need to add (or delete) others. (For additional help revising your drafts, turn to Chapter 5.)

★ CHAPTER 3 SUMMARY

Here is a brief restatement of what you should know about the paragraphs in the body of your essay:

1. Each body paragraph usually contains one major point in the discussion promised by the thesis statement.

2. Each major point is presented in the topic sentence of a paragraph.

3. Each paragraph should be adequately developed with clear supporting detail.

4. Every sentence in the paragraph should support the topic sentence.

5. There should be an orderly, logical flow from sentence to sentence and from thought to thought.

6. The sequence of your essay's paragraphs should be logical and effective.

7. There should be a smooth flow from paragraph to paragraph.

8. The body paragraphs should successfully persuade your reader that the opinion expressed in your thesis is valid.

Chapter 4

Beginnings and Endings

As you work on your rough drafts, you might think of your essay as a coherent, unified whole composed of three main parts: the introduction (lead-in, thesis, and essay map), the body (paragraphs with supporting evidence), and the conclusion (final address to the reader). These three parts should flow smoothly into one another, presenting the reader with an organized, logical discussion. The following pages will suggest ways to begin, end, and also name your essay effectively.

■ How to Write a Good Lead-in

The first few sentences of your essay are particularly important; first impressions, as you know, are often lasting ones. The beginning of your essay, then, must catch the readers' attention and make them want to keep reading. Recall the way you read a magazine: if you are like most people, you probably skim the magazine, reading a paragraph or two of each article that looks promising. If the first few paragraphs hold your interest, you read on. When you write your own introductory paragraph, assume that you have only a few sentences to attract your reader. Consequently, you must pay particular attention to making those first lines especially interesting and well written.

In some essays, your thesis statement alone may be controversial or striking enough to capture the readers. At other times, however, you will want to use the introductory device called a *lead-in*.* The lead-in (1) catches the readers' attention; (2) announces the subject

---

* Do note that for some writing assignments, such as certain kinds of technical reports, attention-grabbing lead-ins are not appropriate. Frequently, these reports are directed toward particular professional audiences and have their own designated format; they often begin, for example, with a statement of the problem under study or with a review of pertinent information or research.

matter and tone of your essay (humorous, satiric, serious, etc.); and (3) sets up, or leads into, the presentation of your thesis and essay map.

Here are some suggestions for and examples of lead-ins:

1. A paradoxical or intriguing statement

> "Eat two chocolate bars and call me in the morning," says the psychiatrist to the patient. Such advice sounds like a sugar fanatic's dream, but recent studies have indeed confirmed that chocolate positively affects depression and anxiety.

2. An arresting statistic or shocking statement

> One of every nine women will develop breast cancer this year, according to a recent report prepared by the Health Information Service.

3. A question

> It is three times the number of people who belong to the Southern Baptist Convention, nine times the number who serve in the U.S. armed forces, and more than twice the number who voted for Barry Goldwater for president in 1964. What is it? It's the number of people in the United States who admit to having smoked marijuana: a massive 70 million.

4. A quotation from a recognized authority, historical figure, or literary source

> Confucius wisely noted that "our greatest glory is not in never falling, but in rising every time we fall." Despite a frustrating series of close losses, my soccer team faced every new game with optimism and determination. My teammates' never-give-up attitudes have shown me that the value of sport is not winning but learning how to face defeat and begin again.

Note too that sometimes writers may challenge the wisdom of authorities or use their words in humorous ways to introduce lighthearted essays:

> When Einstein wrote that the "most beautiful thing we can experience is the mysterious," I don't believe he was thinking about the mystery smell coming from our attic last summer.

5. A relevant story, joke, or anecdote

> Writer and witty critic Dorothy Parker was once assigned a remote, out-of-the-way office. According to the story, she became so lonely, so desperate for company, that she ultimately painted "Gentlemen" on the door. Although this university is large, no one on this campus needs to feel as isolated as Parker obviously did: our excellent Student Activity Office offers numerous clubs, programs, and volunteer groups to involve students of all interests.

6. A description, often used for emotional appeal

> With one eye blackened, one arm in a cast, and third-degree burns on both her legs, the pretty, blond two-year-old seeks corners of rooms, refuses to speak, and shakes violently at the sound of loud noises. Tammy is not the victim of a war or a natural disaster; rather, she is the helpless victim of her parents, one of the thousands of children who suffer daily from America's hidden crime, child abuse.

7. A factual statement or a summary who-what-where-when-why lead-in

> Texas's first execution of a woman in twenty-two years occurred September 17 at the Huntsville Unit of the state's Department of Corrections, despite the protests of various human rights groups around the country.

8. An analogy or comparison

> The Romans kept geese on their Capitol Hill to cackle alarm in the event of attack by night. Modern Americans, despite their technology, have hardly improved on that old system of protection. According to the latest Safety Council report, almost any door with a standard lock can be opened easily with a common plastic credit card.

9. A contrast or a before-and-after scenario

> I used to search for toast in the supermarket. I used to think "blackened"—as in blackened Cajun shrimp—referred to the way I cooked anything in a skillet. "Poached" could only have legal ramifications. But all that has changed! Attending a class in basic cooking this summer has transformed the way I purchase, prepare, and even talk about food.

10. A personal experience

> I realized times were changing for women when I overheard my six-year-old nephew speaking to my sister, a prominent New York lawyer. As we left her elaborate, luxurious office one evening, Tommy looked up at his mother and queried, "Mommy, can little boys grow up to be lawyers, too?"

11. A catalog of relevant examples or facts

> A two-hundred-pound teenager quit school because no desk would hold her. A three-hundred-pound chef who could no longer stand on his feet was fired. A three-hundred-fifty-pound truck driver broke furniture in his friends' houses. All these people are now living healthier, happier, and thinner lives, thanks to the remarkable intestinal bypass surgery first developed in 1967.

12. Statement of a problem or a popular misconception

> Some people believe that poetry is written only by aging beatniks or solemn, mournful men and women with suicidal tendencies. The Poetry in the Schools Program is working hard to correct that erroneous point of view.

13. Brief dialogue to introduce the topic

> "Be bold! You can do it!" said my roommate again and again during the weeks before choir tryouts, despite my whimpering cries of "I can't, I can't." For a shy person like me, the thought of singing in a public audition was agony. But thanks to the ABC Relaxation Method suggested by the Counseling Center, I performed so well I was chosen for a solo. The ABC method, incorporating visualization and proper breathing techniques, is a helpful process every shy person should practice regularly.

14. A proverb, maxim, or motto

> "One falsehood spoils a thousand truths," says the African proverb. Caught in the biggest lie of his political career, once-popular local mayor Paul TerGhist is learning the meaning of this old saying the hard way, as his former friends and supporters are now deserting him.

15. A recognition, revelation, or insight

> As someone who earned "A's" throughout my Spanish classes, I thought I had a good grasp of the language. However, immersion in the Tres Amigos Building Project in Monterrey, Mexico, over Spring Break this year showed me I had much to learn about conversational speech patterns.

Thinking of a good lead-in is often difficult when you sit down to begin your essay. Many writers, in fact, skip the lead-in until the first draft is written. They compose their working thesis first and then write the body of the essay, saving the lead-in and conclusion for last. As you write the middle of your essay, you may discover an especially interesting piece of information you might want to save to use as your lead-in.

■ Avoiding Errors in Lead-ins

In addition to the previous suggestions, here is some advice to help you avoid common lead-in errors:

Make sure your lead-in introduces your thesis. A frequent weakness in introductory paragraphs is an interesting lead-in but no smooth or clear transition to the thesis statement. To avoid a gap or awkward jump in thought in your introductory paragraph, you may need to add a connecting sentence or phrase between your lead-in and thesis. Study the following paragraph, which uses a comparison as its lead-in. The italicized transitional sentence takes the reader from a general comment about Americans who use wheelchairs to information about those in Smallville, smoothly preparing the reader for the thesis that follows.

Lead-in
Transitional sentence
Thesis

> In the 1950s African Americans demanded the right to sit anywhere they pleased on public buses. Today, Americans who use wheelchairs are fighting for the right to board those same buses. *Here in Smallville, the lack of proper boarding facilities often denies disabled citizens basic transportation to jobs, grocery stores, and medical centers.* To give people in wheelchairs the same opportunities as other residents, the City Council should vote the funds necessary to convert the public transportation system.

Keep your lead-in brief. Long lead-ins in short essays often give the appearance of a tail wagging the dog. Use a brief, attention-catching hook to set up your thesis; don't make your introduction the biggest part of your essay.

Don't begin with an apology or complaint. Such statements as "It's difficult to find much information on this topic . . ." and "This controversy is hard to understand, but . . ." do nothing to entice your reader.

Don't assume your audience already knows your subject matter. Identify the pertinent facts even though you know your teacher knows the assignment. ("The biggest problem with the new requirement . . . ." What requirement?) If you are writing about a particular piece of literature or art, identify the title of the work and its author or artist, using the full name in the first reference.

Stay clear of overused lead-ins. If composition teachers had a nickel for every essay that began with a dry dictionary definition, they could all retire to Bermuda. Leave Webster's alone and find a livelier way to begin. Asking a question as your lead-in is becoming overworked, too, so use it only when it is obviously the best choice for your opener.

■ **PRACTICING WHAT YOU'VE LEARNED**

Describe the lead-ins in the following paragraphs. Did any of the writers blend more than one kind of lead-in?

1. In the sixth century, Lao-Tzu, the father of Taoism, described the "good traveler" as someone who has "no fixed plans and is not intent on arriving." If that ancient Chinese philosopher is correct, then my aimless but eventful wanderings across the South last fall qualify me as a World-Class Traveler.

2. Ever wonder if those long hours hitting the books are worth it? Do grades really matter to employers? According to a survey by the National Association of Colleges and Employers, the answer is . . . yes. Strong grades and a go-getter attitude are the keys to securing a good job after college.

3. An average can of soda may contain ten or more teaspoons of sugar. If you are one of the college students who drinks a can or two of pop everyday, you could be consuming as much as thirty-two pounds of sugar every year! Cutting back on soft drinks is an easy way people can achieve a healthier diet.

4. I used to think bees were my friends. They make the honey I like to eat, and they help pollinate the flowers I like to smell. But after being stung multiple times and spending three days in the hospital last summer, I have come to see the little creatures in a totally different light. For those of us who are allergic to their venom, bees are flying killers whose buzz sends us scurrying for cover.

5. On May 6, 1937, the *Hindenburg*, a luxurious German airship with cabins for fifty, exploded into flames as it tried to land in New Jersey, killing thirty-six people and ending zeppelin passenger service forever. Theories about the cause of this mysterious explosion include lightning and static electricity, but the most intriguing explanation involves sabotage and betrayal.

© Baldwin H. Ward & Kathryn C. Ward/CORBIS

■ **ASSIGNMENT**

Find three good lead-ins from essays, magazine articles, or newspaper feature stories. Identify the kinds of lead-ins you found, and tell why you think each effectively catches the reader's attention and sets up the thesis.

■ How to Write a Good Concluding Paragraph

Like a good story, a good essay should not stop in the middle. It should have a satisfying conclusion, one that gives the reader a sense of completion on the subject. Don't allow your essay to drop off or fade out at the end—instead, use the concluding paragraph to emphasize the validity and importance of your thinking. Remember that the concluding paragraph is your last chance to convince the reader. (As one cynical but realistic student pointed out, the conclusion may be the last part of your essay the teacher reads before putting a grade on your paper.) Therefore, make your conclusion count.

Some people feel that writing an essay shares a characteristic with a romantic fling—both activities are frequently easier to begin than they are to end. If you find, as many writers do, that you often struggle while searching for an exit with the proper emphasis and grace, here are some suggestions, by no means exhaustive, that might spark some good ideas for your conclusions:

1. A summary of the thesis and the essay's major points (most useful in long essays)

   > The destruction of the rainforests must be stopped. Although developers protest that they are bringing much-needed financial aid into these traditionally poverty-stricken areas, no amount of money can compensate for what is being lost. Without the rainforests, we are not only contributing to the global warming of the entire planet, we are losing indigenous trees and plants that might someday provide new medicines or vaccines for diseases. Moreover, the replacement of indigenous peoples with corporation-run ranches robs the world of cultural diversity. For the sake of the planet's well-being, Project Rainforest should be implemented.

2. An evaluation of the importance of the essay's subject

   > These amazing, controversial photographs of the comet will continue to be the subject of debate because, according to some scientists, they yield the most important clues yet revealed about the origins of our universe.

3. A statement of the essay's broader implications

   > Because these studies of feline leukemia may someday play a crucial role in the discovery of a cure for AIDS in human beings, the experiments, as expensive as they are, must continue.

4. A recommendation or call to action

   > The specific details surrounding the death of World War II hero Raoul Wallenberg are still unknown. Although Russia has recently admitted—after fifty years of denial—that Wallenberg was murdered by the KGB in 1947, such a confession is not enough. We must write our congressional representatives today urging their support for the new Swedish commission investigating the circumstances of his death. No hero deserves less.

5. A warning based on the essay's thesis

   > Understanding the politics that led to Hiroshima is essential for all Americans—indeed, for all the world's peoples. Without such knowledge, the frightful possibility exists that somewhere, sometime, someone might drop the bomb again.

6. A quotation from an authority or someone whose insight emphasizes the main point

   > Even though I didn't win the fiction contest, I learned so much about my own powers of creativity. I'm proud that I pushed myself in new directions. I know now I will always agree with Herman Melville, whose writing was unappreciated in his own time, that "it is better to struggle with originality than to succeed in imitation."

7. An anecdote or brief example that emphasizes or sums up the point of the essay

> Bette Davis's role on and off the screen as the catty, wisecracking woman of steel helped make her an enduring star. After all, no audience, past or present, could ever resist a dame who drags on a cigarette and then mutters about a passing starlet, "There goes a good time that was had by all."

8. An image or description that lends finality to the essay

> As the last of the Big Screen's giant ants are incinerated by the army scientist, one can almost hear the movie audiences of the 1950s breathing a collective sigh of relief, secure in the knowledge that once again the threat of nuclear radiation had been vanquished by the efforts of the U.S. military.

(For another brief image that captures the essence of an essay, see also the "open house" scene that concludes "To Bid the World Farewell," page 210.)

9. A rhetorical question that makes the readers think about the essay's main point

> No one wants to see hostages put in danger. But what nation can afford to let terrorists know they can get away with blackmail?

10. A forecast based on the essay's thesis

> Soap operas will continue to be popular not only because they distract us from our daily chores but also because they present life as we want it to be: fast-paced, glamorous, and full of exciting characters.

11. An ironic twist, witticism, pun, or playful use of words (often more appropriate in lighthearted essays)

> After analyzing and understanding the causes of my procrastination, I now feel better, more determined to change my behavior. In fact, I've decided that today is the day for decisive action! I will choose a major! Hmmmm . . . or maybe not. I need to think about it some more. I'll get back to you, okay? Tomorrow. Really.

12. Return to the technique used in your lead-in (answer a question you asked, circle back to a story, extend a quotation, etc.)

> So was Dorothy right in *The Wizard of Oz*? After the lonely summer I spent in Wyoming, mending barbed-wire fences, wrestling angry calves, and nursing painful injuries, I could think of nothing else on the long bus trip back to my parents' house. As eager as I had been to leave, I couldn't wait to get back there. It wasn't Kansas, but Dorothy and I knew the truth: there's no place like home.

Hint: After reading the suggestions above, if you are still struggling with your conclusion, turn back to the advice for writing lead-ins, on pages 79–82. One of the suggestions there may trigger a useful idea for closing your essay. In fact, following a first draft, you may decide that the technique you chose to open your essay might be used more effectively to conclude it.

■ Avoiding Errors in Conclusions

Try to omit the following common errors in your concluding paragraphs:

Avoid a boring, mechanical ending. One of the most frequent weaknesses in student essays is the conclusion that merely restates the thesis, word for word. A brief essay of 500 to 750 words rarely requires a flat, point-by-point conclusion; in fact, such an ending often insults the readers' intelligence by implying that their attention spans are extremely short. Only after reading long essays do most readers need a precise recap of all the writer's main ideas. Instead of recopying your thesis and essay map, try finding an original, emphatic way to conclude your essay—or as a well-known newspaper columnist described it, a good ending should snap with grace and authority, like the close of an expensive sports car door.

Don't introduce new points or irrelevant material. Treat the major points of your essay in separate body paragraphs rather than in your exit. Stay focused on your essay's specific thesis and purpose; don't allow any unimportant or off-subject comments to drift into your concluding remarks.

Don't tack on a conclusion. There should be a smooth, logical flow of thought from your last body paragraph into your concluding statements.

Don't change your stance. Sometimes writers who have been critical of something throughout their essays will soften their stance or offer apologies in their last paragraph. For instance, someone complaining about the poor quality of a particular college course might abruptly conclude with statements that declare the class wasn't so bad after all, maybe she should have worked harder, or maybe she really did learn something after all. Such reneging may seem polite, but in actuality it undercuts the thesis and confuses the reader who has taken the writer's criticisms seriously. Instead of contradicting themselves, writers should stand their ground, forget about puffy clichés or "niceties," and find an emphatic way to conclude that is consistent with their thesis.

Avoid trite expressions. Don't begin your conclusion by declaring, "in conclusion," "in summary," or "as you can see, this essay proves my thesis that . . . ." End your essay so that the reader clearly senses completion; don't merely announce that you're finished.

Don't insult or anger your reader. No matter how right you feel you are, resist the temptation to set up an "either-or" conclusion in an argumentative essay: either you agree with me or you are an ignorant/wrong/selfish/immoral person. Don't exaggerate your claims or moralize excessively as you exit. Remember that your purpose is to inform and persuade your readers, not to annoy them to the point of rejecting your thesis out of sheer irritation. Conclude on a positive note, one that encourages readers to see matters your way.

▪ PRACTICING WHAT YOU'VE LEARNED

Identify the weaknesses you see in the following conclusions. How might these writers revise to create more satisfactory endings for their essays?

1. My thesis in this essay stated that I believe that having to change schools does not harm children for three reasons. Children at new schools learn how to make new friends. They learn how to get along with a variety of people. They also learn about different teaching styles. For these three reasons, I believe that having to change schools does not harm children.

2. "A journey of a thousand miles begins with a single step." As I discussed in this causal analysis essay, I would have never started painting again if I hadn't gone back to school. I'm the first to admit that it was a long, hard road to get my degree, and sometimes I really questioned the value of certain courses I had to take (like algebra, for example, which I think is a totally useless course for artists. The entire math requirement needs revision, in my opinion). But going back to school was the right choice for me and, who knows, maybe it would be for others.

3. In conclusion, as I have shown here, our country's forest conservation policies are just plain stupid. If you don't stand up and join the fight against them, I hope you will enjoy living in a tent because pretty soon there isn't going to be any lumber for houses left. After selling out to the tree-huggers, will you be able to look at yourself in the mirror?

▪ ASSIGNMENT

Find three good concluding paragraphs. Identify each kind of conclusion, and tell why you think it is an effective ending for the essay or article.

▪ How to Write a Good Title

As in the case of lead-ins, your title may be written at any time, but many writers prefer to finish their essays before naming them. A good title is similar to a good newspaper headline in that it attracts the readers' interest and makes them want to investigate the essay. Like the lead-in, the title helps announce the tone of the essay. An informal or humorous essay, for instance, might have a catchy, funny title. Some titles show the writer's wit and love of wordplay; a survey of recent magazines revealed these titles: "Bittersweet News about Saccharin," "Coffee: New Grounds for Concern," and "The Scoop on the Best Ice Cream."

On the other hand, a serious, informative essay should have a more formal title that suggests its content as clearly and specifically as possible. Let's suppose, for example, that you are researching the meaning of color in dreams, and you see an article in a database list titled merely "Dreams." You don't know whether you should bother to read it. To avoid such confusion in your own essay and to encourage readers' interest, always use a specific title: "Interpreting Animal Imagery in Dreams," "Dream Research: An Aid to Diagnosing Depression," and so forth. Moreover, if your subject matter is controversial, let the reader know which side you're on (e.g., "The Advantages of Solar Power"). Never substitute a mere label, such as "Football Games" or "Euthanasia," for a meaningful title. And never, never label your essays "Theme One" or "Comparison and Contrast Essay." In all your writing, including the title, use your creativity to attract the readers' attention and to invite their interest in your ideas.

If you're unsure about how to present your title, here are three basic rules:

1. Your own title should not be underlined or put in quotation marks. It should be written at the top of page one of your essay or on an appropriate cover sheet with no special marks of punctuation.

2. Capitalize the first, last, and important words of your title. Generally, do not capitalize such words as "an," "and," "a," or "the," or prepositions, unless they appear as the first or last words of the title or follow a colon within the title.

3. Sometimes writers craft a title that presents a word or phrase followed by a colon introducing a definition, a revealing image, a question, or some other kind of explanatory material to interest the reader.

   Examples   *JFK: Reckless Youth*
   "Memories Carved in Stone: Tennessee Pioneer Memorials"
   "Intervention in Iran: A Recipe for Disaster"
   "Yoga: Does Twisting Like a Pretzel Really Help?"

You may use such titles to clarify a work's scope or perhaps to set the appropriate tone for your reader, but be careful not to overuse this structure. (Note that the word after the colon is capitalized as if it were the first word of the title.)

■ PRACTICING WHAT YOU'VE LEARNED

Describe any weaknesses you see in the following titles. How might each one be revised to clarify its essay's content and to attract more reader interest?

1. Advice for College Freshmen
2. Essay Assignment #3: "Review of a Favorite Movie"
3. Learning to Play Texas Hold'em
4. A Comparison of Two Heroes
5. The Problem of Abandoned Pets and Its Solution
6. Steroids and Athletes Today
7. The Effects of Three Popular Diets
8. The Best Notebook Computer on the Market
9. An Explanation of the Human Genome Project
10. My Interpretation of Auden's "The Unknown Citizen"

▪ ASSIGNMENT

Read one of the student or professional essays in this text and evaluate the title. Explain why you think the title is/is not effective. Or, if you prefer, write a new title for one of the essays in this book. Why is your choice as effective as (or even better than) that of the original writer?

▪ APPLYING WHAT YOU'VE LEARNED TO *YOUR* WRITING

Look at the draft of the essay you are currently working on, and ask yourself these questions:

- Does the opening of my essay make my reader want to continue reading? Does the lead-in smoothly set up my thesis, or do I need to add some sort of transition to help move the reader to my main idea? Is the lead-in appropriate in terms of the tone and length of my essay?

- Does the conclusion of my essay offer an emphatic ending, one that is consistent with my essay's purpose? Have I avoided a mechanical, trite, or tacked-on closing paragraph? Have I refrained from adding a new point in my conclusion that belongs in the body of my essay or in another essay?

- Does my title interest my reader? Are its content and tone appropriate for this particular essay?

If you have answered "no" to any of these questions, you should continue revising your essay. (For more help revising your prose, turn to Chapter 5.)

★ CHAPTER 4 SUMMARY

Here is a brief restatement of what you should remember about writing introductions, conclusions, and titles:

1. Many essays will profit from a lead-in, the first sentences of the introductory paragraph that attract the reader's attention and smoothly set up the thesis statement.

2. Essays should end convincingly, without being repetitive or trite, with thoughts that emphasize the writer's main purpose.

3. Titles should invite the reader's interest by indicating the general nature of the essay's content and its tone.

C h a p t e r 5

Drafting and Revising: Creative Thinking, Critical Thinking

There is no good writing, only rewriting.
—JAMES THURBER

When I say writing, O, believe me, it is rewriting that I have chiefly in mind.
—ROBERT LOUIS STEVENSON

The absolute necessity of revision cannot be overemphasized. All good writers rethink, rearrange, and rewrite large portions of their prose. The French novelist Colette, for instance, wrote everything over and over. In fact, she often spent an entire morning working on a single page. Hemingway, to cite another example, rewrote the ending to *A Farewell to Arms* thirty-nine times "to get the words right." Although no one expects you to make thirty-nine drafts of each essay, the point is clear: writing well means revising. **All good writers revise their prose.**

■ What Is Revision?

Revision is a *thinking process* that occurs any time you are working on a writing project. It means looking at your writing with a "fresh eye"—that is, reseeing your writing in ways that will enable you to make more effective choices throughout your essay. Revision often entails rethinking what you have written and asking yourself questions about its effectiveness; it involves discovery as well as change. As you write, new ideas surface, prompting you to revise what you have planned or have just written. Or perhaps these new ideas will cause changes in earlier parts of your essay. In some cases, your new ideas will encourage you to begin an entirely new draft with a different focus or approach. Revision means making important decisions about the best ways to focus, organize, develop, clarify, and emphasize your ideas.

When Does Revision Occur?

Revision, as previously noted, occurs throughout your writing process. Early on, you are revising as you sort through ideas to write about, and you almost certainly revise as you define your purpose and audience and sharpen your thesis. Some revising may be done in your head, and some may be on paper or computer screen as you plan, sketch, or "discovery-write" your ideas. Later, during drafting, revision becomes more individualized and complex. Many writers find themselves sweeping back and forth over their papers, writing for a bit and then rereading what they wrote, making changes, and then moving ahead. Some writers like to revise "lumps," or pieces of writing, perhaps reviewing one major idea or paragraph at a time. Frequently, writers discover that a better idea is occurring almost at the very moment they are putting another thought on paper. And virtually all writers revise after "reseeing" a draft in its entirety.

Revision, then, occurs before drafting, during drafting, between parts of drafts, and at the ends of drafts. You can revise a word, a sentence, a paragraph, or an entire essay. If you are like most writers, you sometimes revise almost automatically as you write (deleting one word or line and quickly replacing it with another as you move on, for example), and at other times you revise very deliberately (concentrating on a conclusion you know is weak, for example). Revision is "rethinking," and that activity can happen any time, in many ways, in any part of your writing.

Myths about Revision

If revision is rethinking, what is it not? Three misconceptions about revision are addressed here.

1. Revision Is Not Autopsy

Revision is not an isolated stage of writing that occurs *only* after your last draft is written or right before your paper is due. Revising is not merely a postmortem procedure, to be performed only after your creative juices have ceased to flow. Good writing, as Thurber noted, *is* revision, and revision occurs throughout the writing process.

2. Revision Is Not Limited to Editing or Proofreading

Too many writers mistakenly equate revision with editing and proofreading. *Editing* means revising for "surface errors"—mistakes in spelling, grammar, punctuation, sentence sense, and word choice. Certainly, good writers comb their papers for such errors, and they edit their prose extensively for clarity, conciseness, and emphasis, too. *Proofreading* to search out and destroy errors and typos that distort meaning or distract the reader is also important. Without question, both editing and proofreading are essential to a polished paper. But revision is not *limited* to such activities. It includes them but also encompasses those larger, global changes writers may make in purpose, focus, organization, and development. Writers who revise effectively not only change words and catch mechanical errors but also typically add, delete, rearrange, and rewrite large chunks of prose. In other words, revision is not cosmetic surgery on a body that may need major resuscitation.

3. Revision Is Not Punishment or Busywork

At one time or another, most of us have found ourselves guilty of racing too quickly through a particular job and then moving on. And perhaps just as often we have found ourselves redoing such jobs because the results were so disappointing. Some people may regard revising in a similar light—as the repeat performance of a job done poorly the first time. But that attitude isn't productive. Revising isn't punishment for failing to produce a perfect first draft. Rarely, if ever, does anyone—even our most admired professional writers—produce the results he or she wants without revising.* Remember that revising is not a tacked-on stage nor is it merely a quick touch-up; it's an integral part of the entire writing process itself. It's an ongoing opportunity to discover, remember, reshape, and refine your ideas.

If you've ever created something you now treasure—a piece of jewelry, furniture, painting, or music—recall the time you put into it. You probably thought about it from several angles, experimented with it, crafted it, worked it through expected and unexpected problems, and smoothed out its minor glitches, all to achieve the results you wanted. Similarly, with each revision you make, your paper becomes clearer, truer, more satisfying to you and to your readers. With practice, you will produce writing you are proud of—and you will discover that revising has become not only an essential but also a natural part of your writing process.

■ Can I Learn to Improve My Revision Skills?

Because revision is such a multifaceted and individual activity, no textbook can guide you through all the rethinking you may do as you move through each sentence of every writing project. But certainly you can learn to improve your ability to think creatively and critically about your prose. To sharpen your thinking and revision skills, this chapter will suggest a step-by-step method of self-questioning designed to help you achieve your writing goals.

---

* All of us have heard stories about famous essays or poems composed at one quick sitting. Bursts of creativity do happen. But it's highly likely that authors of such pieces revise extensively in their heads before they write. They rattle ideas around in their brains for such a prolonged period that the actual writing does in fact flow easily or may even seem "dictated" by an inner voice. This sort of lengthy internal "cooking" may work well at various times for you, too.

■ Preparing to Draft: Some Time-Saving Hints

Before you begin drafting (either a "discovery" draft or a draft from your working thesis), remember this important piece of advice: no part of your draft is sacred or permanent. No matter what you write at this point, you can always change it. Drafting is discovering and recollecting as well as developing ideas from your earlier plans. Take the pressure off yourself: no one expects blue-ribbon prose in early drafts. (If you can't seem to get going or if you do become stuck along the way, try turning to pages 112–115 of this chapter for suggestions to help you confront your case of Writer's Block.)

At this point, too, you might consider the actual format of your drafts. Because you will be making many changes in your writing, you may find revising less cumbersome and time-consuming if you prepare your manuscripts as described below and in the following section on word processors.

1. If you are handwriting your first drafts, always write on one side of your paper only, in case you want to cut and tape together portions of drafts or you want to experiment with interchanging parts of a particular draft. (If you have written on both sides, you may have to recopy the parts of your essay you want to save; your time is better spent creating and revising.)

2. Leave big margins on *both* sides of any handwritten pages so you can add information later or jot down new ideas as they occur. (Some writers also skip lines for this reason. If you choose to write on every other line, however, do remember that you may not be getting a true picture of your paragraph development or essay length. A handwritten double-spaced body paragraph, for example, may appear skimpy in your typed final copy.)

3. Devise a system of symbols (circles, stars, checks, asterisks, etc.) that will remind you of changes you want to make later. For example, if you're in hot pursuit of a great idea but can't think of the exact word you want, put down a word that's close, circle it (or type three XXXs by it), and go on so that your thinking is not derailed. Similarly, a check in the margin might mean "return to this tangled sentence." A question mark might mean a fuzzy idea, and a star, a great idea that needs expanding. A system of symbols can save you from agonizing over every inch of your essay while you are still trying to discover and clarify your ideas.

4. If your ideas are flowing well but you realize you need more supporting evidence for some of your points, consider leaving some blank spots to fill in later. For example, let's say you are writing about the role of television in our presidential elections; your ideas are good, but in a particular body paragraph you decide some statistics on commercial frequency would be most convincing. Or perhaps you need to cite an example of a particular kind of advertisement, but you just can't think of a good one at that moment. Leave a spot for the piece of evidence with a key word or two to remind you of what's needed, and keep writing. Later, when you come back to that spot, you can add the appropriate support; if you can't find or think of the right supporting evidence to insert, you may decide to omit that point.

5. If you do decide to rewrite or omit something—a sentence or an entire passage—in a handwritten draft, mark a single "X" or line through it lightly.

Don't scratch it out or destroy it completely; you may realize later that you want to reinsert the material there or move it to another, better place. If you are composing on a computer, italicize or put brackets around material you may want to use elsewhere. Or consider moving a larger chunk of prose to a "holding page" or to the end of the current draft so you can take another look at it later.

6. If you begin with a handwritten draft, do eventually work on a typed copy. The more compact spacing of typed prose allows you to see more clearly the relationship of the parts in your essay, making it easier for you to organize and develop your ideas. It is also far more likely that you will catch spelling and other mechanical errors in a printed draft.

7. Always keep your notes, outlines, drafts, and an extra copy of your final paper. Never burn your bridges—or your manuscripts! Sometimes essays change directions, and writers find they can return to prewriting or earlier drafts to recover ideas, once rejected, that now work well. Drafts also may contain ideas that didn't work in one paper but that look like great starts for another assignment. Tracking revisions from draft to draft can give writers a sense of accomplishment and insight into their composing processes. And drafts can be good insurance in case final copies of papers are lost or accidentally destroyed.

Additional Suggestions for Writers with Word Processors

If you have access to a computer and any of the many word-processing programs available today, you probably have already discovered how helpful this technology can be to writers in all stages of the writing process. You can, for example, compose and store your prewriting activities, journal entries, notes, or good ideas in various files until you need to recall certain information, and you can easily produce extra copies of your drafts or finished essays without having to search out a copy machine and correct change. Spell-checkers and dictionaries can help you correct many of your errors and typos.

But the most important use of the computer to a writer may be what it can do as you draft and revise your prose. A word-processing program enables you to add, delete, or change words easily; it allows you to move words, sentences, and even paragraphs or larger pieces of your essay. On a computer, for example, you can play "what if" by dropping below what you have written and phrasing your idea in another way. With some programs, you can even compare drafts side by side or with special "windows" that help you see your choices more clearly. In other words, computers can help us as writers do the kind of deep-structure revision necessary to produce our best, most effective prose—the kind of major changes that, in the past, we may have been hesitant to make because of the time involved in recopying or retyping major portions of our drafts.

Although computers have made composing and revising easier and more effective for many writers, such technology provides its own special temptations and potential problems. Here, in addition to the hints in the previous section, are a few more suggestions for drafting and revising your essay on a computer:

1. To avoid the "agony of delete," always save what you have composed every ten minutes or so, and do print out or make a disk copy after each drafting session in case your system crashes or gobbles your work. Remember that all sorts of events, from electrical storms to carpet cleaning, have caused the tiny leprechauns in computers to behave badly; having copies of your notes and latest revisions, either as printouts or on disk, will help you reconstruct your work should disaster strike. (Also, if you are working on multiple writing tasks, as most students are, or if you are just the forgetful type, develop the habit of noting on each print copy the name you have given the file. Doing so may save you from a frustrating search through your list of existing documents, especially if several days have elapsed between drafts.)

2. Do learn to use the editing tools that your word-processing program offers. In addition to allowing you to make changes and move text, most programs offer a dictionary to help you check the proper spelling, meaning, and use of your words; a thesaurus can help you expand your vocabulary, avoid repetition of words, or find just the right word to express the shade of meaning you want. Even the "word count" command can help writers who want to trim the fat from their essays.

One of the most prized tools the computer offers writers is the spell-checker. For poor spellers and bad typists, the invention of the spell-checker ranks right up there with penicillin as a boon to humankind. The spell-checker performs minor miracles as it asks writers to reconsider certain words as typed on the page. If you have one available, by all means run it! But be aware of its limitations: spell-checkers highlight only words whose order of assembled letters they do not recognize or whose capitalization they question. They do not recognize confused words (its/it's, you're/your, their/there, to/too), incorrect usage of words, or typos that are correctly spelled words. To underscore this point, here's a sample of writing that any spell-checker would happily pass over:

> Eye have a knew spell checker
> That tells me wrong from write;
> It marks four me miss steaks
> My ayes kin knot high light.
>
> I no its let her perfect,
> Sew why due I all ways get
> Re quests to proof reed bet her
> Win my checker says I'm set?

The message of this brilliantly crafted poem? Don't rely on your spell-checker to catch all the errors in your final draft! Learn to edit, question your word choice, and proofread carefully with your own eyes and brain. (The same advice holds true for grammar-check and "style" programs, too. Although such programs have improved over the past several years, they are still limited in their ability to catch errors and see distinctions among usage and punctuation choices. Such programs may help you take a second look at your grammar, punctuation, or word choice, but do not rely on *any* computer program to do your editing and proofreading work for you.)

3. Use the computer to help you double-check for your own common errors. By using the "search," "find," or similar command, writers can highlight words they know they frequently misuse. For example, on a final sweep of editing, you might take one last look at each highlighted "its" you wrote to determine whether the usage truly calls for the possessive pronoun "its" or rather should be the contraction for "it is" (it's). Or perhaps you have an ongoing struggle with the uses of "affect" and "effect" and know that you have used these words often in your essay of causal analysis. Reviewing your word-choice decisions in the proofreading stage could make an important difference to your readers, who wish to travel smoothly through the ideas in your essay without annoying errors flagging down their attention. Also consider searching for and replacing words that you know you overuse or those that are lazy or vague. For example, until you break yourself of the habit, highlight any use of the word "thing." In each case, are you really discussing an unknown quantity—or do you need to press yourself to find a more specific or vivid word to communicate what you mean?

4. Even if you are comfortable drafting on your computer, resist doing all your work there. It's a good idea from time to time to read your screen version in its printed form—the format your readers will most likely see. Many—if not most—writers move back and forth multiple times between the computer screen and printed copies of their drafts. Experiment to discover the best ways for you to revise. Remember that a neatly typed draft can look professional but still need much rethinking, restructuring, and polishing!

■ Writing Centers, Computer Labs, and Computer Classrooms

Today many schools have professionally staffed writing centers and computer labs open to composition students. The writing center or laboratory computers may have a variety of software designed to help you brainstorm, focus your ideas, organize a working structure, compose your drafts, revise your essay, and proofread. These computers also can help you to research a topic by allowing you to check information available in your campus library as well as providing access to other libraries and sources on the Internet. Many writing centers have special tutors on hand to answer your questions about your drafts as well as to explain effective uses of the available computer programs. In addition, some schools now have labs and special classrooms in which the computers are part of a network, linked together so that a specific group of writers can communicate with each other and/or with their instructor. In such a lab or classroom, for example, students might read each other's drafts and make suggestions or post comments about a current reading assignment on an electronic bulletin board for their classmates to consider.

Whether the program you are using at home or at school is a series of simple commands or an elaborate instructional system, make a point of getting to know how to use the computer in the most effective ways. Study the advice that accompanies your word-processing program (or one of the many self-help manuals now on the market), and don't be afraid to ask your instructor or computer-lab tutor for assistance. The more you practice using your program to help you organize, develop, and revise your prose, the better your writing will be.

■ A Revision Process for Your Drafts

Let's assume at this point that you have completed a draft, using the first four chapters of this book as a guide. You feel you've chosen an interesting topic and collected some good ideas. Perhaps the ideas came quickly or perhaps you had to coax them. However your thoughts came, they're now in print—you have a draft with meaning and a general order, although it's probably much rougher in some spots than in others. Now it's time to "resee" this draft in a comprehensive way.

But wait. If possible, put a night's sleep or at least a few hours between this draft and the advice that appears on the next few pages. All writers become tired when they work on any project for too long at one sitting, and then they lose a sense of perspective. When you've looked at a piece of prose again and again, you may begin to read what's written in your head instead of what's on the page—that is, you may begin to "fill in" for yourself, reading into your prose what you meant to say rather than what your reader will actually see. Always try to start your writing process early enough to give yourself a few breaks from the action. You'll find that you will be better able to evaluate the strengths and weaknesses of your prose when you are fresh.

When you do return to your draft, *don't try to look at all the parts of your paper, from ideas to organization to mechanics, at the same time.* Trying to resee everything at once is rarely possible and will only overload and frustrate you. It may cause you to overlook some important part of your paper that needs your full attention. Overload can also block your creative ideas. Therefore, instead of trying to revise an entire draft in one swoop, break your revising process into a series of smaller, more manageable steps. Here is a suggested process:

I.	rethink	purpose, thesis, and audience
II.	rethink	ideas and evidence
III.	rethink	organization
IV.	rethink	clarity and style
V.	edit	grammar, punctuation, and spelling
VI.	proofread	entire essay

IMPORTANT: Please note that these steps are not necessarily distinct, nor must you always follow this suggested order. You certainly might, for instance, add details to a paragraph when you decide to move or reorder it. Or you might replace a vague word with a specific one after thinking about your audience and their needs. After strengthening a particular point, you might decide to offer it last, and therefore you rearrange the order of your paragraphs. In other words, the steps offered above are not part of a forced march—they are here simply to remind you to rethink and improve any part of your essay that needs work.

Now let's look at each of the steps in the revision process suggested above in more detail.

I. Revising for Purpose, Thesis, and Audience

To be effective, writers need a clear sense of purpose and audience. Their essays must present (or clearly imply) a main idea or thesis designed to fulfill that purpose and to inform their audience. As you reread your draft, ask yourself the following questions:

- Have I fulfilled the objectives of my assignment? (For example, if you were asked to analyze the causes of a problem, did you merely describe or summarize it instead?)

- Did I follow directions carefully? (If you were given a three-part assignment, did you treat all parts as requested?)

- Do I understand the purpose of my essay? Am I trying to inform, persuade, or amuse my readers? Spur them to action? Convince them to change their minds? Give them a new idea? Am I myself clear about my exact intent—what I want to do or say—in this essay?

- Does my essay reflect my clearly understood purpose by offering an appropriately narrowed and focused thesis? (After reading through your essay once, could a reader easily state its purpose and main point?)

- Do I have a clear picture of my audience—their character, knowledge, and expectations?

- Have I addressed both my purpose and my readers' needs by selecting appropriate strategies of development for my essay? (For example, would it be better to write an essay primarily developed with examples illustrating the community's need for a new hospital, or should you present a more formal argument that also rebuffs objections to the project? Should you narrate the story of your accident or analyze its effects on your family?)

If you feel that your draft needs work in any of these areas, make changes. You might find it helpful to review Chapters 1 and 2 of this text to guide you as you revise.

II. Revising for Ideas and Evidence

If you're satisfied that your purpose and thesis are clear to your readers, begin to look closely at the development of your essay's ideas.

You want your readers to accept your thesis. To achieve this goal, you must offer body paragraphs whose major points clearly support that main idea. As you examine the body of your essay, you might ask yourself questions such as these:

- Is there a clear relationship between my thesis and each of the major points presented in the body of my essay? That is, does each major point in my essay further my readers' understanding, and thus their acceptance, of my thesis's general claim?

- Did I write myself into a new or slightly different position as I drafted my essay? If so, do I need to begin another draft with a new working thesis?

- Have I included all the major points necessary to the readers' understanding of my subject or have I omitted pertinent ones? (On the other hand, have I included major ideas that aren't relevant or that actually belong in a different essay?)

- Are my major points located and stated clearly in specific language so that readers can easily see what position I am taking in each part of my discussion?

If you are happy with your choice and presentation of the major ideas in the body of your essay, it's time to look closely at the evidence you are offering to support those ideas (which, in turn, support the claim of your thesis). To choose the best supporting evidence for their major points, effective writers use *critical thinking skills*.

What Is Critical Thinking?

Critical thinking means the ability to analyze and evaluate our own ideas and those of others. Because we are constantly bombarded today with all kinds of information and differing points of view, we need skills to examine ideas carefully before we accept or reject them.

Here's a common situation in which critical thinking comes into play: two of your friends are arguing over the use of fetal tissue in medical research. Each friend has many points to offer; each is presenting statistics, examples of actual case studies, the words of experts, and hypothetical situations that might arise. Many of the statistics and experts on one side of the argument seem to contradict directly the figures and authorities on the other side. Which side do you take? Why? Are there other points of view to consider? How can you know what to think?

Every day we are faced with just such decisions. We must be able to judge intelligently the merits of what we hear and read before we can feel confident about what we think of a particular issue. We must practice analyzing our beliefs and those held by others to evaluate the reasons for maintaining those views. To think critically about ideas doesn't mean being constantly hostile or negative; it simply means that we need to examine opinions closely and carefully before we accept them.

Thinking Critically as a Writer

As a writer, you will be thinking critically in two important ways. First, you will need to think critically about any information you may be collecting to use as evidence in your essay. You will, for example, need to be a critical reader as you consider information from books, journals, or electronic sources. You almost certainly will need to be a critical listener as you hear other people talk about their experiences and beliefs.

As you draft and revise your essay, you must become a critical thinker in a second way: you must become your own toughest reader-critic. To convince your readers that your essay has merit, you must stand back and assess objectively what you have written. Are your ideas clear not only to you but to your readers as well? Will readers find your opinions well developed, logical, and supported? In other words, to revise more effectively, try role-playing one of your own most thoughtful critical readers, someone who will be closely examining the ideas and evidence in your essay before agreeing with its position.

Here are six suggestions to help you think critically as you draft and revise:

1. Learn to distinguish fact from opinion. A *fact* is an accepted truth whose verification is not affected by its source. No matter who presents it, a fact remains true. We accept some statements as facts because we can test them personally (fire is hot) or because they have been verified frequently by others (penguins live in Antarctica). We accept as fact, for example, that President John F. Kennedy was killed on November 22, 1963, in Dallas, Texas, while riding in a motorcade. However, even though much investigation and debate have focused on the assassination, the question of who was responsible for the murder is for many people still a matter of *opinion*. Most people believe that Lee Harvey Oswald was the lone gunman; others insist that there were two shooters; still others claim involvement by a foreign government, the Mafia, or even the CIA. Opinions, then, are often based on personal feelings or beliefs or on one's interpretation of information. As you think about your evidence, be careful that you don't present your opinions as facts accepted by everyone. Opinions are debatable, and therefore you must always support them before your readers will be convinced.

2. Support your opinions with evidence. To support your opinions, you must offer evidence of one or more kinds. You have a variety of options to choose from. You might support one idea by using personal experiences. Or you might describe the experiences of friends or family. In another place you might decide to offer detailed examples or to cite statistics or to quote an expert on your subject. You can also use hypothetical examples, researched material, vivid descriptions, reasoned arguments, revealing comparisons, case studies, or testimony of relevant participants, just to name a few other strategies. Consider your purpose and your audience, review the possibilities, and choose the most effective kind of support. The more convincing the support, the more likely your readers are to accept your opinions as true. (If you need to review some sample paragraphs developed by various types of evidence, turn to pages 58–61 of Chapter 3.)

3. Evaluate the strength of your evidence. As you choose your evidence, you should consider its value for the particular point it will support. Scrutinize the nature and source of your evidence carefully. If you are using examples, do they clearly illustrate your claim? Does this example or a different one (or both?) provide the best illustration of your particular point? Is description alone enough support here? Are your statistics or researched material from a reliable, current source? Was information from your research collected in a careful, professional way? Are your experts unbiased authorities in the field under discussion? Where did your experts obtain their information? (For example, are you claiming that crystals possess healing powers because a woman on a talk show said so and she sounded reasonable to you? Just how much do you know about the source of a particular website?) Asking yourself the kinds of questions posed here (and others suggested throughout Part Two of this textbook) will help you develop a critical eye for choosing the best evidence to support your opinions.

4. Use enough specific supporting evidence. Readers need to see strong, relevant supporting evidence throughout your essay. You must be sure, therefore, that you have enough clearly stated evidence for each of your major points. If you present, for instance, too few examples or only a vague reference to an event that supports one of your ideas, a reader may remain unconvinced or may even be confused. As you revise, ask yourself questions such as these: "Do I need to provide additional information here?" "Do I need more details to develop the supporting evidence already present?" "Is any of my evidence clouded by vague or fuzzy language?" If you feel additional supporting evidence or details are needed, take another look at any prewriting you did or use one of the "pump-primer" techniques described in Chapter 1 now to discover some new creative thoughts. For some topics, you may need to do more research or interviewing to find the information you need. (Writers occasionally need to prune ideas too, especially if they're repetitious or off the topic. But, in general, most early drafts are thin or overly general and will profit from more, rather than less, specific supporting evidence.)

5. Watch for biases and strong emotions that may undermine evidence. As you think critically about evidence you are using, monitor any biases and emotional attitudes that may distort information you wish to incorporate into your essay. If you are using personal experiences, for example, have you calmed down enough from your anger over your landlord's actions to write about the clash in a rational, persuasive way? In an essay criticizing a particular product, are you so familiar with the frustrating item that you are making ambiguous claims? (If you write, "The new instructions for use are more confusing than ever," have you shown that they were confusing in the first place? Or why they are more so now?) Be sensitive to any racial, ethnic, cultural, religious, or gender-based assumptions you or your sources may have. Opinions based on generalizations and stereotypes ("Japanese cars are good buys because Asians are more efficient workers than Americans"; "Women should stay home because they are better with children than men") are not convincing to thinking readers.

6. Check your evidence for logical fallacies. Thinking critically about your drafts should help you support your ideas with reasonable, logical explanations and arguments. Logical fallacies are common errors in reasoning that good writers try to avoid. Those fallacies found most often today are explained on pages 286–289 of this text; reviewing them will enable you to identify problems in logic that might appear in the writing of others or in your own drafts.

Critical thinking is not, of course, limited to the six suggestions offered here. But by practicing this advice, you will begin to develop and sharpen analytical skills that should improve any writing project.

III. Revising for Organization

In reality, you have probably already made several changes in the order and organization of ideas in your draft. As noted before, it's likely that when you thought about your essay's meaning—its major points and their supporting evidence—you also thought about the arrangement of those ideas. As you take another look at your draft's organization, use these questions as a guide:

- Am I satisfied with the organizational strategy I selected for my purpose? (For example, would an essay developed primarily by comparison and contrast achieve your purpose better than a narrative approach?)
- Are my major points ordered in a logical, easy-to-follow pattern? Would readers understand my thinking better if certain paragraphs or major ideas were rearranged? Added? Divided? Omitted? Expanded?

- Are my major points presented in topic sentences that state each important idea clearly and specifically? (If any of your topic sentences are implied rather than stated, are you absolutely, 100 percent sure that your ideas cannot be overlooked or even slightly misunderstood by your readers?)

- Is there a smooth flow between my major ideas? Between paragraphs? Within paragraphs? Have I used enough transitional devices to guide the reader along?

- Are any parts of my essay out of proportion? Too long or too brief to do their job effectively?

- Do my title and lead-in draw readers into the essay and toward my thesis?

- Does my conclusion end my discussion thoughtfully? Emphatically or memorably?

Don't be afraid to restructure your drafts. Most good writers rearrange and recast large portions of their prose. Reviewing Chapters 3 and 4 may help you address questions about organization, beginnings, or endings.

IV. Revising for Clarity and Style

As you've revised for purpose, ideas, and organization, you have also taken steps to clarify your prose. Making a special point now of focusing on sentences and word choice will ensure your readers' complete understanding of your thinking. Read through your draft, asking these kinds of questions:

- Is each of my sentences as clear and precise as it could be for readers who do not know what I know? Are there sentences that contain misplaced words or convoluted phrases that might cause confusion?

- Are there any sentences that are unnecessarily wordy? Is there deadwood that could be eliminated? (Remember that concise prose is more effective than wordy, "fat" prose because readers can more easily find and follow key ideas and terms. Nearly every writer has a wordiness problem that chokes communication, so now is the season to prune.)

- Do any sentences run on for too long to be fully understood? Can any repetitive or choppy sentences be combined to achieve clarity and a pleasing variation of sentence style? (To help you decide whether you need to combine sentences, you might try this experiment. Select a body paragraph and count the number of words it contains. Then count the number of sentences; divide the number of words by the number of sentences to discover the average number of words per sentence. If your score is less than 15–18, you might need to combine *some* sentences. Good prose offers a variety of sentence lengths and patterns.)

- Are all my words and their connotations accurate and appropriate?

- Can I clarify and energize my prose by adding "showing" details and by replacing bland, vague words with vivid, specific ones? By using active verbs rather than passive ones?

- Can I eliminate any pretentious or unnecessary jargon or language that's inappropriate for my audience? Replace clichés and trite expressions with fresh, original phrases?

- Is my voice authentic, or am I trying to sound like someone else? Is my tone reasonable, honest, and consistent?

The issues raised by these questions—and many others—are discussed in detail in Chapters 6 and 7, on effective sentences and words, which offer more advice on clarifying language and improving style.

V. Editing for Errors

Writers who are proud of the choices they've made in content, organization, and style are, to use a baseball metaphor, rounding third base and heading for home. But there's more to be done. Shift from a baseball metaphor to car maintenance for a moment. All good essays are not only fine-tuned but also waxed and polished—they are edited and proofread repeatedly for errors until they shine. To help you polish your prose by correcting errors in punctuation, grammar, spelling, and diction, here are some hints for effective editing:

Read aloud. In addition to repeatedly reading your draft silently, reading your draft aloud is a good technique because it allows your ears to hear ungrammatical "clunks" or unintended gaps in sense or sound you may otherwise miss. (Reading aloud may also flag omitted words. If, for example, the mother had reread this note to her child's teacher, she might have noticed a missing word: "Please excuse Ian for being. It was his father's fault.")

Know your enemies. Learn to identify your particularly troublesome areas in punctuation and grammar, and then read through your draft for one of these problems at a time: once for fragments, once for comma splices, once for run-ons, and so on. (If you try to look for too many errors at each reading, you'll probably miss quite a few.)

Read backwards. Try reading your draft one sentence at a time starting at the *end* of your essay and working toward the beginning. Don't read each sentence word-for-word backwards—just read the essay one sentence at a time from back to front. When writers try to edit (or proofread) starting at the beginning of their essays, they tend to begin thinking about the ideas they're reading rather than concentrating on the task of editing for errors. By reading one sentence at a time from the back, you will find that the sentences will still make sense but that you are less likely to wander away from the job at hand.

Learn some tricks. There are special techniques for treating some punctuation and grammar problems. If you have trouble with comma splices, for example, turn to the FANBOYS hint on page 137. If fragments plague your writing, try the "It is true that" test explained on pages 121–122. Consider designating a special part of your journal or class notebook to record in your own words these tricks and other useful pieces of advice so that you can refer to them easily and often.

Eliminate common irritants. Review your draft for those diction and mechanical errors many readers find especially annoying because they often reflect sheer carelessness. For example, look at these frequently confused words: *it's/its, your/you're, there/their/they're, who's/whose* (other often-confused words are listed on page 146). Some readers are ready for a national march to protest the public's abandonment of the apostrophe, the Amelia Earhart of punctuation. (Apostrophes *can* change the meaning of sentences: "The teacher called the students names." Was the instructor being rude or just taking roll?) It's a grammatical jungle out there, so be sensitive to your weary readers.

Use your tools. Keep your dictionary handy to check the spelling, usage, and meanings of words in doubt. A thesaurus can also be useful if you can restrain any tendencies you might have for growing overly exotic prose. If you are using a word processor with a spell-checker, by all means run it after your last revisions are completed. Do remember, as noted earlier in this chapter, that such programs only flag words whose spelling they don't recognize; they will not alert you to omitted or confused words (*affect/effect*), nor will they signal when you've typed in a wrong, but correctly spelled, word (*form* for *from*).

Use Part Four of this text to help resolve any questions you may have about grammar, mechanics, and spelling. Advice on untangling sentences and clarifying word choice in Chapters 6 and 7 may be useful, too.

VI. Proofreading

Proofread your final draft several times, putting as much time between the last two readings as possible. Fresh eyes catch more typographical or careless errors. Remember that typing errors—even the simple transposing of letters—can change the meaning of an entire thought and occasionally bring unintended humor to your prose. (Imagine, for example, the surprise of restaurant owners whose new lease instructed them to "Please sing the terms of the agreement." Or consider the ramifications of the newspaper ad offering "Great dames for sale" or the 1716 Bible whose advice "sin no more" was misprinted as "sin on more.")

Make sure, too, that your paper looks professional before you turn it in. You wouldn't, after all, expect to be taken seriously if you went to an executive job interview dressed in cutoffs. Turning in a paper with a coffee stain or ink smear on it has about the same effect as a blob of spinach in your teeth—it distracts folks from hearing what you have to say. If your final draft has typos or small blemishes, you may use correction fluid to conceal them; but if you've patched so frequently that your paper resembles the medicine-dotted face of a kindergartner with chicken pox, reprint or photocopy your pages for a fresh look.

Check to be sure you've formatted your paper exactly as your assignment requested. Some instructors ask for a title page; others want folders containing all your drafts and prewriting. Most teachers appreciate typed papers with pages that are numbered, ordered correctly, paper clipped or stapled, with clean edges (no sheets violently ripped from a spiral notebook still dribbling angry confetti down one side; no pages mutilated at the corners by the useless "tear-and-fold-tab" technique). Putting your name on each page will identify your work if papers from a particular class are accidentally mixed up.

> ☑ As it's often been said, essays are never really done—only due. Take a last reading using the checklist that follows, make some notes on your progress as a writer and thinker, and congratulate yourself on your fine efforts and accomplishment.

■ A Final Checklist for Your Essay

If you have written an effective essay, you should be able to answer "yes" to the following questions:

1. Do I feel I have something important to say to my reader?

2. Am I sincerely committed to communicating with my reader and not just with myself?

3. Have I considered my audience's needs? (See Chapter 1.)

4. Do my title and lead-in attract the reader's attention and help set up my thesis? (See Chapter 4.)

5. Does my thesis statement assert one main, clearly focused idea? (See Chapter 2.)

6. Does my thesis and/or essay map give the reader an indication of what points the essay will cover? (See Chapter 2.)

7. Do my body paragraphs contain the essential points in the essay's discussion, and are those points expressed in clearly stated or implied topic sentences? (See Chapter 3.)

8. Is each major point in my essay well developed with enough detailed supporting evidence? (See Chapter 3.)

9. Does each body paragraph have unity and coherence? (See Chapter 3.)

10. Are all the paragraphs in my essay smoothly linked in a logical order? (See Chapter 3.)

11. Does my concluding paragraph provide a suitable ending for the essay? (See Chapter 4.)

12. Are all my sentences clear, concise, and coherent? (See Chapter 6.)

13. Are my words accurate, necessary, and meaningful? (See Chapter 7.)

14. Have I edited and proofread for errors in grammar, punctuation, spelling, and typing? (See Part Four.)

And most important:

15. Has my essay been effectively revised so that I am proud of this piece of writing?

■ PRACTICING WHAT YOU'VE LEARNED

The draft of the following student essay has been annotated by its own writer according to some—*but not all*—of the questions presented in this chapter's discussion of revision. As you read the draft and the writer's marginal comments, think of specific suggestions you might offer to help this writer improve her essay. What changes, in addition to the ones mentioned here, would you encourage this writer to make? What strengths do you see in this draft?

DORM LIFE

My title and lead-in are too bland to attract reader's attention.

Would my thesis be clearer if I said —— what I did find?

My supporting examples could use more "showing" details so the readers can really see the unfriendliness.

Contradicts my point

This paragraph has some specific details, but it rambles and repeats ideas. Needs tighter organization.

Contradicts my ——— ¶'s point

Dorm life is not at all what I had expected it to be. I had anticipated meeting friendly people, quiet hours for studying, eating decent food, and having wild parties on weekends. My dreams, I soon found out, were simply illusions, erroneous perceptions of reality.

My roommate, Kathy, and I live in Holland Hall on the third floor. The people on our dorm floor are about as unfriendly as they can possibly be. I wonder whether or not they're just shy and afraid or if they are simply snobs. Some girls, for example, ignore my roommate and me when we say "hello." Occasionally, they stare straight ahead and act like we aren't even there. Other girls respond, but it's as if they do it out of a sense of duty rather than being just friendly. The guys seem nice, but some are just as afraid or snobby as the girls.

I remember signing up for "quiet hours" when I put in my application for a dorm room last December. Unfortunately, I was assigned to a floor that doesn't have any quiet hours at all. I am a person who requires peace and quiet when studying or reading. The girls in all the rooms around us love to stay up until early in the morning and yell and turn up their music full blast. They turn music on at about eight o'clock at night and turn it off early in the morning. There is always at least one girl who has music playing at maximum volume. Now, I am very appreciative of music, but listening to hard rock until three in the morning isn't really my idea of what fun is. The girls right across from us usually play Sheryl Crow or the Dixie Chicks, and I enjoy them. On the other hand, though, the girls on either side of our room love to listen to Slipknot or System of a Down into the wee hours of the morning. It is these girls who run up and down the hall, yell at each other, laugh obnoxiously, and try to attract attention. All this continuous racket makes it nearly impossible to study, read, or get any sleep. Kathy and I usually end up going to the library or student cafeteria to study. As far as sleep goes, it doesn't matter what time we go to bed, but rather it depends on how noisy it is and how late the music is on. Sometimes the noise gets so loud and goes on for so long that even when it stops, my ears are ringing and my stomach keeps churning. It is on nights like this that I never go to sleep. I wish the people here were a little more considerate of the people around them.

Parties, on weekends, are supposedly the most important part of dorm life. Parties provide the opportunity to meet others and have a good time. Holland Hall has had two parties that are even worth mentioning. One of them was a Fifties dance held in the courtyard approximately three weeks ago. Unfortunately, all the other dormitories, the fraternities, and the sororities heard about it, and by eight o'clock at night there were masses of people. It was so packed that it was hard to move around. The other party, much to my dismay, turned out to be a luau party. I do not really care for roast pig, and my stomach turned from the scent of it when I entered the room. Our floor never has parties. Everyone leaves their doors open, turns up the music, and yells back and forth. I suppose that there will be more floor parties once everyone becomes adjusted to this life and begins to socialize.

This paragraph doesn't support my thesis claim—do I mean the dorm has no good parties or not enough parties? Rethink so my point is clear.

Dorm food is what I anticipated it would be, terrible, and I was right, it is awful. Breakfast is probably the hardest meal to digest. The bacon and sausage are cold, slightly uncooked, and very greasy. Sometimes, it's as though I am eating pure grease. The eggs look and taste like nothing I ever had before. They look like plastic and they are never hot. I had eggs once, and I vowed I would never have another one as long as I lived in Holland Hall. The most enjoyable part of breakfast is the orange juice. It's always cold and it seems to be fresh. No one can say dorm food is totally boring because the cooks break up the monotony of the same food by serving "mystery meat" at least once every two weeks. This puts a little excitement in the student's day because everyone cracks jokes and wonders just what's in this "mystery meat." I think a lot of students are afraid to ask, fearful of the answer, and simply make snide remarks and shovel it in.

As stated, this topic sentence contradicts my thesis.

Some good examples— could I use even more descriptive language?

Unity?

All in all, I believe dorm life isn't too great, even though there are some good times. Even though I complain about dorm food, the people, the parties, and everything else, I am glad I am here. I am happy because I have learned a lot about other people, responsibilities, consideration, and I've even learned a lot about myself.

Can I conclude emphatically without switching positions?

■ Benefiting from Revision Workshops

Many writing courses today include revision workshops in which students comment helpfully on one another's drafts. This sort of revision activity may also be called peer editing, classroom critique, or reader review. Peer workshops may be arranged in a variety of ways, though frequently students will work in pairs or in small groups of three to five. Sometimes writers will simply talk about their papers or read them aloud; at other times students will be asked to write suggestions on one another's drafts. Sometimes instructors will give student-reviewers a list of questions to answer; at other times, the writers themselves will voice their concerns directly to their reviewers. Although most revision workshops still take place in the classroom, some composition programs today have the electronic means to post students' drafts on protected course sites so that peer-reviewers can comment on them out of class as well. Structured in many effective ways, peer workshops can be extremely valuable to writers, who will invariably profit from seeing their drafts from a reader's point of view.

Students taking part in revision workshops for the first time often have questions about the reviewing process. Some student-reviewers may feel uneasy about their role, wondering, "What if I can't think of any suggestions for the writer? How can I tell someone that the essay is really terrible? What if I sense something's wrong but I'm not sure what it is—or how to fix it?" Writers, too, may feel apprehensive or even occasionally defensive about receiving criticism of their papers. Because these concerns are genuine and widespread, here is some advice to help you get the most out of your participation in revision workshops, in the role of writer or reviewer.

When you are the **writer**:

1. Develop a constructive attitude. Admittedly, receiving criticism—especially on a creation that has required hard work—can sometimes be difficult, particularly if your self-image has become mixed up with your drafts. Try to realize that your reviewer is not criticizing *you* personally but rather is trying to help you by offering fresh insights. All drafts can be improved, and no writer need feel embarrassed about seeking or receiving advice. (Take comfort in the words of writer Somerset Maugham: "Only the mediocre person is always at his best.") See the workshop as a nonthreatening opportunity to reconsider your prose and improve your audience awareness.

2. Come prepared. If your workshop structure permits, tell your reviewer what sort of help you need at this point in your drafting or revising process. Ask for suggestions to fix a particularly troublesome area, or ask for feedback on a choice you've made but are feeling unsure of. Don't hesitate to ask your reviewer for assistance with any part of your essay.

3. Evaluate suggestions carefully. Writing isn't math; most of the time there are no absolutely right or wrong answers—just better or worse rhetorical choices. That is, there are many ways to communicate an idea to a set of readers. You, as the writer, must decide on an effective way, the way that best serves your purpose and your readers' needs. Sometimes your reviewer will suggest a change that is brilliant or one so obviously right you will wonder why in the world you didn't think of it yourself. At other times you may weigh your reviewer's suggestion and decide that your original choice is just as good or perhaps even better. Be open to suggestions, but learn to trust thyself as well.

4. Find the good in bad advice. Occasionally, you may have a reviewer who seems to miss a crucial point or misunderstands your purpose entirely, whose suggestions for revising your paper seem uniformly unproductive for one reason or another. You certainly shouldn't take bad advice—but do think about the issues it raises. Although it's helpful to receive a dynamite suggestion you can incorporate immediately, the real value of a revision workshop is its ability to encourage you to rethink your prose. Readers' responses (yes, even the bizarre ones) challenge writers to take still another look at their rhetorical choices and ask themselves, "Is this clear after all? Does this example really work here? Did something in my essay throw this reader off the track?" Revision workshops offer you benefits, even if you ultimately decide to reject many of your reviewer's suggestions.

When you are the **reviewer**:

1. Develop a constructive attitude. Sometimes it's hard to give honest criticism—most of us are uncomfortable when we think we might hurt someone's feelings—but remember that the writer has resolved to develop a professional attitude, too. The writer expects (and is sometimes desperately begging for) sincere feedback, so be honest as you offer your best advice.

2. Be clear and specific. Vague or flippant responses ("Confusing"; "Huh?") don't help writers know what or how to revise. Try putting some of your comments into this format: your response to X, the reason for your response, a request for change, and, if possible, a specific suggestion for the change. ("I'm confused when you say you enjoy some parts of breakfast because this seems to contradict your thesis claim of 'wretched dorm food.' Would it be clearer to modify your thesis to exclude breakfast or to revise this paragraph to include only discussion of the rubbery eggs?")

3. Address important issues. Unless you have workshop directions that request certain tasks, read through the draft entirely at least once and then comment on the larger issues first. Writers want to know if they are achieving their overall purpose, if their thesis is clear and convincing, if their major points and evidence make sense, and if their paper seems logical and ordered. Editing tips are fine, too, but because workshops encourage authors to rewrite large portions of their prose, attention to minor details may be less valuable early on than feedback on ideas, organization, and development. (Of course, an editing workshop later in the revision process may be exclusively focused on sentence and word problems. Workshops may be designed to address specific problems that writers face.)

4. Encourage the writer. Writers with confidence write and revise better than insecure or angry writers. Praise honestly wherever you can, as specifically as you can. When weaknesses do appear, show the writer that you know she or he is capable of doing better work by linking the weakness to a strength elsewhere in the draft. ("Could you add more 'showing' details here so that your picture of the dentist is as vivid as your description of the nurse?") Substitute specific responses and suggestions for one-word labels such as "awk" (awkward) or "unclear." Even positive labels don't always help writers repeat effective techniques. ("Good!" enthusiastically inscribed in the margin by a well-developed paragraph feels nice but might cause the writer to wonder, "'Good' what? Good point? Good supporting evidence? Good detail? How can I do 'good' again if I don't know exactly what it is?")

5. Understand your role as critical reader. Sometimes it's easy for a reviewer to take ownership of someone else's paper. Keep the writer's purpose in mind as you respond; don't insist on revisions that produce the essay that's in *your* head. Be sensitive to your own voice and language as a reviewer. Instead of making authoritative pronouncements that might offend, ask reader-based questions ("Will all your readers know the meaning of this technical term?" "Would some readers profit from a brief history of this controversy?"). If you're unsure about a possible error, request verification ("Could you recheck this quotation? Its wording here is confusing me because . . ."). Practice offering criticism in language that acknowledges the writer's hard work and accentuates the positive nature of revision ("Would citing last year's budget figures make your good argument against the fish market even stronger?").

Last, always look over your own draft in light of the insightful suggestions you are offering your classmates. You may feel at first that it is far simpler to analyze someone else's writing than your own. As you participate in revision workshops, however, you will find it increasingly easy to transfer those same critical reading skills to your own work. Becoming a good reader-reviewer for your composition colleagues can be an important part of your training as a first-rate writer.

■ PRACTICING WHAT YOU'VE LEARNED

A. Assume that the following essay is a draft written by one of your classmates who has asked you for help during a class workshop. Using your best critical thinking skills, offer some marginal comments and questions that will guide this writer through an effective revision process.

MAYBE YOU SHOULDN'T GO AWAY TO COLLEGE

Going away to college is not for everyone. There are good reasons why a student might choose to live at home and attend a local school. Money, finding stability while changes are occurring, and accepting responsibility are three to consider.

Money is likely to be most important. Not only is tuition more expensive, but extra money is needed for room and board. Whether room and board is a dorm or an apartment, the expense is great.

Most students never stop to consider that the money that could be saved from room and board may be better spent in future years on graduate school, which is likely to be more important in their careers.

Going to school is a time of many changes anyway, without adding the pressure of a new city or even a new state. Finding stability will be hard enough, without going from home to a dorm. Starting college could be an emotional time for some, and the security of their home and family might make everything easier.

When students decide to go away to school, sometimes because their friends are going away, or maybe because the school is their parents' alma mater, something that all need to decide is whether or not they can accept the responsibility of a completely new way of life.

Everyone feels as if they are ready for total independence when they decide to go away to college, but is breaking away when they are just beginning to set their futures a good idea?

Going away to school may be the right road for some, but those who feel that they are not ready might start looking to a future that is just around the corner.

B. Continue to practice your revision skills by writing a one-to-two-page evaluation of the letter that follows. Help out poor Bubba by telling him what he might do in another draft to accomplish his purpose more effectively and better address his audience. Has he, for example, made the best choices in organization, selection and development of ideas, paragraph structure, and diction? Discuss why and how his letter needs revision.

Dear Mom and Dad,

This week at college has been very interesting.

My roommate is gone and so is my wallet and computer. I tried to tell the police that the stacks of phony $3 bills by his copier weren't mine but I don't know if they believed me.

And, hey, the car thing isn't my fault either. Despite the testimony of all those witnesses. Who knew the entire back end would crumple like that? The other guy's lawyer will be in touch.

Without any transportation, I don't know when I can come home. Maybe at Thanksgiving. The doctor says the rash shouldn't be contagious by then. The arm, after the fight at the party, is another matter altogether.

I have a new girlfriend! Bambi's real nice and the age difference between us is no big deal. I hope you like her, despite how you feel about tattoos. I have a funny story to tell you about how the stuff in her face set off the airport metal detector last weekend. I just wish her sick grandmother didn't need me to help out so much with her expensive operation. Bambi and her brother are pressuring me a lot.

As you can plainly see, I need more financial help! Please send money right away!

Your devoted son,
Bubba

■ ASSIGNMENT

Select a body paragraph from "Dorm Life" (pages 107–108) or "Maybe You Shouldn't Go Away to College" (page 111) and revise it, making any changes in focus, organization, development, sentence construction, or word choice you think necessary. (Feel free to elaborate on, eliminate, or change the content to improve the paragraph's effectiveness.)

■ Some Last Advice: How to Play with Your Mental Blocks

Every writer, sooner or later, suffers from some form of Writer's Block, the inability to think of or organize ideas. Symptoms may include sweaty palms, pencil chewing, and a pronounced tendency to suddenly clean out closets. Although not every "cure" works for everyone, here are a few suggestions to help minimize your misery:

Try to give yourself as much time as possible to write your essay. Don't try to write the entire paper in one sitting at the last minute. By doing so, you place yourself under too much pressure. Writer's Block often accompanies the "up against the wall" feeling that strikes at 2:00 A.M. the morning your essay is due at 9:00. Rome wasn't constructed in a day, and neither are most good essays.

Because most of us have had more experience talking than writing, try verbalizing your ideas. Sometimes it's helpful to discuss your ideas with friends or classmates. Their questions and comments (not to mention their sympathy for your temporary block) will often trigger the thoughts you need to begin writing again. In some cases, especially if you're stuck while drafting an argument or persuasive paper, it's useful to ask someone to role-play your Cranky Opposition. Forcing yourself to answer his or her objections to your position might lead you out of your bog-down into new or stronger points to include in your draft.

When an irresistible force meets an immovable object, something's going to give. Conquer the task: break the paper into manageable bits. Instead of drooping with despair over the thought of a ten-page research paper, think of it as a series of small parts (explanation of the problem, review of current research, possible solutions, etc.). Then tackle one part at a time, and reward yourself when that section is done.

Sometimes Writer's Block makes you want to . . .

The Scream, 1893, by Edvard Munch

Get the juices flowing and the pen (or keys) moving. Try writing the easiest or shortest part of your essay first. A feeling of accomplishment may give you the boost of confidence you need to undertake the other, more difficult sections. If no part looks easy or inviting, try more prewriting exercises, as described in Chapter 1, until you feel prepared to begin the essay itself.

Play "Let's Make a Deal" with yourself. Sometimes we just can't face the failure that we are predicting for ourselves. Strike a bargain with yourself: promise yourself that you are going to work on your paper for only twenty minutes—absolutely, positively only twenty minutes, not a second more, no sir, no way. If in twenty minutes, you're onto something good, ignore your promise to yourself and keep going. If you're not, then leave and come back for another twenty-minute session later (if you started early enough, you can do this without increasing your anxiety).

Give yourself permission to write garbage. Take the pressure off yourself by agreeing in advance to tear up the first page or two of whatever you write. You can always change your mind if the trash turns out to be treasure. If it isn't, so what? You said you were going to tear it up anyway.

Imagine that your brain is a water faucet. If you're like most people, you've probably lived in a house or apartment containing a faucet that needed to run for a few minutes before the hot water came out. Think of your brain in the same way, and do some other, easier writing task to warm up. Write a letter, send an e-mail, make a grocery list, copy notes, whatever, to get your brain running. When you turn to your essay, your ideas may be hotter than you thought.

Remove the threat by addressing a friendly face. Sometimes we can't write because we are too worried about what someone else will think about us, or maybe we can't write because we can't figure out who would want to read this stuff anyway. Instead of writing into a void or to an audience that seems threatening, try writing to a friend. Imagine what that friend's responses might be and try to elaborate or clarify wherever necessary. If it helps, write the first draft as a letter ("Dear Clyde, I want to tell you what happened to me last week . . ."), and then redraft your ideas as an essay when you've found your purpose and focus, making whatever changes in tone or development are necessary to fit your real audience.

If Writer's Block does hit, remember that it is a temporary bogdown, not a permanent one. Other writers have had it—and survived to write again. Try leaving your draft and taking a walk outdoors or at least into another room. Think about your readers—what should they know or feel at this point in your essay? As you walk, try to complete this sentence: "What I am trying to say is . . . ." Keep repeating this phrase and your responses aloud until you find the answer you want.

Sometimes while you're blocked at one point, a bright idea for another part of your essay will pop into your head. If possible, skip the section that has you stuck, and start working on the new part. (At least jot down the new idea somewhere so it won't be lost when you need it later.)

"Feelings, woo-o-o, nothing more than feelings . . ." You've hit a wall: you now despise your essay topic; you can't face that draft one more time. Turn that fear and loathing into something more positive. Put the draft away. Go to a blank page or screen and pour out your feelings toward your essay's *subject*. Why did you care about this topic in the first place? What's meaningful about it? Why did you want others to think about it? Reconnecting with your subject matter, rather than arm wrestling the same draft again and again, may suggest a new start with a clearer purpose. (And if this suggestion doesn't work, you may have at least helped yourself to a good night's rest. According to studies by James Pennebaker, a University of Texas psychology professor, writing about your feelings "reduces stress and allows for better sleep." A good snooze may be just what you need to tackle your essay with renewed energy.)

Change partners and dance. If you're thoroughly overcome by the vast white wasteland on the desk (or screen) before you, get up and do something else for a while. Exercise, balance your checkbook, or put on music and dance. (Mystery writer Agatha Christie claimed she did her best planning while washing the dishes.) Give your mind a break and refresh your spirit. When you come back to the paper, you may be surprised to discover that your subconscious writer has been working while the rest of you played.

Here's the single most important piece of advice to remember: relax. No one—not even the very best professional writer—produces perfect prose every time pen hits paper. If you're blocked, you may be trying too hard; if your expectations of your first draft are too high, you may not be able to write at all for fear of failure. You just might be holding yourself back by being a perfectionist at this point. You can always revise and polish your prose in another draft—the first important step is jotting down your ideas. Remember that once the first word or phrase appears on your blank page or screen, a major battle has been won.

⭐ CHAPTER 5 SUMMARY

Here is a brief summary of what you should remember about revising your writing:

1. Revision is an activity that occurs in all stages of the writing process.

2. All good writers revise and polish their prose.

3. Revision is not merely editing or last-minute proofreading; it involves important decisions about the essay's ideas, organization, and development.

4. To revise effectively, novice writers might review their drafts in stages to avoid the frustration that comes with trying to fix everything at once.

5. Critical thinking skills are vitally important today to all good readers and writers.

6. Most writers experience Writer's Block at some time but live through it to write again.

Chapter 6

Effective Sentences

An insurance agent was shocked to open his mail one morning and read the following note from one of his clients: "In accordance with your instructions, I have given birth to twins in the enclosed envelope." However, he might not have been more surprised than the congregation who read this announcement in their church bulletin: "There will be a discussion tomorrow on the problem of adultery in the minister's office." Or the patrons of a health club who learned that "guest passes will not be given to members until the manager has punched each of them first."

Certainly, there were no babies born in an envelope, nor was there adultery in the minister's office, and one doubts that the club manager was planning to assault the membership. But the implications (and the unintended humor) are nevertheless present— solely because of the faulty ways in which the sentences were constructed.

To improve your own writing, you must express your thoughts in clear, coherent sentences that produce precisely the reader response you want. Effective sentences are similar to the threads in a piece of knitting or weaving: each thread helps form the larger design; if any one thread becomes tangled or lost, the pattern becomes muddled. In an essay, the same is true: if any sentence is fuzzy or obscure, the reader may lose the point of your discussion and in some cases never bother to regain it. Therefore, to retain your reader, you must concentrate on writing informative, effective sentences that continuously clarify the purpose of your essay.

Many problems in sentence clarity involve errors in grammar, punctuation, word choice, and usage; the most common of these errors are discussed in Chapter 7, "Word Logic," and throughout Part Four, the handbook section of this text. In this chapter you'll find some general suggestions for writing clear, concise, engaging sentences. However, *don't try to apply all the rules to the first draft of your essay.* Revising sentences before your ideas are firmly in place may be a waste of effort if your essay's stance or structure changes. Concentrate your efforts in early drafts on your thesis, the development of your important supporting points, and the essay's general organization; then, in a later draft, rework your sentences so that each one is informative and clear. Your reader reads only the words on the page, not those in your mind—so it's up to you to make sure the sentences in your essay express the thoughts in your head as closely and vividly as possible.

© Robert Brenner/PhotoEdit

✓ **REMEMBER:** All good writers revise and polish their sentences.

■ Developing a Clear Style

When you are ready to revise the sentences in your rough draft for clarity, try to follow the following six rules.

Give Your Sentences Content

Fuzzy sentences are often the result of fuzzy thinking. When you examine your sentences, ask yourself, "Do I know what I'm talking about here? Or are my sentences vague or confusing because I'm really not sure what my point is or where it's going?" Look at this list of content-poor sentences taken from student essays; how could you put more information into each one?

> If you were to observe a karate class, you would become familiar with all the aspects that make it up.

> The meaning of the poem isn't very clear the first time you read it, but after several readings, the poet's meaning comes through.

> One important factor that is the basis for determining a true friend is the ability that person has for being a real human being.

> Listening is important because we all need to be able to sit and hear all that is said to us.

Don't pad your paragraphs with sentences that run in circles, leading nowhere; rethink your ideas and revise your writing so that every sentence—like each brick in a wall—contributes to the construction of a solid discussion. In other words, commit yourself to a position and make each sentence contain information pertinent to your point; leave the job of padding to mattress manufacturers.

Sometimes, however, you may have a definite idea in mind but still continue to write "empty sentences"—statements that alone do not contain enough information to make a specific point in your discussion. Frequently, an empty sentence can be revised by combining it with the sentence that follows, as shown in the examples here. The empty, or overly general, sentences are underlined.

Poor	<u>There are many kinds of beautiful tropical fish.</u> The kind most popular with aquarium owners is the angelfish.
Better	Of the many kinds of beautiful tropical fish, the angelfish is the most popular with aquarium owners.
Poor	<u>D. W. Griffith introduced many new cinematic techniques.</u> Some of these techniques were contrast editing, close-ups, fade-outs, and freeze-frame shots.
Better	D. W. Griffith made movie history by introducing such new cinematic techniques as contrast editing, close-ups, fade-outs, and the freeze-frame shot.
Poor	<u>There is a national organization called The Couch Potatoes.</u> The group's 8,000 members are devoted television watchers.
Better	The Couch Potatoes is a national organization whose 8,000 members are devoted television watchers.

For more help on combining sentences, see pages 136–140.

Make Your Sentences Specific

In addition to containing an informative, complete thought, each of your sentences should give readers enough clear details for them to "see" the picture you are creating. Sentences full of vague words produce blurry, boring prose and drowsy readers. Remember your reaction the last time you asked a friend about a recent vacation? If the only response you received was something like, "Oh, it was great—a lot of fun," you probably yawned and proceeded quickly to a new topic. But if your friend had begun an exciting account of a wilderness rafting trip, with detailed stories about narrow escapes from freezing white water, treacherous rocks, and uncharted whirlpools, you'd probably have stopped and listened. The same principle works in your writing—clear, specific details are the only sure way to attract and hold the reader's interest. Therefore, make each sentence contribute something new and interesting to the overall discussion.

The following examples first show sentences that are far too vague to sustain anyone's attention. Rewritten, these sentences contain specific details that add clarity and interest:

Vague	She went home in a bad mood. [What kind of a bad mood? How did she act or look?]
Specific	She stomped home, hands jammed in her pockets, angrily kicking rocks, dogs, small children, and anything else that crossed her path.
Vague	His neighbor bought a really nice old desk. [Why nice? How old? What kind of desk?]
Specific	His neighbor bought a solid-oak rolltop desk made in 1885 that contains a secret drawer triggered by a hidden spring.

Vague   My roommate is truly horrible. ["Horrible" in what ways? To what
                   extent? Do you "see" this person?]
Specific   My thoughtless roommate leaves dirty dishes under the bed, sweaty
                   clothes in the closet, and toenail clippings in the sink.

For more help selecting specific "showing" words, see pages 132–133 in this chapter
and pages 153–156 in Chapter 7.

Avoid Overpacking Your Sentences

Because our society is becoming increasingly specialized and highly technical, we tend to
equate complexity with excellence and simplicity with simplemindedness. This assump-
tion is unfortunate because it often leads to a preference for unnecessarily complicated
and even contorted writing. In a recent survey, for example, a student chose a sample of
bureaucratic hogwash over several well-written paragraphs, explaining his choice by saying that it must have been better because he didn't understand it.

Our best writers have always worked hard to present their ideas simply and specifically
so that their readers could easily understand them. Mark Twain, for instance, once praised
a young author this way: "I notice that you use plain simple language, short words, and
brief sentences. This is the way to write English. It is the modern way and the best way.
Stick to it." And when a critic asked Hemingway to define his theory of writing, he replied,
"[I] put down what I see and what I feel in the best and simplest way I can tell it."

In your own writing, therefore, work for a simple, direct style. Avoid sentences that are
overpacked (too many ideas or too much information at once) as in the following example on racquetball:

> John told Phil that to achieve more control over the ball, he should practice flicking or
> snapping his wrist, because this action is faster in the close shots and placing a shot requires
> only a slight change of the wrist's angle instead of an acute movement of the whole arm,
> which gives a player less reaction time.

To make the overpacked sentence easier to understand, try dividing the ideas into two or
more sentences:

> John told Phil that to achieve more control over the ball, he should practice flicking or
> snapping his wrist, because this action is faster in the close shots. Placing a shot requires only
> a slight change of the wrist's angle instead of an acute movement of the whole arm, which
> gives a player less reaction time.

Don't ever run the risk of losing your reader in a sentence that says too much to
comprehend in one bite. This confusing notice, for example, came from a well-known
credit card company:

> The Minimum Payment Due each month shall be reduced by the amounts paid in excess
> of the Minimum Payment Due during the previous three months which have not already
> been so applied in determining the Minimum Payment Due in such earlier months, unless
> you have exceeded your line of credit or have paid the entire New Balance shown on your
> billing statement.

Or consider the confusion of soccer players whose coach warned them in this manner:

> It is also a dangerous feeling to consider that where we are in the league is of acceptable standard because standard is relevant to the standards we have set, which thereby may well indicate that we have not aspired to the standard which we set ourselves.

Try too for a straightforward construction. This sentence by Ronald Reagan early in his campaign for the presidency, for example, takes far too many twists and turns for anyone to follow it easily on the first reading:

> My goal is an America where something or anything that is done to or for anyone is done neither because of nor in spite of any difference between them, racially, religiously or ethnic-origin-wise.

If any sentences in your rough draft are overpacked or contorted, try rephrasing your meaning in shorter sentences and then combining thoughts where most appropriate. (Help with sentence variety may be found on pages 136–140 of this chapter.)

Fix Fragments

Rather than creating overpacked sentences, some writers have the opposite problem. They write *sentence fragments*, dropping thoughts here or there without forming them into complete, comprehensible grammatical units. Such fragments are confusing to readers, who must struggle to fill in the connecting link between the writer's ideas.

A complete sentence has both a subject (the thing that performs the action or maintains the state of being) and a predicate (the verb and any modifiers or complements). A sentence fragment is often missing its subject, as shown below.

Fragment	David bought a gopher ranch. *Hoping to strike it rich.*
Correct	David bought a gopher ranch, hoping to strike it rich.
Correct	David bought a gopher ranch. He hoped to strike it rich.

Other fragments have the essential sentence components but are considered fragments because they begin with a subordinating conjunction (such as "although," "if," or "when") or a relative pronoun (such as "who," "which," "whose," or "that").

Fragment	David bought a gopher ranch. *Although he knew nothing about rodents.*
Correct	David bought a gopher ranch, although he knew nothing about rodents.
Fragment	David bought a gopher ranch. *Which was for sale at a low price.*
Correct	David bought a gopher ranch, which was for sale at a low price.

If you are having problems recognizing whether a group of words is a fragment or a complete sentence, try the "It is true that" test. When you suspect a fragment, say, "It is true that" in front of words in question. In most cases, a complete sentence will still make sense, but a fragment will not.*

It is true that . . . David bought a gopher ranch. [Makes sense: complete sentence]
It is true that . . . hoping to strike it rich. [No sense: fragment]
It is true that . . . which was for sale at a low price. [No sense: fragment]

Although they can appear anywhere, fragments most often "belong" to the thought in front of them. To make a fragment fully meaningful, consider connecting it to the preceding or following sentence, as appropriate, or simply rewrite it as a complete sentence (for examples, see the first two "Correct" sentences in this section).

In some cases a writer will intentionally use a fragment for a particular purpose, often for emphasis or to create a specific tone ("She felt rotten. Worse than rotten. Miserable-rotten."). But unless you clearly know how to use a fragment for effect and are certain that the tone it creates is appropriate for your essay and audience, stick to writing complete sentences.

For more help with fragments, see pages 536–537 in the Handbook. See also pages 137–140 in this chapter, which will suggest ways to combine thoughts through coordination and subordination. (If you need advice about correcting other common sentence problems, such as run-ons or comma splices, consult pages 538–539 in the Handbook.)

Pay Attention to Word Order

The correct word order is crucial for clarity. Always place a modifier (a word or group of words that affects the meaning of another word) near the word it modifies. The position of a modifier can completely change the meaning of your sentence; for example, each sentence presented here offers a different idea because of the placement of the modifier "only."

1. Eliza said she loves only me.
   [Eliza loves me and no one else.]
2. Only Eliza said she loves me.
   [No other person said she loves me.]
3. Eliza said only that she loves me.
   [Eliza said she loves me, but said nothing other than that.]
4. Eliza said only she loves me.
   [Eliza said no one else loves me.]

To avoid confusion, therefore, place your modifiers close to the words or phrases they describe.

A modifier that seems to modify the wrong part of a sentence is called "misplaced." Not only can misplaced modifiers change or distort the meaning of your sentence, they can also provide unintentional humor, as illustrated by the following excerpt from the 1929 Marx Brothers' movie *The Cocoanuts*:

Woman: There's a man waiting outside to see you with a black mustache.
Groucho: Tell him I've already got one.

---

*The "It is true that" test does not work on questions, elliptical responses or exclamations (such as "Hello," "Yes," "Help!"), or commands ("Go to your room right now").

Of course, the woman didn't mean to imply that the man outside was waiting with (that is, accompanied by) a mustache; she meant to say, "There's a man with a black mustache who is waiting outside."

A poster advertising a lecture on campus provided this opportunity for humor: "Professor Elizabeth Sewell will discuss the latest appearance of Halley's Comet in room 104." Under the announcement a local wit had scribbled, "Shall we reserve room 105 for the tail?" Or take the case of this startling headline: "Calf Born to Rancher with Two Heads."

Here are some other examples of misplaced modifiers:

Misplaced	Dilapidated and almost an eyesore, Shirley bought the old house to restore it to its original beauty. [Did the writer mean that Shirley needed a beauty treatment?]
Revised	Shirley bought the old house, which was dilapidated and almost an eyesore, to restore it to its original beauty.
Misplaced	Because she is now thoroughly housebroken, Sarah can take her dog almost anywhere she goes. [Did the writer mean that Sarah once had an embarrassing problem?]
Revised	Because she is now thoroughly housebroken, Sarah's dog can accompany her almost anywhere she goes.
Misplaced	Three family members were found bound and gagged by the grandmother. [Did the writer mean that the grandmother had taken up a life of crime?]
Revised	The grandmother found the three family members who had been bound and gagged.
Misplaced	The lost child was finally found wandering in a frozen farmer's field. [Did the writer mean to say that the farmer was that cold?]
Revised	The lost child was finally found wandering in a farmer's frozen field.

In each of the preceding examples the writer forgot to place the modifying phrase so that it modifies the correct word. In most cases, a sentence with a misplaced modifier can be corrected easily by moving the word or phrase closer to the word that should be modified.

In some sentences, however, the word being modified is missing entirely. Such a phrase is called a "dangling modifier." Think of these phrases as poor orphans, waiting out in the cold, without a parent to accompany them. Most of these errors can be corrected by adding the missing "parent"—the word(s) described by the phrase. Here are some examples followed by their revisions:

Dangling	Waving farewell, the plane began to roll down the runway. [Did the writer mean the plane was waving farewell?]
Revised	Waving farewell, <u>we</u> watched as the plane began to roll down the runway.
Dangling	After spending hours planting dozens of strawberry plants, the gophers came back to the garden and ate every one of them. [Did the writer mean that the gophers had a good meal after putting in such hard work?]
Revised	After spending hours planting dozens of strawberry plants, <u>Ralph</u> realized that the gophers had come back to the garden and eaten every one of them.

Dangling	While telling a joke to my roommate, a cockroach walked across my soufflé. [Did the writer mean that the cockroach was a comedian?]
Revised	While telling a joke to my roommate, <u>I</u> noticed a cockroach walking across my soufflé.
Dangling	Having tucked the children into bed, the cat was put out for the night. [Did the writer mean that the family pet had taken up nanny duties?]
Revised	Having tucked the children into bed, <u>Mother and Father</u> put the cat out for the night.

Misplaced and dangling modifiers (and many other kinds of sentence errors) often occur as you write your first "idea" drafts. Later, when you are satisfied with your content and organization, you can smooth out these confusing or unintentionally humorous constructions. At first you may agree with well-known essayist Annie Dillard, who notes that writing sometimes feels like alligator wrestling: "With your two bare hands, you hold and fight a sentence's head while its tail tries to knock you over." By practicing good revision skills, however, you soon should be able to wrestle your sentence problems to the ground. (For additional examples of misplaced and dangling modifiers, see pages 534–535 in Part Four.)

Avoid Mixed Constructions and Faulty Predication

Sometimes you may begin with a sentence pattern in mind and then shift, midsentence, to another pattern—a change that often results in a generally confusing sentence. In many of these cases, you will find that the subject of your sentence simply doesn't fit with the rest of the sentence (the predicate). Look at the following examples and note their corrections:

Faulty	Financial aid is a growing problem for many college students. [Financial aid itself isn't a problem; rather, it's the lack of aid.]
Revised	College students are finding it harder to obtain financial aid.
Faulty	Pregnant cows are required to teach a portion of two courses in Animal Science, AS100 (Breeding of Livestock) and AS200 (Problems in Reproduction of Cattle). [Obviously, the cows will not be the instructors for the classes.]
Revised	The Animal Science Department needs to purchase pregnant cows for use in two courses, AS100 (Breeding of Livestock) and AS200 (Problems in Reproduction of Cattle).
Faulty	Love is when you start rehearsing dinner-date conversation before breakfast. [A thing is never a "when" or a "where"; rewrite all "is when" or "is where" constructions.]
Revised	You're in love if you start rehearsing dinner-date conversation before breakfast.
Faulty	My math grade is why I'm so depressed.
Revised	I'm so depressed because of my math grade. [A grade is not a "why"; rewrite "is why" constructions.]
Faulty	"Fans, don't fail to miss tomorrow's game." [A contorted line from Dizzy Dean, baseball star and sportscaster]
Revised	"Fans, don't miss tomorrow's game."

Many mixed constructions occur when a writer is in a hurry; read your rough drafts carefully to see if you have sentences in which you started one pattern but switched to another. (For more help on faulty predications and mixed constructions, see pages 542–543 in Part Four.)

Clear, straightforward sentences keep readers from feeling as though they are lost in an Escher maze. *Convex and Concave*, 1955 by M.C. Escher

ARS NYI/Art Resource, NY

■ PRACTICING WHAT YOU'VE LEARNED

A. In this exercise you will find sentences that are vague, confused, overpacked, or fragmented. Rewrite so that each thought is clear, complete, and specific. You may combine or divide sentences and replace vague language to improve clarity.

1. Roger was an awesome guy who was really a big part of his company.

2. There's a new detective show on television. Starring Phil Noir. It is set in the 1940s.

3. I can't help but wonder whether or not he isn't unwelcome.

4. The book *Biofeedback: How to Stop It* is a good one because of all the ideas the writer put into it.

5. Sarah's room is always a huge disaster. According to her mother.

6. Afraid poor repair service will ruin your next road trip? Come to the Fix-It Shop and be sure. If your car has a worn-out part, we'll replace it with one just like it.

7. I've signed up for a course at my local college. It is "Cultivating the Mold in Your Refrigerator for Fun and Profit."

8. For some people, reading your horoscope is a fun way to learn stuff about your life. Although some people think it's too weird.

9. I'm not sure but I think that Lois is the author of *The Underachiever's Guide to Very Small Business Opportunities* or is she the writer of *Whine Your Way to Success* because I know she's written several books since she's having an autograph party at the campus bookstore either this afternoon or tomorrow.

10. Upon being asked if she would like to live forever, one contestant in the 1994 Miss USA contest replied: "I would not live forever, because we should not live forever, because if we were supposed to live forever, then we would live forever, but we cannot live forever, which is why I would not live forever."

B. The following sentences contain misplaced words and phrases as well as other faulty constructions. Revise them so that each sentence is clear.

1. If you are accosted in the subway at night, you should learn to escape harm from the police.

2. The bride was escorted down the aisle by her stepfather wearing an antique family wedding gown.

3. Almost dead for five years now, I miss my dog so much.

4. For sale: unique gifts for that special, hard-to-find person in your life.

5. The reason why I finally got my leg operated on over Thanksgiving break is because it had been hanging over my head for years.

6. We need to hire two three-year-old teachers for preschool kids who don't smoke.

7. The story of Rip Van Winkle is one of the dangers endured by those who oversleep.

8. We gave our waterbed to friends we didn't want anymore.

9. People who are allergic to chocolate and children under 6 should not be given the new vaccine.

10. At 7:00 A.M., Kate starts preparing for another busy day as an executive in her luxurious bathroom.

■ Developing a Concise Style

Almost all writing suffers from wordiness—the tendency to use more words than necessary. When useless words weigh down your prose, the meaning is often lost, confused, or hidden. Flabby prose calls for a reducing plan: put those obese sentences on a diet by cutting out unnecessary words, just as you avoid eating too many fatty foods to keep yourself at a healthy weight. Mushy prose is ponderous and boring; crisp, to-the-point writing, on the other hand, is both accessible and pleasing. Beware, however, a temptation to overdiet—you don't want your prose to become so thin or brief that your meaning disappears completely. Therefore, cut out only the *unessential* words and phrases.

Wordy prose is frequently the result of using one or more of the following: (1) deadwood constructions, (2) redundancies, (3) passive constructions, and (4) pretentious diction.

Avoid Deadwood Constructions

Always try to cut empty "deadwood" from your sentences. Having a clear, concise style does not mean limiting your writing to choppy, childish Dick-and-Jane sentences; it only means that all unnecessary words, phrases, and clauses should be deleted. Here are some sentences containing common deadwood constructions and ways they may be pruned:

Poor	The *reason* the starving novelist drove fifty miles to a new restaurant was *because* it was serving his favorite chicken dish, Pullet Surprise. ["The reason . . . was because" is both wordy and ungrammatical. If you have a reason, you don't need a "reason because."]
Revised	The starving novelist drove fifty miles to a new restaurant because it was serving his favorite chicken dish, Pullet Surprise.
Poor	The land settlement *was an example where* my client, Ms. Patti O. Furniture, did not receive fair treatment.
Revised	The land settlement was unfair to my client, Ms. Patti O. Furniture.
Poor	Because *of the fact that* his surfboard business failed after only a month, my brother decided to leave Minnesota.
Revised	Because his surfboard business failed after only a month, my brother decided to leave Minnesota.

Other notorious deadwood constructions include the following:

regardless of the fact that	(use "although")
due to the fact that	(use "because")
the reason is that	(omit)
as to whether or not to	(omit "as to" and "or not")
at this point in time	(use "now" or "today")
it is believed that	(use a specific subject and "believes")
concerning the matter of	(use "about")
by means of	(use "by")
these are the kinds of . . . that	(use "these" plus a specific noun)
on account of	(use "because")

Watch a tendency to tack on empty "fillers" that stretch one word into a phrase:

Wordy	Each candidate will be evaluated *on an individual basis.*
Concise	Each candidate will be evaluated *individually.*
Wordy	Television does not portray violence in a *realistic fashion.*
Concise	Television does not portray violence *realistically.*
Wordy	The New York blackout produced a *crisis-type situation.*
Concise	The New York blackout produced a *crisis.*

To retain your reader's interest and improve the flow of your prose, trim all the fat from your sentences.

"There are," "It is." These introductory phrases are often space wasters. When possible, omit them or replace them with specific subjects, as shown in the following:

Wordy	*There are* ten dental students on Full-Bite Scholarships attending this university.
Revised	Ten dental students on Full-Bite Scholarships attend this university.
Wordy	*It is* true that the County Fair still offers many fun contests, including the ever-popular map fold-off.
Revised	The County Fair still offers many fun contests, including the ever-popular map fold-off.

"Who" and "which" clauses. Some "who" and "which" clauses are unnecessary and may be turned into modifiers placed before the noun:

Wordy	The getaway car, *which* was stolen, turned the corner.
Revised	The stolen getaway car turned the corner.
Wordy	The chef, *who* was depressed, ordered his noisy lobsters to simmer down.
Revised	The depressed chef ordered his noisy lobsters to simmer down.

When adjective clauses are necessary, the words "who" and "which" may sometimes be omitted:

Wordy	Sarah Bellam, *who* is a local English teacher, was delighted to hear that she had won the annual lottery, *which* is sponsored by the Shirley Jackson Foundation.
Revised	Sarah Bellam, a local English teacher, was delighted to hear that she had won the annual lottery, sponsored by the Shirley Jackson Foundation.

"To be." Most "to be" phrases are unnecessary and ought not to be. Delete them every time you can.

Wordy	She seems *to be* angry.
Revised	She seems angry.

Wordy	Herb's charisma-bypass operation proved *to be* successful.
Revised	Herb's charisma-bypass operation proved successful.
Wordy	The new governor wanted his archenemy, the local movie critic, *to be* arrested.
Revised	The new governor wanted his archenemy, the local movie critic, arrested.

"Of" and infinitive phrases. Many "of" and infinitive ("to" plus verb) phrases may be omitted or revised by using possessives, adjectives, and verbs, as shown below:

Wordy	At the time *of registration*, students are required *to make* payment *of their library fees.*
Revised	At registration students must pay their library fees.
Wordy	The producer fired the mother *of the director of the movie.*
Revised	The producer fired the movie director's mother.

Including deadwood phrases makes your prose puffy; streamline your sentences to present a simple, direct style.

Avoid Redundancy

Many flabby sentences contain *redundancies* (words that repeat the same idea or whose meanings overlap). Consider the following examples, currently popular in the Department of Redundancy Department:

In this *day and age*, people expect to live at least seventy years. ["Day" and "age" present a similar idea. "Today" is less wordy.]

He repeated the winning bingo number *over again*. ["Repeated" means "to say again," so there is no need for "over again."]

The *group* consensus *of opinion* was that the pizza crust tasted like cardboard. ["Consensus" means "collective opinion," so it's unnecessary to add "group" or repeat "opinion."]

She thought his hot-lava necklaces were *really very* unique. [Because "unique" means "being the only one of its kind," the quality described by "unique" cannot vary in degree. Avoid adding modifiers such as "very," "most," or "somewhat" to the word "unique."]

Some other common redundancies include the following:

reverted ~~back~~	~~new~~ innovation
reflected ~~back~~	red ~~in color~~
retreated ~~back~~	burned ~~down~~ / ~~up~~
fell ~~down~~	~~pair of~~ twins / ~~two~~ twins
climb ~~up~~	~~resulting~~ effect (or "result")
a ~~true~~ fact	~~final~~ outcome
large ~~in size~~	at this point ~~in time~~ (or "now")
joined ~~up~~	8 P.M. ~~at night~~

Carefully Consider Your Passive Verbs

When the subject of the sentence performs the action, the verb is *active;* when the subject of the sentence is acted on, the verb is *passive.* You can recognize some sentences with passive verbs because they often contain the word "by," telling who performed the action.

Passive	The wedding date *was announced* by the young couple.
Active	The young couple *announced* their wedding date.
Passive	His letter of resignation *was accepted* by the Board of Trustees.
Active	The Board of Trustees *accepted* his letter of resignation.
Passive	The trivia contest *was won* by the popular Boulder team, The Godzillas Must Be Crazy.
Active	The popular Boulder team, The Godzillas Must Be Crazy, *won* the trivia contest.

In addition to being wordy and weak, passive sentences often disguise the performer of the action in question. You might have heard a politician, for example, say something similar to this: "It was decided this year to give all the senators an increase in salary." The question of *who* decided to raise salaries remains foggy—perhaps purposefully so. In your own prose, however, you should strive for clarity and directness; therefore, use active verbs as often as you can except when you wish to stress the person or thing that receives the action, as shown in the following examples:

Their first baby was delivered September 30, 1980, by a local midwife.

The elderly man was struck by a drunk driver.

Special note: Authorities in some professional and technical fields prefer the passive construction because they wish to put emphasis on the experiment or process rather than on the people performing the action. If the passive voice is preferred in your field, you should abide by that convention when you are writing reports or papers for your professional colleagues.

Avoid Pretentiousness

Another enemy of clear, concise prose is *pretentiousness.* Pompous, inflated language surrounds us, and because too many people think it sounds learned or official, we may be tempted to use it when we want to impress others with our writing. But as George Orwell, author of *1984,* noted, an inflated style is like "a cuttlefish squirting out ink." If you want your prose easily understood, write as clearly and plainly as possible.

To illustrate how confusing pretentious writing can be, here is a copy of a government memo announcing a blackout order, issued in 1942 during World War II:

Such preparations shall be made as will completely obscure all Federal buildings and non-Federal buildings occupied by the Federal government during an air raid for any period of time from visibility by reason of internal or external illumination.

President Franklin Roosevelt intervened and rewrote the order in plain English, clarifying its message and reducing the number of words by half:

> Tell them that in buildings where they have to keep the work going to put something across the windows.

By translating the obscure original memo into easily understandable language, Roosevelt demonstrated that a natural prose style can communicate necessary information to readers more quickly and efficiently than bureaucratic jargon. (For more advice on ridding your prose of jargon, see pages 156–158.)

✓ **REMEMBER:** In other—shorter—words, to attract and hold your readers' attention, to communicate clearly and quickly, make your sentences as informative, straightforward, specific, and concise as possible.

■ **PRACTICING WHAT YOU'VE LEARNED**

The following sentences are filled with deadwood, redundancies, awkward phrases, and passive constructions. Rewrite each one so that it is concise and direct.

1. In point of fact, the main reason he lost the editing job was primarily because of his being too careless and sloppy in his proofreading work.

2. It was revealed to us by staff members today that there were many adults at the company picnic throwing their trash on the ground as well as their children.

3. My brother Austin, who happens to be older than me, can't drive to work this week due to the fact that he was in a wreck in his car at 2:00 A.M. early Saturday morning.

4. In this modern world of today, we often criticize or disapprove of advertising that is thought to be damaging to women by representing them in an unfair way.

5. When the prosecution tried to introduce the old antique gun, this was objected to by the attorney defending the two twin brothers.

6. It seems to me in my opinion that what the poet is trying to get across to the reader in the poem "Now Is the Winter of Our Discount Tent" is her feeling of disgust with camping.

7. We very often felt that although we expressed our deepest concerns and feelings to our boss, she often just sat there and gave us the real impression that she was taking what we said in a very serious manner although, in our opinion, she did not really and truly care about our concerns.

8. It is a true fact that certainly bears repeating over and over again that learning computer skills and word processing can help you perform in a more efficient way at work and school and also can save you lots of time in daily life too.

9. Personally, I believe that there are too many people who go to eat out in restaurants who always feel they must continually assert their superior natures by acting in a rude, nasty fashion to the people who are employed to wait on their tables.

10. In order to enhance my opportunities for advancement in the workplace at this point in time, I arrived at the decision to seek the hand of my employer's daughter in the state of matrimony.

■ **ASSIGNMENT**

Write a paragraph of at least five sentences as clearly and concisely as you can. Then rewrite this paragraph, filling it with as many vague words, redundancies, and deadwood constructions as possible. Exchange this rewritten paragraph for a similarly faulty one written by a classmate; give yourselves fifteen minutes to "translate" each other's sentences into effective prose. Compare the translations to the original paragraphs. Which version is clearer? Why?

■ Developing a Lively Style

Good writing demands clarity and conciseness—but that's not all. Good prose must also be lively, engaging, and interesting. It should excite, intrigue, and charm; each line should seduce the reader into the next. Consider, for example, a dull article you've read lately. It may have been written clearly, but perhaps it failed to interest or inform because of its insufferably bland tone; by the time you finished a few pages, you had discovered a new cure for insomnia.

You can prevent your readers from succumbing to a similar case of the blahs by developing a vigorous prose style that continually surprises and pleases them. As one writer has pointed out, all subjects—with the possible exceptions of sex and money—are dull until somebody makes them interesting. As you revise your rough drafts, remember: bored readers are not born but made. Therefore, here are some practical suggestions to help you transform ho-hum prose into lively sentences and paragraphs:

Use specific, descriptive verbs.   Avoid bland verbs that must be supplemented by modifiers.

Bland	His fist *broke* the window *into many little pieces.*
Better	His fist *shattered* the window.
Bland	Dr. Love *asked* his congregation about donating money to his "love mission" *over and over again.*
Better	Dr. Love *hounded* his congregation into donating money to his "love mission."

Bland	The exhausted runner *went* up the last hill *in an unsteady way.*
Better	The exhausted runner *staggered* up the last hill.

To cut wordiness that weighs down your prose, try to use an active verb instead of a noun plus a colorless verb such as "to be," "to have," "to get," "to do," and "to make." Avoid unnecessary uses of "got."

Wordy	At first the players and managers *had an argument* over the money, but finally they *came to an agreement that got* the contract dispute settled.
Better	At first the players and managers *argued* over the money, but finally they *settled* the contract dispute.
Wordy	The executives *made the decision* to *have another meeting* on Tuesday.
Better	The executives *decided* to *meet again* on Tuesday.
Wordy	The family *made many enjoyable trips* to Hawaii before their daughter *got married* there in 2002.
Better	The family *enjoyed* many trips to Hawaii before their daughter *married* there in 2002.

Use specific, precise modifiers that help the reader see, hear, or feel what you are describing. Adjectives such as "good," "bad," "many," "more," "great," "a lot," "important," and "interesting" are too vague to paint the reader a clear picture. Similarly, the adverbs "very," "really," "too," and "quite" are overused and add little to sentence clarity. The following are examples of weak sentences and their revisions:

Imprecise	The potion changed the scientist into a *really old* man.
Better	The potion changed the scientist into a *one-hundred-year-old* man.
Imprecise	Marcia is a *very interesting* person.
Better	Marcia is *witty, intelligent,* and *talented.*
Imprecise	The vegetables tasted *funny.*
Better	The vegetables tasted *like moss mixed with Krazy Glue.*

(For more advice on using specific, colorful words, see pages 153–156 in Chapter 7.)

Emphasize people when possible. Try to focus on human beings rather than abstractions whenever you can. Next to our fascinating selves, we most enjoy hearing about other people. Although all the sentences in the first paragraph below are correct, the second one, revised by a class of composition students at Brown University, is clearer and more useful because the jargon has been eliminated and the focus changed from the tuition rules to the students.

Original	Tuition regulations currently in effect provide that payment of the annual tuition entitles an undergraduate-degree candidate to full-time enrollment, which is defined as registration for three, four, or five courses per semester. This means that at no time may an undergraduate student's official registration for courses drop below three without a dean's permission for part-time status and that at no time may the official course registration exceed five. (Brown University Course Announcement)

Revised	If students pay their tuition, they may enroll in three, four, or five courses per semester. Fewer than three or more than five can be taken only with a dean's permission.

Here's a similar example with a bureaucratic focus rather than a personal one:

Original	The salary deflations will most seriously impact the secondary educational profession.
Revised	High school teachers will suffer the biggest salary reductions.

Obviously, the revised sentence is the more easily understood of the two because the reader knows exactly who will be affected by the pay cuts. In your own prose, wherever appropriate, try to replace vague abstractions, such as "society," "culture," "administrative concerns," and "programmatic expectations," with the human beings you're thinking about. In other words, remember to talk *to* people *about* people.

Vary your sentence style. The only torture worse than listening to someone's nails scraping across a blackboard is being forced to read a paragraph full of identically constructed sentences. To illustrate this point, the following are a few sentences composed in the all-too-common "subject + predicate" pattern:

Soccer is the most popular sport in the world. Soccer exists in almost every country. Soccer players are sometimes more famous than movie stars. Soccer teams compete every few years for the World Soccer Cup. Soccer fans often riot if their team loses. Soccer fans even commit suicide. Soccer is the only game in the world that makes people so crazy.

Excruciatingly painful, yes? Each of us has a tendency to repeat a particular sentence pattern (though the choppy "subject + predicate" is by far the most popular); you can often detect your own by reading your prose aloud. To avoid overdosing your readers with the same pattern, vary the length, arrangement, and complexity of your sentences. Of course, this doesn't mean that you should contort your sentences merely for the sake of illustrating variety; just read your rough draft aloud, listening carefully to the rhythm of your prose so you can revise any monotonous passages or disharmonious sounds. (Try also to avoid the hiccup syndrome, in which you begin a sentence with the same word that ends the preceding sentence: "The first president to install a telephone on his desk was Herbert *Hoover. Hoover* refused to use the telephone booth outside his office.")

Avoid overuse of any one kind of construction in the same sentence. Don't, for example, pile up too many negatives, "who" or "which" clauses, and prepositional or infinitive phrases in one sentence.

He *couldn't* tell whether she *didn't* want him to go or *not.*

I gave the money to my brother, *who* returned it to the bank president, *who* said the decision to prosecute was up to the sheriff, *who* was out of town.

I went to the florist *for* my roommate *for* a dozen roses *for* his date.

Try also to avoid stockpiling nouns, one on top of another, so that your sentences are difficult to read. Although some nouns may be used as adjectives to modify other nouns ("book mark," "gasoline pump," "food processor"), too many nouns grouped together sound awkward and confuse readers. If you have run too many nouns together, try using prepositional phrases ("an income tax bill discussion" becomes "discussion of an income tax bill") or changing the order or vocabulary of the sentence:

Confusing	The legislators are currently considering the *liability insurance multiple-choice premium proposal.*
Clearer	The legislators are currently considering the proposal that suggests *multiple-choice premiums* for *liability insurance.*
Confusing	We're concerned about the low *female labor force participation figures* in our department.
Clearer	We're concerned about the low *number of women working* in our department.

Don't change your point of view between or within sentences. If, for example, you begin your essay discussing students as "they," don't switch midway—or midsentence—to "we" or "you."

Inconsistent	Students pay tuition, which should entitle *them* to some voice in the university's administration. Therefore, *we* deserve one student on the Board of Regents.
Consistent	Students pay tuition, which should entitle *them* to some voice in the university's administration. Therefore, *they* deserve one student on the Board of Regents.
Inconsistent	*I* like my photography class because *we* learn how to restore *our* old photos and how to take better color portraits of *your* family.
Consistent	*I* like my photography class because *I'm* learning how to restore *my* old photos and how to take better color portraits of *my* family.

Perhaps this is a good place to dispel the myth that the pronoun "I" should never be used in an essay; on the contrary, many of our best essays have been written in the first person. Some of your former teachers may have discouraged the use of "I" for these two reasons: (1) personal opinion does not belong in the essay, and (2) writing in the first person often produces too many empty phrases, such as "I think that" and "I believe that." Nevertheless, if the personal point of view is appropriate in a particular assignment, you may use the first person in moderation, making sure that every other sentence doesn't begin with "I" plus a verb.

▪ PRACTICING WHAT YOU'VE LEARNED

Replace the following underlined words so that the sentences are clear and vivid. In addition, rephrase any awkward constructions or unnecessarily abstract words you find.

1. Judging from the <u>crazy</u> sound of the reactor, it isn't obvious to me that nuclear power as we know it today isn't a technology with a less than wonderful future.

2. The City Council felt <u>bad</u> because the revised tourist development activities grant fund application form letters were mailed without stamps.

3. To watch Jim Bob eat pork chops was <u>most interesting</u>.

4. For sale: <u>very nice</u> antique bureau suitable for ladies or gentlemen with thick legs and extra-large side handles.

5. We <u>don't want anybody to not</u> have fun.

6. My roommate is <u>sort of different</u>, but he's a <u>good</u> guy at heart.

7. After reading the <u>great</u> new book, *The Looter's Guide to Riot-Prone Cities*, Eddie <u>asked to have</u> a transfer <u>really soon</u>.

8. The wild oats soup was <u>fantastic</u>, so we drank <u>a lot of it very fast</u>.

9. When his new cat Chairman Meow won the pet show, owner Warren Peace got <u>pretty excited</u>.

10. The new diet <u>made me feel awful</u>, and it <u>did many horrible things</u> to my body. ▪

▪ ASSIGNMENT

Find a short piece of writing you think is too bland, boring, vague, or confusing. (Possible sources: your college catalog, a business contract, a form letter, or your student health insurance policy.) In a well-written paragraph of your own, identify the sample's major problems, and offer some specific suggestions for improving the writing. (If time permits, read aloud several of the samples, and vote one the winner of the Most Lifeless Prose Award.) ▪

▪ Developing an Emphatic Style

Some words and phrases in your sentences are more important than others and therefore need more emphasis. Three ways to vary emphasis are by (1) word order, (2) coordination, and (3) subordination.

Word Order

The arrangement of words in a sentence can determine which ideas receive the most emphasis. To stress a word or phrase, place it at the end of the sentence or at the beginning of the sentence. Accordingly, a word or phrase receives least emphasis when buried in the middle of the sentence. Compare the following examples, in which the word "murder" receives varying degrees of emphasis:

Least emphatic	For Colonel Mustard *murder* was the only solution.
Emphatic	*Murder* was Colonel Mustard's only solution.
Most Emphatic	Colonel Mustard knew only one solution: *murder.*

Another use of word order to vary emphasis is *inversion*, taking a word out of its natural or usual position in a sentence and relocating it in an unexpected place.

Usual order	Parents who give their children both roots and wings are *wise.*
Inverted order	*Wise* are the parents who give their children both roots and wings.

Not all your sentences will contain words that need special emphasis; good writing generally contains a mix of some sentences in natural order and others rearranged for special effects.

Coordination

When you want to stress two closely related ideas equally, coordinate them.* In coordination, you join two sentences with a coordinating conjunction. To remember the coordinating conjunctions ("for," "and," "nor," "but," "or," "yet," "so"), think of the acronym FANBOYS; then always join two sentences with a comma and one of the FANBOYS. Here are two samples:

Choppy	The most popular girl's name today is Emily. The most popular boy's name today is Jacob.
Coordinated	The most popular girl's name today is Emily, *and* the most popular boy's name is Jacob.
Choppy	Imelda brought home a pair of ruby slippers. Ferdinand made her return them.
Coordinated	Imelda brought home a pair of ruby slippers, *but* Ferdinand made her return them.

You can use coordination to show a relationship between ideas and to add variety to your sentence structures. Be careful, however, to select the right words while linking ideas, unlike the sentence that appeared in a church newsletter: "The ladies of the church have discarded clothing of all kinds, and they have been inspected by the minister." In other words, writers often need to slow down and make sure their thoughts are not joined in unclear or even unintentionally humorous ways: "For those of you who have children and don't know it, we have a nursery downstairs."

Sometimes when writers are in a hurry, they join ideas that are clearly related in their own minds but whose relationship is confusing to the reader:

Confusing	My laboratory report isn't finished, and today my sister is leaving for a visit home.
Clear	I'm still working on my laboratory report, so I won't be able to catch a ride home with my sister who's leaving today.

---

* To remember that the term "coordination" refers to equally weighted ideas, think of other words with the prefix "co" such as "copilots," "co-authors," or "cooperation."

You should also avoid using coordinating conjunctions to string too many ideas together like linked sausages:

Poor	We went inside the famous cave and the guide turned off the lights and we saw the rocks that glowed.
Revised	After we went inside the famous cave, the guide turned off the lights so we could see the rocks that glowed.

Subordination

Some sentences contain one main statement and one or more less emphasized elements; the less important ideas are subordinate to, or are dependent on, the sentence's main idea.* Subordinating conjunctions introducing dependent clauses show a variety of relationships between the clauses and the main part of the sentence. Here are four examples of subordinating conjunctions and their uses:

1. To show time without subordination	Superman stopped changing his clothes. He realized the phone booth was made of glass.
with subordination	Superman stopped changing his clothes *when* he realized the phone booth was made of glass.
2. To show cause without subordination	The country-western singer failed to gain success in Nashville. She sadly returned to Snooker Hollow to work in the sequin mines.
with subordination	*Because* the country-western singer failed to gain success in Nashville, she sadly returned to Snooker Hollow to work in the sequin mines.
3. To show condition without subordination	Susan ought to study the art of tattooing. She will work with colorful people.
with subordination	*If* Susan studies the art of tattooing, she will work with colorful people.
4. To show place without subordination	Bulldozers are smashing the old movie theater. That's the place I first saw Roy Rogers and Dale Evans ride into the sunset.
with subordination	Bulldozers are smashing the old movie theater *where* I first saw Roy Rogers and Dale Evans ride into the sunset.

Subordination is especially useful in ridding your prose of choppy Dick-and-Jane sentences and those "empty sentences" discussed on pages 118–119. Here are some examples of choppy, weak sentences and their revisions, which contain subordinate clauses:

Choppy	Lew makes bagels on Tuesday. Lines in front of his store are a block long.
Revised	When Lew makes bagels on Tuesday, lines in front of his store are a block long.

---

* To remember that the term "subordination" refers to sentences containing dependent elements, think of such words as "a subordinate" (someone who works for someone else) or a post office "substation" (a less important branch of the main post office).

| **Choppy** | I have fond memories of Zilker Park. My husband and I met there. |
| **Revised** | I have fond memories of Zilker Park because my husband and I met there. |

Effective use of subordination is one of the marks of a sophisticated writer because it presents adequate information in one smooth flow instead of in monotonous drips. Subordination, like coordination, also adds variety to your sentence construction.

Generally, when you subordinate one idea, you emphasize another, so to avoid the tail-wagging-the-dog problem, put your important idea in the main clause. Also, don't let your most important idea become buried under an avalanche of subordinate clauses, as in the sentence that follows:

> *When* he was told by his boss, *who* had always treated him fairly, *that* he was being fired from a job *that* he had held for twenty years at a factory *where* he enjoyed working *because* the pay was good, Henry felt angry and frustrated.

Practice blending choppy sentences by studying the following sentence-combining exercise. In this exercise, a description of a popular movie or book has been chopped into simple sentences and then combined into one complex sentence.

1. *Psycho* (1960)
   Norman Bates manages a motel.
   It is remote.
   It is dangerous.
   Norman has a mother.
   She seems overly fond of knives.
   He tries to protect his mom.

   In a remote—and dangerous—motel, manager Norman Bates tries to protect his mother, who seems overly fond of knives.

2. *King Kong* (1933)
   A showman goes to the jungle.
   He captures an ape.
   The ape is a giant.
   The ape is taken to New York City.
   He escapes.
   He dies fighting for a young woman.
   He loves her.
   She is beautiful.

   A giant ape, captured in the jungle by a showman, is taken to New York City, where he escapes but dies fighting for the beautiful young woman he loves.

3. *Casablanca* (1942)
   Rick is an American.
   He is cynical.
   He owns a café.
   He lives in Casablanca.
   He meets his former love.

She is married.
Her husband is a French resistance fighter.
Rick helps the couple.
He regains self-respect.

When Rick, a cynical American café-owner in Casablanca, helps his former love and her husband, a French resistance fighter, he regains his self-respect.

Please note that the sentences in these exercises may be combined effectively in a number of ways. For instance, the description of *King Kong* might be rewritten this way: "After a showman captures him in the jungle, a giant ape escapes in New York City but dies fighting for the love of a beautiful young woman." How might you rewrite the other two sample sentences?

■ PRACTICING WHAT YOU'VE LEARNED

A. Revise the following sentences so that the underlined words receive more emphasis.

1. A remark attributed to the one-time heavyweight boxing champion <u>Joe Louis</u> is "I don't really like money, but it quiets my nerves."

2. According to recent polls, <u>television</u> is where most Americans get their news.

3. Of all the world's problems, it is <u>hunger</u> that is most urgent.

4. I enjoyed visiting many foreign countries last year, <u>Greece</u> being my favorite of all of them.

5. The annoying habit of <u>knuckle-cracking</u> is something I can't stand.

B. Combine the following sentences using coordination or subordination.

1. The guru rejected his dentist's offer of novocaine. He could transcend dental medication.

2. John failed his literature test. John incorrectly identified Harper Lee as the author of the south-of-the-border classic *Tequila Mockingbird*.

3. Peggy Sue's house burned. She dialed a "9." She couldn't find "11" on the dial.

4. The police had only a few clues. They suspected Jean and David had strangled each other in a desperate struggle over control of the thermostat.

5. Bubba's favorite movie is *Sorority Babes in the Slimeball Bowl-O-Rama* (1988). A film critic called it "a pinhead chiller."

6. We're going to the new Psychoanalysis Restaurant. Their menu includes banana split personality, repressed duck, shrimp basket case, and self-expresso.

7. Kato lost the junior high spelling bee. He could not spell *DNA*.

8. Colorado hosts an annual BobFest to honor all people named Bob. Events include playing softbob, bobbing for apples, listening to bob-pipes, and eating bob-e-que.

9. The earthquake shook the city. Louise was practicing primal-scream therapy at the time.

10. In 1789 many Parisians bought a new perfume called "Guillotine." They wanted to be on the cutting edge of fashion.

C. Combine the following simple sentences into one complex sentence. See if you can guess the name of the book or movie described in the sentences. (Answers appear on page 143.)

1. A boy runs away from home.
   His companion is a runaway slave.
   He lives on a raft.
   The raft is on the Mississippi River.
   He has many adventures.
   The boy learns many lessons.
   Some lessons are about human kindness.
   Some lessons are about friendship.

2. A young man returns from prison.
   He returns to his family.
   His family lives in the Dust Bowl.
   The family decides to move.
   The family expects to find jobs in California.
   The family finds intolerance.
   They also find dishonest employers.

3. A scientist is obsessed.
   He wants to re-create life.
   He creates a monster.
   The monster rebels against the scientist.
   The monster kills his creator.
   The villagers revolt.
   The villagers storm the castle.

■ ASSIGNMENT

A. Make up your own sentence-combining exercise by finding or writing one-sentence descriptions of popular or recent movies, books, or television shows. Divide the complex sentences into simple sentences and exchange papers with a classmate. Give yourselves ten minutes to combine sentences and guess the titles.

B. The following two paragraphs are poorly written because of their choppy, wordy, and monotonous sentences. Rewrite each passage so that it is clear, lively, and emphatic.

1. There is a new invention on the market. It is called a "dieter's conscience." It is a small box to be installed in one's refrigerator. When the door of the refrigerator is opened by you, a tape recorder begins to start. A really loud voice yells, "You eating again? No wonder you're getting fat." Then the very loud voice says, "Close the door; it's getting warm." Then the voice laughs a lot in an insane and crazy fashion. The idea is one that is designed to mock people into a habit of stopping eating.

2. In this modern world of today, man has come up with another new invention. This invention is called the "Talking Tombstone." It is made by the Gone-But-Not-Forgotten Company, which is located in Burbank, California. This company makes a tombstone that has a device in it that makes the tombstone appear to be talking aloud in a realistic fashion when people go close by it. The reason is that the device is really a recording machine that is turned on due to the simple fact of the heat of the bodies of the people who go by. The closer the people get, the louder the sound the tombstone makes. It is this device that individual persons who want to leave messages after death may utilize. A hypochondriac, to cite one example, might leave a recording of a message that says over and over again in a really loud voice, "See, I told you I was sick!" It may be assumed by one and all that this new invention will be a serious aspect of the whole death situation in the foreseeable future.

■ APPLYING WHAT YOU'VE LEARNED TO *YOUR* WRITING

If you have drafted a piece of writing and are satisfied with your essay's ideas and organization, begin revising your sentences for clarity, conciseness, and emphasis. As you move through your draft, think about your readers. Ask yourself, "Are any of my sentences too vague, overpacked, or contorted for my readers to understand? Can I clarify any of my ideas by using more precise language or by revising confusing or fragmented sentence constructions?"

If you can't easily untangle a jumbled sentence, try following the sentence-combining exercise described on page 141 of this chapter—but in reverse. Instead of combining ideas, break your thought into a series of simpler sentences. Think about what you want to say, and put the person or thing of most importance in the *subject* position at the beginning of the sentences. Then select a verb and a brief phrase to complete each of the sentences. You will most likely need several of these simpler constructions to communicate the complexity of your original thought. Once you have your thought broken into smaller, simpler units, carefully begin to combine some of them as you strive for clarity and sentence variety. If you are concerned about fragment sentences, use the "It is true that" test described on pages 121–122.

Remember that it's not enough for you, the writer, to understand what your sentences mean—your readers must be able to follow your ideas, too. When in doubt, always revise your writing so that it is clear, concise, and inviting. (For more help, turn to Chapter 5, on revision.)

⭐ **CHAPTER 6 SUMMARY**

Here is a brief summary of what you should remember about writing effective sentences:

1. All good writers revise and polish their sentences.

2. You can help clarify your ideas for your readers by writing sentences that are informative, straightforward, and precise.

3. You can communicate your ideas more easily to your readers if you cut out deadwood, redundancies, confusing passives, and pretentious language.

4. You can maintain your readers' interest in your ideas if you cultivate an engaging style offering a variety of pleasing sentence constructions.

Answers to sentence-combining exercise (p. 141):
1. *Huckleberry Finn*
2. *The Grapes of Wrath*
3. *Frankenstein*

Chapter 7

Word Logic

The English language contains over a half million words—quite a selection for you as a writer to choose from. But such a wide choice can make you feel like a starving person confronting a six-page, fancy French menu. Which choice is best? How do I choose? Is the choice so important?

Word choice can make an enormous difference in the quality of your writing for at least one obvious reason: if you substitute an incorrect or vague word for the right one, you risk being misunderstood. Ages ago Confucius noted the same point: "If language is incorrect, then what is said is not meant. If what is said is not meant, then what ought to be done remains undone." It isn't enough that you know what you mean; you must transfer your thoughts onto paper in the proper words so that others clearly understand your ideas.

To help you avoid possible paralysis from indecision over word choice, this chapter offers some practical suggestions for selecting words that are not only accurate and appropriate but also memorable and persuasive.

■ Selecting the Correct Words

Accuracy: Confused Words

Unless I get a bank loan soon, I will be forced to lead an *immortal* life.

Dobermans make good pets if you train them with enough *patients*.

He dreamed of eating *desert* after *desert*.

She had dieted for so long that she had become *emancipated.*

The young man was completely in *ah* of the actress's beauty.

Socrates died from an overdose of *wedlock.*

The preceding sentences share a common problem: each one contains an error in word choice. In each sentence, the italicized word is incorrect, causing the sentence to be nonsensical or silly. (Consider a sign recently posted in a local night spot: "No miners allowed." Did the owner think the lights on their hats would bother the other customers? Did the student with "duel majors" imagine that his two areas of study were squaring off with pistols at twenty paces?) To avoid such confusion in word choice, check your words for *accuracy.* Select words whose precise meaning, usage, and spelling you know; consult your dictionary for any words whose definitions (or spellings) are fuzzy to you. As Mark Twain noted, the difference between the right word and the wrong one is the difference between lightning and the lightning bug.

Here is a list of words that are often confused in writing. Use your dictionary to determine the meanings or usage of any word unfamiliar to you.

its/it's	lead/led	choose/chose
to/too/two	cite/sight/site	accept/except
there/their/they're	affect/effect	council/counsel
your/you're	good/well	reign/rein
complement/compliment	who's/whose	lose/loose
stationary/stationery	lay/lie	precede/proceed
capitol/capital	than/then	illusion/allusion
principal/principle	insure/ensure	farther/further

Special note: Some "confused" words don't even exist! Here are four commonly used non-existent words and their correct counterparts:

No Such Word or Spelling	Use Instead
irregardless	regardless
alright	all right
alot	a lot
its'	its or it's

Accuracy: Idiomatic Phrases

Occasionally, you may have an essay returned to you with words marked "awkward diction" or "idiom." In English, as in all languages, we have word groupings that seem governed by no particular logic except the ever-popular "that's-the-way-we-say-it" rule. Many of these idiomatic expressions involve prepositions that novice writers sometimes confuse or misuse. Some common idiomatic errors and their corrected forms are listed here.

regardless ~~to~~ of	different ~~than to~~ from	relate ~~with~~ to
insight ~~of~~ into	must ~~of~~ have known	capable ~~to~~ of
similar ~~with~~ to	superior ~~than~~ to	aptitude ~~toward~~ for
comply ~~to~~ with	~~to~~ in my opinion	prior ~~than~~ to
off ~~of~~	meet ~~to~~ her standards	should ~~of~~ have

To avoid idiomatic errors, consult your dictionary and read your essay aloud; often your ears will catch mistakes in usage that your eyes have overlooked.*

Levels of Language

In addition to choosing the correct word, you should select words whose status is suited to your purpose. For convenience here, language has been classified into three categories, or levels, of usage: (1) colloquial, (2) informal, and (3) formal.

Colloquial language is the kind of speech you use most often in conversation with your friends, classmates, and family. It may not always be grammatically correct ("it's me"); it may include fragments, contractions, some slang, words identified as nonstandard by the dictionary (such as "yuck" or "lousy"), and shortened or abbreviated words ("grad school," "photos," "TV"). Colloquial speech is everyday language, and although you may use it in some writing (personal letters, journals, memos, and so forth), you should think carefully about using colloquial language in most college essays or in professional letters, reports, or papers because such a choice implies a casual relationship between writer and reader.

Informal language is called for in most college and professional assignments. The tone is more formal than in colloquial writing or speech; no slang or nonstandard words are permissible. Informal writing consistently uses correct grammar; fragments are used for special effect or not at all. Authorities disagree on the use of contractions in informal writing: some say avoid them entirely; others say they're permissible; still others advocate using them only to avoid stilted phrases ("let's go," for example, is preferable to "let us go"). Most, if not all, of your essays in English classes will be written in informal language.

Formal language is found in important documents and in serious, often ceremonial, speeches. Characteristics include an elevated—but not pretentious—tone, no contractions, and correct grammar. Formal writing often uses inverted word order and balanced sentence

---

*You may not immediately recognize what's wrong with words your teacher has labeled "diction" or "idiom." If you're uncertain about an error, ask your teacher for clarification; after all, if you don't know what's wrong with your prose, you can't avoid the mistake again. To illustrate this point, here's a true story: A bright young woman was having trouble with prepositional phrases in her essays, and although her professor repeatedly marked her incorrect expressions with the marginal note "idiom," she never improved. Finally, one day near the end of the term, she approached her teacher in tears and wailed, "Professor Jones, I know I'm not a very good writer, but must you write 'idiot,' 'idiot,' 'idiot' all over my papers?" The moral of this story is simple: it's easy to misunderstand a correction or misread your teacher's writing. Because you can't improve until you know what's wrong, always ask when you're in doubt.

structure. John F. Kennedy's 1960 Inaugural Address, for example, was written in a formal style ("Ask not what your country can do for you; ask what you can do for your country"). Most people rarely, if ever, need to write formally; if you are called on to do so, however, be careful to avoid diction that sounds pretentious, pompous, or phony.

Tone

Tone is a general word that describes writers' attitudes toward their subject matter and audience. There are as many different kinds of tones as there are emotions. Depending on how the writer feels, an essay's "voice" may sound light-hearted, indignant, sarcastic, or solemn, to name but a few of the possible choices. In addition to presenting a specific attitude, a good writer gains credibility by maintaining a tone that is generally reasonable, sincere, and authentic.

Although it is impossible to analyze all the various kinds of tones one finds in essays, it is nevertheless beneficial to discuss some of those that repeatedly give writers trouble. Here are some tones that should be used carefully or avoided altogether:

Invective

Invective is unrestrained anger, usually expressed in the form of violent accusation or denunciation. Let's suppose, for example, you hear a friend argue, "Anyone who votes for Joe Smith is a Fascist pig." If you are considering voting for Smith, you are probably offended by your friend's abusive tone. Raging emotion, after all, does not sway the opinions of intelligent people; they need to hear the facts presented in a calm, clear discussion. Therefore, in your own writing, aim for a reasonable tone. You want your readers to think, "Now here is someone with a good understanding of the situation, who has evaluated it with an unbiased, analytical mind." Keeping a controlled tone doesn't mean you shouldn't feel strongly about your subject—on the contrary, you certainly should—but you should realize that a hysterical or outraged tone defeats your purpose by causing you to sound irrational and therefore untrustworthy. For this reason, you should avoid using profanity in your essays; the shock value of an obscenity is probably not worth what you might lose in credibility. The most effective way to make your point is by persuading, not offending, your reader.

Sarcasm

In most of your writing you'll discover that a little sarcasm—bitter, derisive remarks—goes a long way. As with invective, too much sarcasm can damage the reasonable tone your essay should present. Instead of saying, "The last time we had a judge like him, people were burned at the stake," give your readers some reasons why you believe the judge is a poor one. Sarcasm can be effective, but realize that it often backfires by causing the writer to sound like a childish name-caller rather than a judicious commentator.

Irony

Irony is a figure of speech whereby the writer or speaker says the opposite of what is meant; for the irony to be successful, however, the audience must understand the writer's true intent. For example, if you have slopped to school in a rainstorm and your drenched teacher enters the classroom saying, "Ah, nothing like this beautiful, sunny weather," you know that your teacher is being ironic. Perhaps one of the most famous cases of irony occurred in 1938, when Sigmund Freud, the famous Viennese psychiatrist, was arrested by the Nazis. After being harassed by the Gestapo, he was released on the condition that he sign a statement swearing he had been treated well by the secret police. Freud signed it, but he added a few words after his signature: "I can heartily recommend the Gestapo to anyone." Looking back, we easily recognize Freud's jab at his captors; the Gestapo, however, apparently overlooked the irony and let him go.

Although irony is often an effective device, it can also cause great confusion, especially when it is written rather than spoken. Unless your readers thoroughly understand your position in the first place, they may become confused by what appears to be a sudden contradiction. Irony that is too subtle, too private, or simply out of context merely complicates the issue. Therefore, you must make certain that your reader has no trouble realizing when your tongue is firmly embedded in your cheek. And unless you are assigned to write an ironic essay (in the same vein, for instance, as Jonathan Swift's "A Modest Proposal"), don't overuse irony, whose effectiveness may be reduced with overkill.

Flippancy or Cuteness

If you sound too flip, hip, or bored in your essay ("People with IQs lower than their sunscreen number will object . . ."), your readers will not take you seriously and, consequently, will disregard whatever you have to say. Writers suffering from cuteness will also antagonize their readers. For example, let's assume you're assigned the topic "Which Person Did the Most to Arouse the Laboring Class in Twentieth-Century England?" and you begin your essay with a discussion of the man who invented the alarm clock. Although that joke might be funny in an appropriate situation, it's not likely to impress your reader, who's looking for serious commentary. How much cuteness is too much is often a matter of taste, but if you have any doubts about the quality of your humor, leave it out. Also, omit personal messages or comic asides to your reader (such as "Ha, ha, just kidding!" or "I knew you'd love this part"). Humor is often effective, but remember that the purpose of any essay is to persuade an audience to accept your thesis, not merely to entertain with freestanding jokes. In other words, if you use humor, make sure it is appropriate for your subject matter and that it works to help you make your point.

Sentimentality

Sentimentality is the excessive show of cheap emotions—"cheap" because they are not deeply felt but evoked by clichés and stock, tear-jerking situations. In the nineteenth century, for example, a typical melodrama played on the sentimentality of the audience by presenting a black-hatted, cold-hearted, mustache-twirling villain tying a golden-haired, pure-hearted "Little Nell" to the railroad tracks after driving her ancient, sickly mother out into a snowdrift. Today, politicians (among others) often appeal to our sentimentality by conjuring up images they feel will move us emotionally rather than rationally to take their side: "My friends," says Senator Stereotype, "this fine nation of ours was founded by men like myself, dedicated to the principles of family, flag, and freedom. Vote for me, and let's get back to those precious basics that make life in America so grand." Such gush is hardly convincing; good writers and speakers use evidence and logical reason to persuade their audience. In personal essays, guard against becoming too carried away by emotion, as did this student: "My dog, Cuddles, is the sweetest, cutest, most precious little puppy dog in the whole wide world, and she will always be my best friend." In addition to sending the reader into sugar shock, this description fails to present any specific reasons why anyone should appreciate Cuddles. In other words, be sincere in your writing, but don't lose so much control of your emotions that you become mushy or maudlin.

Preachiness

Even if you are so convinced of the rightness of your position that a burning bush couldn't change your mind, try not to sound smug about it. No one likes to be lectured by someone perched atop the mountain of morality. Instead of preaching, adopt a tone that says, "I believe my position is correct, and I am glad to have this opportunity to explain why." Then give your reasons and meet objections in a positive but not holier-than-thou manner.

Pomposity

The "voice" of your essay should sound as natural as possible; don't strain to sound scholarly, scientific, or sophisticated. If you write "My summer sojourn through the Western states of this grand country was immensely pleasurable" instead of "My vacation last summer in the Rockies was fun," you sound merely phony, not dignified and learned. Select only words you know and can use easily. Never write anything you wouldn't say in an intelligent classroom conversation. (For more information on correcting pretentious writing, see pages 130–131 and pages 156–159.)

> ✓ To achieve the appropriate tone, be as sincere, forthright, and reasonable as you can. Let the tone of your essay establish a basis of mutual respect between you and your reader.

Connotation and Denotation

A word's *denotation* refers to its literal meaning, the meaning defined by the dictionary; a word's *connotation* refers to the emotional associations surrounding its meaning. For example, "home" and "residence" both may be defined as the place where one lives, but "home" carries connotations of warmth, security, and family that "residence" lacks. Similarly, "old" and "antique" have similar denotative meanings, but "antique" has the more positive connotation because it suggests something that also has value. Reporters and journalists do the same job, but the latter name somehow seems to indicate someone more sophisticated and professional. Because many words with similar denotative meanings do carry different connotations, good writers must be careful with their word choice. *Select only words whose connotations fit your purpose.* If, for example, you want to describe your grandmother in a positive way as someone who stands up for herself, you might refer to her as "assertive" or "feisty"; if you want to present her negatively, you might call her "aggressive" or "pushy."

In addition to selecting words with the appropriate connotations for your purpose, be careful to avoid offending your audience with particular connotations. For instance, if you were trying to persuade a group of politically conservative doctors to accept your stand on a national health-care program, you would not want to refer to your opposition as "right-wingers" or "reactionaries," extremist terms that have negative connotations. Remember, you want to inform and persuade your audience, not antagonize them.

You should also be alert to the use of words with emotionally charged connotations, especially in advertising and propaganda of various kinds. Car manufacturers, for example, have often used names of swift, bold, or graceful animals (Jaguar, Cougar, Impala) to sway prospective buyers; cosmetics manufacturers have taken advantage of the trend toward lighter makeup by associating such words as "nature," "natural," and "healthy glow" with their products. Diet-conscious Americans are now deluged with "light" and "organic" food products. Politicians, too, are heavy users of connotation; they often drop in emotionally positive, but virtually meaningless, words and phrases such as "defender of the American Way," "friend of the common man," and "visionary" to describe themselves, while tagging their opponents with such negative, emotionally charged labels as "radical," "elitist," and "anti-family." Intelligent readers, like intelligent voters and consumers, want more than emotion-laden words; they want facts and logical argument. Therefore, as a good writer, you should use connotation as only one of many persuasive devices to enhance your presentation of evidence; never depend solely on an emotional appeal to convince your audience that your position—or thesis—is correct.

▪ PRACTICING WHAT YOU'VE LEARNED

A. Some of the following underlined words are used incorrectly; some are correct. Substitute the accurate word wherever necessary.

1. Vacations of <u>to</u> weeks with <u>to</u> friends are always <u>to</u> short, and although <u>you're</u> <u>to</u> tired <u>to</u> return to work, <u>your</u> <u>to</u> broke not <u>to</u>.

2. The professor, <u>whose</u> famous for his <u>photogenic</u> memory, graciously <u>excepted</u> a large <u>amount</u> of <u>complements</u>.

3. <u>Its</u> <u>to</u> bad you don't like <u>they're</u> brand of <u>genetic</u> paper towels since <u>their</u> giving six <u>roles</u> of it <u>to</u> you for <u>you're</u> camping trip.

4. The finances of the chicken ranch are in <u>fowl</u> shape because the hens are <u>lying</u> down on the job.

5. Sara June said she deserved an "A" in math, <u>irregardless</u> of her 59 average in the <u>coarse</u>, but her arguments were in <u>vein</u>.

6. Does the pamphlet "Ridding Your Home of Pesky <u>Aunts</u>" belong in the domestic-relations area of the public library?

7. Did the high school <u>principal</u> <u>loose</u> <u>you're</u> heavy <u>medal</u> CD and <u>it's</u> case <u>too</u>?

8. The new city <u>counsel</u> parade ordinance will <u>effect</u> everyone in the <u>capitol</u> city <u>except</u> members of the Lawn Chair Marching Band.

B. The following sentences contain words and phrases that interfere with the sincere, reasonable tone good writers try to create. Rewrite each sentence, replacing sentimentality, cuteness, and pretentiousness with more appropriate language.

1. The last dying rays of day were quickly ebbing in the West as if to signal the feline to begin its lonely vigil.

2. Because of seasonal unproductivity, it has been deemed an unfortunate fiscal necessity to terminate your valuable association with our store in order to meet our projected growth estimates.

3. I was desirous of acquiring knowledge about members of our lower income brackets.

4. If the bill to legalize marijuana is passed, we can safely assume that the whole country will soon be going to pot (heh, heh!).

5. I just love to look at those little critters with their itty-bitty mousey eyes.

C. In each of the following groups of words, identify the words with the most pleasing and the least positive (or even negative) connotations.

1. dull/drab/quiet/boring/colorless/serene

2. slender/slim/skinny/thin/slight/anorexic

3. famous/notorious/well known/infamous

4. wealthy/opulent/rich/affluent/privileged

5. teacher/instructor/educator/professor/lecturer

D. Replace the underlined words in the following sentences with words that arouse more positive feelings:

1. The stench from Jean's kitchen meant that dinner was ready and was about to be served.

2. My neighbor was a fat spinster lady known for finding cheap deals on the Internet.

3. The coach had rigid rules for all her players.

4. His obsession with his yard pleased the city's beautification committee.

5. The slick car salesman made a pitch to the old geezer who walked in the door.

6. Textbook writers admit to having a few bizarre habits.

7. Carol was a mediocre student.

8. His odd clothes made Mary think he was a bum.

9. The High Priest explained his tribe's superstitions.

10. Many of the board members were amazed to see how Algernon dominated the meeting.

■ Selecting the Best Words

In addition to selecting the correct word and appropriate tone, good writers choose words that firmly implant their ideas in the minds of their readers. The best prose not only makes cogent points but also states these points memorably. To help you select the best words to express your ideas, the following is a list of do's and don't's covering the most common diction (word choice) problems in students' writing today.

Do make your words as precise as possible. Always choose vigorous, active verbs and colorful, specific nouns and modifiers. "The big tree was hit by lightning," for example, is not as informative or interesting as "Lightning splintered the neighbors' thirty-foot oak." *Don't* use words whose meanings are unclear:

Vague Verbs

Unclear	She *got involved* in a lawsuit. [How?]
Clear	She is suing her dentist for filling the wrong tooth.
Unclear	Tom can *relate* to Jennifer. [What's the relationship?]
Clear	Tom understands Jennifer's financial problem.
Unclear	He won't *deal* with his ex-wife. [In what way?]
Clear	He refuses to speak to his ex-wife.
Unclear	Clyde *participated* in an off-Broadway play. [How?]
Clear	Clyde held the cue cards for the actors in an off-Broadway play.

Vague Nouns

Unclear	The burglar took several valuable *things* from our house.* [What items?]
Clear	The burglar took a *television,* a *DVD player,* and a *microwave oven* from our house.
Unclear	When I have my car serviced, there is always *trouble.* [What kind?]
Clear	When I have my car serviced, *the mechanics always find additional repairs and never have the car ready when it is promised.*
Unclear	When I have *problems,* I always call my friends for advice. [What problems?]
Clear	*If my girlfriend breaks up with me, my roof needs repairing, or my dog needs surgery,* I always call my friends for advice.
Unclear	I like to have *fun* while I'm on vacation. [What sort of activities?]
Clear	I like to *eat in fancy restaurants, fly stunt kites,* and *walk along the beach* when I'm on vacation.

---

* Advice that bears repeating: banish the word "thing" from your writing. In nine out of ten cases it is a lazy substitute for some other word. Unless you mean a nameless inanimate object, replace "thing" with the specific word it represents.

Vague Modifiers

Unclear	His *terrible* explanation left me *very* confused. [Why "terrible"? How confused?]
Clear	His *disorganized* explanation left me *too confused to begin the project.*
Unclear	The boxer hit the punching bag *really* hard. [How hard?]
Clear	The boxer hit the punching bag *so hard it split open.*
Unclear	*Casablanca* is a *good* movie *with something for everyone.* [Why "good" and for everyone?]
Clear	*Casablanca* is a *witty, sentimental* movie that *successfully combines an adventure story and a romance.*

To help you recognize the difference between general and specific language, consider the following series of words:

General→ →**Specific**

food→snack food→chips→potato chips→Red Hot Jalapeño Potato Chips

car→red car→red sports car→classic red Corvette→1966 red Corvette convertible

building→house→old house→big old fancy house→19th-century Victorian mansion

The preceding examples illustrate varying degrees of generality, with the words becoming more specific as they move to the right. Sometimes in your writing you will, of course, need to use general words to communicate your thought. However, most writers need practice finding specific language to substitute for bland, vague, or overly general diction that doesn't clearly present the precise picture the writer has in mind. For instance, look at the difference between these two sentences:

- My date arrived at the restaurant in an older car and then surprised us by ordering snack food.

- My date arrived at the restaurant in a rusted-out, bumperless '52 Cadillac DeVille and then surprised us by ordering only a small bowl of organic cheese puffs.

Which description better conveys the start of an unusual evening? Which sentence would make you want to hear more?

Not all occasions call for specific details, to be sure. Don't add details that merely clutter if they aren't important to the idea or mood you are creating. If all your readers need to know is "I ate dinner alone and went to bed early," you don't need to write "Alone, I ate a dinner of lasagna, green salad, and ice cream before putting on my Gap cowgirl pajamas and going to sleep under my yellow comforter at 9 o'clock."

Most of the time, however, writers can improve their drafts by giving their language a close look, considering places where a vigorous verb or a "showing" adjective or a specific noun might make an enormous difference to the reader. As you revise and polish your own essays, ask yourself if you can clarify and enliven your writing by replacing dull, lifeless words with engaging, vivid, specific ones. Challenge yourself to find the best words possible—it's a writing habit that produces effective, reader-pleasing results. (For more help in converting vague sentences to clear, inviting prose, see pages 119–120 in Chapter 6.)

Do make your word choices as fresh and original as possible. Instead of saying, "My hometown is very quiet," you might say, "My hometown's definition of an orgy is a light burning after midnight." In other words, if you can make your readers admire and remember your prose, you have a better chance of persuading them to accept your ideas.

Conversely, to avoid ho-hum prose, *don't* fill your sentences with clichés and platitudes—overworked phrases that cause your writing to sound lifeless and trite. Although we use clichés in everyday conversation, good writers avoid them in writing because (1) they are often vague or imprecise (just how pretty is "pretty as a picture?") and (2) they are used so frequently that they rob your prose style of personality and uniqueness ("It was raining cats and dogs"—does that phrase help your reader "see" the particular rainstorm you're trying to describe?).

Novice writers often include trite expressions because they do not recognize them as clichés; therefore, here is a partial list (there are literally thousands more) of phrases to avoid. Instead of using a cliché, try substituting an original phrase to describe what you see or feel. Never try to disguise a cliché by putting it in quotation marks—a baboon in dark glasses and a wig is still a baboon.

crack of dawn	needle in a haystack	gentle as a lamb
a crying shame	bed of roses	blind as a bat
white as a sheet	cold as ice	strong as an ox
depths of despair	hard as nails	sober as a judge
dead of night	white as snow	didn't sleep a wink
shadow of a doubt	almighty dollar	face the music
hear a pin drop	busy as a bee	out like a light
blessed event	to make a long story short	the last straw
first and foremost	pale as a ghost	solid as a rock

It would be impossible, of course, to memorize all the clichés and trite expressions in our language, but do check your prose for recognizable, overworked phrases so that your words will not be predictable and, consequently, dull. If you aren't sure whether a phrase is a cliché, but you've heard it used frequently, your prose will probably be stronger if you substitute an original phrase for the suspected one.

Some overused words and phrases might better be called "Insta-Prose" rather than clichés. Similar to those instant "just add water and stir" food mixes on grocery shelves, Insta-Prose occurs when writers grab for the closest words within thought-reach rather than taking time to create an original phrase or image. It's easy, for example, to recognize such overused phrases as "last but not least," "easier said than done," and "when all was said and done." But Insta-Prose may pop up in essays almost without a writer's awareness. For instance, using your very first thoughts, fill in the blanks in the following sentence:

> After years of service, my old car finally _____, _____, and _____ by the side of the road.

If your immediate responses were the three words printed at the bottom of page 168, don't be surprised! Most people who have taken this simple test responded that way too, either entirely or in part. So what's the problem, you might ask. The writer describing the car wanted her readers to see *her* particular old car, not some bland image identically reproduced in her readers' minds. To show readers her car—as opposed to thousands of

other old cars—she needs to substitute specific, "showing" language for the Insta-Prose.*
(Retest yourself: what might she have said about this car that would allow you, the reader,
to see what happened that day?)

As a writer, you also want your readers to "see" your specific idea and be engaged by
your prose rather than skipping over canned-bland images. When you are drafting for
ideas early in the writing process, Insta-Prose pours out—and that's to be expected
because you are still discovering your thoughts. But, later, when you revise your drafts, be
sensitive to predictable language in all its forms. Stamp out Insta-Prose! Cook up some
fresh language to delight your reader.

Don't use trendy expressions or slang in your essays. Slang generally consists of commonly used words made up by special groups to communicate among themselves. Slang
has many origins, from sports to space travel; for example, surfers gave us the expression
"to wipe out" (to fail), soldiers lent "snafu" (from the first letters of "situation normal—
all fouled up"), and astronauts provided "A-OK" (all systems working).

Although slang often gives our speech color and vigor, it is unacceptable in most writing
assignments for several reasons. First, slang is often part of a private language understood
only by members of a particular professional, social, or age group. Second, slang often
presents a vague picture or one that changes meanings from person to person or from context to context. More than likely, each person has a unique definition for a particular slang
expression, and although these definitions may overlap, they are not precisely the same.
Consequently, your reader could interpret your words in one way whereas you mean them
in another, a dilemma that might result in total miscommunication.

Too often, beginning writers rely on vague, popular phrases ("The party was way awesome") instead of thinking of specific words to explain specific ideas. Slang expressions
frequently contain nontraditional grammar and diction that is inappropriate for college
work. Moreover, slang becomes dated quickly, and almost nothing sounds worse than
yesterday's "in" expressions. (Can you seriously imagine calling a friend "Daddy-O" or
telling someone you're "feelin' groovy"?)

Try to write so that your prose will be as fresh and pleasing ten years from now as it is today.
Don't allow slang to give your writing a tone that detracts from a serious discussion. Putting
slang in quotation marks isn't the solution—omit the slang and use precise words instead.

Do select simple, direct words your readers can easily understand. Don't use pompous or
pseudo-sophisticated language in place of plain speech. Wherever possible, avoid *jargon*—
that is, words and phrases that are unnecessarily technical, pretentious, or abstract.

Technical jargon—terms specific to one area of study or specialization—should be
omitted or clearly defined in essays directed to a general audience because such language is often inaccessible to anyone outside the writer's particular field. By now, most of
us are familiar with bureaucratese, journalese, and psychobabble, in addition to gobbledygook from business, politics, advertising, and education. If, for example, you worry

---

* Some prose is so familiar that it is now a joke. The phrase "It was a dark and stormy night," the beginning of an 1830 novel by Edward George Bulwer-Lytton, has been parodied in the *Peanuts* comic strip
(plagiarized without shame by Snoopy). It also prompted a bad-writing contest sponsored since 1982 by
the English Department at San José State University, in which entrants are challenged to "compose the
opening sentence to the worst of all possible novels."

that "a self-actualized person such as yourself cannot transcend either your hostile environment or your passive-aggressive behavior to make a commitment to a viable lifestyle and meaningful interpersonal relationships," you are indulging in psychological or sociological jargon; if you "review existing mechanisms of consumer input, thruput, and output via the consumer communications channel module," you are speaking business jargon. Although most professions do have their own terms, you should limit your use of specialized language to writing aimed solely at your professional colleagues; always try to avoid technical jargon in prose directed at a general audience.

Today the term "jargon" also refers to prose containing an abundance of abstract, pretentious, multisyllabic words. The use of this kind of jargon often betrays a writer's attempt to sound sophisticated and intellectual; actually, it only confuses meaning and delays communication. Here, for instance, is a sample of incomprehensible jargon from a college president who obviously prefers twenty-five-cent words to simple, straightforward, nickel ones: "We will divert the force of this fiscal stress into leverage energy and pry important budgetary considerations and control out of our fiscal and administrative procedures." Or look at the thirty-eight-word definition of "exit" written by an Occupational Safety and Health Administration bureaucrat: "That portion of a means of egress which is separated from all spaces of the building or structure by construction or equipment as required in this subpart to provide a protected way of travel to the exit discharge." Such language is not only pretentious and confusing but almost comic in its wordiness.

Legal jargon, complicating even the smallest transaction, has become so incomprehensible that some lawmakers and consumers have begun to fight back. Today in Texas, for example, any firm lending $500 or less must use a model plain-English contract or submit its contract for approval to the Office of Consumer Credit. The new, user-friendly contract replaces "Upon any such default, and at any time thereafter, Secured party may declare the entire balance of the indebtedness secured hereby, plus any other sums owed hereunder, immediately due and payable without demand or notice, less any refund due, and Secured Party shall have all the remedies of the Uniform Commercial Code" with a clear, easy-to-understand statement: "If I break any of my promises in this document, you can demand that I immediately pay all that I owe." Hooray for the gobbledygook squashers in the Lone Star State!

To avoid such verbal litter in your own writing, follow these rules:

1. Always select the plainest, most direct words you know.

Jargon	The editor wanted to halt the proliferation of the product because she discovered an error on the page that terminates the volume.
Revised	The editor wanted to stop publishing the book because she found an error on the last page.

2. Replace nominalizations (nouns that are made from verbs and adjectives, usually by adding endings such as *-tion, -ism, -ness,* or *-al*) with simpler verbs and nouns.

Jargon	The departmental head has come to the recognition that the utilization of verbose verbalization renders informational content inaccessible.
Revised	The head of the department recognizes that wordiness confuses meaning.

3. Avoid adding *-ize* or *-wise* to verbs and adverbs.

Jargon	*Weatherwise*, it looked like a good day to *finalize* her report on wind tunnels.
Revised	The day's clear weather would help her finish her report on wind tunnels.

4. Drop out meaningless tack-on words such as "factor," "aspect," and "situation."

Jargon	The convenience *factor* of the neighborhood grocery store is one *aspect* of its success.
Revised	The convenience of the neighborhood grocery store contributes to its success.

Remember that good writing is clear and direct, never wordy, cloudy, or ostentatious. (For more hints on developing a clear style, see pages 118–125.)

Do call things by their proper names. Don't sugarcoat your terms by substituting *euphemisms*—words that sound nice or pretty applied to subjects some people find distasteful. For example, you've probably heard someone say, "she passed away" instead of "she died" or "he was under the influence of alcohol" instead of "he was drunk." Flight attendants refer to a "water landing" rather than an ocean crash. "Senior Citizens" (or, worse, the "chronologically advantaged") may receive special discounts. Often, euphemisms are used to soften names of jobs: "sanitary engineer" for garbage collector, "field representative" for salesperson, "information processor" for typist, "vehicle appearance specialist" for car washer, and so forth.

Some euphemisms are dated and now seem plain silly: in Victorian times, for example, the word "leg" was considered unmentionable in polite company, so people spoke of "piano limbs" and asked for the "first joint" of a chicken. The phrases "white meat" and "dark meat" were euphemisms some people used to avoid asking for a piece of chicken breast or thigh.

Today, euphemisms still abound. Though our generation is perhaps more direct about sex and death, many current euphemisms gloss over unpleasant or unpopular business, military, and political practices. Some stockbrokers, for example, once referred to an October market crash as "a fourth-quarter equity retreat," and General Motors didn't really shut down one of its plants—the closing was merely a "volume-related production schedule adjustment." Similarly, Chrysler didn't lay off workers; it simply "initiated a career alternative enhancement program." Nuclear power plants no longer have dumps; they have "containment facilities" with radiation "migration" rather than leaks and "inventory discrepancies" rather than thefts of plutonium. Simple products are now complex technology: clocks are "analog temporal displacement monitors," toothbrushes are "home plaque removal instruments," sinks are part of the "hygienic hand-washing media," and pencils are "portable hand-held communications inscribers." Vinyl is now "vegetarian leather."

Euphemisms abound in governments and official agencies when those in charge try to hide or disguise the truth from the public. On the national level, a former budget director gave us "revenue enhancements" instead of new taxes, and a former Secretary of Health, Education, and Welfare once tried to camouflage cuts in social services by calling them "advance downward adjustments." Wiretaps once became "technical collection sources" used by "special investigators units" instead of burglars, and plain lying became on one important occasion merely "plausible deniability." Other lies or exaggerations have been "strategic misrepresentations" and convenient "reality augmentations." Interestingly enough, even Washington staff members in charge of prettying up the truth for the public have earned their own euphemistic title: "spin doctors."

In a large Southwestern city, people might have been surprised to learn that there were no potholes in the streets—only "pavement deficiencies." Garbage no longer stinks; instead, it "exceeds the odor threshold." In some jails, a difficult prisoner who once might have been sent to solitary confinement is now placed in the "meditation room" or the "adjustment center." In some hospitals, sick people do not die—they experience "negative patient care outcome"; if they died because of a doctor's mistake, they underwent a "diagnostic misadventure of a high magnitude." Incidentally, those patients who survive no longer receive greeting cards; instead, they open "social expression products." During their recovery, patients might watch the "choreographed reality" of TV wrestling, while their dogs enjoy "play activities" at a local "pet lodge."

Perhaps the military is the all-time winner of the "substitute-a-euphemism" contest. Over the years, the military has used a variety of words, such as "neutralization," "pacification," and "liberation," to mean the invasion and destruction of other countries and governments. During the first Gulf War with Iraq, for example, bombs that fell on civilians were referred to as "incontinent ordnance," with the dead becoming "collateral damage." Earlier, to avoid publicizing a retreat, the military simply called for "backloading our augmentation personnel." On the less serious side, the Navy changes ocean waves into "climatic disturbances at the air-sea interface," and the Army, not to be outdone, transforms the lowly shovel into a "combat emplacement evacuator."*

Although many euphemisms seem funny and harmless, too many of them are not, because people—often those with power to shape public opinion—have intentionally designed them to obscure the reality of a particular situation or choice of action. Because euphemisms can be used unscrupulously to manipulate people, you should always avoid them in your own prose and be suspicious of them in the writing of others. As Aldous Huxley, author of *Brave New World*, noted, "An education for freedom is, among other things, an education in the proper uses of language."

In addition to weakening the credibility of one's ideas, euphemisms can make prose unnecessarily abstract, wordy, pretentious, or even silly. For a clear and natural prose style, use terms that are straightforward and simple. In other words, call a spade a spade, not "an implement for use in horticultural environments."

Avoid sexist language. Most people will agree that language helps shape thought. Consequently, writers should avoid using language that promotes any kind of exclusion or demeaning gender stereotypes. In particular, sexist language, by consistently identifying certain groups, jobs, or actions as male, subtly suggests that only men, rather than both men and women, appear in those roles. To make your writing as inclusive and unbiased as possible, here are some simple suggestions for writing non-sexist prose:

---

* For more examples of euphemisms and doublespeak, see the "To the Student" essay in the front of this text.

1. Try using plural nouns to eliminate the need for the singular pronouns "he" and "she":

Original	Today's *doctor* knows *he* must carry extra malpractice insurance.
Revision	Today's *doctors* know *they* must carry extra malpractice insurance.

2. Try substituting gender-neutral occupational titles for those ending in "man" or "woman":

Original	The *fireman* and the *saleslady* watched the *policeman* arrest the former *chairman* of the Physics Department.
Revision	The *firefighter* and the *sales clerk* watched the *police officer* arrest the former *chair* of the Physics Department.

3. Don't contribute to stereotyping by assigning particular roles solely to men or women:

Original	*Mothers* concerned about the possibility of Reyes syndrome should avoid giving aspirin to their sick children.
Revision	*Parents* concerned about the possibility of Reyes syndrome should avoid giving aspirin to their sick children.

4. Try substituting such words as "people," "persons," "one," "voters," "workers," "students," and so on, for "man" or "woman":

Original	Any *man* who wants to become a corporation executive before thirty should buy this book.
Revision	*Anyone* who wants to become a corporation executive before thirty should buy this book.

5. Don't use inappropriate diminutives:

Original	In the annual office picture, the photographer asked the men to stand behind the *girls*.
Revision	In the annual office picture, the photographer asked the men to stand behind the *women*.

6. Consider avoiding words that use "man" to describe the characteristics of a group or that refer to people in general.

Original	Rebuilding the space shuttle will call for extra money and *manpower*, but such an endeavor will benefit *mankind* in the generations to come.
Revision	Rebuilding the space shuttle will call for extra money and *employees*, but such an endeavor will benefit future *generations*.

   Similarly, substitute more specific words for "man" used as a verb or as an adjective.

Original	We needed someone to *man* the booth at the fair where we were selling *man-made* opals.
Revision	We needed someone to *staff* the booth at the fair where we were selling *synthetic* opals.

7. Be consistent in your treatment of men's and women's names, marital status, professional titles, and physical appearances:

Original	Neither Herman Melville, the inspired novelist, nor *Miss* Emily Dickinson, the *spinster poetess* of Amherst, gained fame or fortune in their lifetimes.
Revision	Neither Herman Melville, the novelist, nor Emily Dickinson, the *poet*, gained fame or fortune in their lifetimes.

8. If a situation demands multiple hypothetical examples, consider including or alternating references to both genders, when appropriate.

Original	In a revision workshop, one writer may request help with *his* concluding paragraph. Another writer may want reaction to *his* essay's introduction.
Revision	In a revision workshop, one writer may request help with *his* concluding paragraph. Another writer may want reaction to *her* essay's introduction.

Revising your writing to eliminate certain kinds of gender-specific references does not mean turning clear phrases into awkward or confusing jumbles of "he/she told him/her that the car was his/hers." By following the previous suggestions, you should be able to make your prose both clear and inoffensive to all members of your audience.*

Do enliven your writing with figurative language, when appropriate. Figurative language produces pictures or images in a reader's mind, often by comparing something unfamiliar to something familiar. The two most common figurative devices are the simile and the metaphor. A *simile* is a comparison between two people, places, feelings, or things, using the word "like" or "as"; a more forceful comparison, omitting the word "like" or "as," is a *metaphor*. Here are two examples:

Simile	George eats his meals like a hog.
Metaphor	George is a hog at mealtime.

In both sentences, George, whose eating habits are unfamiliar to the reader, is likened to a hog, whose sloppy manners are generally well known. By comparing George to a hog, the writer gives the reader a clear picture of George at the table. Figurative language not only can help you present your ideas in clear, concrete, economical ways but also can make your prose more memorable—especially if the image or picture you present is a fresh, arresting one. Here are some examples of striking images designed to catch the reader's attention and to clarify the writer's point:

- An hour away from him felt like a month in the country.
- The atmosphere of the meeting room was as tense as a World Series game tied in the ninth inning.

---

* Some writers now use "s/he" to promote gender inclusivity in their informal prose. Be aware, however, that this usage is nontraditional and not accepted universally. Always check with your instructors, or the publication for which you are writing, for the appropriate and preferred style.

- The woman's earrings were as big as butter plates.
- The angry accusation flew like a spear: once thrown, it could not be retrieved and it cut deeply.
- Out of the night came the convoy of brown trucks, modern-day buffalo thundering single-file across the prairie, eyes on fire.
- Behind her broad polished desk, Matilda was a queen bee with a swarm of office drones buzzing at her door.
- The factory squatted on the bank of the river like a huge black toad.

Sometimes, in appropriate writing situations, exaggerated similes and metaphors may be used humorously to underscore a particular point: "I felt so stupid that day. I'm sure my colleagues thought my brain was so small that if they placed it on the head of a pin, it would roll around like a marble on a six-lane highway."

Figurative language can spice up your prose, but like any spice, it can be misused, thus spoiling your soup. Therefore, don't overuse figurative language; not every point needs a metaphor or simile for clarity or emphasis. Too many images are confusing. Moreover, don't use stale images. (Clichés—discussed on pages 155–156—are often tired metaphors or similes: snake in the grass, hot as fire, quiet as a mouse, etc.) If you can't catch your readers' attention with a fresh picture, don't bore them with a stale one.

Finally, don't mix images—this too often results in a confusing or unintentionally comic scene. For example, a former mayor of Denver once responded to a question about city fiscal requirements this way: "I think the proper approach is to go through this Garden of Gethsemane that we're in now, give birth to a budget that will come out of it, and then start putting our ducks in order with an appeal and the backup we would need to get something done at the state level." Or consider the defense attorney who didn't particularly like his client's plea-bargaining deal but nevertheless announced, "Given the attitude of the normal jury on this type of crime, I feel we would be paddling up a stream behind the eight ball." Perhaps a newspaper columnist wins the prize for confusion with this triple-decker: "The Assemblymen also were miffed at their Senate counterparts because they have refused to bite the bullet that now seems to have grown to the size of a millstone to the Assemblymen whose necks are on the line."

Business is a series of battles.
We make the chariots.   ✈ UNITED
A STAR ALLIANCE MEMBER   It's time to fly.

Advertising often uses figurative language to sell products. What is the metaphor in this ad?

Think of figurative language as you might regard a fine cologne on the person sitting next to you in a crowded theater: just enough is engaging; too much is overpowering.

(For more discussion of similes, metaphors, and other figurative language, see pages 316–317 in Chapter 11.)

Do vary your word choice so that your prose does not sound wordy, repetitious, or monotonous. Consider the following sentence:

> According to child psychologists, depriving a child of sensory stimulation in the earliest stages of childhood can cause the child brain damage.

Reworded, the following sentence eliminates the tiresome, unnecessary repetition of the word "child":

> According to child psychologists, depriving infants of sensory stimulation can cause brain damage.

By omitting or changing repeated words, you can add variety and crispness to your prose. Of course, don't ever change your words or sentence structure to achieve variety at the expense of clarity or precision; at all times, your goal is to make your prose clear to your readers.

Do remember that wordiness is a major problem for all writers, even the professionals. State your thoughts directly and specifically in as few words as necessary to communicate your meaning clearly. In addition to the advice given here on avoiding wordy or vague jargon, euphemisms, and clichés, you might also review the sections on simplicity and conciseness in Chapter 6.

✓ **THE MOST IMPORTANT KEY TO EFFECTIVE WORD CHOICE IS REVISION.**
As you write your first draft, don't fret about selecting the best words to communicate your ideas; in later drafts, one of your main tasks will be replacing the inaccurate or imprecise words with better ones. (Dorothy Parker, famous for her witty essays, once lamented, "I can't write five words but that I change seven.") All good writers rewrite, so revise your prose to make each word count.

▪ PRACTICING WHAT YOU'VE LEARNED

A. Underline the vague nouns, verbs, and modifiers in the sentences that follow. Then rewrite each sentence so that it says something clear and specific.

   1. The experiment had very bad results.

   2. The speaker came up with some odd items.

3. The house was big, old, and ugly.

4. The man was a nice guy with a good personality.

5. I felt that the whole ordeal was quite an experience.

6. The machine we got was missing a few things.

7. The woman was really something special.

8. The classroom material wasn't interesting.

9. The child made a lot of very loud noises.

10. The cost of the unusual meal was amazing.

B. Rewrite the following sentences, eliminating all clichés, slang, mixed metaphors, euphemisms, and sexist language you find.

1. When the stewardess didn't return from the little girl's room, we agreed that she was slow as molasses.

2. Anyone who wants to be elected the next congressman from our state must clearly recognize that our tourist industry is sitting on a launching pad, ready to flex its muscles and become a dynamo.

3. It goes without saying that all of us silver foxes over the ripe old age of 65 should exercise our most sacred democratic privilege every November.

4. I thought the whole deal was sweet, but then my sister goes "whatever"; I think she got a special delivery from the duh truck.

5. After all is said and done, agricultural producers may be forced to relocate to urban environments, settling in substandard housing with other members of the disadvantaged class until the day they expire.

6. Both Ron Howard and Shirley Temple were popular child actors; as adults, Howard moved on to directing movies, but Shirley left show business to serve Old Glory by becoming ambassadoress to Ghana and Czechoslovakia, believe it or not.

7. Each commander realizes that he might one day be called upon to use the peacekeepers to depopulate an emerging nation in a lethal intervention.

8. Although Jack once regarded her as sweet and innocent, he knew then and there that Jill was really a wolf in sheep's clothing with a heart of stone.

9. The city councilman was stewing in his juices when he learned that his goals-impaired son had been arrested for fooling around with the funds for the fiscal underachievers' home.

10. The automobile company sent a complimentary letter warning that driving their preowned 2002 cars with the factory-installed set of bearings could adversely affect vehicle control.

C. Rewrite the following sentences, replacing jargon and cloudy, repetitive language with clear, precise words and phrases.

1. To maintain a state of high-level wellness, one should use a wooden interdental stimulator at least once a day and avoid spending time at fake-bake salons.

2. According to the military, one should not attempt a predawn vertical insertion without an aerodynamic personnel decelerator because it could lead to sudden deceleration trauma upon landing.

3. American Airlines' passengers can now arrive and depart planes on customer conveyance mobile lounges.

4. If you are in the armed services, you should avoid receiving a ballistically induced aperture in the subcutaneous environment that might lead to your being terminated with extreme prejudice.

5. The U.S. Embassy in Budapest once warned its employees: "It must be assumed that available casual indigenous female companions work for or cooperate with the Hungarian government security establishment."

6. At a 2003 press conference on the war in Iraq, Defense Secretary Donald Rumsfeld announced the following: "Reports that say something hasn't happened are always interesting to me, because as we know, there are known knowns, there are things we know we know. We also know there are known unknowns; that is to say we know there are some things we do not know. But there are also unknown unknowns— the ones we don't know we don't know."*

7. The employee was outplaced for failing to optimize productivity and for a series of misstatements regarding his higher education performance evaluation documents as inscribed on his résumé.

8. "We expect the states to show us whether or not we're achieving simple objectives—like literacy, literacy in math, [and] the ability to read and write." —George W. Bush, 2005

9. All of us could relate to Mabel's essay on the significant educational factors involved in the revenue enhancement tax-base erosion control program.

10. "We were not micromanaging Grenada intelligencewise until about that time frame," said Admiral Wesley L. McDonald, when asked what was happening on the island just prior to the United States' 1983 rescue mission.

---

*Incidentally, this comment won Rumsfeld the "Foot in Mouth" prize for the most confusing public statement of the year, awarded by Britain's Plain English Campaign, a group dedicated to ridding the language of jargon and legalese.

■ **ASSIGNMENT**

A. The following recipe, which first appeared in *The Washington Post*, pokes fun at bureaucratic jargon. See if you can translate the bureaucratese into clear, simple instructions. Then look at your writing to make certain that you are not guilty of using similar gobbledygook in your own prose.

Input to Output, 35 Minutes

For government employees and bureaucrats who have problems with standard recipes, here's one that should make the grade—a classic version of the chocolate-chip cookie translated for easy reading.

Total Lead Time: 35 minutes.

Inputs:
1 cup packed brown sugar
½ cup granulated sugar
½ cup softened butter
½ cup shortening
2 eggs
1½ teaspoons vanilla
2½ cups all-purpose flour
1 teaspoon baking soda
½ teaspoon salt
12-ounce package semi-sweet chocolate pieces
1 cup chopped walnuts or pecans

Guidance:
After procurement actions, decontainerize inputs. Perform measurement tasks on a case-by-case basis. In a mixing type bowl, impact heavily on brown sugar, granulated sugar, softened butter and shortening. Coordinate the interface of eggs and vanilla, avoiding an overrun scenario to the best of your skills and abilities.

At this point in time, leverage flour, baking soda and salt into a bowl and aggregate. Equalize with prior mixture and develop intense and continuous liaison among inputs until well-coordinated. Associate key chocolate and nut subsystems and execute stirring operations.

Within this time frame, take action to prepare the heating environment for throughput by manually setting the oven baking unit by hand to a temperature of 375 degrees Fahrenheit (190 Celsius). Drop mixture in an ongoing fashion from a teaspoon implement onto an ungreased cookie sheet at intervals sufficient enough apart to permit total and permanent separation of throughputs to the maximum extent practicable under operating conditions.

Position cookie sheet in a bake situation and survey for 8 to 10 minutes or until cooking action terminates. Initiate coordination of outputs within the cooling rack function. Containerize, wrap in red tape and disseminate to authorized staff personnel on a timely and expeditious basis.

Output:
Six dozen official government chocolate-chip cookie units.

B. Fill in the blanks with colorful words. Make the paragraph as interesting, exciting, or humorous as you can. Avoid clichés and Insta-Prose (those predictable phrases that first come to mind). Make your responses original and creative.

As midnight approached, Janet and Brad _____ toward the _____ mansion to escape the _____ storm. Their _____ car had _____ on the road nearby. The night was _____, and Brad _____ at the shadows with _____ and _____. As they _____ up the _____ steps to the _____ door, the _____ wind was filled with _____ and _____ sounds. Janet _____ on the door, and moments later, it opened to reveal the _____ scientist, with a face like a _____. Brad and Janet _____ at each other and then _____ (complete this sentence and then end the paragraph and the story).

C. To continue practicing effective word choice, turn to one of the many paintings or photographs in this text. Write several sentences that vividly describe the image you see. For instance, how might you describe the scene of New Orleans during Hurricane Katrina's destruction (page 478)? Or the woman's face in *Migrant Mother* (page 330)? What sensory details might be appropriate in a description of *Moonrise, Hernandez, New Mexico, 1941* (page 478)? (For a list of all artworks in this text, see the page following the table of contents.)

■ **APPLYING WHAT YOU'VE LEARNED TO *YOUR* WRITING**

If you have drafted a piece of writing and you are satisfied with the development and organization of your ideas, you may want to begin revising your word choice. First, read your draft for accuracy, looking up in your dictionary any words you suspect may have been used incorrectly. Then focus your attention on your draft's tone, on the "voice" your words are creating. Have you selected the right words for your purpose, subject, and audience?

If you need a word with a slightly different connotation, use your thesaurus to suggest choices (for example, is the person you're discussing best described as smart, intellectual, studious, or wise?). Next, go on a Bland Verb Hunt. Try to replace at least five colorless verbs (such as "are," "get," or "make") with active, vivid ones. Revise vague nouns ("thing") and dull adjectives ("very," "really"); if you're stuck, think of words with strong sensory appeal (sight, smell, taste, sound, touch) to enliven your prose. Last, mine-sweep for any clichés, slang, or jargon. Make each word count: each choice should clarify, not muddy, your meaning.

★ CHAPTER 7 SUMMARY

Here is a brief restatement of what you should remember about word choice:

1. Consult a dictionary if you are in doubt about the meaning or usage of a particular word.

2. Choose words that are appropriate for your purpose and audience.

3. Choose words that are clear, specific, and fresh rather than vague, bland, or clichéd.

4. Avoid language that is sexist or trendy or that tries to disguise meaning with jargon or euphemisms.

5. Work for prose that is concise rather than wordy, precise rather than fuzzy.

Answer for page 155:
Most people respond with "coughed, sputtered, and died."

Chapter 8

The Reading-Writing Connection

It's hardly surprising that good readers often become good writers themselves. Good readers note effectiveness in the writing of others and use these observations to help clarify their own ideas and rhetorical choices about organization, development, and style. Analogies abound in every skill: singers listen to vocalists they admire, tennis players watch championship matches, actors evaluate their colleagues' award-winning performances, medical students observe famous surgeons, all with an eye to improving their own craft. Therefore, to help you become a better writer, your instructor may ask you to study some of the professional essays included in other sections of this text. Learning to read these essays analytically will help when you face your own writing decisions. To sharpen your reading skills, follow the steps suggested in this chapter. After practicing these steps several times, you should discover that the process is becoming a natural part of your reading experience.

■ How Can Reading Well Help Me Become a Better Writer?

Close reading of the professional essays in this text should help you become a better writer in several ways. First, understanding the opinions expressed in these essays may spark interesting ideas for your own essays; second, discovering the various ways other writers have organized and explained their material should give you some new ideas about selecting your own strategies and supporting evidence. Familiarizing yourself with

© Michael Newman/PhotoEdit

the effective stylistic devices and diction of other writers may also encourage you to use language in ways you've never tried before.

Perhaps most important, analyzing the prose of others should make you more aware of the writing process itself. Each writer represented in this text faced a series of decisions regarding organization, development, and style, just as you do when you write. By asking questions (Why did the writer begin the essay this way? Why compare this event to that one? Why use a personal example in that paragraph?), you will begin to see how the writer put the essay together—and that knowledge will help you plan and shape your own essay. Questioning the rhetorical choices of other writers should also help you revise your prose because it promotes the habit of asking yourself questions that consider the reader's point of view (Does the point in paragraph 3 need more evidence to convince my reader? Will the reader be confused if I don't add a smoother transition from paragraph 4 to 5? Does the conclusion fall flat?).

In other words, the skills you practice as an analytical reader are those you'll use as a good writer.

■ How Can I Become an Analytical Reader?

Becoming an analytical reader may, at first, demand more time—and involvement— than you have previously devoted to a reading assignment. Analytical reading requires more than allowing your eyes to pass over the words on the page; it's not like channel-surfing through late-night TV shows, stopping here or there as interest strikes. Analytical reading asks you not only to understand the writer's ideas, but also to consider *how* those ideas were presented, *why* the writer presented them that way, and whether that presentation was *effective*. Consequently, to improve your understanding of the reading-writing connection, you should plan on two readings of the assigned essay, some note-taking, and some marking of the text (called *annotating*). This procedure may seem challenging at first, but the benefits to you as both reader and writer will be well worth the extra minutes.

Steps to Reading Well

1. Before you begin the essay itself, note the *publication information* and *biographical data* on the author in the paragraph that precedes each selection in this text. Where and when was the essay originally published? Was it directed toward a particular or a general audience? Was it written in response to some event or controversy? Is the essay still timely or is it dated? Does the author seem qualified to write about this subject? Does the introduction offer any other information that might help you assess the essay's effectiveness?

2. Next, note the *title* of the essay. Does it draw you into the essay? Does it suggest a particular tone or image?

3. You're now ready to begin your first reading of the essay. Some readers like to read through the essay without stopping; others feel comfortable at this point underlining a few main ideas or making checks in the margins. You may also have to make a dictionary stop if words you don't know appear in key places in the essay. Many times you can figure out definitions from context—that is, from the words and ideas surrounding the unknown word—but don't miss the point of a major part of an essay because of failure to recognize an important word, especially if that word is repeated or emphasized in some way.

When you finish this reading, write a sentence or two summarizing your general impression of the essay's content or ideas. Consider the author's *purpose:* what do you think the writer was trying to do? Overall, how well did he or she succeed? (A typical response might be "argued for tuition hike—unconvincing, boring—too many confusing statistics.")

Now prepare to take another, closer look at the essay. Make some notes in the margins or in another convenient place as you respond to the following questions. Remember that analytical reading is not a horse race: there are no trophies for finishing quickly! Fight the bad habit of galloping at breakneck speed through an essay; slow down to admire the verbal roses the writer has tried to place in your path.

4. Look at the *title* (again) and at the essay's *introductory paragraph(s).* Did they effectively set up your expectations? Introduce the essay's topic, main idea, tone? (Would some other title or introductory "hook" have worked better?)

5. Locate the writer's main point or *thesis*; this idea may be stated plainly or it may be clearly implied. If you didn't mark this idea on your first reading, do so now by placing a "T" in the margin so you can refer to the thesis easily. (If the thesis is implied, you may wish to mark places that you think most clearly indicate the writer's stance.)

6. As you reread the essay, look for important statements that support or illustrate the thesis. (As you know, these are often found as *topic sentences* occurring near the beginning or end of the body paragraphs.) Try numbering these supporting points or ideas and jotting a key word by each one in the margin.

7. As you identify each important supporting point, ask yourself how the writer develops, explains, or argues that idea. For example, does the writer clarify or support the point by providing examples, testimony, or statistics? By comparing or contrasting one idea to another? By showing a cause-effect relationship? Some other method? A combination of methods? A writer may use one or many methods of development, but each major point in an essay should be explained clearly and logically. Make brief marginal notes to indicate how well you think the writer has succeeded ("convincing example," "generalization without support," "questionable authority cited," "good comparison," etc.). Practice using marginal symbols, such as stars (for especially effective statements, descriptions, arguments) or question marks (for passages you think are confusing, untrue, or exaggerated). Make up your own set of symbols to help yourself remember your evaluations of the writer's ideas and techniques.

8. Look back over the essay's general *organization*. Did the writer use one of the expository, descriptive, narrative, or argumentative strategies to structure the essay? Some combination of strategies? Was this choice effective? (Always consider alternative ways: would another choice have allowed the writer to make his or her main point more emphatically? Why or why not?)

9. Does the essay flow logically and coherently? If you are having trouble with *unity* or *coherence* in your own essays, look closely at the transitional devices used in a few paragraphs; bracketing transitional words or phrases you see might show you how the writer achieved a sense of unity and flow.

10. Consider the writer's *style* and the essay's *tone*. Does the writer use figurative language in an arresting way? Specialized diction for a particular purpose? Repetition of words or phrases? Any especially effective sentence patterns? Does the writer's tone of voice come through clearly? Is the essay serious, humorous, angry, consoling, happy, sad, sarcastic, or something else? Is the tone appropriate for the purpose and audience of this essay? Writers use a variety of stylistic devices to create prose that is vivid and memorable; you might mark new uses of language you would like to try in essays of your own.

Now is also the time to look up meanings of any words you felt you could skip during your first time through the essay, especially if you sense that these words are important to the writer's tone or use of imagery.

Once you have completed these steps and added any other comments that seem important to the analysis of the essay, review your notes. Is this an effective essay? Is the essay's thesis explained or supported adequately with enough logically developed points and evidence? Is the essay organized as effectively as it could have been? What strengths and weaknesses did you find after this analytical reading? Has your original evaluation of this essay changed in any way? If so, write a new assessment, adding any other notes you want to help you remember your evaluation of this essay.

Finally, after this close reading of the essay, did you discover any new ideas, strategies, or techniques you might incorporate into *your* current piece of writing?

■ Sample Annotated Essay

Here is a professional essay annotated according to the steps listed on the previous pages.

By closely reading and annotating the professional essays in this text, you can improve your own writing in numerous ways. Once you have practiced analyzing essays by other writers, you may discover that you can assess your own drafts' strengths and weaknesses with more confidence.

■ Our Youth Should Serve

Steven Muller

title forecasts thesis

Steven Muller is President Emeritus of the Johns Hopkins University, founded in *educator*
1876 in Baltimore, Maryland. This essay first appeared in *Newsweek* in 1978 and *general audience*
has been reprinted often.

1   Too many young men and women now leave school without a
well-developed sense of purpose. If they go right to work after high
school, many are not properly prepared for careers. But if they enter
college instead, many do not really know what to study or what to do
afterward. Our society does not seem to be doing much to encourage   *Introductory*
and use the best instincts and talents of our young.   *paragraphs*

2   On the other hand, I see the growing problems of each year's new   *present the*
generation of high-school graduates. After twelve years of schooling—   *problem*
and television—many of them want to participate actively in society;
but they face either a job with a limited future or more years in educational institutions. Many are wonderfully idealistic: they have talent
and energy to offer, and they seek the meaning in their lives that
comes from giving of oneself to the common good. But they feel
almost rejected by a society that has too few jobs to offer them and   *Problem for youth:*
that asks nothing of them except to avoid trouble. They want to be   *idealism, talent,*
part of a new solution; instead society perceives them as a problem.   *and energy but*
They seek a cause; but their elders preach only self-advancement.   *too few jobs*
They need experience on which to base choice; yet society seems to   *and too little*
put a premium on the earliest possible choice, based inescapably on   *experience*
the least experience.

3   On the other hand, I see an American society sadly in need of   *Problem for society:*
social services that we can afford less and less at prevailing costs of   *social services are*
labor. Some tasks are necessary but constitute no career; they should   *needed but labor*
be carried out, but not as anyone's lifetime occupation. Our democracy   *costs are high*
profoundly needs public spirit, but the economy of our labor system
primarily encourages self-interest. The Federal government spends
billions on opportunity grants for post-secondary education, but
some of us wonder about money given on the basis only of need. We
ask the young to volunteer for national defense, but not for the   *✱ Thesis: Youth*
improvement of our society. As public spirit and public services   *should volunteer to*
decline, so does the quality of life. So I ask myself why cannot we put   *serve America's*
it all together and ask our young people to volunteer in peacetime to   *public service needs*
serve America.

4   I recognize that at first mention, universal national youth service   *¶ clarifies proposal by*
may sound too much like compulsory military service or the Hitler   *contrast : not like*
Youth or the Komsomol. I do not believe it has to be like that at all.   *military, not political,*
It need not require uniforms or camps, nor a vast new Federal   *not required*
bureaucracy, nor vast new public expenditures. And it should certainly   *(Komsomol: youth*
not be compulsory.   *section of the Soviet*
    Communist Party)

5   A voluntary program of universal national youth service does of course require compelling <u>incentives</u>. Two could be provided. Guaranteed <u>job training</u> would be one. Substantial <u>Federal assistance</u> toward <u>post-secondary education</u> would be the other. This would mean that today's complex measures of Federal aid to students would be ended, and that there would also be no need for tuition tax credits for post-secondary education. Instead, prospective students would <u>*earn* their assistance</u> for post-secondary education by volunteering for national service, and only those who earned assistance would receive it. Present Federal expenditures for the assistance of students in post-secondary education would be converted into a <u>simple grant program</u>, modeled on the post–World War II GI Bill of Rights.

6   But what, you say, would <u>huge numbers of high-school graduates do as volunteers in national service?</u> They could be interns in public agencies, local, state, and national. They could staff day-care programs, neighborhood health centers, centers to counsel and work with children; help to maintain public facilities, including highways, railbeds, waterways and airports; engage in neighborhood-renewal projects, both physical and social. Some would elect military service, others the Peace Corps. Except for the latter two alternatives and others like them, they could <u>live anywhere</u> they pleased. They would not wear uniforms. They would be employed and supervised by people already employed locally in public-agency careers.

7   Volunteers would be <u>paid only a subsistence wage</u>, because they would receive the benefits of job training (not necessarily confined to one task) as well as assistance toward post-secondary education if they were so motivated and qualified. If cheap mass <u>housing</u> for some groups of volunteers were needed, supervised participants in the program could rebuild decayed dwellings in metropolitan areas. . . .

8   The (direct benefits) of such a universal national-youth-service program would be significant. Every young man and woman would face a <u>meaningful role in society</u> after high school. Everyone would receive <u>job training</u>, and the right to <u>earn assistance</u> toward post-secondary education. Those going on to <u>post-secondary education</u> would have their education interrupted by a constructive <u>work experience</u>. There is (evidence) that they would thereby <u>become more highly motivated and successful students,</u> particularly if their work experience related closely to subsequent vocational interests. Many participants might <u>locate careers</u> by means of their national-service assignments.

9   <u>No union jobs need be lost,</u> because skilled workers would be needed to give job training. Many <u>public services</u> would be performed by <u>cheap labor</u>, but there would be no youth army. And the intangible <u>indirect benefits</u> would be the greatest of all. Young people could regard themselves as more <u>useful and needed</u>. They could serve this country for a <u>two-year period</u> as volunteers, and earn job

Margin annotations:

1. Incentives
—job training
— Federal money for college

Comparison: education grants like those given to returning WWII soldiers

2. Kinds of jobs

Examples

3. Support costs
—wages
—housing
problem?

* 4. Direct benefits for youth:
—meaningful role in society
—job training
—money for education
—work experience
—success in school
—career direction

such as?

Addresses possible criticism

training and/or assistance toward post-secondary education. There is more self-esteem and motivation in earned than in unearned benefits. Universal national youth service may be no panacea. But in my opinion the idea merits serious and imaginative consideration.

Conclusion summarizes advantages, emphasizes the benefit of earning self-esteem, and calls for consideration of this proposal

First impression: Muller proposes a volunteer youth corps to provide some public services. Many benefits for both country and young people.

Notes: Muller uses comparisons, contrasts, and examples to explain the proposed youth corps, and he clearly shows the benefits (training, grants, self-esteem). His arguments might be even more effective if he had added some specific examples and testimony from students and people in social services. Or maybe from participants in similar kinds of programs, such as VISTA?

(panacea: cure for all ills)

Personal response: Although the low wages might be a problem for many people, I like this program. It might have helped me decide on a career path sooner and definitely would help with tuition now.

Select one of the professional essays reprinted in this text, and annotate it according to the steps described in this chapter. Note at least one strength in the essay that you would like to incorporate into your own writing.

Select one of the professional essays in this text to read analytically and annotate. Then write a one-page explanation of the essay's major strengths (or weaknesses), showing how the writer's rhetorical choices affected you, the reader.

■ Writing a Summary

Frequently, writing teachers will ask students to read an essay and briefly summarize it. A *summary* is an objective, condensed version of a reading selection, containing the author's main ideas. Although summaries are always more concise than the original texts, the length of a particular summary often depends on the length and complexity of the original reading and the purpose of the summary.

Learning to summarize reading material is a valuable skill, useful in many classes and in professional work. In one of your college classes, for example, your instructor might ask you to summarize an article pertinent to an upcoming lecture or class discussion, thus ensuring that you have thoroughly understood the information; at other times, you may need to summarize material for your own research. On a job, you might want to share a summary of an important report with colleagues, or you might be asked to present a summary of project results to your boss.

Because summarizing is such a useful skill, here are a few guidelines:

1. Read the selection carefully, as many times as it takes for you to understand and identify the author's thesis and main ideas. You might underline or take notes on the key ideas as you read, using the suggestions in the previous pages of this chapter to help you.

2. When you begin to draft your summary, always include the author's name and the title of the original text in your first sentence. Many times it's important to include the source of the work and its publication date, too.

3. Using your own words, present the author's thesis and other main ideas in a few concise sentences. Do not merely copy sentences directly from the original text. Use your own words to convey the main ideas as clearly and concisely as possible.

4. Omit all references to the supporting examples and details in the selection, unless you have been instructed to include these.

5. If, for clarity or emphasis, you do need to include an exact word or phrase from the original text, be certain to enclose the words in quotation marks.

6. Do not give your own opinion or interpretation of the material you are summarizing. Your goal is an objective, accurate, condensed overview of the selection that does not reveal your attitude toward the ideas presented.

To illustrate the preceding guidelines, here is a brief summary of the essay that appears on pages 173–175 of this chapter.

In the *Newsweek* essay "Our Youth Should Serve," Steven Muller proposes a voluntary youth corps that would address America's need for social services and benefit our nation's youth. Muller, a former university president, believes the talents of too many bright, idealistic, but inexperienced high school graduates are wasted because the students must choose too soon between a low-paying job or more education with an undefined goal. Muller argues that a voluntary, non-partisan civilian youth corps would provide cheap labor for short-term public service projects while offering young people job training, work experience, assistance toward post-secondary education, and a sense of self-esteem.

Note that the writer of the summary did not offer her opinion of Muller's proposal, but, instead, objectively presented the essay's main ideas.

For additional discussion clarifying the difference between *summary* and *paraphrase*, see pages 385–386 in Chapter 14. For suggestions on writing the assignment known as the "summary-and-response essay," see pages 430–432 in Chapter 15; this section also contains a sample student paper written in response to Steven Muller's essay "Our Youth Should Serve."

■ **PRACTICING WHAT YOU'VE LEARNED**

Read one of the professional essays in this textbook, and annotate it according to the steps outlined earlier in this chapter. After you are sure you clearly understand the author's thesis and main ideas, write a one-paragraph summary of the essay. Use your own words to convey the essay's main ideas, but remember to remain objective in your summary. ■

■ Benefiting from Class Discussions

If you have been practicing the steps for close reading of essays, you are on your way to becoming a better writer. By analyzing the rhetorical choices of other writers, you are gathering new ideas and techniques as well as improving your ability to look thoughtfully at your own drafts. To continue this progress, your composition instructor may devote class time to discussing sample professional or student essays that appear in this text.

Active participation in these discussions will contribute to your growth as a writer as you share ideas about effective prose with your classmates. To benefit from such discussions, consider these suggestions for improving your classroom skills:

Try to arrive a few minutes before class begins so that you can look over the reading and your marginal notes (and any other homework assigned to accompany the essay, such as questions or a summary).* Remind yourself that it is time to become an "active listener," so if sitting by friends or near a window is a distraction, move to another seat. Sitting up front is encouraged not only because you can hear your instructor better, but also because he or she can see and hear you more clearly if you have questions. (Be sure you have turned off your cell phone, pager, or any other electronic device, and remember that gum-popping, pencil tapping, and knuckle-cracking may lead to bad-karma thoughts from nearby students who are also trying to listen without distraction.)

During the class period, your teacher may ask for responses to questions that follow selected essays in this text or he or she may pose new questions. If you've prepared by closely reading and annotating the assigned essay as outlined on pages 173–175, you should be able to join these discussions. Listen carefully to your classmates' opinions; offer your own insights and be willing to voice agreement or polite disagreement. If participating in class makes you so nervous you fear you will break out in spots, prepare one or two comments out of class in such clear detail that speaking about them will be easier for you, and then volunteer when those topics arise in the discussion. Don't hesitate to ask questions or request additional explanations; remember that if you don't

---

* If you're having a difficult time remembering details about the essays you've been assigned to read, try the split-page journal technique, described on page 27.

understand something, it's a good bet others in the class are puzzled too.

As discussion of a sample essay unfolds, practice thinking critically on two levels. First, think of the essay as a draft in which the writer made certain choices to communicate meaning, just as you do in your essays. Trading ideas with your classmates may help you see why the writer chose as he or she did—and whether those decisions work effectively. As you gain a clear understanding of the strengths and weaknesses in the sample essay, move to the second level by considering the choices you are making in your own writing. For example, if you struggle with conclusions to your essays, listen attentively to the discussion of the writer's choice and then consider whether this kind of ending might work in your essay. If a writer has failed to provide enough examples or details to

© Erich Lessing / Art Resource, NY

If we are what we eat, are we also what we read? Reading can transform writers . . .

illustrate a particular point, think about a paragraph in your current rough draft. Do you now see a similar problem in need of revision? In other words, as you and your classmates analyze essays in class, *actively make the essential connection between the readings and your own work.*

To remember important points in any class discussion, sharpen your note-taking skills. If you use a notebook for this course, you may find it helpful to leave a wide margin on the left side of your paper, giving yourself space to write key words, questions, or ideas for your own writing. Start each day's notes on a new page with the day's date to help you locate material later. Acquire the habit of stapling or taping handouts to blank pages that immediately follow notes from a particular class period (handouts stuck in your textbook or in your backpack are easily lost). As you take notes, pay special attention to any words your teacher considers significant enough to write on the board and to those concepts that merit treatment in handouts or other visual aids (transparencies, slides, PowerPoint, etc.). Be sensitive to the verbal cues your instructor uses to emphasize essential material (words such as "key terms," "main reasons," and "central idea," as well as repetition and even a louder tone of voice).

Because class discussion often moves quickly, you'll need to develop a shorthand method of note-taking. Some students write out an important term the first time (development) and then abbreviate it thereafter (dev). You can devise your own system of symbols but included here are some abbreviations common to note-taking you may find handy. Most of these abbreviations are for notes only, although some (such as e.g., i.e., cf., and ca.) may be used in college and professional writing; consult your instructor or the appropriate style manual if you are in doubt.

b/c = because	→ = causes, leads to, produces
b/4 = before	cf. = compare
w/ = with	↑ = increases, higher than
w/o = without	↓ = decreases, lower than
w/i = within	esp. = especially
e.g. = for example	re = regarding
i.e. = that is	ca. = approximately (use with dates or figures)
& = and	∴ = therefore
@ = at	≠ = not equal to, not the same, differs from
# = number	N.B. = "nota bene," Latin for "note well"

Later, after class, you may want to underline, star, or highlight important material. Fill in any gaps and rewrite any illegible words now before you forget what you meant. Use the wide left-hand margin to make some notes about applying the ideas and techniques discussed in class to your own writing. Reread these notes before you begin drafting or revising your essay.

Here's the last, and possibly most important, piece of advice for every student of writing: *attend every class session*! There is a logical progression in all composition courses; each day's lesson emphasizes and builds on the previous one. By conscientiously attending every class discussion and actively participating in your own learning process, you *will* improve your writing skills.

★ CHAPTER 8 SUMMARY

1. Reading and analyzing essays can improve your writing skills.

2. Learning to recognize and evaluate the strategies and stylistic techniques of other writers will help you plan and shape your own essays.

3. Reading analytically takes time and practice but is well worth the extra effort.

4. Learning to summarize reading material accurately and objectively is an important skill, useful in school and at work.

5. Active participation in class discussions of sample essays can help you strengthen your own writing.

★ PART ONE SUMMARY: THE BASICS OF THE SHORT ESSAY

Here are ten suggestions to keep in mind while you are working on the rough drafts of your essay:

1. Be confident that you have something important and interesting to say.

2. Identify your particular audience and become determined to communicate effectively with them.

3. Use prewriting techniques to help you focus on one main idea that will become the thesis of your essay.

4. Organize your essay's points logically, in a persuasive and coherent order.

5. Develop each of your ideas with enough evidence and specific details.

6. Delete any irrelevant material that disrupts the smooth flow from idea to idea.

7. Compose sentences that are clear, concise, and informative; choose accurate, vivid words.

8. Improve your writing by learning to read analytically.

9. Revise your prose.

10. Revise your prose!

Part 2

Purposes, Modes, and Strategies

Communication may be divided into four types (or "modes" as they are often called): exposition, argumentation, description, and narration. Although each one will be explained in greater detail in this section of the text, the four modes may be defined briefly as follows:

Exposition
The writer intends to explain or inform.

Argumentation
The writer intends to convince or persuade.

Description
The writer intends to create in words a picture of a person, place, object, or feeling.

Narration
The writer intends to tell a story or recount an event.

Although we commonly refer to exposition, argumentation, description, and narration as the basic types of prose, in reality it is difficult to find any one mode in a pure form. In fact, almost all essays are combinations of two or more modes; it would be virtually impossible, for instance, to write a story—narration—without including description or to argue without also giving some information. Nevertheless, by determining a writer's main purpose, we can usually identify an essay or prose piece as primarily exposition, argumentation, description, or narration. In other words, an article may include a brief description of a new mousetrap, but if the writer's main intention is to explain how the trap works, then we may designate the essay as exposition. In most cases, the primary mode of any essay will be readily apparent to the reader.

In Part Two of this text, you will study each of the four modes in detail and learn some of the patterns of development, called *strategies*, that will enable you to write the kind of prose most frequently demanded in college and professional work. Mastering the most common prose patterns in their simplest forms now will help you successfully assess and organize any kind of complex writing assignment you may face in the future. Chapter 13 concludes this section by discussing the more complex essay, developed through use of multiple strategies. ∎

Chapter 9

Exposition

Exposition refers to prose whose primary purpose is giving information. Some familiar examples of expository writing include encyclopedias, dictionaries, news magazines, and textbooks. In addition, much of your own college work may be classified as exposition: book reports, political analyses, laboratory and business reports, and most essay exams, to cite only a few of the possibilities.

Although expository writing does present information, a good expository essay is more than a collection of facts, figures, and details. First, each essay should contain a thesis statement clarifying the writer's purpose and position. Then the essay should be organized so that the body paragraphs explain and support that thesis. In an expository essay the writer says, in effect, here are the facts *as I see them;* therefore, the writer's main purpose is not only to inform readers but also to convince them that this essay explains the subject matter in the clearest, most logical way.

■ The Strategies of Exposition

There are a variety of ways to organize an expository essay, depending on your purpose. The most common strategies, or patterns, of organization include development by *example, process analysis, comparison and contrast, definition, classification,* and *causal analysis.* However, an essay is rarely developed completely by a single strategy (an essay developed by comparison and contrast, for instance, may also contain examples; a classification essay may contain definitions, and so forth); therefore, as in the case of the four modes, we identify the kind of expository essay by its *primary* strategy of development. To help you understand every expository strategy thoroughly before going on to the next, each is presented here separately. Each discussion section follows a similar pattern, which includes explanation of the strategy, advice on developing your essay, a list of essay topics, a topic proposal sheet, a revision checklist, sample essays (by students and by professional writers), and a progress report.

■ Strategy One: Development by Example

Perhaps you've heard a friend complain lately about a roommate. "Tina is an inconsiderate boor, impossible to live with," she cries. Your natural response might be to question your friend's rather broad accusation: "What makes her so terrible? What does she do that's so bad?" Your friend might then respond with specific examples of Tina's insensitivity: she never washes her dishes, she ties up the telephone for hours, and she borrows clothes without asking. By citing several examples, your friend clarifies and supports her general criticism of Tina, thus enabling you to understand her point of view.

Examples in an essay work precisely the same way as in the hypothetical story above: they *support, clarify, interest,* and *persuade.*

In your writing assignments, you might want to assert that dorm food is cruel and inhuman punishment, that recycling is a profitable hobby, or that the cost of housing is rising dramatically. But without some carefully chosen examples to show the truth of your statements, these remain unsupported generalities or mere opinions. Your task, then, is to provide enough specific examples to support your general statements, to make them both clear and convincing. Here is a statement offering the reader only hazy generalities:

> Our locally supported TV channel presents a variety of excellent educational shows. The shows are informative on lots of different subjects for both children and adults. The information they offer makes channel 19 well worth the public funds that support it.

Rewritten, the same paragraph explains its point clearly through the use of specific examples:

> Our locally supported TV channel presents a variety of excellent educational shows. For example, young children can learn their alphabet and numbers from *Sesame Street;* imaginative older children can be encouraged to create by watching *Kids' Writes*, a show on which four hosts read and act out stories written and sent in by youngsters from eight to fourteen. Adults may enjoy learning about antiques and collectibles from a program called *The Collector;* each week the show features an in-depth look at buying, selling, trading, and displaying collectible items, from Depression glass to teddy bears to Shaker furniture. Those folks wishing to become handy around the home can use information on repairs from plumbing to wiring on *This Old House*, while the nonmusical can learn the difference between scat singing and arias on such programs as *Jazz!* and *Opera Today*. Money-minded viewers may profit from the tips dropped by stockbrokers who appear on *Wall Street Week*. The information offered makes these and other educational shows on channel 19 well worth the public funds that support the station.

Although the preceding example is based on real shows, you may also use personal experiences, hypothetical situations, anecdotes, research material, facts, testimony, or any combination thereof, to explain, illustrate, or support the points in your essays.

In some cases you may find that a series of short examples fits your purpose, illustrating clearly the idea you are presenting to your reader:

> In the earlier years of Hollywood, actors aspiring to become movie stars often adopted new names that they believed sounded more attractive to the public. Frances Ethel Gumm, for instance, decided to change her name to Judy Garland long before she flew over any rainbows, and Alexander Archibald Leach became Cary Grant on his way from England to America. Alexandra Cymboliak and Merle Johnson, Jr., might not have set teenage hearts throbbing in the early 1960s, but Sandra Dee and Troy Donahue certainly did. Although some names were changed to achieve a smoother flow (Frederic Austerlitz to Fred Astaire, for example), some may have also been changed to ensure a good fit on movie theater marquees as well as a place in their audience's memory: the teenage Turner girl, Julia Jean Mildred Frances, for instance, became just Lana.

Or you may decide that two or three examples explained in some detail provide the best support for your topic, rather than a series of short examples. In the paragraph that follows, the writer chose to develop two examples to illustrate her point about the unusual dog her family owned when she was a young girl in the late 1970s:

> Our family dog Sparky always let us know when he wasn't getting enough attention. For instance, if he thought we were away from home too much, he'd perform his record trick. While we were out, Sparky would push an album out of the record rack and then tap the album cover in just such a way that the record would roll out. Then he would chomp the record! We'd return to find our favorite LP (somehow, always our current favorite) chewed into tiny bits of black vinyl scattered about the room. Another popular Sparky trick was the cat-sit. If the family was peacefully settled on the porch, not playing with him, Sparky would grab the family cat by the ear and drag her over to the steps, whereupon he would sit on top of her until someone paid attention to him. He never hurt the cat; he simply sat on her as one would sit on a fine cushion, with her head poking out under his tail, and a silly grin on his face that said, "See, if you'd play with me, I wouldn't get into such mischief."

You may also find that in some cases, one long, detailed example (called an *extended example*) is more useful than several shorter ones. If you were writing a paragraph urging the traffic department to install a stop sign at a particularly dangerous corner, you probably should cite numerous examples of accidents there. On the other hand, if you were praising a certain kind of local architecture, you might select one representative house and discuss it in detail. In the following paragraph, for instance, the writer might have supported his main point by citing a number of cases in which lives had been saved by seat belts; he chose instead to offer one detailed example, in the form of a personal experience:

> Wearing seat belts can protect people from injury, even in serious accidents. I know because seat belts saved me and my Dad two years ago when we were driving to see my grandparents who live in California. Because of the distance, we had to travel late on a rainy, foggy Saturday night. My Dad was driving, but what he didn't know was that there was a car a short way behind us driven by a drunk who was following our car's tail lights in order to keep himself on the road. About midnight, my Dad decided to check the map to make sure we were headed in the right direction, so he signaled, pulled over to the shoulder, and began to stop. Unfortunately for us, the drunk didn't see the signal and moved his car over to the shoulder thinking that the main road must have curved slightly since our car had gone that way. As Dad slowed our car, the other car plowed into us at a speed estimated later by the police as over eighty miles an hour. The car hit us like Babe Ruth's bat hitting a slow pitch; the force of the speeding car slammed us hard into the dashboard but not through the windshield and out onto the rocky shoulder, because, lucky for us, we were wearing our seat belts. The highway patrol, who arrived quickly on the scene, testified later at the other driver's trial that without question my Dad and I would have been seriously injured, if not killed, had it not been for our seat belts restraining us in the front seat.

The story of the accident illustrates the writer's claim that seat belts can save lives; without such an example, the writer's statement would be only an unsupported generalization.

In addition to making general statements specific and thus more convincing, good examples can explain and clarify unfamiliar, abstract, or difficult concepts for the reader. For instance, Newton's law of gravity might be more easily understood once it is explained through the simple, familiar example of an apple falling from a tree.

Moreover, clear examples can add to your prose vivid details that hold the reader's attention while you explain your points. A general statement decrying animal abuse, for instance, may be more effective accompanied by several examples detailing the brutal treatment of one particular laboratory's research animals.

The use of good examples is not, however, limited only to essays primarily developed by example. In reality, you will probably use examples in every essay you write. You couldn't, for instance, write an essay classifying kinds of popular movies without including examples to help identify your categories. Similarly, you couldn't write an essay defining the characteristics of a good teacher or comparing two kinds of cars without ample use of specific examples. To illustrate the importance of examples in all patterns of essay development, here are two excerpts from student essays reprinted in other parts of this textbook. The first excerpt comes from an essay classifying the Native American eras at Mesa Verde National Park (pages 253–256). In his discussion of a particular time period, the writer uses Balcony House pueblo as an example illustrating the Ancestral Puebloans' skills in building construction.

> The third period lasted until 1300 c.e. and saw the innovation of pueblos, or groups of dwellings, instead of single-family units. Nearly eight hundred dwellings show the large number of people who inhabited the complex, tunneled houses,

shops, storage rooms, courtyards, and community centers whose masonry walls, often elaborately decorated, were three and four stories high. At the spacious Balcony House pueblo, for example, an adobe court lies beneath another vaulted roof; on three sides stand two-story houses with balconies that lead from one room to the next. In back of the court is a spring, and along the front side is a low wall that kept the children from falling down the seven-hundred-foot cliff to the canyon floor below. Balcony House pueblo also contains two kivas, circular subterranean ceremonial chambers that show the importance of fellowship and religion to the people of this era.

Another student uses a personal example to help her support a point in her essay that contrasts a local food co-op to a big chain grocery store (pages 221–224). By using her friend's experience as an example, the writer shows the reader how a co-op can assist local producers in the community:

Direct selling offers two advantages for producers: they get a better price for their wares than by selling them through a middleman, and at the same time they establish an independent reputation for their business, which can be immensely valuable to their success later on. In Fort Collins, for example, Luna tofu (bean curd) stands out as an excellent illustration of this kind of mutual support. Several years ago my friend Carol Jones began making tofu in small batches to sell to the co-op as a way to earn a part-time income as well as to contribute to the co-op. Her enterprise has now grown so well that last year her husband quit his job to go into business with her full time. She currently sells to distributors and independent stores from here to Denver; even Lane Grocer, which earlier would not consider selling her tofu even on a trial basis, is now thinking about changing its policy.

Learning to support, explain, or clarify your assertions by clear, thoughtful examples will help you develop virtually every piece of writing you are assigned, both in school and on the job. Development by example is the most widely used of all the expository strategies and by far the most important.

Developing Your Essay

An essay developed by example is one of the easiest to organize. In most cases, your first paragraph will present your thesis; each body paragraph will contain a topic sentence and as many effectively arranged examples as necessary to explain or support each major point; your last paragraph will conclude your essay in some appropriate way. Although the general organization is fairly simple, you should revise the examples in your rough draft by asking these questions:

Are all my examples relevant? Each specific example should support, clarify, or explain the general statement it illustrates; each example should provide readers with additional insight into the subject under discussion. Keep the purpose of your paragraphs in mind: don't wander off into an analysis of the causes of theft on your campus if you are only supposed to show various examples of it. Keep your audience in mind, too: which examples will provide the kinds of information that your particular readers need to understand your point?

Are my examples well chosen? To persuade your readers to accept your opinion, you should select those examples that are the strongest and most convincing. Let's say you were writing a research paper exposing a government agency's wastefulness. To illustrate your claim, you would select those cases that most obviously show gross or ridiculous expenditures rather than asking your readers to consider some unnecessary but minor expenses. And you would try to select cases that represent recent or current examples of wastefulness rather than discussing expenditures too dated to be persuasive. In other words, when you have a number of examples to choose from, evaluate them and then select the best ones to support your point.

Are there enough examples to make each point clear and persuasive? Put yourself in your reader's place: would you be convinced with three brief examples? Five? One extended example? Two? Use your own judgment, but be careful to support or explain your major points adequately. It's better to risk overexplaining than to leave your reader confused or unconvinced.

Problems to Avoid

By far, the most common weakness in essays developed by example is a lack of specific detail. Too often, novice writers present a sufficient number of relevant, well-chosen examples, but the illustrations themselves are too general, vague, or brief to be helpful. Examples should be clear, specific, and adequately detailed so that the reader receives the full persuasive impact of each one. For instance, in an essay claiming that junior high football has become too violent, don't merely say, "Too many players were hurt last year." Such a statement only hints; it lacks enough development to be fully effective. Go into more detail by giving actual examples of jammed fingers, wrenched backs, fractured legs, crushed kneecaps, and broken dreams. Present these examples in specific, vivid language; once your readers begin to "see" that field covered with blood and bruised bodies, you'll have less trouble convincing them that your point of view is accurate. (For more help incorporating specific details into your paragraph development, review pages 58–61 in Chapter 3.)

The second biggest problem in example essays is the lack of coherence. The reader should never sense an interruption in the flow of thought from one example to the next in paragraphs containing more than one example. Each body paragraph of this kind should be more than a topic sentence and a choppy list of examples. You should first arrange the examples in an order that best explains the major point presented by your topic sentence; then carefully check to make sure each example is smoothly connected in thought to the statements preceding and following it. You can avoid a listing effect by using transitional devices where necessary to ensure easy movement from example to example and from point to point. A few common transitional words often found in essays of example include "for instance," "for example," "to illustrate," "another," and "in addition." (For a list of other transitional words and additional help on writing coherent paragraphs, review pages 68–73 and pages 77–78.)

■ Essay Topics

Use the following statements as prompts to help you discover a focused essay topic of your own design. For additional ideas, turn to the "Suggestions for Writing" section following the professional essay (page 196).

1. Failure is a better teacher than success.

2. First impressions are often the best/worst means of judging people.

3. Road rage is worse today than ever.

4. My fear of flying (or some other fear) prevents me from living a normal life.

5. The willingness to undertake adventure is a necessary part of a happy existence.

6. Everyone should see/flee this movie. (See Chapter 17 for help with this topic.)

7. Complaining can produce unforeseen results.

8. Travel can be the best medicine.

9. Consumers are often at the mercy of unscrupulous companies.

10. Visits to the doctor/dentist/veterinarian can prove more traumatic than the illness.

11. Failure to keep my mouth shut (or some other bad habit) leads me into trouble.

12. Participation in (a particular sport, club, hobby, event) teaches valuable lessons.

13. Modern technology can produce more inconvenience than convenience.

14. Job hunting today is a difficult process.

15. Moving frequently has its advantages (or disadvantages).

16. Good deeds can backfire (or make a wonderful difference).

17. Many required courses are/are not relevant to a student's education.

18. High schools do/do not adequately prepare students for college.

19. One important event can change the course of a life.

20. To encourage people to use their products or services, companies often offer advertisements containing examples of satisfied customers or clients. Analyze the ad that follows plus one of your own choosing that is also developed by examples. As you look at each ad, consider: how and why are the examples used? Are the examples well chosen for the particular target audience? Are

there too many or too few? Overall, what part does the use of example play in the success of the ad? (Hint: In your search for other ads using examples, you might turn to pages 300–302 in this text for some possible choices.)

JACQUELINE GOLSON, CERVICAL CANCER

LUIS RIVERA, BRAIN CANCER

PATTY HILL, PANCREATIC CANCER

SANDY PIERCE, MELANOMA

Cancer strikes indiscriminately. When it does, it's critical to choose the best team possible to help you in your battle. These people were once faced with just such decisions. They didn't ask for cancer. But they did ask lots of questions. And in doing so, they chose the nation's number-one rated cancer hospital as their ally. It's a decision they'll celebrate for the rest of their lives.

THE UNIVERSITY OF TEXAS
MD ANDERSON
CANCER CENTER
Making Cancer History

WHEN YOU'RE READY TO FIGHT, CALL 1-800-392-1611 OR VISIT WWW.MDANDERSON.ORG.
RATED THE NUMBER-ONE CANCER HOSPITAL IN AMERICA BY *U.S.NEWS & WORLD REPORT.*

DVR

Courtesy of M.D. Anderson Cancer Center

A Topic Proposal for Your Essay

Selecting the right subject matter is important to every writer. To help you clarify your ideas and strengthen your commitment to your topic, here is a proposal sheet that asks you to describe some of your preliminary ideas about your subject before you begin drafting.

Although your ideas may change as you draft (they will almost certainly become more refined), thinking through your choice of topic now may help you avoid several false starts.

1. In a few words, identify the subject of your essay as you have narrowed and focused it for this assignment. Write a rough statement of your opinion or attitude toward this topic.

2. Why are you interested in this topic? Do you have a personal or professional connection to the subject? State at least one reason for your choice of topic.

3. Is this a significant topic of interest to others? Why? Who specifically might find it interesting, informative, or entertaining?

4. Describe in one or two sentences the primary effect you would like to have on your audience. After they read your essay, what do you want your audience to think, feel, or do? (In other words, what is your *purpose* in writing this essay?)

5. Writers use examples to explain and clarify their ideas. Briefly list two or three examples you might develop in your essay to support discussion of your chosen topic.

6. What difficulties, if any, might this topic present during your drafting? For example, do you know enough about this topic to illustrate it with specific rather than vague examples? Might the topic still be too broad or unfocused for this assignment? Revise your topic now or make notes for an appropriate plan of action to resolve any difficulties you foresee.

■ Sample Student Essay

Study the use of specific examples in the brief student essay that follows. If the writer were to revise this essay, where might he add more examples or details?

RIVER RAFTING TEACHES WORTHWHILE LESSONS

Paragraphs in the Sample Student Essays are numbered for ease of discussion; do not number your own paragraphs.

1   Sun-warmed water slaps you in the face, the blazing sun beats down on your shoulders, and canyon walls speed by as you race down rolling waves of water. No experience can equal that of river rafting. In addition to being fun and exciting, rafting has many educational advantages as well, especially for those involved in school-sponsored rafting trips. River trips teach students how to prevent some of the environmental destruction that concerns the park officials, and, in addition, river trips teach students to work together in a way few other experiences can.

Introduction: A description

Thesis

Essay map

2   The most important lesson a rafting trip teaches students is respect for the environment. When students are exposed to the outdoors, they can better learn to appreciate its beauty and feel the need to preserve it. For example, I went on a rafting trip three summers ago with the biology department at my high school. Our trip lasted seven days down the Green River through the isolated Desolation Canyon in Utah. After the first day of rafting, I found myself surrounded by steep canyon walls and saw virtually no evidence of human life. The starkly beautiful, unspoiled atmosphere soon became a major influence on us during the trip. By the second day I saw classmates, whom I had previously seen fill an entire room with candy wrappers and empty soda cans, voluntarily inspecting our campsite for trash. And when twenty-four high school students sacrifice washing their hair for the sake of a suds-less and thus healthier river, some new, better attitudes about the environment have definitely been established.

Topic sentence one: Trip teaches respect for environment

Two brief examples illustrating respect:
1. Cleaning up trash
2. Foregoing suds in river

3   In addition to the respect for nature a rafting trip encourages, it also teaches the importance of group cooperation. Since school-associated trips put students in command of the raft, the students find that in order to stay in control, each member must be reliable, be able to do his or her own part, and be alert to the actions of others. These skills are quickly learned when students see the consequences of noncooperation. Usually this occurs the first day, when the left side of the raft paddles in one direction, and the right the other way, and half the crew ends up seasick from going in circles. An even better illustration is another experience I had on my river trip. Because an upcoming rapid was usually not too rough, our instructor said a few of us could jump out and swim in it. Instead of deciding as a group who should go, though, five eager swimmers bailed out. This left me, our angry instructor, and another student to steer the raft. As it turned

Topic sentence two: Trip teaches cooperation

Two examples of the need for cooperation:

1. Difficulties in paddling raft

2. A near accident

out, the rapid was fairly rough, and we soon found ourselves heading straight for a huge hole (a hole is formed from swirling funnel-like currents and can pull a raft under). The combined effort of the three of us was not enough to get the raft completely clear of the hole, and the raft tipped up vertically on its side, spilling us into the river. Luckily, no one was hurt, and the raft did not topple over, but the near loss of our food rations for the next five days, not to mention the raft itself, was enough to make us all more willing to work as a group in the future.

4   Despite the obvious benefits rafting offers, the number of river permits issued to school groups continues to decline because of financial cutbacks. It is a shame that those in charge of these cutbacks do not realize that in addition to having fun and making discoveries about themselves, students are learning valuable lessons through rafting trips—lessons that may help preserve the rivers for future rafters.

Conclusion: Importance of lessons

Professional Essay*

■ So What's So Bad about Being So-So?

Lisa Wilson Strick

Lisa Wilson Strick is a freelance writer who publishes in a variety of magazines, frequently on the subjects of family and education. She is co-author of *Learning Disabilities, A to Z: A Parent's Complete Guide to Learning Disabilities from Preschool to Adulthood* (1997). This essay first appeared in *Woman's Day* in 1984.

1   The other afternoon I was playing the piano when my seven-year-old walked in. He stopped and listened awhile, then said: "Gee, Mom, you don't play that thing very well, do you?"

_____

* To help you read this essay analytically, review pages 170–172.

2   No, I don't. I am a piano lesson dropout. The fine points of fingering totally escape me. I play everything at half-speed, with many errant notes. My performance would make any serious music student wince, but I don't care. I've enjoyed playing the piano badly for years.

3   I also enjoy singing badly and drawing badly. (I used to enjoy sewing badly, but I've been doing that so long that I finally got pretty good at it.) I'm not ashamed of my incompetence in these areas. I do one or two other things well and that should be enough for anybody. But it gets boring doing the same things over and over. Every now and then it's fun to try something new.

4   Unfortunately, doing things badly has gone out of style. It used to be a mark of class if a lady or a gentleman sang a little, painted a little, played the violin a little. You didn't have to be *good* at it; the point was to be fortunate enough to have the leisure time for such pursuits. But in today's competitive world we have to be "experts"—even in our hobbies. You can't tone up your body by pulling on your sneakers and slogging around the block a couple of times anymore. Why? Because you'll be laughed off the street by the "serious" runners—the ones who log twenty-plus miles a week in their headbands, sixty-dollar running suits and fancy shoes. The shoes are really a big deal. If you say you're thinking about taking up almost any sport, the first thing the aficionados will ask is what you plan to do about shoes. Leather or canvas? What type of soles? Which brand? This is not the time to mention that the gym shoes you wore in high school are still in pretty good shape. As far as sports enthusiasts are concerned, if you don't have the latest shoes you are hopelessly committed to mediocrity.

5   The runners aren't nearly so snobbish as the dance freaks, however. In case you didn't know, "going dancing" no longer means putting on a pretty dress and doing a few turns around the ballroom with your favorite man on Saturday night. "Dancing" means squeezing into tights and a leotard and leg warmers, then sweating through six hours of warm-ups and five hours of ballet and four hours of jazz classes. Every week. Never tell anyone that you "like to dance" unless this is the sort of activity you enjoy. (At least the costume isn't so costly, as dancers seem to be cultivating a riches-to-rags look lately.)

6   We used to do these things for fun or simply to relax. Now the competition you face in your hobbies is likely to be worse than anything you run into on the job. "Oh, you've taken up knitting," a friend recently said to me. "Let me show you the adorable cable-knit, popcorn-stitched cardigan with twelve tiny reindeer prancing across the yoke that I made for my daughter. I dyed the yarn myself." Now why did she have to go and do that? I was getting a kick out of watching my yellow stockinette muffler grow a couple of inches a week up till then. And all I wanted was something to keep my hands busy while I watched television anyway.

7   Have you noticed what this is doing to our children? "We don't want that dodo on our soccer team," I overheard a ten-year-old sneer the other day. "He doesn't know a goal kick from a head shot." As it happens, the boy was talking about my son, who did not—like some of his friends—start soccer instruction at age three (along with pre-school diving, creative writing and Suzuki clarinet). I'm sorry, Son, I guess I blew it. In *my* day when we played softball on the corner lot, we expected to give a little instruction to the younger kids who didn't know how. It didn't matter if they were terrible; we weren't out to slaughter the other team. Sometimes we didn't even keep score. To us,

sports were just a way of having a *good time*. Of course we didn't have some of the nifty things kids have today—such as matching uniforms and professional coaches. All we had was a bunch of kids of various ages who enjoyed each other's company.

8   I don't think kids have as much fun as they used to. Competition keeps getting in the way. The daughter of a neighbor is a nervous wreck worrying about getting into the *best* gymnastics school. "I was a late starter," she told me, "and I only get to practice five or six hours a week, so my technique may not be up to their standards." The child is nine. She doesn't want to *be* a gymnast when she grows up; she wants to be a nurse. I asked what she likes to do for fun in her free time. She seemed to think it was an odd question. "Well, I don't actually *have* a lot of free time," she said. "I mean homework and gymnastics and flute lessons kind of eat it all up. I have flute lessons three times a week now, so I have a good shot at getting into the all-state orchestra."

9   Ambition, drive and the desire to excel are all admirable within limits, but I don't know where the limits are anymore. I know a woman who has always wanted to learn a foreign language. For years she has complained that she hasn't the time to study one. I've pointed out that an evening course in French or Italian would take only a couple of hours a week, but she keeps putting it off. I suspect that what she hasn't got the time for is to become completely fluent within the year—and that any lesser level of accomplishment would embarrass her. Instead she spends her evenings watching reruns on television and tidying up her closets—occupations at which no particular expertise is expected.

10   I know others who are avoiding activities they might enjoy because they lack the time or the energy to tackle them "seriously." It strikes me as so silly. We are talking about *recreation*. I have nothing against self-improvement. But when I hear a teenager muttering "practice makes perfect" as he grimly makes his four-hundred-and-twenty-seventh try at hooking the basketball into the net left-handed, I wonder if some of us aren't improving ourselves right into the loony bin.

11   I think it's time we put a stop to all this. For sanity's sake, each of us should vow to take up something new this week—and to make sure we never master it completely. Sing along with grand opera. Make peculiar-looking objects out of clay. I can tell you from experience that fallen soufflés still taste pretty good. The point is to enjoy being a beginner again; to rediscover the joy of creative fooling around. If you find it difficult, ask any two-year-old to teach you. Two-year-olds have a gift for tackling the impossible with zest; repeated failure hardly discourages them at all.

12   As for me, I'm getting a little out of shape so I'm looking into tennis. A lot of people I know enjoy it, and it doesn't look too hard. Given a couple of lessons I should be stumbling gracelessly around the court and playing badly in no time at all.

Questions on Content, Structure, and Style

1. Why does Strick begin her essay with the comment from her son and the list of activities she does badly?

2. What is Strick's thesis? Is it specifically stated or clearly implied?

3. What examples does Strick offer to illustrate her belief that we no longer take up hobbies for fun? Are there enough well-chosen examples to make her position clear?

4. What is the effect, according to Strick, of too much competition on kids? In what ways does she show this effect?

5. Does Strick use enough details in her examples to make them clear, vivid, and persuasive? Point out some of her details to support your answer.

6. What does Strick gain by using dialogue in some of her examples?

7. What solution to the problem does Strick offer? How does she clarify her suggestion?

8. Characterize the tone of Strick's essay. Is it appropriate for her purpose and for her intended audience? Why or why not?

9. Evaluate Strick's conclusion. Does it effectively wrap up the essay?

10. Do you agree or disagree with Strick? What examples could you offer to support your position?

Suggestions for Writing

Try using Lisa Strick's essay "So What's So Bad about Being So-So?" as a stepping-stone, moving from one or more of her ideas to a subject for your own essay. For instance, you might write an essay based on your personal experience that illustrates or challenges Strick's view that competition is taking all the fun out of recreation. Or perhaps Strick's advice urging her readers to undertake new activities might lead you to an essay about your best or worst "beginner" experience. Look through Strick's essay once more to find other springboard ideas for *your* writing.

Vocabulary*

errant (2)   mediocrity (4)   fluent (9)
incompetence (3)   excel (9)   zest (11)
aficionados (4)

■ A REVISION WORKSHEET

As you write your rough drafts, consult Chapter 5 for guidance through the revision process. In addition, here are a few questions to ask yourself as you revise your example essay:

1. Is the essay's thesis clear to the reader?

2. Do the topic sentences support the thesis?

3. Does each body paragraph contain examples that effectively illustrate the claim of the topic sentence rather than offering mere generalities?

4. Are there enough well-chosen examples to make each point clear and convincing?

---

* Numbers in parentheses following vocabulary words refer to paragraphs in the essay.

5. Is each example developed in enough specific detail? Where could more details be added? More precise language?

6. If a paragraph contains multiple examples, are they arranged in the most effective order, with a smooth transition from one to another?

7. If a paragraph contains an extended example, does the discussion flow logically and with coherence?

After you've revised your essay extensively, you might exchange rough drafts with a classmate and answer these questions for each other, making specific suggestions for improvement wherever appropriate. (For advice on productive participation in classroom workshops, see pages 108–111.)

Reviewing Your Progress

After you have completed your essay developed by examples, take a moment to measure your progress as a writer by responding to the following questions. Such analysis will help you to recognize growth in your writing skills and may enable you to identify areas that are still problematic.

1. What is the best feature of your essay? Why?

2. After considering your essay's supporting examples, which one do you think most effectively explains or illustrates your ideas? Why?

3. What part of your essay gave you the most trouble? How did you overcome the problem?

4. If you had more time to work on this essay, what would receive additional attention? Why?

5. What did you learn about your topic from writing this essay? About yourself as a writer?

■ Strategy Two: Development by Process Analysis

Process analysis identifies and explains what steps must be taken to complete an operation or procedure. There are two kinds of process analysis essays: directional and informative.

A *directional process* tells the reader how to do or make something. In simple words, it gives directions. You are more familiar with directional process than you might think. For example, when you open a telephone book or cell phone user's guide, you may see pages explaining how to make a multiparty call. When you tell friends how to find your house, you're asking them to follow a directional process. If you use a computer, you can learn how to transfer files or download attachments or any one of hundreds of other options by following step-by-step directions often found on a "Help" menu. The most widely read books in American libraries fall into the how-to-do-it (or how-to-fix-it) category: how to wire a house, how to repair a car, how to play winning poker, how to become a millionaire overnight, and so forth. And almost every home contains at least one cookbook full of recipes providing directions for preparing various dishes. (Even Part One of this text is, in detailed fashion, a directional process telling how to write a short essay, beginning with the selection of a topic and concluding with advice on revision.)

An *informative process* tells the reader how something is or was made or done or how something works. Informative process differs from directional process in that it is not designed primarily to tell people how to do it; instead, it describes the steps by which someone other than the reader does or makes something (or how something was made or done in the past). For example, an informative process essay might describe how scientists discovered polio vaccine, how a bill passes through Congress, how chewing gum is made, how roller blades were invented, or how an engine propels a jet. In other words, this type of essay gives information on processes that are not intended to be—or cannot be—duplicated by the individual reader.

Developing Your Essay

Of all the expository essays, students usually agree that the process paper is the easiest to organize, mainly because it is presented in simple, chronological steps. To prepare a well-written process essay, however, you should remember the following advice:

Select an appropriate subject. First, make sure you know your subject thoroughly; one fuzzy step could wreck your entire process. Second, choose a process that is simple and short enough to describe in detail. In a 500-to-800-word essay, for instance, it's better to describe how to build a ship in a bottle than how to construct a life-size replica of Noah's Ark. On the other hand, don't choose a process so simpleminded, mundane, or mechanical that it insults your readers' intelligence or bores them silly. (Some years ago at a large state university, students were directed to write a process essay on "How to Sharpen a Pencil"; with the assignment of such stirring, creative topics, it's a wonder that particular English department produced any majors at all that year.)

Describe any necessary equipment and define special terms. In some process essays, you will need to indicate what equipment, ingredients, or tools are required. Such information is often provided in a paragraph following the thesis, before the process itself is described; in other cases the explanation of proper equipment is presented as the need arises in each step of the process. As the writer, you must decide which method is best for your subject. The same is true for any terms that need defining. Don't lose your reader by using terms only you, the specialist, can comprehend. Always remember that you're trying to tell people about a process they don't understand.

State your steps in a logical, chronological order. Obviously, if someone wanted to know how to bake bread, you wouldn't begin with "Put the prepared dough in the oven." Start at the beginning and carefully follow through, step by step, until the process is completed. Don't omit any steps or directions, no matter how seemingly insignificant. Without complete instructions, for example, the would-be baker might end up with a gob of dough rather than a loaf of bread—simply because the directions didn't say to heat the oven to a certain temperature.

Explain each step clearly, sufficiently, and accurately. If you've ever tried to assemble a child's toy or a piece of furniture, you probably already know how frustrating—and infuriating—it is to work from vague, inadequate directions. Save your readers from tears and tantrums by describing each step in your process as clearly as possible. Use enough specific details to distinguish one step from another. As the readers finish each step, they should know how the subject matter is supposed to look, feel, smell, taste, or sound at that stage of the process. You might also explain why each step is necessary ("Cutting back the young avocado stem is necessary to prevent a spindly plant"; "Senator Snort then had to win over the chair of the Arms Committee to be sure his bill would go to the Senate floor for a vote"). In some cases, especially in directional processes, it's helpful to give warnings ("When you begin tightrope walking, the condition of your shoes is critical; make sure the soles are not uneven or slick") or descriptions of errors and how to rectify them ("If you pass a white church, you've gone a block too far, so turn right at the church and circle back on Candle Lane"; "If the sauce appears thin, add one teaspoon more of cornstarch to thicken the gravy").

Organize your steps effectively. If you have a few big steps in your process, you probably will devote a paragraph to each one. On the other hand, if you have several small steps, you should organize them into a few manageable units. For example, in the essay "How to Prepare Fresh Fish," the list of small steps on the left has been grouped into three larger units, each of which becomes a body paragraph:

1. scaling	I. Cleaning
2. beheading	A. scaling
3. gutting	B. beheading
4. washing	C. gutting
5. seasoning	II. Cooking
6. breading	A. washing
7. frying	B. seasoning
8. draining	C. breading
9. portioning	D. frying
10. garnishing	III. Serving
	A. draining
	B. portioning
	C. garnishing

In addition, don't forget to use enough transitional devices between steps to avoid the effect of a mechanical list. Some frequently used linking words in process essays include the following:

next	first, second, third, etc.
then	at this point
now	following
to begin	when
finally	at last
before	afterward

Vary your transitional words sufficiently so that your steps are not linked by a monotonous repetition of "and then" or "next."

Problems to Avoid

Don't forget to include a thesis. You already know, of course, that every essay needs a thesis, but the advice bears repeating here because for some reason some writers often omit the statement in their process essays. Your thesis might be (1) your reason for presenting this process—why you feel it's important or necessary for the readers to know it ("Because rescue squads often arrive too late, every adult should know how to administer CPR to accident victims") or (2) an assertion about the nature of the process itself ("Needlepoint is a simple, restful, fun hobby for both men and women"). Here are some other subjects and sample theses:

- Donating blood is not the painful process one might suspect.
- The raid on Pearl Harbor wasn't altogether unexpected.
- Returning to school as an older-than-average student isn't as difficult as it may look.
- Sponsoring a five-mile run can be a fun way for your club or student organization to raise money for local charities.
- Challenging a speeding ticket is a time-consuming, energy-draining, but financially rewarding endeavor.
- The series of public protests that led to the return of the traditional Coca-Cola was an unparalleled success in the history of American consumerism.

Presenting a thesis and referring to it appropriately gives your essay unity and coherence, as well as ensuring against a monotonous list of steps.

Pay special attention to your conclusion. Don't allow your essay to grind to an abrupt halt after the final step. You might conclude the essay by telling the significance of the completed process or by explaining other uses it may have. Or, if it is appropriate, finish your essay with an amusing story or emphatic comment. However you conclude, leave the reader with a feeling of satisfaction, with a sense of having completed an interesting procedure. (For more information on writing good conclusions, see pages 84–87.)

■ ESSAY TOPICS

Here are suggested topics for both directional and informative process essays. Some of the topics may be used in humorous essays, such as "How to Flunk a Test," "How to Remain a Bench Warmer," or "How to Say Nothing in Eight Hundred Words." For additional ideas, turn to the "Suggestions for Writing" sections following the professional essays (page 211 and page 214).

1. How you arrived at a major decision or solved an important problem
2. How to survive some aspect of a first year at college
3. How to begin a collection or hobby or acquire a skill
4. How to buy a computer, CD player, camera, or other recreational product
5. How a popular product or fad originated or grew
6. How to manage stress, stagefright, homesickness, or an irrational fear

7. How something in nature works or was formed

8. How a company makes or sells a product

9. How a piece of equipment or a machine works

10. How to cure a cold, the hiccups, insomnia, or some other common ailment

11. How to get in shape/develop physical fitness

12. How to stop smoking (or break some other bad habit)

13. How to select a car (new or used), house, apartment, roommate

14. How to earn money quickly or easily (and legally)

15. How a famous invention or discovery occurred

16. How to lodge a complaint and win

17. How to succeed or fail in a job or class (or in some other important endeavor)

18. How to build or repair some small item

19. How to plan the perfect party, wedding, holiday, birthday, or some other celebration

20. How a historical event occurred or an important law was passed (e.g., Rosa Parks's arrest; the 1773 Boston Tea Party; the passage of Title IX, ensuring equal athletic opportunities for female students)

© Bettmann/CORBIS

Rosa Parks, whose refusal to give up her bus seat in Montgomery, Alabama, in 1955 helped to ignite the Civil Rights Movement.

A Topic Proposal for Your Essay

Selecting the right subject matter is important to every writer. To help you clarify your ideas and strengthen your commitment to your topic, here is a proposal sheet that asks you to describe some of your preliminary ideas about your subject before you begin drafting. Although your ideas may change as you write (they will almost certainly become more refined), thinking through your choice of topic now may help you avoid several false starts.

1. What process will you explain in your essay? Is it a directional or an informative process? Can you address the complexity of this process in a short essay?

2. Why did you select this topic? Are you personally or professionally interested in this process? Cite at least one reason for your choice.

3. Why do you think this topic would be of interest to others? Who might find it especially informative or enjoyable?

4. Describe in one or two sentences the ideal response from your readers. What would you like them to do or know after reading about your topic?

5. List at least three of the larger steps or stages in the process.

6. What difficulties might this topic present during your drafting? Will this topic require any additional research on your part?

■ Sample Student Essay

The following essay is a directional process telling readers how to run a successful garage sale. To make the instructions clear and enjoyable, the writer described seven steps and offered many specific examples, details, and warnings.

CATCHING GARAGE SALE FEVER

Introduction:
A series of
questions to
hook the reader

1   Ever need some easy money fast? To repay those incredible overdue library fines you ran up writing your last research paper? Or to raise money for that much-needed vacation to Mexico you put on credit cards last Spring Break? Or maybe you feel you simply have to clear out some junk before the piles block the remaining sunlight from your windows? Whether the problem is cash flow or trash flow, you can solve it easily by holding what is fast becoming an all-American sport: the weekend garage sale. As a veteran of some half-dozen successful

ventures, I can testify that garage sales are the easiest way to make quick money, with a minimum of physical labor and the maximum of fun.

Thesis

2   Most garage sale "experts" start getting ready at least two weeks before the sale by taking inventory. Look through your closets and junk drawers to see if you actually have enough items to make a sale worthwhile. If all you have is a mass of miscellaneous small items, think about waiting or joining a friend's sale, because you do need at least a couple of larger items (furniture is always a big seller) to draw customers initially. Also, consider whether the season is appropriate for your items: sun dresses and shorts, for example, sell better in the spring and summer; coats and boots in the fall. As you collect your items, don't underestimate the "saleability" of some of your junk—the hideous purple china bulldog Aunt Clara gave you for Christmas five years ago may be perfect for someone's Ugly Mutt Collection.

Step one: Taking inventory

3   As you sort through your closets, begin thinking about the time and place of your sale. First, decide if you want a one- or two-day sale. If you opt for only one day, Saturdays are generally best because most people are free that day. Plan to start early—by 8 A.M. if possible—because the experienced buyers get up and get going so they can hit more sales that way. Unless you have nothing else to do that day, plan to end your sale by mid-afternoon; most people have run out of buying energy (or money) by 3 P.M. Deciding on the location of your sale depends, of course, on your housing situation, but you still might need to make some choices. For instance, do you want to put your items out in a driveway, a front yard, or actually in the garage (weather might affect this decision)? Or perhaps a side yard gets more passers-by? Wherever you decide, be sure that there are plenty of

Step two: Deciding when and where

places for customers to park close by without blocking your neighbors' driveways.

Step three: Advertising the sale

4   Unless you live in a very small town or on a very busy street, you'll probably want to place an inexpensive ad in the "garage sale" column of your local newspaper, scheduled to run a day or two before, and the day of, your sale. Your ad should tell the times and place of the sale (give brief directions or mention landmarks if the location is hard to find) as well as a short list of some of your items. Few people will turn out for "household goods" alone; some popular items include bookcases, antiques, books, fans, jewelry, toys, baby equipment, and name-brand clothes. One other piece of advice about the ad copy: it should include the phrase "no early sales" unless you want to be awakened at 6:30 A.M., as I was one Saturday, by a bunch of semi-pro garage sale buyers milling restlessly around in your yard, looking like zombies out of a George Romero horror movie. In addition to your newspaper ad, you may also wish to put up posters in places frequented by lots of people; laundromats and grocery stores often have bulletin boards for such announcements. You can also put up signs on nearby well-traveled streets, but one warning: in some towns it's illegal to post anything on utility poles or traffic signs, so be sure to check your local ordinances first.

A warning

Another warning

Step four: Pricing the merchandise

5   Tagging your items with their prices is the least fun, and it can take a day or a week depending on how many items you have and how much time each day you can devote to the project. You can buy sheets of little white stickers or use pieces of masking tape to stick on the prices, but if you want to save time, consider grouping some items and selling them all for the same price—all shirts, for example, are 50¢. Be realistic about your prices; the handcrafted rug from Greece may have been expensive and important to you, but to others, it's a worn

doormat. Some experts suggest pricing your articles at about one-fourth their original value, unless you have special reasons not to (an antique or a popular collectors' item, for instance, may be more valuable now than when you bought it). Remember that you can always come down on your prices if someone is interested in a particular item.

6   By the day before your sale you should have all your items clean and tagged. One of the beauties of a garage sale is that there's very little equipment to collect. You'll need tables, benches, or boards supported by bricks to display your goods; a rope tied from side to side of your garage can double as a clothes rack. Try to spread out your merchandise rather than dumping articles in deep boxes; customers don't want to feel like they're rummaging through a trash barrel. Most important, you'll need a chair and a table to hold some sort of money box, preferably one with a lock. The afternoon before the sale, take a trip to the bank if you need to, to make sure you have enough one-dollar bills and coins to make plenty of change. The evening before the sale, set up your items on your display benches in the garage or indoors near the site of your sale so that you can quickly set things out in the morning. Get a good night's sleep so you can get up to open on time: the early bird does get the sales in this business.

Step five: Setting up your sale

A note on equipment

7   The sale itself is, of course, the real fun. Half the enjoyment is haggling with the customers, so be prepared to joke and visit with the shoppers. Watching the different kinds of people who show up is also a kick—you can get a cross section from college students on a tight budget to harried mothers toting four kids to real eccentrics in fancy cars who will argue about the price of a 75¢ item (if you're a creative writer, don't forget to take notes for your next novel). If the action

Step six: Running the sale

slows in the afternoon, you can resort to a half-price or two-for-one sale by posting a large sign to that effect; many shoppers can't resist a sale at a sale!

Step seven: Closing up

8   By late afternoon you should be richer and junk-free, at least to some extent. If you do have items left after the half-price sale, decide whether you want to box them up for the next sale or drop them by a charitable organization such as Goodwill (some organizations will even pick up your donations; others have convenient drop boxes). After you've taken your articles inside, don't forget to take down any signs you've posted in the neighborhood; old, withered garage sale signs fluttering in the breeze are an eyesore. Last, sit down and count your profits, so you can go out in the evening to celebrate a successful business venture.

Conclusion: A summary of the benefits and a humorous warning

9   The money you make is, of course, the biggest incentive for having one or two sales a year. But the combination of money, clean closets, and memories of the characters you met can be irresistible. Garage sales can rapidly get in your blood; once you hold a successful one, you're tempted to have another as soon as the junk starts to mount up. And having sales somehow leads to attending them too, as it becomes fun to see what other folks are selling at bargain prices. So be forewarned: you too can be transformed into a garage sale junkie, traveling with a now-popular car bumper sticker that proudly proclaims to the world: "Caution! I brake for garage sales"!

■ Professional Essays*

Because there are two kinds of process essays, informative and directional, this section presents two professional essays so that each type is illustrated.

_____

* To help you read these essays analytically, review pages 170–172.

I. The Informative Process Essay

■ To Bid the World Farewell

Jessica Mitford

As an investigative reporter, Jessica Mitford wrote many articles and books, including *Kind and Unusual Punishment: The Prison Business* (1973), *A Fine Old Conflict* (1977), *Poison Penmanship* (1979), and *The American Way of Birth* (1979). This essay is from her best-selling book *The American Way of Death* (1963), which scrutinizes the funeral industry.

1   Embalming is indeed a most extraordinary procedure, and one must wonder at the docility of Americans who each year pay hundreds of millions of dollars for its perpetuation, blissfully ignorant of what it is all about, what is done, how it is done. Not one in ten thousand has any idea of what actually takes place. Books on the subject are extremely hard to come by. They are not to be found in most libraries or bookshops.

2   In an era when huge television audiences watch surgical operations in the comfort of their living rooms, when, thanks to the animated cartoon, the geography of the digestive system has become familiar territory even to the nursery school set, and in a land where the satisfaction of curiosity about almost all matters is a national pastime, the secrecy surrounding embalming can, surely, hardly be attributed to the inherent gruesomeness of the subject. Custom in this regard has within this century suffered a complete reversal. In the early days of American embalming, when it was performed in the home of the deceased, it was almost mandatory for some relative to stay by the embalmer's side and witness the procedure. Today, family members who might wish to be in attendance would certainly be dissuaded by the funeral director. All others, except apprentices, are excluded by law from the preparation room.

3   A close look at what does actually take place may explain in large measure the undertaker's intractable reticence concerning a procedure that has become his major *raison d'être*. Is it possible he fears that public information about embalming might lead patrons to wonder if they really want this service? If the funeral men are loath to discuss the subject outside the trade, the reader may, understandably, be equally loath to go on reading at this point. For those who have the stomach for it, let us part the formaldehyde curtain. . . .

4   The body is first laid out in the undertaker's morgue—or rather, Mr. Jones is reposing in the preparation room—to be readied to bid the world farewell.

5   The preparation room in any of the better funeral establishments has the tiled and sterile look of a surgery, and indeed the embalmer-restorative artist who does his chores there is beginning to adopt the term "dermasurgeon" (appropriately corrupted by some mortician-writers as "demisurgeon") to describe his calling. His equipment, consisting of scalpels, scissors, augers, forceps, clamps, needles, pumps, tubes, bowls and basins, is crudely imitative of the surgeon's as is his technique, acquired in a nine- or twelve-month post-high-school course in an embalming school. He is supplied by an advanced chemical industry with a bewildering array of fluids, sprays, pastes, oils, powders, creams, to fix or soften tissue, shrink or distend it as needed, dry it here, restore the moisture there. There are cosmetics, waxes and paints

to fill and cover features, even plaster of Paris to replace entire limbs. There are ingenious aids to prop and stabilize the cadaver: a Vari-Pose Head Rest, the Edwards Arm and Hand Positioner, the Repose Block (to support the shoulders during the embalming), and the Throop Foot Positioner, which resembles an old-fashioned stocks.

6   Mr. John H. Eckels, president of the Eckels College of Mortuary Science, thus describes the first part of the embalming procedure: "In the hands of a skilled practitioner, this work may be done in a comparatively short time and without mutilating the body other than by slight incision—so slight that it scarcely would cause serious inconvenience if made upon a living person. It is necessary to remove the blood, and doing this not only helps in the disinfecting, but removes the principal cause of disfigurement due to discoloration."

7   Another textbook discusses the all-important time element: "The earlier this is done, the better, for every hour that elapses between death and embalming will add to the problems and complications encountered. . . ." Just how soon should one get going on the embalming? The author tells us, "On the basis of such scanty information made available to this profession through its rudimentary and haphazard system of technical research, we must conclude that the best results are to be obtained if the subject is embalmed before life is completely extinct—that is, before cellular death has occurred. In the average case, this would mean within an hour after somatic death." For those who feel that there is something a little rudimentary, not to say haphazard, about this advice, a comforting thought is offered by another writer. Speaking of fears entertained in early days of premature burial, he points out, "One of the effects of embalming by chemical injection, however, has been to dispel fears of live burial." How true; once the blood is removed, chances of live burial are indeed remote.

8   To return to Mr. Jones, the blood is drained out through the veins and replaced by embalming fluid pumped in through the arteries. As noted in *The Principles and Practices of Embalming*, "every operator has a favorite injection and drainage point—a fact which becomes a handicap only if he fails or refuses to forsake his favorites when conditions demand it." Typical favorites are the carotid artery, femoral artery, jugular vein, subclavian vein. There are various choices of embalming fluid. If Flextone is used, it will produce a "mild flexible rigidity. The skin retains a velvety softness, the tissues are rubbery and pliable. Ideal for women and children." It may be blended with B. and G. Products Company's Lyf-Lyk tint, which is guaranteed to reproduce "nature's own skin texture . . . the velvety appearance of living tissue." Suntone comes in three separate tints: Suntan; Special Cosmetic Tint, a pink shade "especially indicated for young female subjects"; and Regular Cosmetic Tint, moderately pink.

9   About three to six gallons of a dyed and perfumed solution of formaldehyde, glycerin, borax, phenol, alcohol and water is soon circulating through Mr. Jones, whose mouth has been sewn together with a "needle directed upward between the upper lip and gum and brought out through the left nostril," with the corners raised slightly "for a more pleasant expression." If he should be bucktoothed, his teeth are cleaned with Bon Ami and coated with colorless nail polish. His eyes, meanwhile, are closed with flesh-tinted eye caps and eye cement.

10   The next step is to have at Mr. Jones with a thing called a trocar. This is a long, hollow needle attached to a tube. It is jabbed into the abdomen, poked around the entrails and chest cavity, the contents of which are pumped out and replaced with "cavity fluid." This done, and the hole in the abdomen sewn up, Mr. Jones' face is

heavily creamed (to protect the skin from burns which may be caused by leakage of the chemicals), and he is covered with a sheet and left unmolested for a while. But not for long—there is more, much more, in store for him. He has been embalmed, but not yet restored, and the best time to start the restorative work is eight to ten hours after embalming, when the tissues have become firm and dry.

11   The object of all this attention to the corpse, it must be remembered, is to make it presentable for viewing in an attitude of healthy repose. "Our customs require the presentation of our dead in the semblance of normality . . . unmarred by the ravages of illness, disease or mutilation," says Mr. J. Sheridan Mayer in his *Restorative Art*. This is rather a large order since few people die in the full bloom of health, unravaged by illness and unmarked by some disfigurement. The funeral industry is equal to the challenge: "In some cases the gruesome appearance of a mutilated or disease-ridden subject may be quite discouraging. The task of restoration may seem impossible and shake the confidence of the embalmer. This is the time for intestinal fortitude and determination. Once the formative work is begun and affected tissues are cleaned or removed, all doubts of success vanish. It is surprising and gratifying to discover the results which may be obtained."

12   The embalmer, having allowed an appropriate interval to elapse, returns to the attack, but now he brings into play the skill and equipment of sculptor and cosmetician. Is a hand missing? Casting one in plaster of Paris is a simple matter. "For replacement purposes, only a cast of the back of the hand is necessary; this is within the ability of the average operator and is quite adequate." If a lip or two, a nose or an ear should be miss-ing, the embalmer has at hand a variety of restorative waxes with which to model replacements. Pores and skin texture are simulated by stippling with a little brush, and over this cosmetics are laid on. Head off? Decapitation cases are rather routinely han-dled. Ragged edges are trimmed, and head joined to torso with a series of splints, wires and sutures. It is a good idea to have a little something at the neck—a scarf or high collar—when time for viewing comes. Swollen mouth? Cut out tissue as needed from inside the lips. If too much is removed, the surface contour can easily be restored by padding with cotton. Swollen necks and cheeks are reduced by removing tissue through vertical incisions made down each side of the neck. "When the deceased is cas-keted, the pillow will hide the suture incisions . . . as an extra precaution against leak-age, the suture may be painted with liquid sealer."

13   The opposite condition is more likely to present itself—that of emaciation. His hypodermic syringe now loaded with massage cream, the embalmer seeks out and fills the hollowed and sunken areas by injection. In this procedure the backs of the hands and fingers and the under-chin area should not be neglected.

14   Positioning the lips is a problem that recurrently challenges the ingenuity of the embalmer. Closed too tightly, they tend to give a stern, even disapproving expression. Ideally, embalmers feel, the lips should give the impression of being ever so slightly parted, the upper lip protruding slightly for a more youthful appearance. This takes some engineering, however, as the lips tend to drift apart. Lip drift can sometimes be remedied by pushing one or two straight pins through the inner margin of the lower lip and then inserting them between the two front teeth. If Mr. Jones happens to have no teeth, the pins can just as easily be anchored in his Armstrong Face Former and Denture Replacer. Another method to maintain lip closure is to dislocate the lower jaw, which is then held in its new

position by a wire run through holes which have been drilled through the upper and lower jaws at the midline. As the French are fond of saying, *il faut souffrir pour être belle.**

15   If Mr. Jones has died of jaundice, the embalming fluid will very likely turn him green. Does this deter the embalmer? Not if he has intestinal fortitude. Masking pastes and cosmetics are heavily laid on, burial garments and casket interiors are color-correlated with particular care, and Jones is displayed beneath rose-colored lights. Friends will say, "How *well* he looks." Death by carbon monoxide, on the other hand, can be rather a good thing from the embalmer's viewpoint: "One advantage is the fact that this type of discoloration is an exaggerated form of a natural pink coloration." This is nice because the healthy glow is already present and needs but little attention.

16   The patching and filling completed, Mr. Jones is now shaved, washed and dressed. Cream-based cosmetic, available in pink, flesh, suntan, brunette and blond, is applied to his hands and face, his hair is shampooed and combed (and, in the case of Mrs. Jones, set), his hands manicured. For the horny-handed son of toil special care must be taken; cream should be applied to remove ingrained grime, and the nails cleaned. "If he were not in the habit of having them manicured in life, trimming and shaping is advised for better appearance—never questioned by kin."

17   Jones is now ready for casketing (this is the present participle of the verb "to casket"). In this operation his right shoulder should be depressed slightly "to turn the body a bit to the right and soften the appearance of lying flat on the back." Positioning the hands is a matter of importance, and special rubber positioning blocks may be used. The hands should be cupped slightly for a more lifelike, relaxed appearance. Proper placement of the body requires a delicate sense of balance. It should lie as high as possible in the casket, yet not so high that the lid, when lowered, will hit the nose. On the other hand, we are cautioned, placing the body too low "creates the impression that the body is in a box."

18   Jones is next wheeled into the appointed slumber room where a few last touches may be added—his favorite pipe placed in his hand or, if he was a great reader, a book propped into position. (In the case of little Master Jones a Teddy bear may be clutched.) Here he will hold open house for a few days, visiting hours 10 A.M. to 9 P.M.

Questions on Content, Structure, and Style

1. By studying the first three paragraphs, summarize both Mitford's reason for explaining the embalming process and her attitude toward undertakers who wish to keep their patrons uninformed about this procedure.

2. Does Mitford use enough specific details to help you visualize each step as it occurs? Point out examples of details that create vivid descriptions by appealing to your sense of sight, smell, or touch.

3. How does the technique of using the hypothetical "Mr. Jones" make the explanation of the process more effective? Why didn't Mitford simply refer to "the corpse" or "a body" throughout her essay?

---

* "One must suffer to be beautiful."

4. What is Mitford's general attitude toward this procedure? The overall tone of the essay? Study Mitford's choice of words and then identify the tone in each of the following passages:

> "The next step is to have at Mr. Jones with a thing called a trocar." (10)*

> "The embalmer, having allowed an appropriate interval to elapse, returns to the attack. . . ." (12)

> "Friends will say, 'How *well* he looks.'" (15)

> "On the other hand, we are cautioned, placing the body too low 'creates the impression that the body is in a box.'" (17)

> "Here he will hold open house for a few days, visiting hours 10 A.M. to 9 P.M." (18)

What other words and passages reveal Mitford's attitude and tone?

5. Why does Mitford repeatedly quote various undertakers and textbooks on the embalming and restorative process ("'needle directed upward between the upper lip and gum and brought out through the left nostril'")? Why is the quotation in paragraph 7 that begins "'On the basis of such scanty information made available to this profession through its rudimentary and haphazard system of technical research'" particularly effective in emphasizing Mitford's attitude toward the funeral industry?

6. What does Mitford gain by quoting euphemisms used by the funeral business, such as "dermasurgeon," "Repose Block," and "slumber room"?

7. What are the connotations of the words "poked," "jabbed," and "left unmolested" in paragraph 10? What effect is Mitford trying to produce with the series of questions (such as "Head off?") in paragraph 12?

8. Does this process flow smoothly from step to step? Identify several transitional devices connecting the paragraphs.

9. Evaluate Mitford's last sentence. Does it successfully sum up the author's attitude and conclude the essay?

10. By supplying information about the embalming process, did Mitford change your attitude toward this procedure or toward the funeral industry? Are there advantages Mitford fails to mention?

Suggestions for Writing

Try using Jessica Mitford's "To Bid the World Farewell" as a stepping-stone to your own writing. Mitford's graphic details and disparaging tone upset some readers who feel funerals are important for the living. If you agree, consider writing an essay that challenges Mitford's position. Or adopt Mitford's role as an investigative reporter exposing a controversial process. For example, how is toxic waste disposed of at the student health center? Dangerous chemicals from science labs? What happens to unclaimed animals at your local shelter? Or try a more lighthearted investigation: just how do they obtain that mystery meat served in the dorm cafeteria? Use Mitford's vivid essay as a guide as you present your discoveries.

---

* Numbers in parentheses following quoted material and vocabulary words refer to paragraphs in the essay.

Vocabulary

docility (1)	*raison d'être* (3)	pliable (8)
perpetuation (1)	ingenious (5)	semblance (11)
inherent (2)	cadaver (5)	ravages (11)
mandatory (2)	somatic (7)	stippling (12)
intractable (3)	rudimentary (7)	emaciation (13)
reticence (3)	dispel (7)	

II. The Directional Process Essay

■ Preparing for the Job Interview: Know Thyself

Katy Piotrowski

Katy Piotrowski, M.Ed., is the owner of JobWorks, through which she provides career and job-search support. Her essay, which originally appeared in 2005 in her "On the Job" column for the Fort Collins, Colorado, *Coloradoan* newspaper, has been slightly revised for this text.

1   "I have a job interview this afternoon!" Shawn told me. "Are you ready for it" I asked. "I'm not sure," she confessed. So, drawing on my work as a career-search consultant, I helped her through an interview-readiness procedure, a quick, six-step process that can successfully prepare almost anyone for an job interview.

2   First, I asked, can you identify the top two or three responsibilities of the job? Shawn hesitated, so I asked her to reread the position description and tell me which parts or key words stood out most. "Evaluating the effectiveness of health-care programs" and "coordinating information exchange in the hospital," she determined. With the key responsibilities in mind, we were ready for the next step. For each of the primary responsibilities, can you describe at least three examples from your past that demonstrate your expertise in those areas? Shawn had one example ready to share, but she needed more. "Tell me about a time when you evaluated the effectiveness of health-care or coordinated information among people or agencies," I prompted her. Within minutes, she'd created a longer list of examples.

3   Moving on, I asked Shawn to think of other experiences in her professional background that would show her as an attractive candidate for this job. Shawn's responses were unfocused, so I taught her a simple three-step STAR process for answering a number of interview questions: 1) describe the **s**ituation or **t**asks, 2) talk about the **a**ctions you took, 3) finish with the **r**esults of your efforts. Try to frame your answers concisely but in a compelling way, using action verbs that show leadership, such as "designed," "coordinated," "implemented," "created," and "managed," when such words are appropriate. Shawn practiced the process, and soon her answers were much more effective.

4   In addition to questions about specific qualifications, interviewers often ask general questions designed to reveal a candidate's "fit" as an employee in their business. "Tell me a little about yourself" is a common request; it may even come at the beginning of an interview when you are the most nervous, so it helps to have some prepared (though not

stiffly memorized) thoughts. Shawn's response included highlights of her work history, information about her education, and a statement about why she was excited about the job opening. Variations on this line of questioning might include "As a worker in this field, what is your greatest strength? Biggest weakness?" or "How have you handled a difficult situation?" Shawn had impressive responses to these kinds of questions; she just needed to practice them several more times.

5   As well as presenting themselves to companies, interviewees also need to know something about the companies to which they are applying. Whether you are asked directly or not, it's important to be acquainted with the goals, products, and services of your prospective employer. A quick online search may lead you to a company web page and any recent publicity. Knowing current information about your prospective employer may better help you respond to questions such as "What knowledge or skills can you bring to our company?" with specific answers that happily fit their needs.

6   Often interviewers' final question may be "Do you have any questions for us?" so the last step in your preparation process calls for thinking of at least one good response. You might ask about the ways this position fits into the larger organization or the company's future plans or ask for more details about the advertised position. You might ask them to describe the most successful employees they've ever hired for this job. (At this time, you probably do not want to negotiate salary, especially if you are an entry-level applicant.) If it seems appropriate, you may also ask how you should proceed: would they prefer for you to contact them or to wait for their response? Is there any other information you can provide that would be helpful in furthering your application for this job? (Don't forget, I reminded Shawn, at the close of your meeting, to thank the interviewers for their time.)

7   Within an hour, following these few steps, Shawn was much more prepared for her interview. Though few people can be totally relaxed during an interview, she was calmed with the knowledge that she was ready to effectively give meaningful responses to a variety of questions. And, yes, she *did* get the job.

Questions on Content, Structure, and Style

1. What process is explained in this essay? What is Piotrowski's main purpose?

2. Although Piotrowski describes her conversation with Shawn, why may this article be considered a directional process essay for its readers?

3. What are the primary steps in this process?

4. Piotrowski uses an actual job applicant, Shawn, to show how the interview-preparation process works. What benefits for the reader does this choice of organization present?

5. Consider ways in which Piotrowski explains each step of the process. How does she clarify her advice by using examples?

6. Cite some ways Piotrowski moves her reader from one step in the preparation process to the next. What transitional words or phrases help guide the reader through the steps?

7. Effective writers of process essays often offer warnings or point out what not to do. Where does Piotrowski use this technique?

8. In paragraph 3, how does Piotrowski use an *acronym* (a word formed from the first letters or parts of other words) to explain her advice?

9. Describe Piotrowski's tone or "voice" in this essay. Is it appropriate and effective? Cite some examples of her language to support your answer.

10. Evaluate Piotrowski's conclusion. How does it wrap up the essay? In particular, what is the effect of the last sentence?

Suggestions for Writing

Try using Piotrowski's essay as a stepping-stone to your own writing. Think of a job that you would like to have soon, perhaps this summer or after you finish your education. Following Piotrowski's procedure for interview preparation, write an essay showing why you are the best candidate for the position. Keep this essay for later use when you face a real interview or for help designing a résumé. (Or, if you prefer, try writing a light-hearted, tongue-in-cheek process essay that makes a serious point by humorously advising readers what *not* to do the workplace: how to not impress your boss, how to not cooperate with your co-workers, how to not get a raise, and so on.)

Vocabulary

expertise (2)
implemented (3)
prospective (5)

▪ A REVISION WORKSHEET

As you write your rough drafts, consult Chapter 5 for guidance through the revision process. In addition, here are a few questions to ask yourself as you revise your process essay:

1. Is the essay's purpose clear to the reader?

2. Has the need for any special equipment been noted and explained adequately? Are all terms unfamiliar to the reader defined clearly?

3. Does the essay include all the steps (and warnings, if appropriate) necessary to understanding the process?

4. Is each step described in enough detail to make it understandable to all readers? Where could more detail be effectively added?

5. Are all the steps in the process presented in an easy-to-follow chronological order, with smooth transitions between steps or stages?

6. Are there any steps that should be combined in a paragraph describing a logical stage in the process?

7. Does the essay have a pleasing conclusion?

After you've revised your essay extensively, you might exchange rough drafts with a classmate and answer these questions for each other, making specific suggestions for improvement wherever appropriate. (For advice on productive participation in classroom workshops, see pages 108–111.)

Reviewing Your Progress

After you have completed your process essay, take a moment to measure your progress as a writer by responding to the following questions. Such analysis will help you to recognize growth in your writing skills and may enable you to identify areas that are still problematic.

1. Which part of your essay is most successful? Why?

2. Select two details that contribute significantly to the clarity of your explanation. Why are these details effective?

3. What part of your essay gave you the most trouble? How did you overcome the problem?

4. If you had more time to work on this essay, what would receive additional attention? Why?

5. What did you learn about your topic from writing this essay? About yourself as a writer?

▪ Strategy Three: Development by Comparison and Contrast

Every day you exercise the mental process of comparison and contrast. When you get up in the morning, for instance, you may contrast two choices of clothing—a short-sleeved shirt versus a long-sleeved one—and then make your decision after hearing the weather forecast. Or you may contrast and choose between Sugar-Coated Plastic Pops and Organic Mullet Kernels for breakfast, between the health advantages of walking to campus and the speed afforded by your car or bicycle. Once on campus, preparing to register, you may first compare both professors and courses; similarly, you probably compared the school you attend now to others before you made your choice. In short, you frequently use the process of comparison and contrast to come to a decision or make a judgment about two or more objects, persons, ideas, or feelings.

When you write a comparison or contrast essay, your opinion about the two elements* in question becomes your thesis statement; the body of the paper then shows why you arrived at that opinion. For example, if your thesis states that Mom's Kum-On-Back Hamburger Haven is preferable to McPhony's Mystery Burger Stand, your body paragraphs might contrast the two restaurants in terms of food, service, and atmosphere, revealing the superiority of Mom's on all three counts.

---

* It is possible to compare or contrast more than two elements. But until you feel confident about the organizational patterns for this kind of essay, you should probably stay with the simpler format.

Developing Your Essay

There are two principal patterns of organization for comparison or contrast essays. For most short papers you should choose one of the patterns and stick with it throughout the essay. Later, if you are assigned a longer essay, you may want to mix the patterns for variety as some professional writers do, but do so only if you can maintain clarity and logical organization.

Pattern One: Point by Point

This method of organization calls for body paragraphs that compare or contrast the two subjects first on point one, then on point two, then point three, and so on. Study the following example:

Thesis: Mom's Hamburger Haven is a better family restaurant than McPhony's because of its superior food, service, and atmosphere.

Point 1:   Food
     A. Mom's
     B. McPhony's

Point 2:   Service
     A. Mom's
     B. McPhony's

Point 3:   Atmosphere
     A. Mom's
     B. McPhony's

Conclusion

If you select this pattern of organization, you must make a smooth transition from subject "A" to subject "B" in each discussion to avoid a choppy seesaw effect. Be consistent: present the same subject first in each discussion of a major point. In the essay outlined above, for instance, Mom's is always introduced before McPhony's.

Pattern Two: The Block

This method of organization presents body paragraphs in which the writer first discusses subject "A" on points one, two, three, and so on, and then discusses subject "B" on the same points. The following model illustrates this Block Pattern:

Thesis: Mom's Hamburger Haven is a better family restaurant than McPhony's because of its superior food, service, and atmosphere.

    A. Mom's
      1. Food
      2. Service
      3. Atmosphere

    B. McPhony's
      1. Food
      2. Service
      3. Atmosphere

Conclusion

If you use the Block Pattern, you should discuss the three points—food, service, atmosphere—in the same order for each subject. In addition, you must include in your discussion of subject "B" specific references to the points you made earlier about subject "A" (see outline). In other words, because your statements about Mom's superior food may be several pages away by the time your comments on McPhony's food appear, the readers may not remember precisely what you said. Gently, unobtrusively, remind them with a specific reference to the earlier discussion. For instance, you might begin your paragraph on McPhony's service like this: "Unlike the friendly, attentive help at Mom's, service at McPhony's features grouchy employees who wait on you as if they consider your presence an intrusion on their privacy." The discussion of atmosphere might begin, "McPhony's atmosphere is as cold, sterile, and plastic as its decor, in contrast to the warm, homey feeling that pervades Mom's." Without such connecting phrases, what should be one unified essay will look more like two distinct mini-essays, forcing readers to do the job of comparing or contrasting for you.

Which Pattern Should You Use?

As you prepare to compose your first draft, you might ask yourself, "Which pattern of organization should I choose—Point by Point or Block?" Indeed, this is not your simple "paper or plastic" supermarket choice. It's an important question—to which there is no single, easy answer.

For most writers, choosing the appropriate pattern of organization involves thinking time in the prewriting stage, before beginning a draft. Many times, your essay's subject matter itself will suggest the most effective method of development. The Block Method might be the better choice when a complete, overall picture of each subject is desirable. For example, you might decide that your "then-and-now" essay (your disastrous first day at a new job contrasted with your success at that job today) would be easier for your readers to understand if your description of "then" (your first day) was presented in its entirety, followed by the contrasting discussion of "now" (current success). Later in this section, you will see that Mark Twain chose this method in his essay "Two Ways of Viewing the River" to contrast his early and later impressions of the Mississippi.

On the other hand, your essay topic might best be discussed by presenting a number of distinct points for the reader to consider one by one. Essays that evaluate, that argue the superiority or advantage of one thing over another ("A cat is a better pet for students than a dog because of X, Y, and Z"), often lend themselves to Point-by-Point Method because each of the writer's claims may be clearly supported by the side-by-side details. "Bringing Back the Joy of Market Day," a student essay in this section, employs this method to emphasize three ways in which a small food cooperative is preferable to a chain grocery store.

However, none of the above advice always holds true. There are no hard-and-fast rules governing this rhetorical choice. Each writer must decide which method of organization works best in any particular comparison/contrast essay. Before drafting begins, therefore, writers are wise to sketch out an informal outline or rough plan using one method and then the other to see which is more effective for their topic, their purpose, and their audience. By spending time in the prewriting stage "auditioning" each method of development, you may spare yourself the frustration of writing an entire draft whose organization doesn't work well for your topic.

Problems to Avoid

The single most serious error is the "so-what" thesis. Writers of comparison and contrast essays often wish to convince their readers that something—a restaurant, a movie, a product—is better (or worse) than something else: "Mom's Haven is a better place to eat than McPhony's." But not all comparison or contrast essays assert the absolute superiority or inferiority of their subjects. Sometimes writers simply want to point out the similarities or differences in two or more people, places, or objects, and that's fine, too—*as long as the writer avoids the "so-what" thesis problem.*

Too often, novice writers will present thesis statements such as "My sister and I are very different" or "Having a blended family with two stepbrothers and stepsisters has advantages and disadvantages for me." To such theses, readers can only respond, "So what? Who cares?" There are many similarities and differences (or advantages and disadvantages) between countless numbers of things—but why should your readers care about those described in your essay? Comparing or contrasting for no apparent reason is a waste of the readers' valuable time; instead, find a purpose that will draw in your audience. You may indeed wish to write an essay contrasting the pros and cons of your blended family, but do it in a way that has a universal appeal or application. For instance, you might revise your thesis to say something like "Although a blended family often does experience petty jealousies and juvenile bickering, the benefits of having stepsiblings as live-in friends far outweigh the problems," and then use your family to show the advantages and disadvantages. In this way, your readers realize they will learn something about the blended family, a common phenomenon today, as well as learning some information about you and your particular family.

Another way to avoid the "so-what" problem is to direct your thesis to a particular audience. For instance, you might say that "Although Stella's Sweatateria and the Fitness Fanatics Gym are similar in their low student-membership prices and excellent instructors, Stella's is the place to go for those seeking a variety of exercise classes rather than hard-core bodybuilding machines." Or your thesis may wish to show a particular relationship between two subjects. Instead of writing "There are many similarities between the movie *Riot of the Killer Snails* and Mary Sheeley's novel *Salt on the Sidewalk*," write "The many similarities in character and plot (the monster, the scientist, and vegetable garden scene) clearly suggest that the movie director was greatly influenced by—if not actually guilty of stealing—parts of Mary Sheeley's novel."

In other words, tell your readers your point and then use comparison or contrast to support that idea; don't just compare or contrast items in a vacuum. Ask yourself, "What is the significant point I want my readers to learn or understand from reading this comparison/contrast essay? Why do they need to know this?"

Describe your subjects clearly and distinctly. To comprehend a difference or a similarity between two things, the reader must first be able to "see" them as you do. Consequently, you should use as many vivid examples and details as possible to describe both your subjects. Beware a tendency to overelaborate on one subject and then grossly skimp on the other, an especially easy trap to fall into in an essay that asserts "X" is preferable to "Y." By giving each side a reasonable treatment, you will do a better job of convincing your reader that you know both sides and have made a valid judgment.

Avoid a choppy essay. Whether you organize your essay by the Point-by-Point Pattern or the Block Pattern, you need to use enough transitional devices to ensure a smooth flow from one subject to another and from one point to the next. Without transitions, your essay may assume the distracting movement of a Ping-Pong game, as you switch back and forth between discussions of your two subjects. Listed below are some appropriate words to link your points:

Comparison	Contrast
also	however
similarly	on the contrary
too	on the other hand
both	in contrast
like	although
not only . . . but also	unlike
have in common	though
share the same	instead of
in the same manner	but

(For a review of other transitional devices, see pages 70–73.)

■ ESSAY TOPICS

Here are some topics that may be compared or contrasted. Remember to narrow your subject, formulate a thesis that presents a clear point, and follow one of the two organizational patterns discussed on pages 216–217. For additional ideas, turn to the "Suggestions for Writing" sections following the professional essays (page 230 and page 232).

1. An expectation and its reality

2. A first impression and a later point of view

3. Two views on a current controversial issue (campus, local, national)

4. Two conflicting theories you are studying in another college course

5. A memory of a person or place and a more recent encounter

6. Coverage of the same story by two newspapers or magazines (the *National Enquirer* and the *Dallas Morning News*, for example, or *Time* and *Newsweek*)

7. A hero today and yesterday

8. Two essays or pieces of literature with similar themes but different styles

9. Two pieces of technology or two pieces of sports equipment (or an older and newer version of a product)

10. Two paintings/photographs/posters (You might select any of the many images in this text; a list of the artworks follows the table of contents. You could choose two portraits or a portrait and a self-portrait [for example, *Migrant Mother, Repose,* or *The Two Fridas*]; two landscapes [*Early Snow, Starry Night,* or *Moonrise, Hernandez, New Mexico*]; two scenes of action [*The Third of May, Tornado over*

Kansas]; two pictures with contrasting themes, styles, or media or two that share certain themes or techniques [the surrealism of *The Persistence of Memory*, *Birthday*, or *The Scream*, for example]. For help writing about artworks, see Chapter 17.)

11. Two solutions to a problem in your professional field

12. One of today's popular entertainments and one from an earlier era

13. Two places you've lived or visited or two schools you've attended

14. Two instructors or coaches whose teaching styles are effective but different

15. Two movies; a book and its movie; a movie and its sequel (For help writing about film, see Chapter 18.)

16. Two jobs, bosses, or employers (or your current job and your dream job)

17. Two places that are special for you in different ways

18. An opinion you held before coming to college that has changed

19. Your attitude toward a social custom or political belief and your parents' (or grandparents') attitude toward that belief or custom

20. An analysis of advertising developed by comparison/contrast or analogy (Consider, for example, the ad shown here. What is its purpose and who is its target audience? How does the ad incorporate the strategy of contrast to sell its product? What other appeals are used? Is this ad effective? Why/why not? For another ad developed by contrast, see page 302.)

A Topic Proposal for Your Essay

Selecting the right subject matter is important to every writer. To help you clarify your ideas and strengthen your commitment to your topic, here is a proposal sheet that asks you to describe some of your preliminary ideas about your subject before you begin drafting. Although your ideas may change as you write (they will almost certainly become more refined), thinking through your choice of topic now may help you avoid several false starts.

1. What two subjects will your essay discuss? In what ways are these subjects similar? Different?

2. Do you plan to compare or contrast your two subjects?

3. Write one or two sentences describing your attitude toward these two subjects. Are you stating a preference for one or are you making some other significant point? In other words, what is the purpose of this essay?

4. Why would other people find this topic interesting and important? Would a particular group of people be more affected by your topic than others? Are you avoiding the "so-what" thesis problem?

5. List three or four points of comparison or contrast that you might include in this essay.

6. What difficulties might this topic present during your drafting? For example, would your topic be best explained using the Block or Point-by-Point Pattern?

■ Sample Student Essays

Because there are two popular ways to develop comparison/contrast essays, this section offers two student essays so that each pattern is illustrated.

I. The Point-by-Point Pattern

Note that this writer takes a definite stand—that local food co-ops are superior to chain grocery stores—and then contrasts two local stores, Lane Grocer and the Fort Collins, Colorado, Co-op, to prove her thesis. She selected the Point-by-Point Pattern to organize her essay, contrasting prices, atmosphere, and benefits to local producers. See if you can identify her transitional devices as well as some of her uses of detail that make the essay more interesting and convincing.

BRINGING BACK THE JOY OF MARKET DAY

1   Now that the old family-run corner grocery is almost extinct, many people are banding together to form their own neighborhood stores as food cooperatives. Locally owned by their members, food

---

Thesis

co-ops such as the one here in Fort Collins are welcome alternatives to the impersonal chain-store markets such as Lane Grocer. In exchange for volunteering a few hours each month, co-op members share savings and a friendly experience while they shop; local producers gain loyal, local support from the members as well as better prices for their goods in return for providing the freshest, purest food possible.

Essay map

Point one: Prices

2   Perhaps the most crucial distinction between the two kinds of stores is that while supermarkets are set up to generate profit for their corporations, co-ops are nonprofit groups whose main purpose is to provide their members and the community with good, inexpensive food and basic household needs. At first glance, supermarkets such as Lane Grocer may appear to be cheaper because they offer so many specials, which they emphasize heavily through ads and in-store promotions. These special deals, known as "loss-leaders" in the retail industry, are more than compensated by the extremely high markups on other products. For example, around Thanksgiving Lane Grocer might have a sale on flour and shortening and then set up the displays with utmost care so that as customers reach for the flour they will be drawn to colorful bottles of pie spices, fancy jars of mincemeat, or maybe an inviting bin of fresh-roasted holiday nuts, all of which may be marked up 100% or more—way above what is being lost on the flour and shortening.

Examples of Lane Grocer's prices contrasted to examples of co-op prices

3   The Fort Collins Co-op rarely bothers with such pricing gimmicks; instead, it tries to have a consistent markup—just enough to meet overhead expenses. The flour at the co-op may cost an extra few cents, but that same fancy spice bottle that costs over $1.00 from the supermarket display can be refilled at the co-op for less than 25¢. The nuts, considered by regular groceries as a seasonal "gourmet" item, are

sold at the co-op for about two-thirds the price. Great savings like these are achieved by buying in bulk and having customers bag their own groceries. Recycled containers are used as much as possible, cutting down substantially on overhead. Buying in bulk may seem awkward at first, but the extra time spent bagging and weighing their own food results in welcome savings for co-op members.

4   Once people have become accustomed to bringing their own containers and taking part in the work at the co-ops, they often find that it's actually more fun to shop in the friendly, relaxed atmosphere of the co-ops. At Lane Grocer, for example, I often find shopping a battle of tangled metal carts wielded by bored customers who are frequently trying to manage one or more cranky children. The long aisles harshly lit by rows of cold fluorescent lights and the bland commercial music don't make the chore of shopping any easier either. On the other hand, the Fort Collins Co-op may not be as expertly planned, but at least the chaos is carried on in a friendly way. Parents especially appreciate that they can safely let their children loose while they shop because in the small, open-spaced co-op even toddlers don't become lost as they do in the aisles of towering supermarket shelves. Moreover, most members are willing to look after the children of other members if necessary. And while they shop, members can choose to listen to the FM radio or simply to enjoy each other's company in relative quiet.

Point two: Atmosphere

Description of Lane Grocer's atmosphere contrasted to description of the co-op's atmosphere

5   As well as benefiting member consumers, co-ops also help small local producers by providing a direct market for their goods. Large chain stores may require minimum wholesale quantities far beyond the capacity of an individual producer, and mass markets like Lane Grocer often feel they are "too big" to negotiate with small local producers. But because of their small, independent nature, co-ops

Point three: Benefits to local producers

No benefits at Lane Grocer contrasted to two benefits at the co-op

welcome the chance to buy direct from the grower or producer. Direct selling offers two advantages for producers: they get a better price for their wares than by selling them through a middleman, and at the same time they establish an independent reputation for their business, which can be immensely valuable to their success later on. In Fort Collins, for example, Luna tofu (bean curd) stands out as an excellent illustration of this kind of mutual support. Several years ago my friend Carol Jones began making tofu in small batches to sell to the co-op as a way to earn a part-time income as well as to contribute to the co-op. Her enterprise has now grown so well that last year her husband quit his job to go into business with her full time. She currently sells to distributors and independent stores from here to Denver; even Lane Grocer, which earlier would not consider selling her tofu even on a trial basis, is now thinking about changing its policy.

Conclusion: Summarizing the advantages of co-ops over chain stores

6   Of course, not all co-ops are like the one here in Fort Collins, but that is one of their best features. Each one reflects the personalities of its members, unlike the supermarket chain stores that vary only slightly. Most important, though, while each has a distinctive character, co-ops share common goals of providing members with high-quality, low-cost food in a friendly, cooperative spirit.

II. The Block Pattern

After thinking through both methods of development, a second student writer chose the Block Pattern to contrast two kinds of backyards. He felt it was more effective to give his readers a complete sense of his first backyard, with its spirit of wildness, instead of addressing each point of the contrast separately, as did the first student writer in this section. Do you agree with his choice? Why or why not? Note, too, the ways in which this writer tries to avoid the "split essay" problem by making clear connections between the new yard and the older one.

BACKYARDS: OLD AND NEW

1   Most of the time I like getting something new—new clothes, new CDs, new video games. I look forward to making new friends and visiting new places. But sometimes new isn't better than old. Five years ago, when my family moved to a house in a new area, I learned that a new, neat backyard can never be as wonderful as a rambling, untamed yard of an older house.

Thesis

2   My first yard, behind our older house, was huge, the size of three normal backyards, but completely irregular in shape. Our property line zagged in and out around old, tall trees in a lot shaped like a large pie piece from which some giant had taken random bites. The left side was taken up by a lopsided garden that sometimes grew tomatoes but mainly wild raspberries, an odd assortment of overgrown bushes, and wildflowers of mismatched shapes and sizes. The middle part had grass and scattered shade trees, some that were good for climbing. The grassy part drifted off into an area with large old evergreen trees surrounded by a tall tangle of vines and bushes that my parents called "the Wild Spot," which they had carefully ignored for years. The whole yard sloped downhill, which with the irregular shape and the trees, made my job of mowing the grass a creative challenge.

Block A: The older, "untamed" backyard

(Landscape variety: Irregular lot size and shape; trees, rambling mix of bushes, flowers, berries, and vines)

3   Despite the mowing problem, there was something magical about that untamed yard. We kids made a path through the Wild Spot and had a secret hideout in the brush. Hidden from adult eyes, my friends and I sat around a pretend fire ring, made up adventures (lost in the jungle!), asked each other Important Questions (better to be a rock star or a baseball player?), and shared our secret fears (being asked to dance). The yard's grassy section was big enough for throwing a football with my

(Family activities)

brother (the here-and-there trees made catching long passes even more spectacular), and my twin sisters invented gymnastic routines that rolled them downhill. Mom picked vegetables and flowers when she felt like it. It seemed like someone, family or friend, was always in our yard doing something fun.

Transition to Block B: The new backyard (contrasting bland landscape)

4   When all the kids were teenagers, my parents finally decided we needed more space, so we moved into a house in a new development. Although the house itself was better (more bathrooms), the new backyard, in comparison to our older one, was a total disappointment. New Backyard was neat, tidy, tiny, flat, square, and completely fenced. There were not only no big old trees for shade or for climbing—there were no trees at all. My parents had to plant a few, which looked like big twigs stuck in the ground. No untamed tangles of bushes and flowers there—only identical fire hydrant-sized shrubs planted evenly every few feet in narrow, even beds along the fence. The rest of this totally flat yard was grass, easy to mow in mere minutes, but no challenge either. No wild berry bushes or rambling vegetable gardens were allowed in the new development. No wild anything at all, to be exact.

(Few activities)

5   Nothing wild and no variety: that was the problem. To put it bluntly, the yard was neat but boring. Every inch of it was open to inspection; it held no secret spaces for the imagination to fill. There was no privacy either as our yard looked directly into the almost duplicate bland yards of the neighbors on all sides. The yard was too small to do any real physical activity in it; going out for a long pass would mean automatic collision with the chain fence in any direction. My sisters' dance routines soon dissolved under our neighbor's eyes, and our tomatoes came from the grocery store. With no hidden nooks, no interesting landscape, and no tumbling space, our family just didn't

go into the backyard very often. Unlike the older, overgrown backyard that was always inviting someone to play, the new backyard wasn't fun for anyone.

6   Over the last five years, the trees have grown and the yard looks better, not so sterile and empty. I guess all new yards are on their way to becoming old yards eventually. But it takes decades and that is too slow for me. New houses have lots of modern conveniences, but I hope if I am lucky enough to own my own place someday, I will remember that when it comes to backyards, old is always better than new.

Conclusion: A future preference based on essay's thesis

Professional Essays*

Because there are two common ways to develop comparison/contrast essays, this section offers two professional essays so that each pattern is illustrated.

I. The Point-by-Point Pattern

■ Grant and Lee: A Study in Contrasts

Bruce Catton

Bruce Catton, an authority on the Civil War, won both the Pulitzer Prize for historical work and the National Book Award in 1955. He wrote numerous books, including *Mr. Lincoln's Army* (1951), *A Stillness at Appomattox* (1953), *Never Call Retreat* (1966), and *Gettysburg: The Final Fury* (1974). This essay is a chapter of *The American Story* (1956), a collection of essays by noted historians.

1   When Ulysses S. Grant and Robert E. Lee met in the parlor of a modest house at Appomattox Court House, Virginia, on April 9, 1865, to work out the terms for the surrender of Lee's Army of Northern Virginia, a great chapter in American life came to a close, and a great new chapter began.

2   These men were bringing the Civil War to its virtual finish. To be sure, other armies had yet to surrender, and for a few days the fugitive Confederate government would struggle desperately and vainly, trying to find some way to go on living now that its chief

* To help you read these essays analytically, review pages 170–172.

support was gone. But in effect it was all over when Grant and Lee signed the papers. And the little room where they wrote out the terms was the scene of one of the poignant, dramatic contrasts in American history.

3   They were two strong men, these oddly different generals, and they represented the strengths of two conflicting currents that, through them, had come into final collision.

4   Back of Robert E. Lee was the notion that the old aristocratic concept might some-how survive and be dominant in American life.

5   Lee was tidewater Virginia, and in his background were family, culture, and tradition . . . the age of chivalry transplanted to a New World which was making its own legends and its own myths. He embodied a way of life that had come down through the age of knighthood and the English country squire. America was a land that was beginning all over again, dedicated to nothing much more complicated than the rather hazy belief that all men had equal rights, and should have an equal chance in the world. In such a land Lee stood for the feeling that it was somehow of advantage to human society to have a pronounced inequality in the social structure. There should be a leisure class, backed by ownership of land; in turn, society itself should be keyed to the land as the chief source of wealth and influence. It would bring forth (according to this ideal) a class of men with a strong sense of obligation to the community; men who lived not to gain advantage for themselves, but to meet the solemn obligations which had been laid on them by the very fact that they were privileged. From them the country would get its leadership; to them it could look for the higher values—of thought, of conduct, of personal deportment—to give it strength and virtue.

6   Lee embodied the noblest elements of this aristocratic ideal. Through him, the landed nobility justified itself. For four years, the Southern states had fought a desperate war to uphold the ideals for which Lee stood. In the end, it almost seemed as if the Confederacy fought for Lee; as if he himself was the Confederacy . . . the best thing that the way of life for which the Confederacy stood could ever have to offer. He had passed into legend before Appomattox. Thousands of tired, underfed, poorly clothed Confederate soldiers, long-since past the simple enthusiasm of the early days of the struggle, somehow considered Lee the symbol of everything for which they had been willing to die. But they could not quite put this feeling into words. If the Lost Cause, sanctified by so much heroism and so many deaths, had a living justification, its justification was General Lee.

7   Grant, the son of a tanner on the Western frontier, was everything Lee was not. He had come up the hard way, and embodied nothing in particular except the eternal toughness and sinewy fiber of the men who grew up beyond the mountains. He was one of a body of men who owed reverence and obeisance to no one, who were self-reliant to a fault, who cared hardly anything for the past but who had a sharp eye for the future.

8   These frontier men were the precise opposites of the tidewater aristocrats. Back of them, in the great surge that had taken people over the Alleghenies and into the opening Western country, there was a deep, implicit dissatisfaction with a past that had settled into grooves. They stood for democracy, not from any reasoned conclu-sion about the proper ordering of human society, but simply because they had grown up in the middle of democracy and knew how it worked. Their society might have privileges, but they would be privileges each man had won for himself. Forms and pat-terns meant nothing. No man was born to anything, except perhaps to a chance to show how far he could rise. Life was competition.

9   Yet along with this feeling had come a deep sense of belonging to a national community. The Westerner who developed a farm, opened a shop, or set up in business as a trader could hope to prosper only as his own community prospered—and his community ran from the Atlantic to the Pacific and from Canada down to Mexico. If the land was settled, with towns and highways and accessible markets, he could better himself. He saw his fate in terms of the nation's own destiny. As its horizons expanded, so did his. He had, in other words, an acute dollars-and-cents stake in the continued growth and development of his country.

10   And that, perhaps, is where the contrast between Grant and Lee becomes most striking. The Virginia aristocrat, inevitably, saw himself in relation to his own region. He lived in a static society which could endure almost anything except change. Instinctively, his first loyalty would go to the locality in which that society existed. He would fight to the limit of endurance to defend it, because in defending it he was defending everything that gave his own life its deepest meaning.

11   The Westerner, on the other hand, would fight with an equal tenacity for the broader concept of society. He fought so because everything he lived by was tied to growth, expansion, and a constantly widening horizon. What he lived by would survive or fall with the nation itself. He could not possibly stand by unmoved in the face of an attempt to destroy the Union. He would combat it with everything he had, because he could only see it as an effort to cut the ground out from under his feet.

12   So Grant and Lee were in complete contrast, representing two diametrically opposed elements in American life. Grant was the modern man emerging; beyond him, ready to come on the stage, was the great age of steel and machinery, of crowded cities and a restless, burgeoning vitality. Lee might have ridden down from the old age of chivalry, lance in hand, silken banner fluttering over his head. Each man was the perfect champion of his cause, drawing both his strengths and his weaknesses from the people he led.

13   Yet it was not all contrast, after all. Different as they were—in background, in personality, in underlying aspiration—these two great soldiers had much in common. Under everything else, they were marvelous fighters. Furthermore, their fighting qualities were really very much alike.

14   Each man had, to begin with, the great virtue of utter tenacity and fidelity. Grant fought his way down the Mississippi Valley in spite of acute personal discouragement and profound military handicaps. Lee hung on in the trenches at Petersburg after hope itself had died. In each man there was an indomitable quality . . . the born fighter's refusal to give up as long as he can still remain on his feet and lift his two fists.

15   Daring and resourcefulness they had, too; the ability to think faster and move faster than the enemy. These were the qualities which gave Lee the dazzling campaigns of Second Manassas and Chancellorsville and won Vicksburg for Grant.

16   Lastly, and perhaps greatest of all, there was the ability, at the end, to turn quickly from war to peace once the fighting was over. Out of the way these two men behaved at Appomattox came the possibility of a peace of reconciliation. It was a possibility not wholly realized, in the years to come, but which did, in the end, help the two sections to become one nation again . . . after a war whose bitterness might have seemed to make such a reunion wholly impossible. No part of either man's life became him more than the part he played in their brief meeting in the McLean house at Appomattox.

Their behavior there put all succeeding generations of Americans in their debt. Two great Americans, Grant and Lee—very different, yet under everything very much alike. Their encounter at Appomattox was one of the great moments of American history.

Questions on Content, Style, and Structure

1. What is Catton's thesis?

2. According to Catton, how did Lee view society? Summarize the aristocratic ideal that Lee symbolized.

3. Who did Grant represent? How did they view the country's social structure?

4. After carefully studying paragraphs 4 through 16, describe the pattern of organization Catton uses to present his discussion.

5. What new means of development begins in paragraph 13?

6. How does Catton avoid the choppy seesaw effect as he compares and contrasts his subjects? Point out ways in which Catton makes a smooth transition from point to point.

7. Evaluate Catton's ability to write unified, coherent paragraphs with clearly stated topic sentences. Are his paragraphs adequately developed with enough specific detail? Cite evidence to support your answer.

8. What is the advantage or disadvantage of having only one sentence in paragraph 3? In paragraph 4?

9. What is Catton's opinion of these men? Select words and passages to support your answer. How does Catton's attitude affect the tone of this essay? Is his tone appropriate? Why or why not?

10. Instead of including a separate paragraph, Catton presents his concluding remarks in paragraph 16, in which he discusses his last major point about Grant and Lee. Many essays lacking concluding paragraphs end too abruptly or merely trail off; how does Catton avoid these weaknesses?

Suggestions for Writing

Try using Bruce Catton's "Grant and Lee: A Study in Contrasts" as a stepping-stone to your writing. Comparing public figures is a familiar activity. People often discuss the styles and merits of various politicians, writers, business leaders, humanitarians, sports celebrities, and media stars. Write your own essay about two public figures who interest you. Similar or different, these people may have lived in the same times (Winston Churchill and Franklin D. Roosevelt, Ernest Hemingway and F. Scott Fitzgerald, Babe Didrikson Zaharias and Babe Ruth), or you might choose two people from different eras (Clara Barton and Mother Teresa, Mozart and Madonna, Susan B. Anthony and Cesar Chavez, Harriet Tubman and Martin Luther King, Jr.). The possibilities are endless and thought-provoking; use your essay to make an interesting specific point about the fascinating (and perhaps heretofore unrecognized) differences/similarities between the people you choose.

Vocabulary

chivalry (5)   tenacity (11)   indomitable (14)
deportment (5)   diametrically (12)   reconciliation (16)
embodied (6)   burgeoning (12)

II. The Block Pattern

■ Two Ways of Viewing the River

Samuel Clemens

Samuel Clemens, whose pen name was Mark Twain, is regarded as one of America's most outstanding writers. Well known for his humorous stories and books, Twain was also a pioneer of fictional realism and local color. His most famous novel, *The Adventures of Huckleberry Finn* (1884), is often hailed as a masterpiece. This selection is from the autobiographical book *Life on the Mississippi* (1883), which recounts Clemens's job as a riverboat pilot.

1   Now when I had mastered the language of this water and had come to know every trifling feature that bordered the great river as familiarly as I knew the letters of the alphabet, I had made a valuable acquisition. But I had lost something, too. I had lost something which could never be restored to me while I lived. All the grace, the beauty, the poetry, had gone out of the majestic river! I still kept in mind a certain wonderful sunset which I witnessed when steamboating was new to me. A broad expanse of the river was turned to blood; in the middle distance the red hue brightened into gold, through which a solitary log came floating, black and conspicuous; in one place a long, slanting mark lay sparkling upon the water; in another the surface was broken by boiling, tumbling rings, that were as many-tinted as an opal; where the ruddy flush was faintest, was a smooth spot that was covered with graceful circles and radiating lines, ever so delicately traced; the shore on our left was densely wooded and the somber shadow that fell from this forest was broken in one place by a long, ruffled trail that shone like silver; and high above the forest wall a clean-stemmed dead tree waved a single leafy bough that glowed like a flame in the unobstructed splendor that was flowing from the sun. There were graceful curves, reflected images, woody heights, soft distances, and over the whole scene, far and near, the dissolving lights drifted steadily, enriching it every passing moment with new marvels of coloring.

2   I stood like one bewitched. I drank it in, in a speechless rapture. The world was new to me and I had never seen anything like this at home. But as I have said, a day came when I began to cease from noting the glories and the charms which the moon and the sun and the twilight wrought upon the river's face; another day came when I ceased altogether to note them. Then, if that sunset scene had been repeated, I should have looked upon it without rapture, and should have commented upon it inwardly after this fashion: "This sun means that we are going to have wind tomorrow; that floating log means that the river is rising, small thanks to it; that slanting mark on the water refers to a bluff reef which is going to kill somebody's steamboat one of these nights, if it keeps on stretching out like that; those tumbling 'boils' show a dissolving bar and a changing channel there; the lines and circles in the slick water over yonder are a warning that that

troublesome place is shoaling up dangerously; that silver streak in the shadow of the forest is the 'break' from a new snag and he has located himself in the very best place he could have found to fish for steamboats; that tall dead tree, with a single living branch, is not going to last long, and then how is a body ever going to get through this blind place at night without the friendly old landmark?"

3   No, the romance and beauty were all gone from the river. All the value any feature of it had for me now was the amount of usefulness it could furnish toward compassing the safe piloting of a steamboat. Since those days, I have pitied doctors from my heart. What does the lovely flush in a beauty's cheek mean to a doctor but a "break" that ripples above some deadly disease? Are not all her visible charms sown thick with what are to him the signs and symbols of hidden decay? Does he ever see her beauty at all, or doesn't he simply view her professionally and comment upon her unwholesome condition all to himself? And doesn't he sometimes wonder whether he has gained most or lost most by learning his trade?

Questions on Content, Structure, and Style

1. What is Clemens contrasting in this essay? Identify his thesis.

2. What organizational pattern does he choose? Why is this an appropriate choice for his purpose?

3. How does Clemens make a smooth transition to his later view of the river?

4. Why does Clemens refer to doctors in paragraph 3?

5. What is the purpose of the questions in paragraph 3? Why is the last question especially important?

6. Characterize the language Clemens uses in his description in paragraph 1. Is his diction appropriate?

7. Point out several examples of similes in paragraph 1. What do they add to the description of the sunset?

8. How does the language in the description in paragraph 2 differ from the diction in paragraph 1? What view of the river is emphasized there?

9. Identify an example of personification in paragraph 2. Why did Clemens add it to his description?

10. Describe the tone of this essay. Does it ever shift?

Suggestions for Writing

Try using Samuel Clemens' "Two Ways of Viewing the River" as a stepping-stone to your own writing. Consider, as Clemens did, writing about a subject before and after you experienced it from a more technically informed point of view. Did your appreciation of your grandmother's quilt increase after you realized how much skill went into making it? Did a starry night have a different appeal after your astronomy course? Did your admiration of a story or poem diminish or increase after you studied its craft? Clemens felt a certain loss came with his expertise, but was this the case in your experience?

Vocabulary

trifling (1)	ruddy (1)
acquisition (1)	wrought (2)
conspicuous (1)	compassing (3)

■ A REVISION WORKSHEET

As you write your rough drafts, consult Chapter 5 for guidance through the revision process. In addition, here are a few questions to ask yourself as you revise your comparison/contrast essay:

1. Does the essay contain a thesis that makes a significant point instead of a "so-what" thesis?

2. Is the material organized into the best pattern for the subject matter?

3. If the essay is developed by the Point-by-Point Pattern, are there enough transitional words used to avoid the see-saw effect?

4. If the essay is developed by the Block Pattern, are there enough transitional devices and references connecting the two subjects to avoid the split-essay problem?

5. Are the points of comparison/contrast presented in a logical, consistent order that the reader can follow easily?

6. Are both subjects given a reasonably balanced treatment?

7. Are both subjects developed in enough specific detail so that the reader clearly understands the comparison or contrast? Where might more detail be added?

After you've revised your essay extensively, you might exchange rough drafts with a classmate and answer these questions for each other, making specific suggestions for improvement wherever appropriate. (For advice on productive participation in classroom workshops, see pages 108–111.)

A Special Kind of Comparison: The Analogy

In the last few pages of this text, you've learned about essays developed by comparison/contrast, which generally point out similarities and differences between two things with enough common ground to merit meaningful discussion (two apartments, two computers, a book and its movie, etc.). In comparison/contrast essays, two subjects ("X" and "Y") are explained to make a point. An *analogy* is slightly different: it is a comparison that uses one thing ("X") only to clarify or argue a second thing ("Y"). In an analogy, one element is the main focus of attention.

You've probably heard several colorful analogies this week. Perhaps a friend who holds a hectic, dead-end job has tried to explain life at that moment by comparing herself to a crazed gerbil on a cage treadmill—always running, getting nowhere, feeling trapped in a never-changing environment. Or perhaps your science teacher explained the behavior of cancer cells by comparing them in several ways to an invading army on a destructive mission. If you read the Preface to this text, you were asked to see your writing instructor as a coach who helps you practice your skills, gives constructive criticism, and encourages your successes. Analogies are plentiful in our conversations and in both our reading and writing.

Writers often find analogies useful in three ways:

1. *To clarify and explain:* Most often writers use analogies to clarify an abstract, unfamiliar, or complex element by comparing it to something that is familiar to the reader, often something that is more concrete or easier to understand. For example, raising children has often been compared to nourishing baby birds, with parents feeding and nurturing but ultimately nudging offspring out of the nest. A relationship might be explained as having grown from a seed that eventually blossomed into a flower (or a weed!). Popular novelist Stephen King has used a roller coaster analogy to explain some people's enjoyment of horror movies.

Frequently, scientific and medical topics profit from analogies that a general audience of readers can more readily understand. A technical discussion of the human eye, for instance, might be explained using the analogy of a camera lens; photosynthesis might compared to the process of baking bread. One biology teacher explains the semipermeability of a cell membrane with a football analogy: the offensive line wants to let out the running back with the ball but keep the defensive line in. In short, analogies can make new or difficult material easier to grasp.

2. *To argue and persuade:* Writers often use analogies to try to convince their audience that what is true about "X" would also be true about "Y" because the two elements have so many important similarities. For example, someone against new anti-drug laws might argue that they are similar to those passed under Prohibition, the banning of alcohol in the 1930s, and thus the drug laws are doomed to failure. Or perhaps a NASA official might argue for more money for space exploration by comparing trips into outer space with those expeditions to the New World by explorers such as Columbus. How convincing an analogy is depends to a large extent on how similar the two elements appear to be. Remember, however, that analogies by themselves cannot *prove* anything; they can merely suggest similarities between two cases or things.

3. *To dramatize or capture an image:* Writers (and speakers) often use analogies because they wish their audience to remember a particular point or to see something in a new way. Using a vivid analogy—sometimes referred to as an extended metaphor or simile—can effectively impress an image upon the reader or listener's mind ("Using crack is like burning down your own house. And the insurance policy ran out a long time ago . . ."). Analogies can be enjoyable too for their sheer inventiveness and their colorful language. Perhaps one of the most well-known analogies in American literature is Thoreau's description, in *Walden*, of a battle between two ant colonies, with the tiny creatures drawn as rival warriors fighting to the death in classical epic style. Analogies may even be used for comic effect in appropriate situations (moving into your basement apartment in sweltering August heat as analogous to a trip to the Underworld, for instance). Fresh, creative analogies can delight your readers and hold their attention.

Although analogies can be helpful and memorable, they can also present problems if they are trite, unclear, or illogical. Analogies can be especially harmful to a writer's credibility in an argument if readers don't see enough logical similarities to make the comparison convincing. Some faulty analogies may seem acceptable on first glance but fall apart when the details of the comparison are considered closely. For example, perhaps you have seen a bumper sticker that reads "Giving money and power to the government is like giving whisky and car keys to teenage boys." Are the two situations really alike? Do government agencies/officials and adolescents share many similarities in maturity, experience, and goals? Does financial support have the same effect as alcohol? If too many points of comparison are weak, readers will not find the analogy persuasive. Or perhaps you have read that "America is like a lifeboat already full of people; letting in more immigrants will cause the boat to sink." If readers do not accept the major premise—that America, a country with many renewable resources, closely resembles a lifeboat, a confined space with unchanging dimensions—they are likely to reject the argument.

Also beware those writers who try to substitute an analogy in place of any other kind of evidence to support their points in an argument, and be especially suspicious of those using analogies as "scare tactics" ("This proposed legislation is just like laws passed in Nazi Germany"). As a writer, use only those analogies that will help your reader understand, remember, or accept your ideas; as a reader, always protect yourself by questioning the validity of the analogy offered to you. (For more on *faulty analogy* as a logical fallacy, see page 289.)

To illustrate use of analogy, here are three examples from professional writers. In each case, what was the writer's purpose? How is "X" used to clarify or argue for "Y"? Which of these analogies do you find the most effective, and why?

> A good lab course is an exercise in *doing* science. As such it differs totally in mission from a good lecture course where the object is learning *about* science. In the same way that one can gain vastly greater insight into music by learning to play an instrument, one can experience the doing of science only by going into the lab and trying one's hand at measurement.
>
> —Miles Pickering, "Are Lab Courses a Waste of Time?"

> For a long time now, since the beginning, in fact, men and women have been sparring and dancing around with each other, each pair trying to get it together and boogie to the tune called Life. For some people, it was always a glide, filled with grace and ease. For most of us, it is a stumble and a struggle, always trying to figure out the next step, until we find a partner whose inconsistencies seem to fit with ours, and the two of us fit into some kind of rhythm. Some couples wind up struggling and pulling at cross purposes; and of course, some people never get out on the floor, just stand alone in the corners, looking hard at the dancers.
>
> — Jay Molishever, "Changing Expectations of Marriage"

> One afternoon while we were there at that lake a thunderstorm came up. It was like the revival of an old melodrama that I had seen long ago with childish awe. The second-act climax of the drama of the electrical disturbance over a lake in America had not changed in any important respect. This was the big scene, still the big scene. The whole thing was so familiar, the first feeling of oppression and heat and a general air around camp of not wanting to go very far away. In midafternoon (it was all the same) a curious darkening of the sky, and a lull in everything that had made life tick; and then the way the boats suddenly swung the other way at their moorings with the coming of a breeze out of the new quarter, and the premonitory rumble. Then the kettle drum, then the snare, then the bass drum and cymbals, then crackling

light against the dark. . . . Afterward the calm, the rain steadily rustling in the calm lake, the return of light and hope and spirits, and the campers running out in joy.

—E. B. White, "Once More to the Lake"

Analogies come in a variety of lengths, from several sentences to an entire essay, depending upon the writer's purpose. As you practice your writing in this composition class, you may find that incorporating an analogy into one of your essays is an effective way to explain, emphasize, or help support an idea. (For more discussion, see page 289.)

Reviewing Your Progress

After you have completed your essay developed by comparison/contrast, take a moment to measure your progress as a writer by responding to the following questions. Such analysis will help you to recognize growth in your writing skills and may enable you to identify areas that are still problematic.

1. Which part of your essay do you like the best? Why?

2. Which point of comparison or contrast do you think is the most successful? Why is it effective?

3. What part of your essay gave you the most trouble? How did you overcome the problem?

4. If you had more time to work on this essay, what would receive additional attention? Why?

5. What did you learn about your topic from writing this essay? About yourself as a writer?

■ Strategy Four: Development by Definition

Frequently in conversation we must stop to ask, "What do you mean by that?" because in some cases our failure to comprehend just one particular term may lead to total misunderstanding. Suppose, for example, in a discussion with a friend, you refer to a new law as a piece of "liberal legislation"; if you and your friend do not share the same definition of "liberal," your remark may be completely misinterpreted. Here's another example: if you ask your grandparents for some dead presidents because you're in desperate need of new bling, will they know to open their wallets for your shopping trip? In other words, a clear understanding of terms or ideas is often essential to meaningful communication.

Sometimes a dictionary definition or a one- or two-sentence explanation is all a term needs (Hemingway, for example, once defined courage as "grace under pressure"). And sometimes a brief, humorous definition can cut right to the heart of the matter (comedian Robin Williams, for instance, once defined "cocaine" as "God's way of saying you're making too much money").*

---

* Even graffiti employ definition. One bathroom wall favorite: "Death is Nature's way of telling you to slow down." Another, obviously written by an English major: "A double negative is a no-no."

Frequently, however, you will find it necessary to provide an *extended definition*—that is, a longer, more detailed explanation that thoroughly defines the subject. Essays of extended definitions are quite common; think, for instance, of the articles you've seen on "mercy killing," "assisted suicide," or abortion that define "life" in a variety of ways. Other recent essays have grappled with defining such complex concepts as free speech, animal rights, pornography, affirmative action, and gun control.

Many national discussions center on controversial definitions. Following the events of September 11, 2001, the "War on Terrorism" has produced a host of terms whose meanings are frequently debated. For example, does legislation such as the USA Patriot Act ensure "homeland security" or legitimize unlawful invasions of privacy? Is "racial profiling" acceptable in the search for terrorists? Is it "patriotic" to oppose military actions of one's country? What is the difference between a "political prisoner," a "detainee," and a "prisoner of war"? Is the CIA involved in "extraordinary rendition," the practice of sending suspects to "black sites" in other countries for extreme, and possibly unlawful, interrogation? Today, perhaps more than ever, we need to clearly understand specific meanings of language before we can make intelligent choices or take appropriate actions.

Why Do We Define?

Essays of extended definition are usually written for one or more of the following reasons:

1. To clarify an abstract term or concept ("hero," "success," "friendship," "loyalty")

2. To provide a personal interpretation of a term that the writer feels is vague, controversial, misused, or misunderstood ("feminist," "eco-terrorist," "Feng Shui," "multiculturalism")

3. To explain a new or unusual term or phrase found in popular culture, slang, dialect, or within a particular geographic area or cultural group ("hip hop," "helicopter parent," "McJobs," "metrosexual," "lagniappe")

4. To make understandable the language or technical terms of a particular field of study, a profession, or an industry ("deconstruction," "identity spoofing," "retinitis pigmentosa," "accelerated amortization")

5. To offer information about a term or an idea to a particular interested audience (antique collectors learning about "Depression glass," movie buffs understanding "film noir")

6. To inform and entertain by presenting the colorful history, uses, effects, or examples of a word, expression, or concept ("comfort food," "Zydeco music," "urban legends," "Kwanzaa")

Developing Your Essay

Here are four suggestions to help you prepare your essay of extended definition:

Know your purpose. Sometimes we need to define a term as clearly and objectively as possible. As a laboratory assistant, for instance, you might need to explain a technical measuring instrument to a group of new students. At other times, however, we may wish to persuade as well as inform our readers. People's interpretations of words, especially abstract or controversial terms, can, and often do, differ greatly depending on their point of view. After all, one person's protest march can be another person's street riot. Consequently, before you begin writing, decide on your purpose. If your readers need objective information only, make your definition as unbiased as you can; if your goal is to convince them that your point of view is the right or best one, you may adopt a variety of persuasive techniques as well as subjective language. For example, readers of a paper entitled "Doc in the Box" should quickly realize that they are not getting an objective treatment of the twenty-four-hour emergency-care offices springing up around the country.

Give your readers a reason to read.   One way to introduce your subject is to explain the previous use, misuse, or misunderstanding of the term; then present your new or better interpretation of the term or concept. An introduction and thesis defining a new word in popular usage might state, "Although people who suffer from weak immune systems might suddenly fear breathing the same air as someone suffering from affluenza, they needn't worry. 'Affluenza' isn't germ-laden; it's simply a colorful term describing the out-of-control consumerism spreading like an epidemic through America today." Or consider this introduction and thesis aimed at a word the writer feels is unclear to many readers: "When the credits roll at the end of a movie, much of the audience may be perplexed to see the job of 'best boy' listed. No, the 'best boy' isn't the nicest kid on the set—he (or she) is, in fact, the key electrician's first assistant, who helps arrange the lights for the movie's director of photography."

Keep your audience in mind to anticipate and avoid problems of clarity.   Because you are trying to present a new or improved definition, you must strive above all for clarity. Ask yourself, "Who is my intended audience? What terms or parts of my definition are strange to them?" You don't help your audience, for example, by defining one campus slang expression in terms of other bits of unfamiliar slang. If, in other words, you discuss "mouse potatoes" as "Google bombers," you may be confusing some readers more than you are informing them. If your assignment doesn't specify a particular audience, you may find it useful to imagine one. You might pretend, for instance, that you're defining current campus slang for your parents, clarifying a local expression for a foreign visitor, or explaining a computer innovation to a technophobic friend. Remember that your definition is effective only if your explanation is clear not just to you but to those unfamiliar with the term or concept under discussion.

Use as many strategies as necessary to clarify your definition.   Depending on your subject, you may use any number of the following methods in your essay to define your term:

1. Describe the parts or distinguishing characteristics*

2. Offer some examples

3. Compare to or contrast with similar terms

4. Explain an operation or a process

5. State some familiar synonyms

---

* With some topics, it may also be useful to describe the genus, class, or species to which the subject belongs.

6. Define by negation (that is, tell what the term doesn't mean)

7. Present the history or trace its development or changes from the original linguistical meaning

8. Discuss causes or effects

9. Identify times/places of use or appearance

10. Associate it with recognizable people, places, or ideas

To illustrate some of the methods suggested here, let's suppose you wanted to write an extended definition of "crossover" country music. You might choose several of these methods:

- Describe the parts: lyrics, musical sound, instruments, typical subject matter
- Compare to or contrast with other kinds of music, such as traditional country music, Western swing, or "pop"
- Give some examples of famous "crossover" country songs and artists
- Trace its historical development from traditional country music to its present state

In the paper on "crossover" country music or in any definition essay, you should, of course, use only those methods that will best define your term. Never include methods purely for the sake of exhibiting a variety of techniques. You, the writer, must decide which method or methods work best, which should receive the most emphasis, and in which order the chosen methods of definition should appear.

Problems to Avoid

Here is a list of "don't's" for the writer of extended definition essays:

Don't present an incomplete definition. An inadequate definition is often the result of choosing a subject too broad or complex for your essay. You probably can't, for instance, do a good job of defining "twentieth-century modern art" in all its varieties in a short essay; you might, however, introduce your reader to some specific school of modern art, such as cubism or surrealism. Always narrow your subject to a manageable size and then define it as thoroughly as possible.

Don't begin every definition essay by quoting Webster. If you must include a standard definition of your term, try to find a unique way of blending it into your discussion, perhaps as a point of contrast to your explanation of the word's meaning. Dictionary definitions are generally so overused as opening sentences that they can drive composition teachers to seek more interesting jobs, such as measuring spaghetti in a pasta factory. Don't bore your audience to death; it's a terrible way to go.

Don't define vaguely or by using generalities. As always, use specific, vivid details to explain your subject. If, for example, you define a shamrock as "a green plant with three leaves," you have also described hundreds of other plants, including poison ivy.

Consequently, you must select details that will make your subject distinct from any other. Including concrete examples is frequently useful in any essay but especially so when you are defining an abstract term, such as "pride," "patriotism," or "prejudice." To make your definition both interesting and clear, always add as many precise details as possible. (For a review of using specific, colorful language, see pages 119–120, 132–133, and 153–156.)

Don't offer circular definitions. To define a poet as "one who writes poetry" or the American Dream as "the dream most Americans hold dear" is about as helpful as a doctor telling a patient, "Your illness is primarily a lack of good health." Explain your subject; don't just rename it.

▪ ESSAY TOPICS

Here are several suggestions for terms whose meanings are often unclear. Narrow any topic that seems too broad for your assignment, and decide before writing whether your definition will be objective or subjective. (Student writers, by the way, often note that abstract concepts are harder to define than the more concrete subjects, so proceed at your own risk, and remember to use plenty of specific detail in your essay.) For additional ideas, turn to the "Suggestions for Writing" section following the professional essay (page 247).

1. A current slang, campus, local, or popular culture expression
2. A term from your field of study
3. A slob (or some other undesirable kind of roommate or friend)
4. Success or failure
5. A good/bad teacher, clerk, coach, friend, parent, date, or spouse
6. Heroism or cowardice
7. A term from science or technology
8. A kind of music, painting, architecture, or dance
9. A social label ("Goth," "Prep," "Skater," etc.)
10. A current fad or style or one from the past
11. A rebel or conformist
12. A family or hometown expression
13. A good/bad restaurant, store, movie theater, nightspot, class
14. Self-respect
15. Prejudice or discrimination
16. An important historical movement or group
17. A controversial political idea or term
18. A term from a hobby or sport

19. A medical term or condition

20. Select a painting or photograph in which you think the artist offers a visual definition of the subject matter. Explain this definition by examining the artist's choice and arrangement of details in the picture. (For example, study George Tooker's painting *The Subway*. What definition of urban life is being presented here? What parts of the picture illustrate and clarify this point of view? Or consider another picture in this text, such as *Migrant Mother* [page 330], *The Scream* [page 113], *The Persistence of Memory* [page 474], or *The Two Fridas* [page 475]).

© 2000, Whitney Museum of American Art. Collection of the Whitney Museum of American Art, New York. Photography by Geoffrey Clements, NY.

The Subway, 1950, by George Tooker

A Topic Proposal for Your Essay

Selecting the right subject matter is important to every writer. To help you clarify your ideas and strengthen your commitment to your topic, here is a proposal sheet that asks you to describe some of your ideas about your subject before you begin drafting. Although your ideas may change as you write (they will almost certainly become more refined), thinking through your topic now may help you avoid several false starts.

1. What subject will your essay define? Will you define this subject objectively or subjectively? Why?

2. Why are you interested in this topic? Do you have a personal or professional connection to the subject? State at least one reason for your choice of topic.

3. Is this a significant topic of interest to others? Why? Who specifically might find it interesting, informative, or entertaining?

4. Is your subject a controversial, ambiguous, or new term? What will readers gain by understanding this term as defined from your point of view?

5. Writers use a variety of techniques to define terms. At this point, list at least two techniques you think you might use to help readers understand your topic.

6. What difficulties, if any, can you foresee during the drafting of this essay? For example, do you need to do any additional reading or interviewing to collect information for your definition?

■ Sample Student Essay

A student with an interest in running wrote the following essay defining "runner's high." Note that he uses several methods to define his subject, one that is difficult to explain to those who have not experienced it firsthand.

BLIND PACES

Introduction: An example and a general definition of the term

1   After running the Mile-Hi ten-kilometer race in my hometown, I spoke with several of the leading runners about their experiences in the race. While most of them agreed that the course, which passed through a beautifully wooded yet overly hilly country area, was difficult, they also agreed that it was one of the best races of their running careers. They could not, however, explain why it was such a wonderful race but could rather only mumble something about the tall trees, cool air, and sandy path. When pressed, most of them didn't even remember specific details about the course, except the start and finish, and ended their descriptions with a blank—but content—stare. This self-satisfied, yet almost indescribable, feeling is often the result of an experienced runner running, a feeling often called, because of its similarities to other euphoric experiences, "runner's high."

2   Because this experience is seemingly impossible to define, perhaps a description of what runner's high is not might, by contrast, lead to a

better understanding of what it is. I clearly remember—about five years ago—when I first took up running. My first day, I donned my tennis shorts, ragged T-shirt, and white discount-store tennis shoes somewhat ashamedly, knowing that they were symbolic of my novice status. I plodded around my block—just over a half mile—in a little more than four minutes, feeling and regretting every painful step. My shins and thighs revolted at every jarring move, and my lungs wheezed uncontrollably, gasping for air, yet denied that basic necessity. Worst of all, I was conscious of every aspect of my existence—from the swinging of my arms to the slap of my feet on the road, and from the sweat dripping into my eyes and ears and mouth, to the frantic inhaling and exhaling of my lungs. I kept my eyes carefully peeled on the horizon or the next turn in the road, judging how far away it was, how long it would take me to get there, and how much torture was left before I reached home. These first few runs were, of course, the worst—as far from any euphoria or "high" as possible. They did, however, slowly become easier as my body became accustomed to running.

Definition by negation, contrast

3   After a few months, in fact, I felt serious enough about this new pursuit to invest in a pair of real running shoes and shorts. Admittedly, these changes added to the comfort of my endeavor, but it wasn't until two full years later that the biggest change occurred—and I experienced my first real "high." It was a fall day. The air was a cool sixty-five degrees, the sun was shining intently, the sky was a clear, crisp blue, and a few dead leaves were scattered across the browning lawn. I stepped out onto the road and headed north towards a nearby park for my routine jog. The next thing I remember, however, was not my run through the park, but rather my return, some forty-two minutes and six miles later, to my house. I woke, as if out of a dream, just as I slowed to a walk, cooling down from my run. The only memory I had of my run

Personal example

was a feeling of floating on air—as if my real self was somewhere above and detached from my body, looking down on my physical self as it went through its blind paces. At first, I felt scared—what if I had run out in front of a car? Would I have even known it? I felt as if I had been asleep or out of control, that my brain had, in some real sense, been turned off.

4   Now, after five years of running and hundreds of such mystical experiences, I realize that I had never lost control while in this euphoric state—and that my brain hadn't been turned off, or, at least, not completely. But what does happen is hard to prove. George Sheehan, in a column for Runner's World, suggests that "altered states," such as runner's high, result from the loss of conscious control, from the temporary cessation of left-brain messages and the

dominance of right-brain activity (the left hemisphere being the seat of reason and rationality; the right, of emotions and inherited archetypal feelings) (14). Another explanation comes from Dr. Jerry Lynch, who argues, in his book The Total Runner, that the "high" results from the secretion of natural opiates, called beta endorphins, in the brain (213). My own explanation draws on both these medical

explanations and is perhaps slightly more mystical. It's just possible that indeed natural opiates do go to work and consequently our brains lose track of the ins and outs of everyday activities—of jobs and classes and responsibilities. And because of this relaxed, drugged state, we are able to reach down into something more fundamental, something that ties us not only to each other but to all creation, here and gone. We rejoin nature, rediscovering the thread that links us to the universe.

5   My explanation is, of course, unscientific and therefore suspect. But I found myself, that day of the Mile-Hi Ten K run, eagerly trying to discuss my experience with the other runners: I wanted desperately to discover

where I had been and what I had been doing during the race for which I received my first trophy. I didn't discover the answer from my fellow runners that day, but it didn't matter. I'm still running and still feeling the glow—whatever it is.

Conclusion: An incomplete understanding doesn't hamper enjoyment

WORKS CITED*

Lynch, Jerry. <u>The Total Runner: A Complete Mind-Body Guide to Optimal Performance</u>. Englewood Cliffs, NJ: Prentice Hall, 1987.

Sheehan, George. "Altered States." <u>Runner's World</u>. Aug. 1988: 14.

Professional Essay†

■ The Munchausen Mystery

Don R. Lipsitt

As a clinical professor of psychiatry at Harvard Medical School, Don R. Lipsitt has written over one hundred articles on mental health and coedited four books, including *Hypochondriasis: Modern Perspectives on an Ancient Malady* (2001) and the *Handbook of Studies on General Hospital Psychiatry* (1991). In 2001 he was awarded a Lifetime Achievement Award from the Association of Academic Psychiatry. He published this article in *Psychology Today* in 1983.

1   In Thomas Mann's *Confessions of Felix Krull, Confidence Man*, young Felix fabricates an illness and convinces both his mother and the family doctor that he is sick. Felix describes the intense pleasure that his performance brings him. "I was delirious with the alternate tension and relaxation necessary to give reality, in my own eyes and others, to a condition that did not exist."

2   I estimate that in any given year in the United States, every general hospital with 100 or more beds admits an average of two patients who deliberately mimic symptoms of disease so convincingly that they deceive reasonably competent physicians. The patients' ages range from 11 to 60, but most are men in their 20s and 30s. Often these strange imposters wander from hospital to hospital, but even if we count only one patient per hospital, we are left with the staggering figure of approximately 4,000 people each year who devote their energies to fooling medical practitioners.

---

* Editor's note: In a formal research paper, the "Works Cited" list appears on a separate page.

† To help you read this essay analytically, review pages 170–172.

If each incurs a cost of $1,000 to $10,000—bills that are not unusual, and that are rarely paid—the annual drain on health services alone is between $4 million and $40 million.

3   What do these people hope to gain? Nothing more, experience and research suggest, than the opportunity to assume the role of patient—in some cases, all the way to the operating table.

4   Unlike hypochondriacs, who really believe that they are ill, these people intentionally use varied and often sophisticated deceptions to duplicate medical problems. These deceptions include: blood "spit up" from a rubber pouch concealed in the mouth; genital bleeding deliberately caused by sharp objects; hypoglycemia (low blood sugar) induced by insulin injections; and skin infections or abscesses caused by injecting oneself with feces, sputum, or laboratory cultures of bacteria. A patient who called himself "the Duncan Hines of American hospitals" logged about 400 admissions in 25 years. Another patient, dubbed the "Indiana cyclone," was hospitalized in at least 12 states and two countries. The dramatic fabrication and extensive wandering often observed in such individuals prompted the late British physician Richard Asher in 1951 to label their "condition" the Munchausen Syndrome, after a flamboyant 18th-century teller of tall tales fictionalized in *The Adventures of Baron von Munchausen*, by Rudolph Erich Raspe. But as Asher himself came to realize, the name is somewhat misleading. While stories of the Baron's escapades are always palpably absurd, the accounts of patients whose condition bears his name are generally quite feasible. "Indeed," says Asher, "it is the credibility of their stories that makes these patients such a perpetual and tedious problem."

5   For obvious reasons, Munchausen patients have been difficult to study—they usually flee once their fictions are exposed. But research to this point provides a minimal portrait. In addition to being primarily men in their 20s and 30s, most have high IQs (as their imaginative inventions indicate), often abuse but are not necessarily addicted to drugs, come from a background in which a doctor was an important figure, are employed in health care, and are productive citizens between episodes.

6   What produces their medical madness? There are three main explanations:

7   The psychoanalytic interpretation draws attention to the unconscious. The Munchausen patient, by feigning illness, presents himself simultaneously as victim and victimizer, and compulsively re-enacts unresolved conflicts: The weak child/patient is challenging and even defying the strong father/surgeon. Paradoxically, the weak patient controls the surgeon/parent—and risks death!—by "making" the doctor perform needless surgery. The psychoanalytic view also sees in the syndrome an attempt to continue into adulthood the game of "doctor," which characterizes a phase of childhood development.

8   A second explanation locates the source of Munchausen behavior in a personality trait known as borderline character disorder. According to Otto Kernberg, a psychoanalyst at Cornell who has most fully researched this trait, the core problems are untamed (often unconscious) rage and chronic feelings of boredom, two emotions that work against each other. The Munchausen character, for example, presents himself as a "sick" patient, a condition that should appeal to a dedicated physician—yet no accepting relationship can grow between a deceptive patient and a suspecting physician who is alternately idealized and despised.

9   The third explanation looks to excessive stress as the trigger that starts Munchausen patients on their medical odyssey. Many of them began their "wandering" and symptom mimicry in response to cumulative major disappointments, losses, or damage to self-image. One patient first sought surgery for questionable persistent stomach pains after being jilted by a medical-student lover, beginning a long string of lies and hospitalizations.

10   We are beginning to identify the reasons for the behavior of Munchausen patients, but we are still far from knowing how to free them of their remarkably creative compulsion for self-destructive behavior.

Questions on Content, Structure, and Style

1. Why does Lipsitt begin his essay with reference to Thomas Mann's character in *Confessions of Felix Krull, Confidence Man?*

2. What effect does the essay's title have on readers? Why didn't Lipsitt simply call this essay "Munchausen Syndrome"?

3. Why does Lipsitt feel this syndrome is important to understand? How does this problem affect the health-care system?

4. Why explain the origin of the syndrome's name?

5. Why does Lipsitt use specific examples of "deceptions" to develop his extended definition?

6. Similarly, why does Lipsitt offer examples of actual patients? Would additional examples be helpful?

7. How does Lipsitt use contrast as a technique of definition in paragraph 4?

8. What other strategy of definition does Lipsitt employ in paragraphs 6–9? Why might readers interested in understanding this syndrome want such discussion?

9. Evaluate the essay's conclusion. Is it an effective choice for this essay?

10. After reading Lipsitt's descriptive details, examples, and analysis, do you feel you now have a general understanding of a new term? If the writer were to expand his definition, what might he add to make your understanding even more complete? More statistics? Case studies? Testimony from doctors or patients themselves?

Suggestions for Writing

Try using Don Lipsitt's "The Munchausen Mystery" as a stepping-stone to your essay. Select a puzzling or "mysterious" subject from a field of study (e.g., black holes in space) or from an interest you have explored (or would like to explore). Write an extended definition, as Lipsitt did, that explains this mystery for your readers. As appropriate, include information about its characteristics, parts, history, possible causes, effects, solutions, benefits, or dangers. Or investigate a well-known mystery, such as Stonehenge, the Bermuda Triangle, the Nazca path drawings, the Marfa lights, King Tut's "curse," Big Foot, the Easter Island statues, or perhaps even a famous local ghost. Remember that your essay should offer in-depth explanation, not just general description.

Vocabulary

fabricates (1)   sputum (4)   psychoanalytic (7)
mimic (2)   palpably (4)   paradoxically (7)
incurs (2)   feasible (4)   odyssey (9)
hypochondriacs (4)

■ A REVISION WORKSHEET

As you write your rough drafts, consult Chapter 5 for guidance through the revision process. In addition, here are a few questions to ask yourself as you revise your extended definition essay:

1. Is the subject narrowed to manageable size, and is the purpose of the definition clear to the readers?

2. If the definition is objective, is the language as neutral as possible?

3. If the definition is subjective, is the point of view obvious to the readers?

4. Are all the words and parts of the definition itself clear to the essay's particular audience?

5. Are there enough explanatory methods (examples, descriptions, history, causes, effects, etc.) used to make the definition clear and informative?

6. Have the various methods been organized and ordered in an effective way?

7. Does the essay contain enough specific details to make the definition clear and distinct rather than vague or circular? Where could additional details be added?

After you've revised your essay extensively, you might exchange rough drafts with a classmate and answer these questions for each other, making specific suggestions for improvement wherever appropriate. (For advice on productive participation in classroom workshops, see pages 108–111.)

Reviewing Your Progress

After you have completed your essay developed by definition, take a moment to measure your progress as a writer by responding to the following questions. Such analysis will help you recognize growth in your writing skills and may enable you to identify areas that are still problematic.

1. What do you like best about your essay? Why?

2. After considering the various methods of definition you used in your essay, which one do you think offered the clearest or most persuasive explanation of your topic? Why was that particular technique effective in this essay?

3. What part of your essay gave you the most trouble? How did you overcome the problem?

4. If you had more time to work on this essay, what would receive additional attention? Why?

5. What did you learn about your topic from writing this essay? About yourself as a writer?

■ Strategy Five: Development by Division and Classification

To make large or complex subjects easier to comprehend, we frequently apply the principles of *division* or *classification*.

Division

Division is the act of separating something into its component parts so that it may be better understood or used by the reader. For example, consider a complex subject such as the national budget. Perhaps you have seen a picture on television or in the newspaper of the budget represented by a circle or a pie that has been divided into parts and labeled: a certain percentage or "slice" of the budget designated for military spending, another slice for social services, another for education, and so on. By studying the budget after it has been divided into its parts, taxpayers may have a better sense of how their money is being spent.

As a student, you see division in action in many of your college courses. A literature teacher, for instance, might approach a particular drama by dividing its plot into stages such as exposition, rising action, climax, falling action, and dénouement. Or your chemistry lab instructor may ask you to break down a substance into its components to learn how the parts interact to form the chemical. Even this textbook is divided into chapters to make it easier for you to use. When you think of *division*, then, think of dividing, separating, or breaking apart one subject (often a large or complex or unfamiliar one) into its parts to help people understand it more easily.

Classification

While the principle of division calls for separating one thing into its parts, *classification* systematically groups a number of things into categories to make the information easier to grasp. Without some sort of imposed system of order, a body of information can be a jumble of facts and figures. For example, at some point you've probably turned to the classified ads in the newspaper; if the ads were not classified into categories such as "houses to rent," "cars for sale," and "help wanted," you would have to search through countless ads to find the service or item you needed.

Classification occurs everywhere around you. As a student, you may be classified as a freshman, sophomore, junior, or senior; you may also be classified by your major. If you vote, you may be categorized as a Democrat, Republican, Independent, Socialist, or something else; if you attend religious services, you may be classified as Baptist, Methodist, Catholic, Jewish, and so on. The books you buy may be grouped and shelved by the bookstore into "mysteries," "Westerns," "biographies," "science fiction," and other categories; the movies you see have already been typed as "G," "PG," "PG-13," "R," or "NC-17." Professionals classify almost every kind of knowledge: ornithologists classify birds; etymologists classify words by origins; botanists classify plants; zoologists classify animals. Remember that *classification* differs from division in that it sorts and organizes *many* things into appropriate groups, types, kinds, or categories. *Division* begins with *one* thing and separates it into its parts.

Developing Your Essay

A classification or division paper is generally easy to develop. Each part or category is identified and described in a major part of the body of the essay. Frequently, one body paragraph will be devoted to each category. Here are three additional hints for writing your essay:

Select one principle of classification or division and stick to it. If you are classifying students by major, for instance, don't suddenly switch to classification by college: French, economics, psychology, *arts and sciences,* math, and chemistry. A similar error occurs in this classification of dogs by breeds because it includes a physical characteristic: spaniels, terriers, *long-haired,* hounds, and retrievers. Decide on what basis of division you will classify or divide your subject and then be consistent throughout your essay.

Make the purpose of your division or classification clear to your audience. Don't just announce that "There are four kinds of 'X'" or that "'Z' has three important parts." Why does your particular audience need this information? Consider these sample thesis statements:

> By recognizing the three kinds of poisonous snakes in this area, campers and backpackers may be able to take the proper medical steps if they are bitten.

> Knowing the four types of spinning reels will allow those new to ice fishing to purchase the equipment best suited to their needs.

> Although karate has become a popular form of exercise as well as of self-defense, few people know what the five levels of achievement—or "belts" as they are called—actually stand for.

Organize your material for a particular purpose and then explain to your readers what that purpose is.

Account for all the parts in your division or classification. Don't, for instance, claim to classify all the evergreen trees native to your hometown and then leave out one or more species. For a short essay, narrow your ruling principle rather than omit categories. You couldn't, for instance, classify all the architectural styles in the United States in a short paper, but you might discuss the major styles on your campus. In the same manner, the enormous task of classifying all types of mental illness might be narrowed to the most common forms of childhood schizophrenia. However you narrow your topic, remember that in a formal classification, all the parts must be accounted for.

Like most rules, the preceding one has an exception. If your instructor permits, you can also write a satirical or humorous classification. In this sort of essay, you make up your own categories as well as your thesis. One writer, for example, recently wrote about the kinds of moviegoers who spoil the show for everyone else, such as "the babbling idiot," "the laughing hyena," and "the wandering dawdler." Another female student described blind dates to avoid, including "Mr. Neanderthal," "Timothy Timid," "Red, the Raging Rebel," and "Frat-Rat Freddie," among others. Still another student classified the various kinds of people who frequent the school library at 2 A.M. In this kind of informal essay, in which you're making a humorous or satirical point about your subject, your classification must be more than random silliness. Effective humor should ultimately make good sense, not nonsense.

Problems to Avoid

Avoid underdeveloped categories. A classification or division essay is not a mechanical list; each category should contain enough specific details to make it clearly recognizable and interesting. To present each category or part, you may draw on the methods of development you already know, such as example, comparison and contrast, and definition. Try to use the same techniques in each category so that no one category or part of your essay seems underdeveloped or unclear.

Avoid indistinct categories. Each category should be a separate unit; there should be no overlap among categories. For example, in a classification of shirts by fabric, the inclusion of flannel with silk, nylon, and cotton is an overlap because flannel is a kind of cotton. Similarly, in a classification of soft drinks by flavor, to include sugar-free with cola, root beer, orange, grape, and so on, is misleading because sugar-free drinks come in many different flavors. In other words, make each category unique.

Avoid too few or too many categories. A classification essay should have at least three categories, avoiding the either-or dichotomy. On the other hand, too many categories give a short essay the appearance of a list rather than a discussion. Whatever the number, don't forget to use transitional devices for easy movement from category to category.

■ ESSAY TOPICS

Narrow and focus your subject by selecting an appropriate principle of division or classification. Some of the suggestions below may be appropriate for humorous essays ("The Three Best Breeds of Cats for Antisocial People"). For additional ideas, see the "Suggestions for Writing" section following the professional essays (pages 258 and 261).

1. Friends or relatives

2. First-year college students

3. Heroes in a particular field

4. Summer or part-time jobs

5. Attitudes toward a current controversy

6. Kinds of popular tattoos

7. Specializations in your field of study

8. Approaches to studying a subject

9. Classmates, roommates, or dates

10. Dogs, cats, birds, or other pets

11. Popular kinds of movies, music, or video games (or types within a larger category: kinds of horror movie monsters or varieties of "heavy-metal" music)

12. Chronic moochers or fibbers

13. Vacations or Spring Break trips

14. Methods of accomplishing a task (ways to conduct an experiment, ways to introduce a bill into Congress)

15. Bosses or co-workers to avoid

16. Kinds of tools or equipment for a particular task in your field of study

17. Theories explaining "X" (the disappearance of the dinosaurs, for example)

18. Diets, exercise, or stress-reduction programs (or their participants)

19. Reasons people participate in some activity (or excuses for not participating)

20. Amateur athletes, coaches, or sports fans (including those you hope aren't sitting next to you at an athletic event)

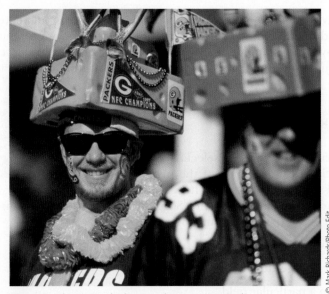

Wisconsin Cheese Heads cheer on the Green Bay Packers.

A Topic Proposal for Your Essay

Selecting the right subject matter is important to every writer. To help you clarify your ideas and strengthen your commitment to your topic, here is a proposal sheet that asks you to describe some of your preliminary ideas about your subject before you begin drafting. Although your ideas may change as you write (they will almost certainly become more refined), thinking through your choice of topic now may help you avoid several false starts.

1. What is the subject of your essay? Will you write an essay of classification or division?

2. What principle of classification or division will you use? Why is this a useful or informative principle for your particular topic and readers?

3. Why are you interested in this topic? Do you have a personal or professional connection to the subject? State at least one reason for your choice of topic.

4. Is this a significant topic of interest to others? Why? Who specifically might find it interesting, informative, or entertaining?

5. List at least three categories you are considering for development in your essay.

6. What difficulties, if any, might arise from this topic during the drafting of your essay? For example, do you know enough about your topic to offer details that will make each of your categories clear and distinct to your readers?

■ Sample Student Essay

In the following essay, the student writer divided the Mesa Verde Native American Era into three time periods that correspond to changes in the people's domestic skills, crafts, and housing. Note the writer's use of description and examples to help the reader distinguish one time period from another.

THE NATIVE AMERICAN ERA AT MESA VERDE

1   Visiting Mesa Verde National Park is a trip back in time to two and a half centuries before Columbus. The park, located in southwestern Colorado, is the setting of a silent stone city, ten ruins built into protective seven-hundred-foot cliffs that housed hundreds of people from the pre-Columbian era to the end of the thirteenth century. Visitors to the park often enjoy its architecture and history more if they know a little about the various people who lived there. The Native American Era may be

Introduction: Establishing a reason for knowing the classification

Principle of division of the Native American Era

divided into three time periods that show growing sophistication in such activities as crafts, hunting, trade, and housing: Basket Maker (1–450 C.E.), Modified Basket Maker (450–750 C.E.), and Pueblo (750–1300 C.E.).*

Time period one: Early cliff life

2   The earliest Mesa Verdeans, the Basket Makers, whose ancestors had been nomads, sought shelter from the dry plains in the cliff caves and became farmers. During growing seasons they climbed up toeholds cut in the cliffs and grew beans and squash on the green mesa above. Settling down also meant more time for crafts. They didn't make pottery yet but instead wove intricate baskets that held water. Instead of depending on raw meats and vegetables, they could now cook food in these baskets by dropping heated rocks into the water. Because the Basket Makers hadn't discovered the bow and arrow yet, they had to rely on the inaccurate spear, which meant little fresh meat and few animal skins. Consequently, they wore little clothing but liked bone, seed, and stone ornaments.

Time period two: New crafts, trade, and housing

3   The second period, 450–750 C.E., saw the invention of pottery, the bow and arrow, and houses. Pottery was apparently learned from other tribes. From crude clay baked in the sun, the Mesa Verdeans advanced to clay mixed with straw and sand and baked in kilns. Paints were concocted from plants and minerals, and the tribe produced a variety of beautifully decorated mugs, bowls, jars, pitchers, and canteens. Such pots meant that water could be stored for longer periods, and perhaps a water supply encouraged more trade with neighboring tribes. These Mesa Verdeans also acquired the bow and arrow, a weapon that improved their hunting skills, and

---

* Last summer I worked at Mesa Verde as a student-guide for the Parks Service; the information in this paper is based on the tour I gave three times a week to hundreds of visitors to the park.

enlarged their wardrobes to include animal skins and feather blankets. Their individual living quarters, called pithouses, consisted of twenty-foot-wide holes in the ground with log, grasses, and earthen framework over them.

4   The third period lasted until 1300 c.e. and saw the innovation of pueblos, or groups of dwellings, instead of single-family units. Nearly eight hundred dwellings show the large number of people who inhabited the complex tunneled houses, shops, storage rooms, courtyards, and community centers whose masonry walls, often elaborately decorated, were three and four stories high. At the spacious Balcony House pueblo, for example, an adobe court lies beneath another vaulted roof; on three sides stand two-story houses with balconies that lead from one room to the next. In back of the court is a spring, and along the front side is a low wall that kept the children from falling down the seven-hundred-foot cliff to the canyon floor below. Balcony House pueblo also contains two kivas, circular subterranean ceremonial chambers that show the importance of fellowship and religion to the people of this era. During this period the Mesa Verdeans were still farmers and potters, but cotton cloth and other nonnative products found at the ruins suggest a healthy trade with the south. But despite the trade goods, sophisticated pottery, and such innovations in clothing as the "disposable" juniper-bark diapers of babies, life was still simple; the Mesa Verdeans had no system of writing, no wheel, and no metal.

> Time period three: Expanded community living and trade

5   Near the end of the thirteenth century, the cliff dwellings became ghost towns. Archaeologists don't know for certain why the Mesa Verdeans left their elaborate homes, but they speculate that a drought that lasted some twenty years may have driven them south

Conclusion: The importance of understanding Mesa Verde's people

into New Mexico and Arizona, where strikingly similar crafts and tools have been found. Regardless of their reason for leaving, they left an amazing architectural and cultural legacy. Learning about the people who lived in Mesa Verde centuries ago provides an even deeper appreciation of the cliff palaces that awe thousands of national park visitors every year.

Professional Essay: Classification*

■ The Plot against People

Russell Baker

Russell Baker has been a journalist and social commentator for over forty years. His "Observer" columns, written for the *New York Times* and syndicated throughout the country, won him both the George Polk Award for Distinguished Commentary and a Pulitzer Prize for journalism. He has published seventeen books, including *Growing Up* (1982), an autobiography that won him a second Pulitzer Prize; *The Good Times* (1989); and *Looking Back* (2002). This essay originally appeared in the *New York Times* in 1968.

1   Inanimate objects are classified into three major categories—those that don't work, those that break down and those that get lost.

2   The goal of all inanimate objects is to resist man and ultimately to defeat him, and the three major classifications are based on the method each object uses to achieve its purpose. As a general rule, any object capable of breaking down at the moment when it is most needed will do so. The automobile is typical of the category.

3   With the cunning typical of its breed, the automobile never breaks down while entering a filling station with a large staff of idle mechanics. It waits until it reaches a downtown intersection in the middle of the rush hour, or until it is fully loaded with family and luggage on the Ohio Turnpike.

4   Thus it creates maximum misery, inconvenience, frustration and irritability among its human cargo, thereby reducing its owner's life span.

5   Washing machines, garbage disposals, lawn mowers, light bulbs, automatic laundry dryers, water pipes, furnaces, electrical fuses, television tubes, hose nozzles, tape

---

* To help you read this essay analytically, review pages 170–172.

recorders, slide projectors—all are in league with the automobile to take their turn at breaking down whenever life threatens to flow smoothly for their human enemies.

6   Many inanimate objects, of course, find it extremely difficult to break down. Pliers, for example, and gloves and keys are almost totally incapable of breaking down. Therefore, they have had to evolve a different technique for resisting man.

7   They get lost. Science has still not solved the mystery of how they do it, and no man has ever caught one of them in the act of getting lost. The most plausible theory is that they have developed a secret method of locomotion which they are able to conceal the instant a human eye falls upon them.

8   It is not uncommon for a pair of pliers to climb all the way from the cellar to the attic in its single-minded determination to raise its owner's blood pressure. Keys have been known to burrow three feet under mattresses. Women's purses, despite their great weight, frequently travel through six or seven rooms to find hiding space under a couch.

9   Scientists have been struck by the fact that things that break down virtually never get lost, while things that get lost hardly ever break down.

10   A furnace, for example, will invariably break down at the depth of the first winter cold wave, but it will never get lost. A woman's purse, which after all does have some inherent capacity for breaking down, hardly ever does; it almost invariably chooses to get lost.

11   Some persons believe this constitutes evidence that inanimate objects are not entirely hostile to man, and that a negotiated peace is possible. After all, they point out, a furnace could infuriate a man even more thoroughly by getting lost than by breaking down, just as a glove could upset him far more by breaking down than by getting lost.

12   Not everyone agrees, however, that this indicates a conciliatory attitude among inanimate objects. Many say it merely proves that furnaces, gloves and pliers are incredibly stupid.

13   The third class of objects—those that don't work—is the most curious of all. These include such objects as barometers, car clocks, cigarette lighters, flashlights and toy-train locomotives. It is inaccurate, of course, to say that they never work. They work once, usually for the first few hours after being brought home, and then quit. Thereafter, they never work again.

14   In fact, it is widely assumed that they are built for the purpose of not working. Some people have reached advanced ages without ever seeing some of these objects—barometers, for example—in working order.

15   Science is utterly baffled by the entire category. There are many theories about it. The most interesting holds that the things that don't work have attained the highest state possible for an inanimate object, the state to which things that break down and things that get lost can still only aspire.

16   They have truly defeated man by conditioning him never to expect anything of them, and in return they have given man the only peace he receives from inanimate society. He does not expect his barometer to work, his electric locomotive to run, his cigarette lighter to light or his flashlight to illuminate, and when they don't, it does not raise his blood pressure.

17   He cannot attain that peace with furnaces and keys and cars and women's purses as long as he demands that they work for their keep.

Questions on Content, Structure, and Style

1. What is Baker's purpose in writing this classification? What reaction do you think Baker wants to evoke from his reading audience?

2. Where is Baker's thesis statement? Would his essay be more effective if his thesis were preceded by a fully developed lead-in? Why or why not?

3. Identify Baker's categories and principle of classification. What do these categories have in common?

4. Why does Baker give examples of items that belong to each category? Does this strengthen his essay? Why or why not?

5. Of the categories of inanimate objects discussed in the essay, which one is most effectively developed? List some examples of details.

6. Consider Baker's use of personification as he talks about inanimate objects. Give some examples of descriptions that give human qualities to these items. What effect does this have on tone and style?

7. How does Baker's word choice affect his tone? Would it be possible to write an effective essay about this subject from a more serious, informative standpoint? Why or why not?

8. What does Baker's title contribute to his tone and his readers' understanding of his classifying principle?

9. If Baker were to revise his essay today, how might he change his word choice in paragraphs 2, 7, 11, 16, and 17 to make his language more gender inclusive?

10. Evaluate Baker's conclusion. Is it effective or too abrupt?

Suggestions for Writing

Try using Russell Baker's "The Plot Against People" as a stepping-stone to your writing. To parallel Baker's criticisms of objects that inflict misery, think about kinds of people or forces that you feel are secretly conspiring to destroy your peace of mind. Consider, for example, kinds of crazed drivers who are contributing to road rage today. Annoying telephone solicitors? Obnoxious waiters or clerks? Grocery shoppers in the checkout line in front of you? Or consider the kinds of rules that govern your life. Inane parking regulations that ensure you will never find a space anywhere near campus? Financial aid red tape only an accounting genius could cut through? Your essay might be humorous, like Baker's, or quite serious, as you expose still another "plot" against humankind.

Vocabulary

inanimate (1)	locomotion (7)	constitutes (11)
cunning (3)	virtually (9)	conciliatory (12)
evolve (6)	inherent (10)	barometer (13)

Professional Essay: Division*

■ A Brush with Reality: Surprises in the Tube

David Bodanis

A former teacher of intellectual history at the University of Oxford, David Bodanis speaks and writes about global trends in science and technology. Four of his books offer revealing insights into our bodies and homes: *The Body Book: A Fantastic Voyage to the World Within* (1984); *The Secret Garden: Dawn to Dusk in the Astonishing Hidden World of the Garden* (1992); *The Secret Family: Twenty-four Hours Inside the Mysterious World of Our Minds and Bodies* (1997); and *The Secret House* (1986), from which this excerpt is taken. His most recent book is *Passionate Minds* (2006).

1 Into the bathroom goes our male resident, and after the most pressing need is satisfied, it's time to brush the teeth. The tube of toothpaste is squeezed, its pinched metal seams are splayed, pressure waves are generated inside, and the paste begins to flow. But what's in this toothpaste, so carefully being extruded out?

2 Water mostly, 30 to 45 percent in most brands: ordinary, everyday simple tap water. It's there because people like to have a big glob of toothpaste to spread on the brush, and water is the cheapest stuff there is when it comes to making big globs. Dripping a bit from the tap onto your brush would cost virtually nothing; whipped in with the rest of the toothpaste the manufacturers can sell it at a neat and accountant-pleasing $2 per pound equivalent. Toothpaste manufacture is a very lucrative occupation.

3 Second to water in quantity is chalk: exactly the same material that schoolteachers use to write on blackboards. It is collected from the crushed remains of long-dead ocean creatures. In the Cretaceous seas chalk particles served as part of the wickedly sharp outer skeleton that these creatures had to wrap around themselves to keep from getting chomped by all the slightly larger other ocean creatures they met. Their massed graves are our present chalk deposits.

4 The individual chalk particles—the size of the smallest mud particles in your garden—have kept their toughness over the aeons, and now on the toothbrush they'll need it. The enamel outer coating of the tooth they'll have to face is the hardest substance in the body—tougher than skull, or bone, or nail. Only the chalk particles in toothpaste can successfully grind into the teeth during brushing, ripping off the surface layers like an abrading wheel grinding down a boulder in a quarry.

5 The craters, slashes, and channels that the chalk tears into the teeth will also remove a certain amount of built-up yellow in the carnage, and it is for that polishing function that it's there. A certain amount of unduly enlarged extra-abrasive chalk fragments tear such cavernous pits into the teeth that future decay bacteria will be able to bunker down there and thrive; the quality control people find it almost impossible to screen out these errant super-chalk pieces, and government regulations allow them to stay in.

* To help you read this essay analytically, review pages 170–172.

6   In case even the gouging doesn't get all the yellow off, another substance is worked into the toothpaste cream. This is titanium dioxide. It comes in tiny spheres, and it's the stuff bobbing around in white wall paint to make it come out white. Splashed around onto your teeth during the brushing it coats much of the yellow that remains. Being water soluble it leaks off in the next few hours and is swallowed, but at least for the quick glance up in the mirror after finishing it will make the user think his teeth are truly white. Some manufacturers add optical whitening dyes—the stuff more commonly found in washing machine bleach—to make extra sure that the glance in the mirror shows reassuring white.

7   These ingredients alone would not make a very attractive concoction. They would stick in the tube like a sloppy white plastic lump, hard to squeeze out as well as revolting to the touch. Few consumers would savor rubbing in a mixture of water, ground-up blackboard chalk, and the whitener from latex paint first thing in the morning. To get around that finicky distaste the manufacturers have mixed in a host of other goodies.

8   To keep the glop from drying out, a mixture including glycerine glycol—related to the most common car antifreeze ingredient—is whipped in with the chalk and water, and to give *that* concoction a bit of substance (all we really have so far is wet colored chalk) a large helping is added of gummy molecules from the seaweed *Chondrus Crispus*. This seaweed ooze spreads in among the chalk, paint, and antifreeze, then stretches itself in all directions to hold the whole mass together. A bit of paraffin oil (the fuel that flickers in camping lamps) is pumped in with it to help the moss ooze keep the whole substance smooth.

9   With the glycol, ooze, and paraffin we're almost there. Only two major chemicals are left to make the refreshing, cleansing substance we know as toothpaste. The ingredients so far are fine for cleaning, but they wouldn't make much of the satisfying foam we have come to expect in the morning brushing.

10   To remedy that, every toothpaste on the market has a big dollop of detergent added too. You've seen the suds detergent will make in a washing machine. The same substance added here will duplicate that inside the mouth. It's not particularly necessary, but it sells.

11   The only problem is that by itself this ingredient tastes, well, too like detergent. It's horribly bitter and harsh. The chalk put in the toothpaste is pretty foul-tasting too for that matter. It's to get around the gustatory discomfort that the manufacturers put in the ingredient they tout perhaps the most of all. This is the flavoring, and it has to be strong. Double-rectified peppermint oil is used—a flavorer so powerful that chemists know better than to sniff it in the raw state in the laboratory. Menthol crystals and saccharin or other sugar simulators are added to complete the camouflage operation.

12   Is that it? Chalk, water, paint, seaweed, antifreeze, paraffin oil, detergent, and peppermint? Not quite. A mix like that would be irresistible to the hundreds of thousands of individual bacteria lying on the surface of even an immaculately cleaned bathroom sink. They would get in, float in the water bubbles, ingest the ooze and paraffin, maybe even spray out enzymes to break down the chalk. The result would be an uninviting mess. The way manufacturers avoid the final obstacle is by putting something in to kill the bacteria. Something good and strong is needed, something that will zap any accidentally intrudant bacteria into oblivion. And that something is formaldehyde—the disinfectant used in anatomy labs.

13   So it's chalk, water, paint, seaweed, antifreeze, paraffin oil, detergent, peppermint, formaldehyde, and fluoride (which can go some way toward preserving children's

teeth)—that's the usual mixture raised to the mouth on the toothbrush for a fresh morning's clean. If it sounds too unfortunate, take heart. Studies show that thorough brushing with just plain water will often do as good a job.

Questions on Content, Structure, and Style

1. How does this essay illustrate division rather than classification?

2. In additional to providing factual information, what is Bodanis's purpose in writing this essay? What response to his subject matter is he trying to produce in his readers?

3. How does Bodanis organize the parts of his division?

4. For what audience is Bodanis writing? How did an awareness of his audience influence his explanations?

5. As a reader, are you confident that Bodanis has accounted for all the parts in the subject of his division? If so, what gives you this sense of confidence?

6. In his explanation of an ingredient, Bodanis sometimes mentions its use in other products. Why does he do so?

7. How does Bodanis employ comparison and cause-and-effect explanations to clarify his subject and inform his readers?

8. What does Bodanis's word choice reveal about his attitude toward toothpaste manufacturing? Cite some examples of Bodanis's vivid language that transform this essay into more than a dry list of chemical ingredients.

9. Why does Bodanis use repetition in paragraphs 9, 12, and 13?

10. Evaluate Bodanis's conclusion. Does it provide an ending that is consistent with Bodanis's tone and point of view throughout the essay? Why/why not?

Suggestions for Writing

Use David Bodanis's essay "A Brush with Reality: Surprises in the Tube" as a stepping-stone to your essay. As a consumer, what other personal products would you like to know more about? What's really in our deodorant, cosmetics, or hair products? Consider any one of the many household cleaners or detergents. Or, if you prefer, think about food as a subject for a division essay. What is in lunch meat? Soft drinks? "Processed cheese food"? Or write an essay that nutritionally analyzes your favorite fast-food dinner. How healthful is a Happy Meal for our nation's children? Make your attitude toward your subject matter unmistakable, as Bodanis did, through your vivid details and word choice.

Vocabulary

splayed (1)	abrading (4)	errant (5)
extruded (1)	carnage (5)	gustatory (11)
lucrative (2)	cavernous (5)	intrudant (12)
aeons (4)		

▪ A REVISION WORKSHEET

As you write your rough drafts, consult Chapter 5 for guidance through the revision process. In addition, here are a few questions to ask yourself as you revise your classification essay:

1. Is the purpose of the essay clear to the reader?

2. Is the principle of classification or division maintained consistently throughout the essay?

3. If the essay presents a formal division or classification, has the subject been narrowed so that all the parts of the subject are accounted for?

4. If the essay presents an informal or humorous division or classification, does the paper nevertheless make a significant or entertaining point?

5. Is each category developed with enough specific detail? Where might more details be effectively added?

6. Is each class distinct, with no overlap among categories?

7. Is the essay organized logically and coherently with smooth transitions between the discussions of the categories?

After you've revised your essay extensively, you might exchange rough drafts with a classmate and answer these questions for each other, making specific suggestions for improvement wherever appropriate. (For advice on productive participation in classroom workshops, see pages 108–111.)

Reviewing Your Progress

After you have completed your essay developed by classification or division, take a moment to measure your progress as a writer by responding to the following questions. Such analysis will help you to recognize growth in your writing skills and may enable you to identify areas that are still problematic.

1. What is the best feature of your essay? Why?

2. Which category do you think is the clearest or most persuasive in your essay? Why does that one stand above the others?

3. What part of your essay gave you the most trouble? How did you overcome the problem?

4. If you had more time to work on this essay, what would receive additional attention? Why?

5. What did you learn about your topic from writing this essay? About yourself as a writer?

■ Strategy Six: Development by Causal Analysis

Causal analysis explains the cause-and-effect relationship between two (or more) elements. When you discuss the condition producing something, you are analyzing *cause;* when you discuss the result produced by something, you are analyzing *effect.* To find examples of causal analysis, you need only look around you. If your car stops running on the way to class, for example, you may discover that the cause was an empty gas tank. On campus, in your history class, you may study the causes of the Civil War; in your economics class, the effects of teenage spending on the cosmetics market; and in your biology class, both the causes and effects of heart disease. Over dinner you may discuss the effects of some crisis in the Middle East on American foreign policy, and as you drift to sleep, you may ponder the effects of your studying—or *not* studying—for your math test tomorrow.

To express it most simply, *cause* asks:

why did "X" happen?

or why does "X" happen?

or why will "X" happen?

Effect, on the other hand, asks:

what did "Y" produce?

or what does "Y" produce?

or what will "Y" produce?

Some essays of causal analysis focus primarily on the cause(s) of something; others mainly analyze the effect(s); still others discuss both causes and effects. If, for example, you wanted to concentrate on the major causes of the Wall Street crash of 1929, you might begin by briefly describing the effects of the crash on the economy, then devote your thesis and the rest of your essay to analyzing the major causes, perhaps allotting one major section (or one paragraph, depending on the complexity of the reasons) to each cause. Conversely, an effect paper might briefly note the causes of the crash and then detail the most important effects. An essay covering both the causes and effects of something often demands a longer paper so that each part will be clear. (Your assignment will frequently indicate which kind of causal analysis to write. However, if the choice is yours, let your interest in the subject be your guide.)

Developing Your Essay

Whether you are writing an essay that primarily discusses either causes or effects, or one that focuses on both, you should follow these rules:

Present a reasonable thesis statement. If your thesis makes dogmatic, unsupportable claims ("Medicare will lead to a complete collapse of quality medical treatment") or overly broad assertions ("Peer pressure causes alcoholism among students"), you won't convince your reader. Limit or qualify your thesis whenever necessary by using such phrases as "may be," "a contributing factor," "one of the main reasons," "two important factors," and so on ("Peer pressure is *one of the major causes* of alcoholism among students").

Limit your essay to a discussion of recent, major causes or effects. In a short paper you generally don't have space to discuss minor or remote causes or effects. If, for example, you analyzed your car wreck, you might decide that the three major causes were defective brakes, a hidden yield sign, and bad weather. A minor, or remote, cause might include being slightly tired because of less-than-usual sleep, less sleep because of staying out late the night before, staying out late because of an out-of-town visitor, and so on—back to the womb. In some cases you may want to mention a few of the indirect causes or effects, but do be reasonable. Concentrate on the most immediate, most important factors. Often, a writer of a 500-to-800-word essay will discuss no more than two, three, or four major causes or effects of something; trying to cover more frequently results in an underdeveloped essay that is not convincing.

Organize your essay clearly. Organization of your causal analysis essay will vary, of course, depending on whether you are focusing on the causes of something or the effects, or both. To avoid becoming tangled in causes and effects, you might try sketching out a drawing of your thesis and essay map before you begin your first draft. Here, for instance, are a couple of sketches for essays you might write on your recent traffic accident:

Thesis Emphasizing the Causes:

Cause (defective brakes)
Cause (hidden yield sign)   produced   Effect (my car wreck)
Cause (bad weather)

Thesis Emphasizing the Effects:

                                        Effect (loss of car)
Cause (my car wreck)   produced   Effect (doctor bills)
                                        Effect (higher insurance rates)

Sometimes you may discover that you can't isolate "the three main causes/effects of 'X'"; some essays do in fact demand a narrative explaining a chain reaction of causes and effects. For example, a paper on the rebellion of the American colonies might show how one unjust British law or restriction after another led to the war for independence. In this kind of causal analysis essay, be careful to limit your subject so that you'll have the space necessary to show your readers how each step in the chain led to the next. Here's a sketch of a slightly different car-wreck paper presented in a narrative or chain-reaction format:

Cause ──────► 1st Effect ──causes──► 2nd Effect ──causes──► 3rd Effect
(bad weather)   (wet brakes)   (car wreck)   (doctor bills)

Sometimes your subject matter will suggest the plan for organizing your causal analysis paper; often, however, you'll have to devote some of your prewriting time to deciding, first, whether you want to emphasize causes or effects and, then, in what arrangement you will present your analysis.

Convince your reader that a causal relationship exists by showing how the relationship works. Let's suppose you are writing an essay in which you want to discuss the three major changes you've undergone since coming to college. Don't just state the changes and describe them; your job is to show the reader how college has *brought about* these changes. If, for instance, your study habits have improved, you must show the reader how the academic demands of your college courses caused you to change your habits; a simple description of your new study techniques is not enough. Remember that a causal analysis essay should stress *how* (and sometimes *why*) "X" caused "Y," rather than merely describing "Y" as it now exists.

Problems to Avoid

Don't oversimplify by assigning one all-encompassing cause to some effect. Most complex subjects have more than one cause (or effect), so make your analysis as complete and objective as you can, especially when dealing with your own problems or beliefs. For example, was that car wreck really caused only by the bad weather—or also because of your carelessness? Did your friend do poorly in astronomy class only because the instructor didn't like her? Before judging a situation too quickly, investigate your own biases. Then provide a thoughtful, thorough analysis, effectively organized to convince your readers of the validity of your viewpoint.

Avoid the *post hoc* fallacy. This error in logic (from the Latin phrase *post hoc, ergo propter hoc,* meaning "after this, therefore because of this") results when we mistake a temporal connection for a causal relationship—or in other words, when we assume that because one event follows another in time, the first event caused the second. Most of our superstitions are *post hoc* fallacies; we now realize that bad luck after walking under a ladder is a matter of coincidence, not cause and effect. The *post hoc* fallacy provided the basis for a rather popular joke in the 1960s' debates over decriminalizing marijuana. Those against argued that marijuana led to heroin because most users of the hard drug had first smoked the weed. The proponents retorted that milk, then, was the real culprit, because both marijuana and heroin users had drunk milk as babies. The point is this: in any causal analysis, you must be able to offer proof or reasoned logic to show that one event *caused* another, not just that it preceded it in time.

Avoid circular logic. Often causal essays seem to chase their own tails when they include such circular statements as "There aren't enough parking spaces for students on campus because there are too many cars." Such a statement merely presents a second half that restates what is already implied in the first half. A revision might say, "There aren't enough parking spaces for students on campus because the parking permits are not distributed fairly." This kind of assertion can be argued specifically and effectively; the other is a dead end.

■ **ESSAY TOPICS**

The following subjects may be developed into essays emphasizing cause or effect, or both. For additional ideas, turn to the "Suggestions for Writing" section following the professional essay (page 273).

1. A pet peeve or bad habit

2. A change of mind about some important issue or belief

3. An accident, illness, or misadventure

4. A family story/tradition or an influential book

5. A trip or an experience in a different country or culture

6. The best gift you ever received or ownership of a particular possession

7. A radical change in your appearance

8. A hobby, sport, or class

9. The best (or worst) advice you ever gave, followed, or rejected

10. An important decision or choice

11. An act of heroism or sacrifice

12. An important idea, event, or discovery in your field of study

13. A superstition or irrational fear

14. A place that is special to you

15. A disappointment or a success

16. Racism or sexism or some other kind of discrimination or prejudice

17. An influential person (teacher, coach, friend, etc.)

18. A political action (campus, local, state, national), historical event, or social movement

19. A popular cultural trend (tattooing, piercing, clothing or hair styles)

20. A piece of visual art promoting a particular cause or point of view (Consider, for example, the famous image of Rosie the Riveter, who first appeared on a poster sponsored by the War Production Committee during World War II. Considering the gender roles of the time, why was such a poster needed? What effects was this image designed to have on both its male and female viewers? What specific elements in this picture produce these effects? What effect does this image have on viewers today? If you prefer, select another visual image reproduced in this text, such as *Migrant Mother* [page 330], or *The Third of May, 1808* [page 470], and analyze its major effects on the viewer. A list of all artworks in this text follows the table of contents. For help writing about art, see Chapter 17.)

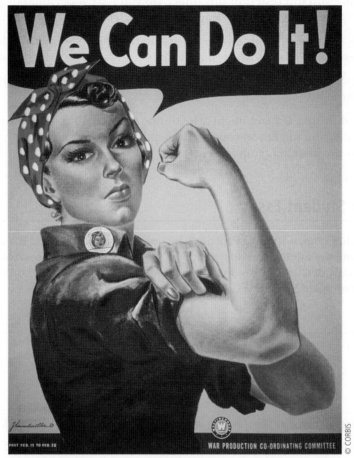

The poster, *Rosie the Riveter*, by graphic artist J. Howard Miller, was created in 1943 as part of a government campaign to encourage women to enter the factory workforce during World War II.

A Topic Proposal for Your Essay

Selecting the right subject matter is important to every writer. To help you clarify your ideas and strengthen your commitment to your topic, here is a proposal sheet that asks you to describe some of your preliminary ideas about your subject before you begin drafting. Although your ideas may change as you write (they will almost certainly become more refined), thinking through your choice of topic now may help you avoid several false starts.

1. What is the subject and purpose of your causal analysis essay? Is this subject appropriately narrowed and focused for a discussion of major causes or effects?

2. Will you develop your essay to emphasize primarily the effects or the causes of your topic? Or is a causal chain the most appropriate method of development?

3. Why are you interested in this topic? Do you have a personal or professional connection to the subject? State at least one reason for your choice of topic.

4. Is this a significant topic of interest to others? Why? Who specifically might find it interesting, informative, or entertaining?

5. List at least two major causes or effects that you might develop in the discussion of your topic.

6. What difficulties, if any, might arise during your drafting on this topic? For example, how might you convince a skeptical reader that your causal relationship is not merely a temporal one?

■ Sample Student Essay

In the following essay, a student explains why working in a local motel damaged her self-esteem, despite her attempts to do a good job. Note that the writer uses many vivid examples and specific details to show the reader how she was treated and, consequently, how such treatment made her feel.

It's Simply Not Worth It

Introduction: Her job as a motel maid

1   It's hard to find a job these days, and with our county's unemployment rate reaching as high as 5 percent, most people feel obligated to "take what they can get." But after working as a maid at a local motel for almost a year and a half, I decided no job is worth keeping if it causes a person to doubt his or her worth. My hard work rarely received recognition or appreciation, I was underpaid, and I was required to perform some of the most disgusting cleaning tasks imaginable. These factors caused me to devalue myself as a person and ultimately motivated me to return to school in hope of regaining my self-respect.

Thesis: No appreciation, low pay, disgusting tasks (causes) produce damaged self-esteem and action (effects)

Cause one: Lack of appreciation

2   It may be obvious to say, but I believe that when a maid's hours of meticulous cleaning are met only with harsh words and complaints, she begins to lose her sense of self-esteem. I recall the care I took in making the motel's beds, imagining them as globs of clay and molding

them into impeccable pieces of art. I would teeter from one side of a bed to the other, over and over again, until I smoothed out every intruding wrinkle or tuck. And the mirrors—I would vigorously massage the glass, erasing any toothpaste splotches or oil smudges that might draw my customer's disapproval. I would scrutinize the mirror first from the left side, then I'd move to the right side, once more to the left until every possible angle ensured an unclouded reflection. And so my efforts went, room after room. But, without fail, each day more than one customer would approach me, not with praise for my tidy beds or spotless mirrors, but with nitpicking complaints that undermined my efforts: "Young lady, I just checked into room 143 and it only has one ashtray. Surely for $69.95 a night you people can afford more ashtrays in the rooms."

3   If it wasn't a guest complaining about ashtrays, it was an impatient customer demanding extra towels or a fussy stay-over insisting his room be cleaned by the time he returned from breakfast at 8:00 A.M. "Can't you come to work early to do it?" he would urge thoughtlessly. Day after day, my spotless rooms went unnoticed, with no spoken rewards for my efforts from either guests or management. Eventually, the ruthless complaints and thankless work began wearing me down. In my mind, I became a servant undeserving of gratitude.

4   The lack of spoken rewards was compounded by the lack of financial rewards. The $6.00/hour appraisal of my worth was simply not enough to support my financial needs or my self-esteem. The measly $3.00 I earned for cleaning one room took a lot of rooms to add up, and by the end of the month I was barely able to pay my bills and buy some food. (My mainstay became ninety-two cent, generic macaroni and cheese dinners.) Because the flow of travelers kept the motel full for only a few months of the year, during some weeks I could only work half time, making a

Cause two: Low pay

mere $480.00 a month. As a result, one month I was forced to request an extension on my rent payment. Unsympathetically, my landlord threatened to evict me if I didn't pay. Embarrassed, yet desperate, I went to a friend and borrowed money. I felt uneasy and awkward and regretted having to beg a friend for money. I felt like a mooch and a bum; I felt degraded. And the constant reminder from management that there were hundreds of people standing in lines who would be more than willing to work for $6.00 an hour only aided in demeaning me further.

Cause three: Repulsive duties

5   In addition to the thankless work and the inadequate salary, I was required to clean some of the most sickening messes. Frequently, conventions for high school clubs booked the motel. Once I opened the door of a conventioneer's room one morning and almost gagged at the odor. I immediately beheld a trail of vomit that began at the bedside and ended just short of the bathroom door. At that moment I cursed the inventor of shag carpet, for I knew it would take hours to comb this mess out of the fibers. On another day I spent thirty minutes dislodging the bed linen from the toilet where it had been stuffed. And I spent what seemed like hours removing from one of my spotless mirrors the lipstick-drawn message that read, "Yorktown Tigers are number one." But these inconsiderate acts were relaying another message, a message I took personally: "Lady, you're not worth the consideration—you're a maid and you're not worth respecting."

Conclusion: Review of the problem and a brief explanation of the solution she chose

6   I've never been afraid to work hard or do jobs that weren't particularly "fun." But the line must be drawn when a person's view of herself becomes clouded with feelings of worthlessness. The thankless efforts, the inadequate wage, and the disgusting work were just parts of a total message that degraded my character and caused me to question my worth. Therefore, I felt compelled to leave this demeaning

job in search of a way to rebuild my self-confidence. Returning to school has done just that for me. As my teachers and fellow students take time to listen to my ideas and compliment my responses, I feel once again like a vital, valued, and worthwhile person. I feel human once more.

Professional Essay*

■ Some Lessons from the Assembly Line

Andrew Braaksma

Andrew Braaksma, from Portage, Michigan, was a junior at the University of Michigan studying history and French in the College of Literature, Science, and Arts, when he won first place in a "Back to School" essay contest sponsored by *Newsweek* magazine. The award-winning essay was then published in *Newsweek's* "My Turn" column on September 12, 2005.

1   Last June, as I stood behind the bright orange guard door of the machine, listening to the crackling hiss of the automatic welders, I thought about how different my life had been just a few weeks earlier. Then, I was writing an essay about French literature to complete my last exam of the spring semester at college. Now I stood in an automotive plant in southwest Michigan, making subassemblies for a car manufacturer.

2   I have worked as a temp in the factories surrounding my hometown every summer since I graduated from high school, but making the transition between school and full-time blue-collar work during the break never gets any easier. For a student like me who considers any class before noon to be uncivilized, getting to a factory by 6 o'clock each morning, where rows of hulking, spark-showering machines have replaced the lush campus and cavernous lecture halls of college life, is torture. There my time is spent stamping, cutting, welding, moving or assembling parts, the rigid work schedules and quotas of the plant making days spent studying and watching "SportsCenter" seem like a million years ago.

3   I chose to do this work, rather than bus tables or fold sweatshirts at the Gap, for the overtime pay and because living at home is infinitely cheaper than living on campus for the summer. My friends who take easier, part-time jobs never seem to understand why I'm so relieved to be back at school in the fall or that my summer vacation has been anything but a vacation.

---

* To help you read this essay analytically, review pages 170–172.

4   There are few things as cocksure as a college student who has never been out in the real world, and people my age always seem to overestimate the value of their time and knowledge. After a particularly exhausting string of 12-hour days at a plastics factory, I remember being shocked at how small my check seemed. I couldn't believe how little I was taking home after all the hours I spent on the sweltering production floor. And all the classes in the world could not have prepared me for my battles with the machine I ran in the plant, which would jam whenever I absent-mindedly put in a part backward or upside down. As frustrating as the work can be, the most stressful thing about blue-collar life is knowing your job could disappear overnight. Issues like downsizing and overseas relocation had always seemed distant to me until my co-workers at one factory told me that the unit I was working in would be shut down within six months and moved to Mexico, where people would work for 60 cents an hour.

5   Factory life has shown me what my future might have been like had I never gone to college in the first place. For me, and probably many of my fellow students, higher education always seemed like a foregone conclusion: I never questioned if I was going to college, just where. No other options ever occurred to me. After working 12-hour shifts in a factory, the other options have become brutally clear. When I'm back at the university, skipping classes and turning in lazy rewrites seems like a cop-out after seeing what I would be doing without school. All the advice and public-service announcements about the value of an education that used to sound trite now ring true.

6   These lessons I am learning, however valuable, are always tinged with a sense of guilt. Many people pass their lives in the places I briefly work, spending 30 years where I spend only two months at a time. When fall comes around, I get to go back to a sunny and beautiful campus, while work in the factories continues. At times I feel almost voyeuristic, like a tourist dropping in where other people make their livelihoods. My lessons about education are learned at the expense of those who weren't fortunate enough to receive one. "This job pays well, but it's hell on the body," said one co-worker. "Study hard and keep reading," she added, nodding at the copy of Jack Kerouac's *On the Road*[*] I had wedged into the space next to my machine so I could read discreetly when the line went down.

7   My experience will stay with me long after I head back to school and spend my wages on books and beer. The things that factory work has taught me—how lucky I am to get an education, how to work hard, how easy it is to lose that work once you have it—are by no means earth-shattering. Everyone has to come to grips with them at some point. How and when I learned these lessons, however, has inspired me to make the most of my college years before I enter the real world for good. Until then, the summer months I spend in the factories will be long, tiring and every bit as educational as a French-lit class.

---

[*] American novelist and poet Jack Kerouac was one of the 1950s "Beat Generation" writers.

Questions on Content, Structure, and Style

1. What cause-effect relationship is presented in this essay? Does this essay focus primarily on causes or effects?

2. What are some of the important lessons Braaksma has learned? Learning these lessons at this point in his life inspired Braaksma in what new way?

3. What strategy does Braaksma use to begin his essay, and why? How is this strategy continued throughout the essay?

4. In paragraph 2, what descriptive details and verbs are particularly effective in characterizing the work that Braaksma did at the factories?

5. What specific examples does Braaksma include to help the reader understand his experiences and reactions?

6. Why does Braaksma often characterize himself and other college students in less than positive ways? Is such a characterization likely to appeal to or offend his readers?

7. Why does Braaksma mention that his lessons are "tinged with sense of guilt"?

8. What does the use of dialogue in paragraph 6 add to this essay?

9. Evaluate Braaksma's conclusion. Why does he refer to his French-lit class?

10. Overall, how effective is Braaksma's essay? Did his causal analysis change or reconfirm any of your beliefs about work or school?

Suggestions for Writing

Use Andrew Braaksma's essay "Some Lessons from the Assembly Line" as a stepping-stone to your essay. If you have held full- or part-time jobs, think of how one affected you in specific ways that led to new insight or encouraged you to take new action. Perhaps your work changed your mind about your major or future profession, or perhaps your job helped you decide to begin or return to school (a topic explored in the student essay on pages 268–271). Or, if you prefer, consider any volunteer work you've done that made a difference in your life or in the lives of others. To help your readers understand the cause-effect relationship you're presenting, be sure to include enough logical explanation and vivid details to show clearly how "X" caused "Y."

Vocabulary

blue-collar (2)	cocksure (4)	voyeuristic (6)
lush (2)	downsizing (4)	discreetly (6)
cavernous (2)	tinged (6)	

■ A REVISION WORKSHEET

As you write your rough drafts, consult Chapter 5 for guidance through the revision process. In addition, here are a few questions to ask yourself as you revise your causal analysis essay:

1. Is the thesis limited to a reasonable claim that can be supported in the essay?

2. Is the organization clear and consistent so that the reader can understand the purpose of the analysis?

3. Does the essay focus on the most important causes or effects, or both?

4. If the essay has a narrative form, is each step in the chain reaction clearly connected to the next?

5. Does the essay convincingly show the reader *how* or *why* relationships between the causes and effects exist, instead of merely naming and describing them?

6. Does the essay provide enough evidence to show the connections between causes and effects? Where could additional details be added to make the relationships clearer?

7. Has the essay avoided the problems of oversimplification, circular logic, and the *post hoc* fallacy?

After you've revised your essay extensively, you might exchange rough drafts with a classmate and answer these questions for each other, making specific suggestions for improvement wherever appropriate. (For advice on productive participation in classroom workshops, see pages 108–111.)

Reviewing Your Progress

After you have completed your essay developed by causal analysis, take a moment to measure your progress as a writer by responding to the following questions. Such analysis will help you to recognize growth in your writing skills and may enable you to identify areas that are still problematic.

1. What do you like best about your essay? Why?

2. After considering your essay's presentation of the major causes or effects, which part of your analysis do you think readers will find the most convincing? Why?

3. What part of your essay gave you the most trouble? How did you overcome the problem?

4. If you had more time to work on this essay, what would receive additional attention? Why?

5. What did you learn about your topic from writing this essay? About yourself as a writer?

Chapter 10

Argumentation

Almost without exception, each of us, every day, argues for or against something with somebody. The discussions may be short and friendly ("Let's go to this restaurant rather than that one") or long and complex ("Mandatory motorcycle helmets are an intrusion on civil rights"). Because we do argue our viewpoints so often, most of us realized long ago that shifting into high whine did not always get us what we wanted. On the contrary, we've learned that we usually have a much better chance at winning a dispute or having our plan adopted or changing someone's mind if we present our side of an issue in a calm, logical fashion, giving sound reasons for our position. This approach is just what a good argumentative essay does: it presents logical reasoning and solid evidence that will persuade your readers to accept your point of view.

Some argumentative essays declare the best solution to a problem ("Raising the drinking age will decrease traffic accidents"); others argue a certain way of looking at an issue ("Beauty pageants degrade women"); still others may urge adoption of a specific plan of action ("Voters should pass ordinance 10 to fund the new ice rink"). Whatever your exact purpose, your argumentative essay should be composed of a clear thesis and body paragraphs that offer enough sensible reasons and persuasive evidence to convince your readers to agree with you.

Developing Your Essay

Here are some suggestions for developing and organizing an effective argumentative essay:

Choose an appropriate topic. Selecting a good topic for any essay is important. Choosing a focused, appropriate topic for your argument essay will save you enormous time and energy even before you begin prewriting. Some subjects are simply too large and complex to be adequately treated in a three-to-five-page argumentative essay; selecting such a subject might produce a rough draft of generalities that will not be persuasive. If you have an interest in a subject that is too general or complex for the length of your assignment, try to find a more focused, specific issue within it to argue. For example, the large, controversial (and rather overdone) subject "capital punishment" might be narrowed and focused to a paper advocating time limits for the death-row appeal process or required use of DNA testing. A general opinion on "unfair college grading" might become a more interesting persuasive essay in which the writer takes a stand on the use of pluses and minuses (A–, B+, B–, etc.) on transcript grades. Your general annoyance with smokers might move from "All smoking should be outlawed forever" to an essay focused on the controversial smoking bans in open-air sports stadiums. In other words, while we certainly do debate large issues in our lives, in a short piece of writing it may be more effective, and often more interesting, to choose a focused topic that will allow for more depth in the arguments. You must ultimately decide whether your choice of subject is appropriate for your assignment, but taking a close, second look at your choice now may save you frustration later.

Explore the possibilities . . . and your opinions. Perhaps you have an interesting subject in mind for your argumentative essay, but you don't as yet have a definite opinion on the controversy. Use this opportunity to explore the subject! Do some research, talk to appropriate people, investigate the issues. By discovering your own position, you can address others who may be similarly uncertain about the subject.

Many times, however, you may want to argue for a belief or position you already hold. But before you proceed, take some time to consider the basis of your strong feelings. Not surprisingly, we humans have been known, on various occasions, to spout out opinions we can't always effectively support when challenged to do so. Sometimes we hold an opinion simply because on the surface it seems to make good sense to us or because it fits comfortably with our other social, ethical, or political beliefs. Or we may have inherited some of our beliefs from our families or friends, or perhaps we borrowed ideas from well-known people we admire. In some cases, we may have held an opinion for so long that we can't remember why we adopted it in the first place. We may also have a purely sentimental or emotional attachment to some idea or position. Whatever the original causes of our beliefs, we need to examine the real reasons for thinking what we do before we can effectively convince others.

If you have a strong opinion you want to write about, try jotting down a list of the reasons or points that support your position. Then study the list—are your points logical and persuasive? Which aren't, and why not? After this bit of prewriting, you may discover that although you believe something strongly, you really don't have the kinds of factual evidence or reasoned arguments you need to support your opinion. In some cases, depending on your topic, you may wish to talk to others who share your position or to research your subject (for help with research or interviewing, see Chapter 14); in other cases, you may just need to think longer and harder about your topic and your reasons for maintaining your attitude toward it. Keep an open mind; your exploration may lead you to a surprising new position. (Remember the words of humorist F. G. Burgess: "If in the last few years you haven't discarded a major opinion or acquired a new one, check your pulse. You may be dead.") But with or without formal research, the better you know your subject, the more confident you will be about writing your argumentative essay.

Anticipate opposing views. An argument assumes that there is more than one side to an issue. To be convincing, you must be aware of your opposition's views on the subject and then organize your essay to answer or counter those views. If you don't have a good sense of the opposition's arguments, you can't effectively persuade your readers to dismiss their objections and see matters your way. Therefore, before you begin your first rough draft, write down all the opposing views you can think of and an answer to each of them so that you will know your subject thoroughly. If you are unfamiliar with the major objections to your position, now is the time to investigate your subject further. (For the sake of clarity throughout this chapter, your act of responding to those arguments against your position will be called *refuting the opposition;* "to refute" means "to prove false or wrong," and that's what you will try to do to some of the arguments of those who disagree with you.)

Know and remember your audience. Although it's important to think about your readers' needs and expectations whenever you write, it is essential to consider carefully the audience of your argumentative essay both before and as you write your rough drafts. Because you are trying to persuade people to adopt some new point of view or perhaps to take some action, you need to decide what kinds of supporting evidence will be most convincing to your particular readers. Try to analyze your audience by asking yourself a series of questions. What do they already know about your topic? What information or terms do they need to know to understand your point of view? What biases might they already have for or against your position? What special concerns might your readers have that influence their receptiveness? To be convincing, you should consider these questions and others by carefully reviewing the discussion of audience on pages 19–22 *before* you begin your drafts.

Decide which points of argument to include. Once you have a good sense of your audience, your own position, and your opposition's strongest arguments, try making a Pro-and-Con Sheet to help you sort out which points you will discuss in your essay.

Let's suppose you want to write an editorial on the sale-of-class-notes controversy at your school. Should professional note-takers be allowed to sit in on a course and then sell their notes to class members? After reviewing the evidence on both sides, you have decided to argue that your school should prohibit professional note-taking services from attending large lecture classes and selling notes. To help yourself begin planning your essay, you list all the pro-and-con arguments you can think of concerning the controversy:

My Side: Against the Sale of Class Notes	My Opposition's Side: For the Sale of Class Notes
1. Unfair advantage for some students in some classes	1. Helps students to get better test, course grades
2. Note-taking is a skill students need to develop	2. Helps students to learn, organize material
3. Rich students can afford and poor can't	3. Helps if you're sick and can't attend class
4. Prevents students from learning to organize for themselves	4. Shows students good models for taking notes and outlining them

My Side: Against the Sale of Class Notes	My Opposition's Side: For the Sale of Class Notes
5. Encourages class cutting	**5.** Other study guides are on the market, why not these?
6. Missing class means no chance to ask questions, participate in discussions	**6.** Gives starving graduate students jobs
7. Notes taken by others are often inaccurate	**7.** No laws against sale of notes, free country
8. Some professors don't like strangers in classroom	
9. Students need to think for themselves	

After making your Pro-and-Con Sheet, look over the list and decide which of your strongest points you want to argue in your paper and also which of your opposition's claims you want to refute. At this point you may also see some arguments on your list that might be combined and some that might be deleted because they're irrelevant or unconvincing. (Be careful not to select more arguments or counter-arguments to discuss than the length of your writing assignment will allow. It's far better to present a persuasive analysis of a few points than it is to give an underdeveloped, shallow treatment of a host of reasons.)

Let's say you want to cover the following points in your essay:

- Professional note-taking services keep students from developing their own thinking and organizational skills (combination of 4 and 9)
- Professional note-taking services discourage class attendance and participation (5 and 6)
- Unfair advantages to some students (1 and 3).

Your assignment calls for an essay of 750 to 1,000 words, so you figure you'll only have space to refute your opposition's strongest claim. You decide to refute this claim:

- Helps students to learn and organize material (2).

The next step is to formulate a working thesis. At this stage, you may find it helpful to put your working thesis in an "although-because" statement so you can clearly see both your opposition's arguments and your own. An "although-because" thesis for the note-taking essay might look something like this:

> *Although* some students maintain that using professional note-taking services helps them learn more, such services should be banned from our campus *because* they prevent students from developing their own thinking and organizational skills, they discourage class attendance, and they give unfair advantages to some students.

Frequently, your "although-because" thesis will be too long and awkward to use in the later drafts of your essay. But for now, it can serve as a guide, allowing you to see your overall position before the writing of the first draft begins. (To practice compiling a Pro-Con List and writing an "although-because" thesis, turn to the exercise on pages 289–290.)

Organize your essay clearly. Although there is no set model of organization for argumentative essays, here are some common patterns that you might use or that you might combine in some effective way.

Important note: For the sake of simplicity, the first two outlines present two of the writer's points and two opposing ideas. Naturally, your essay may contain any number of points and refuted points, depending on the complexity of your subject and the assigned length of your essay.

In Pattern A, you devote the first few body paragraphs to arguing points on your side and then turn to refuting or answering the opposition's claims.

Pattern A: Thesis

Body paragraph 1: you present your first point and its supporting evidence

Body paragraph 2: you present your second point and its supporting evidence

Body paragraph 3: you refute your opposition's first point

Body paragraph 4: you refute your opposition's second point

Conclusion

Sometimes you may wish to clear away the opposition's claims before you present the arguments for your side. To do so, you might select Pattern B:

Pattern B: Thesis

Body paragraph 1: you refute your opposition's first point

Body paragraph 2: you refute your opposition's second point

Body paragraph 3: you present your first point and its supporting evidence

Body paragraph 4: you present your second point and its supporting evidence

Conclusion

In some cases, you may find that the main arguments you want to present are the very same ones that will refute or answer your opposition's primary claims. If so, try Pattern C, which allows each of your argumentative points to refute one of your opposition's claims in the same paragraph:

Pattern C: Thesis

Body paragraph 1: you present your first point and its supporting evidence, which also refutes one of your opposition's claims

Body paragraph 2: you present a second point and its supporting evidence, which also refutes a second opposition claim

Body paragraph 3: you present a third point and its supporting evidence, which also refutes a third opposition claim

Conclusion

Now you might be thinking, "What if my position on a topic as yet has no opposition?" Remember that almost all issues have more than one side, so try to anticipate objections and then answer them. For example, you might first present a thesis that calls for a new traffic signal at a dangerous intersection in your town and then address hypothetical counter-arguments, such as "The City Council may say that a stop light at Lemay and

Columbia will cost too much, but the cost in lives will be much greater" or "Commuters may complain that a traffic light there will slow the continuous flow of north-south traffic, but it is precisely the uninterrupted nature of this road that encourages motorists to speed." By answering hypothetical objections, you impress your readers by showing them you've thought through your position thoroughly before you asked them to consider your point of view.

You might also be thinking, "What if my opposition actually has a valid objection, a legitimate point of criticism? Should I ignore it?" Hoping that an obviously strong opposing point will just go away is like hoping the IRS will cancel income taxes this year—a nice thought but hardly likely. Don't ignore your opposition's good point; instead, acknowledge it, but then go on quickly to show your readers why that reason, though valid, isn't compelling enough by itself to motivate people to adopt your opposition's entire position. Or you might concede that one point while simultaneously showing why your position isn't really in conflict with that criticism, but rather with other, more important, parts of your opponent's viewpoint. By admitting that you see some validity in your opposition's argument, you can again show your readers that you are both fair-minded and informed about all aspects of the controversy.

If you are feeling confident about your ability to organize an argumentative essay, you might try some combination of patterns, if your material allows such a treatment. For example, you might have a strong point to argue, another point that simultaneously answers one of your opposition's strongest claims, and another opposition point you want to refute. Your essay organization might look like this:

Combination: Thesis

Body paragraph 1: a point for your side

Body paragraph 2: one of your points, which also refutes an opposition claim

Body paragraph 3: your refutation of another opposition claim

Conclusion

In other words, you can organize your essay in a variety of ways as long as your paper is logical and clear. Study your Pro-and-Con Sheet and then decide which organization best presents the arguments and counter-arguments you want to include. Try sketching out your essay following each of the patterns; look carefully to see which pattern (or variation of one of the patterns) seems to put forward your particular material most persuasively, with the least repetition or confusion. Sometimes your essay's material will clearly fall into a particular pattern of organization, so your choice will be easy. More often, however, you will have to arrange and rearrange your ideas and counter-arguments until you see the best approach. Don't be discouraged if you decide to change patterns after you've begun a rough draft; what matters is finding the most effective way to persuade the reader to your side.

If no organizational pattern seems to fit at first, ask yourself which of your points or counter-arguments is the strongest or most important. Try putting that point in one of the two most emphatic places: either first or last. Sometimes your most important discussion will lead the way to your other points and, consequently, should be introduced first; perhaps more often, effective writers and speakers build up to their strongest point, presenting it last as the climax of their argument. Again, the choice depends on your material itself, though it's rare that you would want to bury your strongest point in the middle of your essay.

Now let's return to the essay on note-taking first discussed on page 279. After selecting the most important arguments and counter-arguments (pages 279–280), let's say that you decide that your main point concerns the development of students' learning skills. Since your opposition claims the contrary, that their service does promote learning, you see that you can make your main point as you refute theirs. But you also wish to include a couple of other points for your side. After trying several patterns, you decide to put the "thinking skills" rebuttal last for emphasis and present your other points first. Consequently, Pattern A best fits your plan. A sketchy outline might look like this:

- *Revised working thesis and essay map:* Professional note-taking services should be banned from our campus. Not only do they give some students unfair advantages and discourage class attendance, they prevent students from developing and practicing good learning skills.

- *Body paragraph 1 (a first point for the writer's side):* Services penalize some students—those who haven't enough money or take other sections or enroll in classes without lectures.

- *Body paragraph 2 (another point for the writer's side):* Services encourage cutting class and so students miss opportunities to ask questions, participate in discussion, talk to instructor, see visual aids, etc.

- *Body paragraph 3 (rebuttal of the opposition's strongest claim):* Services claim they help students learn more, but they don't because they're doing the work students ought to be doing themselves. Students must learn to think and organize for themselves.

Once you have a general notion of where your essay is going, plan to spend some more time thinking about ways to make each of your points clear, logical, and persuasive to your particular audience. (If you wish to see how one student actually developed an essay based on the preceding outline, turn to the sample student paper on pages 293–295.)

Argue your ideas logically. To convince your readers, you must provide sufficient reasons for your position. You must give more than mere opinion—you must offer logical arguments to back up your assertions. Some of the possible ways of supporting your ideas should already be familiar to you from writing expository essays; listed here are several methods and illustrations:

1. Give examples (real or hypothetical): "Cutting class because you have access to professional notes can be harmful; for instance, you might miss seeing some slides or graphics essential to your understanding of the lecture."

2. Present a comparison or contrast: "In contrast to reading 'canned' notes, outlining your own notes helps you remember the material."

3. Show a cause-and-effect relationship: "Dependence on professional notes may mean that some students will never learn to organize their own responses to classroom discussions."

4. Argue by definition: "Passively reading through professional notes isn't a learning experience in which one's mind is engaged."

The well-thought-out arguments you choose to support your case may be called *logical appeals* because they appeal to, and depend on, your readers' ability to reason and to recognize good sense when they see it. But there is another kind of appeal often used today: the *emotional appeal*.

Emotional appeals are designed to persuade people by playing on their feelings rather than appealing to their intellect. Rather than using thoughtful, logical reasoning to support their claims, writers and speakers using *only* emotional appeals often try to accomplish their goals by distracting or misleading their audiences. Frequently, emotional appeals are characterized by language that plays on people's fears, material desires, prejudices, or sympathies; such language often triggers highly favorable or unfavorable responses to a subject. For instance, emotional appeals are used constantly in advertising, where feel-good images, music, and slogans ("Come to Marlboro Country"; "The Heartbeat of America Is Today's Chevy Truck") are designed to sway potential customers to a product without them thinking about it too much. Some politicians also rely heavily on emotional appeals, often using scare tactics to disguise a situation or to lead people away from questioning the logic of a particular issue.

But in some cases, emotional appeals can be used for legitimate purposes. Good writers should always be aware of their audience's needs, values, and states of mind, and they may be more persuasive on occasion if they can frame their arguments in ways that appeal to both their readers' logic and their emotions. For example, when Martin Luther King, Jr., delivered his famous "I Have a Dream" speech to the crowds gathered in Washington, D. C., in 1963 and described his vision of little children of different races walking hand in hand, being judged not "by the color of their skin but by the content of their character," he certainly spoke with passion that was aimed at the hearts of his listeners. But King was not using an emotional appeal to keep his audience from thinking about his message; on the contrary, he presented powerful emotional images that he hoped would inspire people to act on what they already thought and felt, their deepest convictions about equality and justice.

Appeals to emotions are tricky: you can use them effectively in conjunction with appeals to logic and with solid evidence, but only if you use them ethically. Too many appeals to the emotions are also overwhelming; readers tire quickly from excessive tugs on the heartstrings. To prevent your readers from suspecting deception or feeling manipulated, support your assertions with as many logical arguments as you can muster, and use emotional appeals only when they legitimately advance your cause.

Offer evidence that effectively supports your claims. In addition to presenting thoughtful, logical reasoning, you may wish to incorporate a variety of convincing evidence to persuade your readers to your side. Your essay might profit from including, where appropriate, some of the following kinds of supporting evidence:

- Personal experiences
- The experiences or testimony of others whose opinions are pertinent to the topic
- Factual information you've gathered from research
- Statistics from current, reliable sources
- Hypothetical examples
- Testimony from authorities and experts
- Charts, graphs, or diagrams

You'll need to spend quite a bit of your prewriting time thinking about the best kinds of evidence to support your case. Remember that not all personal experiences or research materials are persuasive. For instance, the experiences we've had (or that our friends have had) may not be representative of a universal experience and consequently may lead to unconvincing generalizations. Even testimony from an authority may not be convincing if the person is not speaking on a topic from his or her field of expertise; famous football players, for instance, don't necessarily know any more about panty hose or soft drinks than anyone else. Always put yourself in the skeptical reader's place and ask, "Does this point convince me? If not, why not?" (For more information on incorporating research material into your essays, see Chapter 14. For more advice on the selection of evidence, see the section on critical thinking in Chapter 5.)

Find the appropriate tone. Sometimes when we argue, it's easy to get carried away. Remember that your goal is to persuade and perhaps change your readers, not alienate them. Instead of laying on insults or sarcasm, present your ideas in a moderate let-us-reason-together spirit. Such a tone will persuade your readers that you are sincere in your attempts to argue as truthfully and fairly as possible. If your readers do not respect you as a reasonable person, they certainly won't be swayed to your side of an issue. Don't preach or pontificate either; no one likes—or respects—a writer with a superior attitude. Write in your natural "voice"; don't adopt a pseudo-intellectual tone. In short, to argue effectively you should sound logical, sincere, and informed. (For additional comments on tone, review pages 148–150.)

Consider using Rogerian techniques, if they are appropriate. In some cases, especially those involving tense situations or highly sensitive issues, you may wish to incorporate some techniques of the noted psychologist Carl Rogers, who developed a procedure for presenting what he called the nonthreatening argument. Rogers believed that people involved in a debate should strive for clear, honest communication so that the problem under discussion could be resolved. Instead of going on the defensive and trying to "win" the argument, each side should try to recognize common ground and then develop a solution that will address the needs of both parties.

A Rogerian argument uses these techniques:

1. A clear, objective statement of the problem or issue
2. A clear, objective summary of the opposition's position that shows you understand its point of view and goals
3. A clear, objective summary of your point of view, stated in nonthreatening language
4. A discussion that emphasizes the beliefs, values, and goals that you and your opposition have in common
5. A description of any of your points that you are willing to concede or compromise
6. An explanation of a plan or proposed solution that meets the needs of both sides

By showing your opposition that you thoroughly understand its position and that you are sincerely trying to effect a solution that is in everyone's—not just your—best interests, you may succeed in some situations that might otherwise be hopeless because of their highly emotional nature. Remember, too, that you can use some of these Rogerian techniques in any kind of argument paper you are writing, if you think they would be effective.

Problems to Avoid

Writers of argumentative essays must appear logical or their readers will reject their point of view. Here is a short list of some of the most common *logical fallacies*—that is, errors in reasoning. Check your rough drafts carefully to avoid these problems.

Students sometimes ask, "If a logical fallacy works, why not use it? Isn't all fair in love, war, and argumentative essays?" The honest answer is maybe. It's quite true that speakers and writers do use faulty logic and irrational emotional appeals to persuade people every day (one needs only to look at television or a newspaper to see example after example). But the cost of the risk is high: if you do try to slide one by your readers and they see through your trick, you will lose your credibility instantly. On the whole, it's far more effective to use logical reasoning and strong evidence to convince your readers to accept your point of view.

■ Common Logical Fallacies

Hasty generalization: The writer bases the argument on insufficient or unrepresentative evidence. Suppose, for example, you have owned two poodles and they have both attacked you. If you declare that all poodles are vicious dogs, you are making a hasty generalization. There are, of course, thousands of poodles who have not attacked anyone. Similarly, you're in error if you interview only campus athletes and then declare, "University students favor a new stadium." What about the opinions of the students who aren't athletes? In other words, when the generalization is drawn from a sample that is too small or select, your conclusion isn't valid.

Non sequitur **("it doesn't follow"): The writer's conclusion is not necessarily a logical result of the facts.** An example of a *non sequitur* occurs when you conclude, "Professor Smith is a famous chemist, so he will be a brilliant chemistry teacher." As you may have realized by now, the fact that someone knows a subject well does not automatically mean that he or she can communicate the information clearly in a classroom; hence, the conclusion is not necessarily valid.

Begging the question: The writer presents as truth what is not yet proven by the argument. For example, in the statement "All useless laws such as Reform Bill 13 should be repealed," the writer has already pronounced the bill useless without assuming responsibility for proving that accusation. Similarly, the statement "Professors on our campus who are using their classroom solely for preaching their political ideas should be fired" begs the question (that is, tries like a beggar to get something for nothing from the reader) because the writer gives no evidence for what must first be argued, not merely asserted—that there are in fact professors on that particular campus using class time solely for spreading their political beliefs.

Red herring: The writer introduces an irrelevant point to divert the readers' attention from the main issue. This term originates from the old tactic used by escaped prisoners, of dragging a smoked herring, a strong-smelling fish, across their trail to confuse tracking dogs by making them follow the wrong scent. For example, roommate A might be criticizing roommate B for his repeated failure to do the dishes when it was his turn. To escape facing the charges, roommate B brings up times in the past when the other roommate failed to repay some money he borrowed. Although roommate A may indeed have a problem with remembering his debts, that discussion isn't relevant to the original argument about sharing the responsibility for the dishes. (By the way, you might have run across a well-known newspaper photograph of a California environmentalist group demonstrating for more protection of dolphins, whales, and other marine life; look closely to see, over in the left corner, almost hidden by the host of placards and banners, a fellow slyly holding up a sign that reads "Save the Red Herring!" Now, who says rhetoricians don't have a good sense of humor?)

Post hoc, ergo propter hoc. See page 265.

Argument *ad hominem* ("to the man"): The writer attacks the opponent's character rather than the opponent's argument. The statement "Dr. Bloom can't be a competent marriage counselor because she's been divorced" may not be valid. Bloom's advice to her clients may be excellent regardless of her own marital status.

Faulty use of authority: The writer relies on "authorities" who are not convincing sources. Although someone may be well known in a particular field, he or she may not be qualified to testify in a different area. A baseball player in an ad for laser surgery may stress his need for correct vision, but he may be no more knowledgeable about eye care than anyone else on the street. In other words, name recognition is not enough. For their testimony to count with readers, authorities must have expertise, credentials, or relevant experience in the area under discussion. (See also pages 285, 380–382, and "transfer of virtue" in the discussion of "bandwagon appeal" on page 288.)

Argument *ad populum* ("to the people"): The writer evades the issues by appealing to readers' emotional reactions to certain subjects. For example, instead of arguing the facts of an issue, a writer might play on the readers' negative response to such words as "communism," "fascism," or "radical," and their positive response to words like "God," "country," "liberty," or "patriotic." In the statement "If you are a true American, you will vote against the referendum on flag burning," the writer avoids any discussion of the merits or weaknesses of the bill and merely substitutes an emotional appeal. Other popular "virtue words" include "duty," "common sense," "courage," and "healthy." (Advertisers, of course, also play on consumers' emotions by filling their ads with pictures of babies, animals, status objects, and sexually attractive men and women.)

Circular thinking. See page 265.

Either/or: The writer tries to convince the readers that there are only two sides to an issue—one right, one wrong. The statement "If you don't go to war against Iceland, you don't love your country" is irrational because it doesn't consider the other possibilities, such as patriotic people's right to oppose war as an expression of love for their country. A classic example of this sort of oversimplification was illustrated in the 1960s' bumper sticker that was popular during the debate over the Vietnam War: "America: Love It or Leave It." Obviously, there are other choices ("Change It or Lose It," for instance, to quote another either/or bumper sticker of that era).

Hypostatization: The writer uses an abstract concept as if it were a concrete reality. Always be suspicious of a writer who frequently relies on statements beginning "History has always taught us . . ." or "Science has proven . . ." or "Research shows . . . ." The implication in each case is that history or science (or any other discipline) has only one voice, one opinion. On the contrary, "history" is written by a multitude of historians who hold a variety of opinions; doctors and scientists also frequently disagree. Instead of generalizing about a particular field, quote a respected authority or simply qualify your statement by referring to "many" or "some" scientists, historians, or other professionals.

Bandwagon appeal: The writer tries to validate a point by intimating that "everyone else believes in this." Such a tactic evades discussion of the issue itself. Advertising often uses this technique: "Everyone who demands real taste smokes Phooey cigarettes"; "Discriminating women use Smacky-Mouth lipstick." (The ultimate in "bandwagon" humor may have appeared on a recent Colorado bumper sticker: "Eat lamb—could 1000s of coyotes be wrong?") A variation of the "bandwagon" fallacy is sometimes referred to as "transfer of virtue," the sharing of light from someone else's sparkle. Advertisers often use this technique by paying attractive models or media stars to endorse their product. The underlying premise is this:

> Popular/beautiful/"cool"/rich people use/buy/wear "X"; if you use "X," you too will be popular/beautiful/etc.

Intelligent readers and consumers know, of course, to suspect such doubtful causal relationships.

Straw man: The writer selects the opposition's weakest or most insignificant point to argue against, to divert the readers' attention from the real issues. Instead of addressing the opposition's best arguments and defeating them, the writer "sets up a straw man"—that is, the writer picks out a trivial (or irrelevant) argument against his or her own position and easily knocks it down, just as one might easily push over a figure made of straw. Perhaps the most famous example of the "straw man" occurred in 1952 when, during his vice-presidential campaign, Richard Nixon was accused of misappropriating campaign funds for his personal use. Addressing the nation on television, Nixon described how his six-year-old daughter, Tricia, had received a little cocker spaniel named Checkers from a Texas supporter. Nixon went on about how much his children loved the dog and how, regardless of what anyone thought, by gosh, he was going to keep that cute dog for little Tricia. Of course, no one was asking Nixon to return the dog; they were asking about the $18,000 in missing campaign funds. But Nixon's canine gift was much easier for him to defend, and the "Checkers" speech is now famous as one of the most notorious "straw man" diversions.

Faulty analogy: The writer uses an extended comparison as proof of a point. Look closely at all extended comparisons and metaphors to see if the two things being compared are really similar. For example, in a recent editorial a woman protested new laws requiring parents to use car seats for small children, arguing that if the state could require the seats, they could just as easily require mothers to breastfeed instead of using formula. Are the two situations alike? Car accidents are the leading cause of death of children under four; is formula deadly? Or perhaps you've read that putting teenagers in sex education classes is like taking an alcoholic to a bar. Is it? Is stem cell research the same as Nazi medical experiments, as the leader of a family-outreach religious group has claimed? If readers don't see a close similarity, the analogy may not be persuasive. Moreover, remember that even though a compelling analogy may suggest similarities, it alone cannot *prove* anything. (For more discussion of analogy, see pages 233–236.)

Quick fix: The writer leans too heavily on catchy phrases or empty slogans. A clever turn of phrase may grab one's attention, but it may lose its persuasiveness when scrutinized closely. For instance, a banner at a recent rally to protest a piece of antigun legislation read, "When guns are outlawed, only outlaws will have guns." Although the sentence had nice balance, it oversimplified the issue. The legislation in question was not trying to outlaw all guns, just the sale of the infamous Saturday Night Specials, most often used in crimes and domestic violence; the sale of guns for sport, such as hunting rifles, would remain legal. Other slogans sound good but are simply irrelevant: a particular soft drink, for example, may be "the real thing," but what drink isn't? Look closely at clever lines substituted for reasoned argument; always demand clear terms and logical explanations.*

■ PRACTICING WHAT YOU'VE LEARNED

A. Imagine that you are writing an argumentative essay addressing the controversial question "Should home-schooled students be allowed to play on public school athletic teams?" You have investigated the topic and have noted the variety of opinions listed here. Arrange the statements into two lists: a "Pro" list (those statements that argue for allowing home schoolers to play) and a "Con" list (those statements that are against allowing home schoolers to play). Cross off any inappropriate or illogical statements you find; combine any opinions that overlap.

    1. Parents of home schoolers pay the same taxes as public school parents.

    2. Public school kids must meet grade requirements to be eligible.

    3. School rules prohibit nonenrolled youth on campus.

---

* Sometimes advertisers get more for their slogans than they bargained for. According to one news source, a popular soft-drink company had to spend millions to revise its slogan after introducing its product into parts of China. Apparently the slogan "Come alive! Join the Blah-Blah-Cola Generation!" translated into some dialects as "Blah-Blah Cola Brings Your Ancestors Back from the Dead"!

4. Home schoolers shouldn't get the benefits of a school they've rejected.

5. Public school kids are bad influences on home schoolers.

6. Home schoolers need the social interaction.

7. Public school teams can always use more good athletes.

8. More students will overburden athletic facilities.

9. Home schoolers miss their public school friends, and vice versa.

10. Ten states allow home schoolers to play on teams.

11. Home schoolers will displace public school students on teams.

12. Public school students have to meet attendance rules to be eligible.

13. Athletic competition is good for everybody.

14. Home schoolers often have controversial political beliefs that will cause fights.

15. Team members need to share the same community on a daily basis.

16. Home schoolers aren't as invested in school pride.

Once you have your two lists, decide your own position on this topic. Then select two points you might use to argue your position and one opposing criticism you might refute. Put your working thesis into an "although-because" format, as explained on page 280. Compare your choices to those of your classmates.

B. Errors in reasoning can cause your reader to doubt your credibility. In the following mock essay, for example, the writer includes a variety of fallacies that undermine his argument; see if you can identify all his errors.

Ban Those Books!

1   A serious problem faces America today, a problem of such grave importance that our very existence as a nation is threatened. We must either cleanse our schools of evil-minded books, or we must reconcile ourselves to seeing our children become welfare moochers and homeless bums.

2   History has shown time and time again that placement of immoral books in our schools is part of an insidious plot designed to weaken the moral fiber of our youth from coast to coast. In Wettuckett, Ohio, for example, the year after books by Mark Twain, such as *Tom Sawyer* and *Huckleberry Finn,* were introduced into the school library by liberal free-thinkers and radicals, the number of students cutting classes rose by 6 percent. And in that same year, the number of high school seniors going on to college dropped from thirty to twenty-two.

3   The reason for this could either be a natural decline in intelligence and morals or the influence of those dirty books that teach our beloved children disrespect and irresponsibility. Since there is no evidence to suggest a natural decline, the conclusion is inescapable: once our children read about Twain's characters skipping school and running away from home, they had to do likewise. If they hadn't read about such undesirable characters as Huckleberry Finn, our innocent children would never have behaved in those ways.

4   Now, I am a simple man, a plain old farm boy—the pseudo-intellectuals call me redneck just like they call you folks. But I can assure you that, redneck or not, I've got the guts to fight moral decay everywhere I find it, and I urge you to do the same. For this reason I want all you good folks to come to the ban-the-books rally this Friday so we can talk it over. I promise you all your right-thinking neighbors will be there.

■ ASSIGNMENT

Search for the following:

1. An example of an advertisement that illustrates one or more of the fallacies or appeals discussed on pages 286–289;

2. An example of illogical or fallacious reasoning in a piece of writing (you might try looking at the editorial page or letters-to-the-editor section of your local or campus newspaper);

3. An example of a logical, persuasive point in a piece of writing.

Be prepared to explain your analyses of your samples, but do not write any sort of identifying label or evaluation on the samples themselves. Bring your ads and pieces of writing to class and exchange them with those of a classmate. After ten minutes, compare notes. Do you and your classmate agree on the evaluation of each sample? Why or why not?

■ ESSAY TOPICS

Write a convincing argument attacking or defending one of the follow-ing statements, or use them to help you think of your own topic. Remember to narrow and focus the topic as necessary. (Note that essays on some of the topics presented here might profit from research material; see Chapter 14 for help.) For additional ideas, see the "Suggestions for Writing" section following the professional essays (page 298).

1. Students should/should not work throughout high school.

2. Expanded guest-worker immigration programs should/should not be implemented in this country.

3. Sixteen-year-olds should/should not be issued limited-privilege or "graduated" driver's licenses.

4. The movie rating system should/should not be revised.

5. All adoption records should/should not be open to adopted people over 18.

6. A school voucher system should/should not be used in this state.

7. Students who do poorly in their academic courses should/should not be allowed to participate in athletic programs.

8. All schools should/should not adopt a "repeat/delete" policy, allowing students to retake a course and substitute a higher grade on their record.

9. Televised instant replays should/should not be used to call plays in football and other sports.

10. Drivers' use of cell phones while vehicles are in motion should/should not be prohibited.

11. Sodas and high-sugar foods should/should not be sold in public school vending machines.

12. Off-road recreational vehicles should/should not be banned from our national parks.

13. Funeral protest bans do/do not infringe on freedom of speech.

14. Public school students should/should not be required to wear uniforms.

15. The electoral system should/should not be used to select the U.S. president.

16. Controversial names or symbols of athletic teams ("Redskins," the Confederate flag, the tomahawk chop) should/should not be changed.

17. A bill increasing the minimum wage (or some other controversial bill or policy) should/should not be approved.

18. Individuals under age 14 charged with crimes should/should not be tried as adults.

19. Men and women in the military should/should not serve in separate units.

20. Advertising for "Product X" rarely/often relies on use of emotional appeals and faulty logic. (Focus on one kind of product—cars, cosmetics, computers, soft drinks, cell phones, etc.—or on one especially popular brand, and collect a number of its ads to analyze. What does your analysis reveal about the major ways the product is advertised to its target audience? Do the ads appeal to consumers' reason or do they employ logical fallacies? Some combination? Which ads are more effective, and why? If it's helpful, consider the appeals of ads reprinted in this text. A list of the ads follows the table of contents.)

A Topic Proposal for Your Essay

Selecting the right subject matter is important to every writer. To help you clarify your ideas and strengthen your commitment to your topic, here is a proposal sheet that asks you to describe some of your preliminary ideas about your subject before you begin drafting. Although your ideas may change as you write (they will almost certainly become more refined), thinking through your choice of topic now may help you avoid several false starts.

1. What is the subject of your argumentative essay? Write a rough statement of your opinion on this subject.

2. Why are you interested in this topic? Is it important to your personal, civic, or professional life? State at least one reason for your choice of topic.

3. Is this a significant topic of interest to others? Why? Is there a particular audience you would like to address?

4. At this point, can you list at least two reasons that support your opinion of your topic?

5. Who opposes your opinion? Can you state clearly at least one of your opposition's major criticisms of your position?

6. What difficulties, if any, might arise during drafting? For example, might you need to collect any additional evidence through reading, research, or interviewing to support your points or to refute your opposition?

■ Sample Student Essay

The student who wrote this essay followed the steps for writing an argumentative paper discussed in this chapter. His intended audience was the readers of his school newspaper, primarily students but instructors as well. To argue his case, he chose Pattern A, presenting two of his own points and then concluding with a rebuttal of an important opposing view. Notice that this writer uses a variety of methods to convince his readers, including hypothetical examples, causal analysis, analogy, and testimony. Does the writer persuade you to his point of view? Which are his strongest and weakest arguments? What might you change to make his essay even more persuasive?

STUDENTS, TAKE NOTE!

1   A walk across campus this week will reveal students, professors, and administrators arguing about class notes like never before. But they're not engaged in intellectual debates over chemical formulas or literary images. They're fighting over the taking of the notes themselves, as professional note-taking services in town are applying for permission to sit in on large lecture courses and then sell their notes to the students in those classes. Although the prospect of having "canned" notes looks inviting to many students, our administration should nevertheless ban these services from campus. Not only do such businesses give certain students unfair advantages and discourage class attendance, but they also prohibit the development of students' important learning skills, despite the services' claims to the contrary.

Introduction: Presenting the controversy

Thesis

Essay map

A point for the writer's position: Note-taking services are unfair to some students

2   What is bothersome for many of us about the professional-notes option is our sense of fair play. Let's face it: like it or not, school is, among other things, a place of competition, as students vie for the best academic records to send to prospective employers, graduate and professional schools, and in some cases, paying parents. In today's classes, all students have an equal opportunity to come to class, take notes, study, and pass or fail on their own merits. But the expensive professional notes, already organized and outlined, may give those with plenty of money some advantages that poorer students—those on scholarships or with families, for example—just can't afford. In addition, the notes may be available only to those students who take certain sections of a course and not others, thus giving some students an extra advantage. The same is true for students who satisfy a requirement by taking one course that has notes available rather than another that has not. Knowing that you're doing your own work may make you feel morally superior to a classmate who isn't, but frankly, on some other level, it just plain feels irritating and unfair, sort of like watching your roommate getting away with plagiarizing his paper for a class after you spent weeks researching yours.

Another point for the writer's position: Professional notes discourage students from attending and participating in class

3   In addition to being a potential source of conflict among students, the professional-note services aren't winning many friends among the faculty, either. Several instructors have complained that the availability of notes will encourage many students, especially the weaker ones, to cut classes, assuming that they have all the material necessary for understanding the lecture, discussion, or lab. But anyone who has ever had to use borrowed notes knows something vital is not there. Someone else's interpretation of the information is often hard or impossible to follow, especially if you must understand complex relationships and problems. Moreover, skipping class may mean missed opportunities for students to ask questions or to participate in experiments or in group discussions, all of which often help clarify concepts under study. Not seeing visual aids or diagrams in person

can also result in problems understanding the material. And, last, missing class can mean failure to become comfortably acquainted with the teacher, which, in turn, may discourage a student from asking for individual help when it's needed. All these possibilities are real; even Jeff Allridge, owner of the Quotable Notes service, has admitted to a campus reporter, "There *is* an incentive to skip class."

4   Despite the admission that professional note-taking encourages class-cutting, the services still promote themselves by claiming that students using their notes learn more. They support this claim by arguing that their notes offer students clearly organized information and, according to one advertising brochure, "good models" for students to follow in other classes. But such arguments miss the larger point: students should be learning how to develop their own note-taking, organizing, and thinking skills rather than swallowing the material whole as neatly packaged and delivered. Memorizing class material as outlined can be important, but it's not really as valuable in the long run as learning how to think about the material and use it to solve problems or come up with new ideas later. Taking your own notes teaches you how to listen and how to spot the important concepts; organizing your own notes teaches you how to pull ideas together in a logical way, all skills students will need in other classes, on jobs, and in life in general. Having memorized the outlines but not really mastered the thinking skills won't help the medical student whose patient's symptoms vary from the textbook description or the engineer whose airplane wings suddenly fail the stress test for no apparent reason.

> Presentation and rebuttal of the opposition's claim that students learn more using professional notes

5   By appealing to students who believe professional notes will help them accomplish their educational goals easier and quicker, a variety of note-taking services now have franchises across the country. But our campus shouldn't allow them to move in. Students need to recognize that the difference between the services' definition of "learning" and the real learning experiences college can provide is of notable importance.

> Conclusion: Restatement of thesis, ending on pun to emphasize the main idea

Professional Essays*

The following essays on school schedules were first published together in *USA Today* in a "Today's Debate" column (January 23, 2006). The first essay represents the views of the newspaper's editorial board; the second essay was written by Paul D. Houston, executive director of the American Association of School Administrators since 1994. Houston has written over two hundred articles on education, collected in two published volumes, and has co-authored three books, the most recent being *The Spiritual Dimension of Leadership* (2006).

Although you may already hold an opinion on this controversy, try to remain objective as you analyze the strengths and weaknesses of both essays. Which points are most and least persuasive, and why?

■ *USA Today*: High Schools, Wake Up!

1   For the typical U.S. high school student, the morning alarm goes off no later than 6:30 A.M. Breakfast (aka "the most important meal of the day") is either scarfed down or skipped altogether. The school bus arrives by 7 A.M., and the first class starts by 7:30 A.M.

2   This schedule works well for sports coaches: With school out by 2:30 P.M., they have plenty of time to whip their teams into shape. It works well for employers and employees. And many work-bound parents like the idea that their kids leave the house before they do.

3   The schedule doesn't work well, however, for the students themselves, who by second period can be seen nodding off at their desks. Sleep researchers side with the teens, whose brains appear wired to stay up later and who require more sleep than do kids of other age groups. Sleep-deprived teens are grouchier, poorer learners, more prone to attention deficit disorders and more likely to cut classes, say sleep researchers from Brown University and the University of Minnesota.

4   So why does nearly every school district in the USA start high school so early? Bus schedules and money.

5   School buses need to make three full cycles to bring elementary, middle and high school students to school. Starting high school later would mean buying more buses and hiring more drivers—or sending younger students to school earlier. Sending the younger students sooner isn't as bad as it sounds. Many are up early anyway. And there's unlikely to be a shortage of parents willing to stand with them at bus stops on dark mornings.

6   School leaders in Edina, Minn., flipped bus schedules nearly a decade ago. For teens and educators there, high school starts at 8:30 A.M. And they're happily sticking with it.

7   Few school districts have followed Edina's lead, however. That's shortsighted. Pushing back high schools' start times can produce:

   ■ Better school attendance. A study of seven Minneapolis high schools that pushed back start times showed higher school attendance in all grades,

---

* For help reading these essays analytically, review pages 170–172.

especially ninth. The same study showed a small improvement in academic performance.

- Happier students and parents. Parents in Edina reported that improved sleep far outweighs concerns over busing, sports and jobs. After one year on the new schedule, 92% of those surveyed approved the change.

- Safer teens. Dumping unsupervised teens onto streets at 2:30 P.M. never made a lot of sense to parents or police. Not only would more teens have less time to get into trouble before adults arrive home, but teens who drive would also be less vulnerable to fatigue-related accidents, sleep experts say.

8   School superintendents defending the status quo cite sports, after-school jobs and school bus schedules. Bus schedules are the only reason to hesitate. Even advocates of pushing back high school start times acknowledge that bus schedules are nightmarishly complicated.

9   But if Edina managed to figure it out, so can other districts. The payoff—more alert, less grumpy teens—is worth the effort, even if the school board needs to pull a few all-nighters to work out the details.

■ Paul D. Houston's Opposing View: Reform No Child's Play

1   The idea that the "early bird gets the worm" might be part of our folklore, but it's the wrong idea for high school students. Recent research on teenagers confirms what most parents already suspected: The teenage brain is unique. Natural sleep patterns for this age group are different, causing teenagers to engage later and stay alert later. This research has some districts rethinking their high school schedules.

2   If teenagers function better with a later start, why don't all schools move in that direction? The answer suggests why education reform can be so difficult. Systemic and social realities can confound change. For example, if the high school schedule is changed, middle and elementary schools also will be affected because they share buses. Imagine younger children standing at bus stops in the dark.

3   Teenagers also play an important role in local economies. Some local school leaders have tried to change high schools' start times only to find overwhelming opposition from local industries that are dependent on student labor or on parents getting to work early in the morning. Some states even dictate school calendars to ensure that teenagers are available to businesses in the summer.

4   High schools do not operate in isolation. All the parts of the system are dynamic and interconnected—from buses to businesses. If we treat the system as a series of independent parts, we sometimes make changes that have unintended consequences. As a result, leaders must view the system comprehensively when making decisions. This means looking at the most current research as well as including the entire community in the process.

5   As with any issue in education reform, good ideas are plentiful, but ways to implement them systemically are far more difficult and far reaching.

Questions on Content, Structure, and Style

1. What is the *USA Today* editorial board's position on later high school start times?

2. For whom does the traditional schedule work well? For whom does it not, and why?

3. Why do the editors specifically refer to sleep researchers at Brown University and the University of Minnesota?

4. According to the editorial board's argument, what benefits will later start times produce?

5. What objections to their position are acknowledged? Are all these objections addressed and resolved?

6. Why do the editors repeatedly refer to the Edina, Minnesota, school district and also to seven other Minneapolis high schools?

7. Although Paul D. Houston begins his essay acknowledging recent sleep research, what problems does he see in the implementation of later start times? Overall, what is his position on this suggested schedule change?

8. How might Houston have strengthened his supporting examples ("Some local school leaders," "Some states") in paragraph 3?

9. Review the conclusions of both essays. Which do you find more effective, and why?

10. Of the two essays, which do you find more persuasive, and why? What specific changes might make each of these essays more convincing?

Suggestions for Writing

Use the essays by the *USA Today*'s editorial board and by Paul D. Houston as a stepping-stone to your essay. Perhaps drawing in part on your response to question 10, write an essay arguing your own position on high school schedules. Or if you prefer, argue for or against some other rule or regulation at a previous or current school that you think affects academic success (a particular course requirement? an attendance policy?). Or perhaps argue for a change in some academic support service or campus office. (For topics that would profit from support from interviews or questionnaires, see the "Conducting Primary Research" section of Chapter 14, pages 371–378).

Vocabulary

USA Today essay:
aka (1)
scarfed (1)
grouchier (3)
prone (3)
shortsighted (7)
status quo (8)

Houston's essay:
folklore (1)
unique (1)
systemic (2)
confound (2)
implement (5)

■ Analyzing Advertisements

Because they are designed to be persuasive, advertisements use a variety of logical and emotional appeals. Ads might be considered arguments in brief form, as they frequently try to convince the public to buy a product, take an action, vote for or against something, join a group, or change an attitude or a behavior. By analyzing the ads that follow, you can practice identifying a variety of persuasive appeals and evaluating their effectiveness. After discussing these ads, apply what you've learned about logical appeals, target audiences, and choice of language to your argumentative essay.*

Conflicting Positions: Gun Control

The three advertisements that follow address the controversial subject of gun control. The first ad is one of a series published by the National Rifle Association (NRA) to tell the public about its organization and its interpretation of the Second Amendment; other ads in this series have featured actor Charlton Heston and author Tom Clancy. The second ad ("Well-Regulated Militia") counters the NRA position. This ad features Sarah Brady, who, following the shooting of her husband, White House Press Secretary James Brady, during an assassination attempt on President Ronald Reagan, became chair of the Center to Prevent Handgun Violence. The third ad uses an expository strategy and statistics to make its point about handgun regulation in America. Analyze the appeals used in each advertisement. Which methods of persuasion do you think are the most effective, and why? Do you find any of the logical fallacies previously described in this chapter?

---

*For additional practice analyzing the arguments and appeals of other advertisements that appear in this text, see pages 162, 190, and 220.

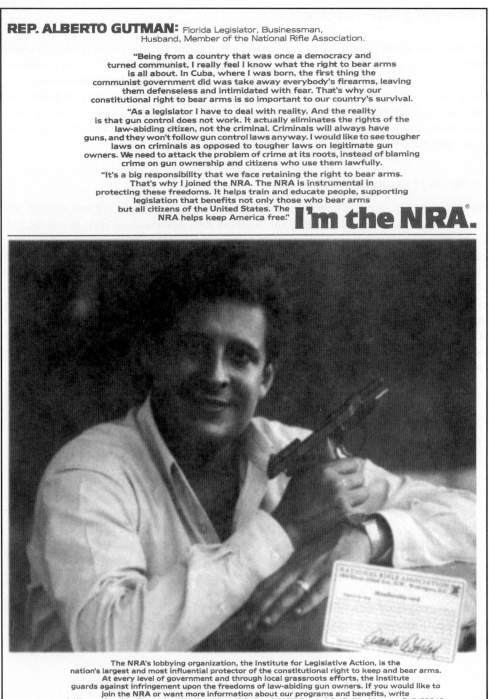

REP. ALBERTO GUTMAN: Florida Legislator, Businessman, Husband, Member of the National Rifle Association.

"Being from a country that was once a democracy and turned communist, I really feel I know what the right to bear arms is all about. In Cuba, where I was born, the first thing the communist government did was take away everybody's firearms, leaving them defenseless and intimidated with fear. That's why our constitutional right to bear arms is so important to our country's survival.

"As a legislator I have to deal with reality. And the reality is that gun control does not work. It actually eliminates the rights of the law-abiding citizen, not the criminal. Criminals will always have guns, and they won't follow gun control laws anyway. I would like to see tougher laws on criminals as opposed to tougher laws on legitimate gun owners. We need to attack the problem of crime at its roots, instead of blaming crime on gun ownership and citizens who use them lawfully.

"It's a big responsibility that we face retaining the right to bear arms. That's why I joined the NRA. The NRA is instrumental in protecting these freedoms. It helps train and educate people, supporting legislation that benefits not only those who bear arms but all citizens of the United States. The NRA helps keep America free." **I'm the NRA.**

The NRA's lobbying organization, the Institute for Legislative Action, is the nation's largest and most influential protector of the constitutional right to keep and bear arms. At every level of government and through local grassroots efforts, the Institute guards against infringement upon the freedoms of law-abiding gun owners. If you would like to join the NRA or want more information about our programs and benefits, write J. Warren Cassidy, Executive Vice President, P.O. Box 37484, Dept. AG-15, Washington, D.C. 20013.

Paid for by the members of the National Rifle Association of America. Copyright 1986.

IS THIS THE "WELL REGULATED MILITIA" PROTECTED BY THE SECOND AMENDMENT?

"A well regulated Militia, being necessary to the security of a free State, the right of the people to keep and bear Arms, shall not be infringed."

—Second Amendment to the U.S. Constitution

For years, the National Rifle Association has spread the myth that gun control laws violate the Second Amendment. Now self-styled "citizen militias" invoke the Second Amendment as they stockpile weapons and train for warfare against what they perceive as a "tyrannical" federal government. The NRA declares that the paramilitary activity of these groups is an exercise of their "right to keep and bear arms." Echoing the extremist rhetoric of the "militias," an NRA official has called the Second Amendment "a loaded gun...held to the head of government." This is a perversion of our Constitution.

When our Founding Fathers wrote the Second Amendment more than 200 years ago, the "well regulated militia" was not a privately organized army formed to resist the government of the United States. It was the military arm of state government, formed to maintain public order.

The Supreme Court has ruled that the "obvious purpose" of the Second Amendment was to protect the "militia which the States were expected to maintain and train," and that "the National Guard is the modern militia."

Because laws regulating firearms do not interfere with the modern militia, no gun control law has ever been overturned by the federal courts on Second Amendment grounds. That's why former Supreme Court Chief Justice Warren Burger has called the NRA's Second Amendment propaganda a "fraud on the American public."

The Second Amendment is not a barrier to reasonable gun control laws. Nor is it a license for those who disagree with government policies to resist them by force of arms. It's time for the NRA to stop its Second Amendment fraud.

The Second Amendment protects the National Guard, not private armies preparing to take the law into their own hands.

Sarah Brady, Chair of the Center to Prevent Handgun Violence

Dear Sarah, I want to support your national education campaign to fight the NRA's Second Amendment fraud. Enclosed is my contribution for:

☐ $15   ☐ $25   ☐ $50   ☐ Other _____

NAME _____

ADDRESS _____

CITY, STATE, ZIP _____

E-MAIL _____

Return to: Center to Prevent Handgun Violence, 1225 Eye Street, NW, Room 1100, Washington, DC 20005

Contributions to the Center to Prevent Handgun Violence are tax-deductible.

☐ I'd like more information on the Second Amendment and the Center to Prevent Handgun Violence.

NAME _____

ADDRESS _____

CITY, STATE, ZIP _____

Return to: Center to Prevent Handgun Violence
1225 Eye Street, NW, Room 1100
Washington, DC 20005

Brought to you by the Center to Prevent Handgun Violence, Sarah Brady, Chair

Courtesy of the Center to Prevent Handgun Violence

TEDDY BEARS
HAVE TO MEET CONSUMER HEALTH & SAFETY STANDARDS

1 At least four types of federal safety standards cover teddy bears: sharp edges and points, small parts, hazardous materials, and flammability.

2 From 1994 to 1997, eight models of teddy bears were recalled by the United States Consumer Product Safety Commission due to possible choking hazards. The total number of teddy bears manufactured during this period was more than 750,000.

3 Teddy bears killed no one in the United States in 1997. From 1994 to 1997 there were 71 toy–related deaths in the United States.

BUT GUNS DON'T!

1 There are no federal safety standards for the domestic manufacture of firearms.

2 No federal health and safety agency has the authority to recall defective firearms or force changes in design.

3 Guns killed 32,436 people in the United States in 1997. From 1994 to 1997 there were 140,938 gun–related deaths in the United States. In 1997, for every time a firearm was used by a civilian to kill in self–defense, there were 4 unintentional deaths, 43 criminal homicides, and 75 suicides involving firearms.

THE SOLUTION

The Firearms Safety and Consumer Protection Act would end the gun industry's deadly exemption from health and safety regulation. Only then will America experience a meaningful reduction in firearms violence.

Violence Policy Center • 1140 19th Street • NW • Suite 600 • Washington • DC • 20036 • www.vpc.org

Competing Products: Sources of Energy

The advertisement by the Metropolitan Energy Council that follows argues for the use of oil to provide heating. What arguments are offered? What emotional appeals does this ad incorporate? To whom are these appeals directed? How does the next ad for Xcel Energy, a large Midwestern and Western natural gas utility company, try to respond to some of the first ad's arguments against using gas heat? Why might Xcel run a newspaper advertisement that appears to be primarily a public safety announcement?

The third advertisement (page 306) is part of a series sponsored by the U. S. Council for Energy Awareness to promote the building of more nuclear energy plants. How does it argue against both oil and gas? What emotional appeals do you see in this ad?

Considering both the language and the visual appeals of all three advertisements, which ad do you find the most persuasive, and why?

"WE COULD MAKE NATURAL GAS SMELL LIKE LILACS OR BACON COOKING IN THE MORNING. BUT THAT WOULDN'T GET YOU OUT OF THE HOUSE."

"Natural gas is naturally odorless. So we mix a harmless chemical in with it that smells like sulfur or rotten eggs. If you ever smell that in your house, you could well have a dangerous gas leak. That's when you have to get everyone out of the house immediately, get to a neighbor's house, and call 1-800-895-2999 to get one of our inspectors over. In an emergency, call 911 first. Most people don't know this either, but if you suspect you have a leak, you should NEVER turn lights or appliances on or off. And NEVER use your phone or cell phone in a house that may be filling with gas. The spark from a switch or phone could cause an explosion. By the same token, don't be lighting a match or opening windows. Just get out of there. Then make that call for help. Remember: Stay away. Stay alive."

Timio, Lead Welder

For more safety tips, visit our website at www.xcelenergy.com.

Xcel Energy

Every time you flip a switch or turn a dial, you tap into the energy of over 12,000 people working to make your life better. Xcel Energy. You get all of our energy.

www.xcelenergy.com   ©2005 Xcel Energy Inc.

Courtesy of Xcel Energy

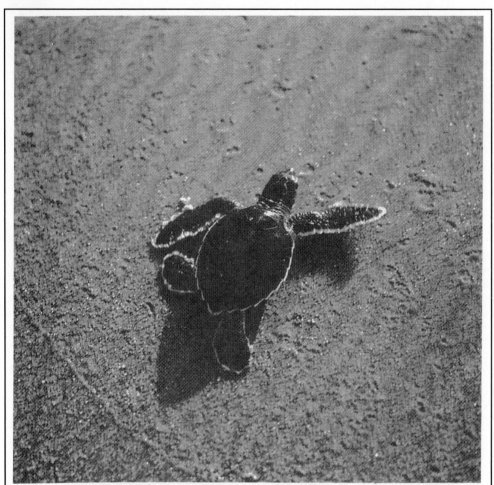

SOME ARGUMENTS FOR NUCLEAR ENERGY ARE SMALLER THAN OTHERS.

Around the nuclear electric plant on Florida's Hutchinson Island, endangered wildlife have a safe haven. The baby sea turtles hatching on nearby beaches are more evidence of the truth about nuclear energy: it peacefully coexists with the environment.

America's 110 operating nuclear plants don't pollute the air, because they don't burn anything to generate electricity. Nor do they eat up valuable natural resources such as oil and natural gas.

Still, more plants are needed—to help satisfy the nation's growing need for electricity without sacrificing the quality of our environment. For a free booklet on nuclear energy, write to the U.S. Council for Energy Awareness, P.O. Box 66080, Dept. TR01, Washington, D.C. 20035.

NUCLEAR ENERGY MEANS CLEANER AIR.

Popular Appeals: Spending Our Money

How do all three of the advertisements that follow employ variations of the "bandwagon" appeal? In the American Century ad, what sort of company identity is created with the story of the boss's lunch? Why might an investment service want this image? To what kind of person does this ad appeal?

The Omega watch ad appeals to a different audience in its use of movie star Pierce Brosnan, known for his portrayal of adventurous characters such as 007 spy James Bond. What effect is "Brosnan's choice" intended to have on the reader? What does the name of the watch style ("Seamaster Aqua Terra") contribute to the appeal of this ad?

The advertisement on page 310, sponsored by People for the Ethical Treatment of Animals (PETA), is one of a series of anti-fur ads featuring media celebrities, such as Oscar-winning Charlize Theron (shown here), Simon Cowell (judge on TV's *American Idol*), and Goran Visnjic (actor on TV show *ER*). In addition to its bandwagon appeal, this ad argues its cause by setting up what comparison or analogy (X is like Y) in the reader's mind? Do you find this ad's argument logical and persuasive? Why or why not? (If it's helpful, review the discussions of analogies on pages 233–236 and 289.)

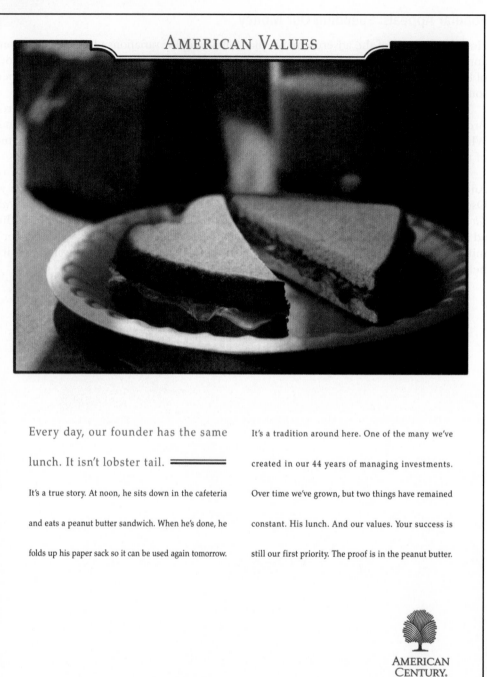

AMERICAN VALUES

Every day, our founder has the same lunch. It isn't lobster tail. ════

It's a true story. At noon, he sits down in the cafeteria and eats a peanut butter sandwich. When he's done, he folds up his paper sack so it can be used again tomorrow.

It's a tradition around here. One of the many we've created in our 44 years of managing investments. Over time we've grown, but two things have remained constant. His lunch. And our values. Your success is still our first priority. The proof is in the peanut butter.

AMERICAN CENTURY.

Investment Managers

American Century Investment Services, Inc. © 2002 American Century Services Corporation

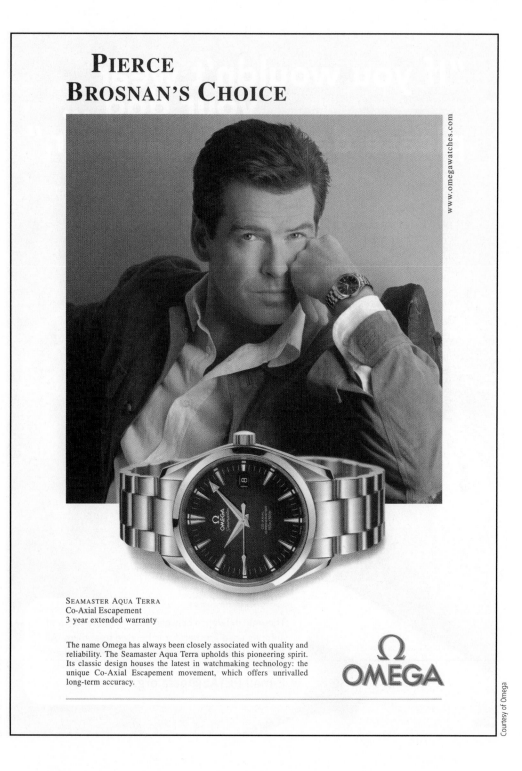

PIERCE
BROSNAN'S CHOICE

www.omegawatches.com

SEAMASTER AQUA TERRA
Co-Axial Escapement
3 year extended warranty

The name Omega has always been closely associated with quality and
reliability. The Seamaster Aqua Terra upholds this pioneering spirit.
Its classic design houses the latest in watchmaking technology: the
unique Co-Axial Escapement movement, which offers unrivalled
long-term accuracy.

Ω
OMEGA

Courtesy of Omega

"If you wouldn't wear your dog ... please don't wear any fur."

—Charlize Theron

The only difference between your "best friend" and animals used for their fur is how we treat them. All animals feel pain and suffer. Receive FREE stickers and information about saving animals. E-mail **PETA2@peta.org.**

peta2.com

▪ A REVISION WORKSHEET

As you write your rough drafts, consult Chapter 5 for guidance through the revision process. In addition, here are a few questions to ask yourself as you revise your argumentative essay:

1. Does this essay present a clear thesis limited to fit the assigned length of this paper?

2. Does this essay contain a number of strong, persuasive points in support of its thesis?

3. Is the essay organized in an easy-to-follow pattern that avoids repetition or confusion?

4. Does the essay present enough supporting evidence to make each of its points convincing? Where could additional examples, factual information, testimony, or other kinds of supporting material be added to make the arguments even more effective?

5. Will all the supporting evidence be clear to the essay's particular audience? Do any terms or examples need additional explanation or special definition?

6. Has at least one major opposing argument been addressed?

7. Does the essay avoid any logical fallacies or problems in tone?

After you've revised your essay extensively, you might exchange rough drafts with a classmate and answer these questions for each other, making specific suggestions for improvement wherever appropriate. (For advice on productive participation in classroom workshops, see pages 108–111.)

Reviewing Your Progress

After you have completed your argument essay, take a moment to measure your progress as a writer by responding to the following questions. Such analysis will help you to recognize growth in your writing skills and may enable you to identify areas that are still problematic.

1. Which part of your essay do you like best? Why?

2. After analyzing your essay's reasoning and evidence, which particular argument or point do you consider the strongest? What makes it so convincing?

3. What part of your essay gave you the most trouble? How did you overcome the problem?

4. If you had more time to work on this essay, what would receive additional attention? Why?

5. What did you learn about your topic from writing this essay? About yourself as a writer?

Chapter 11

Description

The writer of description creates a word-picture of people, places, objects, and emotions, using a careful selection of details to make an impression on the reader. If you have already written expository or argumentative essays in your composition course, you almost certainly have written some descriptive prose. Nearly every essay, after all, calls for some kind of description; for example, in the student comparison/contrast essay (pages 221–224) the writer describes two kinds of stores; in the professional process essay (pages 207–210) the writer describes the embalming procedure in great detail. To help you write better description in your other essays, however, you may want to practice writing descriptive paragraphs or a short descriptive essay.

■ How to Write Effective Description

When descriptive prose is called for in your writing, consider these four basic suggestions:

Recognize your purpose. Description is not free-floating; it appears in your writing for a particular reason: to help you inform, clarify, persuade, or create a mood. In some essays you will want your description as *objective*—without personal impressions—as you can make it; for example, you might describe a scientific experiment or a business transaction in straight factual detail. Other times, however, you will want to convey a particular attitude toward your subject; this approach to description is called *subjective* or *impressionistic*. Note the differences between the following two descriptions of a tall, thin boy: the objective writer sticks to the facts by saying, "The eighteen-year-old boy was 6'1" and weighed 155 pounds," whereas the subjective writer gives an impressionistic description: "The young boy was as tall and scrawny as a birch tree in winter." Before you begin describing anything, you must first decide your purpose and whether it calls for objective or subjective reporting.

Describe clearly, using specific details. To make any description clear to your reader, you must include a sufficient number of details that are specific rather than fuzzy or vague. If, for example, your family dog were missing, you wouldn't call the animal shelter to ask if they'd seen a "big brown dog with a short tail"—naturally, you'd mention every distinguishing detail about your pet you could think of: size, color, breed, cut of ears, and special markings. Similarly, if your car were stolen, you'd give the police as clear and as complete a description of your vehicle as possible. Look at the following sentence. Does it clearly identify a vaulting horse?

> A vaulting horse is a thing usually found in gyms that has four legs and a beam and is used by gymnasts making jumps.

If you didn't already know what a vaulting horse was, you might have trouble picking it out in a gymnasium crowded with equipment. A description with additional details would help you locate it:

> A vaulting horse is a piece of equipment used by gymnasts during competition to help propel them into the air when they perform any of a variety of leaps known as vaults. The gymnasts usually approach the vaulting horse from a running start and then place their hands on the horse for support or for a push off as they perform their vaults. The horse itself resembles a carpenter's sawhorse, but the main beam is made of padded leather rather than wood. The rectangular beam is approximately 5 feet, 3 inches long and 13½ inches wide. Supported by four legs usually made of steel, the padded leather beam is approximately 4 feet, ½ inch above the floor in men's competitions and 3 feet, 7 inches in women's competitions. The padded leather beam has two white lines marking off three sections on top: the croup, the saddle, and the neck. The two end sections—the croup and the neck—are each 15½ inches long. Gymnasts place their hands on the neck or croup, depending on the type of vault they are attempting.

Moreover, the reader cannot imagine your subject clearly if your description is couched in vague generalities. The following sentence, for example, presents only a hazy picture:

> Larry is a sloppy dresser.

Revised, the picture is now sharply in focus:

> Larry wears dirty, baggy pants, shirts too small to stay tucked in, socks that fail to match his pants or each other, and a stained coat the Salvation Army rejected as a donation.

Specific details can turn cloudy prose into crisp, clear images that can be reproduced in the mind like photographs.

Select only appropriate details. In any description the choice of details depends largely on the writer's purpose and audience. However, many descriptions—especially the more subjective ones—will present a *dominant impression;* that is, the writer selects primarily those details that communicate a particular mood or feeling to the reader. The dominant impression is the controlling focus of a description; for example, if you wrote a description of your grandmother to show her thoughtfulness, you would select only those details that convey an impression of a sweet, kindly old lady. Here are two brief descriptions illustrating the concept of dominant impression. The first writer tries to create a mood of mystery:

> Down a black winding road stands the abandoned old mansion, silhouetted against the cloud-shrouded moon, creaking and moaning in the wet, chill wind.

The second writer tries to present a feeling of joy and innocence.

> A dozen kites filled the spring air, and around the bright picnic tables spread with hot dogs, hamburgers, and slices of watermelon, Tom and Annie played away the warm April day.

In the description of the deserted mansion, the writer would have violated the impression of mystery had the sentence read,

> Down the black winding road stands the abandoned old mansion, surrounded by bright, multicolored tulips in early bloom.

Including the cheerful flowers as a detail in the description destroys the dominant mood of bleakness and mystery. Similarly, the second example would be spoiled had the writer ended it this way:

> Tom and Annie played away the warm April day until Tom got so sunburned he became ill and had to go home.

Therefore, remember to select only those details that advance your descriptive purpose. Omit any details you consider unimportant or distracting.

See if you can determine the dominant impression of each of the following descriptions:

> The wind had curled up to sleep in the distant mountains. Leaves hung limp and motionless from the silent trees, while birds perched on the branches like little statues. As I sat on the edge of the clearing, holding my breath, I could hear a squirrel scampering through the underbrush. Somewhere far away a dog barked twice, and then the woods were hushed once more.

> This poor thing has seen better days, but one should expect the sofa in a fraternity house den to be well worn. The large, plump, brown corduroy pillows strewn lazily on the floor and propped comfortably against the threadbare arms bear the pencil-point scars of frustrated students and foam-bleeding cuts of multiple pillow wars. No fewer than four pairs of rotting Nikes stand twenty-four-hour guard at the corners of its carefully mended frame. Obviously the relaxed, inviting appearance masks the permanent odors of cheap cigars from Thursday night poker parties; at least two or three guests each week-end sift through the popcorn kernels and Doritos crumbs, sprawl face down, and pass out for a nap. However, frequent inhabitants have learned to avoid the dark stains courtesy of the house pup and the red-punch designs of the chapter klutz. Habitually, they strategically lunge over the back of the sofa to an unsoiled area easily identifiable in flight by the large depression left by

previous regulars. The quiet *hmmph* of the cushions and harmonious squeal of the exhausted springs signal a perfect landing and utter a warm greeting from an old and faithful friend.

Make your descriptions vivid. By using clear, precise words, you can improve any kind of writing. Chapters 7 (on words) and 6 (on sentences) offer a variety of tips on clarifying your prose style. In addition to the advice given there, here are two other ways to enliven your descriptions, particularly those that call for a subjective approach:

Use sensory details. If it's appropriate, try using images that appeal to your readers' five senses. If, for example, you are describing your broken leg and the ensuing stay in a hospital, tell your readers how the place smelled, how it looked, what your cast felt like, how your pills tasted, and what noises you heard. Here are some specific examples using sensory details:

Sight	The clean white corridors of the hospital resembled the set of a sci-fi movie, with everyone scurrying around in identical starched uniforms.
Hearing	At night, the only sounds I heard were the quiet squeakings of sensible white shoes as the nurses made their rounds.
Smell	The green beans on the hospital cafeteria tray smelled stale and waxy, like crayons.
Touch	The hospital bed sheet felt as rough and heavy as a feed sack.
Taste	Every four hours they gave me an enormous gray pill whose aftertaste reminded me of the stale licorice my great-aunt kept in candy dishes around her house.

By appealing to the readers' senses, you better enable them to imagine the subject you are describing. Joseph Conrad, the famous nineteenth-century novelist, agreed, believing that all art "appeals primarily to the senses, and the artistic aim when expressing itself in written words must also make its appeal through the senses, if its highest desire is to reach the secret spring of responsive emotions." In other words, to make your readers feel, first make them "see."

Use figurative language when appropriate. As you may recall from Chapter 7, figurative language produces images or pictures in the readers' minds, helping them to understand unfamiliar or abstract subjects. Here are some devices you might use to clarify or spice up your prose:

1. Simile: a comparison between two things using the words "like" or "as" (see also pages 161–162)

   Example   Seeing exactly the video game he wanted, he moved as quickly as a starving teenager spotting pie in a refrigerator full of leftover vegetables.

2. Metaphor: a direct comparison between two things that does not use "like" or "as" (see also pages 161–162)

   Example   I was a puppet with my father controlling all the financial strings.

3. Personification: the attribution of human characteristics and emotions to inanimate objects, animals, or abstract ideas

   Example   The old teddy bear sat in a corner, dozing serenely before the fireplace.

4. Hyperbole: intentional exaggeration or overstatement for emphasis or humor

   Example   The cockroaches in my kitchen had now grown to the size of carry-on luggage.

5. Understatement: intentional representation of a subject as less important than the facts would warrant (see also irony, pages 148–149)

   Example   "The reports of my death are greatly exaggerated."—Mark Twain

6. Synecdoche: a part of something used to represent the whole

   Example   A hundred tired feet hit the dance floor for one last jitterbug. [Here "feet" stand for the dancing couples themselves.]

7. Allusion: a brief reference to real or fictitious people, places, events, or things to produce certain associations in the reader's mind

   Example   She proofread her essay again and again, searching for errors with the tenacity of Captain Ahab. [Ahab, the ship captain in the novel *Moby-Dick*, was obsessively devoted to hunting the white whale.]

Using figures of speech in appropriate places can make your descriptions clear, lively, and memorable. (For additional examples, see pages 161–162.)

Problems to Avoid

Keep in mind these three pieces of advice to solve problems that frequently arise in description:

Remember your audience. Sometimes the object of our description is so clear in our minds that we forget that our readers haven't seen it, too. Consequently, the description we write turns out to be vague, bland, or skimpy ("The big tree was beautiful"). Ask yourself about your audience: what do they need to know to see this sight as clearly as I do? Then fill in your description with ample, precise details that reveal the best picture possible. Don't forget to define or explain any terms you use that may be puzzling to your audience. (For more advice on clear, vivid language, see Chapter 7.)

Avoid an erratic organization of details. Too often, descriptions are a hodgepodge of details, jotted down randomly. When you write a lengthy description, you should select a plan that will arrange your details in an orderly fashion. Depending on your subject matter and your purpose, you might adopt a plan calling for a description of something from top to bottom, left to right, front to back, and so on. For example, a description of a woman might begin at the head and move to the feet; furniture in a room might be described as your eyes move from one side of the room to another. A second plan for arranging details presents the subject's outstanding characteristics first and then fills in the lesser information; a child's red hair, for example, might be his most striking feature and therefore would be described first. A third plan presents details in the order you see them approaching: dust, then a car, then details about the car, its occupants, and so on. Or you might describe a subject as it unfolds chronologically, as in some kind of process or operation. Regardless of which plan of organization you choose, the reader should feel a sense of order in your description.

Avoid any sudden change in perspective. If, for example, you are describing the White House from the outside, don't suddenly include details that could be seen only from the inside. Similarly, if you are describing a car from a distance, you might be able to tell the car's model, year, and color, but you could hardly describe the upholstery or reveal the mileage. It is, of course, possible for you—or your observer—to approach or move around the subject of your description, but the reader must be aware of this movement. Any shift in point of view must be presented clearly and logically, with no sudden, confusing leaps from a front to a back view, from outside to inside, and so on.

▪ PRACTICING WHAT YOU'VE LEARNED

A. The following commentary, published in the *New York Times* in 2005, was written by Verlyn Klinkenborg, author of *The Rural Life* (2002) and other books, essays, and articles. Analyze the effectiveness of this brief description: what was the writer's purpose? Is the description objective or subjective? Why does this choice fit the writer's purpose? Does Klinkenborg succeed in recreating his view of the old nickel? Point out some of the details that help the reader understand the differences he sees in the two coins.

[Editor's note: In 2006 the U.S. Mint decided that the popular design of the old buffalo nickel, described in this essay, should appear again, but this time the images of the buffalo and the Native American chief grace the nation's first pure gold coin. Slightly larger and thicker than a Kennedy half-dollar, the coin is designated a $50 gold piece.]

▪ The (Old) Buffalo Nickel

1   Last week, the United States Mint released a new nickel, the third in its Westward Journey series.* On the obverse is a portrait of Thomas Jefferson, who seems to loom into the porthole of the coin. The word "Liberty" appears in a facsimile of Jefferson's handwriting and is dwarfed by "In God We Trust." On the reverse, a bison stands on a small patch of prairie, fenced in by the words "United States of America," which nearly surround him. It is perhaps a meaningless artifact of design that this bison is facing to the right.

2   The new buffalo nickel is, of course, meant to recall the old buffalo nickel, which was minted in Philadelphia, Denver and San Francisco between 1913 and 1938. That nickel was one of the most attractive coins ever issued in this country. A stern, almost oversized profile of an Indian chief appeared on the obverse—the most lifelike portrait of a Native American ever to appear on the United States coinage. The bison on the reverse was not as naturalistic as the one that appears on the new nickel, but he was

---

* This series commemorated the 200th anniversary of the Lewis and Clark expedition, dispatched by Thomas Jefferson in 1803 to chart the unexplored western and northwestern parts of our country.

far more dominant. The coin can barely contain the creature. His head seems to be bowed to fit within the curvature of the rim, and you can almost sense a breadth of prairie lying beyond him. He faces left, and he could, if he wanted, graze his way out from under the words "United States of America," which are over his back.

3   The mint distributed more than 1.2 billion of those nickels, and they have nearly all been retired. But even in the early 1960's, you could still find a buffalo nickel in your change from time to time. It was always an occasion to stop and look closely. This was a coin that worked in a purely iconographic fashion. It had a visual economy that is still moving. In the face of that Indian and the somber mass of that bison, you can visualize the tragic undertone of American history. To come upon a buffalo nickel—one of the old ones—in your pocket was to come upon a work of art.

© Royalty-Free/Corbis

B. Choose sensory details (sight, taste, smell, touch, and hearing) and/or figurative language (similes, metaphors, personification, etc.) to vividly describe each of the following. Avoid clichés and Insta-prose by creating memorable new images (serious or humorous) for your reader.

1. A dessert

2. A pair of jeans

3. A pet

4. The floor of a theater following a kids' movie

5. A sunset

6. February

7. A sound in nature or the city

8. Your favorite pillow

9. A dentist's office

10. Yourself in either a happy or grouchy mood

■ ASSIGNMENT

Use the painting below to practice your descriptive writing skills. Often influenced by his Russian-Jewish heritage, artist Marc Chagall (1887–1985) painted this picture titled *Birthday* in 1915. Describe what you feel is the dominant mood of this picture, pointing out some of the details that communicate that tone to you. Consider the painting's people, setting, colors, and even shapes. In a short descriptive essay, re-create this painting as you see it for someone unfamiliar with the work. To get you started, ponder this: some viewers have questioned whether the male figure is "floating on air" with happiness or is instead an imaginary guest, perhaps even someone deceased. What do *you* think? (For more help writing about art, see Chapter 17.)

Birthday (L'Anniversaire), 1915, by Marc Chagall

■ ESSAY TOPICS

Here are some suggestions for a descriptive paragraph or essay; focus your topic to fit your assignment. Don't forget that every description, whether objective or subjective, has a purpose and that your details should support that purpose. For additional ideas, see "Suggestions for Writing" on page 329.

1. A favorite painting, photograph, or sculpture (Or choose one of the many artworks in this textbook. A list of art works in this text follows the table of contents.)

2. One dish or foodstuff that should be forever banned

3. A piece of equipment important to your major, a hobby, or a favorite sport

4. A campus or local character

5. Your best/worst job

6. Yourself (how you looked at a certain age or on a memorable occasion or in a particular photograph)

7. Your most precious material possession

8. The ugliest/most beautiful place on your campus or in town

9. A holiday, celebration, or ritual in your family

10. Your first or worst car or apartment

11. A piece of clothing that reveals the real "you" (or a favorite costume)

12. A common object with uncommon beauty (See the essay on the buffalo nickel, pages 318–319, for inspiration.)

13. An original poster for a movie, concert, or campus event

14. Your favorite recreation area (beach, hiking trail, park, etc.)

15. An unforgettable moment

16. An event, element, or creature in nature

17. A shopping mall, student cafeteria, or other crowded public place

18. The inside of your refrigerator, closet, or some other equally loathsome place in your home

19. A treasure from a personal collection or a family heirloom

20. Your Special Place (Perhaps your place offers you solitude, beauty, or renewed energy. The scene below was painted ten times by nineteenth-century artist Claude Monet, who loved this tranquil lily pond near his farmhouse in France. Re-create your special place for your readers by choosing the right descriptive words, just as Monet did with each brush stroke of color.)

The Water-Lily Pond, 1899, by Claude Monet

A Topic Proposal for Your Essay

Selecting the right subject matter is important to every writer. To help you clarify your ideas and strengthen your commitment to your topic, here is a proposal sheet that asks you to describe some of your preliminary ideas about your subject before you begin drafting.

Although your ideas may change as you write (they will almost certainly become more refined), thinking through your choice of topic now may help you avoid several false starts.

1. What subject will your essay describe? Will you describe this subject objectively or subjectively? Why?

2. Why are you interested in this topic? Do you have a personal or professional connection to the subject? State at least one reason for your choice of topic.

3. Is this a significant topic of interest to others? Why? Who specifically might find it interesting, informative, or entertaining?

4. What is the main purpose of your description? In one or two sentences describe the major effect you'd like your descriptive essay to have on your readers. What would you like for them to understand or "see" about your subject?

5. List at least three details that you think will help clarify your subject for your readers.

6. What difficulties, if any, might arise during drafting? For example, what organizational strategy might you think about now that would allow you to guide your readers through your description in a coherent way?

■ Sample Student Essay

In her descriptive essay, this student writer recalls her childhood days at the home of her grandparents to make a point about growing up. Notice that the writer uses both figurative language and contrasting images to help her readers understand her point of view.

TREECLIMBING

1   It was Mike's eighteenth birthday and he was having a little bit of a breakdown. "When was the last time you made cloud pictures?" he asked me absently as he stared up at the ceiling before class started. Before I could answer, he continued, "Did you know that by the time you're an adult, you've lost 85 percent of your imagination?" He paused. "I don't want to grow up." Although I doubted the authenticity of his facts, I

Introduction: The conversation that triggers her memory

understood that Mike—the hopeless romantic with his long ponytail, sullen black clothes, and glinting dark eyes—was caught in a Peter Pan complex. He drew those eyes from the ceiling and focused on me: "There are two types of children. Tree children and dirt children. Kids playing will either climb trees or play in the dirt. Tree children are the dreamers—the hopeful, creative dreamers. Dirt children, they just stay on the ground. Stick to the rules." He trailed off, and then picked up again: "I'm a tree child. I want to make cloud pictures and climb trees. And I don't ever want to come down." Mike's story reminded me of my own days as a tree child, and of the inevitable fall from the tree to the ground.

2   My childhood was a playground for imagination. Summers were spent surrounded by family at my grandparents' house in Milwaukee, Wisconsin. The rambling Lannonstone bungalow was located on North 46th Street at Burleigh, a block away from center-city Milwaukee, two blocks from Schuster's department store and the Pfister hotel. In the winter, all the houses looked alike, rigid and militant, like white-bearded old generals with icicles hanging from their moustaches. One European-styled house after the other lined the streets in strict parallel formation, block after block.

The grandparents' neighborhood remembered in military images and sensory details

3   But in the summer it was different . . . softer. No subzero winds blew lonely down the back alley. Instead, kids played stickball in it. I had elegant, grass-stained tea parties with a neighborhood girl named Shelly, while my grandfather worked in his thriving vegetable garden among the honeybees, and watched sprouts grow. An ever-present warming smell of yeast filtered down every street as the nearby breweries pumped a constant flow of fresh beer. Above, the summer sky looked like an Easter egg God had dipped in blue dye.

4   Those summer trips to Milwaukee were greatly anticipated events back then. My brother and I itched with repressed energy throughout the long plane ride from the West Coast. We couldn't wait to see Grandma and Papa.

We couldn't wait to see what presents Papa had for us. We couldn't wait to slide down the steep, blue-carpeted staircase on our bottoms, and then on our stomachs. Most of all, we couldn't wait to go down to the basement.

Use of parallel sentences to emphasize anticipation

5   The basement was better than a toy store. Yes, the old-fashioned milk cabinet in the kitchen wall was enchanting, and the laundry chute was fun because it was big enough to throw down Ernie, my stuffed dog companion, so my brother could catch him below in the laundry room, as our voices echoed up and down the chute. But the basement was better than all of these, better even than sliding down those stairs on rug-burned bottoms.

6   It was always deliciously cool down in the basement. Since the house was built in the 1930s, there was no air conditioning. Upstairs, we slept in hot, heavy rooms. My nightgown stuck to the sheets, and I would lie awake, listening to crickets, inhaling the beer-sweet smell of the summer night, hoping for a cool breeze. Nights were forgotten, however, as my brother and I spent hours every day in the basement. There were seven rooms in the basement; some darker rooms I had waited years to explore. There was always a jumbled heap of toys in the middle room, most of which were leftovers from my father's own basement days. It was a child's safe haven; it was a sacred place.

The basement in contrast to other parts of the house

7   The hours spent in the basement were times of a gloriously secure childhood. Empires were created in a day with faded colored building blocks. New territories were annexed when either my brother or I got the courage to venture into one of those Other Rooms—the dark, musty ones without windows—and then scamper back to report of any sightings of monsters or other horrific childhood creatures. In those basement days everything seemed safe and wholesome and secure, with my family surrounding me, protecting me. Like childhood itself, entering the basement was like entering another dimension.

Adventures in the basement

8   Last summer I returned to Milwaukee to help my grandparents pack to move into an apartment. I went back at 17 to find the house—my kingdom—up for sale. I found another cycle coming to a close, and I found myself separated from what I had once known. I looked at the house. It was old; it was crumbling; it needed paint. I looked down the back alley and saw nothing but trash and weeds. I walked to the corner and saw smoke-choked, dirty streets and thick bars in shop windows, nothing more than another worn-out midwestern factory city. I went back to the house and down to the basement, alone.

The house and neighborhood years later

9   It was gray and dark. Dust filtered through a single feeble sunbeam from a cracked window pane. It was empty, except for the overwhelming musty smell. The toys were gone, either packed or thrown away. As I walked in and out of rooms, the quietness filled my ears, but in the back of my head the sounds of childhood laughter and chatter played like an old recording.

The basement years later

10   The dark rooms were filled not with monsters but with remnants of my grandfather's business. A neon sign was propped against the wall in a corner: Ben Strauss Plumbing. Piles of heavy pipes and metal machine parts lay scattered about on shelves. A dusty purple ribbon was thumbtacked to a door. It said SHOOT THE WORKS in white letters. I gently took it down. The ribbon hangs on my door at home now, and out of context it somehow is not quite so awe-inspiring and mystifying as it once was. However, it does serve its purpose, permanently connecting me to my memories.

11   All children are tree children, I believe. The basement used to be my tree, the place I could dream in. That last summer I found myself, much to Mike's disappointment, quite mature, quite adult. Maybe Mike fell from his tree and was bruised. Climbing down from that tree doesn't have to be something to be afraid of. One needn't hide in the tree for fear of touching the ground and forgetting how to climb back up when necessary. I think there is a way to balance the two extremes. Climb down

Conclusion: A return to the introduction's images and some advice

gracefully as you grow up, and if you fall, don't land in quicksand. I like to think I'm more of a shrubbery child: not so low as to get stuck in the mud and just high enough to look at the sky and make cloud pictures.

Professional Essay*

■ Still Learning from My Mother

Cliff Schneider

Cliff Schneider is a graduate of Cornell and a retired freshwater fisheries biologist, who worked for the Department of Environmental Conservation in New York. Much of his research and writing has focused on his work studying Lake Ontario. This essay, a personal tribute to his seventy-nine-year-old mother, was first published in the "My Turn" column of *Newsweek* magazine, in March 2000.

1   When I was a young boy growing up on New York's Long Island in the 1950s, it was common to see boys and their fathers gathering in the roads in front of their homes on warm summer evenings to "have a catch." That was the term we had for tossing a baseball while we talked about school, jobs and life in general. Although my dad and I had many catches together, my most memorable ones were with my mother. She would happily grab a glove, run out to the road and then fire fast balls at me that cracked my glove and left my hand stinging. She never showed any motherly concern, though, just a broad grin with the tip of her tongue exposed in the corner of her mouth. This was her game face. I can still recall how delighted I was tossing the ball with Mom and hearing the comments from my friends and neighbors: "Where did your mother learn to throw a ball like that?"

2   My mother, you see, was a jock long before Title IX unleashed the explosion of modern women's athletics. She lettered in field hockey and basketball while attending Hofstra University in the late 1930s. This was a time when it wasn't very fashionable for women to go running after a ball and work up a sweat. Luckily for me, Mom never worried about what was fashionable. She loved sports, loved being active and, most of all, loved the competition. Mom was kind to her kids until we played ball. Then we'd notice this gleam in her eye, the broad grin and the familiar tongue that told us she was ready for action and ready to have some fun. No matter what game she played, Mom had class. She played hard, she laughed a lot and, win or lose, she was always gracious.

---

* To help you read this essay analytically, review pages 170–172. For two other professional essays in Part Two that make extensive use of description, see "To Bid the World Farewell" (pages 207–210) and "Two Ways of Viewing the River" (pages 231–232).

3   The years have diminished Mom's physical abilities, as they would have for anyone who is about to become an octogenarian. Her back is a little bent, and she complains occasionally about her hip. Her biggest concession to the aging process, however, is that she has had to lighten up on her bowling ball. As a young mother in suburban bowling leagues she toted a 15-pound ball, carried a 160 average and had a high game of 212. As she's grown older, her scores have declined. In recent years she's had to start using an eight-pound ball, which she protests is too light and "doesn't give enough pin action."

4   For years I have had to listen to my mother's perennial battle cry as she begins each new bowling season—"This is the year I'm going to bowl a 200 game!" I've always smiled and nodded in agreement, which was my way of acknowledging her determination. During our regular Thursday-evening phone conversations (she bowls on Thursdays), she gives me a frame-by-frame description of her games, and gripes that she can't bowl the way she used to. She almost always slips in the comment "I'm going to make 200 if it kills me." I try to explain that she should be satisfied that she is at least able to play the game. "Try to make some concession to your age, Mom," I say. Of course, she will have none of this talk and this year bought a 10-pound ball in pursuit of her dream. Vince Lombardi would be proud.

5   A week after she started bowling with her new ball, I called to check on her progress. She no sooner said "Hi" than I could tell something big had happened in her life. I could feel the smile all the way from Hendersonville, N.C., to upstate New York. I shouted, "You bowled a 200 game!" knowing it could be the only reason for such a happy voice. She corrected me: "Not a 200 game; I got a 220." It was her highest score ever! She gave me a strike-by-strike description of her game, and we both celebrated over the phone. As she signed off and said her goodbyes, I could still sense the smile on her face. Her grin will probably fade in another month or two.

6   After some reflection, I am amazed by my mother's accomplishment. Whether it is baseball, tennis, golf or even bowling, I have never heard of anyone's peaking at 79. Yes, there is some degree of luck in every game, but in Mom's case she had the best game of her life because she persevered. Mom's achievement has lifted her spirits and made her feel young again. For someone who is too frequently reminded that she can't do what she used to, this experience could not have come at a better time in her life. I guess I'm not surprised that I can still learn from Mom—that you are never too old to dream and never too old to realize those dreams. I am not surprised, either, that in our most recent calls she talks about bowling a 250 game.

Questions on Content, Structure, and Style

1.   Is Schneider's description of his mother primarily objective or subjective? Cite an example of his language to support your answer.

2.   Why was his mother's behavior unusual in the 1950s? What does "before Title IX" (paragraph 2) mean?

3.   What "dominant impression" of his mother does Schneider present in this essay? What are some of the details Schneider provides to help us understand this woman's character?

4. How does Schneider physically describe his mother so that readers can easily imagine those early games of catch? Why does she have "class"?

5. Examine some of Schneider's word choices. What, for example, is the effect of writing that his mother would "fire fast balls at me that cracked my glove and left my hand stinging" (paragraph 1) instead of "mom could throw very hard"?

6. What does his mother's "perennial battle cry" at age 79 reveal about her? Why does Schneider think Vince Lombardi—the football coach who holds the record for the most NFL wins—would be proud of her?

7. What does Schneider's occasional use of dialogue add to this essay? Why, for example, does he quote his neighbors in paragraph 1 and his mother in paragraphs 3 and 4?

8. Why does Schneider organize his essay by starting with a description of his mother's younger days and concluding with a reference to "a 250 game"? How does this organization contribute to our understanding of his mother?

9. What has Schneider learned from his mother? In what way is this lesson an important part of this essay's purpose?

10. Did Schneider successfully create a picture of his mother? Could you suggest some ways he might improve his description? What language might have been more specific or vivid?

Suggestions for Writing

Try using Cliff Schneider's "Still Learning from My Mother" as a stepping-stone to your essay. Describe an unusual-but-wonderful relative or friend you admire for a particular trait. Consider including ample physical details, dialogue, and actions illustrating personality, as Schneider did, to make your description of this person vivid for your reader. Or write a description of an ancestor whose photograph has always intrigued you. What is the dominant impression of this picture? What does this person's face (or posture or choice of clothing) say to you about his or her character or style?

Perhaps you might choose to describe another mother figure, whose face is forever identified with the Great Depression. In 1936 photographer Dorothea Lange stopped on a dirt road in California to take a half-dozen pictures of a thirty-two-year-old woman and her children as they huddled in the rain under a lean-to tent. The woman told Lange they had been living off birds the children had killed and that she had just sold the tires off their car to buy food. Why do you think *Migrant Mother*, shown on page 330, is considered one of the most affecting photographs of all time?

Vocabulary

Title IX (2)	octogenarian (3)	toted (3)
diminished (3)	concession (3)	perennial (4)

Migrant Mother, 1936, by Dorothea Lange

■ A REVISION WORKSHEET

As you write your rough drafts, consult Chapter 5 for guidance through the revision process. In addition, here are a few questions to ask yourself as you revise your description:

1. Is the descriptive essay's purpose clear to the reader?
2. Are there enough specific details in the description to make the subject matter distinct to readers who are unfamiliar with the scene, person, or object? Where might more detail be added?
3. Are the details arranged in an order that's easy to follow?
4. If the assignment called for an objective description, are the details as "neutral" as possible?

5. If the assignment called for a subjective description, does the writer's particular attitude come through clearly with a consistent use of well-chosen details or imagery?

6. Could any sensory details or figurative language be added to help the reader "see" the subject matter?

7. Does this essay end with an appropriate conclusion or does description merely stop?

After you've revised your essay extensively, you might exchange rough drafts with a classmate and answer these questions for each other, making specific suggestions for improvement wherever appropriate. (For advice on productive participation in classroom workshops, see pages 108–111.)

Reviewing Your Progress

After you have completed your descriptive essay, take a moment to measure your progress as a writer by responding to the following questions. Such analysis will help you recognize growth in your writing skills and may enable you to identify areas that are still problematic.

1. What is the best part of your essay? Why?

2. Which one descriptive detail or image do you think is the clearest or most vivid in your essay? Why does that one stand above the others?

3. What part of your essay gave you the most trouble? How did you overcome the problem?

4. If you had more time to work on this essay, what would receive additional attention? Why?

5. What did you learn about your topic from writing this essay? About yourself as a writer?

Chapter 12

Narration

When many people hear the word "narrative," they think of a made-up story. But not all stories are fiction. In this chapter we are not concerned with writing literary short stories—that's a skill to develop in a creative writing class—but rather with nonfiction *expository narratives,* stories that are used to explain or prove a point. We most often use two kinds of these stories:

1. the *extended narrative*—a long episode that by itself illustrates or supports an essay's thesis
2. the *brief narrative*—a shorter incident that is often used in a body paragraph to support or illustrate a particular point in an essay.

Let's suppose, for example, you wanted to write an essay showing how confusing the registration system is at your school. To illustrate the problems vividly, you might devote your entire essay to the retelling of a friend's seven-hour experience signing up for classes last fall, thus making use of extended narration. Or take another example: in an argumentative essay advocating mandatory use of side-door air bags in automobiles, you might include a brief narrative about a car wreck to support a paragraph's point about air bags' ability to save lives. Regardless of which type of narrative best fits your purpose, the telling of a story or an incident can be an interesting, persuasive means of informing your readers.

■ Writing the Effective Narrative Essay

Know your purpose. What are you trying to accomplish by writing this narrative essay? Are you, for example, offering an *objective* retelling of a historical event (the dropping of the atomic bomb) to inform your readers who may not be acquainted with the facts? Or are you presenting a *subjective* narrative, which persuasively tells a story (Susan B. Anthony's arrest for voting) from a clearly defined point of view? Perhaps your narrative is a personal story, whose lesson you wish readers to share. Whatever your choice—an objective, factual retelling or a subjective interpretation—your narrative's purpose should be clear to your readers, who should never reach the end of the story wondering "What was that all about?" Knowing your purpose will help you select the information and language best suited to meet your audience's needs.

Present your main point clearly. To ensure that readers understand their purpose, many writers first state a thesis claim followed by a narrative that supports it. Sometimes writers begin with their narrative and use their concluding paragraph to state or sum up the point or "lesson" of their story. Still others choose to imply a main point or attitude through the unfolding action and choice of descriptive details. An implied thesis is always riskier than a stated one, so unless you are absolutely convinced that your readers could not possibly fail to see your point, work on finding a smooth way to incorporate a statement of your main idea into your essay.

Follow a logical time sequence. Many narrative essays—and virtually all brief stories used in other kinds of essays—follow a chronological order, presenting actions as they naturally occur in the story. Occasionally, however, a writer will use the flashback technique, which takes the readers back in time to reveal an event that occurred before the present scene of the essay. If you decide to use shifts in time, use transitional phrases or other signals to ensure that your readers don't become confused or lost.

Use sensory details to hold your readers' interest. For example, if the setting plays an important role in your story, describe it in vivid terms so that your readers can imagine the scene easily. Suppose you are pointing out the necessity of life preservers on sailboats by telling the story of how you spent a stormy night in the lake, clinging to a capsized boat. To convince your readers, let them "feel" the stinging rain and the icy current trying to drag you under; let them "see" the black waves and the dark menacing sky; let them "hear" the howling wind and the gradual splitting apart of the boat. Effective narration often depends on effective description, and effective description depends on vivid, specific detail. (For more help on writing description, see Chapter 11; review Chapter 7 for advice on word choice.)

Create authentic characters. Again, the use of detail is crucial. Your readers should be able to visualize the people (or animals) in your narrative clearly; if your important characters are drawn too thinly or if they seem phony or stereotyped, your readers will not fully grasp the meaning of your story. Show your readers the major characters as you see them by commenting unobtrusively on their appearances, speech, and actions. In addition, a successful narrative may depend on the reader's understanding of people's motives—why they act the way they do in certain situations. A narrative about your hometown's grouchiest miser who suddenly donated a large sum of money to a poor family isn't very believable unless we know the motive behind the action. In other words, let your readers know what is happening to whom by explaining or showing why.

Use dialogue realistically. Writers often use dialogue, their characters' spoken words, to reveal action or personality traits of the speakers. By presenting conversations, writers show rather than tell, often creating emphasis or a more dramatic effect. Dialogue may also help readers identify with or feel closer to the characters or action by creating a sense of "you-are-there." If your narrative would profit from dialogue, be certain the word choice and the manner of speaking are in keeping with each character's education, background, age, location, and so forth. Don't, for example, put a sophisticated philosophical treatise into the mouth of a ten-year-old boy or the latest campus slang into the speech of a fifty-year-old auto mechanic from Two Egg, Florida. Also, make sure that your dialogue doesn't sound wooden or phony. The right dialogue can help make your story more realistic and interesting, provided that the conversations are essential to the narrative and are not merely padding the plot. (For an example of dialogue in a narrative, read Maya Angelou's "Sister Flowers," on pages 341–345. For help in punctuating dialogue, see pages 558–559 in Part Four.)

Problems to Avoid

Weak, boring narratives are often the result of problems with subject matter or poor pacing; therefore, you should keep in mind the following advice:

Choose your subject carefully. Most of the best narrative essays come from personal experience or study, and the reason is fairly obvious: it's difficult to write convincingly about something you've never seen or done or read about. You probably couldn't, for instance, write a realistic account of a bullfight unless you'd seen one or at least had studied the subject in great detail. The simplest, easiest, most interesting nonfiction narrative you can write is likely to be about an event with which you are personally familiar. This doesn't mean that you can't improvise many details or create a hypothetical story to illustrate a point. Even so, you will probably still have more success basing your narrative— real or hypothetical—on something or someone you know well.

Limit your scope. When you wish to use an extended narrative to illustrate a thesis, don't select an event or series of actions whose retelling will be too long or complex for your assignment. In general, it's better to select one episode and flesh it out with many specific details so that your readers can clearly see your point. For instance, you may have had many rewarding experiences during the summer you worked as a lifeguard, but you can't tell them all. Instead, you might focus on one experience that captures the essence of your attitude toward your job—say, the time you saved a child from drowning—and present the story so vividly that the readers can easily understand your point of view.

Don't let your story lag or wander. At some time you've probably listened to a storyteller who became stuck on some insignificant detail ("Was it Friday or Saturday the letter came? Let's see now . . ."; "Then Joe said to me—no, it was Sally—no, wait, it was . . ."). And you've probably also heard bores who insist on making a short story long by including too many unimportant details or digressions. These mistakes ruin the *pacing* of their stories; in other words, the story's tempo or movement becomes bogged down until the readers are bored witless. To avoid creating a sleeping tonic in word form, dismiss all unessential information and focus your attention—and use of detail—on the important events, people, and places. Skip uneventful periods of time by using such phrases as "A week went by before Mr. Smith called . . ." or "Later that evening, around nine o'clock . . . ." In short, keep the story moving quickly enough to hold the readers' interest. Moreover, use a variety of transitional devices to move the readers from one action to another; don't rely continuously on the "and then . . . and then . . ." method.

■ PRACTICING WHAT YOU'VE LEARNED

To practice collecting details that will strengthen your narrative, try this activity. First, study the painting below, *Tornado Over Kansas* by John Steuart Curry, and then list as many specific, descriptive details about the scene as you can see or imagine. For example, what do details about the setting and the

Tornado Over Kansas, 1929, by John Steuart Curry

family's appearance reveal about these people and where they live? What unusual noises, colors, and smells might be present and how might they be vividly described? What does each person's facial expression and body language tell you about his or her thoughts at this very moment? What words might be spoken by each person and in what tone of voice? What role do the animals play in this scene?

Now think of a time in which you experienced a narrow escape or conquered a fearful moment, some event in your life that might be retold in an exciting narrative essay. Using the impressions recorded from the painting as a guide to prompt your memory, compile a similar list of vivid, sensory details describing the people, setting, dialogue, and action at the most dramatic point of your story.

■ ESSAY TOPICS

Use one of the following topics to suggest an essay that is developed by narration. Remember that each essay must have a clear purpose. For additional ideas, see the "Suggestions for Writing" section following the professional essay (page 346).

1. An act of courage or devotion
2. An event of historical, medical, or scientific importance
3. An interaction that changed your thinking on a particular subject
4. Your best holiday; special occasion; first or last day (school, job, camp, etc.)
5. A family story passed down through the generations
6. Your worst accident or brush with danger
7. An unforgettable childhood experience
8. A memorable event governed by nature or an entertaining pet story
9. A time you gained self-confidence or changed your self-image
10. A meaningful event experienced in another culture or country
11. The day everything went wrong (or right)
12. An event that led to an important decision
13. Your experience with prejudice or with an act of charity or friendship
14. Giving in to or resisting peer pressure
15. A gain or loss of something or someone important
16. A risk that paid off (or a triumph against the odds)
17. A nonacademic lesson learned at school, on a job, or on a team
18. An episode marking your passage from one stage of your life to another
19. A habit that got you into (or out of) trouble

20. Your day on September 11, 2001, or on some other memorable date, showing how the events informed or changed you

The destruction of the World Trade Center Towers, September 11, 2001

A Topic Proposal for Your Essay

Selecting the right subject matter is important to every writer. To help you clarify your ideas and strengthen your commitment to your topic, here is a proposal sheet that asks you to describe some of your preliminary ideas about your subject before you begin drafting. Although your ideas may change as you write (they will almost certainly become more refined), thinking through your choice of topic now may help you avoid several false starts.

1. In a sentence or two, briefly state the subject of your narrative. Did you or someone you know participate in this story?

2. Why did you select this narrative? Does it have importance for you personally, academically, or professionally? In some other way? Explain your reason, or purpose, for telling this story.

3. Will others be informed or entertained by this story? Who might be especially interested in hearing your narrative? Why?

4. What is the primary effect you would like your narrative to have on your readers? What would you like them to feel or think about after they read your story? Why?

5. What is the critical moment in your story? At what point, in other words, does the action reach its peak? Summarize this moment in a few descriptive words.

6. What difficulties, if any, might this narrative present as you are drafting? For example, if the story you want to tell is long or complex, how might you focus on the main action and pace it appropriately?

■ Sample Student Essay

In this narrative a student uses a story about a sick but fierce dog to show how she learned a valuable lesson in her job as a veterinarian's assistant. Notice the student's good use of vivid details that make this well-paced story both clear and interesting.

NEVER UNDERESTIMATE THE LITTLE THINGS

1   When I went to work as a veterinarian's assistant for Dr. Sam Holt and Dr. Jack Gunn last summer, I was under the false impression that the hardest part of veterinary surgery would be the actual performance of an operation. The small chores demanded before this feat didn't occur to me as being of any importance. As it happened, I had been in the veterinary clinic only a total of four hours before I met a little animal who convinced me that the operation itself was probably the easiest part of treatment. This animal, to whom I owe thanks for so enlightening me, was a chocolate-colored chihuahua of tiny size and immense perversity named Smokey.

Introduction: A misconception

Thesis: Small preliminary details can be as important as the major action

2   Smokey could have very easily passed for some creature from another planet. It wasn't so much his gaunt little frame and overly large head, or his bony paws with nearly saberlike claws, as it was his grossly infected eyes. Those once-shining eyes were now distorted and swollen into grotesque balls of septic, sightless flesh. The only vague similarity they had to what we'd normally think of as the organs of vision was a slightly upraised dot, all that was left of the pupil, in the center of a pink and purply marble. As if that were not enough, Smokey had a temper to match his ugly sight. He also had surprisingly good aim, considering his largely diminished vision, toward any moving object that happened to place itself unwisely before his ever-inquisitive nose; with sudden and wholly vicious intent, he would snap and snarl at whatever blocked the little light that could filter through his swollen and ruptured blood vessels. Truly, in many respects, Smokey was a fearful dog to behold.

Description of the main character: His appearance

His personality

3   Such an appearance and personality did nothing to encourage my

The difficulty
of moving the
dog to the
surgery room

already flagging confidence in my capabilities as a vet's assistant. How was I
supposed to get that little demon out of his cage? Jack had casually
requested that I bring Smokey to the surgery room, but did he really expect
me to put my hands into the cage of that devil dog? I suppose it must have
been my anxious expression that saved me, for as I turned uncertainly
toward the kennel, Jack chuckled nonchalantly and accompanied me to
demonstrate how professionals in his line of work dealt with professionals
in Smokey's. He took a small rope about four feet long with a no-choke
noose at one end and unlatched Smokey's cage. Then cautiously he reached
in and dangled the noose before the dog's snarling jaws. Since Smokey
could only barely see what he was biting at, his attacks were directed
haphazardly in a semicircle around his body. The tiny area of his cage led to
his capture, for during one of Smokey's forward lunges, Jack dropped the
noose over his head and moved the struggling creature out onto the floor.
The fight had only just begun for Smokey, however, and he braced his feet
against the slippery linoleum tiling and forced us to drag him, like a little
pull toy on a string, to the surgery.

4   Once Smokey was in the surgery, however, the question that hung

The difficulty
of moving the
dog to the
table

before our eyes like a veritable presence was how to get the dog from the
floor to the table. Simply picking him up and plopping him down was out
of the question. One glance at the quivering little figure emitting ominous
and throaty warnings was enough to assure us of that. Realizing that the
game was over, Jack grimly handed me the rope and reached for a muzzle.
It was a doomed attempt from the start: the closer Jack dangled the tiny
leather cup to the dog's nose, the more violent did Smokey's contortions
and rage-filled cries become and the more frantic our efforts became to
try to keep our feet and fingers clear of the angry jaws. Deciding that a
firmer method had to be used, Jack instructed me to raise the rope up
high enough so that Smokey would have to stand on his hind legs. This

greatly reduced his maneuverability but served to increase his tenacity, for at this the little dog nearly went into paroxysms of frustration and rage. In his struggles, however, Smokey caught his forepaw on his swollen eye, and the blood that had been building up pressure behind the fragile cornea burst out and dripped to the floor. In the midst of our surprise and the twinge of panic startling the three of us, Jack saw his chance and swiftly muzzled the animal and lifted him to the operating table.

5   Even at that point it wasn't easy to put the now terrified dog to sleep. He fought the local anesthesia and caused Jack to curse as he was forced to give Smokey more of the drug than should have been necessary for such a small beast. After what seemed an eternity, Smokey lay prone on the table, breathing deeply and emitting soft snores and gentle whines. We also breathed deeply in relief, and I relaxed to watch fascinated, while Jack performed a very delicate operation quite smoothly and without mishap.

The difficulty of putting the dog to sleep before the surgery

6   Such was my harrowing induction into the life of a veterinary surgeon. But Smokey did teach me a valuable lesson that has proven its importance to me many times since: wherever animals are concerned, even the smallest detail is important and should never be taken for granted.

Conclusion: The lesson she learned

Professional Essay*

■ Sister Flowers

Maya Angelou

Maya Angelou is an American author, actor, civil-rights activist, poet, and professor. Recipient of many honorary degrees and awards, she was given the Presidential Medal of Arts in 2000. Angelou has written multiple volumes of poetry and a series of popular autobiographical works. This essay is a chapter from her first memoir, *I Know Why the Caged Bird Sings* (1969). Recent works include *A Song Flung Up to Heaven* (2002) and *Amazing Peace* (2005).

---

* To help you read this essay analytically, review pages 170–172.

1   For nearly a year, I sopped around the house, the Store, the school and the church, like an old biscuit, dirty and inedible. Then I met, or rather got to know, the lady who threw me my first life line.

2   Mrs. Bertha Flowers was the aristocrat of Black Stamps. She had the grace of control to appear warm in the coldest weather, and on the Arkansas summer days it seemed she had a private breeze which swirled around, cooling her. She was thin without the taut look of wiry people, and her printed voile dresses and flowered hats were as right for her as denim overalls for a farmer. She was our side's answer to the richest white woman in town.

3   Her skin was a rich black that would have peeled like a plum if snagged, but then no one would have thought of getting close enough to Mrs. Flowers to ruffle her dress, let alone snag her skin. She didn't encourage familiarity. She wore gloves too.

4   I don't think I ever saw Mrs. Flowers laugh, but she smiled often. A slow widening of her thin black lips to show even, small white teeth, then the slow effortless closing. When she chose to smile on me, I always wanted to thank her. The action was so graceful and inclusively benign.

5   She was one of the few gentlewomen I have ever known, and has remained throughout my life the measure of what a human being can be.

6   Momma* had a strange relationship with her. Most often when she passed on the road in front of the Store, she spoke to Momma in that soft yet carrying voice, "Good day, Mrs. Henderson." Momma responded with "How you, Sister Flowers?"

7   Mrs. Flowers didn't belong to our church, nor was she Momma's familiar. Why on earth did she insist on calling her Sister Flowers? Shame made me want to hide my face. Mrs. Flowers deserved better than to be called Sister. Then, Momma left out the verb. Why not ask, "How *are* you, *Mrs.* Flowers?" With the unbalanced passion of the young, I hated her for showing her ignorance to Mrs. Flowers. It didn't occur to me for many years that they were as alike as sisters, separated only by formal education.

8   Although I was upset, neither of the women was in the least shaken by what I thought an unceremonious greeting. Mrs. Flowers would continue her easy gait up the hill to her little bungalow, and Momma kept on shelling peas or doing whatever had brought her to the front porch.

9   Occasionally, though, Mrs. Flowers would drift off the road and down to the Store and Momma would say to me, "Sister, you go on and play." As she left I would hear the beginning of an intimate conversation. Momma persistently using the wrong verb, or none at all.

10   "Brother and Sister Wilcox is sho'ly the meanest—" "Is," Momma? "Is"? Oh, please, not "is," Momma, for two or more. But they talked, and from the side of the building where I waited for the ground to open up and swallow me, I heard the soft-voiced Mrs. Flowers and the textured voice of my grandmother merging and melting. They were interrupted from time to time by giggles that must have come from Mrs. Flowers (Momma never giggled in her life). Then she was gone.

11   She appealed to me because she was like people I had never met personally. Like women in English novels who walked the moors (whatever they were) with their loyal dogs racing at a respectful distance. Like the women who sat in front of roaring fireplaces, drinking tea incessantly from silver trays full of scones and crumpets. Women

---

* "Momma" was the grandmother who raised Angelou and her brother in Stamps, Arkansas; she was the respected owner of a general store.

who walked over the "heath" and read morocco-bound books and had two last names divided by a hyphen. It would be safe to say that she made me proud to be Negro, just by being herself.

12   She acted just as refined as whitefolks in the movies and books and she was more beautiful, for none of them could have come near that warm color without looking gray by comparison.

13   I was fortunate that I never saw her in the company of po-whitefolks. For since they tend to think of their whiteness as an evenizer, I'm certain that I would have had to hear her spoken to commonly as Bertha, and my image of her would have been shattered like the unmendable Humpty-Dumpty.

14   One summer afternoon, sweet-milk fresh in my memory, she stopped at the Store to buy provisions. Another Negro woman of her health and age would have been expected to carry the paper sacks home in one hand, but Momma said, "Sister Flowers, I'll send Bailey* up to your house with these things."

15   She smiled that slow dragging smile, "Thank you, Mrs. Henderson. I'd prefer Marguerite, though." My name was beautiful when she said it. "I've been meaning to talk to her, anyway." They gave each other age-group looks.

16   Momma said, "Well, that's all right then. Sister, go and change your dress. You going to Sister Flowers'."

17   The chifforobe was a maze. What on earth did one put on to go to Mrs. Flowers' house? I knew I shouldn't put on a Sunday dress. It might be sacrilegious. Certainly not a house dress, since I was already wearing a fresh one. I chose a school dress, naturally. It was formal without suggesting that going to Mrs. Flowers' house was equivalent to attending church.

18   I trusted myself back into the Store.

19   "Now, don't you look nice." I had chosen the right thing, for once. . . .

20   There was a little path beside the rocky road, and Mrs. Flowers walked in front swinging her arms and picking her way over the stones.

21   She said, without turning her head, to me, "I hear you're doing very good school work, Marguerite, but that it's all written. The teachers report that they have trouble getting you to talk in class." We passed the triangular farm on our left and the path widened to allow us to walk together. I hung back in the separate unasked and unanswerable questions.

22   "Come and walk along with me, Marguerite." I couldn't have refused even if I wanted to. She pronounced my name so nicely. Or more correctly, she spoke each word with such clarity that I was certain a foreigner who didn't understand English could have understood her.

23   "Now no one is going to make you talk—possibly no one can. But bear in mind, language is man's way of communicating with his fellow man and it is language alone which separates him from the lower animals." That was a totally new idea to me, and I would need time to think about it.

24   "Your grandmother says you read a lot. Every chance you get. That's good, but not good enough. Words mean more than what is set down on paper. It takes the human voice to infuse them with the shades of deeper meaning."

25   I memorized the part about the human voice infusing words. It seemed so valid and poetic.

---

* Angelou's brother

26   She said she was going to give me some books and that I not only must read them, I must read them aloud. She suggested that I try to make a sentence sound in as many different ways as possible.

27   "I'll accept no excuse if you return a book to me that has been badly handled." My imagination boggled at the punishment I would deserve if in fact I did abuse a book of Mrs. Flowers'. Death would be too kind and brief.

28   The odors in the house surprised me. Somehow I had never connected Mrs. Flowers with food or eating or any other common experience of common people. There must have been an outhouse, too, but my mind never recorded it.

29   The sweet scent of vanilla had met us as she opened the door.

30   "I made tea cookies this morning. You see, I had planned to invite you for cookies and lemonade so we could have this little chat. The lemonade is in the icebox."

31   It followed that Mrs. Flowers would have ice on an ordinary day, when most families in our town bought ice late on Saturdays only a few times during the summer to be used in the wooden ice-cream freezers.

32   She took the bags from me and disappeared through the kitchen door. I looked around the room that I had never in my wildest fantasies imagined I would see. Browned photographs leered or threatened from the walls and the white, freshly done curtains pushed against themselves and against the wind. I wanted to gobble up the room entire and take it to Bailey, who would help me analyze and enjoy it.

33   "Have a seat, Marguerite. Over there by the table." She carried a platter covered with a tea towel. Although she warned that she hadn't tried her hand at baking sweets for some time, I was certain that like everything else about her the cookies would be perfect.

34   They were flat round wafers, slightly browned on the edges and butter-yellow in the center. With the cold lemonade they were sufficient for childhood's lifelong diet. Remembering my manners, I took nice little lady-like bites off the edges. She said she had made them expressly for me and that she had a few in the kitchen that I could take home to my brother. So I jammed one whole cake in my mouth and the rough crumbs scratched the insides of my jaws, and if I hadn't had to swallow, it would have been a dream come true.

35   As I ate she began the first of what we later called "my lessons in living." She said that I must always be intolerant of ignorance but understanding of illiteracy. That some people, unable to go to school, were more educated and even more intelligent than college professors. She encouraged me to listen carefully to what country people called mother wit. That in those homely sayings was couched the collective wisdom of generations.

36   When I finished the cookies she brushed off the table and brought a thick, small book from the bookcase. I had read *A Tale of Two Cities* and found it up to my standards as a romantic novel. She opened the first page and I heard poetry for the first time in my life.

37   "It was the best of times and the worst of times. . . ." Her voice slid in and curved down through and over the words. She was nearly singing. I wanted to look at the pages. Were they the same that I had read? Or were there notes, music, lined on the pages, as in a hymn book? Her sounds began cascading gently. I knew from listening to a thousand preachers that she was nearing the end of her reading, and I hadn't really heard, heard to understand, a single word.

38   "How do you like that?"

39   It occurred to me that she expected a response. The sweet vanilla flavor was still on my tongue and her reading was a wonder in my ears. I had to speak.

40   I said, "Yes, ma'am." It was the least I could do, but it was the most also.

41   "There's one more thing. Take this book of poems and memorize one for me. Next time you pay me a visit, I want you to recite."

42   I have tried often to search behind the sophistication of years for the enchantment I so easily found in those gifts. The essence escapes but its aura remains. To be allowed, no, invited, into the private lives of strangers, and to share their joys and fears, was a chance to exchange the Southern bitter wormwood for a cup of mead with Beowulf or a hot cup of tea and milk with Oliver Twist. When I said aloud, "It is a far, far better thing that I do, than I have ever done . . ." tears of love filled my eyes at my selflessness.

43   On that first day, I ran down the hill and into the road (few cars ever came along it) and had the good sense to stop running before I reached the Store.

44   I was liked, and what a difference it made. I was respected not as Mrs. Henderson's grandchild or Bailey's sister but for just being Marguerite Johnson.

45   Childhood's logic never asks to be proved (all conclusions are absolute). I didn't question why Mrs. Flowers had singled me out for attention, nor did it occur to me that Momma might have asked her to give me a little talking to. All I cared about was that she had made tea cookies for *me* and read to *me* from her favorite book. It was enough to prove that she liked me.

Questions on Content, Structure, and Style

1. What is Angelou's main purpose in this narrative? What does she want to show about Sister Flowers' effect on her?

2. How does Angelou use sensory details and imagery in paragraphs 2–4 to introduce Mrs. Flowers' character?

3. Why does Angelou emphasize the embarrassment she felt when Momma talked to Mrs. Flowers? What do these conversations reveal about Angelou's attitude toward her grandmother at this time?

4. As an adult, what does Angelou suspect about her grandmother's relationship to Mrs. Flowers that she didn't see as a child?

5. Why was Angelou impressed by Mrs. Flowers? To what kinds of women is she compared? Why is Angelou glad she had never seen Mrs. Flowers spoken to by white people?

6. What sort of young girl was Angelou before she became friends with Mrs. Flowers? Cite some evidence from the essay that supports your view of her character.

7. How does the description of Mrs. Flowers' house and possessions help communicate Angelou's childhood reverence for this woman? Why were the cookies and lemonade so important?

8. Why does Angelou choose to use dialogue in paragraphs 37–41 instead of just describing the scene?

9. Does Angelou use enough vivid details to make her narrative seem believable and her characters realistic? Cite two or three examples of descriptive language that you think are particularly effective.

10. Why does Angelou include paragraphs 42, 44, and 45 at the end of her essay? Would the extent of Mrs. Flowers' impact on the author be as clearly understood without them?

Suggestions for Writing

Try using Maya Angelou's "Sister Flowers" as a stepping-stone to your writing. Think of an adult who helped, guided, or "rescued" you when you were a child or young teen. How did this person make a difference in your life? This person might be a relative, a teacher, a neighbor, a coach, a friend's parent. Tell a story that captures an important moment in your relationship with this person: your first meeting, a crucial event, or an incident that crystallized your awareness of this person's influence on you. Or perhaps you have played an important role in the life of a child or older person. In either case, what insight about the value of intergenerational relationships might your narrative offer?

Vocabulary

voile (2)	chifforobe (17)	homely (35)
benign (4)	infuse (24)	aura (42)
gait (8)	boggled (27)	wormwood (42)
morocco-bound (11)	leered (32)	mead (42)

■ A REVISION WORKSHEET

As you write your rough drafts, consult Chapter 5 for guidance through the revision process. In addition, here are a few questions to ask yourself as you revise your narrative:

1. Is the narrative essay's purpose clear to the reader?

2. Is the thesis plainly stated or at least clearly implied?

3. Does the narrative convincingly support or illustrate its intended point? If not, how might the story be changed?

4. Does the story maintain a logical point of view and an understandable order of action? Are there enough transitional devices used to give the story a smooth flow?

5. Are the characters, actions, and settings presented in enough vivid detail to make them clear and believable? Where could more detail be effectively added? Would use of dialogue be appropriate?

6. Is the story coherent and well paced or does it wander or bog down in places because of irrelevant or repetitious details? What might be condensed or cut? Could any bland or wordy description be replaced?

7. Does the essay end in a satisfying way or does the action stop too abruptly?

After you've revised your essay extensively, you might exchange rough drafts with a classmate and answer these questions for each other, making specific suggestions for improvement wherever appropriate. (For advice on productive participation in classroom workshops, see pages 108–111.)

Reviewing Your Progress

After you have completed your narrative essay, take a moment to measure your progress as a writer by responding to the following questions. Such analysis will help you to recognize growth in your writing skills and may enable you to identify areas that are still problematic.

1. What do you like best about your narrative essay? Why?

2. After reading through your essay, select the description, detail, or piece of dialogue that you think best characterizes a major figure or most effectively advances the action in your story. Explain the reason for your choice in one or two sentences.

3. What part of your essay gave you the most trouble? How did you overcome the problem?

4. If you had more time to work on this essay, what would receive additional attention? Why?

5. What did you learn about your topic from writing this essay? About yourself as a writer?

Chapter 13

Writing Essays Using Multiple Strategies

In Part Two of this text you have been studying essays developed primarily by a single mode or expository strategy. You may have, for example, written essays primarily developed by multiple examples, process analysis, or comparison/contrast. Concentrating on a single strategy in your essays has allowed you to practice, in a focused way, each of the patterns of development most often used in writing tasks. Although practicing each strategy in isolation this way is somewhat artificial, it is the easiest, simplest way to master the common organizational patterns. Consider the parallels to learning almost any skill: before you attempt a complex dive with spins and flips, you first practice each maneuver separately. Having understood and mastered the individual strategies of development, you should feel confident about facing any writing situation, including those that would most profit from incorporating multiple strategies to accomplish their goal.

Most essays *do* call upon multiple strategies of development to achieve their purpose, a reality you have probably discovered for yourself as you studied various essays in this text. In fact, you may have found it difficult—or impossible—to avoid combining modes and strategies in your own essays. As noted in the introduction to Part Two, writers virtually always blend strategies, using examples in their comparisons, description in their definitions, causal analysis in their arguments, and so on. Therein is the heart of the matter: the single patterns of development you have been practicing are *thinking* strategies—ways of considering a subject and generating ideas—as well as organizing tools. In most writing situations, writers study their tasks and choose the strategies that will *most effectively* accomplish their purpose.

In addition, some writing tasks, often the longer ones, will clearly profit from combining multiple strategies in distinct ways to thoroughly address the essay's subject, purpose, and audience. Suppose, for example, you are given a problem-solving assignment in a business class: selling the City Council on a plan to build a student housing project in a particular neighborhood. You might call on your writing resources and use multiple strategies to

- Describe the project
- Explain the causes (the need for such a project)
- Argue its strengths; deflect opposing arguments
- Contrast it to other housing options
- Cite similar successful examples in other towns
- Explain its long-term beneficial effects on tenants, neighbors, businesses, etc.

Or perhaps you are investigating recent disciplinary action taken against Colorado high school seniors for decorating their graduation gowns. Your essay might combine strategies by first presenting examples of the controversy, explaining its causes and effects, and then contrasting the opinions of administrators, students, and parents. You might even conclude with a suggested process for avoiding future problems. In other words, many essay assignments—including the widely assigned summary-response paper*—might call for a multi-strategy response.

As a writer who now knows how to use a variety of thinking and organizational methods, you can assess any writing situation and select the strategy—or strategies—that will work best for your topic, purpose, and audience.

Choosing the Best Strategies

To help you choose the best means of development for your essay, here is a brief review of the modes and strategies accompanied by some pertinent questions:

1. Example: Would real or hypothetical illustrations make my subject more easily understood?
2. Process: Would a step-by-step procedural analysis clarify my subject?
3. Comparison/Contrast: Would aligning or juxtaposing my subject to something else be helpful?
4. Definition: Would my subject profit from an extended explanation of its meaning?
5. Division/Classification: Would separating my subject into its component parts or grouping its parts into categories be useful?
6. Causal Analysis: Would explaining causes or effects add important information?
7. Argument: Would my position be advanced by offering logical reasons and/or addressing objections?

---

* For an in-depth look at this popular assignment, see pages 430–432.

8. Description: Would vivid details, sensory images, or figurative language help readers visualize my subject?

9. Narrative: Would a story best illustrate some idea or aspect of my subject?

Try using these questions as prompts to help you generate ideas and select those strategies that best accomplish your purpose.

Problems to Avoid

Avoid overkill. Being prepared to use any of the writing strategies is akin to carrying many tools in your carpenter's bag. But just because you own many tools doesn't mean you must use all of them in one project; rather, you select only the ones you need for the specific job at hand. If you do decide to use multiple strategies in a particular essay, avoid a hodgepodge of information that runs in too many directions. Sometimes your essay's prescribed length means you cannot present all you know; again, let your main purpose guide you to including the best or most important ideas.

Organize logically. If you decide that multiple strategies will work best, you must find an appropriate order and coherent flow for your essay. In the hypothetical problem-solving essay on the housing project mentioned earlier, for instance, the writer must decide whether the long-term effects of the project should be discussed earlier or later in the paper. In the student essay that follows, the writer struggled with the question of putting kinds of vegetarians before or after discussion of reasons for adopting vegetarianism. There are no easy answers to such questions—each writer must experiment with outlines and rough drafts to find the most successful arrangement, one that will offer the most effective response to the particular material, the essay's purpose, and the audience's needs. Be patient as you try various ways of combining strategies into a coherent rather than choppy paper.

■ Sample Student Essay

In the essay that follows, the student writer responds to an assignment that asked her to write about an important belief or distinguishing aspect of her life. The purpose, audience, and development of her essay were left to her; the length was designated at 750 to 1,000 words. As a confirmed vegetarian for well over a decade, she often found herself questioned about her beliefs. After deciding to clarify (and encourage) vegetarianism for an audience of interested but often puzzled fellow students, she developed her essay by drawing on many strategies, including causal analysis, example, classification, contrast, argument, and process analysis. Because she found her early draft too long, the writer edited out an extended narrative telling the story of her own "conversion" to vegetarianism, viewing that section as less central to her essay's main purpose than the other parts.

Pass the Broccoli—Please!

1   What do Benjamin Franklin, Charles Darwin, Leonardo da Vinci, Percy Bysshe Shelley, Mohandas Gandhi, Albert Einstein, and I have in common? In addition to being great thinkers, of course, we are all vegetarians, people who have rejected the practice of eating animals. Vegetarianism is growing rapidly in America today, but some people continue to see it as a strange choice. If you are thinking of making this decision yourself or are merely curious, taking time to learn about vegetarianism is worthwhile.

2   In a land where hamburgers, pepperoni pizza, and fried chicken are among our favorite foods, just why do Americans become vegetarians anyway? Worldwide, vegetarianism is often part of religious faith, especially to Buddhists, Hindus, and others whose spiritual beliefs emphasize nonviolence, karma, and reincarnation. But in this country the reasons for becoming vegetarian are more diverse. Some people cite ecological reasons, arguing that vegetarianism is best for our planet because it takes less land and food to raise vegetables and grain than livestock. Others choose vegetarianism because of health reasons. Repeated studies by groups such as the American Heart Association and the American Medical Association show that diets lower in animal fats and higher in fiber decrease the risk of heart disease, cancer, diabetes, hypertension, and osteoporosis.

3   Still other people's ethical beliefs bring them to vegetarianism. These people object to the ways that some animals, such as cows and chickens, are confined and are often fed various chemicals, such as growth hormones, antibiotics, and tranquilizers. They object to the procedures of slaughterhouses. They object to killing animals for consumption or for their decorative body parts (hides, fur, skins, tusks, feathers, etc.) and to their use in science or

Introduction:
Famous examples

Thesis, purpose,
audience

Contrast to
other parts
of the world

Causal analysis:
3 reasons

cosmetic experiments. These vegetarians believe that animals feel fear and pain and that it is morally wrong for one species to inflict unnecessary suffering on another. I count myself among this group; consequently, my vegetarian choices extend to wearing no leather or fur and I do not use household or cosmetic products tested on animals.

Personal example

4   Regardless of reasons for our choice, all vegetarians reject eating meat. However, there are actually several kinds of vegetarians, with the majority falling into three categories:

1. Ovo-lacto vegetarians eat milk, cheese, eggs, and honey;
2. Lacto vegetarians do not eat eggs but may keep other dairy products in their diet;
3. Vegans do not eat dairy products or any animal by-products whatsoever.

Classification: Three types

Many people, including myself, begin as ovo-lacto vegetarians but eventually become vegans, considered the most complete or pure type.

5   Perhaps the most common objection to any type of vegetarianism comes from a misconception about deficiencies in the diet, particularly protein. But it is a mistake to think only meat offers us protein. Vegetarians who eat dairy products, grains, vegetables, beans, and nuts receive more than enough nutrients, including protein. In fact, according to the cookbook The Higher Taste, cheese, peanuts, and lentils contain more protein per ounce than hamburger, pork, or a porterhouse steak. Many medical experts think that Americans actually eat too much protein, as seen in the revised food pyramid that now calls for an increase in vegetables, fruits, and grains over meat and dairy products. A vegetarian diet will not make someone a limp weakling. Kevin Eubanks, Tonight Show band leader, is, for

Argument: Refutation, evidence, examples

example, not only a busy musician but also a weightlifter. Some members of the Denver Broncos football team, according to their manager, no longer eat red meat at their training table.

6   For those who would like to give vegetarianism a try, here are a few suggestions for getting started:

Process:
4 steps to begin

1. Explore your motives. If you are only becoming a vegetarian to please a friend, for example, you won't stick with it. Be honest with yourself: the reasons behind your choice have a lot to do with your commitment.

2. Read more. The library can provide you with answers to your questions and concerns. There are hundreds of books full of ecological, medical, and ethical arguments for vegetarianism.

(More argument and examples)

3. Eat! Another popular misconception is that vegetarianism means a life of eating tasteless grass; nothing could be less true. Visit a vegetarian restaurant several times to see how many delicious dishes are available. Even grocery stores now carry a variety of vegetarian entrees. Or try one of the many vegetarian cookbooks on the market today. You may be surprised to discover that tofu enchiladas, soy burgers, and stuffed eggplant taste better than you could ever imagine.

4. Start slowly. You don't have to become a vegan overnight if it doesn't feel right. Some people begin by excluding just red meat from their diets. Feeling good as time goes by can direct your choices. Books, such as <u>The Beginning Vegetarian</u>, and magazines, such as <u>Vegetarian Times</u>, can offer encouragement.

7   It's never too late to change your lifestyle. Nobel Prize–winning author Isaac Bashevis Singer became a vegetarian at age fifty-eight.

Making this choice now may allow you to live longer and feel better. In fifty years you may be like playwright George Bernard Shaw, who at twenty-five was warned against a vegetarian diet. As a vigorous old man, Shaw wanted to tell all those people they were wrong, but noted he couldn't: "They all passed away years ago"!

Conclusion: Additional famous examples, witty quotation

Professional Essay*

▪ Don't Let Stereotypes Warp Your Judgments

Robert L. Heilbroner

Robert L. Heilbroner was a Professor of Economics at the New School for Social Research in New York City for over fifty years. He was well known for his *New Yorker* essays and for over twenty books, including *The Worldly Philosophers* (1953), whose revised editions are still widely used in economics classes. This essay, published in *Reader's Digest*, uses multiple strategies to expose a social problem, explain its causes and effects, and offer some practical suggestions for change.

1   Is a girl called Gloria apt to be better-looking than one called Bertha? Are criminals more likely to be dark than blond? Can you tell a good deal about someone's personality from hearing his voice briefly over the phone? Can a person's nationality be pretty accurately guessed from his photograph? Does the fact that someone wears glasses imply that he is intelligent?

2   The answer to all these questions is obviously, "No."

3   Yet, from all the evidence at hand, most of us believe these things. Ask any college boy if he'd rather take his chances with a Gloria or a Bertha, or ask a college

Can you find Cuthbert?

---
* For help reading this essay analytically, review pages 170–172.

girl if she'd rather blind-date a Richard or a Cuthbert. In fact, you don't have to ask: college students in questionnaires have revealed that names conjure up the same images in their minds as they do in yours—and for as little reason.

4   Look into the favorite suspects of persons who report "suspicious characters" and you will find a large percentage of them to be "swarthy" or "dark and foreign-looking"—despite the testimony of criminologists that criminals do *not* tend to be dark, foreign or "wild-eyed." Delve into the main asset of a telephone stock swindler and you will find it to be a marvelously confidence-inspiring telephone "personality." And whereas we all think we know what an Italian or a Swede looks like, it is the sad fact that when a group of Nebraska students sought to match faces and nationalities of 15 European countries, they were scored wrong in 93 percent of their identifications. Finally, for all the fact that horn-rimmed glasses have now become the standard television sign of an "intellectual," optometrists know that the main thing that distinguishes people with glasses is just bad eyes.

5   Stereotypes are a kind of gossip about the world, a gossip that makes us prejudge people before we ever lay eyes on them. Hence it is not surprising that stereotypes have something to do with the dark world of prejudice. Explore most prejudices (note that the word means prejudgment) and you will find a cruel stereotype at the core of each one.

6   For it is the extraordinary fact that once we have typecast the world, we tend to see people in terms of our standardized pictures. In another demonstration of the power of stereotypes to affect our vision, a number of Columbia and Barnard students were shown 30 photographs of pretty but unidentified girls, and asked to rate each in terms of "general liking," "intelligence," "beauty" and so on. Two months later, the same group were shown the same photographs, this time with fictitious Irish, Italian, Jewish and "American" names attached to the pictures. Right away the ratings changed. Faces which were now seen as representing a national group went down in looks and still farther down in likability, while the "American" girls suddenly looked decidedly prettier and nicer.

7   Why is it that we stereotype the world in such irrational and harmful fashion? In part, we begin to type-cast people in our childhood years. Early in life, as every parent whose child has watched a TV Western knows, we learn to spot the Good Guys from the Bad Guys. Some years ago, a social psychologist showed very clearly how powerful these stereotypes of childhood vision are. He secretly asked the most popular youngsters in an elementary school to make errors in their morning gym exercises. Afterwards, he asked the class if anyone had noticed any mistakes during gym period. Oh, yes, said the children. But it was the *unpopular* members of the class—the "bad guys"—they remembered as being out of step.

8   We not only grow up with standardized pictures forming inside of us, but as grown-ups we are constantly having them thrust upon us. Some of them, like the half-joking, half-serious stereotypes of mothers-in-law, or country yokels, or psychiatrists, are dinned into us by the stock jokes we hear and repeat. In fact, without such stereotypes, there would be a lot fewer jokes. Still other stereotypes are perpetuated by the advertisements we read, the movies we see, the books we read.

9   And finally, we tend to stereotype because it helps us make sense out of a highly confusing world, a world which William James* once described as "one great, blooming, buzzing confusion." It is a curious fact that if we don't *know* what we're looking at, we are often quite literally unable to *see* what we're looking at. People who recover their sight after a lifetime of blindness actually cannot at first tell a triangle from a square. A visitor to a factory sees only noisy chaos where the superintendent sees a perfectly synchronized flow of work. As Walter Lippmann† has said, "For the most part we do not first see, and then define; we define first, and then we see."

10   Stereotypes are one way in which we "define" the world in order to see it. They classify the infinite variety of human beings into a convenient handful of "types" towards whom we learn to act in stereotyped fashion. Life would be a wearing process if we had to start from scratch with each and every human contact. Stereotypes economize on our mental effort by covering up the blooming, buzzing confusion with big recognizable cutouts. They save us the "trouble" of finding out what the world is like—they give it its accustomed look.

11   Thus the trouble is that stereotypes make us mentally lazy. As S. I. Hayakawa, the authority on semantics, has written: "The danger of stereotypes lies not in their existence, but in the fact that they become for all people some of the time, and for some people all the time, *substitutes for observation*." Worse yet, stereotypes get in the way of our judgment, even when we do observe the world. Someone who has formed rigid preconceptions of all Latins as "excitable," or all teenagers as "wild," doesn't alter his point of view when he meets a calm and deliberate Genoese,‡ or a serious-minded high school student. He brushes them aside as "exceptions that prove the rule." And, of course, if he meets someone true to type, he stands triumphantly vindicated. "They're all like that," he proclaims, having encountered an excited Latin, an ill-behaved adolescent.

12   Hence, quite aside from the injustice which stereotypes do to others, they impoverish ourselves. A person who lumps the world into simple categories, who type-casts all labor leaders as "racketeers," all businessmen as "reactionaries," all Harvard men as "snobs," and all Frenchmen as "sexy," is in danger of becoming a stereotype himself. He loses his capacity to be himself—which is to say, to see the world in his own absolutely unique, inimitable and independent fashion.

13   Instead, he votes for the man who fits his standardized picture of what a candidate "should" look like or sound like, buys the goods that someone in his "situation" in life "should" own, lives the life that others define for him. The mark of the stereotype person is that he never surprises us, that we do indeed have him "typed." And no one fits this strait-jacket so perfectly as someone whose opinions about *other people* are fixed and inflexible.

14   Impoverishing as they are, stereotypes are not easy to get rid of. The world we type-cast may be no better than a Grade B movie, but at least we know what to expect of our stock characters. When we let them act for themselves in the strangely unpredictable way that people do act, who knows but that many of our fondest convictions will be proved wrong?

---

* William James (1842–1910) was an American philosopher and psychologist.

† Walter Lippmann was a twentieth-century American journalist.

‡ "Genoese" refers to a citizen of Genoa, Italy.

15   Nor do we suddenly drop our standardized pictures for a blinding vision of the Truth. Sharp swings of ideas about people often just substitute one stereotype for another. The true process of change is a slow one that adds bits and pieces of reality to the pictures in our heads, until gradually they take on some of the blurriness of life itself. Little by little, we learn not that Jews and Negroes and Catholics and Puerto Ricans are "just like everybody else"—for that, too, is a stereotype—but that each and every one of them is unique, special, different and individual. Often we do not even know that we have let a stereotype lapse until we hear someone saying, "all so-and-so's are like such-and-such," and we hear ourselves saying, "Well—maybe."

16   Can we speed the process along? Of course we can.

17   First, we can become *aware* of the standardized pictures in our heads, in other peoples' heads, in the world around us.

18   Second, we can become suspicious of all judgments that we allow exceptions to "prove." There is no more chastening thought than that in the vast intellectual adventure of science, it takes but one tiny exception to topple a whole edifice of ideas.

19   Third, we can learn to be chary of generalizations about people. As F. Scott Fitzgerald* once wrote: "Begin with an individual, and before you know it you have created a type; begin with a type, and you find you have created—nothing."

20   Most of the time, when we type-cast the world, we are not in fact generalizing about people at all. We are only revealing the embarrassing facts about the pictures that hang in the gallery of stereotypes in our own heads.

Questions on Content, Structure, and Style

1. Why does Heilbroner begin his essay with a series of questions, references to criminal reports, and the Nebraska study? How does this introduction set up Heilbroner's thesis?

2. How does Heilbroner define stereotypes in paragraph 5? What do the studies at Barnard and Columbia University and at the elementary school (paragraph 7) illustrate about prejudice?

3. Why does Heilbroner use "we" and "us" so often in this essay instead of referring to "people who stereotype"? Is his choice a good one?

4. What explanation of causes does Heilbroner offer? How do stereotypes contribute to the ways we try to "define" the world?

5. In addition to the injustice inflicted on others, what negative effects does stereotyping have on those who employ it?

6. Throughout his essay, Heilbroner uses vivid, specific examples, both real and hypothetical. Cite and explain some of his most effective uses of this strategy.

7. Why does Heilbroner include a three-step process near the end of his essay?

8. Why does Heilbroner quote such well-known figures as William James, S. I. Hayakawa, Walter Lippmann, and F. Scott Fitzgerald in various places in his essay? What purposes do their words serve?

---

* F. Scott Fitzgerald (1896–1940) was an American writer, best known for his novel *The Great Gatsby*.

9. Evaluate this essay's conclusion. How does Heilbroner use figurative language to make a memorable last impression on his readers?

10. List the main strategies Heilbroner uses to develop his essay. Which do you find the most effective? If Heilbroner were to extend his essay, what other strategies might he incorporate in his exploration of stereotyping?

Suggestions for Writing

Try using Robert Heilbroner's "Don't Let Stereotypes Warp Your Judgments" as a stepping-stone to an essay of your own. Have you ever been the victim of someone's irrational or harmful stereotyping? Has anyone ever devalued your job or belittled your choice of activities? Or have you yourself been guilty of misjudging someone else? Remember that not all stereotypes are racial or ethnic; typecasting surrounds economic status (the "welfare moocher"), gender (the "dumb blonde"), locations (the redneck Texan), professions (the mousey accountant), and extracurricular activities (the "jock"), to name only a few areas. Write an essay that explores the topic of stereotyping or prejudice; use any of the modes or strategies you find helpful. You might, for example, describe an incident, discuss causes or effects, argue for ways to solve the problem, or explain steps you once took to escape "the gallery of stereotypes" in your own head.

Vocabulary

swarthy (4)	semantics (11)	chastening (18)
dinned (8)	vindicated (11)	edifice (18)
perpetuated (8)	impoverish (12)	chary (19)
synchronized (9)		

■ A REVISION WORKSHEET

As you write your rough drafts, consult Chapter 5 for guidance through the revision process. In addition, here are a few questions to ask yourself before and during the early stages of your writing:

1. What is my main purpose in writing this particular essay? Who is my audience?

2. Does my assignment or the subject itself suggest a primary method of development or would combining several strategies be more effective?

3. Have I considered my subject from multiple directions, as suggested by the questions on pages 350–351?

4. Have I selected the best strategies to meet the needs of my particular audience?

5. Would blending strategies help my readers understand my topic and my essay's purpose? Or am I trying to include too many approaches, move in too many directions, resulting in an essay that seems too scattered?

6. Have I considered an effective order for the strategies I've chosen? Do the parts of my essay flow together smoothly?

7. Have I avoided common weaknesses such as vague examples, fuzzy directions, circular definitions, overlapping categories, or logical fallacies, as discussed in the "Problems to Avoid" sections of Chapters 9–12?

After you've revised your essay extensively, you might exchange rough drafts with a classmate and answer these questions for each other, making specific suggestions for improvement wherever appropriate. (For advice on productive participation in classroom workshops, see pages 108–111.)

Reviewing Your Progress

After you have completed your essay, take a moment to measure your progress as a writer by responding to the following questions. Such analysis will help you recognize growth in your writing skills and may enable you to identify areas that are still problematic.

1. What do you like best about your essay? Why?

2. After considering the multiple strategies of development used in your essay, which one do you find most effective and why?

3. What part of your essay gave you the most trouble? How did you overcome the problem?

4. If you had more time to work on this essay, what would receive additional attention? Why?

5. What did you learn about your topic from writing this essay? About yourself as a writer?

Part 3

Special Assignments

The third section of this text addresses several kinds of assignments frequently included in many composition classes. Chapter 14 will first explain ways to conduct formal research on a topic and then show you how to best incorporate your research into your essay. "Writing in Class: Exams and 'Response' Essays" confronts the anxiety that writing under pressure may bring by helping you respond quickly but effectively to a variety of timed essays and exams. This chapter also addresses one of the most widely used in-class assignments, the summary-response (or reaction) essay. Chapter 16, "Writing about Literature," illustrates several uses of poetry and short stories in the composition classroom and provides some guidelines for both close reading and analytical thinking. A new chapter, Chapter 17, "Writing about Visual Arts," offers suggestions for essays analyzing paintings, photographs, and sculptures. Chapter 18, "Writing about Film," is focused on thoughtful analysis of movies. The last chapter in Part Three, "Writing in the World of Work," presents advice for effective business letters, memos, electronic-mail messages, and résumés.

If you have worked through Parts One and Two of this book, you have already practiced many of the skills demanded by these special assignments. Information in the next six chapters will build on what you already know about good writing. ∎

Chapter 14

Writing a Paper Using Research

Although the words "research paper" have been known to produce anxiety worse than that caused by the sound of a dentist's drill, you should try to relax. A research paper is similar to the kinds of expository and argumentative essays described in the earlier parts of this book, the difference being the use of documented source material to support, illustrate, or explain your ideas. Research papers still call for thesis statements, logical sequences of paragraphs, well-developed evidence, smooth conclusions—or in other words, all the skills you've been practicing throughout this book. By citing sources in your essays or reports, you merely show your readers that you have investigated your ideas and found support for them. In addition, using sources affords your readers the opportunity to look into your subject further if they so desire, consulting your references for additional information.

The process described in the next few pages should help you write a paper using research that is carefully and effectively documented. This chapter also contains sample citation forms for a variety of research sources, illustrated by sample student writing using both MLA and APA styles.

■ Focusing Your Topic

In some cases, you will be assigned your topic, and you will be able to begin your research right away. In other cases, however, you may be encouraged to select your own subject, or you may be given a general subject ("health-care reform," "recycling," "U.S. immigration policies") that you must narrow and then focus into a specific, manageable topic. If the topic is your choice, you need to do some preliminary thinking about what interests you; as in any assignment, you should make the essay a learning experience from which both you and your readers will profit. Therefore, you may want to brainstorm for a while on your general subject before you go to the library, asking yourself questions about what you already know and don't know. Some of the most interesting papers are argumentative essays in which writers set about to find an answer to a controversy or to find support for a solution they suspected might work. Other papers, sometimes called "research reports," expose, explain, or summarize a situation or a problem for their audience.

Throughout this chapter, we will track the research and writing process of Amy Lawrence, a composition student whose writing assignment called for an essay presenting her view of a controversy in her major field of study. As a history major, Amy is particularly interested in the Russian Revolution of 1918, when the Romanov family, the last ruling family of Russia, was assassinated by the Bolsheviks, the Communist revolutionaries led by Lenin. The long-standing controversy surrounding the assassination of Czar Nicholas II and his family focused on the question of whether the two youngest Romanov children, the beautiful Anastasia and the sickly Alexei, escaped execution. A series of forensic and historical discoveries concerning the controversy had made news in the 1990s, so Amy decided to investigate the Romanov assassination for her topic. Because she already had some general knowledge of the controversy, Amy was able to think about her topic in terms of some specific *research questions:* What would research tell her about the possibility of the Romanov children's escape? Would the new forensic evidence support the theory of an escape—or would it put such a claim to rest forever? (Amy's completed essay appears on pages 410–418.)

■ Beginning Your Library Research

Once you have a general topic (and perhaps have some research questions in mind), your next step is familiarizing yourself with the school or public library where you may do all or part of your research. Most college libraries today have both print and electronic resources to offer researchers, as well as access to the Internet. Your library most likely has an online central information system, which may include a catalog of its holdings, a number of selected databases, gateways to other libraries, and other kinds of resources. With appropriate computer connections, this system may be accessed from other places on or off campus, which is handy for those times when you cannot be in the library.

Most libraries also have information (printed or online) that will indicate the location of important areas, and almost all have reference librarians who can explain the various kinds of programs and resources available to you. The smartest step you may take is asking a librarian for help before you begin searching. Library staff members may be able to save you enormous amounts of research time by pointing you in just the right direction. Do not be shy about asking the library staff for help at any point during your research!

Once you are familiar with your library, you may find it useful to consult one or more of the following research tools.

General Reference Works

If you need a general overview of your subject, or perhaps some background or historical information, you might begin your library research by consulting an encyclopedia, a collection of biographical entries, or even a statistical or demographic yearbook. You might use a comprehensive or specialized dictionary if your search turns up terms that are unfamiliar to you. These and many other library reference guides (in print and online) may also help you find a specific focus for your essay if you feel your topic is still too large or undefined at this point.

Online Catalogs

Today the online catalog has replaced the print catalog system as the primary guide to a library's holdings. You can access a library's catalog through on-site computer terminals or, in many cases, connect from off-site locations through the Internet to the library's web page.

Most computer catalogs allow you to look for information by subject, author, and title as well as by keyword(s), by the ISBN (publisher's book number), by the call number, or by a series title (Time-Life books, for example). On-screen prompts will guide you through the process of searching. Because no two library catalog systems are exactly alike, never hesitate to ask a librarian for help if you need it.

Unless you are already familiar with authorities or their works on your topic, you might begin your search by typing in keywords or your general subject. For example, Amy Lawrence began her research on the Romanov assassination by searching with the keywords Nicholas II, Czar of Russia. After typing in her keywords, she discovered that the library had several books on the czar; one book looked especially promising, so she pulled up the following screen to see more information.

KEYWORD ▼	Nicholas II, Czar of Russia,	View Entire Collection ▼	Search

Record 3 of 5

Author	Radzinsky, Edvard.
Title	**The last Czar: the life and death of Nicholas II**
Publisher	New York: Anchor Books: Doubleday, 1992

LOCATION	CALL#	LAST CHECKED IN	STATUS
HRMY Nonfiction	947.083 Radzinsky, E. 1992	02-28-06	Checked In

Edition	1st Anchor Books ed.
Descript	vi, 475 p., [24] p. of plates : ill., maps : 24 cm.
Subject	Nicholas II, Emperor of Russia, 1868–1918 – Assassination
	Nicholas II, Emperor of Russia, 1868–1918 – Family
Note	Originally published: New York : Doubleday, 1992.
Bibliog.	Includes bibliographical references (p. [453]-457) and index.
ISBN	0385469624 : $14.95 ($18.95 Can.)

If you find a relevant book, as Amy did, look at the catalog record's *Subject* line to see additional headings ("Nicholas II, Emperor of Russia, 1868–1918—Assassination") that may lead you to other useful books. Often these subject headings are linked in the online catalog, and, by clicking on one, you will be taken to books on the topic. Once you have a call number for a particular book, a library map will help you find its location on the shelves.

Indexes

Indexes list magazines, journals, newspapers, audio and video sources, books, and collections that contain material you may wish to consult. All of these indexes are now available as online databases that are updated frequently.

Using the most appropriate index may save you valuable time as you research your subject. For example, if you think your topic has been the subject of general-interest magazines, you might consult the *Reader's Guide to Periodical Literature*; for newspaper articles, you might check the *New York Times Index* or the *National Newspaper Index*. Most specialized disciplines have their own indexes: the *Humanities Index*, the *Art Index*, the *Music Index*, the *Social Science Index*, the *Business Periodicals Index*, the *Applied Science and Technology Index*, and so on.

Databases

Most libraries across the country subscribe to different information services that will lead researchers to appropriate databases for their subjects. A *database* allows users to scan electronic indexes that list thousands of bibliographic sources, abstracts, summaries, and texts.

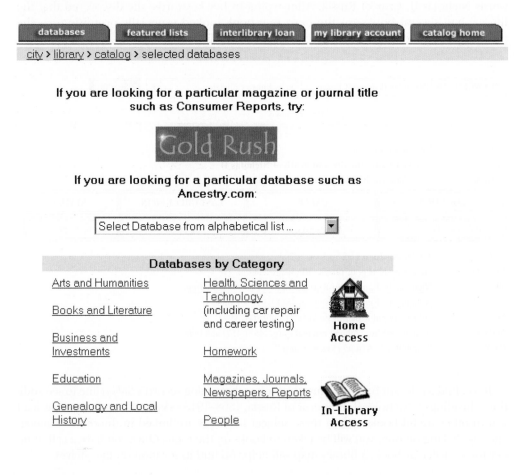

After you access your library's database information screen, you will find some general interest indexes and others that are more specialized. Page 366 shows a database screen from a shared city and community college library in Colorado.

Perhaps most helpful will be *full-text databases* that offer access to numerous academic and professional journals as well as magazines and newspapers. For example, under "Arts and Humanities," you might find this useful database:

> Proquest—Magazine and newspaper articles from over 1,500 indexed publications, many of which are available in full text and full image format.

InfoTrac is another highly useful database that offers full-text articles from nearly 6,000 newspapers, general-interest magazines, trade publications, and scholarly journals. You can now conveniently access InfoTrac™ College Edition from your own web browser; a free four-month subscription is offered by Thomson Learning. (For more information, please consult your instructor.)

Online databases are updated frequently and may therefore provide you with the most current sources for your research. Do note, however, that because libraries contract and pay a fee for database services, they must restrict some database access to on-site use or use by particular patrons (for example, enrolled students only at a campus library). Know, too, that each database may have its own search method. Always ask a librarian to help if you are struggling with a database search.

As you search your electronic sources, remember that you may have to try a variety of keywords (and their synonyms) to find what you need. Sometimes your keyword search may turn up too few leads—and sometimes you may be overwhelmed with too many matches! (For example, when Amy Lawrence typed in the keyword "Anastasia," she discovered too many irrelevant entries focusing on Hollywood movies about the princess.) To save time and effort, you may be able to broaden or narrow your search by typing in words called *Boolean operators*,* as illustrated below:

AND (Nicholas II AND Anastasia)—narrows your search to those references containing both terms

OR (Nicholas II OR Anastasia)—broadens search to find items containing either term

NOT (Anastasia NOT movie)—excludes items irrelevant to your search

NEAR (Nicholas II NEAR assassination)—finds references in which the terms occur within a set number of words (This option is not always available.)

Not all databases respond to Boolean operators, however, so it's always best to consult the searching advice offered by your particular information system.

---

* Named for the nineteenth-century British mathematician and logician George Boole

Here is the InfoTrac College Edition "keyword" search screen Amy used to look for more information on the important Romanov DNA tests:

INFOTRAC COLLEGE EDITION

Keyword search

Click in the entry box and enter search term(s)

| Romanov AND DNA | Search | Clear Form |

Search for words ⦿ in title, citation, abstract ◯ in entire article content
Type words to search for. You can use AND, OR, NOT. Results are sorted by date.

The InfoTrac College Edition search for "Romanov and DNA" produced these two titles, whose full-text articles Amy found useful.

INFOTRAC COLLEGE EDITION

Keyword search (in title, citation, abstract): Romanov AND DNA

——————— **Citations 1 to 2** ———————

☐ Mark all items on this page

☐ 🗎 **DNA test confirms dead czar's identity.** (former Russian Czar Nicholas Romanov II)
Mark   (Biology)(Brief Article)
            Science News April 20, 1996 v149 n16 p255(1) (385 words)

☐ 🗎 **Royal D-loops.** (remains of Russian Czar Nicholas II and family proved authentic with
Mark   DNA) (1993 - The Year in Science) Josie Glausiusz.
            Discover Jan 1994 v15 n1 p90(1) (474 words)

Once you have found useful information, remember that libraries have printers available to print out the on-screen data you wish to keep; you may have to pay a small fee for this printing, so it's a good idea to take some cash along, preferably in correct change. (Sometimes library users with personal computers at home can avoid this expense by e-mailing data to themselves.)

And once again, the very best advice bears repeating: never hesitate to ask your library staff for help.

The Internet

You may have access to the Internet through your library, through your school network, or through a personal account with a service provider of your choice. The Internet can offer great research opportunities, but in many cases, it may only supplement—not replace—the information you will need to collect through library sources.

The most effective approach to discovering useful material on the Internet may be through the use of search engines that produce a list of potential electronic documents or websites in response to your search. After you type in your keyword(s), the search engine explores its database for word or phrase matches; it then presents you with a list of potential sources, which include the Internet addresses (called URLs— "uniform resource locators"). You may access the sources that seem most promising (often those that appear first on the list), and you may also connect to other material by clicking on any highlighted words (hypertext links) appearing within the text of a particular document. At this time, the most popular search engine is Google, but there are many, many more worldwide, including Yahoo!, AlltheWeb, and Ask; some systems, such as Dogpile, MetaCrawler, and KartOO, search multiple engines at once. Because each search engine pulls its results from a different (but often overlapping) pool of web pages, and because each one offers distinct "extra features," it pays to try more than one. (If you aren't satisfied with your results, try another set of keywords before moving on.)

Most search engines have their own searching tips; to improve your chances for success, it's well worth the time to read the advice on conducting advanced searches. For example, Google and Yahoo! search focus results by allowing you to fill in such fields as "exact phrase," "all of the words," "at least one of the words," or "none of the words." Other options will narrow the search by designating certain languages, specific dates, or particular kinds of materials. (Google Scholar, for example, will search among academic books, journals, theses, and abstracts.)

Some search engines allow use of Boolean operators (see page 367) to narrow or broaden your search. Some allow the use of plus and minus signs to show connected terms or unwanted matches:

Anastasia + Nicholas II (find sources containing both terms)

Anastasia – movie (find sources about Anastasia but exclude those that include the word "movie")

Some programs request quotation marks around a key term of multiple words ("Anne Frank"); some are case sensitive (capitalize proper nouns or not?); some use truncation to find various forms of a word (myth* will return *mythology* and *mythical*). Other search engines, such as Ask (formerly Ask Jeeves), allow users to ask questions in natural language ("Who was Marie Romanov?"). As technology continues to improve, searching will no doubt become easier, so always take a moment to look at each search engine's current directions.

Here is one more hint for searching the web: sometimes you can guess the URL you need. Simply fill in the name of a specific company, college, agency, or organization. Do not skip spaces between words (usnews.com).

Businesses: www.name of company.com

Universities: www.name of college.edu

Government agencies: www.name of agency.gov

Organizations: www.name of organization.org

You may also consult specialized directories to discover the addresses you need.

Once you find a useful document, you may print it, add the reference to your "book-mark" or "favorites" list, or copy it to a file if you are using your own computer. Whether at the library or at home, always keep a list of your important sites, their addresses, and the date you accessed them. You may need this information for an easy return to a particular document and also for your working bibliography.

To explore other ways to use the Internet for research, check your library's home page, which most likely will offer links to helpful search advice.

Words of Caution for Internet Users: Be Afraid, Be Very Afraid . . . .

The Internet offers researchers a wealth of information incredibly fast. However, the Internet poses problems, too. It may offer a great deal of information on your essay topic—but it may not offer the *best* information, which might be found in a classic text on your library shelf. Background information or historical perspective may not be available; website information may be out of date. Moreover, simply finding the specific information you need can be frustrating and time-consuming, especially if your keywords and links don't lead in useful directions. The information superhighway is congested with scores of irrelevant distractions, so beware the wild web chase.

There is, however, another much more serious problem: not all material found on the Internet is accurate or reliable. When an article is printed in a respected journal, for example, readers have assurances that editors have reviewed the information, writers have checked their facts, and authorities have been quoted correctly. However, websites may be created by anyone on any subject, from gene splicing to Elvis sightings, without any sort of editorial review. Opinions—wise or crackpot—may be presented as facts; rumors may be presented as reality. Because there is no "quality control" of websites, writers of research papers must evaluate their sources extremely carefully to avoid gathering unreliable information. Always ask these questions of each source:

- What is the purpose of this website? (To inform, persuade, market a product or service, share an interest, entertain?) To whom is this site primarily directed, and why?

- Who is the sponsor, author, or creator of the site? (A business, an educational institution, a nonprofit organization, a government agency, a news bureau, an individual?) Is the sponsor or author known and respected in the particular content area?

- Does the sponsor or author reveal a clear bias or strong opinion? Does such a slant undercut the usefulness of the information?

- When was this site produced? When was it last updated or revised? If links exist, are they still viable? Up to date?

- Is the information accurate? How might the material be cross-checked and verified?

If you have doubts about the accuracy of any material you discover on the Internet, find another authoritative source to validate the information or omit it from your essay. Following the guidelines on pages 380–383 will help you evaluate *all* your potential research sources.

Special Collections

Your library may contain special collections that will help you research your subject. Some libraries, for example, have extensive collections of government documents or educational materials or newspapers from foreign cities. Other libraries may have invested in manuscripts from famous authors or in a series of works on a particular subject, such as your state's history. Remember, too, that some libraries contain collections of early films, rare recordings, or unique photographs. Consult your librarian or the information sources describing your library's special holdings.

■ Conducting Primary Research

To illustrate and support their points, most writers of research papers draw heavily on material found in articles, books, and other library sources. However, researchers sometimes find it useful to gather their own information. Collecting data firsthand is called *primary research*, and it is valuable because it provides information not available from other sources.

Students often conduct primary research in a variety of college classes. For example, a chemistry major may gain new knowledge from a lab experiment; an English major may discover original insights reading a work of literature; a political science major may produce thoughtful analysis after studying local election results. In each case, the investigator collects information that was not already in existence.

Although there are many ways to conduct primary research, this section will present suggestions for conducting two strategies composition students may find most helpful: the *interview* and the *questionnaire*.

The Personal Interview

Depending on your choice of topic, you may find all the information you need for your essay by exploring sources through library and online research. However, sometimes you may discover that an authority on your subject lives in your town or works on your campus. In this case, you may wish to conduct a *personal interview* to gather valuable information for your essay.

Preparation is the key word governing a good interview. Here are some suggestions to help you collect useful data in the most effective way possible.

Before You Interview:

1. *Know your purpose.* If you have only a vague notion of why you are talking to the interviewee, you will waste everyone's time as the conversation roams like a lost hiker wandering from one clearing to the next. A close look at your essay's outline or your early drafts should tell you why and how this person might contribute to your research. Be certain that the person you have selected for an interview is, in fact, the best source for the kind of information you are seeking. For example, if you are writing a paper on the campus program that assists students with learning disabilities, you might interview the program's director to obtain expert opinion; on the other hand, if you wish to know some specific ways in which the program has helped its participants, you might interview a student actively involved in the program for his or her personal response.

2. *Make an appointment.* Calling for an interview may make you a bit nervous, but remember that most people like to be asked for their opinions and are usually willing to help students with their research, if their schedules permit. Be sure the interviewee understands who you are, why you are asking for an interview, and approximately how much time you are requesting. Whenever possible, allow the interviewee to select the hour and place most convenient for him or her. Do adjust your schedule to give yourself time after the meeting in case the interview runs long and to allow yourself a few minutes to review and fill in your notes.

3. *Educate yourself.* Before the interview, read about your topic and your interviewee. You want to appear knowledgeable about your subject; you can also save time by skipping questions that have already been answered in print. Busy experts appreciate not having to explain basic information that you could have—and should have—already looked up.

4. *Plan some questions.* Unless you have an excellent memory, it is best to jot down some specific questions to which you can refer during the interview. Some interviewers write each question at the top of an index card, and then use the rest of the card for their notes on the answer. Others use a notebook in which they write a question (or key words) at the top of each page. Try to create questions that are specific, clear, and logically ordered. Avoid "yes/no" questions that don't lead to discussion. If you have a complicated or convoluted issue you want to discuss, try breaking it into a series of simpler questions that can be tackled by the interviewee one at a time.

During the Interview:

5. *Make a good first impression.* Always arrive on time, prepared with pens, paper, or other documents you need. Some interviewers like to use a recorder, but you first must secure your interviewee's permission to use this equipment. (A recorder makes some people uncomfortably self-conscious and hesitant to speak freely, so consider whether the accuracy it may provide is more important than the spontaneity it may kill.) Always begin by thanking your interviewee for his or her time and briefly say again why you think he or she can provide helpful information to you.

6. *Ask, listen, ask.* Begin asking your prepared questions, but don't rush through them. Listen attentively to your interviewee's answers, and although it takes practice, try to maintain eye contact as you jot down abbreviated notes on the answers. Allow the interviewee to do almost all the talking; after all, you are there to collect information, not participate in a debate. Do politely ask for clarification (unfamiliar terms, spelling of names, unclear references, and so on) when you need it.

7. *Be flexible.* Sometimes your interviewee will talk about something fascinating that never occurred to you when you prepared your original list of questions. Be ready to adapt your plan and ask new questions that follow up on unexpected commentary.

8. *Silence is Golden but . . .* If an interviewee is quiet or hesitates to give the kind of detailed responses you are seeking, you may need to use phrases of this kind to draw out longer answers:

   Can you elaborate on that?

   Tell me more about X.

   Why did you think that?

   How did you react to that?

   When did you realize . . . ?

   Why do you believe that?

   What's your reading of that situation?

   Would you explain that for me?

   As you ask for more details, try to use a friendly, conversational tone that will put your interviewee at ease.
   　　On the other hand, sometimes interviewees talk too much! They become stuck on one aspect of a topic, going into unnecessary depth, or perhaps they begin to drift off the subject completely. Be courteous but firm in your resolve to redirect the flow of conversation. To get back to your topic, you may need to re-ask the original question, using slightly different words.

9. *Conclude thoughtfully.* At the end of the interview, ask for any additional comments the interviewee would like to offer and for any information (or other sources) he or she thinks you might find useful. Ask the interviewee if you may contact him or her again if you should have another brief question; if such permission is granted, ask for the best means of contact (a telephone number or e-mail address). Give the interviewee your most sincere thanks for his or her time and assistance.

After the Interview:

10. *Review your notes immediately.* Fill in gaps in your notes while your memory is fresh, and write out acronyms or abbreviations whose meanings you might forget in a few days. Make some notes to yourself about using the information in your essay.

Later, if the interview figures prominently in your essay, consider sending your interviewee a copy of your work. Within days of the interview, however, it is ALWAYS polite to send your interviewee a short thank-you note, acknowledging his or her help with your research project.

The Questionnaire

A questionnaire is a series of questions or statements designed to obtain people's opinions about certain ideas, products, issues, activities, or even other people. You have, no doubt, responded to a number of questionnaires yourself: in your school, you may have filled out course evaluation forms; in a store, you may have answered questions about a new product or service; at home, you may have replied to political pollsters or participated in a marketing survey.

Designing effective questionnaires is a complex business. There are, in fact, entire college courses devoted to the analysis and development of polls and surveys, courses often required for marketing majors and political science students. As daunting as composing a questionnaire may sound, student writers often find it useful to conduct small-scale surveys to gain wider opinions on a topic under research. For example, let's assume you've been assigned a paper calling for a specific recommendation to improve a campus service or agency. You have chosen the composition computer lab and, although you have a few ideas of your own, you think it would be valuable to know what other users of the lab would most like to see changed. You design a questionnaire asking lab users to identify their chief areas of concern, and, using that information, you write a persuasive essay calling for a specific change.

Here are some suggestions for designing, administering, and analyzing questionnaires, whose results might prove useful in your research.

Developing the Questionnaire

1. *Know your purpose and identify your target audience.* Writers of effective questionnaires have a specific goal in mind; articulating that goal clearly in writing will help you create the best survey questions. Ask yourself: what do I most want to know from this particular group of people? Which group of people will give me the information I want? Hint: Asking a particular population (computer lab users) to focus on a single issue (computer lab hours) will often produce the most precise responses.

2. *Encourage participation.* At the top of your questionnaire, briefly state your purpose and your request for response, giving pertinent (but not personal) information. People are more likely to participate if they know who is conducting the survey ("student in English 121"), what you want ("collecting composition students' opinions on . . ."), and how the results will be used ("data for essay whose purpose is . . ."). Some respondents will be naturally sympathetic to a hard-working student; others may need an answer to "what's in this for me?" If it's appropriate, you can appeal to your respondents' sense of the Common Good. In the case of the computer lab survey, for example, respondents might be encouraged to answer the questions if they thought the essay's recommendations would actually go to the lab supervisor, thus creating the possibility of improved service for all.

3. *Choose the most effective type of questionnaire for your purpose.* There are several kinds of questions or statements you may use to generate information; in a short survey choose only one or two types to avoid confusing your participants.

Common methods include the following:

- **Yes/No answers**
  Example   Do you use the computer lab at least once a week?
                 ( ) Yes
                 ( ) No

- **Multiple Choice**
  Example   Check one answer. How often do you use the computer lab?
                 ( ) Once a week?
                 ( ) Twice a week?
                 ( ) More than twice a week?

- **Checklist**
  Example   Check all the statements with which you agree.
                 ____ The current lab hours of operation are convenient for me.
                 ____ The lab should be open on the weekends.
                 ____ The lab needs extended evening hours.
  Etc.

- **Rank Order**
  Example   In the list below, identify the issues most important to you by marking the most important as "1" and the least important as "5."
                 ____ Hours of operation
                 ____ Updated equipment
                 ____ Technical assistance available
  Etc.

- **Rating System**
  Example   Rate the following statements as SA (Strongly Agree), A (Agree), D (Disagree), SD (Strongly Disagree), N (No Opinion).
                 ____ The lab should be open on the weekends.
                 ____ The lab should be open later at night.
                 ____ The lab should have extended hours during final exams.
  Etc.

- **Open Questions**
  Example   If you could change the lab's hours of operation, what would an ideal schedule look like for you? Why would these hours be better than the current schedule?

Designers of questionnaires should note that although open questions may produce the most interesting answers to read, they are also the most difficult to tally objectively. Multiple-choice questionnaires may be the easiest to score, and their numbers may quickly be converted to percentages.

Once you have decided which method will best retrieve the kind of information you are seeking, clearly state the directions for following that method at the top of your questionnaire, after your statement of purpose. Consider using bold type to emphasize any important words in the instructions.

4. *Watch your language.* It's unfortunately easy to confuse your respondents or "contaminate" your survey with careless use of words or phrases. Avoid problems by remembering the following advice:

- Clarify vague references and avoid abbreviations your participants may not know.

Unclear	Are you in favor of or opposed to the proposed SB128?
Better	Are you in favor of or opposed to Colorado Senate Bill 128, which would raise the technology fees at this college by 2 percent?

- Rewrite any "loaded" questions or leading statements that attempt to shape the respondent's answer.

Biased	Should the university continue to waste your money on new, overpriced computer equipment?
Objective	Should the university purchase new computer equipment?

- Ask for one piece of information at a time.

Double question	Are the technical assistants at the lab helpful and friendly? Yes/No [Respondents might find the assistants friendly but not particularly helpful, or vice versa, so a single "yes" or a "no" answer would be misleading.]
Better questions	Do you find the technical assistants at the lab helpful? Yes/No Do you find the technical assistants in the lab friendly? Yes/No

5. *Keep it short, simple, and smooth.* People often cooperate with pollsters, but they don't want to be imposed on for too long. After you've drafted a number of potential questions for your survey, cut your list down to the most important ones. Unless you have an overwhelming reason to ignore this advice, limit your questionnaire to a single page. (Some pollsters also advise placing your most important questions first, in case respondents tire of answering and turn in incomplete forms.) Ask your questions in the clearest, most direct way possible to get the most straightforward answers.* Just as you know how to write coherent, smoothly linked paragraphs in your essays, group questions logically to move your respondents' thoughts easily from issue to issue.

---

* Some national pollsters believe that to obtain the most truthful responses, questionnaires should be answered anonymously; others suggest making signatures optional.

Administering the Questionnaire

6. *Secure a valid sampling.* To get meaningful responses, you must survey the right people, ones with the knowledge or opinions that matter to your research. But at this point you must also ask yourself two other vitally important questions: are the people taking my survey truly representative of my target group as a whole? Does my sample—the number of people contacted—comprise a large enough part of the target group to merit the conclusions I might draw from their comments?

   For valid results, first make sure that you are taking a *random sample*; that is, you must ensure that each member of the population has a fair and equal chance of being selected. In a survey on the computer center hours, for example, you would not get an accurate cross-section of opinions if you sampled only the work-study students staffing the lab or your best friends who feel as you do. Similarly, if you sample only a tiny fraction of the students who use the lab, your results will not provide strong support for any broad claims about student opinion. As you prepare to distribute your questionnaire, be sure you will address a significant number of randomly selected people who compose a cross section of your target group.

7. *Perform a test run.* If time permits, ask several people in your target group to take the survey before you distribute it widely. If the questionnaire has problems or confusing spots, they will surface in time for you to fix them.

8. *Be prepared.* Plan ahead to discover how to best distribute your questionnaires. If you are handing them out on school or private property, be sure you have permission to do so. If you are placing the questionnaires in a public place for respondents to pick up at their leisure, think about a secure drop-box for completed surveys that you can empty frequently. (If your respondents are answering by hand, don't forget to provide an extra-large number of pencils or pens as they do "walk off" with great regularity.)

Totaling and Reporting Results

9. *Analyze your responses.* Depending on your method of surveying, you may simply add up the totals for each answer (in multiple-choice or checklist questionnaires, for example), or you may need to spend some time pondering the nuances of written comments. All returned, completed questionnaires must be included in your analysis. If you wish to convert questionnaire numbers into percentages, divide the number of responses to a particular answer by the total number of questionnaires returned and then multiply that figure by 100 (Example: Five responses to one multiple choice answer out of 25 questionnaires would be .20; multiplying .20 × 100 = 20%). As you study your results, look for emerging patterns and repeated ideas. What conclusions can you draw based on these responses?

10. *Accurately report your findings.* If you base your essay's assertions, arguments, conclusions, or recommendations on your quetionnaire's results, your readers will certainly need a clear understanding of how those results were obtained. To be persuaded that your research is valid, they may wish to know how the questionnaire was designed and why, how many were distributed and completed, how the respondents were chosen, and other such information. Such explanations may

appear within the body of your essay or in appropriately marked sections (such as "Purpose and Design," "Results," "Recommendations") or in an appendix; in all cases, always attach a blank sample copy of the questionnaire to your essay.

Conducting research through the distribution of a questionnaire is a challenging but fascinating way to collect information about current unexplored topics. If you have collected data that would be valuable to people on your campus, at your work, or in your community, by all means communicate it to them. Your primary research, and your conclusions, could help someone make an important decision.

■ Preparing a Working Bibliography

As you search for information about your essay topic, keep a list of sources that you may want to use in your essay. This list, called a *working bibliography*, will grow as you discover potential sources, and it may shrink if you delete references that aren't useful. Ultimately, this working bibliography will become the list of references presented at the end of your essay.

There are several ways to record your sources. Some students prefer to make an index card for each title; others compile a list in a research notebook; still others prefer to create a computer file or a folder of printouts. As you add sources to your working bibliography, note the following information as appropriate.

Book

1. Author's or editor's full name (and name of translator if given)
2. Complete title, including subtitle if one exists
3. Edition number
4. Volume number and the total number of volumes if the book is part of a series
5. Publisher
6. City of publication
7. Date of publication
8. Library call number or location of source
9. Chapter title or page numbers of the information you need

Article in a Journal, Magazine, or Newspaper

1. Author's full name (if given)
2. Title of the article
3. Title of the journal, magazine, or newspaper
4. Volume and issue number of the journal or magazine
5. Date of publication
6. Page numbers of the article (section and page numbers for newspaper)

Electronic Sources

1. Author's full name or name of sponsoring organization
2. Title of document

3. Information about print publication (book: place, publisher, date; periodical: title, volume and issue if given, date, pages)

4. Information about electronic publication (source, such as database or website; name of service; date of publication or most recent update)

5. Access information (URL and date of access)

Interview

1. Interviewee's name and title

2. Interviewee's organization or company, job description, or other information regarding his or her expertise, including pertinent publications, studies, presentations, etc.

3. Subject of interview

4. Date, place, and method of interview (e.g., in person, by telephone, by e-mail)

Here are four sample index cards that might appear in Amy Lawrence's working bibliography:

Book

> *Radzinsky, Edvard*
>
> *The Last Czar: The Life and Death of Nicholas II*
>
> *Doubleday Publishers, 1992*
>
> *New York, New York*
>
> *pp. 8–10, 315–434*   *Translated by*
>
> *call number: AN947.083*   *Marian Schwartz*
>
> *(CSU Library, East Wing)*

Article in Magazine

> *Elliott, Dorinda*
>
> *"The Legacy of the Last Czar"*
>
> *Newsweek, pp. 60–61*   *Vol. 120*
>
> *Sept. 21, 1992*   *Issue 12*

Electronic Source

> Varoli, John
>
> "Nemtsov: Bury Czar in St. Petersburg July 17"
>
> <u>St. Petersburg Times</u>
>
> St. Petersburg, Russia
>
> Feb. 9–15, 1998
>
> <http://www.spb.ru/times/336–337/nemtsov.html>
>
> Internet   (date of access: 2/26/06)

Interview

> Wheeler, Anne (Dr.)
>
> Professor of History
> Department of History
> Colorado State University
>
> Teaches H456, Russian History and Culture
>
> Interview subject: Romanov assassination
> In-person interview: Feb. 15, 2006
> Office of Dr. Wheeler, Clark 305, campus, Ft. Collins, CO

■ Choosing and Evaluating Your Sources

After you have found a number of promising sources, take a closer look at them. The strength and credibility of your research paper will depend directly on the strength and credibility of your sources. In short, a research paper built on shaky, unreliable sources will not convince a thoughtful reader. Even one suspect piece of evidence may lead your reader to wonder about the validity of other parts of your essay.

To help you choose your print and online sources, ask yourself the following questions as you try to decide which facts, figures, and testimonies will best support or illustrate your ideas.

What do I know about the author? Does this person have any expertise or particular knowledge about the subject matter? If the author of an article about nuclear fusion is a physics professor at a respected university, her views may be more informed than those of a writer of popular science. Although books and scholarly journals generally cite their author's qualifications, the credentials of journalists and magazine writers may be harder to evaluate. Internet sources, as mentioned earlier, may be highly suspect. In cases in which the background of a writer is unknown, you might examine the writer's use of his or her own sources. Can sources for specific data or opinions be checked or verified? In addition, the objectivity of the author must be considered: some authors are clearly biased and may even stand to gain economically or politically from taking a particular point of view. The president of a tobacco company, for instance, might insist that secondary smoke from the cigarettes of others will not harm nonsmokers, but does he or she have an objective opinion? Try to present evidence only from those authors whose views will sway your intelligent readers.

What do I know about the publisher? Who published your sources? Major, well-known publishing houses can be one indication of a book's credibility. (If you are unfamiliar with a particular publisher, consult a librarian or professor in that field.) Be aware that there are many publishers who publish books supporting only a specific viewpoint; similarly, many organizations support websites to further their causes. The bias in such sources may limit their usefulness to your research.

For periodicals, consider the nature of the journal, magazine, or newspaper. Who is its intended audience? A highly technical paper on sickle-cell anemia, for example, might be weakened by citing a very general discussion of the disease from *Health Digest*; an article from the *Journal of the American Medical Association*, however, might be valuable. Is it a publication known to be fairly objective (the *New York Times*) or does it have a particular cause to support (the *National Sierra Club Bulletin*)? Looking at the masthead of a journal or other publication will often tell you whether articles are subjected to stringent review before acceptance for publication. In general, articles published in "open" or nonselective publications should be examined closely for credibility. For example, the newsletter for MENSA—a well-known international society for individuals who have documented IQs in the top 2 percent of the population—once created a furor when an article appeared recommending the euthanasia of the mentally and physically disabled, the homeless, and other so-called "nonproductive" members of society. The newsletter editor's explanation was that all articles submitted for publication were generally accepted.

Is my research reasonably balanced? Your treatment of your subject—especially if it is a controversial one—should show your readers that you investigated all sides of the issue before reaching a conclusion. If your sources are drawn only from authorities well known for voicing one position, your readers may be skeptical about the quality of your research. For instance, if in a paper arguing against a new gun-control measure, you cite only the opinions voiced by the officers of the National Rifle Association, you may antagonize the reader who wants a thorough analysis of all sides of the question. Do use sources that support your position, but don't overload your argument with obviously biased sources.

Are my sources reporting valid research? Is your source the original researcher or is he or she reporting someone else's study?* If the information is being reported second-hand, has your source been accurate and clear? Is the original source named or referenced in some way so that the information could be checked?

A thorough researcher might note the names of authorities frequently cited by other writers or researchers and try to obtain the original works by those authorities. This tip was useful for Amy Lawrence as she found the researcher Robert K. Massie mentioned in a number of magazine articles. Once she obtained a copy of his often-quoted book, she had additional information to consider for her paper.

Look too at the way information in your source was obtained in the first place. Did the original researchers themselves draw logical conclusions from their evidence? Did they run their study or project in a fair, impartial way? For example, a survey of people whose names were obtained from the rolls of the Democratic party will hardly constitute a representative sampling of voters' opinions on an upcoming election.

Moreover, be especially careful with statistics because they can be manipulated quite easily to give a distorted picture. A recent survey, for instance, asked a large sample of people to rate a number of American cities based on questions dealing with quality of life. Pittsburgh—a lovely city to be sure—came out the winner, but only if one agrees that all the questions should be weighted equally; that is, the figures gave Pittsburgh the highest score only if one rates "weather" as equally important as "educational opportunities," "number of crimes," "cultural opportunities," and other factors. In short, always evaluate the quality of your sources' research and the validity of their conclusions before you decide to incorporate their findings into your own paper. (And don't forget Mark Twain's reference to "lies, damned lies, and statistics.")

Are my sources still current? Although some famous experiments or studies have withstood the years, many topics demand research as current as possible. What was written two years or or even two weeks ago may have been disproved or surpassed since, especially in our rapidly changing political world and ever-expanding fields of technology. A paper on the status of the U.S. space program, for example, demands recent sources, and research on personal computer use in the United States would be severely weakened by the use of a text published as recently as 2005 for "current" statistics.

If they're appropriate, journals and other periodicals may contain more up-to-date reports than books printed several years ago; library database searches can often provide the most current information. On the other hand, you certainly shouldn't ignore a "classic" study on your subject, especially if it is the one against which all the other studies are measured. A student researching the life of Abraham Lincoln, for instance, might find Carl Sandburg's multivolume biography of over 65 years ago as valuable as more recent works. Be aware, too, that even though websites can be continually revised, they are sometimes neglected; always check to see if a "last updated" date has been posted or if the material contains current dates or references. In some cases, an elusive "last update" may be determined by typing the following in the address field: javascript:alert(document:lastModified).

---

* Interviews, surveys, studies, and experiments conducted firsthand are referred to as *primary sources*; reports and studies written by someone other than the original researcher are called *secondary sources*.

> ✓ **REMEMBER:** For more advice to help you think critically about your sources, see Chapter 5.

▪ Preparing an Annotated Bibliography

While you are gathering and assessing your sources, you may be asked to compile an annotated bibliography—a description of each important source that includes the basic bibliographic facts as well as a brief summary of each entry's content. After reading multiple articles or books on your subject over a period of days or even weeks, you may discover that the information you've found has begun to blur together in your head. Annotating each of your sources will help you remember the specific data in each one so that you can locate the material later in the planning and drafting stages of your writing process.

Here is a sample taken from Amy Lawrence's annotated bibliography:

Elliott, Dorinda. "The Legacy of the Last Czar." <u>Newsweek</u> 21 Sept. 1992: 60-61.

  Elliot offers the results of early forensic analysis of the Romanov grave site and a brief description of the events surrounding the executions. The article quotes forensic experts and historians and includes the views of Russian citizens on the significance of finding and identifying the remains of the Romanov family.

Compiling an annotated bibliography will also give you a clear sense of how complete and balanced your sources are in support of your ideas, perhaps revealing gaps in your evidence that need to be filled with additional research data. Later, when your essay is finished, your annotated bibliography might provide a useful reference for any of your readers who are interested in exploring your subject in more depth.

▪ Taking Notes

As you evaluate and select those sources that are both reliable and useful, you will begin taking notes on their information. Most researchers use one or more of the following three methods of note-taking.

1. Some students prefer to make their notes on index cards rather than on notebook paper because a stack of cards may be added to, subtracted from, or shuffled around more easily when it's time to plan the essay. You may find it useful to label each card with a short topic heading that corresponds to a major idea in your essay. Then, as you read, put pertinent information on its appropriate card. Be sure to identify the source of all your notes. (Hint 1: If you have used bibliography cards, take your notes on cards of different sizes or colors to avoid any confusion; write on only one side of each card so that all your information will be in sight when you draft your essay.)

2. Other students rely on photocopies or printouts of sources, highlighting or underlining important details. (Hint 2: Copy a source's title page and other front matter so that you can clip complete bibliographic information to your pages.)

3. Students with personal computers may prefer to store their notes as computer files because of the easy transfer of quoted material from file to essay draft. (Hint 3: Always make a hard copy of your notes and back up your files frequently in case of a crash!) You will probably find yourself taking notes by hand on those occasions when you are without your computer (library, classroom, interview, public speech, etc.), so carry index cards with you and transcribe your notes into your files later.

Whichever note-taking method you choose, always remember to record bibliographic information and the specific page numbers (in printed sources) or paragraph numbers (in some electronic sources) from which your material is taken. Your notes may be one of the following kinds:

1. *Direct quotations.* When you use material word for word, you must always enclose it in quotation marks and note the precise page number of the quotation, if given.* If the quoted material runs from one printed page onto another, use some sort of signal to yourself, such as a slash bar (child/abuse) or arrow ($\rightarrow$ p. 162) at the break so if you use only part of the quoted material in your paper, you will know on which page it appeared. If the quoted material contains odd, archaic, or incorrect spelling, punctuation marks, or grammar, insert the word *sic* in brackets next to the item in question; [*sic*] means "this is the way I found it in the original text," and such a symbol will remind you later that you did not miscopy the quotation. Otherwise, always double-check to make sure you did copy the material accurately and completely to avoid having to come back to the source as you prepare your essay. If the material you want to quote is lengthy or complex, you will find it easier—though not cheaper—to photocopy (or print out) the text rather than transcribe it.

2. *Paraphrase.* You paraphrase when you put into your own words what someone else has written or said. Please note: *paraphrased ideas are borrowed ideas, not your original thoughts, and, consequently, they must be attributed to their owner just as direct quotations are.*

To remind yourself that certain information in your notes is paraphrased, always introduce it with some sort of notation, such as a handwritten Ⓟ or a typed P//. Quotation marks will always tell you what you borrowed directly, but sometimes when writers take notes one week and write their first draft a week or two later, they cannot remember if a note was paraphrased or if it was an original thought. Writers occasionally plagiarize unintentionally because they erroneously believe that only direct quotations and statistics must be attributed to their proper sources, so make your notes as clear as possible. (For more information on avoiding plagiarism, see pages 388–390.)

3. *Summary.* You may wish to condense a piece of writing so you can offer it as support for your own ideas. Using your own words, you should present in shorter form the writer's thesis and supporting ideas. You may find it helpful to include a

---

* All tables, graphs, and charts that you copy must also be directly attributed to their sources, though you do not enclose graphics in quotation marks.

few direct quotations in your summary to retain the flavor of the original work. Of course, you will tell your readers what you are summarizing and by whom it was written. Remember to make a note (sum:) to yourself to indicate summarized, rather than original, material. (For more information on writing a summary, see also pages 175–176.)

4. *Your own ideas.* Your notes may also contain your personal comments (judgments, flashes of brilliance, questions, notions of how to use something you've just read, notes to yourself about connections between sources, and so forth) that will aid you in the writing of your paper. In handwritten notes, you might jot these down in a different-colored pen or put them in brackets that you've initialed, so that you will recognize them later as your own responses.

Distinguishing Paraphrase from Summary

Because novice writers sometimes have a hard time understanding the difference between paraphrase and summary, here is an explanation and a sample of each. The original paragraph that appears here was taken from a magazine article describing an important 1984 study still frequently cited:

> Another successful approach to the prevention of criminality has been to target very young children in a school setting before problems arise. The Perry Preschool Program, started 22 years ago in a low socioeconomic area of Ypsilanti, Michigan, has offered some of the most solid evidence to date that early intervention through a high-quality preschool program can significantly alter a child's life. A study released this fall tells what happened to 123 disadvantaged children from preschool age to present. The detention and arrest rate for the 58 children who had attended the preschool program was 31 percent, compared to 51 percent for the 65 who did not. Similarly, those in the preschool program were more likely to have graduated from high school, have enrolled in postsecondary education programs and be employed, and less likely to have become pregnant as teenagers.
>
> —from "Arresting Delinquency,"
> Dan Hurley, <u>Psychology Today</u>,
> March 1985, page 66

Paraphrase

A *paraphrase* puts the information in the researcher's own words, but it does follow the order of the original text, and it does include the important details:

> Quality preschooling for high-risk children may help stop crime before it starts. A 1984 study from the Perry Preschool Program located in a poor area of Ypsilanti, Michigan, showed that of 123 socially and economically disadvantaged children, the 58 who attended preschool had an arrest rate of 31 percent compared to 51 percent for those 65 who did not attend. The adults with preschool experience had also graduated from high school in larger numbers; in addition, more of them had attended postsecondary education programs, were employed, and had avoided teenage pregnancy (Hurley 66).

Summary

A *summary* is generally much shorter than the original; the researcher picks out the key ideas but often omits many of the supporting details:

> A 1984 study from the Perry Preschool Program in Michigan suggests that disadvantaged children who attend preschool are less likely to be arrested as adults. They choose more education, have better employment records, and avoid teenage pregnancy more often than those without preschool (Hurley 66).

☑ **REMEMBER:** Both paraphrased and summarized ideas must be attributed to their sources, even if you do not reproduce exact words or figures.

■ Incorporating Your Source Material

Be aware that a research paper is not a massive collection of quotations and paraphrased or summarized ideas glued together with a few transitional phrases. It is, instead, an essay in which you offer *your* thesis and ideas based on and supported by your research. Consequently, you will need to incorporate and blend in your reference material in a variety of smooth, persuasive ways. Here are some suggestions:

Use your sources in a clear, logical way. Make certain that you understand your source material well enough to use it in support of your own thoughts. Once you have selected the best references to use, be as convincing as possible. Ask yourself if you're using enough evidence and if the information you're offering really does clearly support your point. As in any essay, you need to avoid oversimplification, hasty generalizations, *non sequiturs*, and other problems in logic (for a review of common logical fallacies, see pages 286–289). Resist the temptation to add quotations, facts, or statistics that are interesting but not really relevant to your paper.

Don't overuse direct quotations. It's best to use a direct quotation *only* when it expresses a point in a far more impressive, emphatic, or concise way than you could say it yourself. Suppose, for instance, you were analyzing the films of a particular director and wanted to include a sample of critical reviews:

> As one movie critic wrote, "This film is really terrible, and people should ignore it" (Dennison 14).

The direct quotation above isn't remarkable and could be easily paraphrased. However, you might be tempted to quote the following line to show your readers an emphatically negative review of this movie:

> As one movie critic wrote, "This film's plot is so idiotic it's clearly intended for people who move their lips not only when they read but also when they watch TV" (Dennison 14).

When you do decide to use direct quotations, don't merely drop them in your prose as if they had fallen from a tall building onto your page. Instead, lead into them smoothly so that they obviously support or clarify what you are saying.

Dropped in	Scientists have been studying the ill effects of nitrites on test animals since 1961. "Nitrites produced malignant tumors in 62 percent of the test animals within six months" (Smith 109).
Better	Scientists have been studying the ill effects of nitrites on test animals since 1961. According to Dr. William Smith, head of the Farrell Institute of Research, who conducted the largest experiment thus far, "Nitrites produced malignant tumors in 62 percent of the test animals within six months" (109).

Vary your sentence pattern when you present your quotations. Here are some sample phrases for quotations:

In her introduction to <u>The Great Gatsby</u>, Professor Wilma Smith points out that Fitzgerald "wrote about himself and produced a narcissistic masterpiece" (5).

Wilma Smith, author of <u>Impact</u>, summarized the situation this way: "Eighty-eight percent of the sales force threaten a walkout" (21).

"Only the President controls the black box," according to the White House Press Secretary Wilma Smith.

As drama critic Wilma Smith observed last year in <u>The Saturday Review</u>, the play was "a rousing failure" (212).

Perhaps the well-known poet Wilma Smith expressed the idea best when she wrote, "Love is a spider waiting to entangle its victims" (14).

"Employment figures are down 3 percent from last year," claimed Senator Wilma Smith, who leads opposition to the tax cut (32).

In other words, don't simply repeat "Wilma Smith said," "John Jones said," "Mary Brown said."

Punctuate your quotations correctly. The proper punctuation will help your reader understand who said what. For information on the appropriate uses of quotation marks surrounding direct quotations, see pages 558–559 in Part Four. If you are incorporating a long quoted passage into your essay, one that appears as more than four typed lines in your manuscript, you should present it in block form without quotation marks, as described on page 393. To omit words in a quoted passage, use ellipsis points, explained on page 567.

Make certain your support is in the paper, not still in your head or back in the original source. Sometimes when you've read a number of persuasive facts in an article or a book, it's easy to forget that your reader doesn't know them as you do now. For instance, the writer of the following paragraph isn't as persuasive as she might be because she hides the support for her controversial point in the reference to the article, forgetting that the reader needs to know what the article actually said:

An organ transplant from one human to another is becoming an everyday occurrence, an operation that is generally applauded by everyone as a life-saving effort. But people are over-looking many of the serious problems that come with the increase in transplant surgery. A study shows that in Asia there may be a risk of traffic in organs on the Black Market. Figures recorded recently are very disturbing (Wood 35).

For the reader to be persuaded, he or she needs to know what the writer learned from the article: What study? What figures and what exactly do they show? Who has recorded these? Is the source reliable? Instead of offering the necessary support in the essay, the writer merely points to the article as proof. Few readers will take the time to look up the article to find the information they need to understand or believe your point. Therefore, when you use source material, always be sure that you have remembered to put your support on the page, *in the essay itself,* for the reader to see. Don't let the essence of your point remain hidden, especially when the claim is controversial.

Don't let reference material dominate your essay. Remember that your reader is interested in *your* thesis and *your* conclusions, not just in a string of references. Use your researched material wisely whenever your statements need clarification, support, or amplification. But don't use quotations, paraphrases, or summarized material at every turn, just to show that you've done your homework.

■ Avoiding Plagiarism

Unfortunately, most discussions of research must include a brief word about plagiarism. Novice writers often unintentionally plagiarize, as noted before, because they fail to recognize the necessity of attributing paraphrased, summarized, and borrowed ideas to their original owners. And indeed it is sometimes difficult after days of research to know exactly what one has read repeatedly and what one originally thought. Also, there's frequently a thin line between general or common knowledge ("Henry Ford was the father of the automobile industry in America") that does not have to be documented and those ideas and statements that do ("USX reported an operating loss of four million in its last quarter"). As a rule of thumb, ask yourself whether the majority of your readers would recognize the fact or opinion you're expressing or if it's repeatedly found in commonly used sources; if so, you may not need to document it. For example, most people would acknowledge that the Wall Street crash of 1929 ushered in the Great Depression of the 1930s, but the exact number of bank foreclosures in 1933 is not common knowledge and, therefore, needs documenting. Similarly, a well-known quotation from the Bible or Mother Goose or even the Declaration of Independence might pass without documentation, but a line from the vice-president's latest speech needs a reference to its source. Remember, too, that much of the material on the Internet is copyrighted. When in doubt, the best choice is to document anything that you feel may be in question.

To help you understand the difference between plagiarism and proper documentation, here is an original passage and both incorrect and correct ways to use it in a paper of your own:

Original   It is a familiar nightmare: a person suffers a heart attack, and as the ambulance fights heavy traffic, the patient dies. In fact, 350,000 American heart-attack victims each year die without ever reaching a hospital. The killer in many cases is ventricular fibrillation, uncoordinated contraction of the heart muscle. Last week a team of Dutch physicians reported in <u>The New England Journal of Medicine</u> that these early deaths can often be prevented by administration of a common heart drug called lidocaine, injected into the patient's shoulder muscle by ambulance paramedics as soon as they arrive on the scene.

—from "First Aid for Heart Attacks,"
<u>Newsweek</u>, November 11, 1985,
page 88

Plagiarized   It is a common nightmare: as the ambulance sits in heavy traffic, a person with a heart attack dies, often a victim of ventricular fibrillation, uncoordinated contraction of the heart muscle. Today, however, these early deaths can often be prevented by an injection into the patient's shoulder of a common heart drug called lidocaine, which may be administered by paramedics on the scene.

This writer has changed some of the words and sentences, but the passage has obviously been borrowed and must be attributed to its source.

Also plagiarized   According to <u>Newsweek</u>, 350,000 American heart attack victims die before reaching help in hospitals ("First Aid for Heart Attacks" 88). However, a common heart drug called lidocaine, which may be injected into the patient by paramedics on the scene of the attack, may save many victims who die en route to doctors and sophisticated life-saving equipment.

This writer did attribute the statistic to its source, but the remainder of the preceding paragraph is still borrowed and must be documented.

Properly documented   Ambulance paramedics can, and often do, play a vital life-saving role today. They are frequently the first medical assistance available, especially to those patients or accident victims far away from hospitals. Moreover, according to a <u>Newsweek</u> report, paramedics are now being trained to administer powerful drugs to help the sick survive until they reach doctors and medical equipment. For instance, paramedics can inject the common heart drug lidocaine into heart attack victims on the scene, an act that may save many of the 350,000 Americans who die of heart attacks before ever reaching a hospital ("First Aid for Heart Attacks" 88).

This writer used the properly documented information to support her own point about paramedics and has not tried to pass off any of the article as her own.

Although plagiarism is often unintentional, it's your job to be as honest and careful as possible. If you're in doubt about your use of a particular idea, consult your instructor for a second opinion.

Here's a suggestion that might help you avoid plagiarizing by accident. When you are drafting your essay and come to a spot in which you want to incorporate the ideas of someone else, think of the borrowed material as if it were in a window.* Always frame the window at the top with some sort of introduction that identifies the author (or source) and frame the window on the bottom with a reference to the location of the material, as illustrated on the following page.

A sample might look like this:

Introductory phrase identifies author

As humorist Mike McGrady once said about housekeeping, "Any job that requires six hours to do and can be undone in six minutes by one small child carrying a plate of crackers and a Monopoly set—this is not a job that will long capture my interest" (13).

Location

Window

In a later draft, you'll probably want to vary your style so that all your borrowed material doesn't appear in exactly the same "window" format (see page 387 for suggestions). But until you acquire the habit of always documenting your sources, you might try using the "window" technique in your early drafts.

* I am indebted to Emeritus Professor John Clark Pratt, Colorado State University, for this useful suggestion. Professor Pratt is the author of *Writing from Scratch: The Essay* (1987) published by Hamilton Press, and the editor of the *Writing from Scratch* series.

■ PRACTICING WHAT YOU'VE LEARNED

As Amy Lawrence researched the Romanov execution, she found the following information about one of the earlier Romanov czars. To practice some of the skills you've learned so far, read the following passage on Alexander II of Russia (1855–1881) and do the tasks that are listed after it.

> Alexander's greatest single achievement was his emancipation of some forty million Russian serfs, a deed which won him the title of "Tsar Liberator." To visit a rural Russian community in the earlier nineteenth century was like stepping back into the Middle Ages. Nine-tenths of the land was held by something less than one hundred thousand noble families. The serfs, attached to the soil, could be sold with the estates to new landlords, conscripted into the nobleman's household to work as domestic servants, or even sent to the factories in the towns for their master's profit. Though some nobles exercised their authority in a kindly and paternal fashion, others overworked their serfs, flogged them cruelly for slight faults, and interfered insolently in their private affairs and family relations. A serf could not marry without his master's consent, could not leave the estate without permission, and might be pursued, brought back, and punished if he sought to escape. He lived at the mercy of his master's caprice.

1. The book from which the preceding passage was taken contains the following information. Select the appropriate information and prepare a working bibliography card.

   A Survey of European Civilization Part Two, Since 1660

   Third Edition
   Houghton Mifflin Company, Publishers
   Boston
   First edition, 1936
   853.21
   1,012 pages
   Authors:
     Wallace K. Ferguson, The University of Western Ontario
     Geoffrey Brun, Formerly Visiting Professor of History, Cornell University
   Indexes: general, list of maps
   Picture Acknowledgments, xxvii
   copyright 1962
   page 716
   44 chapters

2. Paraphrase the first four sentences of the passage.

3. Summarize the passage, but do not quote from it.

4. Select an important idea from the passage to quote directly and lead into the quotation with a smooth acknowledgment of its source.

5. Select an idea or a quotation from the passage and use it as support for a point of your own, being careful not to plagiarize the borrowed material.

- **ASSIGNMENT**

1. In your library, look up a newspaper* from any city or state and find the issue published on the day of your birth or on some other significant date. Prepare a bibliography card and then summarize an important article from the front page. (Don't forget to acknowledge the source of your summary.)

2. To practice searching for and choosing source material, find three recent works on your essay topic available in your library. If you don't have an essay topic yet, pick a subject that interests you, one that is likely to appear in both print and electronic sources (Baseball Hall of Fame, stamp collecting, the Titanic disaster, king cobras, etc.). If possible, try to find three different kinds of sources, such as a book, a journal or magazine article, and a website. After you have recorded bibliographic information for each source, locate and evaluate the works. Do all of these sources provide relevant, reliable information? In a few sentences explain why you believe each one would or would not be an appropriate source for your research essay. ■

■ Choosing the Documentation Style for Your Essay

Once you begin to write your paper incorporating your source material, you need to know how to show your readers where your material came from. You may have already learned a documentation system in a previous writing class, but because today's researchers and scholars use a number of different documentation styles, it's important that you know which style is appropriate for your current essay. In some cases, your instructors (or the audience for whom you are writing) will designate a particular style; at other times, the choice will be yours.

In this chapter, we will look at two widely used systems—MLA style and APA style—and also briefly review the use of the traditional footnote/bibliography format.

MLA Style

Most instructors in the humanities assign the documentation form prescribed by the Modern Language Association of America (MLA). Since 1984, the MLA has recommended a form of documentation that no longer uses traditional footnotes or endnotes to show references.† The current form calls for *parenthetical documentation*, most often consisting of the author's last name and the appropriate page number(s) in parentheses immediately following the source material in your paper. At the end of your discussion, readers may find complete bibliographic information for each source on a "Works Cited" page, a list of all the sources in your essay.

---

* If the newspaper is not accessible you might substitute a weekly news magazine, such as *Time* or *Newsweek*.

† If you wish a more detailed description of the current MLA form, ask your local bookstore or library for the *MLA Handbook for Writers of Research Papers*, 6th ed. (New York: MLA, 2003) and also the *MLA Style Manual and Guide to Scholarly Publishing*, 2nd ed. (New York: MLA, 1998). The most up-to-date documentation information may be found on the MLA website <http://www.mla.org>.

MLA Citations in Your Essay

Here are some guidelines for using the MLA parenthetical reference form within your paper.

1. If you use a source by one author, place the author's name and page number after the quoted, paraphrased, or summarized material. Note that the parentheses go *before* the end punctuation, and there is no punctuation between the author's name and the page number. (Use the author's name and omit the page reference when citing a complete work or a one-page work.)

   Example   Although pop art often resembles the comic strip, it owes a debt to such painters as Magritte, Matisse, and de Kooning (Rose 184).

2. If you use a source by one author and give credit to that author by name in your paper, you need only give the page number in the parentheses.

   Example   According to art critic Barbara Rose, pop art owes a large debt to such painters as Magritte, Matisse, and de Kooning (184).

3. If you are directly quoting material of more than four typed lines, indent the material one inch (or ten spaces) from the left margin, double-space, and do not use quotation marks. Do not change the right margin. Note that in this case, the parentheses appear *after* the punctuation that ends the quoted material.

   Example   In addition to causing tragedy for others, Crane's characters who are motivated by a desire to appear heroic to their peers may also cause themselves serious trouble. For example, Collins, another Civil War private, almost causes his own death because of his vain desire to act bravely in front of his fellow Union soldiers. (Hall 16)

4. If you are citing more than one work by the same author, include a short title in the parentheses.

   Example   Within 50 years, the Inca and Aztec civilizations were defeated and overthrown by outside invaders (Thomas, <u>Lost Cultures</u> 198).

5. If you are citing a work by two or three authors, use all last names and the page number.

   Examples   Prisons today are overcrowded to the point of emergency; conditions could not be worse, and the state budget for prison reforms is at an all-time low (Smith and Jones 72).

Human infants grow quickly, with most babies doubling their birth weight in the first six months of life and tripling their weight by their first birthday (Pantell, Fries, and Vickery 52).

6. For more than three authors, use all the last names or use the last name of the first author plus *et al.* (Latin for "and others") and the page number. There is no comma after the author's name.

Example   Casualties of World War II during 1940-45 amounted to more than twenty-five million soldiers and civilians (Blum et al. 779).

7. If you cite a work that has no named author, use the work's title and the page number.

Example   Each year 350,000 Americans will die of a heart attack before reaching a hospital ("First Aid for Heart Attacks" 88).

8. If the work you are citing appears in a series, include the volume and page number with the author's name.

Example   On August 28, 1963, King delivered his "I Have A Dream" address to more than 200,000 civil rights supporters in Washington, DC, a speech that added momentum to the passage of the 1964 Civil Rights Act (Lopez 1:270).

9. If your source is an electronic document, treat it as you would a print source. If you are citing an entire work from an electronic source that has no page, paragraph, or screen numbers, it is preferable to use the name of the author or editor in the text, rather than in a parenthetical reference. If the author's or editor's name is unavailable, use a short reference to the works's title.

Example   Cannon College Economics Professor John Thompson argues a different view of the Chinese role in Indonesia's economy.

Some electronic documents include paragraph or screen numbers. When citing these documents, include the appropriate number, preceded by *par.* or *pars.* for paragraph(s), or *screen.*

Example   The Chinese in Indonesia account for only 4% of the population but control 70% of the economy (Thompson, par. 6).

10. If the material you are citing contains a passage quoted from another source, indicate the use of the quotation in the parentheses.

Example   According to George Orwell, "Good writing is like a window-pane" (qtd. in Murray 142).

11. If the work you are citing is a nonprint source with no reference markers, such as an interview, lecture, television show, film, or performance, include in the text the name of the person or the title (i.e., <u>60 Minutes</u>) that begins the corresponding entry in the Works Cited list.

Example   In a March 5, 2003, telephone interview, ZipDrive president Charles Byrd denied persistent rumors of an impending merger.

Compiling a Works Cited List: MLA Style

If you are using the MLA format, at the end of your essay you should include a *Works Cited* page—a formal listing of the sources you used in your essay. (If you wish to show all the sources you consulted, but did not cite, add a *Works Consulted* page.) Arrange the entries alphabetically by the authors' last names; if no name is given, arrange your sources by the first important word of the title. Double-space each entry, and double-space between entries. If an entry takes more than one line, indent the subsequent lines one-half inch (or five spaces). Current MLA guidelines indicate one space following punctuation marks. (Some instructors still prefer two spaces, however, so you might check with your teacher on this issue.) See the sample entries that follow.

Sample Entries: MLA Style

Here are some sample entries to help you prepare a Works Cited page according to the MLA guidelines. Please note that MLA style recommends shortened forms of publishers' names: Holt for Holt, Rinehart & Winston; UP for University Press; and so forth. Also, omit business descriptions, such as Inc., Co., Press, or House.

Remember, too, when you type your paper, the titles of books and journals should be underlined even though you may see them printed in books or magazines in italics. The titles of articles, essays, and chapters should be enclosed in quotation marks. All important words in titles are capitalized.

Books

- Book with one author

    Keillor, Garrison. <u>WLT: A Radio Romance</u>. New York: Viking, 1991.

- Two books by the same author

    List books alphabetically by title. After the first entry, use three hyphens in place of the author's name.

    Keillor, Garrison. <u>Leaving Home</u>. New York: Viking, 1987.

    ---. <u>WLT: A Radio Romance</u>. New York: Viking, 1991.

- Book with two or three authors

  Note that only the name of the first author is inverted.

  Pizzo, Stephen, and Paul Muolo. <u>Profiting from the Bank and Savings and Loan Crisis</u>. New York: Harper, 1993.

- Book with more than three authors

  You may use *et al.* for the other names or you may give all names in full in the order they appear on the book's title page.

  Guerin, Wilfred L., et al. <u>A Handbook of Critical Approaches to Literature</u>. New York: Harper, 1979.

- Book with author and editor

  Chaucer, Geoffrey. <u>The Tales of Canterbury</u>. Ed. Robert Pratt. Boston: Houghton, 1974.

- Book with corporate authorship

  National Fire Safety Council. <u>Stopping Arson before It Starts</u>. Washington: Edmondson, 1992.

- Book with an editor

  Knappman, Edward W., ed. <u>Great American Trials: From Salem Witchcraft to Rodney King</u>. Detroit: Visible Ink, 1994.

- Selection or chapter from an anthology or a collection with an editor

  Chopin, Kate. "La Belle Zoraide." <u>Classic American Women Writers</u>. Ed. Cynthia Griffin Wolff. New York: Harper, 1980. 250-73.

- One volume of a multivolume work

  Delaney, John J., ed. <u>Encyclopedia of Saints</u>. Vol. 4. New York: Doubleday, 1998.

- Work in more than one volume

  If the volumes were published over a period of years, give the inclusive dates at the end of the citation.

  Piepkorn, Arthur C. <u>Profiles in Belief: The Religious Bodies of the United States and Canada</u>. 2 vols. New York: Harper, 1976-78.

- Work in a series

  Berg, Barbara L. <u>The Remembered Gate: Origins of American Feminism</u>. Urban Life in Amer. Ser. 3. New York: Oxford UP, 1978.

- Translation

  Radzinsky, Edvard. <u>The Last Czar: The Life and Death of Nicholas II</u>. Trans. Marian
    Schwartz. New York: Doubleday, 1992.

- Reprint

  Note that this citation presents two dates: the date of original publication (1873) and the date of the reprinted work (1978).

  Thaxter, Celia. <u>Among the Isles of Shoals</u>. 1873. Ed. Leslie Dunn. Hampton, NH:
    Heritage, 1978.

- An introduction, preface, foreword, or afterword

  Begin the citation with the name of the writer of the section you are citing; then identify the section but do not underline or use quotation marks around the word. Next, give the name of the book and the name of its author, preceded by the word "By" as shown below.

  Soloman, Barbara H. Introduction. <u>Herland</u>. By Charlotte Perkins Gilman. New
    York: Penguin, 1992. xi-xxxi.

Periodicals (Magazines, Journals, Newspapers)

If an article is not printed on consecutive pages, use the first page number and a plus sign.

- Signed article in a monthly magazine

  Kaminer, Wendy. "Feminism's Identity Crisis." <u>Atlantic</u> Oct. 1993: 51+.

- Unsigned article in a weekly magazine

  "The Wedding." <u>The New Yorker</u> 11 Sept. 1989: 34-35.

- Signed article in a journal

  Lockwood, Thomas. "Divided Attention in <u>Persuasion</u>." <u>Nineteenth-Century
    Fiction</u> 33 (1978): 309-23.

- A review

  Spudis, Paul. Rev. of <u>To a Rocky Moon: A Geologist's History of Lunar Exploration</u>,
    by Don E. Wilhelms. <u>Natural History</u> Jan. 1994: 66-69.

- Signed article in newspaper

  Friedman, Thomas. "World Answer to Jobs: Schooling." <u>Denver Post</u>
    16 Mar. 1994: B9+.

- Unsigned article in newspaper

  "Blackhawks Shut Down Gretsky, Kings, 4–0." <u>Washington Post</u> 11 Mar. 1994: C4.

- Unsigned editorial in newspaper

  If the newspaper's city of publication is not clear from the title, put the location in brackets following the paper's name, as shown in the entry below.

  "Give Life after Death." Editorial. <u>Coloradoan</u> [Ft. Collins, CO] 23 Dec. 1995: A4.

- A letter to the newspaper

  Byrd, Charles. Letter. <u>Denver Post</u> 10 May 2004: A10.

Encyclopedias, Pamphlets, Dissertations

Use full publication information for reference works, such as encyclopedias and dictionaries, unless they are familiar and often revised. Delete volume and page numbers if the information is in alphabetical order.

- Signed article in an encyclopedia (full reference)

  Collins, Dean R. "Light Amplifier." <u>McGraw-Hill Encyclopedia of Science and Technology</u>. Ed. Justin Thyme. 3 vols. Boston: McGraw, 1997.

- Unsigned article in a well-known encyclopedia

  "Sailfish." <u>Encyclopedia Britannica</u>. 18th ed. 1998.

- A pamphlet

  Young, Leslie. <u>Baby Care Essentials for the New Mother</u>. Austin: Hall, 2006.

- A government document

  United States. National Institute on Drug Abuse. <u>Drug Abuse Prevention</u>. Washington: GPO, 1980.

- Unpublished dissertations and theses

  Harmon, Gail A. "Poor Writing Skills at the College Level: A Program for Correction." Diss. U of Colorado, 2006.

Films, Television, Radio, Performances, Recordings

- A film

  Begin with the title (underlined) followed by the director, the distributor, and the year of release. You may also include other data, such as the star performers, writer, or producer.

<u>Schindler's List</u>. Dir. Steven Spielberg. Perf. Liam Neeson and Ben Kingsley.
Universal, 1993.

If you are referring to the contribution of a particular individual, such as the director, writer, actor, or composer, begin with that person's name. Cite a videocassette, DVD, or laser disc as a film but also include the medium, its distributor, and its distribution date.

Spielberg, Steven, dir. <u>Schindler's List</u>. Perf. Liam Neeson and Ben Kingsley. 1993.
DVD. Universal. 2004.

- A television or radio show

<u>Innovation</u>. WNET, Newark. 12 Oct. 1985.

If your reference is to a particular episode or person associated with the show, cite that name first, before the show's name.

"General Stonewall Jackson." <u>Civil War Journal</u>. Arts and Entertainment Network.
10 June 1992.

Moyers, Bill, writ. and narr. <u>Bill Moyers' Journal</u>. PBS. WABC, Denver. 30 Sept. 1980.

- Performances (plays, concerts, ballets, operas)

<u>Julius Caesar</u>. By William Shakespeare. Dir. Andrew St. John. Perf. Patrick Stewart.
Booth Theater, New York. 13 Oct. 1982.

If you are referring to the contribution of a particular person associated with the performance, put that person's name first.

Shao, En, cond. <u>Wiegenlied</u>. By Franz Schubert. Perf. Clare Stollak. Colorado
Symphony Orch. Boettcher Concert Hall, Denver. 18 Mar. 1994.

- A recording
If your source is not a compact disc, include the type of medium.

Marsalis, Wynton. "Oh, But on the Third Day." Rec. 27-28 Oct. 1988. <u>The Majesty
of the Blues</u>. Audiocassette. Columbia, 1989.

Letters, Lectures, and Speeches

- An unpublished letter, archived

Steinbeck, John. Letter to Elizabeth R. Otis. 11 Nov. 1944. Steinbeck Collection.
Stanford U Lib., Stanford, CA.

- A letter received by the author

Hall, Katherine. Letter to the author. 10 May 2006.

- A lecture or speech

    Give the speaker's name and the title of the talk first, before the sponsoring organization (or occasion) and location. If there is no title, substitute the appropriate label, such as "lecture" or "speech."

    Dippity, Sarah N. "The Importance of Prewriting." CLAS Convention. President

    Hotel, Colorado Springs. 15 Feb. 2006.

Interviews

- A published interview

    (Cite the person interviewed first and the title of the interview, if any. Use the word "Interview" if the interview has no title. The interviewer's name may be added if known and relevant. Conclude with publication information.)

    Mailer, Norman. "Dialogue with Mailer." With Andrew Gordon. Berkeley Times

    15 Jan. 1969: A12.

- A personal interview

    Give the name of the person interviewed, the kind of interview, and the date.

    Adkins, Camille. Personal interview. 11 Jan. 2006.

    Payne, Linda. Telephone interview. 13 Apr. 2006.

Electronic Sources: MLA Style

The purpose of a citation for an electronic source is the same as that for printed matter: identification of the source and the best way to locate it. All citations basically name the author and the work and identify publication information. Citations for various types of electronic sources, however, must also include different kinds of additional information—such as network addresses—to help researchers locate the sources in the easiest way.

It's important to remember, too, that forms of electronic sources continue to change rapidly. As technology expands, new ways of documenting electronic sources must also be created. The problem is further complicated by the fact that some sources will not supply all the information you might like to include in your citation. In these cases, you simply have to do the best you can by citing what is available.

The guidelines and sample entries that follow are designed merely as an introduction to citing electronic sources according to MLA style. If you need additional help citing other kinds of electronic sources, consult the most up-to-the-minute documentation guide available, such as the current *MLA Handbook for Writers of Research Papers* or the MLA website.

Before looking at the sample citations given here, you should be familiar with the following information regarding dates, addresses, and reference markers in online sources.

Use of multiple dates. Because online sources may change or be revised, a citation may contain more than one date. Your citation may present, for example, the original date of a document if it appeared previously in print form, the date of its electronic publication, or the date of its "latest update." Your entry should also include a "date of access," indicating the day you found the particular source.

Use of network addresses. The *MLA Handbook* recommends inclusion of network addresses (URLs) in citations of online works. Enclose URLs in angle brackets, and, if you must divide an address at the end of a line, break it only after a slash mark. Do not use a hyphen at the break as this will distort the address. URLs are often long and easy to misread, so take extra time to ensure that you are copying them correctly.

Important note: Many online databases and some online library catalogs now include a persistent link or URL to their records; do use this link in your citations for online works.

Use of reference markers. Unfortunately, many online sources do not use markers such as page or paragraph numbers. If such information is available to you, include it in your citations by all means; if it does not exist, readers must fend for themselves when accessing your sources. (Some readers might locate particular information in a document by using the "Find" tool in their computer program, but this option is not always available or useful.)

Scholarly Projects or Information Databases

An entry for an entire online scholarly project or information database may include the following information, *if available*: title of the project or database, editor's name, electronic publication information (including version number, publication date or latest update, name and place of sponsoring organization), date of access, and network address.

> American Memory Project. 15 Nov. 2000. Lib. of Congress, Washington. 10 Jan. 2004
>   <http://rs6.loc.gov/amhome.html>.
>
> Granger's World of Poetry. 1999. Columbia UP. 10 Dec. 2003 <http://www.
>   grangers.org>.

Documents within a Library or Subscription Database

To cite a source that you have found through one of your library's databases, begin with the author's name, if given. Follow the author's name with the name of the document, its publication information, the name of the database (underlined), the name of the subscription service, the name of the library you used (with its city, state abbreviation, or both if useful), and the date of access. If possible, conclude with the URL of the document; however, if the URL is impractically long, you may use the URL of the site's search page, as shown below. If no service URL is available, you may simply end with the date of access.

> Smith, Lucinda. "Was She Anastasia or a World-Class Imposter?" Denver Post 18 July
>   1993: 5D. ProQuest News & Magazines. ProQuest. Fort Collins Public Lib.,
>   Fort Collins, CO. 28 Feb. 2006 <http://0-proquest.umi.com.dalva.fcgov.com/>.

If you are using a source from a personal subscription service (e.g., America Online) that allows you to search by keyword, end the citation by writing "Keyword:" followed by the word itself.

> "Pneumonia." Compton's Encyclopedia Online. Vers. 3.0. 2003. America Online. 2
>   May 2006. Keyword: Compton's.

Articles in Online Periodicals (Magazines, Journals, Newspapers)

In citing online periodicals, begin with the author's name; if no author is given, begin with the title of the article. Continue with the name of the periodical (underlined), volume and issue number (if given), date of publication, the number range or total number of pages or paragraphs (if available), date of access, and network address (or persistent URL if the database supplies one).

- Signed article in a magazine

  Goodman, David. "Forced Labor." <u>Mother Jones Interactive</u> Jan.-Feb. 2001. 2 Jan.

  2004 <http://www.motherjones.com/mother_jones/JFOL/labor.html>.

- Unsigned article in a magazine

  "School Violence." <u>U.S. News Online</u> 6 July 2000. 21 Nov. 2005 <http://

  www.usnews.com/usnews/news/ctshoot.htm>.

- Article in a journal

  Cummings, Robert. "Liberty and History in Jonson's 'Invitation to Supper.'" <u>Studies

  in English Literature</u> 40.1 (2000). 29 Dec. 2005 <http://muse.jhu.edu/

  journals/studies_in_english_literature/vo40/40.1/cummings.html>.

- Article in a newspaper or on a newswire

  Kitner, John. "Widespread Opposition to Mideast Plan on Both Sides." <u>New York

  Times on the Web</u> 31 Dec. 2000. 1 Jan. 2006 <http://www.nytimes.com/

  2000/12/31/world/31MIDE.html/>.

- An editorial

  "Success at Last." Editorial. <u>Front Range Times: Electronic Edition</u> 18 Jan. 2001. 12

  Feb. 2006 <http://www.frtimes.com/ed/2001/01/18/p04.html>.

- A review

  Ebert, Roger. Rev. of <u>What Women Want</u>, dir. Nancy Meyers. <u>Chicago Sun-Times

  Online</u> 15 Dec. 2000. 31 Dec. 2005 <http://www.suntimes.com/output/

  ebert1/want15f.html>.

Personal or Professional Websites

In citing websites, begin with the name of the person who created the site, if appropriate. If no name is given, begin with the title of the site (underlined) or a description, such as "home page" (but do not underline or enclose a description in quotation marks).

Continue with date of publication, or latest update, if given; the name of any organization associated with the site; date of access; and the network address.

> Czepiel, Brad. Home page. 11 Mar. 2003. 22 Apr. 2006 <http://
>
> www.chass.ucolorado.co:7070/~BC/>.

> Department of English Home Page. May 1999. Colorado State U. 9 Jan. 2006
>
> <http://colostate.edu/depts/English/english_ie4.htm>.

Note that in the first example, the phrase "home page" is used as a description of a personal website and is therefore *not* underlined; in the second example, "Home Page" is part of the site's title and *is* underlined.

To cite a home page for an academic course, begin the entry with the instructor's name, followed by the name of the course (do not underline or place in quotation marks). Continue with a description such as "Course home page" (again, do not underline or place in quotation marks), the dates of the course, the names of the department and the institution, the date of access, and the network address.

> Wheeler, Jane. Advanced Expository Writing. Course home page. Jan.-May 2006.
>
> Dept. of English, Colorado State U. 10 Apr. 2006 <http://writing.colostate.edu./
>
> JWheeler/ENG301A/002/Index.htm>.

Online Books

The texts of some books are now available online. Begin the citation with the author's name, the book's name, and any publication information given in the source (city of publication, publisher, date). Then list the title of the site (underlined), the name of the editor (if given), and the electronic publication information. Conclude with the date of access and the network address of the book itself, if possible.

> Baum, Frank L. Glinda of Oz. 1920. Project Gutenberg. Ed. Frances Stewart. June
>
> 1997. 6 May 2006 <ftp://ftp.archive.org/pub/etex/etex97/14woz10h.htm>.

Nonperiodical Publications on CD-ROM, Diskette, or Magnetic Tape

Nonperiodical electronic citations are similar to those for a print book, but also include the medium of publication (CD-ROM, diskette, magnetic tape). If you are citing a specific entry, article, essay, poem, or short story, enclose the title in quotation marks.

> "Acupuncture." Oxford English Dictionary. 2nd ed. CD-ROM. Oxford UP, 1992.

E-Mail Communications

Begin with the name of the writer of the message, followed by the title taken from the subject line (if given), type of communication and its recipient, and date of the message.

> Clinton, Hillary. "Election News." E-mail to Jean Wyrick. 31 Oct. 2005.

APA Style

The American Psychological Association (APA) recommends a documentation style for research papers in the social sciences.* Your instructors in psychology and sociology classes, for example, may prefer that you use the APA form when you write essays for them.

The APA style is similar to the MLA style in that it calls for parenthetical documentation within the essay itself, although the information cited in the parentheses differs slightly from that presented according to the MLA format. For example, you will note that in the APA style the date of publication follows the author's last name and precedes the page number in the parentheses. Instead of a Works Cited page, the APA style uses a References page at the end of the essay to list those sources cited in the text. A Bibliography page lists all works that were consulted. Another important difference concerns capitalization of book and article titles in the reference list: in the MLA style, all important words are capitalized, but in the APA style, only proper names, the first word of titles, and the first word appearing after a colon are capitalized.

APA Citations in Your Essay

Here are some guidelines for using the APA parenthetical form within your paper:

1. APA style typically calls for an "author-publication year" method of citation, with the name and date inserted in the text at an appropriate place in the reference.

   Examples   A recent study (Jones, 2006) found no discernible differences in the absentee rate of men and women students on the main campus.

   Jones (2006) contrasted the absentee rates of men and women students on the main campus but found no discernible differences.

2. When you are quoting directly, place the author's name, the publication year, and the page number in parentheses following the quoted material. Note that in APA style, you place commas between the items in the parentheses, and you do include the "p." abbreviation for "page" (these are omitted in MLA style).

   Example   One crucial step in developing an anti-social personality may, in fact, be "the experience of being caught in some act and consequently being publicly labeled as a deviant" (Becker, 1983, p. 31).

3. If you use a print source by one author and give credit to that author by name within your paper, you need give only the date and the page number in parentheses. Note that the publication date follows directly after the name of the author.

   Example   According to Green (1994), gang members from upper-class families are rarely convicted for their crimes and are "almost never labeled as delinquent" (p.101).

---

* If you wish a more detailed description of the APA style, you might order a copy of the *Publication Manual of the American Psychological Association*, 5th ed. (Washington, DC: American Psychological Association, 2001). The most up-to-date documentation forms may be found on the APA website <http://www.apastyle.org>.

4. If you are citing a work with more than two authors, but fewer than six, list all names in the first reference; in subsequent references, use only the first author's last name and *et al.* (which means "and others"). For six or more authors, use only the last name of the first author followed by *et al.* for all citations, including the first. Note the use of "&" instead of "and" within parentheses.

Example   *First reference:* After divorce, men's standard of living generally rises some 75% whereas women's falls to approximately 35% of what it once was (Bird, Gordon, & Smith, 1992, p. 203).

Subsequent references: Almost half of all the poor households in America today are headed by single women, most of whom are supporting a number of children (Bird et al., 1992, p. 285).

5. If you cite a work that has a corporate author, cite the group responsible for producing the work.

Example   In contrast, the State Highway Research Commision (2004) argues, "The return to the sixty-five-mile-an-hour speed limit on some of our state's highways has resulted in an increase in traffic fatalities" (p. 3).

6. Private interviews, e-mail messages, and other personal communications should be referred to in your text but *not* in your reference list. Provide the initials and last name of the communicator, the words "personal communication," and the date in your paper.

Example   A. E. Wheeler acknowledged that until the most recent DNA work, most historians rejected belief in the Romanov children's escape (personal communication, February 23, 2006).

Compiling a Reference List: APA Style

If you are using the APA style, at the end of your essay you should include a page labeled References—a formal listing of the sources you cited in your essay. Arrange the entries alphabetically by the authors' last names; use initials for the authors' first and middle names. All authors' names are inverted (Forst, M. L.; Hall, S. L.). If there are two or more works by one author, list them chronologically, beginning with the earliest publication date. If an author published two or more works in the same year, the first reference is designated *a*, the second *b*, and so on (Feinstein 1999a; Feinstein 1999b).

If a work has more than six authors, APA lists the first six and then follows with "et al." (not italicized or within quotation marks).

Remember that in APA style, you italicize books and journal titles, volume numbers, and their associated punctuation, but you do not put the names of articles in quotation marks. Although you do capitalize the major words in the titles of magazines, newspapers, and journals, you do not capitalize any words in the titles of books or articles except the first word in each title, the first word following a colon, and all proper names. Write out the names of publishers, including the words "Books" and "Press," but omit terms such as "Co." or "Inc."

Sample Entries: APA Style

Books

- Book with one author

  Gould, S. J. (1985). *The flamingo's smile*. New York: W. W. Norton.

- Book with two authors

  Forst, M. L., & Blomquist, M. (1991). *Missing children: Rhetoric and reality*.
  New York: Lexington Books.

- Books by one author published in the same year

  Hall, S. L. (1980a). *Attention deficit disorder*. Denver: Bald Mountain Press.

  Hall, S. L. (1980b). *Taming your adolescent*. Detroit: Morrison Books.

- Book with an editor

  Banks, A. S. (Ed.). (1988). *Political handbook of the world*. Binghamton, NY: CSA
  Publications.

- Selection or chapter from collection with an editor

  Newcomb, T. M. (1958). Attitude development as a function of reference groups:
  The Bennington study. In E. Maccoby, T. M. Newcomb, & E. L. Hartley (Eds.),
  Readings in social psychology (pp. 10–12). New York: Holt, Rinehart and
  Winston.

- A book with a corporate author

  Mentoring Group. (1997). *The new mentors and protégés: How to succeed with
  the new mentoring partnerships*. Grass Valley, CA: Author.

Articles (In Print)

Note that when a volume number appears, it is italicized, as is all associated punctuation. Use *p.* or *pp.* with page numbers in newspapers but not in magazines or journals. Do not abbreviate names of the months.

- An article in a magazine

  Langer, E. T. (1989, May). The mindset of health. *Psychology Today, 48*, 1138-1241.

■ An article in a journal

> Nyden, P. W. (1985). Democratizing organizations: A case study of a union reform movement. *American Journal of Sociology, 90,* 1119-1203.

■ An article in a newspaper, author cited

> Noble, K. B. (1986, September 1). For ex-Hormel workers, no forgive and forget. *New York Times*, p. A5.

■ An article in a newspaper, no author given

> Fire claims historic café. (June 12, 2006). *The Red Feather News*, p. 1.

Electronic Sources: APA Style

The most current guidelines for electronic citations appear on the APA website at <http://www.apastyle.org/elecsource.html>. Note that unlike MLA style, APA does not put a period at the end of the URLs nor enclose them in angle brackets. Break a URL only after a slash mark or a period.

Internet Article Based on a Print Source

Most articles currently retrieved from online publications in psychology and the behavioral sciences are duplicates of those in print. However, if you have viewed the article only in its electronic form, add "Electronic version" in brackets after the article's title.

> Merrill, A. (2006). Use of group activities in first-year seminars [Electronic version]. *Journal of Nursing Instruction, 2,* 31-33.

If you are citing an online article that does differ from the print version (e.g., different format, additional information), add the date you retrieved the document from the URL. Note that a period does not follow the URL.

> Merrill, A. (2006). Use of group activities in first-year seminars. *Journal of Nursing Instruction, 2,* 31-33. Retrieved April 10, 2006, from http://jni.org/articles.html

Article in an Internet-Only Journal

> Keen, M. L. (2005, April 5). Yoga for migraine headache relief. *Prevention & Treatment, 2,* Article 0001a. Retrieved December 29, 2005, from http://journalsapa.org/prevention/volume2/pre00030001a.html

Article Retrieved from a Database

> Hall, K. E., Lind, S., & Michael, A. (2004). Sibling rivalry in adolescents. *Journal of American Psychology, 22,* 121-124. Retrieved February 26, 2006, from PsycARTICLES database.

Footnote and Bibliography Form

Most research papers today use a parenthetical documentation style, as illustrated in the MLA and APA sections of this chapter. However, in the event you face a writing situation that calls for use of traditional footnotes and bibliography page, here is a brief description of that format. This section will also help you understand the citation system of older documents you may be reading, especially those using Latin abbreviations.

If you are writing a paper using this format, each idea you borrow and each quotation you include must be attributed to its author(s) in a footnote that appears at the bottom of the appropriate page.* Number your footnotes consecutively throughout the essay (do not start over with "1" on each new page), and place the number in the text to the right of and slightly above the end of the passage, whether it is a direct quotation, a paraphrase, or a summary. Place the corresponding superscript number, indented (one-half inch or five spaces), before the note at the bottom of the page. Single-space each entry, and double-space after each footnote if more than one appears on the same page. Once you have provided a first full reference, subsequent footnotes for that source may include only the author's last name and page number. (See examples below. Please note that today many word-processing programs include a function for formatting footnotes.)

You may notice the use of Latin abbreviations in the notes of some documents, such as *ibid.* ("in the same place") and *op. cit.* ("in the work cited"). In such documents, *ibid.* follows a footnote as a substitute for the author's name, title, and publication information; there will be a new page number only if the reference differs from the one in the previous footnote. Writers use *op. cit.* with the author's name to substitute for the title in later references.

In the Bibliography at the end of the document, sources are listed by author in alphabetical order (or by title if no author is given).

First footnote reference	[5]Garrison Keillor, <u>Leaving Home</u> (New York: Viking, 1987) 23.
Next footnote	[6]Keillor 79.
Later reference	[12]Keillor 135.
Bibliographic entry	Keillor, Garrison. <u>Leaving Home</u>. New York: Viking, 1987.

■ Using Supplementary Notes

Sometimes when writers of research papers wish to give their readers additional information about their topic or about a particular piece of source material, they include *supplementary notes.* If you are using the MLA or APA format, these notes should be indicated by using a superscript number in your text (The study seemed incomplete at the time of its publication.[2]); the explanations appear on a page called "Notes" (MLA) or "Footnotes" (APA) that immediately follows the end of your essay. If you are using traditional footnote form, simply include the supplementary notes in your list of footnotes at the bottom of the page or in the list of endnotes following your essay's conclusion.

---

* Some documents use endnotes that appear in a list on a page immediately following the end of the essay, before the bibliography page.

Supplementary notes can offer a wide variety of additional information.

Examples

[1]For a different interpretation of this imagery, see Spiller 63-67.

[2]Simon and Brown have also contributed to this area of investigation. For a description of their results, see <u>Report on the Star Wars Project</u> 98-102.

[3]It is important to note here that Brown's study followed Smith's by at least six months.

[4]Later in his report Carducci himself contradicts his earlier evaluation by saying, "Our experiment was contaminated from the beginning" (319).

Use supplementary notes only when you think the additional information would be truly valuable to your readers. Obviously, information critical to your essay's points should go in the appropriate body paragraphs. (See page 416 for additional examples.)

■ Sample Student Paper Using MLA Style

Here is the result of Amy Lawrence's research into the latest forensic and historical discoveries concerning the 1918 Romanov assassination. As you read her essay, ask yourself how effectively she uses research material to explain and support her view of the controversy surrounding the assassination and possible escape. Do you find her essay informative? Interesting? Convincing? Point out major strengths and weaknesses that you see. Does her method of structuring her essay—the step-by-step revelation of the new "clues"—add to her argument?

Remember that the paragraphs in Amy's essay have been numbered for easy reference during class discussion. Do *not* number the paragraphs in your own essay.

The Romanovs: Olga, Marie, Czar Nicholas II, Czarina Alexandra, Anastasia, Alexei, and Tatiana

1"   ½"

Lawrence 1

1" Amy Lawrence

Professor Adams   Double-space

English 1012   1"

Indent   13 March 2006
½" or 5
spaces
A Possibility of Survival:

The Mysterious Fate of Anastasia and Alexei

1   The mystery has raged for over eighty years. According to the

history books, in 1918 Bolshevik revolutionaries brutally executed all

Introduction: seven members of the Russian royal family, the Romanovs.
History of the
controversy   Immediately following the murders, however, rumors appeared
and the
research   claiming that one, or perhaps two, of the Romanov children had
questions
escaped the assassination. Is there any evidence to support even the

possibility that seventeen-year-old Anastasia and thirteen-year-old

Alexei were somehow secreted away from the murder scene? Or is

this merely a romantic story that has been repeated generation after

generation?

2   Over the years, many people have come forth to claim their

identities as either Anastasia or Alexei. Movies, plays, and even a ballet

have repeatedly captured the public's fascination with this story that

just won't die.[1] Until recently, many dismissed the story entirely as pure

fiction. However, political changes in the Soviet Union during the

1990s produced a government that is more open to research into the

haunting Romanov mystery. Today, historical information and

improved forensic research have provided exciting evidence that points

to a new conclusion based on facts, not rumors. It is indeed possible

Thesis   that Anastasia and Alexei survived the execution designed to end the

Romanov dynasty forever.

3   The first break in solving the mystery came in 1989 when the

1"

Lawrence 2

Russian government released important information about the
Romanovs' mass grave. Although the rumors had always insisted that
discovery of the secret grave would confirm that two Romanovs had
escaped, the location of the grave had never been revealed. In 1976 a
Soviet writer claimed that he had uncovered the common grave in
woods near the murder site, but its location was kept secret by the
Communist government (Kurth 100). The 1989 revelation of this
grave site was important to Romanov scholars because it did support
the often-retold escape stories: although <u>eleven</u> people were reported
executed (seven Romanov family members and four attendants), only
<u>nine</u> bodies were found in the grave (Massie 43). But was this really
the Romanov grave?

4   The next important historical information came in 1992 from
Edvard Radzinsky, a Russian playwright whose research on the
Romanovs could now be published. Radzinsky had spent two decades
studying the Central State Archives in Moscow, discovering the
unread diaries of the murdered Czar Nicholas II and Czarina
Alexandra and, even more important, the previously secret
"Yurovsky note." Yakov Yurovsky was the leader of the execution
squad, and his statement contained not only his description of the
horrible night but also testimony from other guards at the scene
(Radzinsky 373). The "Yurovsky note" clearly emphasized the chaos of
the execution and contributed to the possible explanation
surrounding the persistent rumors of two survivors.

5   According to Yurovsky, in the early hours of July 17, 1918, the
Romanov family--the Czar, the Czarina, four daughters, and son--were
taken with their personal physician and three servants into the
cellar in the house where they had been held prisoners by the

Release of
evidence: The
grave site

More historical
information
uncovered: The
"Yurovsky note"

revolutionaries.[2] During the executions, the room filled with smoke and noise, and the bullets seemed to be oddly ricocheting, "jumping around the room like hail" (qtd. in Radzinsky 389). Although many bullets were fired at close range, Yurovsky mentions that the deaths of all five children were strangely hard to accomplish. Finally, as the guards hurriedly prepared to load the bodies onto a waiting truck, one of the guards heard a daughter cry out and then it was discovered that, amazingly, all the daughters were still alive (391). The daughters were then supposedly murdered by a drunken guard with a bayonet, who again experienced difficulty: "the point would not go through [the] corset" (qtd. in Radzinsky 391).

6   What the guards did NOT know until much later (at the grave site) was that at least three of the daughters, and possibly all the children, were wearing "corsets made of a solid mass of diamonds" (Radzinsky 373). The hidden Romanov jewels had acted like bullet-proof vests and were the reason the bullets and bayonet were deflected (373). Radzinsky argues that the chaos of the dark night, the drunken state of nervous, hurried guards, and the protective corsets cast serious doubt on the success of all the murder attempts (392).

7   The trip to the grave site was not smooth either. The truck broke down twice, and it was hard to move the bodies from the truck through the woods to the actual grave site. Yurovsky wrote that to lighten the load two bodies were cremated, supposedly the Czarina and her son, but he also claims that by mistake the family maid was confused with Czarina Alexandra (Radzinsky 410). Although the cremation story would account for the two bodies missing in the common grave, no remains or signs of a cremation site have ever been found. Consequently, many

Lawrence 4

Romanov researchers have another explanation. They argue that the two youngest Romanovs, wounded but still alive thanks to their protective corsets of jewels, were secretly removed from the truck during a breakdown by guards who regretted their part in the killing of the Romanov children (Smith). After all, why stop to burn only two bodies? Why just two and not all? Wouldn't such a cremation have taken valuable time and attracted attention? Why choose the boy and not Nicholas, the hated Czar? Could Yurovsky have been covering up the fact that by the time they reached the grave site two bodies were missing--the boy and a female (Radzinsky 416)?

8   Although the newly recovered historical evidence added important pieces, it did not solve the puzzle. However, forensic research, using techniques not available until 1993, began to shed light on the decades-old controversy. An international team of geneticists conducted DNA analysis on the nine recovered skeletons. Through mitochondrial-DNA sequencing, a process that analyzes DNA strains, and comparison to DNA samples donated by living relatives of the Romanovs, the team concluded in July 1993 that the skeletons were indeed the remains of five members of the Romanov family and four members of their household staff (Dricks). Yurovsky's story about the cremation of the maid was therefore not true--two <u>Romanovs</u> were missing!

> New forensic research:
> 1. DNA analysis

9   Taking the next step, scientists used computer modeling to superimpose facial photographs onto the skulls to determine structural matches that would tell which family members the skeletons actually were. The computer technology and dental work positively identified the Czar and Czarina as two of the bodies. Then more news: all of the

> 2. Computer modeling

Lawrence 5

remaining Romanov skeletons were of young females (Elliott 61). Alexei, the heir to the throne, was one of the missing--just as the rumors have always claimed.

10   To discover if the missing daughter was in fact Anastasia, the scientists compared the size and age of the girls to the skeletons. More controversy erupted. Although some Russian scientists argued that the missing skeleton was that of daughter Marie, Dr. William Maples, head of the American forensics team, strongly disagreed. According to Dr. Maples, all the skeletons were too tall and too developed to be Anastasia: "The bones we have show completed growth, which indicates more mature individuals" (qtd. in Toufexis 65). Dr. Peter Gill, head of the British Forensic Science Service that also studied the bones, agreed (O'Sullivan 6). According to these respected scientists, Anastasia was definitely not in the grave.

11   Six more years of sophisticated scientific experiments followed these initial studies; DNA tests were replicated and results confirmed (Glausiusz). Finally, in February 1998, a special federal commission chaired by First Deputy Prime Minister Boris Nemtsov officially announced its findings to Russian President Boris Yeltsin and the world: the bones were, beyond a shadow of scientific doubt, those of the Romanovs--but the bodies of Alexei and one sister (Anastasia?) remained unaccounted for (Varoli).[3]

12   Throughout the years, stories speculating on the Romanov assassination have always focused on the survival of the beautiful Anastasia and her sickly brother, Alexei, often describing a devoted guard smuggling them out through dark woods or secret passages. Doubters have always said that the stories were folktales not worth serious investigation. American and British forensic research, however,

3. Skeletal measurements

More tests lead to official announcement

Lawrence 6

argues this much: the real fate of Anastasia and Alexei is still unknown.

Therefore, their survival of the execution is still a possibility. Finally,

after the decades of rumors, there is a scientific basis for continuing the

search for the missing Romanovs. Someday, the mystery of their fate

will be solved and the controversy will rest in peace.

Conclusion: The search should continue

Lawrence 7

Notes

[1] The best-known story was told by Anna Anderson, a woman found in Berlin in 1920, who convinced many people throughout the world that she was indeed Anastasia. In 1956 her story was made into a popular movie starring Ingrid Bergman (Smith). The most recent treatment is the 1997 animated Fox film <u>Anastasia</u>, in which the young girl is saved by a servant boy, loses her memory, but is ultimately restored to her true identity (Rhodes).

[2] The Russian revolutionaries wanted to be rid of Czar Nicholas II and the entire Romanov family, which had ruled Russia since 1613. The Bolsheviks had held the family captive, charging Nicholas II with responsibility for Russia's poverty and social problems during World War I ("Romanov").

[3] The bones were officially buried on July 17, 1998, in the Peter and Paul Cathedral in St. Petersburg, resting place of all the Romanov czars since Peter the Great. The date marked the eightieth anniversary of the Romanov execution (Caryl).

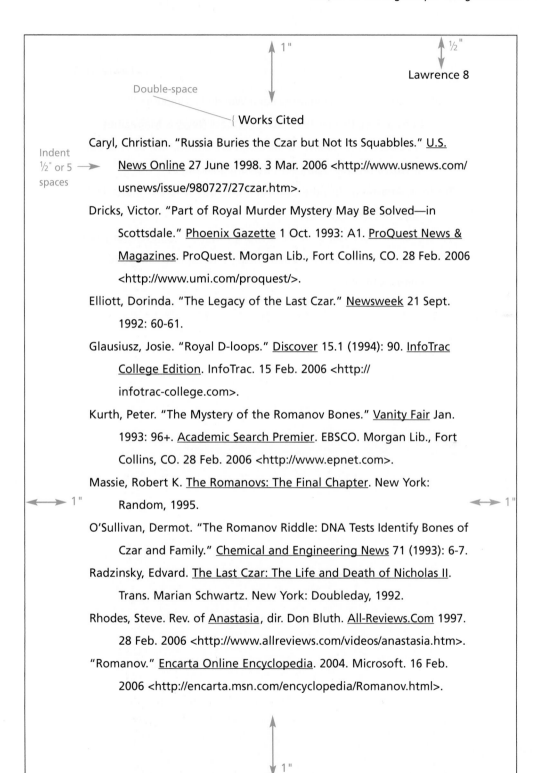

1"   ½"

Lawrence 8

Double-space

Works Cited

Indent ½" or 5 spaces →

Caryl, Christian. "Russia Buries the Czar but Not Its Squabbles." <u>U.S.</u>
<u>News Online</u> 27 June 1998. 3 Mar. 2006 <http://www.usnews.com/
usnews/issue/980727/27czar.htm>.

Dricks, Victor. "Part of Royal Murder Mystery May Be Solved—in
Scottsdale." <u>Phoenix Gazette</u> 1 Oct. 1993: A1. <u>ProQuest News &</u>
<u>Magazines</u>. ProQuest. Morgan Lib., Fort Collins, CO. 28 Feb. 2006
<http://www.umi.com/proquest/>.

Elliott, Dorinda. "The Legacy of the Last Czar." <u>Newsweek</u> 21 Sept.
1992: 60-61.

Glausiusz, Josie. "Royal D-loops." <u>Discover</u> 15.1 (1994): 90. <u>InfoTrac</u>
<u>College Edition</u>. InfoTrac. 15 Feb. 2006 <http://
infotrac-college.com>.

Kurth, Peter. "The Mystery of the Romanov Bones." <u>Vanity Fair</u> Jan.
1993: 96+. <u>Academic Search Premier</u>. EBSCO. Morgan Lib., Fort
Collins, CO. 28 Feb. 2006 <http://www.epnet.com>.

Massie, Robert K. <u>The Romanovs: The Final Chapter</u>. New York:
Random, 1995.

← 1"   1" →

O'Sullivan, Dermot. "The Romanov Riddle: DNA Tests Identify Bones of
Czar and Family." <u>Chemical and Engineering News</u> 71 (1993): 6-7.

Radzinsky, Edvard. <u>The Last Czar: The Life and Death of Nicholas II</u>.
Trans. Marian Schwartz. New York: Doubleday, 1992.

Rhodes, Steve. Rev. of <u>Anastasia</u>, dir. Don Bluth. <u>All-Reviews.Com</u> 1997.
28 Feb. 2006 <http://www.allreviews.com/videos/anastasia.htm>.

"Romanov." <u>Encarta Online Encyclopedia</u>. 2004. Microsoft. 16 Feb.
2006 <http://encarta.msn.com/encyclopedia/Romanov.html>.

1"

Smith, Lucinda. "Was She Anastasia or a World-Class Imposter?"
Denver Post 18 July 1993: 5D. ProQuest News & Magazines.
ProQuest. Fort Collins Public Lib., Fort Collins, CO. 28 Feb. 2006
<http://0-proquest.umi.com.dalva.fcgov.com/>.

Toufexis, Anastasia. "It's the Czar All Right, but Where's Anastasia?"
Time 14 Sept. 1992: 65.

Varoli, John. "Bury Tsar in St. Petersburg July 17." St. Petersburg Times
9-16 Feb. 1998. 26 Feb. 2006 <http://www.spb.ru/times/336-337/
nemtsov.html>.

■ Student Sample Using APA Style

To illustrate some of the important differences between MLA and APA documentation styles, here is a paragraph from the previous student essay as it would appear using APA guidelines. Following that paragraph is a sample References page, showing how the sources in a MLA's Works Cited list (pages 417–418) would be presented in APA style.

Paragraph 10

To discover if the missing daughter was in fact Anastasia, the scientists compared the size and age of the girls to the skeletons. More controversy erupted. Although some Russian scientists argued that the missing skeleton was that of daughter Marie, Dr. William Maples, head of the American forensics team, strongly disagreed. According to Dr. Maples, all the skeletons were too tall and too developed to be Anastasia: "The bones we have show completed growth, which indicates more mature individuals" (Toufexis, 1992, p. 65). Dr. Peter Gill, head of the British Forensic Science Service that also studied the bones, agreed (O'Sullivan, 1993, p. 6). According to these respected scientists, Anastasia was definitely not in the grave.

References

Caryl, C. (1988, June 27). Russia buries the czar but not its squabbles [Electronic version]. *U.S. News Online, 124.* Retrieved March 3, 2006, from http://www.usnews.com/usnews/issue/980727/27czar.htm

Dricks, V. (1993, October 1). Part of royal murder mystery may be solved—in Scottsdale. *Phoenix Gazette,* p. A1. Retrieved February 28, 2006, from ProQuest News & Magazine database.

Elliot, D. (1992, September 21). The legacy of the last czar. *Newsweek, 120,* 60-61.

Glausiusz, J. (1994). Royal d-loops. *Discover, 15,* 90. Retrieved February 15, 2006, from InfoTrac College Edition database.

Kurth, P. (1993, January). The mystery of the Romanov bones. *Vanity Fair, 56,* 96-103. Retrieved February 28, 2006, from Academic Search Premier database.

Massie, R. K. (1995). *The Romanovs: The final chapter.* New York: Random House.

O'Sullivan, D. (1993). The Romanov riddle: DNA tests identify bones of czar and family. *Chemical and Engineering News, 71,* 6-7.

Radzinsky, E. (1992). *The last czar: The life and death of Nicholas II* (Marian Schwartz, Trans.). New York: Doubleday.

Rhodes, S. (1997). [Review of the motion picture *Anastasia*]. *All-Reviews.Com.* Retrieved February 28, 2006, from http://www.allreviews.com/videos/anastasia.htm

Romanov. (2004). In *Encarta Online Encyclopedia.* Retrieved February 16, 2006, from http://encarta.msn.com/encyclopedia/Romanov.html

Smith, L. (1993, July 18). Was she Anastasia or a world-class imposter? *The Denver Post*, p. 5D. Retrieved February 28, 2006, from ProQuest News & Magazines database.

Toufexis, A. (1992, September 14). It's the czar all right, but where's Anastasia? *Time*, *140*, 65.

Varoli, J. (1998, February 9-16). Bury tsar in St. Petersburg July 17. *The St. Petersburg Times*, p. A2. Retrieved February 26, 2006, from http://www.spb.ru/times/336-337/nemtsov.html

Chapter 15

Writing in Class: Exams and "Response" Essays

In-class writing assignments call for good writing skills, analytical reading skills, and confidence. When you write essays out of class, you have the luxury of time: you can mull over your ideas, talk about them with friends or classmates, prewrite, plan, revise, or even start over if you wish. Because essay assignments written in class must be planned and composed on the spot under the pressure of a time limit, they may induce anxiety in some students. (One composition-class student characterized his feelings of terror this way: "I felt like a slug caught in a sudden salt storm!")

Never fear! Hope reigns! By remembering what you already know about writing the short essay and by learning to analyze quickly the demands of the task you face, you can substantially reduce your anxiety level. With practice, you may discover that in-class writing assignments are not nearly as threatening as you may have once thought.

■ Steps to Writing Well under Pressure

1. After you are assigned in-class writing, your first step is to **clarify for yourself the kind of task you face.** Sometimes your instructor will tell you about the assignment's format or general design in advance. Other times, however, figuring out the demands of the assignment on the spot and following the instructions carefully will be part of the task itself. Understanding the kind of exam or essay question you face will help you prepare your response and boost your confidence. Here are some common formats for in-class assignments that call for your writing skills:

- **Short-answer exam questions**

    Your instructor might give an exam that asks you to write a well-developed paragraph or two to identify, define, or explain a term or idea. For example, a political science instructor might ask for paragraphs explaining the importance of certain treaties or laws; a literature teacher might ask for paragraphs that explain the significance of certain lines, characters, or symbols in a particular work; a science instructor might ask for extended definitions of important biological terms, and so on. The paragraph skills you learned in Chapter 3—focus, development, unity, and coherence—are all relevant here.

- **Essay exam questions**

    Frequently, questions appear on exams that call for more detailed discussion of specific material studied in a course. An essay question on a history exam might ask you to "Explain the major causes of the Civil War." Or in biology you might be asked to "Trace a drop of blood on its circulatory journey from the human heart throughout the body." You would be expected to shape your answer into a multi-paragraphed essay developed clearly in an easy-to-follow organizational pattern.

- **"Prompted" essays**

    Perhaps the most common in-class assignment in composition classes asks students to respond thoughtfully to some *prompt*—that is, students are asked to give their own opinion about a specific topic presented in a written passage or question, such as "Do you think teenage consumers are too influenced by television?" Other times, students will be asked to read a quotation or proverb ("All that glitters is not gold") and then respond in a personal essay. Other prompts include a statement of a current controversy (students should/should not be assessed a special fee for athletics on this campus) or the description of a hypothetical problem (the developer of a discount superstore has applied for a building permit on the edge of a wildlife preserve). Each student is responsible for explaining and supporting his or her position on the topic presented by the prompt.

- **Summary-and-response essays**

    Some in-class essays ask students to do more than voice their opinions in response to a short prompt. One common assignment is known as the *summary-and-response* essay or the *summary-reaction* essay. Students first read an essay by a professional writer (the reading may be done either in or out of class, depending on the instructor's preference). Once in class, students write an essay that begins with a clear summary of the essay they have just read (an activity that demonstrates analytical reading abilities), and then they present a reasoned argument that agrees or disagrees with the professional essay's ideas. Summary-and-response essays are often used as entrance or exit exams for composition classes at many schools throughout the country because they allow students to display both reading and writing skills. Because the summary-and-response essay is so frequently assigned today, additional discussion, illustrated by a student paper, is provided on pages 430–432 of this chapter.

There are numerous kinds and combinations of essay exams and in-class writing assignments. You can best prepare yourself mentally if you know in advance the purpose and format of the writing task you will face. If possible, ask your instructor to clarify the nature of your assignment before you come to class to write. (Also, some teachers allow students to bring dictionaries, outlines, or notes to class, but others don't. Consult your instructor.)

2. Arrive prepared. Before class, determine what items you need to take to respond to your writing assignment. For example, do you need loose paper or an exam book or will paper be provided? (If you are writing on your own notebook paper, always bring a paper clip or, better, one of those mini-staplers to fasten your pages together.) Were you asked to bring a copy of a reading or essay questions that were handed out in advance? Are dictionaries permitted? Note cards? The two essential items for every in-class assignment, regardless of type, are a watch, to help you gauge your writing time, and extra pens, to rescue you when yours inevitably runs dry. Having adequate supplies on hand keeps you from rustling around to borrow from your neighbors, which not only costs you valuable minutes but also disturbs the other writers around you. In addition, speaking to your classmates, especially during an examination, may be erroneously perceived as scholastic dishonesty. To avoid all such problems, bring the right tools to class.

Perhaps this is also a good place to say a little more about classroom atmosphere. Students often complain about their classmates' annoying behaviors during in-class writing assignments or examinations. Repeated pen-clicking, gum snapping, or chair kicking can make life miserable for other writers in the room. Empty pop cans noisily clanking down aisles, musical cell phones, beeping watches, and even crinkling candy wrappers can distract and derail someone else's complex thought. Please be *courteous:* leave the snack bar at home, spit out that gum, and turn off electronic equipment.

One more piece of advice: many in-class writing situations are "closed door." That is, at the appointed time for the class or exam to begin, the door is closed and no one is permitted to enter late. Consequently, try to arrive at least five minutes early, in case your instructor's watch is faster than yours but also to have the extra minutes to settle yourself mentally as well as physically. ("Closed door" may also mean that no one is permitted to leave and return to the room during the writing session, even for restroom trips, so think carefully about that extra cup of coffee or can of pop just before your class.)

3. Once you are in class ready to write, **read the entire assignment with great care.** First, underline *key words* that are important to the subject matter of your essay; then circle the *directional words* that give you clues to the method of development you might use to organize your response.

Example   Explain the effects of the Triangle Shirtwaist Factory fire on child-labor laws in America from 1912 to 1915.

Example   In *The Grapes of Wrath*, John Steinbeck criticizes the unfair treatment of farmworkers by California land owners. Illustrate this criticism with three examples from the novel.

To help you identify some of the frequently used directional words and understand the approaches they suggest, study the following chart.

Directional Word or Phrase	Suggested Method of Development
Illustrate . . . Provide examples of . . . Show a number of . . . Support with references to . . .	Example
Explain the steps . . . Explain the procedure . . . Outline the sequence of . . . Trace the events . . . Review the series of . . . Give the history of . . .	Process or Narration
Discuss the effects of . . . Show the consequences of . . . Give the reasons for . . . Explain why . . . Discuss the causes of . . . Show the influence of . . .	Causal Analysis
Compare the following . . .* Contrast the positions of . . .* Show the differences between . . . Discuss the advantages and disadvantages . . . Show the similarities among . . . Relate X to Y . . .	Comparison/Contrast
Describe the following . . . Re-create the scene . . . Discuss in detail . . . Explain the features of . . .	Description
Agree or disagree . . . Defend or attack . . . Offer proof . . . Present evidence . . . Criticize . . . Evaluate . . . State reasons for . . . Justify your answer . . . What if . . .	Argument
Discuss the types of . . . Show the kinds of . . . Analyze the parts of . . . Classify the following . . .	Classification/ Division
Define . . . Explain the meaning of . . . Identify the following . . . Give the origins of the term . . .	Definition

* Remember that the directional word "compare" may indicate a discussion of both similarities and differences; the directional word "contrast" focuses only on the differences.

Note that essay questions may demand more than one pattern of development in your response:

Explain the meaning of the term "hospice" and show the differences between the Hospice Movement in Great Britain and that in the United States. [definition and contrast]

Discuss Weber's three types of authority, giving examples of societies that illustrate each type. [classification and example]

Explain President Truman's reasons for bombing Japan during World War II and then defend or attack Truman's decision. [causal analysis and argument]

Learning to quickly recognize key directional words will help you organize as you begin to focus your essay. Always read the assignment at least twice and ask your instructor for clarification if some part of the assignment seems confusing to you.

4. Once you have read and fully understood the purpose and direction of your assignment, **prepare to write.** The following advice may be helpful:

- Think positively: remind yourself that the task you face is not unknown to you. You are being asked to write—yes, quickly—the same kind of essay that you have been practicing in your composition class. You *CAN* do this!

- If you are writing an in-class essay, take the first few minutes to think and plan. Many times it's helpful to formulate a thesis in a direct rephrasing of the exam question or "prompt" you have been assigned. For example:

    Assignment: After reading "How to Make People Smaller Than They Are" by Norman Cousins, write an essay agreeing or disagreeing with Cousins's suggestions for improving higher education today.

    Thesis: In his essay "How to Make People Smaller Than They Are," author Norman Cousins convincingly argues for requiring additional liberal arts courses for all students in college today. His suggestions for improving higher education are uniformly excellent and should be implemented immediately.

    Assignment: Discuss Weber's three types of authority, giving examples to clarify your answer.

    Thesis: Weber's three types of authority are traditional authority, charismatic authority, and legal authority. The three types may be exemplified, respectively, by the 19th-century absolute monarchs of Europe, by a variety of religious groups, and by the constitutional government of the United States.

- After deciding on your thesis, jot down on scratch paper a brief plan or outline that sketches out the main points that will appear in the body of your essay. You might scribble a few key words to remind yourself of the supporting evidence or important details you will use. Don't get too bogged down in detailed outlining—just use enough words to help you stay on track.

- You might also budget your time now—thinking "by 2:30 I should be done with two points in my discussion." Although such figuring is approximate at best, having a general schedule in mind might keep you from drifting or spending too much time on the first parts of your essay. In most cases, you should assume you will not be able to write a rough draft of your essay and then have the time to massively reorganize as you recopy it.

© Stockbyte/SuperStock

5. As you **begin writing,** remember what you have learned about paragraphing, topic sentences, and supporting evidence. If you have been given multiple tasks, be sure that you are responding to all parts of the assignment. If the assignment asks you to present your own opinion, focus your answer accordingly. In timed-writing situations, you can't take on the world, but you can offer intelligent commentary on selected ideas. If you only have an hour or less to complete your essay, consider aiming for three well-developed points of discussion. You may be writing a rather conventional five-paragraph essay, but such a clear pattern of organization frequently works best when nervous writers are under pressure and time is short.

Two more suggestions:

- It may be a good idea to write on one side of your paper only, leaving wide margins on both sides; consider, too, leaving extra lines between paragraphs. If you discover that you have time after finishing your essay, you might wish to add additional information to your exam answer or perhaps another persuasive example to a body paragraph. Leaving plenty of blank spaces will allow you to insert information neatly instead of jamming in handwriting too small for your instructor to decipher.

- If you are writing an essay (rather than a short answer), do try to conclude in a satisfactory way. Your conclusion may be brief, but even a few sentences are better than an abrupt midsentence halt when time runs out.

6. In the time remaining after writing the complete draft of your essay, **read what you have written.** Aim for sufficient, appropriate content and clear organization. Insert, delete, or make changes neatly. Once you are reasonably satisfied with the essay's content and flow, take a few minutes to proofread and edit. Although most instructors do not expect an in-class essay to be as polished as one written out of class, you are responsible for the best spelling, grammar, and punctuation you can muster under the circumstances. Take care to apply what you know to sentence problems, especially the run-ons, comma splices, and twisted predicates that tend to surface when writers are composing in a hurry. After all, information too deeply hidden in a contorted sentence is information that may not be counted in your favor.

7. Tips. Before you turn in your work, be sure your name is on every page of your essay or exam so your instructor will know whom to praise for a job well done. If appropriate, include other pertinent information, such as your class section number or your student number. Number and clip or staple the loose pages of your essay or exam (do *not* rely on folded corners to hold your pages together!).

Problems to Avoid

Misreading the assignment. Always read the directions and the assignment completely and carefully before you start prewriting. Mark key and directional words. Do you have multiple tasks? Consider numbering the tasks to avoid overlooking any parts. Important choices to make? Neatly put a line through the options you don't want. Grossly misreading your assignment may give you as much chance at success as a pig at a barbecue.

Incomplete essay. Don't begin writing an in-class essay without a plan, even if you are excited about the topic and want to dive right in. Having a plan and budgeting your time accordingly will avoid the common problem of not finishing, which, in the end, may cost you dearly. Don't allow yourself to ramble off on a tangent in one part of the assignment. Stay focused on your plan and complete the entire essay or exam. If you have left blank space as described previously, you can return to a part of the essay to add more information if time permits. Wear a watch and consult it regularly! Don't depend on a classmate or your instructor to advise you of the time remaining.

Composition amnesia. Writing essays under time pressure causes some students suddenly to forget everything they ever knew about essay organization. This memory loss often wreaks havoc on paragraphing skills, resulting in a half-dozen one- and two-sentence string-bean paragraphs without adequate development; at other times, it results in one long super-paragraph that stretches for pages before the eye like the Mohave Desert, no relief or rest stop in sight. Emphasize your good ideas by presenting them in a recognizable organizational structure, just as you would do in an out-of-class assignment.

Gorilla generalizations. Perhaps the biggest problem instructors find is the lack of adequate, specific evidence to explain or support shaggy, gorilla-sized generalities roaming aimlessly through students' essays. If, for example, you argue, "Team sports are good for kids because they build character," *why* do you believe this? What particular character traits do you mean? Can you offer a personal example or a hypothetical case to clarify and support your claim? Remember what you learned in Chapter 3 about using evidence—examples, personal experience, testimony—to illustrate or back up any general claims you are making. Your goal is to be as clear and persuasive as you can be—*show* what you know!

■ PRACTICING WHAT YOU'VE LEARNED

Underline the key words and circle the directional words or phrases in the following assignments. What pattern(s) of development are suggested in each assignment?

1. Discuss three examples of flower imagery as they clarify the major themes of Toni Morrison's novel *The Bluest Eye*.

2. Trace the events that led to the Bay of Pigs invasion of Cuba.

3. Discuss Louis B. Mayer's major influences on the American film industry during the "Golden Age of Moviemaking."

4. Agree or disagree with the following statement: "The 1957 launching of the Russian satellite Sputnik caused important changes in the American educational system."

5. Consider the similarities and differences between the expressionistic techniques of American painters Jaune Quick-to-See Smith and Audrey Flack. Illustrate your answer with references to important works of both artists.

■ ASSIGNMENT

Practice planning an in-class essay by selecting one of the quotations on pages 43–45 in Chapter 2 as a brief "prompt" for a personal opinion essay developed by any method(s) you find appropriate. Allow yourself only ten minutes to write a working thesis and a sketch outline for your essay. Would you then be ready to turn your plan into a clearly organized and well-developed in-class essay? Continue to practice responding to the prompts in Chapter 2 until you gain confidence in your ability to think, plan, and write under time pressure.

■ Writing the Summary-and-Response Essay

The "summary-and-response essay" is such a common assignment today that it merits additional discussion and illustration. As noted earlier in this chapter, this kind of assignment frequently asks students to read a professional article, summarize its thesis and main points, and write a response expressing agreement or disagreement with the article's ideas.

You may have had experience with some form of this assignment before now. Many college entrance examinations have adopted this kind of essay to evaluate both reading comprehension and writing skills. Many colleges also use this format as their composition placement exam, to direct students into the appropriate writing class. Still other schools employ this kind of essay as a final exam or exit test for their composition requirement. And although this format is often assigned as in-class writing, it certainly is not limited to this use. Many composition classes and other academic courses include this type of essay as an out-of-class paper.

Though the format of this assignment may vary slightly depending on its purpose and occasion, throughout your college and professional life you will almost certainly be asked on more than one occasion to read information, summarize it for others, and then present your reaction to its ideas. To help you prepare for this kind of thinking and writing activity, here are a few suggestions, divided into three sections for clarity:

Reading the Assignment and the Article

1. Read your assignment's directions carefully to discover exactly what you are being asked to do. For example, are you being asked to present a one-paragraph summary of a professional article first and then write a personal response? Or are you being asked to respond to the professional article's major points one at a time? Perhaps you are being asked to critique the author's style as well as ideas. Because formats vary, be sure you understand your complete assignment—all its required parts—before you begin writing.

2. Before you can intelligently respond to any reading you need to thoroughly understand its ideas. To review suggestions for close reading, take the time now to review Chapter 8, "The Reading-Writing Connection," in this text. This chapter will help you identify and evaluate an article's thesis, main points, supporting evidence, and other rhetorical techniques.

3. If you are given an article to read out of class, study it carefully, annotating it as outlined in Chapter 8. If reading the article is part of the in-class activity, you may have only enough time to read it carefully once, underlining and annotating as you move through each paragraph. Minimally, you should mark the thesis and the main ideas of the body paragraphs. Underline or star important claims or supporting evidence. Are the claims logical and well supported, or does the author rely on generalizations or other faulty reasoning? Overall, do you agree or disagree with the article? Would you call it a weak or strong piece of writing? Why? (For help evaluating claims and supporting evidence, review the discussion of logical fallacies in Chapter 10, pages 286–289.)

Writing the Summary Section*

If you are to begin with a brief summary of the article, follow the guidelines listed under "Writing a Summary" on pages 175–176 of Chapter 8. Remember that a good summary presents the author's name and full title of the article in the first sentence, which also frequently presents the article's thesis (In his article "Free Speech on Campus," author Clarence Page argues that . . .). The next sentences of your summary should present the article's main ideas, found in the article's body paragraphs. Unless you need to quote a word or phrase for clarity or emphasis, use your own words to present a concise version of the article. Normally, your summary will be an objective treatment of the article's ideas, so save your opinions for the "response" section.

Writing the Response Section

1. Before you begin writing the "response" part of your essay, look at the underlining and any marginal notes you made on the article. What was your general assessment of the article? Do you agree or disagree with the author? Perhaps you only agree with some points and disagree with others? Or perhaps you agree with the main ideas but think that this particular essay is a weak defense of those ideas? After looking over the article and your notes, decide on your overall reaction to this article. This assessment will become your thesis in the "response" portion of your essay.

2. Once you have a working thesis in mind, plan the rest of your essay. For example, if you disagree with the article, you might want to note two or three reasons you

---

* To avoid confusion in this discussion between the professional essay used as a prompt and the student's response essay, the word "article" will be used to refer to the professional reading.

reject the author's opinion; these reasons may become the basis for your own body paragraphs. Important: Be sure you have evidence of your own to support your positions. Responding with personal examples is perhaps the most common kind of support for essays written in class, but if you know facts, statistics, testimony, or other information that would support your position, you may certainly include them.

3. If you have begun your essay with a summary, start the next paragraph with a sentence that clearly indicates the "response" section is now beginning. Present a smooth transition to your thesis and consider using an "essay map" to indicate to your readers the points you will discuss.

Example   Although in his article "Test!" Paul Perez correctly identifies a growing drug problem in our public schools, his plan to drug-test all students involved in campus activities should be rejected. Such a test could not be implemented fairly and is an unreasonable invasion of students' privacy.

4. In each of your own body paragraphs make clear which of the author's claims or ideas you are refuting or supporting by using "tag lines" to remind the reader.

Example   Although Foxcroft argues that the proposed tuition increase will not discourage prospective students, she fails to understand the economic situation of most IBC applicants, who are sacrificing income to return to school. In a recent survey . . . .

5. Once you have signaled the point in question and stated your position, develop each body paragraph with enough specific supporting evidence to make your claim convincing. If you disagree with a point, you must show why and present your position logically (you may wish to review Chapter 10 on argument). If you agree with the article, beware a tendency to simply restate the positions with which you are in agreement ("I think Brower is right when she says housing is too expensive on campus. She is also right about the lack of housing choices . . ."). Find examples, reasons, or information that lend support to the points that you and the author think are valid.

6. Many assignments call for a straightforward personal opinion or "agree-disagree" response. In other assignments, you may be given the option of criticizing or praising an author's logic, style, or even tone. You might, for example, show that a particular argument is ineffective because it is based on a mass of overstated generalities, or you might show why the author's sarcastic tone alienates the reader. On the other hand, an author might deserve credit for a particularly effective supporting example or a brilliantly clever turn of phrase that captures the essence of an idea. Always check your assignment to see if this sort of critique is welcome or even required in your response.

7. Don't forget to write a brief concluding paragraph. If appropriate, you might emphasize the value of the article in question, or call for action for or against its ideas, or project its effects into the future (other suggestions for conclusions appear in Chapter 4). However you end your essay, your conclusion should always be consistent with your overall assessment of the article and its ideas.

■ Sample Student Essay

The essay that follows was written by a student who was assigned the article "Our Youth Should Serve" by Steven Muller (pages 173–175 in Chapter 8) and then asked to write a one-paragraph summary and a response essay, expressing her opinion of the article's proposal. Although the student thought the article itself could have been stronger, she liked Muller's suggestion for a volunteer youth service. Her approval of his proposal became her essay's thesis, which she then developed through use of her own experience.

After you read Muller's article and the student's summary-and-response essay, what suggestions for revision might you offer her?

YOUTH SERVICE: AN IDEA WHOSE TIME HAS COME

1   In "Our Youth Should Serve," former university president Steven Muller proposes a national volunteer youth service. This program would perform some of our country's public service tasks and also help high school graduates who have to choose between low-paying jobs or starting college with no clear direction. Although the pay would be low, volunteers would benefit through job training and by earning federal grants for college. Muller also argues that youth service would motivate volunteers to become better students and perhaps help them find a career. The greatest benefit, according to Muller, would be the self-esteem volunteers would gain from earning these benefits themselves.

Summary

2   Although Muller's article might have been more persuasive with some specific examples supporting its claims, Muller's national volunteer youth service is still a good idea, especially for students who have no money for college and no work experience. I was one of those students, and because of the year I spent after high school graduation working in a boring, dead-end job, I believe the Youth Service should be started as soon as possible.

Response begins

Thesis

3   After I graduated from high school, I didn't go to college because I didn't have any money saved and I was tired of school. I decided to work for a while to save up, but I didn't have any training for

Response to
the benefit
of earning
grant money

anything so I took a minimum-wage sales job in a mall clothing store.
I had to look good for work, but since my wardrobe consisted of jeans
and T-shirts, I had to buy new clothes. With clothes and transportation
to work and other bills, I was barely breaking even. If I had been in
Muller's program, my pay would also have been low but at least I
would have been earning grant money for college at the same time.

Response
to the
benefits of
meaningful
work, skills

4   Muller also makes a good point about people needing to feel that
what they are doing is important or meaningful. My job at the store
wasn't meaningful or challenging; it was, in fact, repetitive and
boring. For example, a typical day during the summer months
consisted of cleaning out dressing rooms and hanging up two-piece
swim suits thrown all over the floor. It took forever to match up the
right size tops and bottoms and then hang them back up on these
crazy little double hangers so that everything was facing the right
way with all the straps untwisted. In the winter it was pants and
sweaters. Unlike Muller's volunteers who would be helping society
while getting some valuable training themselves, I wasn't contributing
to anything meaningful, and I sure wasn't learning any skills for a
better future.

5   It didn't take me long to figure out that I wanted more out of life
than a low-paying, boring, going-nowhere job. So I talked to a
counselor here at Logan [Community College] who helped me explore

Response
to career
benefits

some of my interests, and now I am enrolled in the pre-nursing
program. In Muller's program I might have discovered this career
earlier by volunteering at a hospital or nursing home, plus getting
some on-the-job experience. I would have tuition grant money
instead of going into major debt from student loans like I am now. I
might also have worked for someone who might even hire me later.

and increased
self-esteem

And I'm absolutely positive I would have felt more useful and had
better self-esteem than I did hanging up clothes for eight months!

6   Although this program wasn't there to help me, my sister is getting ready to graduate and she is in the same situation I was two years ago—no money, no skills, no solid future goals. If Muller's program existed today, I'd tell her to look into it. The benefits of college money, job training, and better self-esteem are just too good to pass up.

Conclusion emphasizes benefits to a future volunteer

■ PRACTICING WHAT YOU'VE LEARNED

A. After reading Steven Muller's article "Our Youth Should Serve" (pages 173–175), write your own summary-and-response essay, drawing on your own knowledge and experience to support or reject his proposed program. In your opinion, would this be a worthwhile, feasible program? Why or why not?

B. Write a response to "Our Youth Should Serve" that presents at least one paragraph critiquing Muller's reasoning, use of supporting evidence, or other methods of persuasion. How might Muller have improved the arguments for his proposed youth service? Did he overlook any major problems or disadvantages that you see? (In other words, if Muller asked you for help during a revision workshop, what major suggestion for change or addition would you offer to assist him in writing a stronger draft?)

■ ASSIGNMENT

Read and annotate the selection "So What's So Bad about Being So-So?" on pages 193–195 of this textbook and then write your own summary-and-response essay, agreeing or disagreeing (wholly or in part) with the writer's view of competition today. Remember to support your position with logical reasons, persuasive examples, or relevant facts. (If you prefer, you may select some other professional essay from this textbook or from another source, such as a newspaper or magazine, but be sure to obtain your instructor's approval of your selection in advance.)

Chapter 16

Writing about Literature

People read literature for many, many reasons, including amusement, comfort, escape, new ideas, exploration of values, intellectual challenge, and on and on. Similarly, people write about literature to accomplish a variety of purposes. Literary essays may inform readers about the ideas in a work, analyze its craft, or focus on the work's relationship to the time or culture in which it was written. Other essays might explore biographical, psychological, archetypal, or personal readings of a work.

Although approaches to literature are diverse and may be studied in depth in other English courses, writing essays about literature is worthwhile in the composition classroom as well. Writing about literature offers an opportunity to practice the important skills of close reading, critical thinking, and effective expression of ideas.

■ Using Literature in the Composition Classroom

Teachers of writing most often use literature in their courses in two ways: as "prompts" to inspire personal essay topics and as subjects of interpretative essays.

1. *Prompts:* You might be asked to read a poem or short story and then use some aspect of it—its ideas or characters, for example—as a springboard to discover an essay topic of your own. For instance, after reading John Updike's "A & P," a story about a rather naive young man who receives a real-world lesson, you might write about a coming-of-age experience you had. Or your teacher might assign Shirley Jackson's "The Lottery" and ask you to agree or disagree with the author's views on unexamined conformity to tradition.

2. *Literary Analysis:* Rather than responding to a piece of literature in a personal essay, you might be assigned a literary analysis, asking you to study a piece of literature and then offer your interpretation—that is, your insight into the work (or some important part of it). Your insight becomes your thesis; the body of your essay explains this reading, supported by textual evidence (material from the work) to help your reader understand your view and perhaps gain greater pleasure in, and appreciation of, the work itself.

Literary analysis assignments may be focused in different ways, as well. Some common examples include essays whose main purpose is to show:

- how the various parts or elements of a piece of literature work together to present the main ideas (for example, how the choices of narrator, stanza form, and figurative language in a poem effectively complement each other);
- how one element fits into the complex whole (for example, how setting contributes to a story);
- how two works or two elements may be profitably read together (two poems with similar ideas but different forms; two characters from one story);
- how one interpretation is more insightful than another reading;
- how a work's value has been overlooked or misunderstood.

There are as many possibilities for essay topics as there are readers!

Regardless of the exact assignment, you should feel confident about writing an essay of literary analysis. Working through Part Two of this text, you have already practiced many of the strategies required. For example, to present a particular reading of a poem, you may organize your discussion by *dividing* it into its major literary elements: point of view, setting, structure, language, and so on. Your essay may offer specific lines or images from the work as *examples* illustrating your reading. Working with more than one piece of literature or literary element calls for *comparison and contrast* techniques. And every paper—whether it is a personal response or literary analysis—uses the skills you learned in Part One of this text: a clear thesis, adequate development of ideas, coherent organization, and effective use of language.

■ Suggestions for Close Reading of Literature

Writing about literature begins with careful reading—and, yes, rereading. The steps suggested here are certainly not exhaustive; one can ask literally hundreds of questions about a complex piece of literature. Rather, these questions are intended to give you a start. Practicing close reading and annotation should help you generate ideas and lead you to additional questions of your own.

Our discussion in this chapter is limited to poems and short stories because composition courses frequently do not have the time to include novels and plays (or long narrative poems, for that matter). However, many of the suggestions for reading short stories and poems may be applied to the reading of longer fiction and drama.

Before you begin reading the suggestions that follow, let's dispel the myth about "hidden meanings." A work of literature is not a trick or puzzle box wherein the author has hidden a message for readers to discover if they can just uncover the right clues. Literary works are open to discussion and interpretation; that's part of their appeal. They contain ideas and images that the author thought important, and some ideas or elements the writer may not have consciously been aware of. You, as the reader, will have insights into a poem or story that your classmates don't. It's your job as the writer of your literary analysis to explain not only *WHAT* you see but also *WHY* and *HOW*, supporting your interpretation in ways that seem reasonable, persuasive, and satisfying to your readers.

■ Steps to Reading a Story

If possible, make your own copy of the story and read with pen in hand. Prepare to make notes, underline important lines, circle revealing words or images, and put stars, question marks, or your own symbols in the margins.

1. Before you begin the piece, read any *biographical information* that may accompany the story. Knowing information about the author and when the story was written or published may offer some insight. Also, note the *title*. Does it offer intriguing hints about the story's content?

2. Read through the story at least once to clearly acquaint yourself with its *plot*, the series of actions and events that make up the narrative. In other words, what happened and to whom? Is there a conflict of some sort? Is it resolved or is the story left open-ended?

3. Many times you'll see words in a story you don't know. Sometimes you can figure them out from their context, but if you find unknown words that might indeed have a critical bearing on your understanding of a character, for example, look these up now.

4. Jot a few notes describing your initial reactions to the story's main idea(s) or major *theme(s)*. (If it's helpful, think of the story in terms of its "about-ness." What do you as reader think this story is about? Loss of innocence? The bitterness of revenge? The power of sympathy? Tragic lack of communication? The wonder of first love?) In other words, what comments or observations does this story make about the human condition?

5. As you review the story, begin to think about its parts, always asking yourself "why?": Why did the author choose to do it this way? What is gained (or lost) by writing it this way? What does "X" contribute to my understanding of the story? You might begin noting *point of view*—that is, who is narrating this story? Is a character telling this story or is it told by an all-knowing (omniscient) narrator? A narrator who is partially omniscient, seeing into the thoughts of only some characters? If the story is told by a character, is this narrator informed and trustworthy or "unreliable" to some degree because of ignorance, bias, psychological state, age (a young child, for example), or some other factor? What is gained through the story's choice of narration?

6. Is the story's *structure* in chronological order, or does the writer shift time sequences through flashbacks or multiple points of view? Does the story contain foreshadowing, early indications in the plot that signal later developments? Again, think about the author's choices in terms of communicating the story's ideas.

7. Think about the *characters,* their personalities, beliefs, motivations. How do they interact? Do any of them change—refuse or fail to change? Look closely at their descriptions, thoughts, and dialogue. Sometimes names are revealing, too.

8. What is the relationship between the *setting* of the story and its action or characters? Remember that setting can include place, time of year, hour of day or night, weather or climate, terrain, culture, and so on. Settings can create mood and even function symbolically to reveal character or foreshadow a coming event.

9. Look closely at the *language* of the story, paying attention to revealing images, metaphors, and similes (for help identifying these, see pages 316–317). Note any use of *symbols*—persons, places, or things that bear a significant meaning beyond their usual meaning. (For example, in a particular story, a dreary rain might be associated with a loss of hope; a soaring bird might emphasize new possibilities.) Overall, would you characterize the story's *style* as realistic or something else? What is the *tone* of the story? Serious? Humorous? Does irony, the discrepancy between appearance and reality, play a part?

10. After you've looked at these and any other important elements of the reading, review your initial reactions. How would you now describe the main ideas or major themes of this story? How do the parts of the story work together to clarify those themes?

Remember to add your own questions to this list, ones that address your specific story in a meaningful way. To continue improving your reading skills, turn to the "Practicing What You've Learned" exercise on pages 455–462, which offers two stories for your analysis. Before you write an essay of literary analysis, see the guidelines on pages 453–455.

■ Annotated Story

Using the preceding guidelines, a composition student annotated the story that follows. Some of the notes she made on imagery became the basis for her short essay, which appears on pages 444–446. Before you read the story, however, cover the marginal notes with a sheet of paper. Then read the story, making your own notes. Next, uncover the student's notes and reread the story. Compare your reactions to those of the student writer. What new or different insights did you have?

■ The Story of an Hour

Kate Chopin

Kate Chopin was a nineteenth-century American writer whose stories appeared in such magazines as the *Atlantic Monthly, Century,* and the *Saturday Evening Post.* She published two collections of short stories and two novels; one of her novels, *The Awakening* (1899), was considered so shocking in its story of a married woman who desired a life of her own that it was removed from some library shelves. "The *similar theme* Story of an Hour" was first published in 1894.

1   Knowing that Mrs. Mallard was afflicted with a heart trouble, *foreshadowing*
great care was taken to break to her as gently as possible the news
of her husband's death.

2   It was her sister Josephine who told her, in broken sentences,
veiled hints that revealed in half concealing. Her husband's friend
Richards was there, too, near her. It was he who had been in the
newspaper office when intelligence of the railroad disaster was
received, with Brently Mallard's name leading the list of "killed."
He had only taken the time to assure himself of its truth by a second telegram, and had hastened to forestall any less careful, less
tender friend in bearing the sad message.

3   She did not hear the story as many women have heard the same,
with a paralyzed inability to accept its significance. She wept at
once, with sudden, wild abandonment, in her sister's arms. When
the storm of grief had spent itself she went away to her room alone. *storm imagery*
She would have no one follow her.

4   There stood, facing the open window, a comfortable, roomy
armchair. Into this she sank, pressed down by a physical exhaus- *Setting: closed*
tion that haunted her body and seemed to reach into her soul. *room but open*
window

5   She could see in the open square before her house the tops of *—spring*
trees that were all aquiver with the new spring life. The delicious breath *—trees, air*
of rain was in the air. In the street below a peddler was crying his wares. *—songs*
The notes of a distant song which some one was singing reached her *—blue sky*
faintly, and countless sparrows were twittering in the eaves.

6   There were patches of blue sky showing here and there through
the clouds that had met and piled each above the other in the west
facing her window.

7   She sat with her head thrown back upon the cushion of the chair
quite motionless, except when a sob came up into her throat and shook *Mrs M.:*
her, as a child who has cried itself to sleep continues to sob in its dreams. *repression and*
strength

8   She was young, with a fair, calm face, whose lines bespoke repression and even a certain strength. But now there was a dull stare in
her eyes, whose gaze was fixed away off yonder on one of those *3rd person*
patches of blue sky. It was not a glance of reflection, but rather indi- *narrator—*
cated a suspension of intelligent thought. *readers know*
her feelings.

9   There was something coming to her and she was waiting for it,
fearfully. What was it? She did not know; it was too subtle and elusive to name. But she felt it, creeping out of the sky, reaching toward *new insight*
her through the sounds, the scents, the color that filled the air. *from spring sky*

10   Now her bosom rose and fell tumultuously. She was beginning to
recognize this thing that was approaching to possess her, and she
was striving to beat it back with her will—as powerless as her two *conflict within*
white slender hands would have been. *herself*

11   When she abandoned herself a little whispered word escaped
her slightly parted lips. She said it over and over under her breath: **Revelation:*
"Free, free, free!" The vacant stare and the look of terror that had *freedom*

followed it went from her eyes. They stayed keen and bright. Her pulses beat fast, and the coursing blood warmed and relaxed every inch of her body.

images of vitality

12   She did not stop to ask if it were not a monstrous joy that held her. A clear and exalted perception enabled her to dismiss the suggestion as trivial.

13   She knew that she would weep again when she saw the kind, tender hands folded in death; the face that had never looked save with love upon her, fixed and gray and dead. But she saw beyond that bitter moment a long procession of years to come that would belong to her absolutely. And she opened and spread her arms out to them in welcome.

more "open" imagery

14   There would be no one to live for during those coming years; she would live for herself. There would be no powerful will bending her in that blind persistence with which men and women believe they have a right to impose a private will upon a fellow creature. A kind intention or a cruel intention made the act seem no less a crime as she looked upon it in that brief moment of illumination.

**self-assertion, wants to control her own life

15   And yet she had loved him—sometimes. Often she had not. What did it matter! What could love, the unsolved mystery, count for in face of this possession of self-assertion which she suddenly recognized as the strongest impulse of her being.

16   "Free! Body and soul free!" she kept whispering.

17   Josephine was kneeling before the closed door with her lips to the keyhole, imploring for admission. "Louise, open the door! I beg; open the door—you will make yourself ill. What are you doing, Louise? For heaven's sake open the door."

closed door, illness imagery vs "elixir of life" (potion that cures all), open window

18   "Go away. I am not making myself ill." No; she was drinking in a very elixir of life through that open window.

19   Her fancy was running riot along those days ahead of her. Spring days, and summer days, and all sorts of days that would be her own. She breathed a quick prayer that life might be long. It was only yesterday she had thought with a shudder that life might be long.

future: seasons of life, growth

20   She arose at length and opened the door to her sister's importunities. There was a feverish triumph in her eyes, and she carried herself unwittingly like a goddess of Victory. She clasped her sister's waist, and together they descended the stairs. Richards stood waiting for them at the bottom.

victory imagery

21   Some one was opening the front door with a latchkey. It was Brently Mallard who entered, a little travel-stained, composedly carrying his gripsack and umbrella. He had been far from the scene of accident, and did not even know there had been one. He stood amazed at Josephine's piercing cry; at Richards' quick motion to screen him from the view of his wife.

Is he associated with rain?

22   But Richards was too late.

23   When the doctors came they said she had died of heart disease—of joy that kills.

Irony: She may die from a "broken" heart all right, but readers know it's not from joy.

Initial Reactions: Mrs. Mallard is sad about her husband's death, though I'm not sure she really loved him all that much. He wasn't a bad guy—she just wants to be a "free" woman, back when women had few rights, little control over their lives. She dies—of shock? disappointment?—when he turns up alive.

After Rereading: I think Chopin wanted readers to see how confined some 19th-century women felt in their traditional roles. I felt sorry for Mrs. Mallard, whose realization that life will not be hers after all is so traumatic that it kills her.

Open window—lets in spring scenes, color, sounds of new life—symbol of future possibilities. Also, lots of sick-versus-well and life-versus-death imagery.

Question: Why is she named "Mallard"—a duck?

Repose, 1911, by John Singer Sargent, presents a portrait of the artist's niece.

■ Sample Student Essay

After studying Chopin's story, this student writer decided to focus her essay on important imagery in the work, to show how contrasting images of illness and health reveal the main character's changes in attitude. Numbers in parentheses following direct quotations refer to the paragraphs in the story.

A BREATH OF FRESH AIR

Introduction: title and author identified; brief summary of plot and theme

In Kate Chopin's 1894 story "The Story of an Hour" a young wife grieves over news of her husband's accidental death but soon discovers herself elated at the prospect of a life under her own control. The story ends tragically when the husband's sudden reappearance causes her weak heart to fail—not from joy—but from the devastating realization that her newfound freedom is lost. To help readers understand Mrs. Mallard's all-too-brief transformation to a hopeful "free" woman, Chopin contrasts images of illness and lifelessness with positive images of vitality and victory.

Thesis

2   In the first line of the story, Mrs. Mallard is associated with illness because of her "heart trouble" (1). Following a "storm of grief" (3) on hearing of her husband's death, she isolates herself in her room, lifeless and numb behind a closed door. Chopin describes Mrs. Mallard as feeling "pressed down" (4) and "haunted" (4), exhausted in body and soul; she sits "motionless" (7) with a "dull stare" (8), except for an occasional sob. The lines in her strong, fair face "bespoke repression" (8) and indeed Mrs. Mallard is a young woman who, only the day before, hopelessly shuddered to think "that life might be long" (19).

Images of illness and lifelessness, illustrated by lines from the story

3   In direct contrast with these images of lifelessness and emotional repression, Chopin introduces images of rebirth and hope. Mrs. Mallard's room has an open window, which becomes the key symbol

in the description of Mrs. Mallard's transformation. Chopin uses the open window to provide Mrs. Mallard with both a view of new life and with fresh air, paralleling the new hopeful feelings that come to her. Through this "open window" (4) Mrs. Mallard sees beyond her house to an "open square" (5) with "trees that were all aquiver with the new spring life" (5). The repetition of the word "open," the budding trees, and the spring season all emphasize the contrast between the world of possibilities and new life and Mrs. Mallard's enclosed room and enclosed spirit. The air after a life-giving spring rain has a "delicious breath" (5), and both people and birds are now singing. "Patches of blue sky" (6) are symbolically breaking through the clouds, but, as yet, Mrs. Mallard can only stare vacantly at the blue sky rather than respond to it.

Contrasting images of rebirth, supported by examples

4   Soon, however, Mrs. Mallard realizes that something—she's not sure what—is "creeping out of the sky, reaching toward her through the sounds, the scents, the color that filled the air" (9). She resists at first but ultimately allows herself the glorious revelation that she is free to live a new life as she, not others, wants it to be. The imagery associated with this revelation shows Mrs. Mallard becoming energized and healthy, in direct contrast to the imagery of lifelessness that characterized her before. The "vacant stare" (11) is replaced by eyes that are "keen and bright" (11). No longer beaten down, "her pulses beat fast, and the coursing blood warmed and relaxed every inch of her body" (11). In contrast to her previous hopeless view of the future, Mrs. Mallard joyfully thinks of the years ahead and "opened and spread her arms out to them in welcome" (13). This open gesture aligns her with the open window and open square, with their images of rebirth and hope.

Contrasting images of vitality, supported by examples and comparison

5   Chopin emphasizes the transformation even further by contrasting Mrs. Mallard's description to her sister Josephine's image of her.

Contrast
of illness
imagery to
images of
health, victory

Symbolically placed on the opposite side of the closed door from the open window and spring sky, her sister tells Mrs. Mallard that "you will make yourself ill" (17). But the images associated with the transformed Mrs. Mallard are not of illness but of health and victory. Through the open window, she is drinking in a "very elixir of life" (18), a potion that restores the sick to health, as she thinks of spring and summer, seasons of fertility and growth. She finally emerges from her room with "triumph in her eyes" (20), carrying herself "like a goddess of Victory" (20).

6   Mrs. Mallard's victory is cut short, however, as the return of Mr. Mallard destroys her hopes for her future life. The image of illness once again prevails, as doctors wrongly attribute her death to "heart disease—of joy that kills" (23). With this ironic last line echoing the story's first line, Chopin's imagery describing her character comes full circle, from illness to life and back to death, to emphasize for readers the tragedy of Mrs. Mallard's momentary gain and then the crushing defeat of her spiritual triumph.

Conclusion:
Restatement of
thesis showing
purpose of the
imagery

■ Steps to Reading a Poem

Close reading of a poem is similar to reading a story in many ways. Again, try to read with pen in hand so you can take notes, circle important words, and make comments in the margins.

1. Pay attention to any *biographical information* on the author and the date of publication, which may give you insight into the poem. Also note the *title*, as it may introduce the poem's main idea or tone.

2. Read through the poem at least twice. Poetry does differ from prose in that poets often compress or turn sentence structure in unusual ways, to create new images and fit rhyme and rhythm patterns. You might find it helpful to try to paraphrase (put into your own words) the lines of shorter poems (or summarize distinct parts) so that you have a clear understanding of the basic content. If you're lost in several lines, try to locate the subject, the verb, and objects of the action or description. And, always, before you begin to analyze a poem, be sure

you know the meaning of *all* the words. Looking up unfamiliar words is critical here—short poems are compact so every word counts.

3. Some poems are *narratives* and contain a plot; others, often referred to as *lyrics,* capture a scene, a series of images, an emotion, or a thought that has universal appeal. At this point, what action, situation, or ideas do you see presented in this poem? Is there a dominant tone or opinion expressed? Make some notes about your initial reactions to the poem's issues, themes, or ideas. As in fiction, poets often offer comments on the human condition or social values.

4. Now begin to analyze the elements of the poem. Identifying the *speaker* (or narrator) of the poem is a good place to start. Is it someone with recognizable characteristics or personality traits? Someone involved in the action of the poem? Young or old? Male or female? Mother, father, lover, friend? Tone of voice (angry, pleading, sad, joyful, etc.)? Remember that a speaker using "I" is not necessarily the poet but rather a persona or role the poet has assumed. Or is the speaker unidentified as she or he unfolds the poem for the reader? And to whom is the poem addressed? A specific person, a group of people, any readers?

5. What is the *setting* or *occasion* of the poem? Is the place, time, season, climate, or historical context important to understanding the poem? Why or why not?

6. What *characters*, if any, appear in the poem? What is the relationship between the speaker and others in the poem? What values, opinions, and motivations do these characters present? What conflicts or changes occur?

7. Look carefully at the poem's *diction* (choice of words). Most poems contain description and figurative language to create imagery, the vivid pictures that create meaning in the reader's mind. Look for similes and metaphors, as illustrated on page 316 and pages 161–162, that make abstract or unfamiliar images clear through comparisons, as well as personification and synecdoche (pages 316–317). Poets often use patterns or groups of *images* to present a dominant impression and concrete objects as *symbols* to represent abstract ideas within the poem (cold rain as death, a spring flower as rebirth). They also use *allusions,* brief references to other well-known persons, places, things, and literary works that shed light on their subject by association (for example, a reference to Romeo and Juliet might suggest ill-fated lovers). Underline or circle those words and images that you find most effective in communicating ideas or emotions.

8. How is the poem *structured?* There are too many poetic forms to define each one here (ballads, sonnets, odes, villanelles, etc.) so you might consult a more detailed handbook to help you identify the characteristics of each one. However, to help you begin, here is a brief introduction. Some poems are written in patterns called "fixed" or "closed" form. They often appear in stanzas, recognizable units often containing the same number of lines and the same rhyme and rhythm pattern in those lines. They often present one main idea per unit and have a space between each one. Some poems are not divided into stanzas but nevertheless have well-known fixed forms, such as the Shakespearean sonnet, which traditionally challenges the poet to write within fourteen lines, in a predictable line rhythm and rhyme scheme. The modern English version of the Japanese haiku (as illustrated on page 465) calls for three lines and seventeen syllables but no rhyme. Other

poems are written in free verse (or "open" form), with no set line length or regular rhyme pattern; these poems may rely on imagery, line lengths, repetition, and sound devices to maintain unity and show progression of ideas.

Study your poem and try to identify its form. How does its structure help communicate its ideas? Why might have the poet chosen this particular structure?

9. *Sound devices* may help unify a poem, establish tone, emphasize a description, and communicate theme. There are many kinds of rhyme (end, internal, slant, etc.), which often help unify or link ideas and parts of poems. For example, stanzas often have set patterns of end rhyme that pull a unit together; a quatrain (four-line stanza), for example, might rhyme *abab,* as shown here:

    | . . . free, | a |
    | . . . sky, | b |
    | . . . sea, | a |
    | . . . fly. | b |

    Four other common sound devices include:

    - *Alliteration:* repetition of consonant sounds at the beginning of words ("The S̲oul s̲elects her own S̲ociety"), often used to link and emphasize a relationship among words;

    - *Assonance:* repetition of vowel sounds ("ch̲ild br̲ide of t̲ime") to link and underscore a relationship among the words;

    - *Onomatopoeia:* a word whose sound echoes, and thus emphasizes, its meaning (buzz, rustle, hiss, boom, sigh);

    - *Repetition:* repetition of the same words, phrases, or lines for unity, emphasis, or musical effect ("Sing on, spring! Sing on, lovers!").

    Sound devices not only unify poems but also add to their communication of images and meaning. Harsh-sounding, monosyllabic words ("the cold stone tomb") may slow lines and create a tone vastly different from one produced by multisyllabic words with soft, flowing sounds. Poets pick their words carefully for their sounds as well as their connotations and denotations. Ask yourself: What sound devices appear in the poem I'm reading, and why?

10. *Rhythm,* the repetition of stresses and pauses, may also play an important part in the creation of tone and meaning. A poem about a square dance, for example, might echo the content by having a number of quick stresses to imitate the music and the caller's voice. You can discover patterns of rhythm in lines of poetry by marking the accented (′) and unaccented (˅) syllables:

    My mistress' eyes are nothing like the sun

    Many poems demand a prescribed rhythm as part of their fixed form; lines from a Shakespearean sonnet, as illustrated above, contain an often-used pattern called *iambic pentameter:* five units (called *feet*) of an unaccented syllable followed by an accented syllable.

    Another device that contributes to the rhythm of a line is the *caesura,* a heavy pause in a line of poetry. Caesuras (indicated by a ‖ mark) may be used to isolate and thus emphasize words or slow the pace. Sometimes they are used to show strong contrasts, as in the following line: "Before, a joy proposed; ‖ behind, a dream." Caesuras may follow punctuation marks such as commas, semicolons, or periods, marks that say "slow down" to the reader.

After you have looked at the various elements of a poem (and there are many others in addition to the ones mentioned here), reassess your initial reaction. Do you understand the poem in a different or better way? Remember that the elements of an effective poem work together, so be sensitive to the poet's choices of point of view, language, structure, and so on. All these choices help communicate the tone and underscore the ideas of the poem. Ask yourself: What is gained through the poet's choice? What might be different—or lost—if the poet had chosen something else?

To continue working on your close-reading skills, you may turn to the "Practicing What You've Learned" exercise on pages 462–464, which includes two poems for your analysis. Before you begin drafting a discussion of a poem, you may find it helpful to read the general guidelines for writing about literature on pages 453–455.

■ Annotated Poem

Using the suggestions of this chapter, a student responded to the Walt Whitman poem "When I Heard the Learn'd Astronomer" on the next page. The student essay on pages 451–453 presents an analysis developed from some of the notes shown there.

Starry Night, 1889, by Vincent Van Gogh

Digital Image © The Museum of Modern Art/Licensed by Scala/Art Resource, NY

■ When I Heard the Learn'd Astronomer

Educated ⟵

⟵ *someone who studies the stars, sky*

Walt Whitman

⟵ *used here too*

Walt Whitman was a nineteenth-century American poet whose free-verse poems often broke with conventional style and subject matter. Some of his most famous poems, including "Song of Myself," "Crossing Brooklyn Ferry," and "Passage to India," extol the virtues of the common people and stress their unity with a universal spirit. This poem was published in 1865.

⟵ *speaker: "I" in audience*

settings: inside lecture hall {

When I heard the learn'd astronomer;
When the proofs, the figures, were ranged in columns
    before me;
When I was shown the charts and diagrams, to
    add, divide, and measure them;
When I, sitting, heard the astronomer, where he
    lectured with much applause in the lecture-room.

} *scientific images, repetition, long lines, slow pace*

outside at night {

5 How soon, unaccountable, I became tired and sick;
Till rising and gliding out, I wander'd off by myself,
In the mystical moist night-air, and from time to time,
Look'd up in perfect silence at the stars.

} *Contrast to 4 lines above: quicker, smoother sounds; nature imagery; appeals to senses, not brain*

assonance

multiple uses of alliteration

Initial Reaction: The speaker of the poem (a student?) is listening to an astronomer's lecture—lots of facts and figures. He gets tired (bored?) and goes outside and looks at the nice night himself.

After rereading: I see two ways of looking at the sky here, two ways of understanding. You can learn academically and you can use your own senses. I think Whitman prefers the personal experience in this case because the language and images are much more positive in the last lines of the poem when the speaker is looking at nature for himself.

The poem shows the contrast between the two ways by using two stanzas with different styles and tones. Cold vs. warm. Passive vs. active. Facts vs. personal experience.

■ Sample Student Essay

After studying the Whitman poem, the student writer wrote this essay to show how many poetic elements work together to present the main idea. Do you agree with his analysis? Which of his claims seems the most or least persuasive, and why? What different interpretation(s) might you suggest?

TWO WAYS OF KNOWING

1   In the poem "When I Heard the Learn'd Astronomer," nineteenth-century American poet Walt Whitman contrasts two ways people may study the world around them. They can approach the world through lectures and facts, and they can experience nature firsthand through their own senses. Through the use of contrasting structures, imagery, diction, and sound devices in this poem, Whitman expresses a strong preference for personal experience.

Introduction: title, author, brief overview of content

Thesis and essay map

2   The poem's structure clearly presents the contrast between the two ways of experiencing the world, or in this specific case, two ways of studying the heavens. The eight-line, free-verse poem breaks into two stanzas, with the first four lines describing an indoor academic setting, followed by a one-line transition to three concluding lines describing an outdoor night scene. The two parts are unified by a first-person narrator who describes and reacts to both scenes.

Two-part structure

3   In the first four lines the narrator is described as sitting in "a lecture-room" (l. 4) as part of an audience listening to an astronomer's talk. The dominant imagery of lines 2–3 is scientific and mathematical: "proofs," "figures," "charts," and "diagrams" are presented so that the audience "may add, divide, and measure them" (l. 3). The words, mostly nouns, appear without any colorful modifiers; the facts and figures are carefully arranged "in columns" (l. 2) for objective analysis. This approach to learning is clearly logical and systematic.

Stanza 1: Inside lecture hall

4   The structure and word choice of the first four lines of the poem also subtly reveal the narrator's attitude toward the lecture, which he finds dry and boring. To emphasize the narrator's emotional uninvolvement with the material, Whitman presents him passively "sitting" (l. 4), subject of the passive verb "was shown" (l. 3). Lines 2,

3, and 4, which describe the lecture, are much longer than the lines in the second stanza, with many caesuras, commas, and semicolons that slow the rhythm and pace (for example, l. 3: "When I was shown the charts and diagrams, to add, divide, and measure them;"). The slow, heavy pace of the lines, coupled with the four repetitions of the introductory "when" phrases, emphasizes the narrator's view of the lecture as long, drawn out, and repetitious. Even though the rest of the audience seems to appreciate the astronomer, giving him "much applause" (l. 4), the narrator becomes restless, "tired and sick" (l. 5), and leaves the lecture hall.

Slow pace to emphasize attitude

5   In the last three lines of the poem, the language and sound devices change dramatically, creating positive images of serenity, wonder, and beauty. The narrator leaves the hall by "rising and gliding out" (l. 6), a light, floating, almost spirit-like image that connects him with the "mystical" (l. 7) nature of the heavens. Whitman also uses assonance (repetition of the "i" sound) to strengthen the connection between the "rising and gliding" narrator and the "mystical . . . night-air" (l. 7). In the lecture hall, the narrator was bored, passive, and removed from nature, but now he is spiritually part of the experience himself.

Stanza 2: Outside under stars

"mystical" imagery

6   Alone outside in the night, away from the noisy lecture hall, the narrator quietly contemplates the wonder of the sky, using his own senses of sight, touch, and hearing to observe the stars and feel the air. Positive words, such as "mystical" (l. 7) and "perfect" (l. 8), describe the scene, whose beauty is immediately accessible rather than filtered through the astronomer's cold "proofs" and "diagrams." Examples of alliteration tie together flowing images of natural beauty and serenity: "*m*ystical *m*oist night-air" (l. 7), "from *t*ime *t*o *t*ime" (l. 7), "*s*ilence at the *s*tars" (l. 8). Whitman's choice of the soft "m" and "s" sounds here

contrasting diction, flowing lines, smooth sounds

also adds to the pleasing fluid rhythm, which stands in direct, positive contrast to the harsher, choppier sounds ("charts," "add," "divide") and slow, heavy pauses found in the poem's first stanza.

7   Through careful selection and juxtaposition of language, sound, and structure in the two parts of this short poem, Whitman contrasts distinct ways of studying the natural world. One may learn as a student of facts and figures or choose instead to give oneself over to the wonders of the immediate experience itself. Within the context of this poem, it's no contest: first-hand natural experience wins easily over diagrams and lectures. Stars, 1; charts and graphs, 0.

Conclusion: Restatement of thesis and poem's main idea

■ Guidelines for Writing about Literature

Here are some suggestions that will improve any essay of literary analysis:

1. **Select a workable topic.** If the choice of subject matter is yours, you must decide if you will approach a work through discussion of several elements or if you will focus on some specific part of it as it relates to the whole work. You must also select a topic that is interesting and meaningful for your readers. If your topic is too obvious or insignificant, your readers will be bored. In other words, your essay should inform your readers and increase their appreciation of the work.

2. **Present a clear thesis.** Remember that your purpose is to provide new insight to your readers. Consequently, they need to know exactly what you see in the work. Don't just announce your topic ("This poem is about love"); rather, put forth your argumentative thesis clearly and specifically ("Through its repeated use of sewing imagery, the story emphasizes the tragedy of a tailor's wasted potential as an artist"). And don't waltz around vaguely talking about something readers may not have seen the first time through ("At first the warehouse scene doesn't look that important, but after reading it a few times you see that it really does contain some of the meaningful ideas in the story"). Get on with it! cries your impatient reader. Tell me what you see!

3. **Follow literary conventions.** Essays of literary analysis have some customs you should follow, unless instructed otherwise. Always include the full name of the author and the work in your introductory paragraph; the author's last name is fine after that. Titles of short poems and stories are enclosed in quotation marks.

Most literary essays are written in present tense ("the poet presents an image of a withered tree"), from third-person point of view rather than the more informal first-person "I." So that your readers may easily follow your discussion, include a copy of the work or at least indicate publication information describing the location of the work (the name of volume, publisher, date, pages, and so forth).

Within your essay, it's also helpful to include a poem's line number following a direct quotation: "the silent schoolyard" (l. 10). Some instructors also request paragraph or page numbers in essays on fiction.

4. **Organize effectively.** Your method of organization may depend heavily on your subject matter. A poem, for example, might be best discussed by devoting a paragraph to each stanza; on the other hand, another work might profit from a paragraph on imagery, another on point of view, another on setting, and so on. You must decide what arrangement makes the best sense for your readers. Experiment by moving your ideas around in your prewriting outlines and drafts.

5. **Use ample evidence.** Remember that you are, in essence, arguing your interpretation—you are saying to your reader, "Understand this work the way I do." Therefore, it is absolutely essential that you offer your reader convincing evidence, based on reasonable readings of words in the work itself. The acceptance of your views depends on your making yourself clear and convincing. To do so, include plenty of references to the work through direct quotation and paraphrase. Don't assume that your reader sees what you see—or sees it in the way you do. You must *fight* for your interpretation by offering clearly explained readings substantiated with references to the work.

   Unsupported claim: Robert feels sorry for himself throughout the story.

   Claim supported with text: Robert's self-pity is evident throughout the story as he repeatedly thinks to himself, "No one on this earth cares about me" (4) and "There isn't a soul I can turn to" (5).

   Ask yourself as you work through your drafts, am I offering enough clear, specific, convincing evidence here to persuade my reader to accept my reading?

6. **Find a pleasing conclusion.** At the end of your literary analysis, readers should feel they have gained new knowledge or understanding of a work or some important part of it. You might choose to wrap up your discussion with a creative restatement of your reading, its relation to the writer's craft, or even your assessment of the work's significance within the author's larger body of writing. However you conclude, the readers should feel intellectually and emotionally satisfied with your discussion.

Problems to Avoid

Don't assign meanings. By far the most common problem in essays of literary analysis involves interpretation without clear explanation of supporting evidence. Remember that your readers may not see what you see in a particular line or paragraph; in fact, they may see something quite different. The burden is on you to show cause—how you derived your reading and why it is a good one. Don't represent claims as truth even if they ever-so-conveniently fit your thesis: "It is clear that the moon is used here as a symbol of her family's loss." Clear to whom besides you? If it helps, each time you make an interpretative claim, imagine a classmate who immediately says, "Uh, sorry, but I don't get it. Show me how you see that?" Or imagine a hostile reader with a completely different reading who sneers, "Oh yeah, says who? Convince me."

Use quoted material effectively. Many times your supporting evidence will come from quotations from the text you're analyzing. But don't just drop a quoted line onto your page, as if it had just tumbled off a high cliff somewhere. You run the risk of your readers reading the quoted material and still not seeing in it what you do. Blend the quoted material smoothly into your prose, in a way that illustrates or supports your clearly stated point:

> *Dropped in:* Miranda is twenty-four years old. "After working for three years on a morning newspaper she had an illusion of maturity and experience" (280). [What exact point do you want your reader to understand?]

> *Point clarified:* Although Miranda is twenty-four and has worked on a newspaper for three years, she is not as worldly wise as she thinks she is, having acquired only the "illusion of maturity and experience" (280).

Review pages 386–387 for some ways to blend your quotations into your prose. Always double-check to ensure you are quoting accurately; refer to pages 393 and 558–559 for help with proper punctuation and block indention of longer quoted material.

Analysis is not plot summary. Sometimes you may want to offer your readers a brief overview of the work before you begin your in-depth analysis. And certainly there will be times in the body of your essay, especially if you are writing about fiction, that you will need to paraphrase actions or descriptions rather than quote long passages directly. Paraphrasing can indeed provide effective support, but do beware a tendency to fall into unproductive plot-telling. Remember that the purpose of your paper is to provide insight into the work's ideas and craft—not merely to present a rehash of the story line. Keep your eye on each of your claims and quote or paraphrase only those particular lines or important passages that illustrate and support your points. Use your editing pen as a sharp stick to beat back plot summary if it begins taking over your paragraphs.

■ PRACTICING WHAT YOU'VE LEARNED: STORIES

Practice your skills of literary analysis on one or both of the following stories. A few questions about each story are offered here to start your thinking.

"Geraldo No Last Name" is an excerpt from Sandra Cisneros' 1984 novel *The House on Mango Street,* which presents a series of vignettes often told by Esperanza, a young girl growing up in a Latino area of Chicago. In this story, Esperanza's older teenage friend Marin has a chance meeting with Geraldo. How does this story comment on stereotyping and human misunderstanding? Overall, what new insights do you think Cisneros wanted her readers to take away from this brief story, and did she succeed? In what way does Geraldo's having no last name universalize this story?

The second story, Edgar Allan Poe's "The Cask of Amontillado," written in 1846, tells of a very different crime. Pay close attention to the story's point of view: why did Poe choose a first-person narrator? Is Montresor a "reliable" narrator? To whom do you think he is telling this story, and when? What criteria for successful revenge does Montresor explain in paragraph 1? Did he achieve these goals? Note too Poe's ample use of irony and sensory details to create the appropriate mood and setting for this tale.

■ Geraldo No Last Name

Sandra Cisneros

Sandra Cisneros is an award-winning author of poetry, short stories, and novels. Best known for *The House on Mango Street* (1984), from which this story is taken, she has also published a collection of stories, *Woman Hollering Creek* (1991); two books of poetry, *My Wicked, Wicked Ways* (1992) and *Loose Woman* (1994); a children's book, *Hairs/Pelitos* (1997); and her most recent novel, *Caramelo* (2002).

1   She met him at a dance. Pretty too, and young. Said he worked in a restaurant, but she can't remember which one. Geraldo. That's all. Green pants and Saturday shirt. Geraldo. That's what he told her.

2   And how was she to know she'd be the last one to see him alive. An accident, don't you know. Hit and run. Marin, she goes to all those dances. Uptown. Logan. Embassy. Palmer. Aragon. Fontana. The Manor. She likes to dance. She knows how to do cumbias and salsas and rancheras even. And he was just someone she danced with. Somebody she met that night. That's right.

3   That's the story. That's what she said again and again. Once to the hospital people and twice to the police. No address. No name. Nothing in his pockets. Ain't it a shame.

4   Only Marin can't explain why it mattered, the hours and hours, for somebody she didn't even know. The hospital emergency room. Nobody but an intern working all alone. And maybe if the surgeon would've come, maybe if he hadn't lost so much blood, if the surgeon had only come, they would know who to notify and where.

5   But what difference does it make? He wasn't anything to her. He wasn't her boyfriend or anything like that. Just another *brazer** who didn't speak English. Just another wetback. You know the kind. The ones who always look ashamed. And what was she doing out at three a.m. anyway? Marin who was sent home with her coat and some aspirin. How does she explain?

6   She met him at a dance. Geraldo in his shiny shirt and green pants. Geraldo going to a dance.

7   What does it matter?

8   They never saw the kitchenettes. They never knew about the two-room flats and sleeping rooms he rented, the weekly money orders sent home, the currency exchange. How could they?

*Slang for migrant worker.

9   His name was Geraldo. And his home is in another country. The ones he left behind are far away, will wonder, shrug, remember. Geraldo—he went north . . . we never heard from him again.

■ The Cask of Amontillado

Edgar Allan Poe

Edgar Allan Poe is best known for shaping the genres of psychological horror tales and detective fiction, but he is also recognized for his romantic poems and his literary criticism. Born in 1806, Poe often quarreled with his adoptive parents; he attended West Point but was discharged for disobedience. Depressed from poverty and his young wife's death, Poe died in 1849 under mysterious circumstances. Other well-known stories include "The Fall of the House of Usher" and "The Murders in the Rue Morgue."

1   The thousand injuries of Fortunato I had borne as I best could, but when he ventured upon insult I vowed revenge. You, who so well know the nature of my soul, will not suppose, however, that I gave utterance to a threat. *At length* I would be avenged; this was a point definitely settled—but the very definitiveness with which it was resolved precluded the idea of risk. I must not only punish but punish with impunity. A wrong is unredressed when retribution overtakes its redresser. It is equally unredressed when the avenger fails to make himself felt as such to him who has done the wrong.

2   It must be understood that neither by word nor deed had I given Fortunato cause to doubt my good will. I continued, as was my wont, to smile in his face, and he did not perceive that my smile *now* was at the thought of his immolation.

3   He had a weak point—this Fortunato—although in other regards he was a man to be respected and even feared. He prided himself on his connoisseurship in wine. Few Italians have the true virtuoso spirit. For the most part their enthusiasm is adopted to suit the time and opportunity, to practise imposture upon the British and Austrian *millionaires*. In painting and gemmary, Fortunato, like his countrymen, was a quack, but in the matter of old wines he was sincere. In this respect I did not differ from him materially;—I was skillful in the Italian vintages myself, and bought largely whenever I could.

4   It was about dusk, one evening during the supreme madness of the carnival season, that I encountered my friend. He accosted me with excessive warmth, for he had been drinking much. The man wore motley.[1] He had on a tight-fitting parti-striped dress, and his head was surmounted by the conical cap and bells. I was so pleased to see him that I thought I should never have done wringing his hand.

5   I said to him—"My dear Fortunato, you are luckily met. How remarkably well you are looking to-day. But I have received a pipe[2] of what passes for Amontillado,[3] and I have my doubts."

---

[1] The multicolored clothes of a court jester.

[2] A cask.

[3] A Spanish sherry.

6   "How?" said he. "Amontillado? A pipe? Impossible! And in the middle of the carnival!"

7   "I have my doubts," I replied; "and I was silly enough to pay the full Amontillado price without consulting you in the matter. You were not to be found, and I was fearful of losing a bargain."

8   "Amontillado!"

9   "I have my doubts."

10   "Amontillado!"

11   "And I must satisfy them."

12   "Amontillado!"

13   "As you are engaged, I am on my way to Luchresi. If any one has a critical turn it is he. He will tell me—"

14   "Luchresi cannot tell Amontillado from Sherry."

15   "And yet some fools will have it that his taste is a match for your own."

16   "Come, let us go."

17   "Whither?"

18   "To your vaults."

19   "My friend, no; I will not impose upon your good nature. I perceive you have an engagement. Luchresi—"

20   "I have no engagement;—come."

21   "My friend, no. It is not the engagement, but the severe cold with which I perceive you are afflicted. The vaults are insufferably damp. They are encrusted with nitre."

22   "Let us go, nevertheless. The cold is merely nothing. Amontillado! You have been imposed upon. And as for Luchresi, he cannot distinguish Sherry from Amontillado."

23   Thus speaking, Fortunato possessed himself of my arm; and putting on a mask of black silk and drawing a *roquelaire*[4] closely about my person, I suffered him to hurry me to my palazzo.

24   There were no attendants at home; they had absconded to make merry in honor of the time. I had told them that I should not return until the morning, and had given them explicit orders not to stir from the house. These orders were sufficient, I well knew, to insure their immediate disappearance, one and all, as soon as my back was turned.

25   I took from their sconces two flambeaux, and giving one to Fortunato, bowed him through several suites of rooms to the archway that led into the vaults. I passed down a long and winding staircase, requesting him to be cautious as he followed. We came at length to the foot of the descent, and stood together upon the damp ground of the catacombs of the Montresors.

26   The gait of my friend was unsteady, and the bells upon his cap jingled as he strode.

27   "The pipe," he said.

28   "It is farther on," said I; "but observe the white web-work which gleams from these cavern walls."

---

[4] A cloak.

29   He turned towards me, and looked into my eyes with two filmy orbs that distilled the rheum of intoxication.

30   "Nitre?" he asked at length.

31   "Nitre," I replied. "How long have you had that cough?"

32   "Ugh! ugh! ugh!—ugh! ugh! ugh!—ugh! ugh! ugh!—ugh! ugh! ugh!—ugh! ugh! ugh!"

33   My poor friend found it impossible to reply for many minutes.

34   "It is nothing," he said at last.

35   "Come," I said, with decision, "we will go back; your health is precious. You are rich, respected, admired, beloved; you are happy, as once I was. You are a man to be missed. For me it is no matter. We will go back; you will be ill, and I cannot be responsible. Besides, there is Luchresi—"

36   "Enough," he said; "the cough is a mere nothing; it will not kill me. I shall not die of a cough."

37   "True—true," I replied; "and, indeed, I had no intention of alarming you unnecessarily—but you should use all proper caution. A draught of this Medoc[5] will defend us from the damps."

38   Here I knocked off the neck of a bottle which I drew from a long row of its fellows that lay upon the mould.

39   "Drink," I said, presenting him with wine.

40   He raised it to his lips with a leer. He paused and nodded to me familiarly, while his bells jingled.

41   "I drink," he said, "to the buried that repose around us."

42   "And I to your long life."

43   He again took my arm, and we proceeded.

44   "These vaults," he said, "are extensive."

45   "The Montresors," I replied, "were a great and numerous family."

46   "I forget your arms."

47   "A huge human foot d'or,[6] in a field azure; the foot crushes a serpent rampant whose fangs are imbedded in the heel."

48   "And the motto?"

49   *"Nemo me impune lacessit."*[7]

50   "Good!" he said.

51   The wine sparkled in his eyes and the bells jingled. My own fancy grew warm with the Medoc. We had passed through long walls of piled skeletons, with casks and puncheons[8] intermingling, into the inmost recesses of the catacombs. I paused again, and this time I made bold to seize Fortunato by an arm above the elbow.

52   "The nitre!" I said; "see, it increases. It hangs like moss upon the vaults. We are below the river's bed. The drops of moisture trickle among the bones. Come, we will go back ere it is too late. Your cough—"

53   "It is nothing," he said; "let us go on. But first, another draught of the Medoc."

---

[5] A French wine.

[6] Of gold.

[7] No one attacks me without punishment.

[8] Barrels.

54   I broke and reached him a flagon of De Grâve.[9] He emptied it at a breath. His eyes flashed with a fierce light. He laughed and threw the bottle upwards with a gesticulation I did not understand.

55   I looked at him in surprise. He repeated the movement—a grotesque one.

56   "You do not comprehend?" he said.

57   "Not I," I replied.

58   "Then you are not of the brotherhood."

59   "How?"

60   "You are not of the masons."[10]

61   "Yes, yes," I said; "yes, yes."

62   "You? Impossible! A mason?"

63   "A mason," I replied.

64   "A sign," he said, "a sign."

65   "It is this," I answered, producing from beneath the folds of my *roquelaire* a trowel.[11]

66   "You jest," he exclaimed, recoiling a few paces. "But let us proceed to the Amontillado."

67   "Be it so," I said, replacing the tool beneath the cloak and again offering him my arm. He leaned upon it heavily. We continued our route in search of the Amontillado. We passed through a range of low arches, descended, passed on, and descending again, arrived at a deep crypt, in which the foulness of the air caused our flambeaux[12] rather to glow than flame.

68   At the most remote end of the crypt there appeared another less spacious. Its walls had been lined with human remains, piled to the vault overhead, in the fashion of the great catacombs of Paris. Three sides of this interior crypt were still ornamented in this manner. From the fourth side the bones had been thrown down, and lay promiscuously upon the earth, forming at one point a mound of some size. Within the wall thus exposed by the displacing of the bones, we perceived a still interior crypt or recess, in depth about four feet, in width three, in height six or seven. It seemed to have been constructed for no especial use within itself, but formed merely the interval between two of the colossal supports of the roof of the catacombs, and was backed by one of their circumscribing walls of solid granite.

69   It was in vain that Fortunato, uplifting his dull torch, endeavored to pry into the depth of the recess. Its termination the feeble light did not enable us to see.

70   "Proceed," I said; "herein is the Amontillado. As for Luchresi—"

71   "He is an ignoramus," interrupted my friend, as he stepped unsteadily forward, while I followed immediately at his heels. In an instant he had reached the extremity of the niche, and finding his progress arrested by the rock, stood

---

[9] A bottle of French wine.

[10] Freemasonry is a centuries-old fraternal organization with secret rituals; the society uses stonemasonry tools as metaphors to convey its philosophy.

[11] A flat-bladed hand tool, such as a stonemason might use to apply cement or mortar.

[12] Torches.

stupidly bewildered. A moment more and I had fettered him to the granite. In its surface were two iron staples, distant from each other about two feet, horizontally. From one of these depended a short chain, from the other a padlock. Throwing the links about his waist, it was but the work of a few seconds to secure it. He was too much astounded to resist. Withdrawing the key I stepped back from the recess.

72   "Pass your hand," I said, "over the wall; you cannot help feeling the nitre. Indeed, it is *very* damp. Once more let me *implore* you to return. No? Then I must positively leave you. But I must first render you all the little attentions in my power."

73   "The Amontillado!" ejaculated my friend, not yet recovered from his astonishment.

74   "True," I replied; "the Amontillado."

75   As I said these words I busied myself among the pile of bones of which I have before spoken. Throwing them aside, I soon uncovered a quantity of building stone and mortar. With these materials and with the aid of my trowel, I began vigorously to wall up the entrance of the niche.

76   I had scarcely laid the first tier of the masonry when I discovered that the intoxication of Fortunato had in a great measure worn off. The earliest indication I had of this was a low moaning cry from the depth of the recess. It was *not* the cry of a drunken man. There was a long and obstinate silence. I laid the second tier, and the third, and the fourth; and then I heard the furious vibrations of the chain. The noise lasted for several minutes, during which, that I might hearken to it with the more satisfaction, I ceased my labors and sat down upon the bones. When at last the clanking subsided, I resumed the trowel, and finished without interruption the fifth, the sixth, and the seventh tier. The wall was now nearly upon a level with my breast. I again paused, and holding the flambeaux over the mason-work, threw a few feeble rays upon the figure within.

77   A succession of loud and shrill screams, bursting suddenly from the throat of the chained form, seemed to thrust me violently back. For a brief moment I hesitated, I trembled. Unsheathing my rapier, I began to grope with it about the recess; but the thought of an instant reassured me. I placed my hand upon the solid fabric of the catacombs, and felt satisfied. I reapproached the wall; I replied to the yells of him who clamoured. I re-echoed, I aided, I surpassed them in volume and in strength. I did this, and the clamourer grew still.

78   It was now midnight, and my task was drawing to a close. I had completed the eighth, the ninth and the tenth tier. I had finished a portion of the last and the eleventh; there remained but a single stone to be fitted and plastered in. I struggled with its weight; I placed it partially in its destined position. But now there came from out the niche a low laugh that erected the hairs upon my head. It was succeeded by a sad voice, which I had difficulty in recognizing as that of the noble Fortunato. The voice said—

79   "Ha! ha! ha!—he! he! he!—a very good joke, indeed—an excellent jest. We will have many a rich laugh about it at the palazzo—he! he! he!—over our wine—he! he! he!"

80   "The Amontillado!" I said.

81   "He! he! he!—he! he! he!—yes, the Amontillado. But is it not getting late? Will not they be awaiting us at the palazzo, the Lady Fortunato and the rest? Let us be gone."

82   "Yes," I said, "let us be gone."

83   *"For the love of God, Montresor!"*

84   "Yes," I said, "for the love of God."

85   But to these words I hearkened in vain for a reply. I grew impatient. I called aloud—

86   "Fortunato!"

87   No answer. I called again—

88   "Fortunato!"

89   No answer still. I thrust a torch through the remaining aperture and let it fall within. There came forth in return only a jingling of the bells. My heart grew sick; it was the dampness of the catacombs that made it so. I hastened to make an end of my labour. I forced the last stone into its position; I plastered it up. Against the new masonry I re-erected the old rampart of bones. For the half of a century no mortal has disturbed them. *In pace requiescat!*[13]

---

[13] May he rest in peace.

■ PRACTICING WHAT YOU'VE LEARNED: POETRY

Practice your skills of literary analysis on one or both of the following poems. A few suggestions are presented here to help you begin your reading.

Consider the point of view in both "Those Winter Sundays" by Robert Hayden and "The Road Not Taken" by Robert Frost. Who is speaking in each poem? How old might each speaker be? What actions are described in each poem? What new insight does each person have? What descriptive words and word-sounds help Hayden present vivid images? How might a reader see Frost's "diverging roads" as a metaphor?

■ Those Winter Sundays

Robert Hayden

Robert Hayden was a poet and professor at Fisk University and at the University of Michigan; he also served as Poetry Consultant to the Library of Congress. *A Ballad of Remembrance* (1962) first won him international honors at the World Festival of Negro Arts in Senegal; many other volumes of poetry followed, including *Words in Mourning Time* (1970), *American Journal* (1978), and *Complete Poems* (1985). This poem originally appeared in *Angle of Ascent, New and Selected Poems* (1975).

Sundays too my father got up early
and put his clothes on in the blueblack cold,
then with cracked hands that ached
from labor in the weekday weather made
5 banked fires blaze. No one ever thanked him.

I'd wake and hear the cold splintering, breaking,
When the rooms were warm, he'd call,
and slowly I would rise and dress,
fearing the chronic angers of that house,

10 Speaking indifferently to him,
who had driven out the cold
and polished my good shoes as well.
What did I know, what did I know
of love's austere and lonely offices?

■ The Road Not Taken

Robert Frost

Robert Frost was a twentieth-century poet whose poems frequently focus on the characters and scenes of New England. Three of his many volumes of poetry won Pulitzer Prizes: *New Hampshire* (1923), *Collected Poems* (1930), and *A Further Range* (1936). Frost taught at Amherst College, Dartmouth, Yale, and Harvard and was one of the founders of the Bread Loaf School of English in Vermont. This poem was first published in 1916.

Two roads diverged in a yellow wood,
And sorry I could not travel both
And be one traveler, long I stood
And looked down one as far as I could
5 To where it bent in the undergrowth;

Then took the other, as just as fair,
And having perhaps the better claim,
Because is was grassy and wanted wear;
Though as for that the passing there
10 Had worn them really about the same,

And both that morning equally lay
In leaves no step had trodden black.
Oh, I kept the first for another day!
Yet knowing how way leads on to way,
15 I doubted if I should ever come back.

I shall be telling this with a sigh
Somewhere ages and ages hence:
Two roads diverged in a wood, and I—
I took the one less traveled by,
20   And that has made all the difference.

■ Suggestions for Writing

The three stories and three poems in this chapter may be used as stepping-stones to your own essays. Here are a variety of suggestions:

1. Write an essay of literary analysis presenting your interpretation of "Geraldo No Last Name," "The Cask of Amontillado," "Those Winter Sundays," or "The Road Not Taken." Support your analysis with ample references to the work you've chosen. Consider, if appropriate, discussion of such elements as point of view, characterization, narrative structure, imagery and diction, among other features.

2. Choose one of the three stories reprinted in this chapter, and write an in-depth analysis showing how one significant part of the story effectively contributes to the reader's understanding and enjoyment. The student essay on pages 444–446, for example, focused on the series of life-death images in "The Story of an Hour." You might consider writing about Poe's creation of his story's setting, the ways Cisneros shifts point of view, or the function of minor characters in the Chopin story. Find a topic that you think illuminates the writer's artistry.

3. Write an essay comparing/contrasting themes and techniques in two of the literary works from this chapter. For example, how do Hayden and Frost use the past in their poems? How do Cisneros and Poe treat the concept of guilt? How are stereotypical roles examined in Chopin's and Cisneros' stories?

4. Use one of the works in this chapter as a "prompt" for your own personal essay. For example, have you ever taken people for granted or devalued their help, as did the narrator in the Hayden poem? Perhaps the Whitman poem reminded you of a time when you learned something through hands-on experience rather than study? Or perhaps the opposite was true: you didn't fully appreciate an experience until you had studied it? Or, if you prefer, use Cisneros' story "Geraldo No Last Name" to start you thinking about a research essay on some specific aspect of the complex immigration situations facing nations today.

5. Writing your own short poem may help you better understand the power and beauty of figurative language. For starters, you might try mastering the modern version of the Japanese *haiku*, an unrhymed poem of only seventeen syllables, divided into three lines of five, seven, and five syllables each. This form challenges the writer to paint a single strong image in the reader's mind.

Here's an example, a prize-winning haiku written by Northern Colorado poet Jane Wheeler, first published by the Poetry in Motion project in 2000. What figure of speech creates the central image?

Haiku: Colorado Nightfall
The gypsy sunset
Sky dances in her fire silks,
Then hides in darkness.

(Hint: If you're stuck for a subject for your haiku, try creating an image that captures the essence of a character appearing in one of the stories or poems in this chapter. Or, if you prefer, create a haiku in response to one of the pictures in this text; a list of artworks follows the table of contents.)

■ Some Last Thoughts about Literature

Here are some thought-provoking observations on reading and writing literature from four very different authors. Have you ever read a book, story, or poem that validated any of these comments for you?

"One reads books in order to gain the privilege of living more than one life. People who don't read are trapped in a mineshaft, even if they think the sun is shining." —Garrison Keillor, contemporary American novelist and story-teller

"A book [is] the axe for the frozen sea inside us." —Franz Kafka, twentieth-century German novelist and short story writer

"Literature doesn't have a country. Shakespeare is an African writer. . . . Dickens' characters are Nigerians. . . . Literature may come from a specific place, but it always lives in its own kingdom." —Ben Okri, contemporary Nigerian poet and novelist

"Occasionally the [Mississippi] river floods . . . but in fact it is not flooding; it is remembering. . . . All water has a perfect memory and is forever trying to get back to where it was. Writers are like that: remembering where we were, what valley we ran through, what the banks were like, the light that was there and the route back to our original place." —Toni Morrison, contemporary American novelist and winner of the Nobel Prize for Literature

Chapter 17

Writing about Visual Arts

Today, more than at any time in the history of the world, we live in a visual culture. On a daily basis we receive information and messages from images on television, on the Internet, in magazines and newspapers, in movies, in galleries, and in advertisements, just to name a few sources. Artistic visual images may enrich our lives by bringing beauty, retrieving memories, posing questions, stirring action, or offering new ideas that awaken our minds to different possibilities.

Learning to analyze visual art is an important skill; understanding how and why images affect us in specific ways helps us evaluate the messages we are being given and our reactions to them. Writing about art is an excellent way to practice careful observation, analytical thinking, and the ability to organize and clearly communicate ideas.

Close scrutiny of visual images is generally a pleasant activity; for example, most of us enjoy looking at the photographs we've taken, the art we hang on our walls, and even the computer desktop wallpaper we've selected. Although there are many kinds of visual arts, this chapter will focus primarily on the analysis of paintings, with additional brief advice about responding to sculpture and photography. Chapter 18 is entirely devoted to writing about film.

To practice applying the advice outlined here, you may find it helpful to look at some of the many artworks reprinted in this and other chapters in this text; a list of paintings and photographs may be found following the table of contents.

Using Visual Arts in the Composition Classroom

Because writing about art is such a good way to practice valuable thinking and writing skills, composition teachers often assign one of the following kinds of essays:

1. *A personal response:* You might be assigned a discussion of a particular picture or be asked to select one of your choice. Your thesis would be your interpretation of the picture, its dominant impression on you as a viewer, and then your essay would offer examples and details from both the picture and your personal associations to explain why you have that response.

2. *A formal analysis:* This kind of essay is similar to the preceding one in that you will state an interpretation, but in this case you will offer support for your view by analyzing, in more detail, various components of the picture, such as point of view, subject matter, shapes, colors, textures, etc., showing the ways these elements effectively work together to create an overall impression, just as parts of a poem work together.

Some formal analyses may incorporate research material to add relevant information about the artist's life or the painting's style. Some essays may include commentary from art critics to support claims; at other times teachers will prefer that students offer only their own interpretations and evidence.

3. *Strategy practice:* To practice your descriptive writing skills, you might be asked to recreate a picture in words for someone who has never seen it. Or you might practice the strategy of comparison/contrast by showing the similarities and/or differences between two works of art: two paintings by different artists, two by the same artist in a different period or style, a painting and a photograph with a similar theme, and so on. In almost any essay that offers an interpretation, you will be practicing the expository strategies of causal analysis (showing how the work affects the viewer) and exemplification (citing supporting details from the work). Offering a bold new or unusual interpretation of a work may allow you to practice your argumentative writing skills, as you persuade readers that previous interpretations are off the mark.

4. *Prompted response:* On some occasions, writing teachers will use visual arts to help writers find their own essay topics. A landscape painting might trigger memories of a special place or trip; a newspaper photograph might inspire research into a current event. Visual images may encourage some writers to write, just as literary prompts may jumpstart others.

Writing about the visual arts is of course not limited to the four kinds of essays described here, and the kinds of essay assignments in composition classes will certainly vary or overlap depending on purpose, audience, subject matter, and scope. All essays focused on visual images will allow you to practice useful thinking and writing skills.

Suggestions for Analyzing Paintings

Critics today continue to debate the existence of "meaning" in art: does it lie solely within the artwork itself? Only in the subjective eyes of the viewer? In the opinion of the artist? Does the concept of "meaning" in art even exist at all? Still others who think and write about art try to find a middle ground, believing that a sensible, enjoyable discussion of a work of art may draw on many factors, including the components of the work, its dominant impression, the response of the viewer, and various kinds of background information about the work, artist, or style.

Depending on the purpose of your assignment, you may find some of a the following suggestions helpful in an analysis of a painting.

1. **Prepare for your viewing.** If you are analyzing an artwork in a museum or gallery, be sure to take a pen and paper for your notes. You may find it helpful to have a picture to take home with you for later reference as you write: some museums may offer inexpensive postcards or pictures of the artwork; some exhibition locations allow photography but others don't (or prohibit flash photography), so be sure to ask first. Copies of well-known paintings may be found in your library's art books or online; this text also offers a number of interesting paintings if the selection of art is up to you.

2. **Note your first impressions.** What are your feelings at first seeing this artwork? Pleasure? Shock? Anger? Laughter? Sadness? Something else or some combination? Are you attracted or repelled? Why? What associations or memories come to you as you see this piece of art? Make some notes about your personal responses.

3. **Record basic information.** What is the name of the painting? Who is the artist? When and where was it created? Was it created for a particular purpose (to celebrate or protest a specific event, for example) or perhaps commissioned (ordered or paid for) by a specific person or group? Of what medium (oil, watercolors, inks, chalk, etc.) is the painting composed? (If your painting is in a museum or gallery, some of this information may appear on a card next to the painting.) Note too if the painting is identified with a particular style of painting, such as Impressionism or Cubism.

4. **Study the subject matter.** Put simply, what is in the picture? People, places, animals, objects, designs? Is there some action captured or is it a picture of a fixed subject? An abstract confluence of shapes and colors?

To help you begin your analysis, see if your painting falls into one of the general categories described in the following pages. Please note, however, that although these categories are common, they are by no means exhaustive.

- *A scene with one or more figures:* Who is in the picture, and what action or activity is taking place? What is the setting (place, year, season, time of day, weather, etc.)? If there are multiple people in the scene, is there a primary character? What is the relationship of the people to each other, and why do you think so? How would you describe the relationship of the viewer to the figure(s) in this picture? For example, is the viewer close to the people or action or is the viewer looking at the scene from a distance? Are the people looking directly at the viewer or away? Is any figure used as a symbol of an abstract concept (liberty, love, youth, etc.)?

  Allow your answers to the preceding questions (and others) to help shape your dominant impression of, and reaction to, the painting you are studying. Consider, for example, the painting *Nighthawks*, by Edward Hopper, on page 482. A student responding to this painting of a late-night diner felt it captured the loneliness people often feel in their lives. The shadowy empty streets, the solitary faceless man at the counter, and the distance from the viewer to the diner are three of several factors contributing to this impression. (For more notes on this painting and a sample student essay developed from those notes, see pages 483 and 484–485.)

Artists may paint scenes of ordinary human life (such as *Nighthawks* or Jacob Lawrence's *The Library*, page 51), or they may choose more turbulent action scenes (such as John S. Curry's *Tornado Over Kansas*, page 336). In addition, artists have frequently painted historical events as they saw or imagined them. For example, in the age before photography, Napoleon paid artist Jacques-Louis David to paint his and Empress Josephine's coronation (when Napoleon's mother couldn't attend the event, David obliged Napoleon by painting her into the scene anyway). In *The Raft of the Medusa*, Theodore Gericault transformed the news story of an 1816 shipwreck into a visual image, showing the wretchedness of survivors adrift at sea. Throughout the ages, many artworks have made clear social or political statements. J. M. W. Turner's *The Slave Ship*, painted in 1840, criticized the English slave trade; Francisco Goya's painting *The Third of May, 1808* (below) focused attention on executions in Spain. Still other paintings present scenes from well-known myths (the birth of Venus), literature (death of Ophelia from *Hamlet*), or cultural or religious events (the crucifixion of Jesus). A little research may help

© Scala / Art Resource, NY

The Third of May, 1808, painted by Francisco Goya in 1814, recorded the mass executions of Spanish civilians who had rebelled against the occupation of Napoleon's French troops; the painting has been called the first modern image of war.

you better understand paintings with historical, political, or literary subject matter.

- *A portrait:* Rather than a broader scene, your painting might be a closer, more focused representation of a particular person.* Is the person well known (e.g., a portrait of George Washington) or specifically identified by name or relationship to the artist (the painter's mother)? Perhaps the artist chose to paint a portrait of someone representing a universal human type (an innocent child, for example). Remember, too, that artists also frequently paint self-portraits, often at different times in their lives. Portraits capture not only faces but also personalities and attitudes; such paintings may also present commentary on the status and values of their subjects, as well as the time and culture in which they live.

  As you study a portrait, note your reaction to the person and consider the following questions: when, where, and for what purpose was this picture painted? Is the subject identified or unidentified? What does the person's facial expression and posture say to you—that is, do the facial features and angle of the body imply power, superiority, gentleness, aloofness, boredom, innocence, or something else? What sort of clothing or accessories (jewelry or hat, for example) characterize this person and his or her social class? Note too both the immediate setting and the background of the portrait. Painters often include objects that offer insight into their subject: books, dogs, and food surrounding a figure in a richly furnished room might reveal a wealthy eighteenth-century landowner with leisure time. Consider too the size of the person within the frame and the direction of the figure's gaze (straight at you or away?), both of which may affect your feelings toward the subject.

  At this point if you wish to practice this advice, turn to *Repose,* a 1911 portrait of his niece by John Singer Sargent, reprinted on page 443 of this text. What is your impression of this woman and her status in life, and how do her expression, posture, clothes, and other details in the portrait communicate that impression? What is the effect of the artist's decision to make her dress occupy so much of the picture?

- *A landscape:* Paintings of nature and other outdoor scenes are generally called "landscapes," even though their specific subject matter varies widely from woods to meadows, mountains, rivers, roads, fields of crops, villages, clouds and sky, and so on. Landscapes may also contain people, animals, and buildings, though these are sometimes included to give the viewer a sense of proportion, emphasizing the majesty or vastness of Nature (a small figure by a tall waterfall, for example).

  If the painting you are analyzing may be considered a landscape, explore the artist's interpretation of this view. Is the scene tranquil and inviting or

---

*A portrait may also contain more than one figure; artists often paint couples, children, entire families, small groups of workers or officials, etc. If there are multiple people in the portrait you are analyzing, take into consideration the connection of the people to each other. Is there, for example, an obvious power relationship captured in the picture?

dark and foreboding? Does it emphasize the calming powers of nature or capture its raw power? Its mystery, its grandeur, or something else? Does the artist seem to invite the viewer to simply enjoy a beautiful natural experience or is there a feeling of paradise lost? Is anything in the picture used symbolically, such as a crossroad or storm? If there are people in the picture, what is their purpose? To show proportion or to illustrate a reaction to the scene? Do the people or buildings emphasize a contrast—perhaps between town and county, civilization and the natural world?

For examples of outdoor scenes, in both painting and photography, look at Caspar David Friedrich's *Early Snow* (page 45), Claude Monet's *The Water-Lily Pond* (page 322), Vincent Van Gogh's *Starry Night* (page 449), and Ansel Adams' *Moonrise, Hernandez, New Mexico* (page 478). How would you describe the mood or dominant effect of each of these works?

■ *A still life:* A painting that closely focuses on objects assembled in a domestic setting, frequently on a table or desk, is called a still life. These paintings often picture food (such as fruits and vegetables), flowers, dishes, glasses, pitchers, silverware, and even the bodies of game animals, such as pheasants or rabbits, that might be incorporated into a meal. Other still lifes* show books, manuscripts, and writing utensils. Some scenes include watches, burned-out candles, overturned glasses, or even a skull to symbolically emphasize the brevity of life or the folly of human vanity. Other pictures are less elaborate, focusing simply on a vase of flowers or bowl of fruit.

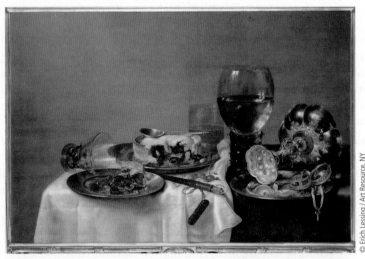

Painted in 1631, *Breakfast Table with Bramble Pie*, by Willem Claesz Heda, is a typical seventeenth-century still life, including both food and elegant tableware, but also a watch and an overturned goblet to remind viewers of the passage of time in the material world.

© Erich Lessing / Art Resource, NY

---

* It may sound odd, but the plural of "still life" is "still lifes," not "still lives."

As you study a still life, identify the common bond of the items in the picture. What is the setting? Is it an orderly or chaotic scene? Are the items elaborate or simple? Still lifes were enormously popular in the seventeenth century, especially among Dutch painters, who often pictured in realistic detail dinner tables overflowing with food to emphasize the rich, varied quality of life. Other table scenes may praise rustic life or emphasize the natural beauty of common objects. In some cases, bread and wine may be used symbolically as religious symbols. As you analyze a still life, don't forget to take note of any background details, including any domestic animals included in the scene.

In 1917 Russian painter Liubov Popova combined colors and geometrical shapes in *Painterly Architectonic,* one of her nonrepresentational works influenced by the Cubist Movement.

The Museum of Modern Art, New York, NY

- *Nonrepresentational art:* Many paintings contain subject matter (people, places, and things) that are easily recognized: a red barn looks like a red barn. Other paintings, sometimes referred to as nonrepresentational or nonobjective art, offer viewers interesting relationships of shapes, colors, and textures rather than realistic pictures of identifiable elements. *Painterly Architectonic* (shown here) by Liubov Popova illustrates this style. The appeal of such a painting relies heavily on the viewer's emotional response to its design. Jackson Pollock's canvases of paint applied in drips and spiraling strings of color and Piet Mondrian's black lines and colored squares are other well-known examples of nonrepresentational art.

Remember that not all paintings fall neatly into the categories described in the last few pages. Even these broad categories may overlap and have multiple variations; for instance, seascapes and city-scapes are first-cousins of landscapes. Despite the artificiality of any such categories, a clear understanding of your painting's subject matter is important before you move on to close study of composition and style.

5. A SPECIAL NOTE: Beyond realism. Suppose for a moment that you have selected a painting to analyze that does indeed present a landscape—but wait, you're thinking, this is no place you—or anyone else—have ever visited. Yes, there's a sea and a cliff in the background, but the foreground is full of strange melting watch faces, and there's a large other-worldly blob-creature lying there too. What kind of landscape is this?

Although all paintings, rendered through each individual artist's eye, are subjective to a degree, some artists move farther away from "realism" than others. Abstract painters, for instance, often forgo realism in an attempt to extract (or "abstract") the essence of the thing they are painting. Pablo Picasso, for example,

Salvador Dali's famous surreal landscape, *The Persistence of Memory* (1931)

painted *The Crying Woman,* easily recognized as a female figure but composed of sharp jagged angles that emphasize her shattered emotions. Other painters known as Surrealists often use highly symbolic objects and strange dreamlike images to create pictures of psychological states or subconscious feelings. This group includes Salvador Dali, whose well-known landscape of melting watches described previously and shown above is called *The Persistence of Memory,* a painting in which Dali said he was trying to "materialize" internal reality (memory) and abstract concepts (passage of time). Painted in 1939, *The Two Fridas* (page 475) is a double self-portrait by artist Frida Kahlo, with exposed heart lines, both connected and severed, communicating multiple identities and loyalties. Using a different symbolic style, Expressionist painter Edvard Munch makes feelings of anguish visible in *The Scream* (page 113).

If you have selected a nonrealistic or highly symbolic painting to analyze, enjoy explaining its unique purpose and style to your readers. (For two other examples of nonrealistic art, see Marc Chagall's *Birthday* on page 320 and Giuseppe Arcimboldo's *The Librarian* on page 178.)

6. Analyze the painting's composition and design. Artists use a variety of materials and techniques to create each work, depending on the painting's subject matter,

The Two Fridas (1939) presents a double self-portrait by Frida Kahlo. Dressed in traditional Tehuana clothing, the Frida on the right holds a small picture of Diego Rivera, the well-known painter from whom Kahlo was recently divorced, with the two figures perhaps symbolically representing the artists's conflicting psychological states at the time.

purpose, mood, and style. The arrangement of elements in the picture, the use of colors, and even the kind of brush strokes are but a few of the many factors that go into the composition of a particular painting.

Although no set of questions will apply to all paintings, the list that follows might help you to begin analyzing your particular picture. First, think about your reaction to the painting, and review any notes you may have about the painting's subject, title, and history. With a sense of the painting's dominant impression or "theme" in mind, explore the effects of the artist's choices. As you address each question, ask yourself WHY the artist chose to paint this way; what was gained by each choice?

- What is the arrangement of the subject matter in this picture? What is the focal point of the picture?
- Are all the elements in the picture equal in size, proportion, and emphasis? Is the composition balanced or dramatically asymmetrical for some reason?

■ Are any of the elements used in a symbolic or nonrealistic way?

■ What role does light and dark play in this picture? Sunlight or shadows?

■ What colors predominate? Are the colors soft, muted, tranquil? Bright, bold, energetic? Cool hues (pale blues and greens, for example) or warm (reds, oranges, yellows)? A mix of shades or unusual colors for special effects?

■ Are the lines and shapes in the picture hard, flat, or geometrical? Or soft and gently sloped? Irregular or curvy, perhaps suggesting motion or action? Is there a pattern of repeated shapes?

■ Are the lines in the picture distinct or are they irregular or broken? Thick or thin?

■ What medium (physical materials) did the artist choose (oil paints, watercolors, tempera, chalk, etc.)? Is the painting on canvas, paper, silk, or some other material?

■ What sort of brush stroke is evident? How is the pigment applied (long flowing strokes, short swirling circles, small dabs, heavy globs, strings of paint, etc., or a combination)?

■ What is the effect of the paint texture (roughness, radiance, translucence, flatness, etc.)?

As was previously noted, this list is by no means comprehensive. Look at your painting again and again, allowing it to suggest other questions and ideas as you study its design. Consider grouping your responses by topics (e.g., the painting's use of colors) so that later, when you are ready to write your essay's first draft, your thoughts may be somewhat organized in support of a larger point. (For a sample of responses to some of the preceding questions, see the notes on *Nighthawks* on page 482.)

7. If possible, identify the painting's period style or "school." Some paintings may be recognized by common characteristics as belonging to a particular group or era of painters. Recognizing your painting as part of, or influenced by, a particular artistic movement may help you better understand important elements of its composition and design. For example, Monet's *The Water-Lily Pond* (page 322) shows variations of color as reflected in natural light that often characterize paintings of the late nineteenth-century movement called Impressionism. Other artistic movements of the last 150 years include Cubism, Surrealism, Art Nouveau, Art Deco, Expressionism, Abstract Expressionism, and Pop Art, to name only a few; art from earlier periods maybe identified with Classical, Romantic, or Renaissance styles, or any one of many others. If you are analyzing a well-known work, art history books or websites may help you identify the major style of your painting.

Once you have studied the subject matter, composition, and style of your painting, reassess your first reactions. Is your interpretation of the painting the same? Has your analysis broadened or changed your understanding or appreciation of the artwork and the ways its parts work together to communicate a dominant impression or main idea?

■ Additional Advice about Sculpture and Photography

Much of the advice for close analysis of paintings can be applied to sculpture and to professional photography. Use as many of the questions in the preceding pages as possible to shed light on the work you have selected. Here are a few more suggestions.

Sculptures may represent a wide variety of forms, including humans, animals, mythical creatures, everyday objects, and abstract or whimsical shapes. Sculptures of the human form or face have been found since the Stone Age, and people continue to be the dominant subject matter of sculpture today.

Some human subjects are specific, well-known people (e.g., Abraham Lincoln); others may honor a group of people (e.g., WW II soldiers); and others may represent universal types (e.g., a young girl on a swing). Some human sculptures, especially ones from earlier Greek, Roman, and Egyptian cultures, maybe idealized (or culturally stylized) to varying degrees, often to express harmony of body and mind, leadership qualities, or even a link to divinity. In addition to a statue's facial features, consider such factors as the pose (standing, sitting, in action?), clothing or drapery, and the size of the figure. In some cases, the advice on analyzing portraits (page 471) may be especially helpful.

Sculptures may be composed of a wide variety of materials, such as marble, bronze, stone, clay, pewter, plaster, wire, or wood, and both the choice of material (its texture, color, and weight) and the sculptor's technique often con-
tribute significantly to the work's dominant impression. Polished white marble, for instance, might be the best choice for a statue of a mythical goddess because of its soft, smooth classical beauty; sturdy, roughed bronze might be better used to communicate the strength and ruggedness of a golden grizzly bear; lightweight plastics or fiberglass might be used appropriately in an abstract sculpture of a kite dancing in the wind. Whether the sculpture is a representational ("realistic"), symbolic, or abstract piece, the selection and treatment of its material are important parts of its effect.

Remember, too, that unlike paintings, sculptures may be seen from multiples angles, so do walk around the artwork, if possible. Does the change in perspectives affect your understanding or appreciation of the work? If the base, pedestal, or wall/ceiling connection is part of the artwork, include its contribution in your analysis. Sometimes, especially in sculpture that has been commissioned for a particular purpose, the site of a sculpture is noteworthy; consider, for example, the kinds of sculpture one might find in a public park as opposed to an older cemetery or college library. How does your piece of sculpture blend with or complement its location?

Photography, like painting, may show people, places, things, or pleasing combinations of colors, shadows, and shapes. Like paintings, photos may tell a story, illustrate or document a news or historical event, capture a mood or feeling, make a political

Some critics see Meta Warrick Fuller's bronze sculpture *Ethiopia Awakening* (1914) as her tribute to a politically emerging Africa; others see a celebration of African-American women who take pride in their heritage. What is your interpretation?

statement, encourage social action, or accomplish some other purpose. Whether you are analyzing an example of photojournalism or a fine art photograph, always collect the identifying information: the name of the photographer, the name of the photograph (if given), the subject matter, the place and date of the photo, the place of first publication or exhibition, and any other pertinent background details.

In addition to analyzing the composition of the photograph using some of the suggestions outlined in previous pages, be aware that the circumstance and method by

Moonrise, Hernandez, New Mexico, 1941, by Ansel Adams

which the photo was made may also affect a viewer's response. Some prize-winning news photographs have been taken on the run in risky circumstances (battle scenes, for example) or as the result of chance meetings (see the story of Dorothea Lange's *Migrant Mother*, page 329); other fine art photographs are the product of long patience waiting for the perfect shot. Still other photos are staged (still lifes such as Edward Weston's peppers) or posed (portraits of William Wegman's costumed dogs). Others are produced with complex camera manipulation or crafted through computer technology to achieve desired effects.

Analysis of photographs also invites special attention to its use of lighting and color or absence of color. A photo taken with black-and-white film produces a different effect from one in high-speed color often used for action shots (compare, for example,

Photojournalist Thomas Dworzak's dramatic picture of both flood and fire in New Orleans following Hurricane Katrina was selected as one of *Time* magazine's "Best Photos of 2005."

Migrant Mother, page 330, or *Moonrise, Hernandez, New Mexico*, page 478, to the color photo of hurricane Katrina's destruction in New Orleans, page 478). Exposure time, depth of field (use of focus), angle and range of vision may also affect an image's appearance and meaning. Although no one expects you to be an expert on cameras or photo technology, do plan to explore the effects on you, the viewer, of the photograph's arrangement of subject matter, sharp/soft or blurry focus, wide or close angle, or any one of many other factors that make the particular picture effective.

As in the discussion of paintings, these suggestions for analyzing photography and sculptures are only a start, prompting your own closer investigation of the work you are analyzing.

■ **PRACTICING WHAT YOU'VE LEARNED**

Using the steps outlined on pages 469–476 in this chapter, practice your analytical skills by responding to a piece of art whose picture is reproduced in this textbook (a list of the artworks follows the table of contents). First, record your selection's title, artist, medium, and other pertinent information; then briefly describe the work. In a few sentences, explain the dominant effect or theme of the artwork as you see it and identify the important elements in the work that support your interpretation. (If you prefer, study the painting *Nighthawks* on page 482 and then compare your responses to those of another student writer whose notes appear on page 483. Were your reactions similar or different? If different, how might you support your interpretation?)

■ Guidelines for Writing about Artworks

Whether you are analyzing a painting, drawing, photograph, or piece of sculpture, you may find the following advice helpful as you write your essay.

1. **In the beginning** . . . Consider starting your essay with a brief interest-catching lead-in, perhaps an arresting descriptive detail, a hint of controversy, or a reference to the artwork's appeal or popularity. However you begin, your introduction should always clearly identify the work by title, full name of the artist, date (if available), and any other information you deem important, such as a painting's period style or a sculpture's location. Remember that names of artworks are always underlined or italicized.

2. **Offer a compelling thesis.** In an essay of analysis, your thesis will be the statement of your thoughtful interpretation of the work—what you see as its dominant effect, theme, main ideas, appeal, or commentary—and your discussion will show how the various elements of the piece work together to suggest that interpretation. In an essay focused on two works, you might show how the selections may be compared or contrasted to better inform the reader about the works' subject matter and/or style (for example, what interesting similarities and differences in subject and style exist in Edvard Munch's *The Scream* [page 113] and George Tooker's *The Subway* [page 241]?).

In some cases, you may find it helpful to include an essay map that will indicate the main topics of discussion. For example, your map might assert that your painting's theme, a commentary on the brutality of war, is best understood through explanation of its violent subject matter, its asymmetrical arrangement of jagged shapes and lines, and its unusual harsh colors.

3. **Present an overview of the work and, if appropriate, include pertinent background information.** Remember that your readers may be unfamiliar with the piece of art. Even though you will be analyzing important elements of it in your body paragraphs, readers may profit from a clear sense of the work in its entirety. In some cases, this overview may effectively appear in a paragraph following your introduction, just as a book or movie review might give a brief plot summary before discussing individual parts of those works. At this point in your essay you might also decide to include other relevant information about the painting's background. For example, if it is a historical painting, you might need to explain the circumstances; if a photograph captures a news event, an explanation of the situation might be in order; a statue of a particular person, real or mythological, may need identification.

4. **Organize your main points effectively.** Because artworks are unique, no one formula exists for organizing the body paragraphs of your essay. Perhaps the most helpful advice suggests that you look closely at the notes you took on the artist's choices of subject matter, composition, and design and then decide which aspects of the artwork play the most important roles in communicating the "meaning" or mood of the piece, as you see it. Try grouping your thoughts about the artwork into logical clusters; for instance, in a particular painting, one cluster might focus on the selection and arrangement of the subject matter while another addresses issues of light, shadow, and intensity of colors. With an appropriate topic sentence to introduce each one, these clusters may be shaped into effective body paragraphs in support of your thesis. In other cases artworks will suggest their own organization and order; for instance, a discussion of a portrait (if it helps, think *Mona Lisa* here) might focus first on the facial expression; then move to a paragraph on the body, clothes and accessories; then to the landscape in the background. Although there are no set blueprints for organizing body paragraphs in essays analyzing visual arts, readers must always feel a sense of coherence and logical order as the essay discussion progresses.

5. **Provide clear supporting evidence.** To help your reader understand—and accept—your interpretative claims, you must provide clear explanations and descriptive details from the artwork. Make your references to particular elements as vivid and specific as possible; describing a storm cloud looming over a ship as "huge" is not as helpful as describing it proportionally as three times the size of the ship, taking over half of the entire canvas. If you sense motion from circular images in the same storm-at-sea picture, show repetition of the shape in rounded waves, billowing sails, and whirling tufts of clouds. Remember that

acceptance of your thesis—your interpretation—depends on your readers' ability to see what you see in the work.

6. **Conclude gracefully.** By the end of your essay your readers should feel that they have acquired insight into a specific work of art, and perhaps even learned new information about an artist or particular artistic style. Your conclusion might reemphasize what you see as the work's purpose or primary appeal or you might point out its influence on other artists or later works. If you know such information, you can "situate" this selection in the artist's larger body of work. However you choose to end your essay, readers should feel they have enjoyed a reasonable, well-written analysis that has provided new understanding and appreciation of the work.

Problems to Avoid

Pay close attention to your assignment. Be sure you clearly understand the *purpose* of your essay. If you have been asked to provide a formal analysis of a painting, one that presents an interpretation by showing how the elements work together in support of that view, do not simply describe the picture. In addition, some assignments encourage research, but others request only personal response. Read your assignment carefully so that you will know exactly how to approach your essay topic. (Note too that in personal response essays, some teachers allow the use of "I," but others don't, preferring more objective references to "viewers" or "observers." Ask you instructor for guidance on this matter.)

Inform and delight readers with your own vivid description. As in any evaluation, whether it discusses a book, movie, restaurant, or artwork, it isn't enough to simply say, "I liked it. It was interesting." As someone sharing your opinion with others, you must work hard to help readers understand your point of view and the reasons for it. Explain your reasoning logically and with ample references to the artwork; be sure that those references are themselves vividly described (yes, the sky in Van Gogh's *Starry Night* [page 449] is blue and green—but what shades of blue and green, and why?). Revise your own bland or fuzzy language by using action verbs and colorful adjectives and adverbs that appeal to your reader's senses. Make your prose as inviting as the artwork you are describing. (For more help strengthening your prose, review pages 118–121 and 153–156.)

■ Annotated Painting: *Nighthawks*

Using this chapter's suggestions for analyzing paintings, a composition student took the following notes on the well-known picture *Nighthawks* (page 482), painted in 1942 by American artist Edward Hopper. Many of these notes were incorporated into the student's essay, on pages 484–485.

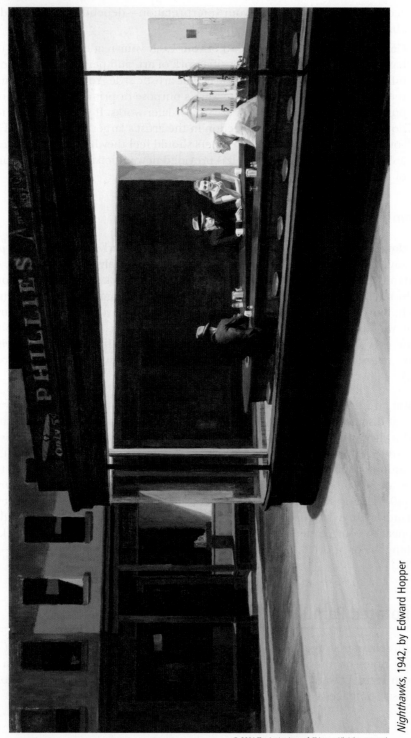

Nighthawks, 1942, by Edward Hopper

Notes

First impressions: I've seen a poster of this painting somewhere. I get feelings of loneliness and depression from this picture but I like it anyway. What are these people's stories?

Basic information: Nighthawks, *Edward Hopper (American artist), 1942, oil paint.*

Subject matter: An all-night café in a city. Four people in the café: a couple, a man by himself, and a counter-guy. In the 1940s because the guys at the counter are wearing '40s hats. Late night — empty streets, dark buildings.

The café is lit up so we can see inside. My eye is drawn to the single guy, maybe because he's in the middle of the picture, but also because he's turned away. He's separate from everyone else. The couple doesn't look too happy but at least they're together.

Colors: Shadows, dark areas, eerie green street and sidewalk. Café's walls — bleached out yellow, plain. All mostly depressing, though café does have light.

Shapes: Lots of long straight lines, rectangle shapes; even the counter and the ceiling are sort of triangle shaped. Sharp edges == harsh city life? Paint is flat, feels cold.

Note: the viewer is way back from the people (more isolation feeling?). No sky, just buildings.

What kind of birds are "nighthawks"?

Reassessment: Picture captures the loneliness of city life — maybe loneliness anywhere? The setting, figures, colors and shapes all add to feeling of isolation. Maybe the light and café represent a small bit of hope in a hard world?

■ Sample Student Essay

After studying the painting *Nighthawks*, the student writer incorporated his notes into this analytical essay, offering his interpretation of the work and showing important ways in which the painting's elements effectively communicate a dominant effect. As you read this essay, what specific details help you understand the writer's main points?

Night in the City and Psyche

1   It's four o'clock in the morning and after studying all night, you stumble out for coffee at an ever-open café. The night outside is cold and dark, the café light is harsh, and slumped on a worn counter stool, you've never felt so alone. Could anyone else possibly understand how this moment feels? American artist Edward Hopper captured just this emotion in his 1942 oil painting, *Nighthawks*. Through skillful arrangement of space, sharp angles, and muted colors, Hopper brilliantly conveys on canvas the sense of isolation and loneliness often experienced in modern life.

Introduction sets the mood

Thesis and essay map

2   *Nighthawks* presents a late-night scene in a city café, surrounded by dark buildings and a deserted street. The viewer, at some distance from the café, can see inside through a large glass window. Only four people are in the café: three customers—a single man and a couple—sitting on bar stools at the counter and a young waiter behind the counter. There is a sense of silence in the picture, a moment frozen in time, as no one is pictured as speaking or moving, except for a slight arm motion of the waiter as he does his job.

Overview of painting

3   To capture the mood of loneliness and separation, Hopper effectively arranges the figures through use of isolating space and distance. Near the center of the painting, Hopper places the single man apart from the others. Alone, faceless, with his back turned to the viewer, he represents every person who has ever felt distanced from other humans, whether it be in a quiet café or a noisy dorm. He isn't interacting with the waiter or the couple, who are not communicating with or even looking at each other. Though they obviously know each other, they look tired, maybe depressed, and have retreated into separate worlds. As important as the isolation of the figures within the café is the distance between the viewer and the scene. Just as the characters do not close the gap between each other, the viewer too is removed, outside the café observing these nighthawks, these solitary nocturnal creatures, like birds in a glass cage.

Point One: Use of space

(figures)

(viewer)

Point Two:
Use of lines,
shapes,
angles

4   Hopper's use of long straight lines and sharp geometrical shapes throughout the picture also communicates the sense of an unfriendly, stark world. Rectangle shapes appear throughout the picture: the plate glass windows; the inside door; the doorway, window, and window sills across the street; and the street, to name a few examples. Long thin lines dominate the scene, visible in window dividers, columns, edges of doors, building trim, and the curb. Even the counter inside the café is a triangle, with a darker triangle inside of it. The angle of the roof makes the wall above the far glass window come to a point, like a thin knife blade. There are few rounded lines in this picture, and there are no trees on the street or decorations on the café walls to soften the scene. Hard buildings and concrete fill the entire canvas out to its edges, stressing again the idea of the city as a cold, confining box.

Point Three:
Use of colors

5   The choice of colors also adds to the depressed mood of the painting. The dark patches, in the shadows on the building across the street and in its windows, emphasize the emptiness of the street. The pale, shadowy green of the sidewalk and street gives the scene an eerie feeling in the late-night hours. The café outside is brown-black, and the counter is also brown; although the walls are lighter, the color is a faded-out yellow. The use of these dark, sickly colors adds to the gloomy atmosphere. However, Hopper does place the couple and the counter-guy in more light than the single man, and the woman's red dress adds a small bit of brighter color. Perhaps Hopper means to suggest that there is still a slight hope if people try to find companionship.

Conclusion:
A quotation
emphasizing
the
painting's
appeal

6   French playwright Jean Anouilh once said, "Life is very nice, but it lacks form. It's the aim of art to give it some." In *Nighthawks* Edward Hopper gives visible form to the feelings of loneliness, an emotion almost everyone has experienced at one time or another. Hopper's painting appeals to viewers because it taps into our own sense of isolation, perhaps subtly encouraging us to reach out to others before it's too late.

■ Suggestions for Writing

1. Write an essay of analysis that presents and supports your interpretation of an artwork you find especially appealing. You might select a favorite painting, a piece of sculpture that is on your campus, or one of the many artworks reproduced in this textbook. (A list of artworks in this text follows the table of contents.) What elements of the piece make it "work" for you? (If you completed the Practice on page 479, you might expand those notes into this essay.)

2. Write an essay that compares/contrasts two artworks in such a way that both of them are clarified for your reader. For example, you might select two landscapes or two portraits and show how the style of each is similar or different, and why each is effective for its purpose. Or perhaps you might argue your preference for one over the other, explaining the reasons for your selection.

3. Write an essay that highlights the differences between two different kinds of art, such as a painting and a sculpture or a painting and a photograph. What advantages does each medium offer its subject?

4. Use this opportunity to investigate a "classic" artwork. Research an admired painting, a famous sculpture, or a Pulitzer Prize–winning photograph and discover why others have found the work so arresting. After reading about your subject (and possibly about its artist), decide if you agree with the comments you found. Do you have a better interpretation to offer?

5. Practice your descriptive writing skills by reproducing in words one of the artworks whose picture appears in this text. Your writing should be so vivid and precise that any reader could identify the artwork you chose. Or, if you prefer, allow one of the artworks in this text to suggest to you a similar scene to describe (for example, you might take a close look at Lawrence's *The Library* [page 51] and then "paint" your own library scene in colorful language).

Chapter 18

Writing about Film

Millions of people see films of one kind or another every day. Because the movie screen has become such an important medium of communication, it is not surprising that so many college courses have added a variety of films—from educational documentaries to commercially produced "Hollywood" movies—to their syllabi.

As you know from visiting your local movie house, a powerful film can move its audience in many emotional and intellectual ways, leading its viewers to thoughtful consideration of its ideas, craft, and construction. Writing about film is simply the next step from something you have probably done for years. Moving from informally talking about a movie with your friends, you can now learn to use your analytical thinking skills to put your ideas into thoughtful essays so that others may respond to them.

■ Using Film in the Composition Classroom

Writing about film in academic classes may take many forms, depending on its purpose and audience and the kind of course in which it is assigned. Here are some of the more common kinds of essay assignments using film found in composition and writing-across-the-disciplines courses:

1. *Prompted Response:* You might be shown a scene, a longer "clip" (that is, multiple shots or scenes), or a short film to help you find an interesting topic for your own writing. For example, a documentary on an inspirational figure might encourage you to write about a personal moment of courage, or you might write an essay about a memorable relative you recall after watching a fictionalized screen character or an interview with a famous author. Or perhaps you might

write about one of the important themes you saw expressed in a movie (for example, the importance of honesty or lessons learned from teamwork). Film, like literature, can be the springboard to all sorts of good essay topics.

2. *Review Essay:* Many composition courses offer students the chance to *evaluate* a commercial movie of their choice or one from an approved list. These review essays focus on why the writer does/does not think the movie is effective and whether it should be recommended to a particular audience. In these essays, writers usually select two or three important criteria by which a film may be judged (such as acting, plot, direction, special effects, etc.) and then offer evidence from the film to illustrate the reasons for their opinions. More than a simple yay/nay pronouncement, this kind of assignment is popular in writing classes because it allows writers to practice basic essay skills: a clear thesis, logical organization of persuasive claims, adequate development in support of those claims, and effective language.

3. *Strategy Practice:* You may also be offered the option of using film as subject matter in your essays as you practice mastering one or more of the organizational strategies discussed in Part Two of this text. For example, if you are practicing comparison/contrast, you might choose to write about a movie version of a literary work, an older movie and its current remake, a movie and its sequel, two movies with similar themes, or a Hollywood treatment of a historical event. Or you might practice causal analysis by explaining why a particular movie is your favorite or by showing how it influenced you at a crucial point in your life. Recalling a film you like (or hate!) can provide you with a wealth of examples and details while you practice developing essays in a number of ways.

4. *Formal Analysis:* Similar to essays of literary analysis discussed in Chapter 16, some assignments call for interpretation of one or more of the elements that make up a film, explaining how those elements help communicate a particular idea or mood. For example, you might analyze the setting in a particular scene and show what it adds to a movie's effectiveness (the house in *The Others*), or you might analyze a minor character to show his or her contribution to the viewer's understanding of the film's major themes (the little girl in the red coat in *Schindler's List*). Other kinds of analysis essay assignments might ask specific questions about a movie's political, cultural, or social ideas ("What criticisms of 1950s' American values does *Dr. Strangelove* offer its viewers?"; "Explain the concept of personal sacrifice as suggested in *It's a Wonderful Life*.").

There are, of course, many other kinds of essays written about film. In Film Studies classes, for example, you will often find students writing essays on film history (the influence of *Star Wars* on subsequent science fiction movies) or on the films of a particular actor or director (Spielberg's body of work), as well as many treatments of technical elements, such as editing, lighting, sound production, and special effects (computer-assisted fight scenes in *The Matrix*; use of innovative camera angles in *Citizen Kane*). These kinds of essay topics are fascinating, but they are often dependent upon expertise gained from research and in-depth study of film theory and production; consequently, they are not usually assigned in composition classes.

■ Guidelines for Writing about Film

Because the purposes of writing about film vary greatly, it is difficult to list suggestions that will apply to all assignments. However, if you are writing a movie review or an essay of film analysis, you may find some of these hints helpful.

1. **Pay close attention to your assignment.** Be sure you have a clear understanding of your purpose and audience. Are you, for example, writing a complete movie review or a more formal analysis of only certain elements? Does your assignment ask you to address any specific questions? Is your intended audience a group of general viewers, perhaps other students in your class, or are you writing for a particular audience, such as parents who might wish to know if this film is appropriate for their young children? Having a good understanding of the goals for this essay will help you focus your attention on the parts of the film relevant to your assignment.

2. **Prepare in advance of your first screening.** If you are writing a movie review or formal analysis, you may need to include certain kinds of production informa-tion about the film. To save time and stress (credits roll by quickly), obtain the information you need before you watch the film. It might be helpful, for exam-ple, to know the names of the director, the major actors, the screenwriter, the studio or film company, and the date of release. Does the movie fall into a par-ticular genre, or category, such as horror, science fiction, mystery, adventure, musical, romantic comedy, or domestic drama? Some combination of genres (comedy-adventure) or a recognizable subcategory of a genre (buddy cops 'n robbers, teen-slasher horror flick, *film noir* mystery)? Some reviewers like to have a brief plot summary before they see the movie; other viewers want to experi-ence the film free of preconceived ideas or expectations. (Hint: If the film is a classic, popular, or current movie, production information is often available online from the many studio, movie review, or film studies websites. Books on film in your library may also provide such information, although they will not contain facts about the most current movies.)

3. **Try to arrange multiple viewing opportunities.** It's difficult to write any kind of detailed treatment of a film you have seen only once, as most viewers need at least one screening just to take in plot and character development. If the choice of film is yours, you may find it much easier to write about one that is on DVD so that you can see it more than once as well as replay specific scenes for closer study. Multiple screenings may be necessary if you plan to quote dialogue, which must be presented accurately. (Remember that all kinds of films may be avail-able, without charge, from your community's public library.)

4. **Take notes as you watch.** It's easier, of course, to take notes while watching a film at home than it is in a darkened movie theater or even in a classroom. But you can do it, even if you have to struggle to decipher some of your scrawl later. As you watch, take notes on the plot or story line, the sequence of events (told chronologically, in flashback, or in some other nontraditional way?), the time and places in which the narrative occurs, the character development and

interactions, and any cinematic elements (camera shots, lighting, sound, etc.) that seem especially striking. Jot down your reactions to key scenes, characters, or lines of dialogue in the film, and make notes on parts you may already know will be important to your particular assignment. As the film unfolds, do you see any commentary on particular values or cultural assumptions?

5. **Make more notes immediately after the screening**. While your memory is fresh, ask and try to answer questions for yourself. Did you like or dislike the film? Mixed reaction? Why? What were the best or worst parts? Try to record some specific reasons for your opinions. Begin to use your critical thinking skills here: what is the film "about"? That is, what larger themes, values, or point of view does this film communicate to its viewers? For example, does this film comment on the triumph of good over evil, the loss of innocence, the search for love in the modern world, materialism in our society? Even movies that one might view as "purely entertainment" have a point of view toward the actions and characters presented in their stories. What is your film saying about certain social, political, or personal values? Is the film positive, satiric, or cynical about these values? Do you agree or disagree with the stances taken in the film?

6. **Review your notes in light of your assignment's purpose**. At this point, do you have enough ideas to draft a tentative thesis (and perhaps an essay map) for your particular assignment? For example, if you are writing a review of a movie, do you have a clear idea of what the movie is about, your evaluation of it, and some reasons to offer for that opinion? You may need to reorganize your notes in order to focus your efforts at this stage. Remember, you can't talk about every aspect of a movie. Often movie review essays in composition classes will focus on two or three main points about the film. To help you select important discussion points, try rearranging your notes into useful groups (for example: notes on acting, notes on the screenplay, notes on the settings). Which ideas look most promising in order to illustrate and support your thesis? (One professional reviewer uses index cards to "bunch together" those notes that might make up a good discussion point; you could also type your notes on a computer and then move the similar notes together to see what you have.)

   At this stage, many writers will have a working thesis in mind but now see the wisdom of screening the movie one or more times to clarify their supporting claims and to collect specific evidence to support those points.

7. **Watch the film again with a more analytical eye**. During this screening (and perhaps during repeated viewings of particular scenes), you can focus your attention on those specific aspects of the film you want to write about in your essay. If you already have a sense of the claims you want to make about the film, collect specific details you might use to illustrate and support your ideas.

   If at this stage you are still searching for your thesis or main supporting points, try posing questions for yourself before you watch the film again. What parts of the film were confusing to you (e.g., a character's decision, an ambiguous ending) and why? Concentrate on the most powerful images that stuck with you from the first viewing. Or try to analyze the three most memorable scenes. What do these images or scenes contribute to your understanding of and response to the film? Why is the film titled as it is? Asking "why" as you watch a second time may uncover interesting questions about the film that your essay will answer, responses that will inform other viewers. (Incidentally, writing analytically about film has much in common with literary analysis, so you may find it helpful to review pages 439–440 in Chapter 16 for some general tips regarding common elements such as characterization, setting, point of view, and narrative structure.)

8. **As you begin to draft, be aware of certain conventions particular to writing about film**. For example, most movie review essays will include a brief summary of the movie's story. It may be clearer for folks who have not seen the movie to read the summary in a paragraph near the essay's beginning, though in some essays the plot may be effectively interwoven throughout the discussion. (*Special note*: If presenting a complete plot summary would give away a surprise ending, the name of the villain, or other information that would diminish the enjoyment of the potential moviegoer, you can acknowledge that you are holding back certain information. Or you can adopt the handy phrase "Spoiler Alert," which professional reviewers use to warn readers to skip the next sentence or two if they wish to remain in the dark about a particular detail.) In addition to a brief summary, reviews usually offer some production information, such as names of the leading actors and director and the year of the film; your essay may also present pertinent background or historical information about the film if it is relevant to the assignment.

    Another consideration for the writer is whether to use "I" in a movie review essay. Although some famous movie reviewers consistently use "I" and "my" in their reviews ("I am putting this movie on my 'All-Time Worst List'"), others do not, so ask your instructor which choice is preferable for your assignment.

9. **Use clear, precise language**. As you draft and revise, assume that your readers have not watched the film and consequently cannot visualize what you have seen unless you help them. Make your discussions as clear as possible, using details and vivid language to re-create the images you are recalling. For ease of discussion, writers on film sometimes make use of a few cinematic terms to help communicate what they saw ("Hollywood ending") or to describe how something was done on the screen ("voice-over"). A glossary at the end of this chapter provides vocabulary that might prove useful as you watch and write about film, though essays for a general audience should not become overly technical.

10. **In your final draft, it's wise to recheck the film to ensure your accuracy**. Be sure that you have the characters' names right and that any lines you quoted are correctly transcribed. (For help punctuating dialogue, see the guidelines for quoted material on pages 558–559 in Part Four.) Remember that the names of films are underlined or printed in italics, not placed within quotation marks.

Watching and thinking about films are enjoyable experiences for most people, and writing analytically about film can extend that pleasure as you offer your thoughtful opinions to others in an organized, persuasive way. Practice your good writing skills as you create an essay worthy of Four Stars!

Problems to Avoid

Don't be tempted to just "pun and run." Movie reviews are rather well known for offering critics the opportunity to throw out witty phrases or memorable one-liners to praise or slash actors, directors, or scripts. You may have read lines similar to "her acting ran the range of emotions from A to B" or "his performance was so wooden you could have boarded up the windows with it." Or perhaps you've just seen a "must flee" rather than a "must see" movie. Puns and vivid figurative language often do add humor and spice that increase our enjoyment of reading a review. However, witty one-liners, as on-target as they may be, are never a substitute for good analysis. Even if you think a movie is so frightfully bad that its screening could be used to extract confessions out of hardened serial killers, you must offer some reasons for your evaluation. It isn't enough to say of a movie, "I just liked it" or "It was a tragic waste of two hours of my life"—explain your judgment and illustrate your claims with ample details from the film.

Keep your primary purpose in mind. Although you may need to include a plot summary in your essay, don't allow it to dominate your discussion. Remember that your larger purpose in a review or analytical essay is to offer an opinion—to give readers your recommendation and/or to interpret some important parts of the film. If your reaction to a film is mixed, you may certainly say so in a review essay as long as you avoid seeming wishy-washy. It's true that most bad films have at least one redeeming feature and many good films have flaws. But even if some aspect of the film bothered you to the point of wanting to pitch your popcorn (an annoying soundtrack, for example), ask yourself if that element alone merits a main point in your discussion. If, in fairness, you feel you must mention a strength in an overall negative review or point out a weakness in a generally positive review, then do so—but keep your main purpose and thesis in mind. Focus your discussion chiefly on those parts of your film that best support your overall evaluation or interpretation.

■ Sample Student Essay

In this essay a student recommends one of his favorite movies to his classmates. According to this writer, his hardest task was describing the mystery's twisting plot without spoiling the movie's surprises for the potential viewers. As you read this review, do you find that his comments encourage you to see this movie?

CATCH THE BLACK BIRD

1   Tired of watching movies with predictable plots, repetitive car chases, and excessive shoot-outs? Bored with lame performances and awful dialogue? As you stroll the aisles at your favorite movie rental store, leave

Introduction:
Questions lead to
thesis and map
(plot, cast, dialogue)

those unoriginal stories and special effects behind. Reach for something new by reaching for something older. If you are looking for a crime caper with surprising plot twists, an unbeatable cast, and some of the best dialogue ever written, reach for The Maltese Falcon (1941).

2   Adapted from the detective novel by Dashiell Hammett, with direction and screenplay by John Huston, The Maltese Falcon is regarded as one of the first and best movies in the *film noir* genre, films popular from the early 1940s to the late 1950s (revisited by Hollywood more recently with L.A. Confidential, Body Heat, and Chinatown). These films typically tell dark stories of urban crime and are filled with seedy characters, often including a hard-boiled detective and a beautiful, treacherous woman. Frequently filmed in shadows and night scenes, these movies have a gritty visual style that emphasizes the bleak and corrupt atmosphere of their stories.

Production and genre information

3   The plot of The Maltese Falcon is complex and unpredictable, mainly because throughout the film almost no character tells the truth the first time around . . . or even the second. The story begins in the office of tough-guy detective Sam Spade and his partner Miles Archer, hired by a beautiful Miss Wonderly to rescue her sister from a hoodlum named Thursby. Archer trails Thursby but is shot (at close range and with his coat buttoned over his gun). Spade is suspected of killing his partner because he has had an affair with Archer's wife, but then Thursby is killed too. The plot twists when Miss Wonderly admits (after trying out a few more phony stories) that she is really a thief named Brigid O'Shaughnessy, who claims she was double-crossed by Thursby, one of a handful of shady characters searching for a statue of a jewel-encrusted bird, now covered with a black veneer. Brigid convinces Spade to help her get the stolen bird, and an uneasy romantic relationship begins to grow. In pursuit of the mysterious falcon, Spade must outwit Brigid's dangerous enemies— the "Fatman," his murderous young henchman Wilmer, and Joel Cairo—not to mention a cop who hates Spade, Archer's angry widow, and Brigid herself. Characters make alliances one minute and then betray each other the next. By the movie's famous ending, Spade faces his toughest moral dilemma: whose side is he on?

Supporting Point One: Surprising plot twists

(Brief summary)

4   But it's not the plot twists that ultimately make this film so watchable—it's the fascinating cast of characters and the actors who play them perfectly. The best is Humphrey Bogart as the archetypal tough guy, whose un-pretty, no-nonsense face is an ideal match for the cold, cynical Spade. Bogart is totally believable as the unsentimental antihero: his reaction to his partner's brutal murder, for example, is a flat "yeah, tough break." Street smart and confident, he won't take guff from the cops, sees through Brigid's various poses, and knows how to manipulate the criminals in his own behalf. In one scene when the Fatman won't deal with him to his liking, he convincingly throws a violent fit of anger, smashes a glass, and stalks out—then grins all the way to the elevator, laughing over his successful act.

Supporting Point Two: Excellent cast

A. Bogart as antihero

5   The villains in the film are quirky and unforgettable too. Sidney Greenstreet is Kaspar Gutman, the huge "Fatman," whose chuckles and nice manners only partially hide his creepy obsession with the Black Bird. Peter Lorre plays bad guy Joel Cairo like a prissy little penguin with lethal craziness. And certainly Mary Astor as Brigid is much more than a Pretty Face. Like a quick-change artist, she's the Good/Bad Girl, who lies, tearfully admits her faults, and then lies again. When "helpless" Brigid begs Sam for protection, he replies, "You won't need much help . . . you're good. It's chiefly in your eyes, I think—and that throb you get in your voice. . . ." It takes a talented actress to play such a convincing liar, especially one who fools the audience every time she opens her mouth.

B. Memorable villains: Greenstreet, Lorre, Astor

6   The best part of the movie, however, may be the fast-paced, witty dialogue, full of wisecracks and sharp retorts. Sam gets most of the good lines, of course. Nobody's fool and slightly corrupt himself, he lets Brigid know he spotted her as a fake in his office from the beginning: "Oh, we didn't exactly believe your story . . . we believed your two hundred dollars." And he coolly answers an accusation of murder with the ironic question, "How'd I kill him, I forget." A lot of the humor is directed at Wilmer, the nasty young thug who is forever being needled by Spade. Relieving Wilmer of all his guns with a simple maneuver, Spade sneers, "Come on, this'll put you in solid with your boss" and then tells the Fatman how Wilmer lost his weapons: "a crippled newsy [newsboy] took 'em away

Supporting Point Three: Witty dialogue (examples)

from him but I made him give them back." To quote the famous lines of the last scene here would give away too much of the film's ending, but Sam's speech to the deceitful Brigid is so full of deliciously cold-blooded (but well-deserved) sarcasm that many film buffs know it by heart.

7   The movie's surprising conclusion wraps up a near-perfect film. Though it's not a warm, happy ending, it's a just one. Sam Spade may not always play fair or by the cops' rules, and he may be tempted by desire and money. Ultimately, however, he must follow a code of his own to maintain self-respect. He remains a hard-core detective to the end. Despite all the copycat detectives in films since 1941, there is truly only one Sam Spade. And as the Fatman explains as he agrees to sell out Wilmer to the cops, "There is only one Maltese falcon." So true, and its story is one of the best movies ever made.

Conclusion: An original hero in a compelling story make a great film

© Bettmann/CORBIS

Humphrey Bogart, Peter Lorre, Mary Astor, and Sydney Greenstreet star in *The Maltese Falcon* (1941).

■ **PRACTICING WHAT YOU'VE LEARNED**

Evaluate the effectiveness of the brief movie review that follows. Does the writer present a clear recommendation and overview of the film? Are all of the reasons for his opinion supported with enough details from the movie, or are you left unconvinced? Why? What changes or additions might make this a more informative, persuasive review?

■ *Cat in the Hat* Coughs Up Mayhem

By David Germain

David Germain writes movie reviews and entertainment features for The Associated Press news organization. This review first appeared in newspapers in November 2003.

1   The cat in the hat has come back, and he might put you and the kids in the mood for an evening alone with Dr. Seuss' original picture book to fumigate the stink of this feline's awful live-action adventure.

2   Shrill, boorish and witless, *Dr. Seuss' The Cat in the Hat* is as scenically crass and cluttered as its predecessor, *Dr. Seuss' How the Grinch Stole Christmas*, the first live adaptation of one of Theodor Geisel's children's tales. Yet *The Cat in the Hat* lacks the one saving grace of that earlier movie, Jim Carrey's whirlwind central character. As the Cat, Mike Myers is irritating and unamusing, caterwauling in a voice that channels Charles Nelson Reilly with traces of Bert Lahr's Cowardly Lion. And while the Grinch was meant to be a little menacing, the Cat ends up a scarier figure thanks to his rather creepy facial design and Myers' overly frisky demeanor, reminiscent of the goofy uncle who should never be left home alone with the kids.

3   First-time director Bo Welch, a production designer whose credits include *Edward Scissorhands* and the *Men in Black* flicks, crafts a visually overbearing movie. The performances he coaxes from Myers and the costars amount to distasteful tumult that's hard to endure. Screenwriters Alec Berg, David Mandel and Jeff Schaffer, who also adapted the *Grinch*, do a miserable job fleshing out the nuggets of Geisel's story to feature length. The characters they add are unpleasant, the expanded story details and sight gags vapid.

4   From a whimsical little rhyme about a feline in striped top hat who teaches two bored siblings a lesson on having fun, the filmmakers have strung together the insufferable story of a single mom (Kelly Preston), her control-freak daughter (Dakota Fanning) and reckless son (Spencer Breslin). The day mom's supposed to play host for her real-estate company's party, she's called in to work, leaving the kids with a narcoleptic baby-sitter and strict orders not to mess up the house. As the children cope with ennui, a sense of neglect and the machinations of mom's vile boyfriend (Alec Baldwin), the Cat pops in to spread mayhem and destruction. The frenzied pace fails to cover up the story's utter emptiness. The *Grinch* at least provided a protagonist with a character arc, who undergoes a real, though cartoonish, transformation. All *The Cat in the Hat* offers is the shallow message that to

have fun, you must know how. Fine for bedtime storybook reading, but piffling on the big screen.

5   The trappings Welch hangs on this thread of story are vulgar, a sensory over-load of garish pastels and cloying characters. Sean Hayes is disagreeable on two fronts, as mom's germ-phobic boss and the voice of the family's whiny computer-animated goldfish. The Cat's helpers, Thing 1 and Thing 2, are in the running for most obnoxious looking and sounding creatures ever to appear in a family film.

6   The most alarming thing is that there's a ready-made sequel with Geisel's follow-up book, *The Cat in the Hat Comes Back*. Here's hoping this screen cat has just one life to live.

■ Suggestions for Writing

1. Select a film that's available on DVD or video, and write a movie review that might appear in your local newspaper, addressed to a general audience. Explain your evaluation of the movie by providing at least two or three important reasons, each supported with details from the film. (Suggestion: As you decide on a movie to review, you might look at the American Film Institute website, containing their list of the top 100 American movies. Although you may not agree with the Institute, this ranking will suggest some films admired over the years by both critics and viewers. Now may be your chance to discover for yourself why a particular movie is considered a classic.)

2. Analyze one of your favorite movies. Write an essay explaining why you find it so satisfying. Or, if you prefer, tackle a movie that seems to be loved (or loathed) by everyone—but you. Write an essay that shows the world why your assessment is the better one.

3. Find a movie review (newspaper, magazine, online) with which you strongly disagree. Write an essay in which your analysis shows why the reviewer is off track in his or her evaluation of this movie.

4. Write an essay comparing/contrasting a literary work (novel, short story, or drama) you know well to its movie version (for example, one of the *Harry Potter* or *Lord of the Rings* movies, *The Grapes of Wrath, Gone with the Wind*), explaining how effectively you think the original story was captured on the Big Screen.

5. Think of a film story (fictional or factual) that deeply impressed you, one that you feel presents a thoughtful message, question, or challenge to its viewers. Explore this idea in a personal essay as it applies to values or choices in your own life. Or perhaps you have seen a film that changed your mind about an important topic. Explain how the film has affected your point of view.

■ Glossary of Film Terms

Camera angle The position of the camera in relation to the subject being filmed. Some common camera angles include the close-up (often of a face), the long shot, and the high angle.

Deus ex machina Refers to use of an improbable plot device to save the hero from a difficult situation (the cavalry or police arrive at just the right moment, for example). The phrase, meaning "god from the machine," came from ancient Greek drama when a crisis was solved by the appearance of a god, lowered onto the stage with ropes or other equipment. Today the term is most often used to criticize an unbelievable rescue in a weak script.

Dialogue The words spoken by the characters in a film.

Editing Technically, editing is the splicing together of different pieces of film. The order in which a filmmaker links shots in a single scene, and then links scenes together, to construct the entire film plays a crucial role in communicating the film's meaning.

Fade A transitional device in which the picture on the screen gradually darkens to black before another scene begins.

Flashback A scene or sequence of scenes that take the story into the past.

Genre Movies may be categorized into recognizable types that share similarities in themes, narrative structures, characters, style, mood, and other characteristics. Some common movie genres include horror, romantic comedy, Westerns, adventure, science fiction, crime, and mystery. Many movies are a blend of more than one genre.

"Guilty Pleasure" Refers to a movie that a reviewer enjoyed in spite of recognizing that the film has serious flaws (a comedy that is fun even though it is over-the-top silly or an action movie that is thrilling even though its special effects are ridiculously unbelievable).

Hero/Antihero The hero of a film is usually a major character who displays worthy values and admirable characteristics, often including courage and self-sacrifice for the good of others. An antihero rejects traditional values or societal norms, but may nevertheless appeal to audiences because of his/her individualism or adherence to a personal code of behavior.

"Hollywood Ending" Refers to a movie's happy ending that often seems contrived or tacked on merely to make audiences feel good as they leave the theater.

Location A film that is shot "on location" is filmed in the geographical area that is present in the story rather than in a studio.

Narrative structure Refers to the way a story's plot line is constructed, through arrangement of scenes and point of view.

Scene A period of screen activity in which the action is usually confined to one time and space.

Sets Constructed physical environments in scenes.

Setting Place and time (year, hour of day, month, season, etc.) of a particular scene or entire film. Lighting and sound effects may influence the mood of a particular setting.

Shot A single image on the screen; a variety of shots may be edited to form a sequence that makes up a scene.

Slow motion Film speed is slowed to produce a desired effect on the audience; frequently used in modern movies to underscore an emotional interaction between characters or to emphasize the horror of tragedy or violence. (In contrast, ***fast motion*** is often used for comedic effect or to show frenzied activity in a passage of time.)

Soft focus Refers to scenes in which the images on the screen appear slightly fuzzy or out of focus to the viewer; often used to create a romantic effect.

Special effects Refers to a variety of methods, from makeup to complex computer technology, used to create characters or scenes that cannot be produced normally (e.g., space travel, superhuman powers, battle scenes, dinosaurs).

"Spoiler Alert" Phrase used by movie reviewers to warn those who have not seen the film that an important plot element (the identity of the murderer, for example) is about to be revealed.

Voice-over Refers to the commentary heard over the screen images, spoken by a narrator or character whose remarks directly address the audience.

Chapter 19

Writing in the
World of Work

Imagine you are a manager of a business who receives the following memo from one of the sales representatives:

> Our biggest customer in Atlanta asked me to forward the shipment to the company warehouse and I said I could not realizing how serious a decision this was I changed my mind. This OK with you?

Did the salesperson mean to say that at first he thought he could send the shipment but then changed his mind? Or did he mean he thought he couldn't but then reconsidered? What would you do as the manager? Probably you would stop your current work and contact the salesperson to clarify the situation before you gave an OK. Because of the unclear communication, this extra effort will cost your business valuable time, energy, and perhaps even customer satisfaction.

The preceding scenario is not far-fetched; unclear writing hurts businesses and organizations in every country in the world. Consequently, here is a bold claim:

> Almost all workplaces today demand employees with good communication skills.

Although specific writing tasks vary from job to job, profession to profession, successful businesses rely on the effective passage of information among managers, coworkers, and customers. No employer ever wants to see confusing reports or puzzling memos that result in lost production time, squandered resources, or aggravated clients. To maximize their organization's efficiency, employers look for and reward employees who can demonstrate the very writing skills you have been practicing in this composition course. Without question, your ability to communicate clearly in precise, organized prose will give you a competitive edge in the world of work.

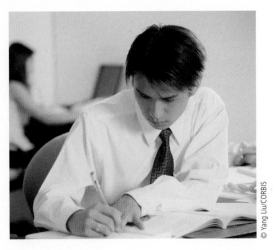

To help you address some of the most common on-the-job writing situations, this chapter offers general guidelines for business letters, office memos, and professional e-mail messages. A special section on the preparation of résumés at the end of the chapter will suggest ways to display your skills to any prospective employer.

■ Composing Business Letters

Letters in the workplace serve many purposes and audiences, so it isn't possible to illustrate each particular kind. However, it is important to note that all good business letters have some effective qualities in common. And although a business letter is clearly not a personal essay, they share many features: consideration of audience, development of a main idea, organized paragraphs, appropriate tone and diction, and clear, concise expression of thoughts.

Before you begin any letter, prewrite by considering these important questions:

1. What is the main purpose of this letter? What do you want this letter to accomplish? Are you applying for a job, requesting material, offering thanks, lodging a complaint? Perhaps it is you who are answering a request for information about a product, procedure, service, or policy. The occasions for written correspondence are too many to list, but each letter should clearly state its purpose for the reader, just as a thesis in an essay presents your main idea.

2. Who is your "audience," the person to whom you are writing? As discussed in detail on pages 19–22 in Chapter 1, effective writers select the kinds of information, the level of complexity, and even the appropriate "voice" in response to their readers' needs, knowledge, and attitudes. Remember that no matter who the recipient of your letter happens to be, all readers want clarity, not confusion; order, not chaos; and useful information, not irrelevant chitchat. Put yourself in the reader's place: what should she or he know, understand, or decide to do after reading this letter?

3. What overall impression of yourself do you want your letter to present? All business correspondence should be courteous, with a tone that shows your appreciation for the reader's time and attention. Achieving this tone may be more difficult if you are writing a letter of complaint, but remember that to accomplish your purpose (a refund or an exchange of a purchase, for example), you

must persuade, not antagonize, your reader. If you're too angry or frustrated to maintain a reasonable tone, give yourself some time to cool off before writing. A respectful tone should not, on the other hand, sound phony or pretentious ("It is indeed regrettable but I must hereby inform you . . ."). Choose the same level of language you would use in one of your polished academic essays. In short, good business writing is clear, courteous, and direct.

Business Letter Format

Most traditional business letters are neatly typed on one side of 8½-by-11-inch white bond paper. Margins are usually set for a minimum of 1¼ inches at the top and at least one inch on the left and right sides and at the bottom. Almost all professional letters now use the "block form"—that is, lines of type are flush with the left margin and paragraphs are not indented. Envelopes should match the letter paper.

Business letters typically have six primary parts:

1. The **heading** of a letter is your address and the date, typed either above the inside address of the letter or in the upper right corner. If the heading is in the upper right position, the longest line should end at the one-inch margin on the right side of the page. All lines in your heading should begin evenly on the left. If you are using letterhead stationery (paper already imprinted with your business name, address, or logo), you need to add only the date.

2. The **inside address** contains the name of the person to whom you are writing, the person's title or position, the name of the company or organization, the full address (street or post office box, city, state, ZIP Code). The first line of the inside address should appear at least two spaces below the last line of the heading. (The inside address information should be repeated exactly on your letter's envelope.)

Correct use of titles and positions can be tricky. Sometimes a person has a title and an additional position; other times, the title is lengthy. In general, if a person's title has more than two words, put it on a separate line:

Professor Linda Payne
Dean, College of Liberal Arts
Colorado State University

Whenever possible, direct your letter to a specific person. If you do not know the name of the person and cannot discover it before your letter must be sent, you may address the correspondence to the position held by the appropriate person(s): General Manager, Graduate Advisor, Personnel Director, City Council, and so forth.

3. The **salutation** is your letter's greeting to your reader. Begin the salutation two spaces down from the inside address, and greet the person formally using the word "Dear" plus title and name (Dear Mr. Smith, Dear Ms. Jones,* Dear Dr. Black). The salutation is traditionally followed by a colon rather than the more informal comma:

Dear Dr. Montoya:
Dear Personnel Director:

A caution: be careful to avoid sexist assumptions in your salutations. If you do not know the gender of the person to whom you are writing (initials and many first names—Chris, Pat, Jordan—are used by both men and women), do some research, if possible. When in doubt, use the title or position and last name (Dear Professor Chieu). Use of the full name (Dear Xin Chieu) or organization name (Dear Safety Council) may be preferable to the impersonal "Dear Sir or Madam," a phrase that seems stilted today.

4. The **text** of your letter refers to the message that appears in the paragraphs. As in essays, think of your text as having a beginning, a middle, and an ending. Although

---

* If you know that the woman you are writing prefers to be addressed as Mrs. X, address her in this way. However, if you do not know her marital status or preferred title, Ms. may be the best choice. If possible, avoid the matter altogether by using her professional title: Dear Professor Smith, Dear Mayor Alvarez.

there is no rule about the number of paragraphs in any business letter, most letters contain the following:

- a first paragraph that clearly states the reason for writing (think about a thesis in an essay);

- one or more paragraphs that present the necessary details or explanation of the reason for writing (think body paragraphs in an essay);

- a last paragraph that sums up the message in a positive way, offers thanks if appropriate, and, on occasion, provides information to help reader and writer make contact (think conclusion in an essay).

Because professional people receive so much mail, business letters should be brief and to the point. *Above all, readers want clarity!* Scrutinize your prose for any words or phrases that might mislead or confuse your reader. Select precise words and create trim sentences that present your message in the clearest, most straightforward way possible. (For help writing clear, concise prose, review Chapters 6 and 7.)

If possible, without sacrificing clarity or necessary information, keep your letter to one page. Single-spaced paragraphs of eight lines or fewer are easiest to read. Skip a space between paragraphs. If you must go to a second page, type your name, the date, and the page number in an upper corner. If you discover that you have only one or two lines to carry over to the second page, try to condense your text or, if you must, squeeze or expand the margins just a bit. Try not to divide paragraphs between pages, and do not split a word between pages. Second and subsequent pages should be plain paper, without letterhead material.

5. The **complimentary closing** of a business letter is a conventional farewell to the reader, typed two spaces below the last line of the text. The two most common phrases for closing formal business correspondence are "Sincerely" and "Yours truly." Stick with these unless you have a more informal relationship with the person you are writing. In those cases, you might use such closings as "Cordially" or "Warm regards." The first letter of the first closing word is capitalized, and the closing is followed by a comma.

6. The **signature** part of a business letter contains both your handwritten name and, beneath that, your typed name (plus your title, if appropriate). Leave approximately four spaces for your handwritten name, which should be written in black ink:

Sincerely,

Jane Doe

Jane Doe
Professor of Philosophy

Do not forget to sign your letter! Such an oversight not only looks careless but may also suggest to the reader that this is merely a mass-produced form letter.

7. Some letters contain additional information below the signature. Typical notes include the word "enclosure" (or "encl.") to indicate inclusion of additional material (which may be named) or a distribution list to indicate other persons who are receiving a copy of this letter. Distribution is indicated by the word "copy" or by the letters *c*, *cc* (for "carbon copy"), or *xc* (for "Xeroxed copy"), followed by a colon and the name(s); if more than one person is listed, the names should appear in alphabetical order.

Copy: Mayor Sue Jones   Enclosure *or* Encl.
        or   *or*
cc: Mayor Sue Jones,   Enclosure: résumé
    Dr. Inga York

If someone else types your letter, put your initials in capital letters, a slash mark, and the typist's initials in lowercase:

JCW/ma

In formal business correspondence, avoid any sort of postscript (P.S.).

Some last advice: Most business letters today are written on a word processor, whose spelling and grammar programs can help writers find and fix typos. But, as in any piece of writing, always proofread for errors carefully—and repeatedly! Never trust your spell-checker to catch all possible errors. Don't undercut the message you are sending by failing to revise misspelled words, inaccurate names, ungrammatical sentences, or sloppy punctuation. Also, be sure to select a clear, traditional type font (such as Times New Roman; no fancy script or gothic styles, please), set in a readable size (at least 12 point), and use only a printer that can produce dark, high-grade type.

■ PRACTICING WHAT YOU'VE LEARNED

Find a recent business letter you or someone you know has received. This letter might be a request for a charitable donation, an announcement of some school policy, a letter of recommendation, or even a parking-violation summons. Assess the effectiveness of the letter: is it clear? Informative? To the point? Write a one-paragraph critique of the letter that identifies both its strengths and any weaknesses you see.

■ ASSIGNMENT

Writing business letters becomes easier with practice. Think of an upcoming occasion that will require you to write a professional letter. Perhaps you are asking for a job or accepting one? Applying for a scholarship, grant, or school loan? Requesting an interview or letter of recommendation? Complaining to your landlord? Ordering or returning a product? The choices are many but try to select a letter that you might indeed send sometime soon. Limit your letter to one page, and revise as many times as necessary to illustrate your good understanding of purpose, audience, format, and style. Don't forget to proofread carefully!

■ Sample Business Letter

Art Tech Studio
802 West Street
Fort Collins, CO 80525
May 10, 2006

Mr. Thomas Valdez
General Manager
Harmony Products, Inc.
645 Monroe Avenue
Little Rock, AR 90056

Dear Mr. Valdez:

Thank you for your May 5 order for twenty of my hand-designed laptop cases and for your advance payment check of $250. I am delighted that your company wishes to stock my painted carrying cases in both your Little Rock and Fayetteville stores.

The cases are being packed in individual boxes this week and should arrive by Air Flight Mail at your main office no later than May 25. If you wish for me to use express-mail for quicker arrival, please let me know.

Many thanks again for your interest in my work and for your recent order. I am planning to attend a marketing seminar in Little Rock, June 5–8; I will call you next week to see if we might arrange a brief meeting at your convenience on one of those days. Until then, should you need to contact me, please call my studio (970/555-6009).

Sincerely,

Rachel Zimmerman

Rachel Zimmerman

Enclosure: receipt

■ Creating Memos

A memo, short for "memorandum," is a common form of communication *within* a business or an organization. Memos are slightly more informal than business letters, and they may be addressed to more than one person (a committee, a sales staff, an advisory board, etc.). Memos may be sent up or down the chain of command at a particular workplace, or they may be distributed laterally, across a department or between offices. Although the format of the paper memo may vary slightly from organization to organization, it often appears arranged in this manner:

TO:	name of recipient(s) and/or title(s)
FROM:	name of sender and title; handwritten initials
DATE:	day, month, year
SUBJECT:	brief identification of the memo's subject matter

The message follows in one or more paragraphs.

Note that the name of the sender is usually accompanied by the sender's handwritten initials, rather than a full signature as in a business letter. Also, in some memos, the term "Re" ("in reference to") may be substituted for the word "Subject."

Many memos are brief, containing important bulletins, announcements, or reminders, as illustrated in this sample:

TO:	Editorial Staff
FROM:	Louise Presaria, Editor-in-Chief *LP*
DATE:	April 22, 2006
RE:	Silver Eagle Award Banquet

Because the current snowstorm is presenting problems with public transportation and also with heating outages in our building, the annual Silver Eagle Banquet originally scheduled for tomorrow night has been postponed for one week. It is now rescheduled for Thursday, April 29, beginning at 7:30 PM, in the Whitaker conference room.

I look forward to seeing you all there. Each of you has done a marvelous job this year and greatly deserves to share the benefits that come with our industry's most prestigious award.

Other in-house memos—those explaining policies or procedures, for example—may be long and complex. Lengthy memos may begin with a summary or statement of general purpose and may use headings (such as "Background Information," "Previous Action," or "Recommendations") to identify various parts of the discussion.

All business memos, regardless of length, share a common goal: the clear, concise communication of useful information from writer to reader.

■ Sending Professional E-Mail

Although the world of work will never be totally paperless, more businesses today are relying on computer-based communications to send or request information, both inside and outside their organizations.

Electronic mail, or e-mail, has a number of advantages over the business letter, memo, and telephone. It's faster and easier than postal service (now known to many as "snail mail"), as you can compose or forward a message to one person or many people, across the building or across the country, and receive a reply almost instantly. Messages may be sent anytime, day or night, and are held until the recipient is able to open them. Unlike the telephone, most e-mail has an "attachments" feature that may contain documents, forms, graphics, or pictures.

Because e-mail is so useful in so many ways to many different kinds of businesses and organizations, there is no one-size-fits-all format. Consequently, it's always a good idea to acquaint yourself with customary use of e-mail at your place of work. In addition, here are some suggestions for improving the quality of all electronic communications:

1. Use a helpful subject line. Successful business leaders today may receive scores of e-mail messages every day, so many that they are tempted to delete any unrecognizable mail that might be "spam" (an unsolicited message or sales offer) or contain a "virus" that might destroy their files. To ensure that your message will be opened and read, always use specific words in the subject line to clearly delineate the central focus or key words of your correspondence ("Project Thunderbolt contracts"). Using a specific subject line will also be helpful if your reader wants to reread your message later and needs to find it quickly in a long list of e-mails.

2. Begin appropriately. Unlike a business letter, e-mail needs no heading or inside address, but a new communication should begin with an appropriate greeting, depending on the formality of the occasion. For example, if you are writing an officer of another company to ask for information, you might begin with a traditional salutation (Dear Mr. Hall:). An informal memo to a coworker might have a more casual greeting, depending on your relationship to that person (Hello, Bill; Good morning, Ms. Merrill). Some companies prefer the standard To-From-Date-Subject memo form discussed earlier in this chapter.

3. Keep your message brief. Long messages are difficult to read on screens; all that scrolling and flipping back and forth to check information can be tiresome. If possible, confine your message to one screen. Working people are busy, so try to follow the advice given previously in this chapter regarding business letters and memos: clearly state your purpose, explain in a concise manner, and conclude gracefully.

4. Make it easy to read. To avoid contributing to your reader's eyestrain, write messages that are visually pleasant. Keep your paragraphs short, and skip lines between each paragraph. If your message is long, break it up with headings, numbered lists, or "bullets." Use a readable, plain font.

5. Check your tone. Your e-mail messages should sound professional and cordial. Unlike personal e-mail, which may contain slang, fragments, asides, or funny graphics, business e-mails should be written in good standard English and be straight to the point. If you're angry, resist the temptation to fly to the computer and "flame"; cool off and compose a thoughtful, persuasive response instead. Be especially careful about the use of irony or humor: without nonverbal clues, readers may misinterpret your words and react in a manner opposite the one you intended. In general, strive for a polite, friendly tone, using the clearest, most precise words you can muster.

6. Sign off. If your e-mail is performing a task similar to that of a business letter, you may wish to close in a traditional way:

Yours truly,

Scott Muranjan

You may also want to create a standard sign-off that not only includes your name but also your title, telephone and fax number, mailing and e-mail address. Such information is helpful for readers who wish to contact you later.

However, if your e-mail is more akin to an informal memo between coworkers, you may find it appropriate to end with a friendly thought or word of thanks and your first name:

I'm looking forward to working with you on the Blue file. See you at Tuesday's meeting.
Scott

Allow your sense of occasion and audience to dictate the kind of closing each e-mail requires.

7. Revise, proofread, copy, send. The very ease of e-mail makes it tempting to send messages that may not be truly ready to go. All your professional correspondence should look just that: professional. Take some time to revise for clarity and tone; always proofread. Double-check figures and dates, and run the spell-checker if you have one. If time permits, print out a "hard copy" of important messages to look over before you hit the Send button. If you need to keep track of your correspondence, make a computer file or a print copy for your office.

Problems to Avoid

Electronic mail has revolutionized the workplace, but it is not without its disadvantages. Computers crash, files vaporize, printers freeze, and so on. Work on developing patience and give yourself time to use other methods of communication if necessary. Meanwhile, here are two other tips:

Business E-mail Is Not Private. Perhaps because of individual passwords or because of experience with sealed postal mail, employees often believe that their e-mail is private correspondence. It is not! Employers have the legal right to read any e-mail sent from their organizations. Moreover, you never know when someone may be peering at a screen over the shoulder of the intended recipient. And there's always the danger of hitting the wrong button, sending your thoughts to an entire list of people when you meant to contact only one. To avoid embarrassing yourself—or even endangering your job—never send inappropriate comments, angry responses, petty remarks, or personal information through your business e-mail. Never send confidential or "top secret" business information through e-mail without proper authorization. Learn to use e-mail in a productive way that protects both you and your organization.

Mind Your Netiquette! Although no one requires that you don your white kid gloves to hit those computer keys, rules of etiquette for e-mail writers are important. Here are a few suggestions for well-behaved writers:

- Don't "shout" your messages in all capital letters. IT'S TOO HARD TO READ A SCREEN FULL OF SAME-SIZED LETTERS. Occasionally, you may type a word in capital letters for emphasis, but use this technique sparingly. (For more advice on proper tone, see previous page.)

- Be cautious about using Internet shorthand or in-house abbreviations ("the TR6 project"), especially in messages to other organizations. If certain shorthand signs or phrases, such as BTW (by the way), FWIW (for what it's worth), or G2G (got to go), are routinely used in casual e-mail at your place of work, feel free to adopt them. However, most business correspondence is more formal and not all abbreviations may be universally recognized. When in doubt, spell it out. Business messages depend on clarity and a mutual understanding of all terms.

- Don't ever, ever use "emoticons" in business writing. Emoticons are typed "smiley" faces read sideways that many people find more annoying than ground glass in a sandwich. Instead of relying on these gaggingly cute symbols to communicate emotions of happiness, sadness, surprise, or irony, find the right words instead. Show off your writing skills, not your ability to group type!

- Never forward anyone else's e-mail message without permission, especially if that message contains controversial and/or hurtful statements or confidential material. (Because other people often break this rule, think twice before *you* write.)

■ Designing Résumés

A résumé is a document that presents a brief summary of your educational background, work experiences, professional skills, special qualifications, and honors; some résumés also contain a brief list of references. You may be asked to submit a résumé on a variety of occasions, most often to supplement your applications for jobs, interviews, promotions, scholarships, grants, fellowships, or other kinds of opportunities. Because prospective employers are the largest target audience for résumés, the following section offers advice to help job seekers design the most effective document possible.

Job seekers most frequently send their résumés with *cover letters* directed to particular employers. To prepare each cover letter, follow the basic steps for writing the traditional business letter, as outlined earlier in this chapter. In the first paragraph, clearly tell your reader why you are writing: the specific job you are applying for and why. Devote one or more paragraphs in the "body" of your letter to noting your education or professional experience or both, explaining why you are a good match for the advertised position or how you might benefit the organization. Your concluding paragraph should express thanks for the employer's consideration and briefly reemphasize your interest in the job; in this paragraph you may also mention contact information or explain access to your credentials file. In some situations, you may indicate your availability for an interview. If the employer is interested, he or she will read your résumé for more details and possibly distribute copies to others involved in the hiring process.

Because employers today may receive hundreds of applications for a single job, it is important to present yourself as positively as possible in your letter and résumé. If your campus has a career center, seek it out as your first step. Career centers often have extraordinary resources: sample cover letters and résumés, hints for interviews, information on electronic job searching, and much more. Because there are multiple ways to arrange a résumé, you will find it useful to familiarize yourself with some representative samples before you begin working on your own.

Although there is no single blueprint for all résumés, there is one guiding principle: *select and arrange your information in the way that most effectively highlights your strengths to your prospective employer.* Think of your résumé as a one-page advertisement for yourself.

To find the best way to "sell" yourself to an employer, you might choose to adopt one of the two most popular arrangement styles:

- *Functional format:* This arrangement places the reader's focus more directly on the job seeker's education and skills than on limited work experience. It is better suited for job seekers who are new graduates or those just entering the workforce. Most résumés of this type are one page.

- *Experiential format:* This style emphasizes professional experience by placing work history in the most prominent position, listing the current or most important employment first. This format might be best for nontraditional students who have a work history before school or for those students who have worked throughout their college careers. If the list of relevant professional experience is lengthy, this kind of résumé may extend to a second page if necessary.

Before you begin drafting your résumé, make a list of the information you want to include. Then think about the best ways to group your material, and select an appropriate title for each section. Some of the common content areas include the following:

1. **Heading.** Located at the top of your résumé, this section identifies you and presents your contact information: your full name, address, phone number, and e-mail address if you have one. You may wish to put your name in slightly bigger type or in bold letters.

2. **Employment objective.** Some job seekers choose to include a statement describing the kind of employment or specific position they are seeking. Others omit this section, making this information clear in their cover letters. If you do

include this section, always substitute a brief, specific objective for trite, overblown language any job seeker in the world might write:

Trite: Seeking employment with a company offering intellectual challenges and opportunities for professional growth

Specific: A microbiology research position in a laboratory or center working on disease prevention and control

If you have the time and resources to customize a résumé for each job announcement you respond to, you can use this section to show that the position you most want matches the one advertised. However, if you plan to use one résumé for a variety of job applications, beware presenting an employment objective so narrowly focused that it excludes you from a particular application pool.

3. **Education.** If you have no relevant or recent work experience, this section might appear next on your résumé. Begin with the highest degree you have earned or are working on; if you are about to graduate, you may present the anticipated graduation date. Include the name of the school and its location and, if relevant, your major, minor, or special concentration. Some students with a "B" or better grade point average also include that information. This section might also contain any professional certificates or licenses (teaching, real estate, counseling, etc.) you have earned or other educational information you deem relevant to a particular job search (internships, research projects, study-abroad programs, honors classes, or other special training).

4. **Professional experience.** If you wish to emphasize your work history, place this section after your heading or employment objective, rather than your educational background. In this section, list the position title, name of employer, city and state, and employment dates, with the most current job or relevant work experience first. Some résumés include brief statements describing the responsibilities or accomplishments of each position; you may list these statements (with "bullets," not numbers) or present brief paragraphs if space is an issue (see page 517 for an example). If you include job descriptions, be specific (prepared monthly payroll for 35 employees) rather than general (performed important financial tasks monthly); use action verbs (supervised, developed, organized, trained, created, etc.) that present your efforts in a strong way. Use past tense verbs for work completed and present tense for current responsibilities.

   Note that résumés traditionally do not use the word "I"; beginning brief descriptive phrases with a strong verb, rather than repeating "I had responsibility for . . . ," saves precious space on a résumé.

5. **Skills.** Because you want to stress your value to a prospective employer, you may wish to note relevant professional skills or special abilities you have to offer. This section may be especially important if you do not have a work history; many recent graduates place this section immediately following the education section to underscore the skills they could bring to the workplace. For example, you might list technical skills you possess or mention expertise in a foreign language if that might look useful to a company with overseas connections.

6. **Honors, awards, activities.** In this section, list those awards, scholarships, honors, and prizes that show others have selected you as an outstanding worker, student, writer, teacher, and so on. Here (or perhaps in a section for related skills

or experiences) you might also add leadership roles in organizations, and even certain kinds of volunteer work, if mentioning these would further your case. Although you don't want to trivialize your résumé by listing irrelevant activities, think hard about your life from a "skills" angle. Coordinating a campus charity project, for example, may indicate just the kinds of managerial skills an employer is looking for. Don't pad your résumé—but don't undersell yourself either.

7. **References.** Some employers ask immediately for references, persons they may contact for more information about you and your work or academic experiences; other employers ask for references later in the hiring process. If references are requested with the initial application letter, the information may be listed at the end of the résumé or on an attached page. Reference information includes the person's full name and title or position, the name and address of the person's business or organization, telephone number, and e-mail address, if available. Do not list friends or neighbors as references; résumé references should be academics or professionals who are familiar with your work.

Critique Your Page Appeal

Once you have decided on your résumé's content, you also need to consider its visual appeal. Because employers often look over résumés quickly, your page should be not only informative but also professional looking and easy to read. Unless you have a compelling reason for another choice, always laser print your résumé on high-quality white or off-white paper. You may highlight your section titles (education, work experiences, skills, etc.) by using boldface or large print, but don't overuse such print. Balance your text and white space in a pleasing arrangement.

If you have problems arranging your material (too much information jammed on the page or so little that your text looks lonely, for example), go back to the career center to look at ways others handled similar problems (some large copy shops also have sample books). A good page design, like a good haircut, can frame your best features in the most engaging way.

Most important: Always proofread your résumé for errors in grammar, punctuation, spelling, spacing, or typing! Because you want your résumé to look as professional as possible, make a point of having several careful (human) readers proofread your final draft.

Problems to Avoid

Remain ethical. Never lie on a résumé! Never, ever! Although you want to present yourself in the best possible ways, never fib about your experience, forge credentials you don't have, take credit for someone else's work, or overstate your participation in a project. No matter what you have heard about "puffery" in résumés ("Everyone exaggerates so why shouldn't I?"), avoid embarrassment (or even legal action) by always telling the truth. Instead of misrepresenting yourself, find ways to identify and arrange your knowledge and skills in ways that best highlight your strengths.

Contact your references in advance. You *must* obtain permission from each person before you list him or her as a reference. Even if you know the person well, use your good manners here: in person or in a politely written note or letter, ask in advance of your job application if you may name him or her as a reference. Once permission is granted, it's smart to give your references your résumé and any other information that might help them help you if they are contacted by a prospective employer. (Although a former boss or teacher may remember you well, they may be hazy about your exact dates of employment or the semester of your course work. Give them a helpful list of places, dates, skills, and—though you may have to overcome your sense of modesty—tactfully remind them of any outstanding work you did.

It's also good manners (and smart) to send your references a thank-you note, expressing your appreciation for their part in your job search (such notes are absolutely *required* if people write letters of recommendation for you). Thank-you notes should be written on stationery and sent through the mail; e-mail notes are not appropriate.

Add personal information thoughtfully. Federal law protects you: employers may not discriminate on the basis of ethnicity, race, religion, age, or gender. You should not include on your résumé any personal information (marital status, number of children, birth date, country of origin, etc.) that is not relevant to the job search. Although you may, if you wish, include information on your résumé about relevant personal interests (travel, theatrical experience, volunteer rescue work, etc.), you should be aware that employers may not consider such details useful. Don't squander your résumé space on unessential information! A better plan: if you've spent a great deal of your time in some after-work or extracurricular activity, identify the *skills* you have developed that will transfer to the workplace (customer relations, public speaking, editing, etc.). Instead of just describing yourself, show prospective employers what you can *do* for them.

Special Note: An increasing number of websites are helping employers and job seekers find each other through the posting of jobs and résumés. If you do post your résumé on such a site, choose your words carefully. Many prospective employers now use applicant-tracking software to look for keywords in résumés to match their needs. For example, a business seeking an accountant to assist its offices in Paris and Rome might flag only those résumés containing the words "CPA," "French," and "Italian." So if you are interested in a particular job advertised on the web, study the language of the job description and consider repeating, where appropriate, its keywords in your résumé.

■ Sample Résumés

The first résumé that follows was designed by a recent college graduate. Because he did not have an extensive work record, he chose a functional format to emphasize his education, business skills, and scholastic honors. The second résumé briefly notes specific skills from previous academic and work experiences that might interest a prospective employer.

■ Sample Résumé #1

Brent Monroe

417 Remington Street
Fort Collins, CO 80525

(970) 555-4567
BCMonroe@aol.com

Education

B.S. in Business Administration, Colorado State University, May 2006. GPA 3.6
A.S., Front Range Community College, May 2004. GPA 3.9

Professional Skills

Accounting

Spreadsheet programs
Amortization schedules
Payroll design and verification
Contracts and invoices

Computer

Word processing: Microsoft Word, WordPerfect
Spreadsheets: Excel, Select
Presentations: PowerPoint
website design

Awards and Activities

Outstanding Student Achievement Award, College of Business, Colorado State
University, 2006
President's Scholarship, Colorado State University, 2005 and 2006
Treasurer, Business Students Association, Colorado State University, 2006

Employment

Assistant Manager, Poppa's Pizza; Ault, Colorado, 6/05-12/06

References

Professor Gwen Lesser
Department of Accounting
Colorado State University
Fort Collins, CO 80523
(970) 555-7890
Glesser@colostate.edu

Professor Ralph Berber
Department of Finance
Colorado State University
Fort Collins, CO 80523
(970) 555-2344
Rberber@colostate.edu

Mr. Randy Attree
Manager, Poppa's Pizza
630 E. Third Street
Ault, CO 80303
(970) 333-4839

■ Sample Résumé #2

ROSEMARY SILVA

3000 Colorado Avenue   (720) 555-6428
Boulder, Colorado 80303   Rosesilva@netscape.net

Objective

To secure a full-time position as an admissions counselor at a mental health or addiction recovery facility

Education

B.A., University of Colorado, Boulder, May 2006. Major: Psychology. Minor: Spanish. GPA: 3.5

Internship and Research Experience

Intern Detoxification Counselor, Twin Lakes Recovery Center, Boulder, Colorado; January-May 2006.

Provided one-on-one counseling for in-patient residents; conducted admission interviews and prepared mental and physical evaluation reports; monitored physical vitals of patients; responded to crisis phone calls from out-patients; performed basic paramedical techniques; referred patients to other community agencies; supplied substance abuse information to patients and families.

Psychology Research Lab Assistant, University of Colorado at Boulder, under the direction of Professor Lois Diamond; September-December 2005.

Helped conduct experiments on CU student-volunteers to measure the relationship of memory and academic success: explained experiment procedures, set up computers, recorded student information, validated research credit slips.

Employment

Night Security Dispatcher, University of Colorado, Boulder, Campus Police Department; May 2004-April 2006.

Accurately received and responded to emergency and non-emergency calls and radio transmissions; communicated emergency information to appropriate agencies, such as Boulder Police and Rape Crisis Center; dispatched security units to handle crisis situations; wrote detailed records of incoming calls, security patrols, and responses.

References Available Upon Request

■ Assignment

Prepare a one-page résumé for your professional use at this time or in the near future. While you are in school, you might use this résumé to apply for a scholarship, an internship, a summer job, or a part-time position. Arrange your information to emphasize your strengths, and don't forget to thoroughly proof-read several times before you print your final draft. (If you keep a copy of this résumé handy and revise it regularly, you will be ready to respond quickly should a job or other opportunity unexpectedly present itself.)

■ Preparing Interview Notes and Post-Interview Letters

If a prospective employer wishes to interview you, sketch out a few notes for yourself before the meeting. Try to anticipate questions you may be asked, such as "What are your strengths as a worker?" and "How would you fit into our organization?" You will feel much more confident if you are prepared to discuss specific experiences that show both your skills and your previous work or school successes. Think about important information you wish your interviewer to know; consider making a brief list of the reasons you are the best candidate for the job. Once you have completed your notes, jot down a few key words on a note card to review just before your appointment so you can easily recall the details you want to provide. (For more good suggestions, turn to "Preparing for the Job Interview: Know Thyself, [pages 212–213], by Katy Piotrowski, a career-search consultant.)

After you interview for a job you want, consider writing a follow-up note to the prospective employer. This letter should be more than a polite thank you for the interview, however. Use the opportunity to again emphasize your skills. Begin by thanking the person for his or her time, but move on to show that you think, now more than ever, that you are the right person for the position and for the organization. Illustrate this claim by showing that during the interview you really listened and observed: "After hearing about your goals for new product X, I know I could contribute because . . . ." Or remind your interviewer of reasons to hire you: "You stressed your company's need for someone with XYZ skills. My internship training in that area . . . ." In other words, use this follow-up letter not only to offer your thanks but also to gently advertise yourself (and your good writing skills) one more time.

Part 4

A Concise Handbook

In this section you will learn to recognize and correct the most common errors in grammar, punctuation, and mechanics. Each error will be explained as simply as possible, with a minimum of technical language. Beside each rule you will find the editing mark or abbreviation that is most often used to identify that error; each rule is also numbered for easy reference. Exercises throughout each chapter will help you practice your grammar and punctuation skills. ■

Chapter 20

Major Errors in Grammar

■ Errors with Verbs

Verbs express action or state of being.

20a Faulty Agreement S-V Agr

Make your verb agree in number with its subject; a singular subject takes a singular verb, and a plural subject takes a plural verb.

Incorrect	*Lester Peabody*, principal of the Kung Fu School of Grammar, *don't* agree that gum chewing should be banned in the classroom.
Correct	*Lester Peabody*, principal of the Kung Fu School of Grammar, *doesn't* agree that gum chewing should be banned in the classroom.
Incorrect	The *actions* of the new senator *hasn't* been consistent with her campaign promises.
Correct	The *actions* of the new senator *haven't* been consistent with her campaign promises.

Compound subjects joined by "and" take a plural verb, unless the subject refers to a single person or a single unit.

Examples	*Bean sprouts* and *tofu are* dishes Jim Bob won't consider eating. ["Bean sprouts" and "tofu" are a compound subject joined by "and"; therefore, use a plural verb.]
	The *winner* and new *champion refuses* to give up the microphone at the news conference. ["Winner" and "champion" refer to a single person; therefore, use a singular verb.]

Listed here are some of the most confusing subject-verb agreement problems:

1. With a collective noun: a singular noun referring to a collection of elements as a unit generally takes a singular verb.

Incorrect	During boring parts of the Transcendental Vegetation lecture, the *class* often *chant* to the music of Norman Bates and the Shower Heads.
Correct	During boring parts of the Transcendental Vegetation lecture, the *class* often *chants* to the music of Norman Bates and the Shower Heads.
Incorrect	The *army* of the new nation *want* shoes, bullets, and weekend passes.
Correct	The *army* of the new nation *wants* shoes, bullets, and weekend passes.

2. With a relative pronoun ("that," "which," and "who") used as a subject: the verb agrees with its antecedent, the word being described.

Incorrect	The boss rejected a shipment of *shirts, which was* torn.
Correct	The boss rejected a shipment of *shirts, which were* torn.

3. With "each," "everybody," "everyone," and "neither" as the subject: use a singular verb even when followed by a plural construction.

Incorrect	*Each* of the children *think* Mom and Dad are automatic teller machines.
Correct	*Each* of the children *thinks* Mom and Dad are automatic teller machines.
Incorrect	Although only a few of the students saw the teacher pull out his hair, *everybody know* why he did it.
Correct	Although only a few of the students saw the teacher pull out his hair, *everybody knows* why he did it.
Incorrect	*Neither have* a dime left by the second of the month.
Correct	*Neither has* a dime left by the second of the month.

4. With "either . . . or" and "neither . . . nor": the verb agrees with the nearer item.

Incorrect	Neither rain nor dogs nor *gloom of night keep* the mail carrier from delivering bills.
Correct	Neither rain nor dogs nor *gloom of night keeps* the mail carrier from delivering bills.
Incorrect	Either Betty or her *neighbors is* hosting a come-as-you-are breakfast.
Correct	Either Betty or her *neighbors are* hosting a come-as-you-are breakfast.

5. With "here is (are)" and "there is (are)": the verb agrees with the number indicated by the subject following the verb.

Incorrect	*There is* only two good *reasons* for missing this law class: death and jury duty.
Correct	*There are* only two good *reasons* for missing this law class: death and jury duty.

Incorrect   To help you do your shopping quickly, Mr. Scrooge, *here are* a *list* of gifts under a dollar.

Correct   To help you do your shopping quickly, Mr. Scrooge, *here is* a *list* of gifts under a dollar.

6. With plural nouns intervening between subject and verb: the verb still agrees with the subject.

Incorrect   The *jungle,* with its poisonous plants, wild animals, and biting insects, *make* Herman long for the sidewalks of Topeka.

Correct   The *jungle,* with its poisonous plants, wild animals, and biting insects, *makes* Herman long for the sidewalks of Topeka.

7. With nouns plural in form but singular in meaning: a singular verb is usually correct.

Examples   *News travels* slowly if it comes through the post office.

Charades is the exhibitionist's game of choice.

Politics is often the rich person's hobby.

8. As you revise your prose, use a dictionary if you need help determining whether a word is singular or plural. For example, two common subject-verb agreement errors occur with the words "media" and "data," which, despite colloquial usage, should be treated as plurals in formal writing.

Correct   The *data were* faulty.

The *media* often *influence* public opinion polls.

■ PRACTICING WHAT YOU'VE LEARNED

Errors with Verbs: Subject-Verb Agreement

The following sentences contain subject-verb agreement errors. Correct the problems by changing the verbs. Some sentences contain more than one error.

1. A recent report on Cuban land crabs show that they can run faster than horses.

2. The team from Snooker Hollow High School are considering switching from basketball to basket weaving because passing athletics are now required for graduation.

3. Neither of the students know that both mystery writer Agatha Christie and inventor Thomas Edison was dyslexic.

4. Each of the twins have read about Joseph Priestley's contribution to the understanding of oxygen, but neither were aware that he also invented the pencil eraser.

5. Clarity in speech and writing are absolutely essential in the business world today.

6. Historical data suggests that the world's first money, in the form of coins, were made in Lydia, a country that is now part of Turkey.

7. Bananas, rich in vitamins and low in fat, is rated the most popular fruit in America.

8. There is many children in this country who appreciate a big plate of hot grits, but none of the Hall kids like this Southern dish.

9. Either the cocker spaniel or the poodle hold the honor of being the most popular breed of dogs in the United States, say the American Kennel Club.

10. Many people considers Johnny Appleseed a mythical figure, but now two local historians, authors of a well-known book on the subject, argues that he was a real person named John Chapman.

20b   Subjunctive   V Sub

When you make a wish or a statement that is contrary to fact, use the subjunctive verb form "were."

Incorrect	I wish I *was* queen so I could levy a tax on men who spit.
Correct	I wish I *were* queen so I could levy a tax on men who spit. [This expresses a wish.]
Incorrect	If "Fightin' Henry" *was* a foot taller and thirty pounds heavier, we would all be in trouble.
Correct	If "Fightin' Henry" *were* a foot taller and thirty pounds heavier, we would all be in trouble. [This proposes a statement contrary to fact.]

20c   Tense Shift   T

In most cases, the first verb in a sentence establishes the tense of any later verb. Keep your verbs within the same time frame to avoid confusing your readers.

Incorrect	Big Joe *saw* the police car coming up behind, so he *turns* into the next alley.
Correct	Big Joe *saw* the police car coming up behind, so he *turned* into the next alley.
Incorrect	Horace *uses* an artificial sweetener in his coffee all day, so he *felt* a pizza and a hot-fudge sundae *were* fine for dinner.
Correct	Horace *uses* an artificial sweetener in his coffee all day, so he *feels* a pizza and a hot-fudge sundae *are* fine for dinner.
Incorrect	Rex the Wonder Horse *was* obviously very smart because he *taps* out the telephone numbers of the stars with his hoof.
Correct	Rex the Wonder Horse *was* obviously very smart because he *tapped* out the telephone numbers of the stars with his hoof.

Split Infinitive   Sp I

Many authorities insist that "to" never be separated from its verb; today, however, some grammarians allow the split infinitive except in the most formal kinds of writing. Nevertheless, because it offends some readers, it is probably best to avoid the construction unless clarity or emphasis is clearly served by its use.

Traditional	A swift kick is needed *to start* the machine properly.
Untraditional	A swift kick is needed *to* properly *start* the machine.
Traditional	The teacher wanted Lori *to communicate* her ideas clearly.
Untraditional	The teacher wanted Lori *to* clearly *communicate* her ideas.

20e Double Negatives   D Neg

1. Rewrite sentences that use two negatives to communicate a single negative idea.

Incorrect	He *don't* need *no* fancy car to impress her.
Correct	He *doesn't* need a fancy car to impress her.
Incorrect	They *couldn't* find *no* record of my purchase.
Correct	They *could* find *no* record of my purchase.
Also Correct	They *couldn't* find *any* record of my purchase.

2. Don't use a negative verb and a negative qualifier ("hardly," "barely," "scarcely") together.

Incorrect	I *can't hardly* wait until Jim Bob gets his jaw out of traction, so I can challenge him to a bubble gum blowing contest.
Correct	I *can hardly* wait until Jim Bob gets his jaw out of traction, so I can challenge him to a bubble gum blowing contest.
Incorrect	Even when he flew his helicopter upside-down over her house, she *wouldn't barely* look at him.
Correct	Even when he flew his helicopter upside-down over her house, she *would barely* look at him.

20f Passive Voice   Pass

"Active voice" refers to sentences in which the subject performs the action. "Passive voice" refers to sentences in which the subject is acted upon.

Active	The police *pulled* over the van full of stolen ski sweaters.
Passive	The van full of stolen ski sweaters *was pulled* over by the police.

The passive voice is a logical construction when the person or thing performing the action is unknown or of lesser importance than the event or action.

Examples	My car was stolen last night.
	The soldier was buried with full military honors.

Some disciplines, particularly those in science and engineering, may prefer the passive voice: "All results were triple verified." Nevertheless, your prose style will improve if you choose strong, active-voice verbs over wordy, awkward, or unclear passive constructions.

Awkward passive construction	The call for volunteers was responded to by many students.
Active verb	Many students responded to the call for volunteers.
Unclear passive construction	Much protest is being voiced over the new electric fireworks. [Who is protesting?]
Active verb	Members of the Fuse Lighters Association are protesting the new electric fireworks.

(For more examples of active- and passive-voice verbs, see page 130.)

20g Irregular Verbs   Irreg V

Most verbs form their past tense by adding "-ed" ("ask/asked," "walk/walked"). However, some verbs form their past tenses by changing a vowel ("begin/began," "write/wrote"); others indicate past tense with an entirely new spelling or word ("go/went," "strike/struck").

Consult your dictionary when you are uncertain of the correct verb form you need. Remember that some verbs simply do not behave themselves!

Incorrect	Irregular verbs have *creeped* into our language.
Correct	Irregular verbs have *crept* into our language.
Incorrect	She *shaked* the piggy bank as hard as she could.
Correct	She *shook* the piggy bank as hard as she could
Incorrect	I don't know the current price of ant farms because I haven't *boughten* one since grade school
Correct	I don't know the current price of ant farms because I haven't *bought* one since grade school.

■ Practicing What You've Learned

Errors with Verbs: Form, Tense Shift, and Double Negatives

A. The following sentences contain incorrect verb forms, tense shifts, and double negatives. Correct any problems you see, and rewrite any sentences whose clarity or conciseness would be improved by using active rather than passive verbs.

    1. He couldn't hardly wait to hear country star Sue Flay sing her version of "I've Been Flushed from the Bathroom of Your Heart."

    2. "If you was in Wyoming and couldn't hear no wind blowing, what would people call you?" asked Jethro. "Dead," replies his buddy Herman.

    3. It was believed by Aztec ruler Montezuma that chocolate had magical powers and can act as an aphrodisiac.

4. Tammy's favorite band is Opie Gone Bad, so she always was buying their concert tickets, even though she can't hardly afford to.

5. Suspicions of arson are being raised by the Fire Department following the burning of the new Chip and Dale Furniture Factory.

B. Revise any incorrect verbs in the following sentences.

1. I seen what she was hiding behind her back.

2. He come around here yesterday asking questions, but we're use to that.

3. Having forget the combination to the safe, the burglar quietly snuck out the back door.

4. Austin don't like to be awokened until noon.

5. The kids done good work all day.

■ Errors with Nouns N

Nouns name people, places, and things ("boy," "kitchen," "car"). Proper nouns name specific people, places, and things ("Zora Neale Hurston," "Texas," "Chevrolet") and are capitalized.

20h Possessive with "-ing" Nouns

When the emphasis is on the action, use the possessive pronoun plus the "-ing" noun.

Example	He hated *my* singing around the house, so I made him live in the garage. [The emphasis is on *singing*.]

When the emphasis is not on the action, you may use a noun or pronoun plus the "-ing" noun.

Example	He hated *me* singing around the house, so I made him live in the garage. [The emphasis is on the person singing—me—not the action; he might have liked someone else singing.]

20i Misuse of Nouns as Adjectives

Some nouns may be used as adjectives modifying other nouns ("horse show," "movie star," "theater seats"). But some nouns used as adjectives sound awkward or like jargon. To avoid such awkwardness, you may need to change the noun to an appropriate adjective or reword the sentence.

Awkward	The group decided to work on local *environment* problems.
Better	The group decided to work on local *environmental* problems.
Jargon	The executive began a *cost estimation comparison study* of the two products.
Better	The executive began a *comparison study* of the two products' costs.

(For more information on ridding your prose of multiple nouns, see page 135.)

20j Plurals of Proper Nouns

Add an "s" to indicate plural proper nouns.

Example   Both *Keishas* volunteered for the charity drive.

The *Halls* were home for the holidays, enjoying their new *Frisbees* every afternoon.

(For practice correcting errors with nouns, turn to pages 531–532.)

■ Errors with Pronouns

A pronoun takes the place of a noun.

20k Faulty Agreement   Pro Agr

A pronoun should agree in number and gender with its antecedent (that is, the word the pronoun stands for).

Incorrect   To get a temperamental *actress* to sign a contract, the director would lock *them* in the dressing room.

Correct   To get a temperamental *actress* to sign a contract, the director would lock *her* in the dressing room.

Use the singular pronoun with "everyone," "anyone," and "each."

Incorrect   When the belly dancer asked for a volunteer partner, *everyone* in the men's gym class raised *their* hand.

Correct   When the belly dancer asked for a volunteer partner, *everyone* in the men's gym class raised *his* hand.

Incorrect   *Each* of the new wives decided to keep *their* own name.

Correct   *Each* of the new wives decided to keep *her* own name.

In the past, writers have traditionally used the masculine pronoun "he" when the gender of the antecedent is unknown, as in the following: "If a *spy* refuses to answer questions, *he* should be forced to watch James Bond movies until *he* cracks." Today, however, some authorities prefer the nonsexist "she or he," even though the construction can be awkward when maintained over a stretch of prose. Perhaps the best solution is to use the impersonal "one" when possible or simply rewrite the sentence in the plural: "If *spies* refuse to answer questions, *they* should be forced to watch James Bond movies until *they* crack." (For more advice and examples, see pages 159–161.)

20l Vague Reference   Ref

Your pronoun references should be clear.

Vague	If the trained seal won't eat its dinner, throw *it* into the lion's cage. [What goes into the lion's cage?]
Clear	If the trained seal won't eat its dinner, throw *the food* into the lion's cage.
Vague	After the dog bit Harry, *he* raised such a fuss at the police station that the sergeant finally had *him* impounded. [Who raised the fuss? Who was impounded?]
Clear	After being bitten, *Harry* raised such a fuss at the police station that the sergeant finally had the *dog* impounded.

Sometimes you must add a word or rewrite the sentence to make the pronoun reference clear:

Vague	I'm a lab instructor in the biology department and am also taking a statistics course. *This* has always been difficult for me. [What is difficult?]
Clear	I'm a lab instructor in the biology department and am also taking statistics, a *course* that has always been difficult for me.
Clear	I'm a lab instructor in the biology department and am also taking a statistics course. Being a teacher and a student at the same time has always been difficult for me.

In many cases, simply inserting a noun after a vague use of "this" or "that" will clarify meaning.

Vague	I visited with my grandmother while we watched the lunar eclipse. That was so special. [What was special? The visit? The eclipse?]
Clear	I visited with my grandmother while we watched the lunar eclipse. That *evening* was so special.

As you revise your prose, train yourself to catch any sentences that begin with "this" or "that" and see whether adding a noun or phrase will help communicate your meaning more effectively.

20m Shift in Pronouns   P Sh

Be consistent in your use of pronouns; don't shift from one person to another.

Incorrect	*One* shouldn't eat pudding with *your* fingers.
Correct	*One* shouldn't eat pudding with *one's* fingers.
Correct	*You* shouldn't eat pudding with *your* fingers.

| Incorrect | *We* left-handed people are at a disadvantage because most of the time *you* can't rent left-handed golf clubs or bowling balls. |
| Correct | *We* left-handed people are at a disadvantage because most of the time *we* can't rent left-handed golf clubs or bowling balls. |

(For additional examples, see page 135.)

20n   Incorrect Case   Ca

1. The case of a pronoun is determined by its function in the particular sentence. If the pronoun is a subject, use the nominative case: "I," "he," "she," "we," and "they"; if the pronoun is an object, use the objective case: "me," "him," "her," "us," and "them." To check your usage, all you need to do in many instances is isolate the pronoun in the manner shown here and determine whether it sounds correct alone.

Incorrect	Give the treasure map to Frankie and *I*.
Isolated	Give the treasure map to *I*. [awkward]
Correct	Give the treasure map to Frankie and *me*.
Incorrect	Bertram and *her* suspect that the moon is hollow.
Isolated	*Her* suspects that the moon is hollow. [awkward]
Correct	Bertram and *she* suspect that the moon is hollow.
Incorrect	The gift is from Annette and *I*.
Isolated	The gift is from *I*. [awkward]
Correct	The gift is from Annette and *me*.

Sometimes the "isolation test" doesn't work, so you just have to remember the rules. A common pronoun problem involves use of the preposition "between" and the choice of "me" or "I." Perhaps you can remember this rule by recalling there is no "I" in "between," only "e's" as in "me."

| Incorrect | Just *between you and I*, the Russian housekeeper is a good cook, but she won't iron curtains. |
| Correct | Just *between you and me*, the Russian housekeeper is a good cook, but she won't iron curtains. |

In other cases, to determine the correct pronoun, you will need to add implied but unstated sentence elements:

Examples	Mother always liked Dickie more than *me*. [Mother liked Dickie more than *she liked* me.]
	She is younger than *I* by three days. [She is younger than I *am* by three days.]
	Telephone exchange: May I speak to Kate? This is *she*. [This is she *speaking*.]

2. To solve the confusing *who/whom* pronoun problem, first determine the case of the pronoun in its own clause in each sentence.

    A. If the pronoun is the subject of a clause, use "who" or "whoever."

Examples   I don't know *who* spread the peanut butter on my English paper. ["Who" is the subject of the verb "spread" in the clause "who spread the peanut butter on my English paper."]
Rachel is a librarian *who* only likes books with pictures. ["Who" is the subject of the verb "likes" in the clause "who only likes books with pictures."]
He will sell secrets to *whoever* offers the largest sum of money. ["Whoever" is the subject of the verb "offers" in the clause "whoever offers the largest sum of money."]

    B. If the pronoun is the object of a verb, use "whom" or "whomever."

Examples   *Whom* am I kicking? ["Whom" is the direct object of the verb "kicking."]
Sid is a man *whom* I distrust. ["Whom" is the direct object of the verb "distrust."]
Whomever he kicked will probably be angry. ["Whomever" is the direct object of the verb "kicked."]

    C. If the pronoun occurs as the object of a preposition, use "whom," especially when the preposition immediately precedes the pronoun.

Examples   *With whom* am I speaking?
To whom is the letter addressed?
Do not ask *for whom* the bell tolls.

20o Incorrect Compound Forms

Compound personal pronouns are formed by adding "-self" or "selves" to some of the simple personal pronouns ("my," "you," "her," "him"). Use a dictionary if you are unsure of a correct form.

Correct   myself, yourself, himself, themselves
Incorrect   hisself, theirselves

■ Practicing What You've Learned

Errors with Nouns and Pronouns

A. In the following sentences, select the proper nouns and pronouns.

    1. Please buy a copy of the book *The Celery Stalks at Midnight* for my sister and (I, me).

    2. Between you and (I, me), some people define a Freudian slip as saying one thing but meaning your mother.

3. (Who, Whom) is the singer of the country song "You Can't Make a Heel Toe the Mark"?

4. Aunt Beulah makes better cookies than (I, me).

5. (Him and me, He and I) are going to the movies to see *Attack of the Killer Crabgrass*.

6. I'm giving my accordion to (whoever, whomever) is carrying a grudge against our new neighbors, the (Smith's, Smiths).

7. The Botox surprise party was given by Paige Turner, Justin Case, and (I, me).

8. She is the kind of person for (who, whom) housework meant sweeping the room with a glance.

9. (Her and him, She and he) are twins; they both like to repair old (Fords, Ford's).

10. The judge of the ugly feet contest announced (his self, him self, himself) the winner.

B. The following sentences contain a variety of errors with nouns and pronouns. Some sentences contain more than one error; skip any correct sentences you may find.

1. Clarence and me have an uncle who is so mean he writes the name of the murderer on the first page of mystery novels that are passed around the family.

2. Of whom did Oscar Wilde once say, "He hasn't a single redeeming vice"?

3. It was a surprise to both Marys and I to learn that Switzerland didn't give women the right to vote until 1971.

4. Each of the young women in the Family Life class decided not to marry after they read that couples today have 2.3 children.

5. Jim Bob explained to Frankie that the best way for him to avoid his recurring nosebleeds was to stay out of his cousin's marital arguments.

6. Those of us who'd had the flu agreed that one can always get a doctor to return your call quicker if you get in the shower, but let's keep this tip confidential between you and I.

7. The stranger gave the free movie tickets to Louise and I after he saw people standing in line to leave the theater.

8. The personnel director told each of the employees, most of who opposed him, to signify their "no" vote by saying, "I resign."

9. A person knows he's in trouble when their salary undergoes a modification reduction adjustment of 50 percent.

10. One of the first movies to gross over one million dollars was *Tarzan of the Apes* (1932), starring Johnny Weismuller, a former Olympic star who became an actor. This didn't happen often in the movie industry at that time.

■ Errors with Adverbs and Adjectives

20p   Incorrect Usage   Adv   Adj

Incorrect use of adverbs and adjectives often occurs when you confuse the two modifiers. Adverbs qualify the meanings of verbs, adjectives, and other adverbs; they often answer the questions "how?" "when?" or "where?" and they frequently end in "ly."

Incorrect	After Kay argued with the mechanic, her car began running *bad*.
Correct	After Kay argued with the mechanic, her car began running *badly*.

Adjectives, on the other hand, commonly describe or qualify the meanings of nouns only.

Example   The *angry* mechanic neglected to put oil into Kay's *old* car.

One of the most confusing pairs of modifiers is "well" and "good." We often use "good" as an adjective modifying a noun and "well" as an adverb modifying a verb.

Examples   *A Sap's Fables* is a *good* book for children, although it is not *well* organized.

Bubba was such a *good* liar his wife had to call in the children at suppertime.

After eating Rocky Mountain oysters, Susie yodels exceptionally *well*.

Did you do *well* on your math test?

If you cannot determine whether a word is an adverb or an adjective, consult your dictionary.

20q   Faulty Comparison   Comp

When you compare two elements to a higher or lower degree, you often add "-er" or "-r" to the adjective.

Incorrect	Of the two sisters, Selene is the *loudest*.
Correct	Of the two sisters, Selene is the *louder*.

When you compare more than two elements, you often add "-est" to the adjective.

Example   Selene is the *loudest* of the four children in the family.

Other adjectives use the words "more," "most," "less," and "least" to indicate comparison.

Examples   Bela Lugosi is *more* handsome than Lon Chaney but *less* handsome than Vincent Price.

Of all the horror film stars, Boris Karloff is the *most* handsome, and Christopher Lee is the *least* handsome.

Beware using a double comparison when it is unnecessary:

| Incorrect | It was the *most saddest* song I've ever heard. |
| Correct | It was the *saddest* song I've ever heard. |

Note, too, that for most authorities, the word "unique" is a special adjective, one without a degree of comparison. Despite common usage to the contrary, an experience or thing may be unique—that is, one of a kind—but it may not be "very unique."

■ PRACTICING WHAT YOU'VE LEARNED

Errors with Adverbs and Adjectives

Choose the correct adverbs and adjectives in the following sentences.

1. After the optometrist pulled her eye tooth, Hortense didn't behave very (good, well) in the waiting room.

2. Which is the (worser, worse, worst) food, liver or buttermilk?

3. I didn't do (good, well) on my nature project because my bonsai sequoia tree grew (bad, badly) in its tiny container.

4. Don't forget to dress (warm, warmly) for the Arctic freestyle race.

5. Of the twins, Teensie is more (funner, fun) than Egore.

6. Watching Joe Bob eat candied fruit flies made Jolene feel (real, really) ill, and his table manners did not make her feel (more better, better).

7. The Roman toothpick holder was (very unique, the uniquest, unique).

8. That was the (funniest, most funniest) flea circus I have ever seen.

9. Does the instructional guide *Bobbing for Doughnuts* still sell (good, well)?

10. The Fighting Mosquitoes were trained (well, good), but they just didn't take practices (serious, seriously).

■ Errors in Modifying Phrases

20r Dangling Modifiers   DM

A modifying—or descriptive—phrase must have a logical relationship to some specific words in the sentence. When those words are omitted, the phrase "dangles" without anything to modify. Dangling modifiers frequently occur at the beginnings of sentences and often can be corrected by adding the proper subjects to the main clauses.

| Dangling | Not knowing how to swim, buying scuba gear was foolish. |
| Correct | Not knowing how to swim, *we* decided that buying scuba gear was foolish. |

Dangling	Feeling too sick to ski, her vacation to the mountains was postponed.
Correct	Feeling too sick to ski, *Laura* postponed her vacation to the mountains.

(For additional examples, see pages 122–124.)

20s Misplaced Modifiers   MM

When modifying words, phrases, or clauses are not placed near the word they describe, confusion or unintentional humor often results.

Misplaced	Teddy swatted the fly still dressed in his pajamas.
Correct	Still dressed in his pajamas, Teddy swatted the fly.
Misplaced	There are many things people won't eat, especially children.
Correct	There are many things people, especially children, won't eat.

(For additional examples, see pages 122–124.)

■ PRACTICING WHAT YOU'VE LEARNED

Errors in Modifying Phrases

Correct the errors in dangling and misplaced modifiers by rearranging or rewriting the following sentences.

1. After boarding Hard Luck Airlines, the meals convinced us to return by ship.

2. Here is the new telephone number for notifying the fire department of any fires that may be attached to your telephone.

3. The prize-winning ice sculptor celebrated her new open-air studio in Aspen, where she lives with her infant daughter, purchased for $10,000.

4. The movie star showed off letters from admirers that were lying all over his desk.

5. Running too fast during a game of "Kick the Can," my face collided with the flagpole.

6. Eloise bought a computer from her neighbor with faulty memory.

7. Baggy, wrinkled, and hopelessly out of style, Jean tossed the skirt from her closet.

8. Forgetting to pack underwear, the suitcase had to be reopened.

9. Blanche plans to teach a course next spring incorporating her research into the mating habits of Big Foot on the campus of Slippery Rock College.

10. After spending all night in the library, Kate's friends knew she'd need a trip to Special Coffee.

11. Squeezing the can, the tomatoes didn't seem ripe to DeeDee.

12. From birth to twelve months, parents don't have to worry about solid food.

13. He didn't think the bicycles would make it over the mountains, being so old.

14. I've read that a number of modern sailors, like Thor Heyerdahl, have sailed primitive vessels across the ocean in books from the public library.

15. Proofreading carefully, dangling modifiers may be spotted and corrected easily.

■ Errors in Sentences

20t   Fragments   Frag

A complete sentence must contain a subject and a verb. A fragment is an incomplete sentence; it is often a participial ("-ing") phrase or dependent clause that belongs to the preceding sentence. To check for fragments, try reading your prose, one sentence at a time, starting at the *end* of your essay. If you find a "sentence" that makes no sense alone, it's probably a fragment that should either be rewritten or connected to another sentence.

Incorrect	Bubba's parents refuse to send him to a psychiatrist. Although they both know he eats shoelaces and light bulbs.
Correct	Bubba's parents refuse to send him to a psychiatrist, although they both know he eats shoelaces and light bulbs.
Incorrect	This recording of the symphony's latest concert is so clear you can hear every sound. Including the coughs and whispers of the audience.
Correct	This recording of the symphony's latest concert is so clear you can hear every sound, including the coughs and whispers of the audience.
Incorrect	At Liz's most recent wedding, the photographer used an instant camera. Because her marriages break up so fast.
Correct	At Liz's most recent wedding, the photographer used an instant camera because her marriages break up so fast.

You can also try this test to see whether a group of words is a fragment: say the phrase "It is true that" in front of the words in question. In most cases, a complete sentence will still make sense, but a fragment won't.

Example	At Liz's most recent wedding, the photographer used an instant camera. Because her marriages break up so fast.
	Which is a fragment?
	It is true that *at Liz's most recent wedding, the photographer used an instant camera.* [This sentence makes sense, so it's not a fragment.]
	It is true that *because her marriages break up so fast.* [Yes, this is a fragment.]

Sentence fragments are often used in conversations ("yes," "maybe," "just a minute") and in informal or personal writing (notes, letters, email, etc.). In some professional and academic writing, *intentional fragments* or abbreviated sentences may be used occasionally for emphasis or to convey a particular tone, such as playfulness, anger, or scorn. However, intentional fragments should be just that: created on purpose to achieve a specific rhetorical goal.

Intentional fragments	After cleaning out the attic, Eloise felt terrible. *Hot. Tired. Cranky with the world.*
	She agreed to hand over the jewels. *Just exactly what he had had in mind all along.*

As a general rule, fragments should be avoided in formal writing. Ask your instructor whether intentional fragments are permitted in your essays.

■ PRACTICING WHAT YOU'VE LEARNED

Fragment Sentence Errors

A. Using the "It is true that" test, identify the fragments and the complete sentences in the following samples.

1. The first drive-in theaters opened in New Jersey in 1933. Which was in the middle of the Great Depression when money was scarce.

2. By 1958 there were over 4,000 drive-ins in the United States. As recorded by the United Drive-in Theatre Owners Association.

3. The number of drive-ins has fallen drastically. Perhaps because escalating land prices make property too valuable for use in this way. Or the fact that they are open only during the summer months in some areas.

4. There are only 430 drive-ins left in the country. Including the American territories.

5. Other outdoor summer activities are also endangered. For instance, the minature golf industry, down from 50,000 courses in the 1930s to fewer than 15,000 today.

B. Rewrite the following sentences so that there are no fragments.

1. The idea of a credit card first appeared in 1887. According to Lawrence M. Ausbel, author of "Credit Cards," in the *McGraw-Hill Encyclopedia of Economics.*

2. Originally an imaginary concept in a futurist novel by Edward Bellamy. The card allowed characters to charge against future earnings.

3. Around the turn of the twentieth century some American stores issued paper or metal "shoppers' plates." Although they were only used by retailers to identify their credit customers.

4. The first real credit card was issued in 1947 by a New York bank and was a success. Despite the fact that customers could only charge purchases in a two-block area in Brooklyn.

5. Travel and entertainment cards soon appeared that allowed customers to charge items and services across the country. For example, the American Express card in 1958 and Carte Blanche in 1959.

20u   Run-On Sentence   R-O

Don't run two sentences together without any punctuation. Use a period, a semicolon, or a comma plus a coordinating conjunction (if appropriate), or subordinate one clause.

Incorrect	The indicted police chief submitted his resignation the mayor accepted it gratefully.
Correct	The indicted police chief submitted his resignation. The mayor accepted it gratefully.
Correct	The indicted police chief submitted his resignation; the mayor accepted it gratefully.
Correct	The indicted police chief submitted his resignation, and the mayor accepted it gratefully.
Correct	When the indicted police chief submitted his resignation, the mayor accepted it gratefully.

Do not try to correct a run-on by inserting a comma between the two sentences; doing so without a coordinating conjunction will produce an error called a *comma splice*, discussed on pages 539 and 547. Punctuate correctly or rewrite the run-on to best communicate your meaning.

Incorrect (run-on)	Victoria Woodhull was the first American woman to run for the presidency she was defeated in 1872 by Ulysses S. Grant.
Incorrect (comma splice)	Victoria Woodhull was the first American woman to run for the presidency, she was defeated in 1872 by Ulysses S. Grant.
Correct	Victoria Woodhull was the first American woman to run for the presidency. She was defeated in 1872 by Ulysses S. Grant.
Correct	Victoria Woodhull was the first American woman to run for the presidency; she was defeated in 1872 by Ulysses S. Grant.
Correct	Victoria Woodhull was the first American woman to run for the presidency, but she was defeated in 1872 by Ulysses S. Grant.
Correct	Victoria Woodhull, the first American woman to run for the presidency, was defeated in 1872 by Ulysses S. Grant.

■ **PRACTICING WHAT YOU'VE LEARNED**

Run-On Errors

Correct the following run-on sentences. Try to use several different methods of correcting the errors.

1. Workers in the United States take an average of thirteen days of vacation a year in Italy they take forty-two.

2. In 1901 a schoolteacher named Annie Edson Taylor became the first person to go over Niagara Falls in a wooden barrel she is the only woman known to have survived this risky adventure.

3. The minister preached his farewell sermon the choir sang "Break Forth into Joy."

4. The first microwave oven marketed in 1959 was a built-in unit it cost a whopping $2,595.

5. Coffee was considered a food in the Middle Ages travelers who found it growing in Ethiopia mixed it with animal fat.

(For additional practice, turn to exercise "B" on pages 551–552.)

20v Comma Splice   CS

A comma splice occurs when two sentences are linked with a comma. To correct this error, you can (1) separate the two sentences with a period, (2) separate the two sentences with a semicolon, (3) insert a coordinating conjunction ("for," "but," "and," "or," "nor," "so," "yet") after the comma, or (4) subordinate one clause.

Incorrect	Grover won a stuffed gila monster at the church raffle, his mother threw it away the next day while he was in school.
Correct	Grover won a stuffed gila monster at the church raffle. His mother threw it away the next day while he was in school.
Correct	Grover won a stuffed gila monster at the church raffle; his mother threw it away the next day while he was in school.
Correct	Grover won a stuffed gila monster at the church raffle, but his mother threw it away the next day while he was in school.
Correct	Although Grover won a stuffed gila monster at the church raffle, his mother threw it away the next day while he was in school.

(For more help on correcting comma splices, see page 547 in the following chapter on punctuation; coordination and subordination are discussed in detail on pages 137–139.)

■ **PRACTICING WHAT YOU'VE LEARNED**

Comma Splice Errors

A. Correct the comma splices that appear in the following sentences. Use more than one method of correcting the errors.

1. Most people know that the likeness of Susan B. Anthony appeared on an American dollar coin in the 1990s, fewer people know exactly who she was or why she is so important.

2. For most of her life Anthony fought for women to obtain the right to vote, she was an organizer of the world's first women's rights convention in 1848.

3. Anthony often risked her safety and her freedom for her beliefs, she was arrested in 1872 for the crime of voting in an election.

4. She also worked to secure laws to protect working women, at that time all of a woman's wages automatically belonged to her husband.

5. Unfortunately, Anthony did not live to see the 1920 passage of the Nineteenth Amendment giving women the right to vote, she died in 1906.

B. Correct any run-on sentences or comma splice errors you see. Skip any correct sentences you find.

1. My mother is very politically conservative, she's written in King George III for president in the last two elections.

2. Mary Lou decided not to eat the alphabet soup the letters spelled out "botulism."

3. A dried gourd containing seeds probably functioned as the first baby rattle, ancient Egyptian wall paintings show babies with such gourds clutched in their fingers.

4. Opportunists who came to the South after the Civil War were often called "carpetbaggers," they carried their belongings in cheaply produced travel bags made of Belgian carpet.

5. A friend of mine offers a good definition of nasty theater critics on opening night, according to him, they're the people who can't wait to stone the first cast.

6. When English scientist James Smithson died in 1829, he willed his entire fortune to the United States to establish a foundation for knowledge, that's how the Smithsonian Institution was started.

7. The word "jack-o'-lantern" may have come from the legend of Irish Jack, a mean old man in life, he was condemned after death to wander the earth carrying a hollow turnip with a lump of burning coal inside.

8. Americans forget how large the blue whale is it has a heart as large as a Volkswagen Beetle and can hold an elephant on its tongue.

9. According to a study by the Fish and Wildlife Service, Americans' favorite animals are dogs, horses, swans, robins, and butterflies; their least favorite are cockroaches, mosquitos, rats, wasps, and rattlesnakes.

10. The famous Eiffel Tower, built for the 1889 Paris Exposition, has inspired many crazy stunts, for example, in 1891 Silvain Dornon climbed the 363 steps on stilts.

20w Faulty Parallelism   //

Parallel thoughts may be expressed in similar grammatical constructions. Repeated sentence elements, such as verbs, nouns, pronouns, and phrases, often appear in parallel form to emphasize meaning and to promote sentence fluency.

Examples

Parallel verbs: In his vaudeville act he *sang, danced,* and *juggled.*

Parallel prepositional phrases: She ran *through the door, across the yard,* and *into the limo.*

You might find it helpful to isolate the repeated elements in a sentence to see whether they are parallel.

She ran

(1) through the door
(2) across the yard   parallel
(3) into the limo

Faulty Parallelism	Boa constrictors like *to lie* in the sun, *to hang* from limbs, and *swallowing* small animals.
Isolated	(1) to lie (2) to hang (3) swallowing [not parallel to #1 and #2]
Revised	Boa constrictors like *to lie* in the sun, *to hang* from limbs, and *to swallow* small animals.
Faulty Parallelism	Whether *working* on his greasy car, *fistfighting* at the hamburger stand, or *in bed,* my brother always kept his hair combed.
Revised	Whether *working* on his greasy car, *fistfighting* at the hamburger stand, or *lounging* in bed, my brother always kept his hair combed.

■ Practicing What You've Learned

Errors in Parallelism

Revise the following sentences so that the parallel ideas are expressed in similar grammatical constructions.

1. Is it true that Superman could leap tall buildings, run faster than a locomotive, and that bullets would bounce off his skin?

2. To celebrate the canned pork product called Spam, we attended the Texas Spamarama Festival to participate in the Spambalaya cook-off, the Spam slab toss, the Spam relay race, and were dancing to such favorites as "Twist and Snout."*

3. My Aunt Clara swears she has seen Elvis snacking at the deli, browsing at the supermarket, munching at the pizza parlor, and in the cookbook section of a local bookstore.

4. According to my husband, summer air in Louisiana is one part oxygen, nine parts water, and the rest is mosquitoes, about 90 percent.

5. Many teachers believe that the most important keys to success for students in college include attending class, keep up with reading assignments, and being brave enough to ask questions.

6. Yoga encourages its participants to work on their flexibility, strength, and how they can reduce their stress levels.

7. Drivers should hang up their cell phones, refrain from eating, and drinking too, leaving the radio buttons alone.

8. Smart people learn from their own mistakes; learning from the mistakes of others is what even smarter people do.

9. Theater class helped me overcome my shyness, make new friends, and my confidence to do other activities was improved.

10. The writer Oscar Wilde, the dancer Isadora Duncan, the painter Max Ernst, and Jim Morrison, who was a rock star, are all buried in the same Paris cemetery.

20x False Predication   Pred

This error occurs when the predicate (that part of the sentence that says something about the subject) doesn't fit properly with the subject. Illogical constructions result.

If it's helpful in some cases, remember that the verbs "is" and "was" often mean "equates to."

Incorrect	Energy is one of the world's biggest problems. ["Energy" itself is not a problem.]
Correct	The lack of fuel for energy is one of the world's biggest problems.

---

* Yes, readers, there really is a Spamarama Festival, a silly outdoor event in Austin, Texas, with music and games (the Spamolympics) for all ages. Held annually around April Fool's Day for over twenty-five years, the Festival raises money for charity.

Incorrect	My roommate is why I'm moving to a new apartment. [A roommate is not a reason.]
Correct	My roommate's habit of talking nonstop is driving me to find a new apartment.
Also Correct	Because of my annoying roommate, I'm moving to a new apartment.
Incorrect	Her first comment after winning the lottery was exciting. [Her comment wasn't exciting; she was excited.]
Correct	Her first comment after winning the lottery expressed her excitement.
Incorrect	True failure is when you make an error and don't learn anything from it. [Avoid all "is when" and "is where" constructions. The subject does not denote a time, so the predicate is faulty.]
Correct	You have truly failed only when you make an error and don't learn anything from it.

(For other examples of faulty predication, see page 124.)

20y Mixed Structure Mix S

"Mixed structure" is a catchall term that applies to a variety of sentence construction errors. Usually, the term refers to a sentence in which the writer begins with one kind of structure and then shifts to another in midsentence. Such a shift often occurs when writers are in a hurry and their minds have already jumped ahead to the next thought.

Confused	By the time one litter of cats is given away seems to bring a new one.
Clear	Giving away one litter of cats seems to tell the mother cat that it's time to produce a new batch.
Confused	The bank robber realized that in his crime spree how very little fun he was having.
Clear	The bank robber realized that he was having very little fun in his crime spree.
Confused	The novel is too confusing for what the author meant.
Clear	The novel is too confused for me to understand what the author meant.
Confused	Children with messages from their parents will be stapled to the bulletin board.
Clear	To find messages from their parents, children should look at the bulletin board.

(For other examples of mixed structure, see page 124.)

■ PRACTICING WHAT YOU'VE LEARNED

Errors of False Predication and Mixed Structure

Rewrite the following sentences so that each one is clear and coherent.

1. The team's quarterback A. M. Hall's broken finger, which sidelined him last week for the Raiders' game, is expected to play in tonight's game.

2. The groom is a graduate of Centerville High School where he lived all his life.

3. On my way to the doctor's office, my universal joint went out, causing even more body damage after hitting the tree.

4. An example of his intelligence is when he brought home a twenty-pound block of ice after ice fishing all day.

5. For those new residents who have children and don't know about it, the town offers low-cost daycare services.

6. According to the nineteenth-century cynic Ambrose Bierce, marriage is when there is "a master, a mistress, and two slaves, making in all, two."

7. Another situation when I get so mad is the plumber showing up three hours late.

8. My drama teacher is a big reason why I am a star today.

9. Some folks argue that sound travels slower than light such as when advice parents give their teenagers doesn't reach them until they're forty.

10. Hearing his cries for help is how he came to be found in a ditch by some stray cows.

Chapter 21

A Concise Guide to Punctuation

Punctuation marks do not exist, as one student recently complained, to make your life complicated. They are used to clarify your written thoughts so that the reader understands your meaning. Just as traffic signs and signals tell a driver to slow down, stop, or go, so punctuation is intended to guide the reader through your prose. Look, for example, at the confusion in the following sentences when the necessary punctuation marks are omitted:

Confusing	Has the tiger been fed Bill? [Bill was the tiger's dinner?]
Clear	Has the tiger been fed, Bill?
Confusing	After we had finished raking the dog jumped into the pile of leaves. [Raking the dog?]
Clear	After we had finished raking, the dog jumped into the pile of leaves.
Confusing	The coach called the swimmers names. [Was the coach fired for verbally abusing the swimmers?]
Clear	The coach called the swimmers' names.

Because punctuation helps you communicate clearly with your reader, you should familiarize yourself with the following rules.

21a The Period (.)   P

1. Use a period to end a sentence that makes a statement.

Examples   Employees at that company are not allowed to go on coffee breaks.
It takes too long to retrain them.

2. Use a period at the end of a sentence that makes a direct command or request.

Examples   Don't walk on the grass.
Please give me your new address.

3. Use a period after initials and many abbreviations.

Examples   W. B. Yeats, 12 A.M., Dr., etc., M.A.

4. Only one period is necessary if the sentence ends with an abbreviation.

Examples   The elephant was delivered C.O.D.
To find a good job, you should obtain a B.S. or B.A.

21b The Question Mark (?)   P

1. Use a question mark after every direct question.

Examples   May I borrow your boots?
Is the sandstorm over now?

2. No question mark is necessary after an indirect question.

Examples   Jean asked why no one makes a paper milk carton that opens
without tearing.
Dave wondered how the television detective always found a parking
place next to the scene of the crime.

21c The Exclamation Point (!)   P

The exclamation point follows words, phrases, or sentences to show strong feelings.

Examples   Fire! Call the rescue squad!
The Broncos finally won the Super Bowl!

■ PRACTICING WHAT YOU'VE LEARNED

Errors Using Periods, Question Marks, and Exclamation Points

Correct the following sentences by adding, deleting, or changing
periods, question marks, or exclamation points, where appropriate.

1. The space program sent some cows into orbit last year I think they are now
known as the herd shot around the world

2. Ms Anita Bath wants to know why erasers never outlast their pencils?

3. Her French class at St Claire's School on First Ave was taught by Madame Beau V Rhee, Ph.D..

4. Where do all the birds go when it's raining

5. I have wonderful news I won the lottery

21d   The Comma (,)   P

1. Use a comma to separate two independent clauses* joined by a coordinating conjunction. To remember the coordinating conjunctions, think of the acronym FANBOYS: "for," "and," "nor," "but," "or," "yet," and "so." Always use one of the FANBOYS and a comma when you join two independent clauses.

Examples   You can bury your savings in the backyard, *but* don't expect Mother Nature to pay interest.

I'm going home tomorrow, *and* I'm never coming back.

After six weeks Louie's diet was making him feel lonely and depressed, *so* he had a bumper sticker printed that said, "Honk if you love groceries."

Do *not* join two sentences with a comma only; such an error is called a *comma splice.* Use a comma plus one of the coordinating conjunctions listed previously, a period, a semicolon, or subordination.

Comma splice	Beatrice washes and grooms the chickens, Samantha feeds the spiders.
Correct	Beatrice washes and grooms the chickens, and Samantha feeds the spiders.
Correct	Beatrice washes and grooms the chickens. Samantha feeds the spiders.
Correct	Beatrice washes and grooms the chickens; Samantha feeds the spiders.
Correct	When Beatrice washes and grooms the chickens, Samantha feeds the spiders.
Comma splice	Jack doesn't like singing groups, he won't go with us to hear Fed Up with People.
Correct	Jack doesn't like singing groups, so he won't go with us to hear Fed Up with People.
Correct	Jack doesn't like singing groups. He won't go with us to hear Fed Up with People.
Correct	Jack doesn't like singing groups; he won't go with us to hear Fed Up with People.
Correct	Because Jack doesn't like singing groups, he won't go with us to hear Fed Up with People.

(For additional help, see page 539; for practice exercises, see pages 540–541 and 551–552.)

---

* An independent clause looks like a complete sentence; it contains a subject and a verb, and it makes sense by itself.

Beware the tricky word "however." "However" is *not* one of the FANBOYS (coordinating conjunctions) and consequently can never be used to join two independent clauses. Incorrect use of "however" most often results in a comma splice.

Comma splice	The police arrested the thief, *however,* they had to release him because the plant wouldn't talk.
Correct	The police arrested the thief; *however,* they had to release him because the plant wouldn't talk.
Also correct	The police arrested the thief. *However,* they had to release him because the plant wouldn't talk.

2. Set off with a comma an introductory phrase or clause.

Examples	After we had finished our laundry, we discovered that one sock was missing.
	According to the owner of the laundromat, customers have conflicting theories about missing laundry.
	For example, one man claims his socks make a break for freedom when no one is watching the dryers.

3. Set off nonessential phrases and clauses. If the information can be omitted without changing the meaning of the main clause, then the phrase or clause is nonessential. Do *not* set off clauses or phrases that are essential to the meaning of the main clause.

Essential	He looked worse than my friend *who gets his clothes from the "lost and found" at the bus station.* [The "who" clause is essential to explain which friend.]
	The storm *that destroyed Mr. Peartree's outhouse* left him speechless with anger. [The "that" clause is essential to explain which storm angered Mr. Peartree.]
	The movie *now showing at the Ritz* is very obscene and very popular. [The participial phrase is essential to identify the particular movie.]
Nonessential	Joe Medusa, *who won the jalapeno-eating contest last year,* is this year's champion cow-chip tosser. [The "who" clause is nonessential because it only supplies additional information to the main clause.]
	Black widow spiders, *which eat their spouses after mating,* are easily identifiable by the orange hourglass design on their abdomens. [The "which" clause is nonessential because it only supplies additional information.]
	The jukebox, *now reappearing in local honky-tonks,* first gained popularity during the 1920s. [The participial phrase is nonessential because it only supplies additional information.]

4. Conjunctive adverbs, such as "however," "moreover," "thus," "consequently," and "therefore," are used to show continuity and are frequently set off by commas when they appear in midsentence.

Examples	She soon discovered, *however,* that he had stolen her monogrammed towels in addition to her pet avocado plant.
	She felt, *consequently,* that he was not trustworthy.

When a conjunctive adverb occurs at the beginning of a sentence, it may be followed by a comma, especially if a pause is intended. If no pause is intended, you may omit the comma, but inserting the comma is never wrong.

Examples   *Thus,* she resolved never to speak to him again.
Thus she resolved never to speak to him again.
Therefore, he resolved never to speak to her again.
Therefore he resolved never to speak to her again.

(For practice of comma rules 1–4, turn to page 551.)

5. Use commas to separate items in a series of words, phrases, or clauses.

Examples   Julio collects coins, stamps, bottle caps, erasers, and pocket lint.

Mrs. Jones chased the burglar out the window, around the ledge, down the fire escape, and into the busy street.

Do note that there is no comma separating "such as" and the first word in the list of items that follow.

Incorrect   Sarah eats a variety of vegetarian foods, such as, tofu, nuts, and fruit.

Correct   Sarah eats a variety of vegetarian foods, such as tofu, nuts, and fruit.

Although journalists and some grammarians permit the omission of the last comma before the "and," many authorities believe the comma is necessary for clarity. For example, how many pints of ice cream are listed in the sentence below?

Please buy the following pints of ice cream: strawberry, peach, coffee, vanilla and chocolate swirl.

Four or five pints? Without a comma before the "and," the reader doesn't know whether vanilla and chocolate swirl are (is?) one item or two. By inserting the last comma, you clarify the sentence:

Please buy the following pints of ice cream: strawberry, peach, coffee, vanilla, and chocolate swirl.

6. Use commas to separate adjectives of equal emphasis that modify the same noun. To determine whether a comma should be used, see if you can insert the word "and" between the adjectives; if the phrase still makes proper sense with the substituted "and," use a comma.

Examples   She finally moved out of her cold, dark apartment.
She finally moved out of her cold and dark apartment.

I have a sweet, handsome husband.
I have a sweet and handsome husband.

He called from a convenient telephone booth.
But not: He called from a convenient and telephone booth. ["Convenient" modifies the unit "telephone booth," so there is no comma.]

Hand me some of that homemade pecan pie.
But not: Hand me some of that homemade and pecan pie. ["Homemade" modifies the unit "pecan pie," so there is no comma.]

7. Set off a direct address with commas.

Examples   Gentlemen, keep your seats.

Car fifty-four, where are you?

Not now, Eleanor, I'm busy.

8. Use commas to set off items in addresses and dates.

Examples   The sheriff followed me from Austin, Texas, to question me about my uncle.

He found me on February 2, 1978, when I stopped in Fairbanks, Alaska, to buy sunscreen.

9. Use commas to set off a degree or title following a name.

Examples   John Dough, M.D., was audited when he reported only $5.68 in taxable income last year.

The Neanderthal Award went to Samuel Lyle, Ph.D.

10. Use commas to set off dialogue from the speaker.

Examples   Alexander announced, "I don't think I want a second helping of possum."

"Eat hearty," said Marie, "because this is the last of the food."

Note that you do not use a comma before an indirect quotation or before titles in quotation marks following the verbs "read," "sang," or "wrote."

Incorrect   Bruce said, that cockroaches have portions of their brains scattered throughout their bodies.

Correct   Bruce said that cockroaches have portions of their brain scattered throughout their bodies.

Incorrect   One panel member read, "Aunt Jennifer's Tigers," and the other sang, "Song for My Father."

Correct   One panel member read "Aunt Jennifer's Tigers," and the other sang "Song for My Father."

11. Use commas to set off "yes," "no," "well," and other weak exclamations.

Examples   Yes, I am in the cat condo business.

No, all the units with decks are sold.

Well, perhaps one with a pool will do.

12. Set off interrupters or parenthetical elements appearing in the middle of a sentence. A parenthetical element is additional information placed as explanation or comment within an already complete sentence. This element may be a word (such as "certainly" or "fortunately"), a phrase ("for example" or "in fact"), or a clause ("I believe" or "you know"). The word, phrase, or clause is parenthetical if the sentence parts before and after it fit together and make sense.

Examples   Jack is, *I think,* still a compulsive gambler.

Harvey, *my brother,* sometimes has breakfast with him.

Jack cannot, *for example,* resist shuffling the toast or dealing the pancakes.

13. Resist the temptation to pepper your prose with commas when you have no good reason to use them. Not all sentences containing "and" take a comma. In the sentence below, for example, "and" separates a compound predicate; it is not used as one of the FANBOYS (a coordinating conjunction) separating two independent clauses.

Incorrect   She ate a biscuit, and drank a cup of tea. [The comma here incorrectly separates the verb "drank" from its subject "she."]

Correct   She ate a biscuit and drank a cup of tea.

On the other hand, writers may use commas when necessary to improve sentence clarity.

Confusing   Unlike Mary Jo never learned to cook.
Clear   Unlike Mary, Jo never learned to cook.

Confusing   Whatever will be will be.
Clear   Whatever will be, will be.

■ PRACTICING WHAT YOU'VE LEARNED

Comma Errors

A. Study the comma rules numbered 1–4 on pages 547–549.
    Correct any comma errors you see in the following sentences.

1. In 1886 temperance leader Harvey Wilcox left Kansas, he purchased 120 acres near Los Angeles to develop a new town.

2. Although there were no holly trees growing in that part of California Mrs. Wilcox named the area Hollywood.

3. Mrs. Wilcox may have named the place after a home, owned by a friend living in Illinois.

4. During the early years settlers who shared the Wilcoxes' values moved to the area and banned the recreational drinking of alcoholic beverages, however, some alcohol consumption was allowed for medicinal purposes.

5. Nevertheless by 1910 the first film studio opened its doors inside a tavern on Sunset Boulevard, within seven short years the quiet community started by the Wilcoxes had vanished.

B. Study the comma rules 5–13 on pages 549–551. Correct any comma errors you see in the following sentences.

1. Yes Hortense in the 1920s young women did indeed cut their hair raise their hemlines dab perfume behind their knees and dance the Charleston.

2. In 1873 Cornell University cancelled the school's first intercollegiate football game with Michigan when the president announced "I will not permit 30 men to travel 400 miles merely to agitate a bag of wind."

3. Jane Marian Donna Ann and Cissy graduated from high school on June 5 1964 in Texarkana Texas in the old Walnut Street Auditorium.

4. "I may be a man of few opinions" said Henry "but I insist that I am neither for nor against apathy."

5. Did you know for instance that early American settlers once thought the tomato was so poisonous they used the plant only for decoration?

C. The following sentences contain many kinds of comma errors, including the comma splice. Correct any errors you see by adding, deleting, or changing the commas as needed.

1. The father decided to recapture his youth, he took his son's car keys away.

2. Although ice cream didn't appear in America until the 1700s our country now leads the world in ice cream consumption, Australia is second I think.

3. Last summer the large friendly family that lives next door flew Discount Airlines and visited three cities on their vacation, however, their suitcases visited five.

4. Researchers in Balboa, Panama have discovered that the poisonous, yellow-belly, sea snake which descended from the cobra, is the most deadly serpent in the world.

5. Lulu Belle, my cousin, spent the week of Sept. 1–7, 1986 in the woods near Dimebox, Texas looking for additions to her extinct, butterfly collection, however she wasn't at all successful in her search.

(For additional practice correcting comma splice errors, see pages 540–541 in Chapter 20.)

21e   The Semicolon (;)   P

1. Use a semicolon to link two closely related independent clauses.

Examples   Anthropologists believe popcorn originated in Mexico; they have found popcorn poppers that are over 1,500 years old.

Kate's mother does not have to begin a jogging program; she gets all the exercise she needs by worrying in place.

Avoid a "semicolon fragment" error by making sure there is an independent clause—a complete sentence, not a fragment—on either side of the semicolon.*

---

* Some folks have noted that the semicolon might be better named the "semi-period" in that it functions like a weak period, joining two complete sentences together but with a weaker stop between thoughts than a period demands.

Semicolon fragment	Cutting your lawn with a push mower burns 420 calories; according to *Vitality* magazine. ["According to *Vitality* magazine" is a fragment. In this case, a comma, not a semicolon, is needed.]
Correct	Cutting your lawn with a push mower burns 420 calories, according to *Vitality* magazine.

If you are unsure about recognizing a fragment, try using the "It is true that" test as described on page 536.

2. Use a semicolon to avoid a comma splice when connecting two independent clauses with words like "however," "moreover," "thus," "therefore," and "consequently."

Examples	Vincent Van Gogh sold only one painting in his entire life; however, in 1987 his *Sunflowers* sold for almost $40 million.
	All Esmeralda's plants die shortly after she gets them home from the store; consequently, she has the best compost heap in town.
	This town is not big enough for both of us; therefore, I suggest we expand the city limits.

3. Use a semicolon in a series between items that already contain internal punctuation.

Examples	Last year the Wildcats suffered enough injuries to keep them from winning the pennant, as Jake Pritchett, third baseman, broke his arm in a fight; Hugh Rosenbloom, starting pitcher, sprained his back on a trampoline; and Boris Baker, star outfielder, ate rotten clams and nearly died.
	Her children were born a year apart: Moe, 1936; Curley, 1937; and Larry, 1938.

■ **PRACTICING WHAT YOU'VE LEARNED**

Semicolon Errors

Correct the sentences that follow by adding, deleting, or changing the semicolons.

1. The soloist sang the well-known hymn "I Will Not Pass This Way Again" at her concert last night the audience was delighted.

2. Apples have long been associated with romance for example, one legend says if you throw an apple peel over your shoulder, it will fall into the shape of your true love's initial.

3. According to an 1863 book of etiquette, the perfect hostess will see to it that the works of male and female authors are properly separated on her bookshelves, however, if the authors happen to be married, their proximity may be tolerated.

4. Today, there are some 60,000 Americans older than 100 in 1960, there were only 3,222; according to *Health* magazine.

5. The sixth-grade drama club will present their interpretation of *Hamlet* tonight in the school cafeteria all parents are invited to see this tragedy.

6. Some inventors who named weapons after themselves include Samuel Colt, the Colt revolver, Henry Deringer, Jr., the derringer pistol, Dr. Richard J. Gatling, the crank machine gun, Col. John T. Thompson, the submachine or "tommy" gun, and Oliver F. Winchester, the repeating rifle.

7. My doctor failed in his career as a kidnapper, no one could read his ransom notes.

8. The highest point in the United States is Mt. McKinley at 20,320 feet, in contrast, the lowest point is Death Valley at 282 feet below sea level.

9. As we drove down the highway, we saw a sign that said "See the World's Largest Prairie Dog Turn Right at This Exit," therefore we immediately stopped to look.

10. The next billboard read "See Live Jackalopes"; making us want to stop again.

21f   The Colon (:)   P

1. Use a colon to introduce a long or formal list, but do not use one after "to be" verbs.

Correct	Please pick up these items at the store: garlic, wolfbane, mirrors, a prayer book, a hammer, and a wooden stake.
Incorrect	Jean is such a bad cook that she thinks the four basic food groups are: canned, frozen, ready-to-mix, and take-out.
Correct	Jean is such a bad cook that she thinks the four basic food groups are canned, frozen, ready-to-mix, and take-out.

Avoid needless colons.

Incorrect	At the store I couldn't find: wolfbane or a wooden stake.
Correct	At the store I couldn't find wolfbane or a wooden stake.

2. A colon may be used to introduce a quotation or definition.

Examples	Nineteenth-century writer Ambrose Bierce offers this definition of a bore: "A person who talks when you wish him to listen."
	Critic Dorothy Parker was unambiguous in her review of the book: "This is not a novel to be tossed aside lightly; it should be thrown with great force."
	In singer Jimmy Buffett's Margaritaville store in Key West, a sign warns: "Shoplifters will be forced to listen to Barry Manilow."

3. Use a colon to introduce a word, phrase, or sentence that emphatically or humorously explains, summarizes, or amplifies the preceding sentence.

Examples   To her delight, we fed our pet lamb her favorite dish: shepherd's pie.

According to Jean, Colorado has four seasons: last winter, this winter, next winter, and July.

After marrying nine times, glamour queen Zsa Zsa Gabor had simple advice for becoming a marvelous housekeeper: every time you leave a relationship, keep the house.

4. Use a colon in the salutations of business or professional correspondence. Colons may also follow headings in memos.

Examples   Dear Professor Stallones:
To: Subject: Date:

▪ PRACTICING WHAT YOU'VE LEARNED

Errors with Colons

Correct the following errors by adding, deleting, or substituting colons for faulty punctuation. Skip any correct sentences.

1. Experts have discovered over thirty different kinds of clouds but have separated them into three main types cirrus, cumulus, and stratus.

2. To those folks who may talk too much, Abraham Lincoln gives the following advice: "It is better to remain silent and be thought a fool than to speak out and remove all doubt."

3. A recent Gallup poll found that Americans consider only one activity more stressful than visiting the dentist hosting a dinner party.

4. Because Hindu custom forbids the eating of beef, McDonald's restaurants in India often feature: veggie-burgers and mutton-burgers.

5. Please remember to buy the following at the pet store, one pound of cat food, two flea collars, kitty fang floss, a bag of catnip, and thirty-six lint rollers.

6. A Director of Academic Services at Pennsylvania State University once nominated this sentence for Punctuation Error of the Year; "I had to leave my good friend's behind and find new ones."

7. Some of the cars manufactured between 1907 and 1912 that didn't achieve the popularity of the Model T were: the Black Crow, the Swallow, the Bugmobile, and the Carnation.

8. There's only one thing that can make our lawn look as good as our neighbor's; snow.

9. In a Thurmont, Maryland, cemetery can be found this epitaph "Here lies an Atheist, all dressed up, and no place to go."

10. George Bernard Shaw, the famous playwright, claimed he wanted the following epitaph on his tombstone: "I knew if I stayed around long enough, something like this would happen."

21g   The Apostrophe (')   AP

1. Use an apostrophe to indicate omitted letters in a contraction ("cannot" = "can't").

Examples   *It's* too bad your car burned.

Wouldn't the insurance company believe your story?

Many people today confuse "it's" (the contraction for "it is") and "its" (the possessive pronoun, which never takes an apostrophe).

Its = shows possession, functioning like "his" or "her"

It's = contraction for "it is"

Examples   The car is old, but *its* paint is new ["Its" shows the car's possession of paint.]

The car is old, but *it's* reliable. ["It's" is a contraction for "it is."]

If you are ever in doubt about your choice, read the sentence aloud, saying the words "it is" in place of the *its/it's* in question. If the sentence becomes nonsensical (The car is old but *it is* coat of paint is new), then the possessive form "its" is probably what you need.

Special note. There is no "its'." No such word exists in the English language! Forget you even thought about it!

2. Add an apostrophe plus "s" to a noun to show possession.

Examples   *Jack's* dog ate the *cat's* dinner.

The *veterinarian's* assistant later doctored the *puppy's* wounds.

3. Add only an apostrophe to a plural noun ending in "s" to show possession.

Examples   Goldilocks invaded the *bears'* house.

She ignored her *parents'* warning about breaking and entering.

4. To show joint possession between two people or things, you need to add an apostrophe and "-s" only to the second noun. To show separate ownership, add an apostrophe plus "-s" to both nouns.

Examples   Isabel and *Sharona's* design project will be presented today. [one project]

Isabel's and *Sharona's* design projects will be presented today. [separate projects]

5. Be careful to avoid adding an apostrophe when the occasion simply calls for the plural use of a word.

Incorrect	*Apple's* are on sale now.
Correct	*Apples* are on sale now.
Incorrect	We ordered *chip's* and dip.
Correct	We ordered *chips* and dip.

6. In some cases you may add an apostrophe plus "s" to a singular word ending in "s," especially when the word is a proper name or for ease of pronunciation.

Examples   *Doris's* name was popular in the 1950s.

The silent screen *actress's* favorite flowers were mums.

7. To avoid confusion, you may use an apostrophe plus "s" to form the plurals of letters, figures, and words discussed as words; no apostrophe is also acceptable.

Examples   He made four "*C's*" last fall. [or "*Cs*"]

The right to resist the draft was a major issue in the *1960's*. [or *1960s*]

You use too many "*and's*" in your sentence. [or "*ands*"]

■ **PRACTICING WHAT YOU'VE LEARNED**

Errors with Apostrophes

A. Correct the apostrophe errors you see in the following phrases.

1. A horses' pajamas

2. The queens throne

3. A families' vacation

4. Ten students grades

5. The Depression of the 1930s' was over.

6. That dress of hers'

7. The childrens' toys

8. Worm's for sale

9. Bill Jones car

10. All essay's are due today.

11. Sign both the painters and the roofer's contracts.

12. Womens hats with feather's for decoration

B. Show that you understand the difference between "it's" and "its" by correcting any errors in the sentences that follow. Skip any correct use you see.

    1. Its unfortunate that the game ended in a tie.

    2. The tree lost its leaves.

    3. Its beginning to feel like fall now.

    4. The library was closing its' doors.

    5. I realize its none of my business.

(For more practice, turn to page 560.)

21h   Quotation Marks (" " and ' ')   P

    1. Use quotation marks to enclose someone's spoken or written words.

Examples   "Watch out for that left hook," said Tinkerbell to Peter Pan, just before his fight with the pirate captain.

                    Upon the opening of the world's first underground passenger train in 1863, the editor of the *London Times* wrote that it was "an insult to common sense to think that people would choose to travel in darkness across London."

Note that when a quotation is interrupted, an extra set of marks should be used.

Examples   "Today, American coins of ten cents or more have grooved edges," explained the numismatist, "because decades ago our government wanted to stop thieves from shaving the edges of silver and gold coins."

    2. Use quotation marks around the titles of essays,[*] articles, chapter headings, short stories, short poems, and songs.

Examples   "How to Paint Ceramic Ashtrays"

                    "The Fall of the House of Usher"

                    "Stopping by Woods on a Snowy Evening"

                    "Yankee Doodle"

    3. You may either underline or place quotation marks around a word, phrase, or letter used as the subject of discussion.

Examples   Never use "however" as a coordinating conjunction.

                    The word "bigwig," meaning an important person, is derived from the large wigs worn by seventeenth-century British judges.

                    Is your middle initial "X" or "Y"?

                    Her use of such adjectives as "drab," "bleak," and "musty" gives the poem a somber tone.

---

[*] Do *not,* however, put quotation marks around your own essay's title on either the title page or the first page of your paper.

4. Place quotation marks around uncommon nicknames and words used ironically. Do not, however, try to apologize for slang or clichés by enclosing them in quotation marks; instead, substitute specific words.

Examples	"Scat-cat" Malone takes candy from babies.
	Her "friend" was an old scarecrow in an abandoned barn.
Slang	After work Chuck liked to "simple out" in front of the television.
Specific	After work Chuck liked to relax by watching old movies on television.

5. The period and the comma go inside quotation marks; the semicolon and the colon go outside. If the quoted material is a question, the question mark goes inside; if the quoted material is a part of a whole sentence that is a question, the mark goes outside. The rules for exclamation points are the same as those for question marks.

Examples	According to cartoonist Matt Groening, "Love is a snowmobile racing across the tundra; suddenly it flips over, pins you underneath, and at night the ice weasels come."
	"Love is a snowmobile racing across the tundra; suddenly it flips over, pins you underneath, and at night the ice weasels come," says cartoonist Matt Groening.
	According to cartoonist Matt Groening, "Love is a snowmobile . . . suddenly it flips over, pins you underneath, and at night the ice weasels come"; Groening also advises that bored friends are one of the first signs that you're in love.
	Did he really say, "At night the ice weasels come"?
	Lisa asked, "Do you think you're in love or just in a snowmobile?"
	As usual, Homer replied, "D'oh!"

6. Use single quotation marks to enclose a quotation (or words requiring quotation marks) within a quotation.

Examples	Professor Hall asked his class, "Do you agree with Samuel Johnson, who once said that a second marriage represents 'the triumph of hope over experience'?"
	"One of my favorite songs is 'In My Life' by the Beatles," said Jane.
	"I'm so proud of the 'A' on my grammar test," Sue told her parents.

7. If you are quoting fewer than four lines of poetry, enclose them within quotation marks, using a slash to indicate each line division.

Example	In possibly the first love poem ever published in America, Anne Bradstreet wrote these opening lines in 1678: "If ever two were one, then surely we. / If ever man were loved by wife, then thee."

■ PRACTICING WHAT YOU'VE LEARNED

Errors with Apostrophes and Quotation Marks

Correct the following errors by adding, changing, or deleting apostrophes and quotation marks.

1. Its true that when famous wit Dorothy Parker was told that President Coolidge, also known as Silent Cal, was dead, she exclaimed, How can they tell?

2. When a woman seated next to Coolidge at a dinner party once told him she had made a bet with a friend that she could get more than two words out of him, he replied You lose.

3. Twenty-one of Elvis Presleys albums have sold over a million copies; twenty of the Beatles albums have also done so.

4. Cinderellas stepmother wasn't pleased that her daughter received an F in her creative writing class on her poem Seven Guys and a Gal, which she had plagiarized from her two friend's Snow White and Dopey.

5. Wasn't it Mae West who said, When choosing between two evils, I always like to try the one I've never tried before? asked Olivia.

6. Horace said Believe me, its to everybodies' advantage to sing the popular song You Stole My Heart and Stomped That Sucker Flat, if thats what the holdup man wants.

7. A scholars research has revealed that the five most commonly used words in written English are the, of, and, a, and to.

8. The triplets mother said that while its' hard for her to choose, O. Henrys famous short story The Ransom of Red Chief is probably her favorite.

9. Despite both her lawyers advice, she used the words terrifying, hideous, and unforgettable to describe her latest flight on Golden Fleece Airways, piloted by Jack One-Eye Marcus.

10. Its clear that Bubba didnt know whether the Christmas' tree thrown in the neighbors yard was ours, theirs', or your's.

21i   Parentheses ( )   P

1. Use parentheses to set off words, dates, or statements that give additional information, explain, or qualify the main thought.

Examples

To encourage sales, some automobile manufacturers name their cars after fast or sleek animals (Impala, Mustang, and Thunderbird, for example).

Popular American author Mark Twain (Samuel Clemens) described many of his childhood experiences in *Tom Sawyer* (1876).

The Ford Motor Company once rejected the name Utopian Turtletop for one of its new cars, choosing instead to call it the Edsel (a name that obviously didn't help sales either).

2. The period comes inside the close parenthesis if a complete sentence is enclosed; it occurs after the close parenthesis when the enclosed matter comes at the end of the main sentence and is only a part of the main sentence.

Examples   The Colorado winters of 1978 and 1979 broke records for low temperatures. (See pages 72–73 for temperature charts.)

Jean hates Colorado winters and would prefer a warmer environment (such as Alaska, the North Pole, or a meat locker in Philadelphia).

3. If you are confused trying to distinguish whether information should be set off by commas, parentheses, or dashes, here are three guidelines:

  a. Use commas to set off information closely related to the rest of the sentence.

Example   When Billy Clyde married Maybelle, his brother's young widow, the family was shocked. [The information identifies Maybelle and tells why the family was shocked.]

  b. Use parentheses to set off information loosely related to the rest of the sentence or material that would disturb the grammatical structure of the main sentence.

Examples   Billy Clyde married Maybelle (his fourth marriage, her second) in Las Vegas on Friday. [The information is merely additional comment not closely related to the meaning of the sentence.]

Billy Clyde married Maybelle (she was previously married to his brother) in Las Vegas on Friday. [The information is an additional comment that would also disturb the grammatical structure of the main sentence were it not enclosed in parentheses.]

  c. Use dashes to set off information dramatically or emphatically.

Example   Billy Clyde eloped with Maybelle—only three days after her husband's funeral—without saying a word to anyone in the family.

4. For clarity, parentheses may be used to set off numbers in a list that appears within prose.

Example   Urban legends are popular stories that almost always share these characteristics: (1) they are spread through person-to-person communication; (2) they are virtually untraceable to a single source, such as a book or newspaper; (3) they involve outlandish, humorous, or terrifying events; and (4) they carry an unstated warning or moral.

5. Parentheses may enclose the first-time use of acronyms (words formed from the initials of several words) or abbreviations.

Examples   National Aeronautics and Space Administration (NASA)
University of California at Los Angeles (UCLA)
Museum of Modern Art (MoMA)

21j   Brackets [ ]   P

1. Use brackets to set off editorial explanations in the work of another writer.

Examples   According to the old letter, the treasure map could be found "in the library taped to the back of the portrait [of Gertrude the Great] that faces north."

The country singer ended the interview by saying, "My biggest hit so far is 'You're the Reason Our Kids Are Ugly' [original version by Sarah Bellham]."

2. Use brackets to set off editorial corrections in quoted material. By placing the bracketed word "sic" (meaning "thus") next to an error, you indicate that the mistake appeared in the original text and that *you* are not misquoting or misspelling.

Examples   The student wrote, "I think it's unfair for teachers to count off for speling [sic]." ["Sic" in brackets indicates that the student who is quoted misspelled the word "spelling."]

The highway advertisement read as follows: "For great stakes [sic], eat at Joe's, located right behind Daisy's Glue Factory." [Here, "sic" in brackets indicates an error in word choice; the restaurant owner incorrectly advertised "stakes" instead of "steaks."]

3. If additional information needs to appear in material already enclosed in parentheses, use brackets to avoid the confusion of double parenthesis marks.

Example   Nineteenth-century author Kate Chopin often found herself in the midst of controversy. (For example, *The Awakening* [1899] was considered so scandalous that it was banned by the St. Louis Library.)

21k   The Dash (—)*   P

1. Use a dash to indicate a strong or sudden shift in thought.

Examples   Now, let's be reasonable—wait, put down that ice pick!

"It's not athlete's foot—it's deadly coreopsis!" cried Dr. Mitty.

2. Use dashes to set off parenthetical matter that deserves more emphasis than parentheses denote.

Examples   Wanda's newest guru—the one who practiced catatonic hedonism—taught her to rest and play at the same time.

He was amazed to learn his test score—a pitiful 43.

(To clear up any confusion over the uses of dashes, commas, and parentheses, see the guidelines on pages 547–551 and 560–561.)

---

* Do not confuse the dash with the hyphen. In typed work, a dash is indicated by *two* bar marks ("--"); one bar mark ("-") indicates a hyphen.

3. Use a dash before a statement that summarizes or amplifies the preceding thought. (Dashes can also be used to introduce a humorous or ironic twist on the first idea in the sentence.)

Examples Aged wine, delicious food, someone else picking up the check—the dinner was perfect.

Not everyone agrees with football coach Vince Lombardi, who said, "Winning isn't everything—it's the only thing."

According to Hollywood star Cher, "The trouble with some women is that they get all excited about nothing—and then marry him."

■ **PRACTICING WHAT YOU'VE LEARNED**

Errors with Parentheses, Brackets, and Dashes

Show that you understand the difference between parentheses, brackets, and dashes by using the best choice in the sentences that follow. Skip any correct sentences you see. (For additional practice, see also the exercise that appears on page 568.)

1. George Eliot (the pen name of Mary Ann Evans) wrote the novel *Middlemarch.*

2. The Apostrophe Protection Society, founded in London in 2001, fights against the gross misuse of this mark of punctuation. Editor's note: For help with apostrophes, see pages 556–557 in this text.

3. A Russian woman holds the record for the highest number of children born to one mother: sixty-nine babies in a total of twenty-seven pregnancies sixteen pairs of twins, seven sets of triplets, and four sets of quadruplets.

4. More men holding first-class tickets on the *Titanic* were saved than childrens (sic) in the third-class section of the ship.

5. Billy Clyde could stay married to Maybelle as long as he played his cards right [his Visa card, his Mastercard, his American Express card.]

21l The Hyphen (-)*   P

1. Use a hyphen to join words into a single adjective before a noun.

Examples a wind-blown wig

the mud-caked sneakers

a made-for-television movie

a well-written essay

a five-year-old boy

---

* Do not confuse the hyphen with the dash. In typed work, a hyphen is indicated by *one* bar mark ("-"); a dash is indicated by *two* bar marks ("--").

Do *not* use a hyphen when the modifier ends in "ly."

Examples   a highly regarded worker

a beautifully landscaped yard

2. Writers who create original compound adjectives often join the words with hyphens.

Examples   Compulsive shoppers suffer from stuff-lust syndrome.

She prefers novels with they-lived-wretchedly-ever-after endings.

3. Some compound words are always spelled with a hyphen; check your dictionary when you're in doubt. Note that compound numbers from twenty-one to ninety-nine use a hyphen.

Examples   mother-in-law

president-elect

runner-up

good-for-nothing

twenty-nine

Compound words made from combining verb forms are frequently hyphenated: The psychiatrist insisted his birthday presents be *shrink-wrapped.*

4. Some words with prefixes use a hyphen; again, check your dictionary if necessary. (Hint: If the second word begins with a capital letter, a hyphen is almost always used.)

Examples   ex-wife

self-esteem

all-American

non-English

5. In a series of compound adjectives, place a space (or a comma and a space, when appropriate) following the hyphen in every item except the last one.

Examples   They surveyed students at both two- and four-year colleges.

She found herself on both the best- and the worst-dressed lists.

He suffered first-, second-, and third-degree burns on his arms.

6. Use a hyphen to mark the separation of syllables when you divide a word at the end of a line. Do not divide one-syllable words; do not leave one or two letters at the end of a line. (In most dictionaries, dots are used to indicate the division of syllables: va • ca • tion.)

Examples   In your essays you should avoid using fragment sentences.

Did your father try to help you with your homework?

■ **PRACTICING WHAT YOU'VE LEARNED**

Errors with Hyphens

Correct the errors in the phrases that follow by adding, deleting, or changing hyphens. Skip any correct uses you see.

1. A first class event
2. The well done steak
3. A self employed person
4. His completely fabricated story
5. Her one word answer
6. Pre-Columbian art
7. A once in a lifetime experience
8. A fifteen year-old girl
9. The overly-excited dog
10. His fifty sixth birthday
11. fourth- and fifth-place trophies
12. The hard boiled detective o-
    mitted an important detail in his re-
    port.

(For additional practice using hyphens, turn to the exercise on page 568.)

21m   Italics (Ital) and Underlining (_____)   P

Today, many style manuals accept the use of italics in printed matter in place of underlining. Other authorities do not; the guidlines of the Modern Language Association, for example, recommend underlining the titles of books. Ask your instructor whether the use of italics or underlining is preferred.

In handwritten material, use underlining in the cases described in the following rules.

   1. Underline, italicize, or place quotation marks around a word, phrase, or letter used as the subject of discussion. Whether you underline, italicize, or use quotation marks, always be consistent. (See also pages 558–559.)

Examples   No matter how I spell <u>offered</u>, it always looks wrong.

Is your middle initial "X" or "Y"?

Her use of such words as *drab*, *bleak*, and *musty* give the poem a somber tone.

2. Underline or italicize the title of books, plays, magazines, newspapers, movies, works of art, television programs (but use quotation marks for individual episodes), airplanes, trains, and ships.

Examples		or	
	Moby Dick		*Moby Dick*
	Reader's Digest		*Reader's Digest*
	Texarkana Gazette		*Texarkana Gazette*
	Gone with the Wind		*Gone with the Wind*
	Mona Lisa		*Mona Lisa*
	60 Minutes		*60 Minutes*
	Spirit of St. Louis		*Spirit of St. Louis*
	Titanic		*Titanic*

Exceptions: Do not italicize or underline the Bible or the titles of legal documents, including the United States Constitution, or the name of your own essay when it appears on your title page. Do not italicize or underline the city in a newspaper title unless the city's name is actually part of the newspaper's title.

3. Underline or italicize foreign words that are not commonly regarded as part of the English language.

Examples   He shrugged and said, "C'est la vie."

Under the "For Sale" sign on the old rusty truck, the farmer had written *caveat emptor*, meaning "let the buyer beware."

4. Use underlining or italics sparingly to show emphasis.

Examples   Everyone was surprised to discover that the butler <u>didn't</u> do it.

"Do you realize that *your* son just ate a piece of my priceless sculpture?" the artist screamed at the museum director.

■ PRACTICING WHAT YOU'VE LEARNED

Errors with Italics and Underlining

Which of the following words should be italicized or underlined in your essay?

1. page six of the New York Times
2. the popular novel The Great Gatsby
3. an article in Time magazine
4. watching the episode The Puffy Shirt on Seinfeld
5. movie stars in The Matrix
6. confusing the words to, too, and two
7. the first act of Death of a Salesman
8. remembering the words to The Star-Spangled Banner
9. the sinking of the Edmund Fitzgerald
10. missing my abuela in Texas

(For additional practice, turn to page 568.)

21n Ellipsis Points (. . . or . . . .)   P

1. To show an omission in quoted material within a sentence, use three periods, with spaces before and after each one.

Original	Every time my father told the children about his having to trudge barefooted to school in the snow, the walk got longer and the snow got deeper.
Quoted with omission	In her autobiography, she wrote, "Every time my father told the children about his having to trudge barefooted to school . . . the snow got deeper."

Note: Never begin a sentence with ellipsis points.

2. Three points with spaces may be used to show an incomplete or interrupted thought.

Example	My wife is an intelligent, beautiful woman who wants me to live a long time. On the other hand, Harry's wife . . . oh, never mind.

3. If you omit any words at the end of a quotation and you are also ending your sentence, use three points plus a fourth to indicate the period. Put a space before the first point.

Example	Lincoln wrote, "Four score and seven years ago our fathers brought forth upon this continent, a new nation . . . ."

4. If the omission of one or more sentences occurs at the end of a quoted sentence, use four points with no space before the first point.

Example	"The Lord is my shepherd; I shall not want. . . . he leadeth me in the paths of righteousness for his name's sake."

5. Use a row of ellipsis points to indicate one or more missing lines of poetry.

Example	Failing to fetch me at first keep encouraged.
	. . . .
	I stop somewhere waiting for you.
	--Walt Whitman, "Song of Myself"

6. Ellipsis points can occasionally be used to show hesitation or a pause in thought.

Example	"Yes, I'm leaving . . . I need to find myself," said Waldo.

21o The Slash (/)   P

1. Use a slash between terms to indicate that either is acceptable. Do not put a space on either side of the slash.

Examples	Bring a salad *and/or* a dessert to share at the picnic.
	Be careful to avoid the *either/or* fallacy in your argument paper.

2. Use a slash to mark line divisions in quoted poetry. Do use a space both before and after the slash.

Example   In this poem Shakespeare describes love as "an ever-fixed mark / That looks on tempests and is never shaken."

■ PRACTICING WHAT YOU'VE LEARNED

Errors with Parentheses, Brackets, Dashes, Hyphens, Italics, Ellipses, and Slashes

Correct the following errors by adding, changing, or deleting parentheses, brackets, dashes, hyphens, italics, ellipsis points, and slashes.

1. Many moviegoers know that the ape in King Kong the original 1933 version, not the re-make was only an eighteen inch tall animated figure, but not everyone realizes that the Red Sea Moses parted in the 1923 movie of The Ten Commandments was a quivering slab of Jell O sliced down-the-middle.

2. We recall the last words of General John B. Sedwick at the Battle of Spotsylvania in 1864: "They couldn't hit an elephant at this dist   ."

3. In a person to person telephone call the twenty five year old starlet promised the hard working gossip columnist that she would "tell the truth . . . and nothing but the truth" about her highly-publicized feud with her exhusband, editor in chief of Meat Eaters Digest.

4. While sailing across the Atlantic on board the celebrity filled yacht Titanic II, Dottie Mae Haskell she's the author of the popular new self help book Finding Wolves to Raise Your Children confided that until recently she thought chutzpah was an Italian side dish.

5. During their twenty four hour sit in at the melt down site, the anti-nuclear protestors began to sing, "Oh, say can you see . . . "

6. Few people know that James Arness later Matt Dillon in the long running television series Gunsmoke got his start by playing the vegetable creature in the postwar monster movie The Thing 1951.

7. If you do not pay your rent on time, your landlord has the right to charge a late fee and-or begin an eviction procedure.

8. A French chemist named Georges Claude invented the first neon sign in 1910. For additional information on his unsuccessful attempts to use seawater to generate electricity, see pages 200–205.

9. When Lucille Ball, star of I Love Lucy, became pregnant with her first child, the network executives decided that the word expecting could be used on the air to refer to her condition, but not the word pregnant.

10. In mystery stories the detective often advises the police to cherchez la femme. Editor's note: Cherchez la femme means "look for the woman."

Chapter 22

A Concise Guide to Mechanics

22a Capitalization   Cap

1. Capitalize the first word of every sentence.

Example   The lazy horse leans against a tree all day.

2. Capitalize proper nouns—the specific names of people, places, and products—and also the adjectives formed from proper nouns.

Examples   John Doe
Austin, Texas
First National Bank
the Eiffel Tower
Chevrolets
Japanese cameras
Spanish class
an English major

3. Always capitalize the days of the week, the names of the months, and holidays.

Examples   Saturday, December 14
                Tuesday's meeting
                Halloween parties

Special events are often capitalized: Super Bowl, World Series, Festival of Lights.

4. Capitalize titles when they are accompanied by proper names.

Examples   President Jones, Major Smith, Governor Brown, Judge Wheeler,
                Professor Plum, Queen Elizabeth

5. Capitalize all the principal words in titles of books, articles, stories, plays, movies, and poems. Prepositions, articles, and conjunctions are not capitalized unless they begin or end the title.

Examples   "The Face on the Barroom Floor"
                A Short History of the Civil War
                For Whom the Bell Tolls

6. Capitalize the first word of a direct quotation.

Examples   Shocked at actor John Barrymore's use of profanity, the woman
                said, "Sir, I'll have you know I'm a lady!"
                Barrymore replied, "Your secret is safe with me."

7. Capitalize "east," "west," "north," and "south" when they refer to particular sections of the country but not when they merely indicate direction.

Examples   The South has produced many excellent writers, including William
                Faulkner and Flannery O'Connor. ["South" here refers to a
                section of the country.]
                If you travel south for ten miles, you'll see the papier-mâché replica of
                the world's largest hamburger. [In this case, "south" is a direction.]

8. Capitalize a title when referring to a particular person;* do not capitalize a title if a pronoun precedes it.

Examples   The President announced a new national holiday honoring Frank
                H. Fleer, inventor of bubble gum.
                The new car Dad bought is guaranteed for 10,000 miles or until
                something goes wrong.
                My mother told us about a Hollywood party during which Zelda
                and F. Scott Fitzgerald collected and boiled all the women's purses.

---

* Some authorities disagree; others consider such capitalization optional.

9. Capitalize important historic movements, documents, and events.

Examples   the Civil Rights Movement

World War I

Impressionism

Declaration of Independence

D-Day

10. Capitalize the names of religions, their followers, revered books, and holidays.

Examples   Islam

Methodists

Torah

Bible

Easter

11. Capitalize the letters that make up abbreviations for organizations, companies, agencies, and well-known people, places, and events.

Examples   NFL

CBS

FEMA

JFK

USA

WW II

■ PRACTICING WHAT YOU'VE LEARNED

Errors with Capitalization

A. Correct the errors in capitalization in the following phrases.

1. delicious chinese food

2. memorial day memories

3. fiery southwestern salsa

4. his latest novel, *the story of a prince among thieves*

5. bible study at the baptist church

6. count Dracula's castle in transylvania

7. african-american heritage

8. a dodge van driven across the golden gate bridge

9. sunday morning news on abc

10. the british daughter-in-law of senator Snort

B. Write a sentence in which of the following pairs of words are capitalized correctly. Example: He joined the U.S. Navy wearing his best white shirt and navy pants.

1. street, Street

2. lake, Lake

3. mustang, Mustang

4. south, South

5. president, President

22b   Abbreviations   Ab

1. Abbreviate the titles "Mr.," "Mrs.," "Ms.," "St.," and "Dr." when they precede names

Examples   Dr. Scott, Ms. Steinham, Mrs. White, St. Jude

2. Abbreviate titles and degrees when they follow names.

Examples   Charles Byrd, Jr.; David Hall, Ph.D.; Dudley Carpenter, D.D.S.

3. You may abbreviate the following in even the most formal writing: A.M. (*ante meridiem*, before noon), P.M. (*post meridiem*, after noon), A.D. (*anno Domini*, in the year of our Lord), B.C. (before Christ), C.E. (common era), B.C.E. (before the common era), etc. (*et cetera*, and others), i.e. (*id est*, that is), and e.g. (*exempli gratia*, for example).

4. In formal writing, do *not* abbreviate the names of days, months, centuries, states, countries, or units of measure. Do *not* use an ampersand (&) unless it is an official part of a title.

Incorrect in formal writing	Tues., Sept., 18th century, Ark., Mex., lbs.
Correct	Tuesday, September, eighteenth century, Arkansas, Mexico, pounds
Incorrect	Tony & Gus went to the store to buy ginseng root.
Correct	Tony *and* Gus went to the A & P to buy ginseng root. [The "&" in "A & P" is correct because it is part of the store's official name.]

5. In formal writing, do *not* abbreviate the words for page, chapter, volume, and so forth, except in footnotes and bibliographies, which have prescribed rules of abbreviation.

6. Except in formal writing, it is often permissible to use abbreviations or acronyms for well-known organizations or people. However, you should spell out the abbreviation the first time, to avoid any confusion.

Examples   Franklin Delano Roosevelt (FDR)
National Public Radio (NPR)
North Atlantic Treaty Organization (NATO)

(For additional information on proper abbreviation, consult your dictionary.)

22c Numbers   Num

1. Use figures for dates; street, room, and apartment numbers; page numbers; telephone numbers; percentages, and decimals.

Examples   April 22, 1946
                      710 West 14th Street
                      page 242
                      room 17
                      476-1423
                      40 percent
                      3.78 GPA

2. Use figures for hours with A.M. and P.M. but write out the time when you use "o'clock."

Examples   8.00 A.M. or 8 A.M.
                      eight o'clock in the morning

3. Some authorities say to spell out numbers that can be expressed in one or two words; others say to spell out numbers under one hundred.

Examples   ten thousand dollars or $10,000
                      twenty-four hours
                      thirty-nine years
                      five partridges
                      $12.99 per pair
                      1,294 essays

4. When several numbers are used in a short passage, use figures.

Examples   In the anchovy-eating contest, Jennifer ate 22, Juan ate 21, Pete ate 16, and I ate 6.

                      According to the U.S. Census Bureau, on an average day 11,000 babies are born, 6,000 people die, 7,000 couples marry, and 3,000 couples divorce.

5. Never begin a sentence with a figure.

Incorrect   50 spectators turned out to watch the surfing exhibition at Niagara Falls.

Correct   Fifty spectators turned out to watch the surfing exhibition at Niagara Falls.

6. When a date containing a day and a year appears within a sentence, always set off the year by placing commas on each side.

Examples   She married her first husband on February 2, 1978, in Texas.

                      The first birth on a commercial airliner occurred on October 28, 1929, as the plane cruised over Miami.

■ PRACTICING WHAT YOU'VE LEARNED

Errors in Capitalization, Abbreviations, and Numbers

Correct the following errors by adding, deleting, or changing capitals, abbreviations, and numbers. Skip any correct words, letters, or numbers you may find.

1. Speaking to students at Gallaudet university, Marian Wright Edelman, Founder and president of the Children's Defense Fund, noted that an american child is born into poverty every thirty seconds, is born to a teen mother every 60 seconds, is abused or neglected every 26 seconds, is arrested for a violent crime every five minutes, and is killed by a gun every two hours.

2. My sister, who lives in the east, was amazed to read studies by Thomas Radecki, MD, showing that 12-year-olds commit 300 percent more murders than did the same age group 30 years ago.

3. In C.E. sixty-seven the roman emperor Nero entered the chariot race at the olympic games, and although he failed to finish the race, the judges unanimously declared him the Winner.

4. According to John Alcock, a Behavioral Ecologist at Arizona State University, in the U.S.A. the chance of being poisoned by a snake is 20 times less than that of being hit by lightning and 300 times less than the risk of being murdered by a fellow American.

5. The official chinese news agency, located in the city of xinhua, estimates that there are ten million guitar players in their country today, an amazing number considering that the instrument was banned during the cultural revolution, which lasted 10 years, from nineteen sixty-six to nineteen seventy-six.

6. 231 electoral votes were cast for James Monroe but only 1 for John Quincy Adams in the 1820 Presidential race.

7. The british soldier T. E. Lawrence, better known as "lawrence of arabia," stood less than 5 ft. 6 in. tall.

8. Drinking a glass of french wine makes me giddy before my 10 a.m. english class, held in wrigley field every other friday except on New Year's day.

9. When a political opponent once called him "two-faced," president Lincoln retorted, "if I had another face, do you think I would wear this one?"

10. Alexander Graham Bell, inventor of the telephone, died on aug. 2, 1922 in nova scotia; 2 days later, on the day of his burial, for 1 minute no telephone in north america was allowed to ring.

22d Spelling   Sp

For some folks, learning to spell correctly is harder than trying to herd cats. Entire books have been written to teach people to become better spellers, and some of these are available at your local bookstore (and, no, not listed under witchcraft). Here, however, are a few suggestions that seem to work for many students:

1. Keep a list of the little beasties you misspell. After a few weeks, you may notice that you tend to misspell the same words again and again or that the words you misspell tend to fit a pattern—that is, you can't remember when the *i* goes before the *e* or when to change the *y* to *i* before *ed*. Try to memorize the words you repeatedly misspell, or at least keep the list somewhere handy so you can refer to it when you're editing your last draft (listing the words on the inside cover of your dictionary also makes sense).

2. Become aware of a few rules that govern some of our spelling in English. For example, many people know the rule in the jingle "*I* before *E* except after *C* or when sounded like *A* as in *neighbor* and *weigh*." Not everyone, however, knows the follow-up line, which contains most of the exceptions to that jingle: "Neither the weird financier nor the foreigner seizes leisure at its height."

3. Here are some other rules, without jingles, for adding suffixes (new endings to words), a common plague for poor spellers:

- Change final *y* to *i* if the *y* follows a consonant.*

  bury → buried

  marry → marries

- But if the suffix is *-ing*, keep the *y*.

  marry + ing = marrying

  worry + ing = worrying

- If the word ends in a single consonant after a single vowel and the accent is on the last syllable, double the consonant before adding the suffix.

  occur → occurred

  cut → cutting

  swim → swimmer

- If a word ends in a silent *e*, drop the *e* before adding *-able* or *-ing*.

  love + able = lovable

  believe + able = believable

4. And here's an easy rule governing the doubling of letters with the addition of prefixes (new beginning syllables): Most of the time, you simply add all the letters you've got when you mix the word and the prefix.

  mis + spell = misspell

  un + natural = unnatural

  re + entry = reentry

---

* Reminder: Consonants are all the letters that are *not* vowels (*a, e, i, o, u*, and sometimes *y*).

5. Teach yourself to spell the words that you miss often by making up your own silly rules or jingles. For instance:

- dessert (one *s* or two?): I always want two helpings so I double the *s*.

- apparently (apparantly?): Ap*parent*ly, my *parent* knows the whole story.

- separate (seperate?): I'd be *a rat* to sep*arat*e from you.

- a lot (or alot?): A cot (not *acot*) provides *a lot* of comfort in a tent.

- all right (or alright?): Think of the rhyme "all right, good night" and remember that both these phrases have two words. (No matter what Roger Daltrey and The Who said, the line should be "The kids are all right"!)

- questionnaire (one *n* or two?): Questio*nn*aires have *n*umerous *n*umbered questions (two *n*'s).

And so on.

6. Proofread your papers carefully. Anything that looks misspelled probably is and deserves to be looked up in your dictionary. Reading your paper one sentence at a time from the end helps, too, because you tend to start thinking about your ideas when you read from the beginning of your paper. If you are writing on a word processor that has a spell-checking program, don't forget to run it; however, do remember that such programs will skip over confused words (*to* for *too*, *there* for *their*) that are spelled correctly.

Although these few suggestions won't completely cure your spelling problems, they can make a dramatic improvement in the quality of your papers and give you the confidence to continue learning and practicing other rules that govern the spelling of our language. Good luck!

Credits

Photos and Advertisements

American Art. Collection of the Whitney Museum of American Art, New York. Photography by Geoffrey Clements, NY.

252 © Mark Richards/PhotoEdit

267 Rosie the Riveter, "We Can Do It" poster by J. Howard Miller, c. 1942 © CORBIS

300 Reprinted with permission of the National Rifle Association

301 Courtesy of the Center to Prevent Handgun Violence

302 Courtesy of the Violence Policy Center, Washington, DC

304 Courtesy of the Metropolitan Energy Council, Inc., Norwood, NJ

305 Courtesy of Xcel Energy

306 This advertisement is provided courtesy of the United States Council for Energy Awareness, Washington, DC

308 Courtesy of American Values

309 Courtesy of Omega

310 Courtesy of PETA, Washington, DC.

318 © Royalty Free/CORBIS

320 Chagall, Marc (1887-1985) *Birthday (L'Anniversaire)*. 1915. Oil on canvas. 31¾ × 39¼". Acquired through the Lillie P. Bliss Bequest. (275.1949) © ARS, NY/Digital Image/ © The Museum of Modern Art/Licensed by SCALA/Art Resource, NY 319

322 © SuperStock

330 Copyright © the Dorothea Lange Collection, Oakland Museum of California.

336 *Tornado over Kansas* by John S. Curry. 1929. Oil on canvas. Hackly Fund Purchase, 1935. Hackney Picture Fund Purchase, Muskegon Museum of Art, Muskegon, Michigan

338 © Reuters NewMedia, Inc./CORBIS

355 © Tom & Dee Ann McCarthy/CORBIS

409 © Bettmann/CORBIS

428 © Stockbyte/SuperStock

443 *Nonchaloir (Repose)* by John Singer Sargent, 1911. Oil on canvas. 63.8 × 76.2 cm (25 12/8" × 30"). National Gallery, Washington, DC. Gift of Curt H. Reisinger. 1948.16.1

449 Vincent van Gogh. *The Starry Night*, 1889, oil on canvas. Museum of Modern Art, New York. Digital Image © The Museum of Modern Art/Licensed by Scala/Art Resource, NY

470 Goya y Lucientes, Francisco de (1746–1828) *Third of May, 1808* (1814). Location: Museo del Prado, Madrid, Spain © Scala / Art Resource, NY

472 Heda, Willem Claesz (1594–1678) *Breakfast Table with Bramble Pie*, 1631. Location: Gemaeldegalerie, Staatliche Kunstsammlungen, Dresden, German © Erich Lessing/Art Resource, NY

473 Popova, Liubov (1889–1924) *Painterly Architectonic*. 1917.Oil on canvas, 31½ × 38⅝". Philip Johnson Fund. (14.1958) Location: The Museum of Modern Art, New York, NY, U.S.A.

474 Dali, Salvador (1904–1989) *The Persistence of Memory*. 1931. Oil on canvas, 9½ × 13". (162.1934). Given anonymously. Location: The Museum of Modern Art, New York, NY, U.S.A. © ARS, NY/Digital Image © The Museum of Modern Art/Licensed by SCALA/Art Resource, NY

Index